THE
SHAAR
PRESS

THE JUDAICA IMPRINT
FOR THOUGHTFUL PEOPLE

of the Fathers

Pirkei Avos with an
insightful and inspiring commentary by

RABBI ABRAHAM J. TWERSKI, M.D.

פרקי אבות

Visions

THE
SHAAR
PRESS

Published by **SHAAR PRESS**
Distributed by MESORAH PUBLICATIONS, LTD.
4401 Second Avenue / Brooklyn, N.Y 11232 / (718) 921-9000

Distributed in Israel by SIFRIATI / A. GITLER
6 Hayarkon Street / Bnei Brak 51127

Distributed in Europe by LEHMANNS
Unit E, Viking Industrial Park, Rolling Mill Road / Jarrow, Tyne and Wear, NE32 3DP/ England

Distributed in Australia and New Zealand by GOLDS WORLD OF JUDAICA
3-13 William Street / Balaclava, Melbourne 3183 / Victoria Australia

Distributed in South Africa by KOLLEL BOOKSHOP
Shop 8A Norwood Hypermarket / Norwood 2196, Johannesburg, South Africa

ISBN: 1-57819-281-1 Hard Cover
ISBN: 1-57819-282-X Paperback

Printed in·the United States of America by Noble Book Press
Custom bound by Sefercraft, Inc. / 4401 Second Avenue / Brooklyn N.Y. 11232

Visions of the Fathers
is lovingly dedicated to my wife,
Geulah *(Gail)*

ৰঙ Preface

"The words of Torah can be compared to a stone crushed by a hammer" (*Rashi, Genesis* 33:20). Just as the stone disintegrates into many fragments, so are the words of Torah subject to countless interpretations, all of which may be valid.

Another analogy might be to a perfect diamond, which scintillates with many colors, or to a kaleidoscope, where every minute turn produces new designs. Whatever the metaphor, we should give much thought to the various interpretations of *Pirkei Avos*, because they can all enrich our lives.

Pirkei Avos (Ethics of the Fathers) has been the subject of many Torah commentaries. Whet follows is a collection of thoughts inspired by this volume of the Talmud, some of which I heard both at my father's Shabbos *shiurim* (lectures) and from various other Torah scholars, and others which I gleaned in my studies.

Wherever I remember the source, I have provided it. However, there are many interpretations whose source I do not recall. A few items, particularly those relating to psychology, may be original, but the vast majority are taken from works of Torah commentaries.

כָּל יִשְׂרָאֵל ◈

Introduction

כָּל יִשְׂרָאֵל יֵשׁ לָהֶם חֵלֶק לָעוֹלָם הַבָּא, שֶׁנֶּאֱמַר:
„וְעַמֵּךְ כֻּלָּם צַדִּיקִים, לְעוֹלָם יִירְשׁוּ
אָרֶץ, נֵצֶר מַטָּעַי, מַעֲשֵׂה יָדַי לְהִתְפָּאֵר.“

Pirkei Avos — Ethics of the Fathers — is the favorite tractate of the Talmud.
Although one is not supposed to show preference for any particular part of
Torah, it is difficult not to single out Ethics of the Fathers as the choice of many
people. During the long summer Shabbos afternoons, the six chapters of Pirkei
Avos are read in all synagogues, and rabbis regularly lecture on its teachings.
Indeed, even the Talmud singles out Pirkei Avos when it says, "If someone
wishes to be truly pious, he should fulfill the teachings of Pirkei Avos (Bava
Kamma 30a). Probably more commentaries have been written on Ethics than
on any other volume of the Talmud.

Given the many anthologies, one might ask — Is there really a need for one
more? The reason I am presenting this book is twofold. Firstly, there are many
wonderful interpretations that have not as yet been made available in English,
and secondly, I have been amazed at the profound understanding our sages
had of human nature and the workings of the human mind. This should have
come as no surprise, because the Talmud says, "Review Torah again and again,
because it contains everything" (Ethics of the Fathers 5:26). One of our Torah
authorities has stated that whatever can be proven to be true and valid in
psychology can be found in Torah literature. Nevertheless, it is exciting to find
that ideas which have relatively recently been espoused by psychology were
contained in the words of our sages 2,000 years ago.

The Midrash states that we were given Torah and mitzvos in order to refine
ourselves (Vayikra Rabbah 13:3). The many works of mussar and Chassidus
concentrate on the development of middos (character traits), and the ultimate
sources of middos can be found in Ethics of the Fathers. But the development
of middos is hardly a simple task. We come into this world with many physical
drives inherent within us. It is a major task to exert restraint on our natural
inclinations, and furthermore to transform them and direct their energies into
the proper channels. A human being is born with various talents and propensi-
ties, but while some of his makeup is predetermined, how he will use his innate
capacities, whether for good or evil, is left totally to bechirah, to one's freedom
of choice.

It has been said that it is easier to learn the entire Talmud than to transform
even a single inborn character trait, yet this is precisely our assignment on earth.

In the account of Creation, God said "Let us make man" (Genesis 1:26).
Why does God use the word "us"? Whose participation in the creation of man
is God seeking? The Baal Shem Tov explains that all other living things were
created in a state of completion. Man, however, was created in a state of
potential. Man was given bechirah. Man may allow himself to be dominated by
his innate drives, in which case he is nothing more than an intellectual animal.

*A*ll Israel has a share in the World to Come, as it is said: And your people are all righteous; they shall inherit the land forever; a branch of My plantings, My handiwork, in which to take pride (Isaiah 60:21).

However, man has the capacity to elevate himself above the animal level to become a spiritual being. This transformation is wholly in the hands of man, since God does not interfere in issues of free choice. *Man, therefore, must participate in his own creation.* God was referring to man's participation when he said, "Let *us* make man." The keen insights of our sages in *Ethics* can guide us in this challenging task.

As a psychiatrist, I often encounter people who have developed problems in life as a result of emotional illnesses. Not all problems are the result of psychological illnesses. Some are essentially maladjustments in life, due to the lack of spiritual perfection. Just as the body will develop symptoms when it is deprived of essential nutrients, the vitamins and minerals which are necessary for proper physical functioning, so will our spirit manifest symptoms when we fail to provide the *neshamah* with its "nutrients." The latter are essentially the *middos* that we are meant to develop.

Many commentaries offer explanations as to why *Ethics of the Fathers* was called *Avos* (Fathers). Perhaps it is because just as it is the obligation of parents to provide their children with all the elements necessary for physical growth and health, so it is a parental duty to provide them with those elements necessary for spiritual development. The principles herein serve this function; hence this tractate is appropriately referred to as *Avos*.

Torah observance requires compliance with halachah. It is a mistake to think that halachah is limited to certain religious rituals, or even to the manifest mitzvos, e.g., Shabbos, kashrus, etc. How we behave in our daily activities and interact with other people is also a matter of halachah. Indeed, proper conduct is a prerequisite for Torah observance, as the Midrash says, "*Derech eretz kadmah laTorah*," decent behavior precedes Torah (*Vayikra Rabbah* 9:3). The guidelines to this aspect of halachah can be found in *Ethics of the Fathers*, and the brilliant interpretations of Torah scholars throughout history have illuminated the content of these six chapters. This volume is presented with the hope that their precious insights and understanding of the psychology of the human being will facilitate our achieving our goal as "a kingdom of *Kohanim* and a sacred people" (*Exodus* 19:6).

כָּל יִשְׂרָאֵל יֵשׁ לָהֶם חֵלֶק לְעוֹלָם הַבָּא

All Israel has a share in the World to Come

---

*T*he recitation of *Pirkei Avos* is usually preceded with this *mishnah* (*Sanhedrin* 90a). "All Israel has a share in the World to Come (Paradise), as it is said, 'And your people are all *tzaddikim* (righteous), they shall inherit the land

forever; a branch of My plantings, My handiwork, in which to take pride'"
(*Isaiah* 60:21). This verse, which promises reward in the Eternal World, may
have been instituted to encourage people to accept the deprivations and
restraints on gratification of their innate drives that may result from
implementation of the principles set down in *Ethics of the Fathers*.

Talmudic commentaries have pointed out an apparent conflict between this
Talmudic statement and others elsewhere in the Talmud which indicate that
certain sinful acts may result in an individual forfeiting his share in the World to
Come.

This apparent contradiction may be reconciled if we translate the words
"*Kol Yisrael*" to mean "the whole of Israel" rather than "everyone of Israel."
In our earthly lives, we find that there are events to which a person may not
gain access as an individual, but only as part of a group. There are others to
which one may be admitted both as an individual or as part of a group. In the
World to Come, both types of admissions occur. A person may merit a portion
of Paradise by his virtuous behavior, and may also share in it as part of the
larger group, *Klal Yisrael*, the whole of Israel. Sinful behavior may indeed
result in the loss of one's individual privileges, but that to which one is entitled
as a part of *Klal Yisrael* is unaffected. Hence, "*Kol Yisrael*," the whole of
Israel, including those who may have forfeited their individual portions,
nevertheless have a collective share in the World to Come. The latter's share
may be lost only if one separates oneself from *Klal Yisrael* and repudiates his
affiliation with the universal household of Israel.

I was thrilled to discover that the great Torah scholar, R' Shlomo Kluger,
states that this is the proper interpretation of this mishnah. He notes that the
syntax is not consistent, because the mishnah should have said either: כָּל
יִשְׂרָאֵל יֵשׁ לָהֶם חֲלָקִים, "all of Israel have *shares*," or: כָּל אֶחָד מִיִּשְׂרָאֵל יֵשׁ לוֹ חֵלֶק,
"everyone in Israel has *his* share." To say כָּל יִשְׂרָאֵל יֵשׁ לָהֶם חֵלֶק can only mean
that *Klal Yisrael*, as a unit, has a *collective share* in the World to Come

There are numerous references in the Talmud indicating that *Klal Yisrael*
never loses Divine favor. Indeed, the Scriptural verse cited above must be
understood in this sense. One can hardly say that Isaiah meant that *every*
individual is a *tzaddik*. Rather, his statement means that *Klal Yisrael*, when
considered as a whole, are *tzaddikim*, and therefore everyone included in the
Klal merits the Eternal World.

It is for this reason that the Talmud states, "Do not withdraw from the
community" (*Ethics of the Fathers* 2:5). The isolated individual may never be
able to stand up under scrutiny, but when one is absorbed in the *Klal*, he is
judged favorably along with the *Klal*. "The virtue of a multitude is very great"
(*Avodah Zarah* 4b), and again, "The prayer of a multitude is never rejected"
(*Berachos* 8a). Once more, "One should always join oneself in prayer with the
community" (*Berachos* 30a). These are but a few of the many references in
the Talmud to the importance of not withdrawing from the group.

R' Akiva stated that the all-encompassing principle of Torah is to love another as oneself (*Jerusalem Talmud*, *Nedarim* 9:4). Feeling close and empathizing with other people is thus a prerequisite for Torah. To the degree that we isolate ourselves and withdraw from others, we weaken our relationship with Torah.

In Chapter Six of *Ethics of the Fathers*, the Talmud lists the prerequisites for acquisition of Torah, and among them is "sharing the burden of others." R' Simchah Zissel points out that the Torah tells us that when Moses was a prince in the court of Pharaoh, he went out among the Israelites and saw their suffering. Rashi comments, "He devoted his eyes and heart to feel with them" (*Exodus* 2:11), and the Midrash adds that he put his shoulder under their burdens to carry with them. His contribution toward relieving their burden may have been minimal, but doing so enabled him to experience their suffering emotionally as well as to understand it intellectually. R' Simchah Zissel states that it was this trait that enabled Moses to be the one who received the Torah, to be the one who transmitted it to Israel, and to become *Moshe Rabbeinu*, the teacher of Torah for all generations to come.

Being part of *Klal Yisrael* is not accomplished by payment of dues to an organization. It requires active participation in promoting the welfare of the community and alleviating its distress. As long as a person is motivated by egocentric drives and is concerned primarily with self-gratification, he will not endure the deprivations of comfort and make the self-sacrifice that being part of *Klal Yisrael* requires. The teachings of *Ethics of the Fathers* are a guide to overcoming the inborn tendencies to gratify the various drives that are part of the human makeup, and they help elevate people to a level of spirituality that will enable them to give of themselves to others.

The human being is comprised of an animal body and a spiritual soul. Animals (with the exception of domesticated pets) are driven solely by their physical drives for gratification, and do not sacrifice their comforts for altruistic goals. The human being exercises the uniqueness of his spirit when he begins to look away from his own needs and desires and looks toward helping others. In instructing us how to develop the finest character traits, *Ethics of the Fathers* teaches us how to be a *mentsch*, a truly *human* being.

פרק ראשון ✥

Chapter One

פרק ראשון

[א] **מֹשֶׁה** קִבֵּל תּוֹרָה מִסִּינַי, וּמְסָרָהּ לִיהוֹשֻׁעַ,

Chapter One

1.

מֹשֶׁה קִבֵּל תּוֹרָה מִסִּינַי
Moses received the Torah
from Sinai

We begin the teachings of *Ethics of the Fathers* with the historical fact of Moses receiving the Torah from God at Sinai. The significance of this historical statement is probably better understood by us today than by our predecessors.

It is generally appreciated that the commandments that comprise the Torah are dependent upon Divine authority. It is by Divine decree that work on *Shabbos* is prohibited, that certain foods are designated as prohibited, and that rituals such as *matzah*, *shofar*, and *succah* are to be observed. Human logic would not lead us to observe these mitzvos. But ethical behavior? Is it not within our own capabilities to determine proper behavior? Can we not conclude on our own that it is improper to kill, to steal, to lie, or to covet someone else's property? Is it not simply a matter of good judgment to honor one's parents or to help the poor? Furthermore, does not the Talmud state that if the Torah had not been given, we would have been obligated to learn propriety from observance of nature, such as the behaviors of doves, cats, ants, etc. (*Eruvin* 100b)? Why must we have recourse to God for ethics, and be bound to these by Divine law?

But let us look at several recent social changes. Just several decades ago, terminating a nonlife-threatening pregnancy was a heinous crime considered tantamount to murder. Today, it is not only acceptable, but has become an inalienable right which should be financed by public funds. How does something undergo so radical a change from a sin to a virtue in so brief a period of time?

Just several years ago, we were struck with horror at the idea of physician-assisted suicide, and euthanasia was considered abominable. Today, under various euphemisms, these have lost their opprobrium. State legislatures are now debating the issue of voluntarily terminating human life. Again, a very radical change of attitude in just a brief period of time.

The reason for this phenomenon is rather simple. Prior to the marvelous advances of medical science, with its wonder drugs, diagnostic tools, and unprecedented surgical procedures, the life span was short. In the early decades of this century, the average life span was 40 years. Infant mortality was high and childhood diseases and tuberculosis truncated many young lives. The community needed people, hence terminating a pregnancy was a crime against society, since it resulted in depriving the community of a vital commodity: *people*.

Today things have changed radically. The average life span is now approach-

Chapter One

1. **M**oses received the Torah from [God Who revealed Himself at Mount] Sinai and transmitted it to Joshua;

---

ing 80 years. Infant mortality is rare, many childhood diseases have been prevented by immunization, and there is not even a single tuberculosis hospital in the country. Television newscasts and daily newspapers repeatedly remind us that the country faces a fiscal crisis due to runaway costs of Medicare and the burgeoning expenditure for Social Security benefits. Young people, who are paying unprecedented amounts of their paycheck into Social Security, are concerned whether there will be anything left for them when they reach retirement age, particularly since they are making such a huge sacrifice to insure comfortable living conditions for today's senior citizens.

Today's society is not in need of more people, hence it can afford to terminate a healthy pregnancy. This may not be a pleasant thought, but society is hardly upset about legitimizing terminating the lives of the elderly whose treatment comprises the major portion of rapidly accelerating medical costs. These heretofore abominations have therefore ascended into a state of acceptability and even desirability.

Yes, the Talmud states that had the Torah not been given we would have been *expected* to learn proper behavior from observation of nature, but would mankind have lived up to these expectations? Social pressures such as those noted above may well have blinded mankind from deriving ethical behavior from observation of animals. Temptation may have led mankind to emulate dogs and tigers rather than doves and ants.

While ethics and morals based on social needs may undergo change, Torah ethics and morals are immutable. No legislature, no rabbinical gathering, not even a Divinely inspired prophet can alter a single word of Torah. What was forbidden in the days of Sinai remains forbidden in the age of computer technology. Torah is identified with God Himself, and both are eternal. The teachings of *Avos* were received by Moses at Sinai and are as eternal and immutable as everything else in the Torah.

וּמְסָרָהּ לִיהוֹשֻׁעַ
and transmitted it to Joshua

The statement that Moses transmitted the Torah to Joshua may be seen as a reinforcement of the Divine origin of Torah. It rebuts the skeptics who question this and ascribe the Torah to Moses' genius, glorifying him as the "great lawgiver." It is a cardinal principle of faith, cited by Rambam, that Moses was *not* the originator of Torah, but a conduit between God and Israel. Perhaps to refute the skeptics, the mishnah states that Moses transmitted the Torah and the leadership of Israel to his student Joshua, rather than to his own sons. Flesh and blood rulers invariably invest their children with their authority. Moses, even though he would have desired this (*Rashi, Numbers* 27:16), was

וִיהוֹשֻׁעַ לִזְקֵנִים, וּזְקֵנִים לִנְבִיאִים, וּנְבִיאִים מְסָרוּהָ לְאַנְשֵׁי כְנֶסֶת הַגְּדוֹלָה. הֵם אָמְרוּ שְׁלֹשָׁה דְבָרִים: הֱווּ מְתוּנִים בַּדִּין, וְהַעֲמִידוּ תַלְמִידִים הַרְבֵּה, וַעֲשׂוּ סְיָג לַתּוֹרָה.

---

told by God that Joshua was to inherit his high position. Hence the transmission to Joshua is further testimony to the Divine origin of Torah.

קִבֵּל . . . וּמְסָרָה
received . . .
and transmitted

Prior to the time of R' Yehudah HaNasi, the Mishnah was not recorded in writing and was studied orally. It was therefore essential that the wording of the Mishnah be concise, so that it would not overtax one's memory. Inasmuch as every word in Talmud is carefully measured, we must pause and reflect on even minor nuances. For example, the mishnah states that Moses *received* the Torah, and *transmitted* it to Joshua. Note that it does not say that Joshua *received* the Torah from Moses; i.e., as a receiver of Torah, Moses appears to have been rather passive, but as a transmitter to Joshua, he was more active. Then we read, "Joshua to the Elders; the Elders to the Prophets," and neither the verb "transmitted" nor "received" is mentioned. Finally, "and the Prophets *transmitted* it to the Men of the Great Assembly," where the verb again appears.

This syntax contains principles of educational psychology. The teacher-student relationship may be one where the student is so eager to learn that he absorbs everything the teacher provides. There may be another relationship in which the teacher may have to exert extra effort to convey his knowledge to the student. There may be a halfway point, when the efforts of each are relatively equal. It is important for instructors to realize their students' capacities and attitudes, so that they may adapt their teaching methods to maximize the learning process.

The Talmudic sages were able to conceptualize how Torah was taught. Moses had totally effaced himself before God, and became a huge receptacle for the Divine wisdom, to the point where "God gave Moses the Torah as a gift" (*Rashi, Exodus* 31:18). Joshua was unable to absorb all of Moses' immense knowledge, and Moses had to be more active in transmitting it. The transmission from Joshua to the Elders and the latter to the Prophets was more or less equally divided between the giver and the recipient, but when prophecy came to an end, the transmission from the Prophets to the Men of the Great Assembly was again a quantum leap, requiring a greater exertion on the part of the instructors.

When there are significant changes in the culture or learning capacity, the methodology for transmission of Torah must adapt in order to maximize learning. Hence, we have the flourishing of yeshivos in the 18th and 19th centuries, and the expansion of Torah academies after the destruction of the Torah centers in the Holocaust.

1/1   *Joshua to the Elders; the Elders to the Prophets; and the Prophets transmitted it to the Men of the Great Assembly. They said three things: Be deliberate in judgment; develop many disciples; and make a [protective] fence for the Torah.*

Torah transmission from generation to generation must never be interrupted, and the substance of Torah never changes. However, we must be alert to what methodologies must be adopted to assure continuity of Torah learning. Thus, in the 1920s R' Meir Shapiro of Lublin instituted *daf yomi*, learning one folio of Talmud each day, which not only increased Talmudic study among the laity, but also introduced a new unifying concept, wherein Jews the world over would be studying the same *daf*. The availability of audiotapes and CD-Rom have put Torah at the fingertips of every Jew who wishes to acquaint himself with Torah study.

By the use of different terms, the mishnah tells us that the *mesorah* (transmission) of Torah is continuous, but that we must utilize whatever teaching techniques are appropriate for different times.

Attention to the nuances of the Talmud may thus provide valuable guidelines for both teachers and students.

וִיהוֹשֻׁעַ לִזְקֵנִים וּזְקֵנִים לִנְבִיאִים
Joshua to the Elders; the Elders to the Prophets

Although the verb "transmitted" is not specifically stated in the transfer from Joshua to the Elders and from the latter to the Prophets, it is nevertheless implied, and it is only of Moses that it is said that he *received* the Torah (i.e., rather than "God transmitted the Torah to Moses").

Some students just love to learn, and some teachers just love to teach. We may all recall instructors who clearly took pleasure in teaching, and who personified the Talmudic statement that "More than the calf wishes to suck, the cow wishes to suckle" (*Pesachim* 112a). This was the exuberance whereby Torah was transmitted with the knowledge of the teachers overflowing onto the students, and this characterized the conveyance of Torah after Moses, where the desire of the teachers to transmit Torah surpassed the students' desire to learn. Moses' thirst and desire for Torah was unparalleled, and indeed, the Midrash states that he was willing to sacrifice his life to obtain the Torah. This is why the mishnah says that Moses *received* the Torah rather than that God *transmitted* the Torah to him. It is because of this unequaled desire for Torah that we refer to it as the "Torah of Moses."

This has served as a prototype for Torah teachers, who have been exuberant in imparting Torah knowledge to their students, and also for the latter, who have had an insatiable craving for it. These attitudes toward Torah have sustained it throughout our history and have given us the great Torah scholars who grace our proud heritage.

This attitude should characterize every teacher of Torah, who should feel the Torah so well up in him as to constitute a pressing urge to share it. He should resemble the nurturing mother, who feels relieved only when her infant takes from her. It is this desire to impart of oneself that has perpetuated Torah throughout our history.

The chain of Torah running throughout history has unfortunately been one of diminishing capacities. As a rule, Torah scholars of a subsequent era may not dispute the opinions of scholars of an earlier era. We assume that the earlier scholars were of a higher spiritual level, which made their insights into Torah more authoritative.

This state of affairs did not have to be. When the Israelites heard the voice of God at Sinai, they asked Moses to intervene on their behalf and impart the Divine word to them, because they felt they could not withstand the immensity of the direct Divine revelation (*Deuteronomy* 5:20-23). Moses was critical of the Israelites for their hesitancy in listening to God Himself (ibid. *Rashi*). The Talmud states that had the Israelites heard the entire Torah directly from God, they would have been free of the *yetzer hara* (evil inclination). The Torah would have been eternally implanted within them, never to be forgotten (*Shir Hashirim Rabbah* 1:15). The worship of a golden calf and the tragedy of the spies (*Numbers* 13-14) would never have occurred. The entire course of Jewish history would have been radically altered.

Why were our ancestors reluctant to hear the voice of God? Because they did not consider themselves worthy and deserving of receiving the greatest of all revelations. This is just one of several incidents where our history has been negatively affected by misguided humility. Moses was the most humble of all men on earth (*Numbers* 12:3), yet he knew that if God wished to speak to him, he was capable of listening to Him. Our ancestors should have reasoned that if God chose to speak with them directly, they were indeed able to receive His word directly. The decrease in Torah knowledge that has occurred throughout our history is a consequence of humility that degenerated into a lowered self-regard.

King Saul forfeited his reign because of misguided humility (*I Samuel* 15:16-28). The Talmud states that the Second Temple was destroyed because of misguided humility (*Gittin* 56a). While vanity is the worst of all character traits and humility is the finest of all traits, we must be guided by the teachings of our great ethicists, so that we do not allow humility to be distorted into pathological low self-esteem.

The works of *mussar* and *chassidus* stress that the *yetzer hara* may impede a person's study of Torah or performance of mitzvos under the guise of providing a pious reprimand, such as, "Who do you think you are to aspire to spiritual greatness? You are a lowly sinner and have no right to such aspirations." It was this manner of wile used by the *yetzer hara* that caused our ancestors to forgo the opportunity of hearing the Torah from God Himself.

We may thus understand the opening mishnah of *Avos*. It is because Moses received the Torah from Sinai and transmitted it to Joshua that we have a progressive decline of Torah scholarship throughout history. Had the Israelites themselves received the Torah from God without Moses as an intermediary, their knowledge of Torah would have been unequivocal and remained permanent throughout history.

It is a common experience that if a person achieves something and has no one to share it with, it is not a satisfying experience. The joy of a scholar in acquiring new knowledge is greatest when he knows he can share it with his students. Moses' enthusiasm in receiving the Torah was intensified because he knew he would have eager students to whom he could teach it. Thus, Moses' fervor at receiving the Torah at Sinai was in part because he knew that he would transmit it to Joshua.

מֹשֶׁה קִבֵּל . . . וּמְסָרָהּ . . .
וּנְבִיאִים מְסָרוּהָ לְאַנְשֵׁי כְנֶסֶת הַגְּדוֹלָה

Moses received . . . and transmitted it . . . and the Prophets transmitted it to the Men of the Great Assembly.

The term *"mesirah"* is used only twice: once in the transmission from Moses to Joshua, and again in the transmission from the Prophets to the Men of the Great Assembly. Although the word *"mesirah"* denotes transmission, its connotation carries an implication of coercion or force (*Rashi, Numbers* 31:5). At these two points in history, the transmission of Torah to the next generation required a greater degree of assertiveness and perhaps even aggressiveness.

Both periods are characterized by a radical, qualitative change. After Moses there would never again be as direct, clear, and unequivocal a revelation of the Divine will. Moses' prophecy was never again equaled (*Numbers* 12:6-8, *Deuteronomy* 34:10). Subsequent prophets were indeed Divinely inspired to interpret their prophetic visions, but the clarity with which Moses received and taught the word of God was never again equaled.

The close of the period of prophecy was again a time when we were deprived of Divine revelation. In both cases, greater recourse to insights derived from Torah study had to compensate for what was lacking in Divine revelation. In both cases the transmission therefore had to be more aggressive in developing the students' grasp of Torah principles. In the transmission from Joshua to the Elders and then to the Prophets there was no such cataclysmic gap, and adequate impartation could occur without extraordinary effort.

This should serve as a lesson for us. There were periods, such as those following the Chmelnicki pogroms and the *Shabtai Zvi* debacle, when extraordinary effort was necessary to preserve Torah, and this is when *Chassidus* emerged. When the secularism of the enlightenment threatened to extinguish the Torah lifestyle, the *mussar* movement materialized. Today, following the unprecedented losses of the Holocaust and the hedonism that arose in the wake of the "God is dead" movement of the '60s, we are again confronted with a cataclysm. In this situation we must redouble our efforts at Torah study and living according to Torah values and *middos* (character traits). Given the rarefaction of morality and ethics that has beset modern civilization, a concerted effort must be made by both parents and teachers to be most assertive in teaching refinement of *middos* to their students and children, not only by didactics, but even more by being role models. We cannot be lax in the teaching of *middos*. Our era is one which requires the dedication entailed in the concept of *mesirah*.

הֱווּ מְתוּנִים בַּדִּין
Be deliberate in judgment

Although this statement would appear to be directed to judges, some commentaries point out that it applies to every individual. All of us are judges, and although we may not render decisions in litigation, we frequently make decisions that affect others as well as ourselves. Hence, guidelines that are appropriate for jurists are equally appropriate for everyone.

"Deliberate in judgment" means not being hasty when making decisions. One might think that a diligent person is one who acts quickly, whereas an indolent person is one who dilly-dallies. While endless procrastination is certainly deplorable, a person who acts quickly without deliberation may actually be more indolent. He may be too lazy to put his mind to use and make the necessary effort to think things through adequately.

A judge may not take a bribe. The Torah states that it is impossible for a person to judge fairly if he has taken a bribe, because he is blinded to the truth and his reasoning is distorted (*Deuteronomy* 16:19). We are often subject to "bribes" in making personal decisions. These bribes consist of the gratification or pleasures that are incidental to a particular act. Our thinking will tend to favor that decision which will satisfy a desire. We are capable of ingenious rationalizations to justify whatever it is we may desire. One recovered alcoholic said, "In all my years of drinking I never once took a drink unless I had decided that it was the right thing to do at the time." King Solomon stated this principle, "All of a person's ways are right in his own eyes" (*Proverbs* 16:2).

Deliberation on a decision enables a person to be aware that he may be biased, but it is no guarantee that he will not delude himself. It is therefore wise, especially when making important life decisions, to seek the advice of someone who is objective and who is unaffected by our biases. We should incorporate such advice in our deliberation.

2. **S**himon the Righteous was [one] of the remnants of the Great Assembly.

The Hebrew word מְתוּנִים that is translated as "be deliberate" also means "be patient." Deliberation requires time as well as effort. If we allow ourselves to be rushed into decisions, we may not have the opportunity to deliberate. Too often we regret having acted in haste, having allowed ourselves to be unduly influenced by the emotions of the moment.

We may not realize that when we judge others, we may be passing judgment on ourselves. The classic example of this is the reprimand of the prophet Nathan to King David over the incident with Bathsheba. Nathan told David about a wealthy person who had abundant livestock, and who stole the sole lamb of a poor neighbor. David, outraged by so crass a crime, exclaimed, "As Hashem lives, any man who does this deserves to die!" Nathan responded, "You are that man" (II Samuel 12:7).

God may give us the opportunity to pass judgment on ourselves. He presents us with situations in which we must make decisions which could apply equally to our own behavior. If we are lenient and considerate, we may receive similar consideration from God. If we are stern and unyielding, we may expect Him to treat us similarly.

It is to our own advantage to be patient and cautious in making decisions that may affect others.

2.

The message of this mishnah can better be appreciated if we place it in its historical framework.

Shimon HaTzaddik was a contemporary of Alexander the Great. He lived in the time when Greek philosophy was flourishing, with the budding of science and the revolutionary concepts of Aristotle. The might of Alexander and the wisdom of Aristotle appeared to be an invincible combination which would transform the civilized world.

Some 2,000 years later, the might of the Greek empire exists only in history, and the remnants of the Acropolis testify to the glory of the Greece that once was but is no longer. Aristotelian science has long since been refuted and replaced. However, the Torah of the Men Of The Great Assembly is still alive and thriving.

It was therefore Shimon HaTzaddik, the man before whom Alexander bowed in reverence at the gates of Jerusalem, who delineated the foundation which can give the world permanence. It is neither the might nor the philosophy of Greece, but rather the Torah, along with the Divine service and the mitzvah of gemilas chassadim. These are still with us today, and will be unto eternity.

הוּא הָיָה אוֹמֵר: עַל שְׁלֹשָׁה דְבָרִים הָעוֹלָם עוֹמֵד: עַל הַתּוֹרָה, וְעַל הָעֲבוֹדָה, וְעַל גְּמִילוּת חֲסָדִים.

עַל שְׁלֹשָׁה דְבָרִים הָעוֹלָם עוֹמֵד:
עַל הַתּוֹרָה, וְעַל הָעֲבוֹדָה, וְעַל גְּמִילוּת חֲסָדִים
The world is based on three things —
on the Torah, on the service [of God],
and upon acts of loving-kindness.

The Talmud lends itself to a variety of interpretations, and in each era we may find an interpretation that is relevant to that particular period of time.

Our predecessors understood the phrase "The world is based (or is supported) on three things" to refer to society or humanity. I.e., civilization can continue only by the merit of observance of the principles of Torah, service of God, and kindness and consideration to other people. It is only today that we may appreciate an interpretation that was unavailable to previous generations.

Rarely does a week go by that we are not made aware that the actual survival of the world is in jeopardy. Our technological advances have indeed given us many blessings and have made life more comfortable in many ways. Unfortunately, this has come at the incredible cost of chemical pollution of our rivers and lakes, seepage of nuclear waste into our drinking water, acid rain, the greenhouse effect of carbon dioxide emissions, and tampering with the ozone layer. The eventual increase in global warming may result in more hurricanes, tornadoes, and flooding. There is destruction of tropical forests, resulting in elimination of various species of animals. There may be other evils which we have not yet discovered. Various efforts have been made to attempt to control this progressive ruin, but they have met with only limited success. The reason? People have an insatiable appetite for wealth, leisure, and greater conveniences. We will obviously not transmit the same world we inherited from our ancestors to future generations.

Humanity is as addicted to gratifying its many desires as the drug addict is to his heroin and cocaine. It is common knowledge that the addict is not deterred from drug use by the knowledge that drugs may destroy him. His craving for the immediate gratification blinds him to the ultimate self-destruction.

This sorry state of affairs is due to the hedonism which prevails today. The goal in life has become pursuit of pleasure with the resultant craving for pleasure being strikingly similar to that of the drug addict.

What if people had more spiritual aspirations rather than simply pursuit of physical pleasures? In the treatment of addiction, the recovery of the addict occurs when the awareness of the destructive progression of his addiction results in his changing his lifestyle to a greater pursuit of spirituality. It is this change in attitude that can curb the self-destruction of the pathological pursuit of pleasure, both in the addict and in humanity as a whole.

If people would adopt the goals in life suggested by the mishnah — to live according to the principles of Torah, to dedicate themselves to the service of

He was accustomed to say: The world is based on three things — on the Torah, on the service [of God], and upon acts of loving-kindness.

God, and to be considerate of others — we could reverse the incessant pattern of environmental erosion that threatens the existence of life on earth. The world could be preserved if we reined in our insatiable appetites for pleasure.

Today we have the novel interpretation of the mishnah, a literal interpretation which was heretofore unthinkable. *The world can be maintained only by three things: Torah, service of God, and consideration of others.* Without these, we may be on a collision course with destiny. The very existence of the world may be brought to an end.

<hr>

הָעוֹלָם עוֹמֵד
The world is based

<hr>

We often find the term "*Olam Over*," a transitory world, applied to our earthly existence, and the term "*Olam Omed*," a permanent world, applied to the Eternal, spiritual World. A life of physical indulgence is indeed transient. You may have enjoyed a delectable meal several days ago, but its enjoyment is long gone, and even the memory of it gives you scant pleasure today. This is equally true of all physical pleasures.

Spiritual fulfillment, however, is of a lasting nature. The mishnah (4:2) says "The reward of a mitzvah is the mitzvah." If, in the past, you gave *tzedakah* and happen to think about it today, you may have a good feeling about what you did then. In addition to the reward you will receive in the Eternal World for having done a mitzvah, the awareness that you have done a mitzvah is its own reward, something which can give you pleasure even during your earthly existence.

The *Maggid* of Vilna gave a unique interpretation to the statement of Solomon in *Ecclesiastes* (1:2), "Nothing of nothingness, all is nothing." The *Maggid* said, " 'Nothing' is a zero. Even a whole string of zeros amounts to nothing. However, if one places the number '1' before the string of zeros, it turns into an astronomical number.

"We may partake of worldly goods purely for physical pleasure, in which case this amounts to nothing. Or, we may do so in order to maintain our bodies in optimum health, so that we may live to fulfill our mission in life: to observe the Torah and mitzvos. The latter is essentially placing the number '1' before the zeros. All mundane activities may then add up to a great amount. Eating, sleeping, and participating in all the activities necessary to preserve life thus become a part of the ultimate goal, and take on a quality of permanence rather than being ephemeral."

Based on this interpretation of *Ecclesiastes*, we can understand the statement of the mishnah. This earthly world can become an עוֹלָם עוֹמֵד, *Olam Omed*, a permanent existence instead of an עוֹלָם עוֹבֵר, *Olam Over,* a transitory world, if we adopt the three principles: Torah, service to God, and acts of consideration and kindness to others. Our earthly life is thus essentially converted into a spiritual life which has an eternal quality.

עַל שְׁלֹשָׁה דְבָרִים הָעוֹלָם עוֹמֵד:
עַל הַתּוֹרָה, וְעַל הָעֲבוֹדָה, וְעַל גְּמִילוּת חֲסָדִים
The world is based on three things —
on the Torah, on the service [of God],
and upon acts of loving-kindness.

R' Yechezkel Landau of Prague (*Noda BeYehudah*) urged his congregants to greater exertion in giving *tzedakah* and doing acts of *chesed*. When he found that his biddings were not being heeded, he closed the local yeshivah and conspicuously wandered the streets as if he had nothing to do.

When he was asked about this unusual behavior, R' Landau said, "The Talmud tells us that there are three pillars that support the world: study of Torah, the Divine service, and acts of *chesed*. If a table which stands on three legs loses one of its legs, it can continue to be used if something is placed under it for support. However, if a second leg is missing, it cannot be supported. The only thing to do is to remove the third leg and set the tabletop on the floor.

"Our Divine service has long been inadequate, but as long as we had two of the three legs intact, Torah and *chesed,* the system could function with some additional support. However, if there are no longer acts of *chesed*, then only one leg (Torah) remains. The system is then nonfunctional, and the only thing to do is to remove the third leg. When the community became lax in acts of *chesed,* my only option was to close the yeshivah, thereby removing the third leg of Torah. If the community will resume doing *chesed*, I will open the yeshivah again."

Close attention to the syntax of this mishnah reveals that an accurate translation is "The world is based on three things: *the* Torah, *the* Divine service, and acts of *chesed.*" The first two have the definite article "the," indicating that there is something particular about these, whereas *chesed* is not preceded by the definite article, which indicates that it can be generic.

The reason for this is that Torah is a virtue only if it is studied for proper reasons; i.e., to fulfill the mitzvah of Torah study and to know what we must do or may not do. If Torah is studied primarily for ego purposes, so that one may be praised and acclaimed as a scholar, this constitutes vanity and is not virtuous. Certainly if Torah is studied for devious reasons, to undermine its authority by seeking to find defects in Torah, it is surely not meritorious. Hence, for Torah to be a virtue, it is *the* Torah that is virtuous, but not *all* Torah.

This is equally true of the Divine service, which nowadays is prayer. Prayer without *kavannah* (concentration) is "like a body without a soul" (*Shelah*), and if one is ostentatious in prayer in order to impress others with one's piety, that prayer is hardly meritorious. It is therefore only *the* proper prayer that is virtuous, but not *all* prayer.

Acts of kindness, however, require no qualification. If one gives *tzedakah*, thereby enabling the poor to have their needs met, the donor's motivation makes little difference. Even if he provides for the needy primarily because he wishes to be acknowledged and praised as a philanthropist, this does not detract from the mitzvah. Hence, *chesed* is generic because **all** *chesed* is a virtue.

We can learn so much from just the presence or absence of a single letter of the alphabet!

There are three essential human relationships: man with God; man with his fellow man; and man with himself. The Divine service binds man to God, and acts of kindness bind man to his fellow man. *Torah enables man to relate to himself.*

It is unfortunate that a person may become alien to himself. This may occur when a person denies part of himself, because there are things that he cannot accept as comprising part of his being. There may be thoughts and feelings which are so reprehensible that one denies having them. I.e., he does not lie about them, but rather is unaware of their existence within him. He simply cannot admit that he can harbor such ideas. In psychology, we refer to this process as *denial,* which is an unconscious mechanism that protects a person from things he does not wish to know.

Denial is a costly defense, as it can give rise to a number of symptoms that can produce emotional discomfort and dysfunction. Denial of a fact is essentially a refutation of reality. It is obvious that a person cannot function properly when he is in denial of reality. Properly understood, Torah can help us overcome some denial.

The Talmud states that when Moses ascended to Heaven to receive the Torah, the angels pleaded with God to give them the Torah and keep it in the celestial spheres rather than give it to mortals. "Humans are far too corrupt, and will violate the Torah," they said. Moses responded, "What is written in the Torah? The Torah forbids swearing falsely. Do you transact business that might cause you to take an oath? The Torah forbids working on Shabbos. Do you do any work from which you must abstain? The Torah commands one to honor his father and mother. Do you have parents? The Torah forbids acts of murder and theft. Are you subject to such temptations?" By pointing out to the heavenly angels that the Torah was not relevant to them, Moses succeeded in bringing it down to us (*Shabbos* 88b).

The message is undeniable. There is no need to forbid any action for which one has no desire. The Torah was given to mortals rather than to heavenly angels precisely because humans are in need of its teachings and its restrictions in order to restrain themselves and to be masters over their emotional impulses.

אַנְטִיגְנוֹס [ג] אִישׁ סוֹכוֹ קִבֵּל מִשִּׁמְעוֹן הַצַּדִּיק.
הוּא הָיָה אוֹמֵר: אַל תִּהְיוּ כַּעֲבָדִים
הַמְשַׁמְּשִׁין אֶת הָרַב עַל מְנָת לְקַבֵּל פְּרָס; אֶלָּא הֱווּ
כַּעֲבָדִים הַמְשַׁמְּשִׁין אֶת הָרַב שֶׁלֹּא עַל מְנָת לְקַבֵּל פְּרָס;

Inasmuch as the Torah was intended for every individual, it follows that every person must have the impulses which the Torah forbids, otherwise the Torah would not be relevant in its entirety to everyone. *The 365 prohibitions in the Torah indicate that a person must have a natural tendency for the prohibited behavior,* otherwise there would not have been a need to restrict them, anymore than there would be a need to restrict the heavenly angels from behaviors to which they are not subject.

One does not need to undergo extensive psychoanalysis to discover what base impulses are contained within human beings. All one needs to do is to read the 365 Torah prohibitions to discover what comprises much of human emotions. We are not only capable of animal impulses, but even of some that are beneath lower forms of life. Hence, if one discovers such urges within oneself, there is no reason to be alarmed or even ashamed. They are just part of the human physical makeup.

However, we are not meant to function at a mere animal level. It is precisely our mission and responsibility to elevate ourselves above our physical being and make our *neshamah* dominant, and we must become master of our physical being rather than its slave. Man is not an angel, devoid of base drives, but neither is he an animal, to give them free rein.

The *Tiferes Yisrael* (*Kiddushin,* end of Chapter 4) relates a story that a desert king heard of the greatness of Moses, and sent his finest artists to bring back a portrait of him. He then submitted the portrait to his physiognomists to study it and describe Moses' character. They reported that the portrait revealed a man who was vain, arrogant, lustful, greedy, and degenerate. Inasmuch as this was in sharp contrast to what he had heard of Moses, the king went to the Israelite encampment to see for himself.

Upon meeting Moses, the king saw that his artists had indeed captured every minute detail, and he could not understand how his physiognomists could be so far off course. Moses explained to him, "Your physiognomists can interpret only the innate characteristics with which a person was born. All they said of me was true insofar as those were the traits I was born with. However, I struggled to overcome them and to transform my character."

A proper understanding of Torah will thus allow a person to accept himself, and make it unnecessary for him to disown any part of his intrinsic being. By the same token, observance of Torah will elevate man to a status superior even to that of angels. Heavenly angels are indeed holy, because that is how they were created. They did not achieve holiness by their own efforts. Man becomes holy by his own efforts, and that is his majesty.

3. **A**ntigonos, *leader of Socho, received the tradition from Shimon the Righteous. He was accustomed to say: Be not as servants who serve the master for the sake of receiving [even a token] reward, but rather, be like servants who serve the master not for the sake of receiving [a token] reward;*

The observance of all three — Torah, the Divine service, and acts of kindness — provide for a wholesome character. Man can then relate properly to God, to his fellow man, and to himself.

3.

אַל תִּהְיוּ כַּעֲבָדִים הַמְשַׁמְּשִׁין
אֶת הָרַב עַל מְנָת לְקַבֵּל פְּרָס
Be not as servants who serve the master for the sake of receiving reward

Although believing that there is reward for mitzvos and punishment for sins is one of the thirteen principles of faith, Antigonos urges us not to allow reward to be the primary motivation for doing mitzvos.

It should be apparent that reward and punishment are essentially juvenile motivations. A small child who runs into the street because he is unaware of the danger of being hit by a car must be scolded and perhaps even spanked. He lacks the capacity to understand a verbal reprimand, and unless he feels the pain of the spanking and associates it with his running out into the street, he might endanger himself again. A more mature person avoids stepping into traffic because he is aware of the risk. There is no need for any punishment to discourage him from doing so.

This is equally true of reward. I recall that as a child I had to be bribed to go to the dentist. I was promised that I could buy a comic book after I left the dentist's office. A mature person knows that he must have proper dental care. He visits the dentist because he wishes to retain his teeth. Hence, while we believe in reward and punishment, we should be mature enough to understand that God is all-perfect and does not need our performance of mitzvos for His own good. "If your sins are abundant, how have you affected Him? If you were righteous, what have you given to Him?" (*Job 35:6-7*).

This may help us understand an otherwise problematic episode in Scripture. The Patriarch Isaac seemingly loved his profligate son Esau, and Rebecca loved the pious Jacob. It is difficult to accept that the saintly Patriarch was deceived by the wily Esau and preferred him to Jacob, although Esau did hunt for food for Isaac. At Rebecca's behest, Jacob disguised himself as Esau and received the blessings intended for his brother. When Isaac discovered the ruse, he shuddered violently, which Rashi explains, "because he saw *Gehinnom* opening beneath him" (*Genesis 1:33*). Was blessing his son Jacob,

albeit by error, so great a devastation as to bring about so violent a reaction?

But let us look at it this way. Contrary to what is generally assumed, the
saintly Patriarch did appreciate the piety of Jacob. He was secure in his knowledge that Jacob would be the one to carry out the Divine mission to establish the
nation of Israel, and that he was the proper heir of the spirituality of Abraham.
Isaac was also aware that Esau was totally devoid of spirituality. Isaac's treatment of Esau was in the hope of salvaging his wayward son, as the Baal Shem
Tov would recommend many centuries later to a man who complained that his
son had strayed from the path of righteousness. "You must show him even
more love than to his brothers," the Baal Shem Tov said.

Isaac knew that Jacob was mature and would lead a righteous life for its own
merits. However, he was reluctant to abandon all hope for Esau. He therefore
tried to win Esau with the same tactics one would use with a child: reward for
doing what is right. Isaac therefore said to Esau, "Look, my child. Mitzvos bring
great rewards, and you will profit by behaving justly. Let me give you an
example. There is a mitzvah to honor your parents. Bring me some tasty food,
and I will reward you with a bountiful blessing. Let this serve as a prototype for
you, that doing mitzvos will bring you reward." This was the Patriarch's final
resort at salvaging Esau.

Rebecca, however, did not want Esau to receive the blessings, regardless of
any arguments to the contrary. Perhaps she knew that Esau was so disinter-
ested in spirituality that not even this tactic would turn him around. She
therefore wished Jacob to receive the blessings he rightfully deserved. Although
Jacob was reluctant to indulge in so juvenile a behavior as seeking rewards for
good deeds, he participated in the ruse only because he was bound to respect
his mother's wishes.

When Isaac discovered that Jacob had come to get the blessings, he concluded that Jacob had regressed to the juvenile behavior of seeking rewards
for mitzvos. This utterly devastated him. He feared that Esau was indeed
a lost cause. He had been secure in the knowledge that Jacob was devoted
to the principles of righteousness, and was the proper father of the nation of
Israel which was to receive the Torah. Not knowing that Jacob was coerced
by his mother to get the blessings, Isaac felt that Jacob had lowered himself
to the level of seeking rewards for doing what was right. If so, there was no
one capable of carrying out the Divine mission assigned to Abraham.
Isaac knew that Esau was a profligate, and now it seemed that Jacob was
immature! No wonder Isaac shuddered and saw "*Gehinnom* open beneath
him."

Antigonos therefore tells us, "Yes, maintain your belief in the principles of
faith, but do not let reward be your primary motivation for doing what is right.
You should function at a much more mature level."

וִיהִי מוֹרָא שָׁמַיִם עֲלֵיכֶם
***And the fear of Heaven
should be upon you.***

Some commentaries question the sequence of Antigonos' statement. To serve God without consideration of reward is a level of *ahavas Hashem*, love for God, which is considered a higher level of spirituality than *yiras Hashem*, reverence of God. Should not the sequence be reversed, that one proceeds from *yirah* to *ahavah*, from reverence to love?

While this is true in one sense, there is nevertheless good reason for emphasizing *yirah after ahavah*. There is an aphorism that "familiarity breeds contempt," and we must be most cautious not to dissipate the attitude of reverence in an intimate relationship.

The Torah teaches us this in the episode where Pharaoh increased the burden on the Israelite slaves after Moses delivered the Divine message to set them free. Moses confronted God with "After I delivered Your message to Pharaoh, he increased the suffering of the Israelites and You did not rescue Your people" (*Exodus* 5:23). The Talmud states that this bold language indicated a lack of proper reverence for God and that this was one of the reasons Moses was not permitted to enter the Promised Land (*Rashi, Exodus* 6:1). The intimate relationship Moses had with God should not have detracted from his reverence.

There is an interesting parallel to this in the Talmudic statement on how a husband should relate to his wife: "He should love her as dearly as he loves himself, and respect her even more than he respects himself" (*Yevamos* 62b). The Talmud was aware that even profound love may not preclude offending the wife with a harsh word or even an insult in a moment of anger. It therefore requires that in addition to love, a husband must maintain a high level of respect for his wife.

This is the message of Antigonos. Whether in the relationship of man to fellow man, man to God, or husband to wife, intimacy should not be permitted to lead to a lack of reverence. Love and respect must go hand in hand.

"And the fear of Heaven should be upon you." How is this relevant to the earlier statement, to de-emphasize reward as a motivation for doing mitzvos?

We generally assume "fear of heaven" or fear of God to refer to fear of transgressing the Divine will. However, there may also be a somewhat different interpretation: to have the fear that heaven has; i.e., to have the fear that God has.

"But that is absurd," you will say. "God has no fears at all." Well, let us see. The Talmud states that everything is in God's control, except whether a person chooses to do right or wrong (*Berachos* 33b). God has left the choice of moral behavior exclusively in the hands of man, and never interferes to stop a person

[ד] **יוֹסֵי** בֶּן יוֹעֶזֶר אִישׁ צְרֵדָה וְיוֹסֵי בֶּן יוֹחָנָן אִישׁ
יְרוּשָׁלַיִם קִבְּלוּ מֵהֶם.
יוֹסֵי בֶּן יוֹעֶזֶר אִישׁ צְרֵדָה אוֹמֵר: יְהִי בֵיתְךָ בֵּית וַעַד
לַחֲכָמִים, וֶהֱוֵי מִתְאַבֵּק בַּעֲפַר רַגְלֵיהֶם, וֶהֱוֵי שׁוֹתֶה בַצָּמָא
אֶת דִּבְרֵיהֶם.

---

from doing wrong. Freedom of choice insofar as right or wrong behavior is concerned is in the hands of the person alone, and God does not control this.

However, God wishes for a person to behave correctly, and violation of the Torah is not only sinful but is detrimental to a person's welfare. When a person does something wrong, God's position is much like that of a parent who watches from afar and sees his little child about to run into the street where he may be hit by a car. All the distraught parent can do from a distance is to shout to the child and hope that the child will hear him and avoid being harmed. However, the father is powerless to restrain him from endangering himself. The parent is seized by the fear that the child will not heed his warning and will indeed endanger himself.

God, too, has such a fear for His children's spiritual welfare. Inasmuch as He allows man to have total freedom regarding moral behavior, He is, as it were, powerless to intervene and restrain him from sin, which is a self-destructive act. Much like the parent, God fears for His children.

We should share in God's fear. We should know that sin is harmful to ourselves, and this is the reason why we should abstain from sin, rather than because of fear of retribution.

In this sense, the latter portion of Antigonos' statement complements the first part. Do not perform mitzvos primarily in anticipation of reward, and do not abstain from sin primarily to avoid retribution. The Midrash states that the mitzvos were given to refine man, and we should obey them with the conviction that they were given to us for our own betterment.

4.

יְהִי בֵיתְךָ בֵּית וַעַד לַחֲכָמִים . . .
וֶהֱוֵי שׁוֹתֶה בַצָּמָא אֶת דִּבְרֵיהֶם
Let your house be a meeting place for Torah scholars . . .
and you shall drink in their words with thirst.

While being in the company of scholars exposes a person to wisdom, there is the possibility that a constant association with scholars may result in one's becoming complacent, losing one's enthusiasm for learning, and perhaps even becoming somewhat bored. There is a Yiddish aphorism: "Even roasted meat can lose its taste if it becomes part of one's regular diet."

4. Yose ben Yoezer, leader of Tz'redah, and Yose ben Yochanan, leader of Jerusalem, received the tradition from them.

Yose ben Yoezer, leader of Tz'redah, says: Let your house be a meeting place for Torah scholars; you shall become dusty in the dust of their feet; and you shall drink in their words with thirst.

The proper attitude toward Torah is stated by Rashi (*Deuteronomy* 11:13), that it should be as new to you as though you first received it today. This is possible only if one has a proper perspective of Torah. It is not unusual for people to nod off during a lecture. This may occur even if the lecturer is an outstanding orator. Attentiveness depends more on the attitude of the student than on the skill of the instructor. If a person was in a precarious situation and someone was giving him instructions on how to save himself, he would certainly remain attentive and listen carefully to every word.

We refer to Torah as "a Torah of life," and if we fully appreciated it as sustaining us in life, we would hardly become complacent. The water we drink today is not noticeably different in taste than the water of yesterday or that of the past years, but if we are very thirsty, it is refreshing and delicious.

Thirst is a sensation that we feel when the body lacks water, and the dehydrated tissues generate a craving for water. "Drink the wisdom of scholars with thirst." The craving for Torah will occur only if one knows how much one is in need of it, and how much one is actually lacking of it. One will never become complacent if one thirsts for Torah.

וֶהֱוֵי שׁוֹתֶה בַצָּמָא אֶת דִּבְרֵיהֶם
And you shall drink in their words with thirst.

If we look closely at the syntax of the mishnah, we will note that it reads, "Drink the words of scholars בַצָּמָא, *with* thirst." The metaphor comparing eagerness to learn with thirst should more accurately have read, כְּצָמֵא, "Drink the words of scholars *as one in* thirst," which would convey the concept of having as intense a desire for knowledge as a thirsty person for water. The expression בַצָּמָא, "*with* thirst," is a bit awkward.

R' Chaim of Volozhin said that there is a reason for this wording. When a thirsty person satisfies his thirst with water, his craving for water disappears. Our desire for knowledge should never be satiated. To the contrary, the more we learn, the more eager we should be to learn yet more. Hence, in contrast to someone with a parched throat, our thirst for knowledge should never be alleviated. Therefore, we should learn *with thirst*, always retaining our craving for wisdom.

אהמר

[ה] **יוֹסֵי** בֶּן יוֹחָנָן אִישׁ יְרוּשָׁלַיִם אוֹמֵר: יְהִי בֵיתְךָ
פָּתוּחַ לָרְוָחָה, וְיִהְיוּ עֲנִיִּים בְּנֵי בֵיתֶךָ, וְאַל
תַּרְבֶּה שִׂיחָה עִם הָאִשָּׁה. בְּאִשְׁתּוֹ אָמְרוּ; קַל וָחֹמֶר

5.

יְהִי בֵיתְךָ פָּתוּחַ לָרְוָחָה
Let your house be open wide

The teaching of Yose ben Yoezer in mishnah 4 might conceivably be misconstrued to mean that one's home should be open *only* to scholars, and that one should not associate with ordinary people. Yose ben Yochanan therefore cautions us to have our homes open to everyone and to welcome unlearned as well as learned people.

The two brothers, the chassidic masters R' Elimelech and R' Zusia, would travel from town to town to encourage people to greater devotion to Torah study and mitzvos. They appeared as itinerant poor people, and no one showed them particular warmth. For lack of better accommodations they often stayed in the local hostel. In one town they were well received by a *melamed* (tutor).

Years later, when their fame as *tzaddikim* had spread, they again came to this town, but this time they came in an impressive horse-drawn carriage. The town's most prominent citizen greeted them and invited them to his spacious home.

R' Zusia politely declined the invitation. "During the years we came as unknown wanderers," he said, "you never welcomed us. *We* have not changed, and the only reason you now invite us is because we came in an impressive carriage. You may therefore take the horses and carriage to your home, and we will again stay with the *melamed,* who accepted us for who we were."

The Torah relates that when the angels came to the Patriarch Abraham they appeared not only in human form, but clad as pagans. Nevertheless, Abraham welcomed them and was hospitable to them. However, when they came to Lot, they appeared as heavenly angels, and this was why Lot welcomed them. As a resident of Sodom, Lot would hardly show hospitality to mere mortals.

The mishnah tells us to keep our homes open to all. While we should indeed show great respect for scholars and learn from them, we should not turn anyone away. Every person should be accorded due dignity.

וְיִהְיוּ עֲנִיִּים בְּנֵי בֵיתֶךָ
Treat the poor as members of your household

The mishnah requires that not only should we be considerate of the poor by helping them, but we should also make them feel comfortable in our homes, as if they were members of our household.

We are often solicited by people who collect money, either for themselves or for charitable institutions. They frequently come to our homes in the evening. It has happened that they are told, "Don't bother me at home. Come to see me at the office tomorrow."

5. **Y**ose ben Yochanan, leader of Jerusalem, says: Let your house be open wide; treat the poor as members of your household; and do not converse excessively with the woman. They said this even about one's own wife; surely it applies to

---

Tzedakah is one of the greatest mitzvos, but proper fulfillment of this mitzvah necessitates more than a monetary gift. It is also necessary to comfort the recipient of alms. His spirit may be crushed by his need to beg, and it is a mitzvah of the highest order to elevate his spirit and give him *tzedakah* with a pleasant attitude. Certainly any remark such as the above is a rebuff and can cause the recipient added distress.

Furthermore, we wish to teach our children the value of the mitzvah of *tzedakah*. They must learn to share and to do so gracefully, else they will be dominated by the innate selfish emotion of greed. If the latter is not overcome, it will result in their being unable to share, which will negatively affect their relationships to others and cause them much unhappiness.

Rather than consider it an imposition, we should appreciate the mitzvah of *tzedakah* and perform it in the manner that will be educational for our children. For example, do not let the solicitor stand in the doorway. Invite him to sit down, and offer him a cup of coffee, or a cold drink in the summer. When he leaves, escort him to the door, and wish him *hatzlachah* (success).

A traveler stopped at the home of R' Naftali Trop and inquired as to whether he could possibly be put up for the night. Since there was not an extra bed available, the Rebbetzin gave him money to take a room at the inn.

When R' Naftali found out about this, he asked, "If this had been a close family member, wouldn't we have somehow accommodated him by making space for him in our home rather than sending him to the inn? This is what we must also do for strangers, because the mishnah says to treat the poor as if they were members of the household. At the very least, he should have been given the option of staying here or going to the inn."

Our *tzaddikim* heeded the words of the mishnah meticulously.

There is no mitzvah that approaches that of *tzedakah*. If we value the opportunity to perform this wonderful mitzvah, our children are apt to do likewise.

וְאַל תַּרְבֶּה שִׂיחָה עִם הָאִשָּׁה
**And do not converse
excessively with the woman.**

This mishnah is sometimes misinterpreted as discouraging communication between husband and wife.

The mishnah discourages *excessive*, i.e., unnecessary, conversation. In mishnah 17 Rabban Shimon ben Gamliel says that he found "nothing better for the body than silence." Clearly R' Shimon does not advocate being mute. Rather, he means to curtail unnecessary talk, and there are no exceptions to this rule.

בְּאֵשֶׁת חֲבֵרוֹ. מִכַּאן אָמְרוּ חֲכָמִים: כָּל הַמַּרְבֶּה שִׂיחָה עִם הָאִשָּׁה — גּוֹרֵם רָעָה לְעַצְמוֹ, וּבוֹטֵל מִדִּבְרֵי תוֹרָה, וְסוֹפוֹ יוֹרֵשׁ גֵּיהִנֹּם.

[ו] **יְהוֹשֻׁעַ** בֶּן פְּרַחְיָה וְנִתַּאי הָאַרְבֵּלִי קִבְּלוּ מֵהֶם.

What constitutes "excessive" talk? Let us look at this statement in the context of the mishnah, which begins with "treat the poor as members of your household," and this is immediately followed by "do not converse excessively with the woman."

Many women prefer to prepare a proper meal for guests, and may be uncomfortable when someone drops in unexpectedly and all they have to serve is leftovers. The mitzvah of *hachnassas orchim*, as demonstrated by the Patriarch Abraham, necessitates that we provide wayfarers with food. For example, if you met a stranger in *shul* and called home saying, "I'm bringing someone home for breakfast," your wife may hurry to put together a proper breakfast, perhaps even jumping in the car to buy lox and cream cheese. This places an unnecessary burden on her, and you may then be hesitant to make this offer. *Hachnassas orchim* does not require lavish meals. It is perfectly adequate if the guest shares with the family whatever there is in the refrigerator and cupboard.

If you met your son and daughter and asked them to stop in for a snack you would hardly call your wife to prepare a lavish meal. "Treat the poor as you would treat the members of your household, and do not converse excessively with the wife." Make *hachnassas orchim* an easy task. Make sure that by notifying your wife that you are bringing a stranger home, you are not causing her to exert herself to prepare for him, because that might discourage you from fulfilling the mitzvah of *hachnassas orchim*.

A second type of "excessive" talk is *lashon hara*. There is a common misconception that telling one's wife something negative about another person is permissible and does not fall into the category of *lashon hara*. This is incorrect.

One evening, R' Shlomo Zalman Auerbach was at home with his wife and sister. His sister inquired about a student in the yeshivah who had been suggested as a *shidduch* (marriage match) for her daughter. "Yes," the rabbi said. "He is a fine young man."

His sister then said that she planned to visit another sibling. When his sister emerged from her sibling's house, she found R' Shlomo Zalman waiting for her. "I came to tell you that the young man about whom you inquired is indeed very fine, but he is not appropriate for your daughter."

"Then why didn't you tell me that before?" the sister asked.

"I couldn't," R' Shlomo Zalman answered, "because my wife was in the

another's wife. Consequently, the Sages said: Anyone who converses excessively with a woman causes evil to himself, neglects Torah study, and will eventually inherit Gehinnom.

6. **Y**ehoshua ben Perachyah and Nittai of Arbel received the tradition from them.

---

room. I am obligated to tell you, because it affects your decision about a *shidduch.* Inasmuch as it does not have a practical application for my wife, her listening to a negative comment about the young man would be *lashon hara.* " This is the kind of talk that the mishnah is restricting.

A person should weigh his words carefully when speaking to others. The mishnah tells us that he should do so, *especially* when speaking with his wife. When speaking to other people, one is more likely to think about what he is about to say, whereas his guard is lowered when speaking to his own wife. Giving some thought to what he is about to say to his wife goes a long way in avoiding abusive language, and in telling her things that might cause her needless worry. There is no reason to tell her something that may be distressing if it serves no purpose.

For example, a man arrives at an important meeting, opens his attaché case for the necessary documents, and discovers to his horror that they are not there! He distinctly remembers preparing them to take along, but he obviously left them on his desk. His wife is not at home to be able to fax them, and it would be pretty difficult to fax almost 200 pages anyway. He apologizes to the other participants at the meeting, and does his best from memory, promising to send them the detailed documents when he returns home. He castigates himself for his negligence in not checking that the papers were in the attaché case before he left.

That evening he calls home. Should he tell his wife that he forgot the papers? She will obviously feel badly about this, but will it do any good? If he thinks that by sharing this with his wife he will feel better, then there may be reason to do so, because spouses should be supportive of each other. If it will not make him feel any better, there is no logic in causing her unnecessary distress.

Or suppose that a friend suffered a misfortune. If the wife's knowing about this may be constructive in any way, as for example, the friend is sitting *shivah* and she can make a condolence call, then there is a purpose in telling her. However, if her knowing about it cannot lead to anything constructive, one should think twice before telling his wife.

These are some examples of "excessive" talk which the mishnah discourages.

יְהוֹשֻׁעַ בֶּן פְּרַחְיָה אוֹמֵר: עֲשֵׂה לְךָ רַב, וּקְנֵה לְךָ חָבֵר,
וֶהֱוֵי דָן אֶת כָּל הָאָדָם לְכַף זְכוּת.

6.

עֲשֵׂה לְךָ רַב
Make a teacher for yourself

I once attended a meeting of recovering alcoholics, and the individual who addressed the gathering was 26 years sober. He said, "Last year my sponsor (mentor in recovery) died, and I was having great difficulty finding someone to be my sponsor. You see, around here there is no one sober longer than I am.

"I mentioned this to a friend who asked, 'Why does your sponsor have to be sober longer than you? All you need is someone who understands alcoholism and the recovery process, and can give you objective feedback.'

"I realized this person was right, and that my search for someone sober longer than me was nothing but an ego trip. I was not going to accept guidance from anyone whom I could not view as being superior to me. I now have a sponsor who is sober only 10 years, whereas I have 26 years."

I had to marvel at this person's sagacity. In the medical profession, I have come across some doctors who bristle at the request to call in a consultant, and who then insist that the consultant must be someone of prominence, such as the chief of the department at the university. To accept consultation from anyone of lesser stature is demeaning to them.

I was in the first few months of my psychiatric training when I received a call from a close acquaintance in New York. Her brother, whom I knew quite well, was suffering from a severe depression. What kind of treatment could I recommend? I told her that as a beginner I was not in a position to make any recommendations. I suggested she consult a psychiatrist in New York. She asked if I knew anyone whom I might refer. I did not know any New York psychiatrists, but on my desk was the text which we were studying written by Dr. Kalinowski of New York, and I suggested she try to get an appointment with him.

About a week later I received a call from Dr. Kalinowski. Inasmuch as the antidepressant medication had not been effective and the depression was severe, he believed that several electroshock treatments would help, and he wanted to know what I thought of this.

"Dr. Kalinowski," I said, "you may have the wrong impression. I am not a psychiatrist, but only in my first year of training. The only thing I know about treatment of depression is what I am learning from your book."

Dr. Kalinowski responded, "Yes, I know treatment, but you have a better knowledge of this man's personality."

"Well, in that case," I said, "although we know that electroshock does not impair the mind, this man has always sought ways of shirking responsibility. I am concerned that he might say, 'You can't expect anything of me. They have tampered with my brain.' "

Yehoshua ben Perachyah says: Make a teacher for your-self; acquire a friend for yourself; and judge everyone fa-vorably.

Dr. Kalinowski said, "Yes, yes. You are right. We will not be able to use electroshock in this case."

I went to my supervisor's office and said, "Guess who called me for a consul-tation!" After I told him the story he smiled and said, "The only one who would feel secure enough to ask the opinion of a first-year resident is the man who wrote the book. He is not worried that this would be a reflection on his competence."

My alcoholic friend was right. The attitude of taking advice only from some-one of promnence and with outstanding credentials is nothing but an ego trip. It is a defensive posture which is undoubtedly the result of nagging feelings of inadequacy. A person with a healthy ego will have no difficulty accepting coun-sel from anyone.

When the chassidic master, R' Bunim of P'shische died, there was a question as to which one of his disciples would assume the leadership. Ultimately the choice was narrowed to two: R' Mendel of Kotzk, and R' Yitzchak Meir of Gur. The two had been bosom friends for years.

The two friends went into the forest where they could hold counsel privately. However, someone eavesdropped and overheard part of the conversation, where one of them said, "Look, it must be either you to me or I to you." Although the two had been peers and had related to each other as equals, they understood that the disciples of Rabbi Bunim needed a leader, and that a division of leadership would splinter the group. Preservation of unity required that one of the two assume the leadership.

When they emerged from the forest, R' Mendel led the way, and R' Yitzchak Meir walked humbly four steps behind. He had accepted R' Mendel as the leader, and the relationship was no longer one of two equals, but one of master to disciple. This, in spite of the fact that R' Yitzchak Meir's scholarship was known to be unparalleled. For the remainder of his life, R' Yitzchak Meir totally effaced himself before someone who had been his equal, and whom he may even have surpassed in some ways.

R' Yitzchak Meir understood and implemented the teaching of this mishnah, not only to accept someone as your teacher, but to *make* someone your teacher.

The expression "make a teacher for yourself" is a bit unusual. One can find a teacher, or acquire a teacher, but how does one "make" someone into a teacher?

The fact is that one can indeed make a teacher. Students who are eager to learn and who pressure the teacher for more knowledge will cause the teacher to learn more and prepare his lectures on a higher level.

Something similar to this can be found in the Talmud which states that each generation receives the leaders it deserves (*Sanhedrin* 38b). This is supported by the Talmudic comment of God telling Moses to "descend from the mountain" when the Israelites worshipped the golden calf (*Exodus* 36:7). The Talmud interprets the Divine words to mean, "Descend from your lofty status. Your greatness was contingent upon the virtue of the Israelites. Now that they have sinned, you have lost your greatness" (*Berachos* 32a).

According to this, the stature of the teacher is dependent on that of the student, who therefore has the capacity to "make" the teacher into a great teacher or otherwise. The mishnah is thus essentially saying, "Behave in such a manner that you *make* your teacher into a great person." The mishnah says to *acquire* a friend, but tells us to *make* a teacher.

As important as it is to have a mentor and to even make someone into one's teacher, it is also important not to lose one's sense of self, and to realize that we must exercise our own capacity for judgment as well. This is a very sensitive point and must be carefully understood, because the possibility of error is considerable.

Ultimately, a person is responsible for his own judgments. In matters of *halachah,* we must defer to the acknowledged authority. We must also set our own opinion aside even in nonhalachic issues if we are specifically instructed to do so by a competent Torah authority. However, we must be careful that we maintain a reasonable attitude of self-reliance.

Perhaps it is an extreme example, but I know of a case of a man who always consulted his Rebbe as to which name to give a newborn child. One time he came to the Rebbe and handed him a *kvittel* (petition) where he listed all his children by name, except for his youngest daughter, who was four months old.

"What is your daughter's name?" the Rebbe asked.

"I have not yet named her," the man replied. "When she was born, I sent a message to the Rebbe asking what name to give her, and since I have not received a reply, I have not named her yet." The Rebbe soundly reprimanded the man for his foolishness.

R' Shimon Shkop was a great Talmudist, who often gave unique interpretations to Talmudical passages. Once, when he requested some paper to write a letter and was given lined paper, he quipped, "Why must I allow someone else to dictate where I should do my writing?"

Responsible behavior requires accepting counsel and deferring to authority, but also not totally surrendering one's own judgment capacities.

וּקְנֵה לְךָ חָבֵר
*Acquire a friend
for yourself*

The literal translation of the mishnah is "*buy* yourself a friend." Since the intent is certainly not to buy friendship with money, what is the medium of payment to purchase friendship?

Rabbi Yosef Yaavetz said, "The price is to adapt yourself to another person's needs, and to be sensitive to his feelings."

When we are rigid in our opinions and refuse to consider the opinions of others, when we look out primarily for our own needs and do not think of the needs of others, we cannot establish a true friendship.

The Hebrew word for friend, *chaver*, comes from the word meaning to connect or to bind together. Two pieces of wood can be glued together only if their surfaces are smooth. If there are protrusions on the surface which prevent a close adhesion, even strong glue cannot bind them together satisfactorily.

To acquire a חָבֵר, *chaver*, we must see that a true חִבּוּר, *chibur*, can take place. If we are self-centered and opinionated, and do not consider the needs of others and respect their opinions, we have "protrusions" and obstacles which make a strong union impossible. Sensitivity to others' needs and tolerance of their opinions can allow a true bond of friendship to form.

It is difficult to think of any guidelines for proper conduct and constructive behavior that could be more important than the words of this mishnah.

As we noted in mishnah 1, we all act as judges and make judgments numerous times each day. A judge cannot come to a just decision if he takes a bribe or has a personal interest in the decision. Similarly, we are often "bribed" by personal interests which can distort our judgment capacity. Certainly if one option is more pleasant or less unpleasant than another, we will favor that option, and we can easily produce abundant reasons supporting that decision. We may make very unwise decisions which we believe are right, because our desire for something causes us to be blind to any negative considerations.

The only way to avoid the pitfall of distorted judgment is to enlist the help of an outside person who is not affected by our own biases. Sometimes this may be a *Rav* or teacher, other times it may be a friend.

The chassidic master R' Elimelech of Lizhensk recommends that we have a trusted friend in whom we can confide, and to whom we can reveal all our thoughts as well as our actions. This is an excellent recommendation that can help us avoid doing things that are detrimental to our own welfare, but to which we may have been blinded by our desires.

וֶהֱוֵי דָן אֶת כָּל הָאָדָם לְכַף זְכוּת
And judge everyone favorably

Judging everyone favorably has advantages over and above facilitating relationships.

The *Baal Shem Tov* interpreted the verse "God is your shadow" (*Psalms*

א/ז [ז] **נִתַּאי** הָאַרְבֵּלִי אוֹמֵר: הַרְחֵק מִשְּׁכֵן רָע, וְאַל תִּתְחַבֵּר לָרָשָׁע, וְאַל תִּתְיָאֵשׁ מִן הַפֻּרְעָנוּת.

121:5) to mean that just as a shadow mimics *every* movement made by the principal, so does God relate to us just as we relate to others. If we are flexible and lenient with other people, then God is lenient to us. If we are stern, rigid, and demanding, then God will act accordingly with us. When we judge other people favorably rather than condemn them, we merit that God will judge us favorably as well.

The latter portion of this mishnah may be related to the earlier portion. If we are guided by our teachers and can confide in our friends, we are more likely to avoid unwarranted criticism of others. The Baal Shem Tov said that the world is but a mirror. Inasmuch as we are unlikely to recognize our own character defects, God allows us to see them in others. When we see faults in others, we should be aware that it is our own reflection that we see, and that these defects are really our own.

One Shabbos the Baal Shem Tov saw a person doing something forbidden. He took this as a sign that he had somehow violated Shabbos himself. Despite a most thorough soul-searching, he could not recall violating the Shabbos. He prayed intensely to be shown where he had done so, and it was revealed to him that he had once stood by silently when someone had said something disrespectful about a Torah scholar. Inasmuch as the *Zohar* states that a Torah scholar has the same *kedushah* (sanctity) as the Shabbos, his failure to defend the honor of the Torah scholar was considered equivalent to a violation of Shabbos. He was therefore given a sign that he had to rectify this defect within himself.

If we fail to identify our own shortcomings, we are likely to see them in others and be critical of them. If we acquire a teacher and friend that can alert us to our own biases and allow us to be more impartial in our judgments, we are far less likely to be condemning of others.

The *Maggid* of Koznitz gives this mishnah a unique interpretation, translating it to read, "And decree all of mankind for a favorable verdict."

The *Maggid* cited the Talmud, which states that a person should think of the entire world as being in an even balance; i.e., having just as many virtuous people as there are sinful people. He should also think of himself as being on an equal balance, having just as many mitzvos as sins. If he does one more mitzvah, he now has a majority of mitzvos and is considered a virtuous person. This, in turn, tips the scales of all mankind because it now makes the number of virtuous people in the entire world a majority over sinners (*Kiddushin* 40b).

7. Nittai *of Arbel says: Distance yourself from a bad neighbor; do not associate with a wicked person; and do not despair of retribution.*

Let no one think that his actions are inconsequential. With just one good deed, says the *Maggid*, you can bring about a favorable decree for all mankind.

7.

הַרְחֵק מִשָּׁכֵן רָע
Distance yourself from a bad neighbor

If we look at the sequence of statements in this mishnah, it seems that the reverse order would have been more appropriate. A person should first be instructed to do simple things, and subsequently go on to more difficult things. The first point should therefore have been, "Do not go out and make friends with bad people," which is much easier to do than to uproot oneself from where one lives if one happens to have bad neighbors. If we take the mishnah literally, relocating one's residence is a major ordeal, as anyone who has moved can testify. Why is the difficult task put first? The answer is that if we are in a corrupt environment, we may so lose our sensitivity to what is good or bad that we may begin associating with the wrong people, *without recognizing that they are a bad influence on us.*

"A bad neighbor" does not necessarily mean the individual living next door, but may mean a corrupt environment. This refers to all varieties of corruption that may surround us. The debauchery that is so prevalent in the electronic and printed media constitute a corrupt environment, and we should avoid exposure to these. Seeing, reading, and hearing indecent things can dull one's sensitivities, and we may find ourselves developing personal relationships with people whose morals and ethics are not quite up to par.

Clinically, I have seen young people who come from fine homes and upright families stray into deplorable lifestyles by associating with a degenerate population. This has become the curse of our times.

I particularly wish to address those families who operate on a double standard, who think that as mature adults they may see or read material that is considered objectionable for children, as long as they monitor their children and do not allow them such experiences. This is a grave mistake. Youngsters will be attracted precisely to whatever interests their parents. It is a well established fact that "Do as I say, not as I do" has the very effect that parents wish to avoid. Children tend to emulate their parents.

Take the words of the mishnah to heart in order to save yourself as well as your children from thoughts, feelings, and behavior that can be self-destructive. Each one of us must make every effort to eradicate the corruption of the environment as best we can.

וְאַל תִּתְחַבֵּר לְרָשָׁע
Do not associate
with a wicked person

As we noted, the word for friendship that is used here is *"chaver"* which means "attachment." There is a mitzvah to help an errant person attain a more spiritual life, and to do so we may befriend people with the goal of helping them to a Torah-observant life. However, there is always the risk that such a relationship may affect one negatively. Frequent exposure to people who are not observant of Torah carries the risk of cooling one's own devotion.

Medical practice may give us a model of proper approach. As health professionals, we try to help people who have a disease, but we take serious precautions not to be infected by diseases which may be contagious. Doctors, dentists, and nurses often wear masks and gloves, because of the risk of contracting a communicable disease. If you wish to influence people who are not observant, that is highly commendable, but you must beware of the reverse influence. Yes, befriend them, but be careful, as the mishnah says, not to "attach" yourself to them. This can be achieved by increasing your own Torah study, greater devotion to performance of mitzvos, intense prayer, and above all by maintaining a close relationship with Torah scholars. In this way you can befriend others and attract them to Torah without being so "attached" to them that you may adopt non-Torah ways.

There is yet another interpretation of this mishnah. We have appliances, such as a vacuum cleaner or a food processor, which have a motor unit and a number of attachments. The unit is the major part of the appliances, and the various attachments are essentially secondary to the motor. They "attach to" the motor, but the motor does not "attach to" them.

What the mishnah is telling us is that if you are in contact with people who do not have a desirable lifestyle, let them "attach to" you, but don't you "attach to" them. Do not lose your identity as the "motor," the major part of the unit.

וְאַל תִּתְיָאֵשׁ מִן הַפֻּרְעָנוּת
And do not despair
of retribution.

The phrase "do not despair of retribution" can be interpreted in two ways. It may mean that we should not be misled by the apparent successes enjoyed by people who we consider undeserving. Or it may mean that if one views himself to be a victim of Divine punishment, he should not lose hope of eventual happiness.

Both interpretations are in keeping with the first part of the mishnah. King David speaks of this in Psalm 92. The simpleton who sees that unscrupulous people prosper does not understand that God is giving the wicked the reward for their few good deeds in this world, and that they will not enjoy any reward in the Eternal World. On the other hand, people who have many mitzvos to their credit, but have a few transgressions, reap the consequences of their sins in this transient world, so that their bliss in the Eternal World will be undisturbed.

The earthly reward for even the slightest mitzvah may be very great. A man once said to R' Levi Yitzchak of Berditchev, "It says in the *Shema* that we will be punished for our sins. But just look at me! I am a sinner, but I have great wealth and a very enjoyable life."

R' Levi Yitzchak responded, "My child, the only way you could make this statement is because you have recited the *Shema*. There is not enough wealth in the entire world to adequately compensate anyone for reciting the *Shema* even a single time."

Although it sometimes tests the strength of one's faith, we should know that the ways of God are ultimately just, even when we are unable to understand why reward or punishment are meted out in certain ways. It is at this time that we must surrender to the infinite wisdom of God.

It is very difficult to find comfort when one is suffering. The Talmud states that whenever R' Yochanan, whose 10 sons had died, encountered someone who had experienced tragedy, he showed them a tiny bone of his youngest child (*Berachos* 5b). R' Yochanan was not saying, "My troubles are worse than yours," because that is a foolish and hollow consolation. What R' Yochanan was saying was that in spite of his severe losses, he did not despair of life and continued with his study and teaching of Torah.

We may not understand why suffering occurs. The Chofetz Chaim referred to the epic of Joseph and his brothers, and pointed out how they were repeatedly bewildered by all that transpired. When Joseph revealed himself to them and said, "I am Joseph," everything suddenly fell into place and was understood. Similarly, the Chofetz Chaim said, when God will reveal Himself to us at the Redemption and say, "I am God," all the heretofore unanswerable questions will be answered at once.

The Chofetz Chaim lived according to his teachings. When his beloved son died, the Chofetz Chaim said, "A human being's love is finite. The love that I previously gave to my son will now be directed to You, God, and I will love You even more."

Several years ago a young child was brought from Israel to undergo open-heart surgery at a hospital in our community. Inasmuch as neither the child nor his parents spoke English, it was arranged among the local people who spoke Hebrew that someone would always be with the child, to make his needs known to the hospital staff and to interpret for them

I happened to be on duty when they took the child to the treatment room for respiratory therapy, to suction the secretions that he could not bring up by coughing. This was a painful procedure, and I had to hold the father's hand while he heard the child crying, *"Abba* (Father)! They are hurting me! Don't let them do this to me!" The father could not restrain himself, and broke into the treatment room, pleading with the child, "Yossi, don't you want to get out of the hospital and come back home? If you have this done, you will be able to come home soon!"

I thought of the repeated sufferings that our people have experienced, and could almost hear God saying, "Don't you want to come home? It is necessary for you to undergo this pain in order for you to return home."

א/ח

[ח] **יְהוּדָה** בֶּן טַבַּאי וְשִׁמְעוֹן בֶּן שָׁטַח קִבְּלוּ מֵהֶם.
יְהוּדָה בֶּן טַבַּאי אוֹמֵר: אַל תַּעַשׂ
עַצְמְךָ כְּעוֹרְכֵי הַדַּיָּנִין; וּכְשֶׁיִּהְיוּ בַּעֲלֵי הַדִּין עוֹמְדִים
לְפָנֶיךָ, יִהְיוּ בְעֵינֶיךָ כִּרְשָׁעִים; וּכְשֶׁנִּפְטָרִים מִלְּפָנֶיךָ,

Of course, the analogy is limited. There was nothing the child's father could
do to hasten the child's return home, whereas God is All-powerful and could
bring us home in a moment without our experiencing any suffering. Why God
allows this to happen is beyond our comprehension, but knowing that God's
love for us surpasses any love that we can possibly imagine should help us
realize that there is a reason why we must undergo these painful ordeals. This
is as true of the individual as of the nation.

The Talmud states that when a person suffers a tragedy he is to recite the
berachah "God is a just judge," and must do so with simchah. Rashi is careful
to explain that in this context simchah does not mean joy, but rather faith and
trust in the Divine judgment (Berachos 60b). It is not considered sinful for a
person to complain to God when he is suffering (Bava Basra 16b), but one
should never despair.

8.

אַל תַּעַשׂ עַצְמְךָ כְּעוֹרְכֵי הַדַּיָּנִין
[When serving as a judge,]
do not act as a lawyer

This mishnah has been variously interpreted,
with all the interpretations concurring that it
means to preserve the integrity of the judicial
system. R' Yaakov Kamenetzky points out the
that authors of this mishnah are R' Shimon ben Shatach and R' Yehudah ben
Tabbai. This is an important observation. The Talmud relates that Yehudah
ben Tabbai condemned to death a witness whose testimony had been proven
false, even though not all of the criteria for a death sentence had been met,
because he wished to refute the position of the Sadducees on the subject of
such witnesses. Shimon ben Shatach minced no words in reprimanding his
friend, whose zeal to discredit the Sadducees led to so tragic an error (Makkos
5b).

No one could have been more unsympathetic to the Sadducees than R'
Shimon ben Shatach, who was a brother-in-law to King Yannai, himself a
Sadducee. In fact, the sole reason R' Shimon was not killed was because he
was under the protection of his sister, the queen. Yet, in spite of his fierce
opposition to the Sadducees, he counseled his friend that one's emotions,
however just, must not be allowed to affect the judicial process.

R' Shimon knew only too well the need to protect the authority and integrity
of the court. As a result of his campaign against witchcraft, there was a conspir-

8. Yehudah ben Tabbai and Shimon ben Shatach received the tradition from them.

Yehudah ben Tabbai says: [When serving as a judge,] do not act as a lawyer; while the litigants stand before you, consider them both as guilty; but when they are dismissed from

---

acy against his son, and a foolproof case was trumped up to condemn his son to death. As the son was being led to his execution, he said, "If I am guilty of this crime, then let my death not absolve me from the sin." The witnesses then recanted their testimony, but it was too late, and the verdict was carried out (*Rashi, Sanhedrin* 44b s.v. דבעיא).

R' Shimon could undoubtedly have intervened to save his son, but the grieving father made the ultimate sacrifice to preserve the authority of the court.

וּכְשֶׁיִּהְיוּ בַּעֲלֵי הַדִּין עוֹמְדִים לְפָנֶיךָ,
יִהְיוּ בְעֵינֶיךָ כִּרְשָׁעִים

While the litigants stand before you, consider them both as guilty

We may postulate it, and the law of the United States certainly dictates that every person should be considered innocent until proven guilty. Why does the mishnah seem to take the opposite point of view, considering both litigants to be guilty until proven otherwise?

What the mishnah is really saying is not to think of anyone as *guilty*, but rather to assume that both litigants are "wrong." There is a sound psychological basis for this.

We should not suspect a person to be willfully and maliciously lying. However, someone who has a personal interest at stake, such as a litigant in a trial, is likely to have a distorted perception. He may actually "know" the facts of the case to be what he would like them to be; i.e., in his favor. There is abundant clinical evidence of people believing something to be true and being ready to defend this position to their very death.

Let me share an interesting experiment with you. The purpose of the experiment was to see whether a person could actually testify under oath that something is true, even if it is known to be false.

In the 1950s a prominent psychiatrist hypnotized a perfectly normal, healthy young man, and told him that there was a communist conspiracy to infiltrate the major networks and to spread communist ideology to the American people.

After emerging from the trance, this young man alerted NBC about this danger. The spokesperson for NBC (who was privy to the experiment) told him that he could not give serious consideration to this accusation unless the man was able to provide evidence to support his allegation. The man eventually told about meetings he had attended, and gave dates, places, and names of people

יִהְיוּ בְעֵינֶיךָ כְּזַכָּאִין, כְּשֶׁקִבְּלוּ עֲלֵיהֶם אֶת הַדִּין.

[ט] **שִׁמְעוֹן** בֶּן שָׁטַח אוֹמֵר: הֱוֵי מַרְבֶּה לַחֲקוֹר אֶת הָעֵדִים; וֶהֱוֵי זָהִיר בִּדְבָרֶיךָ, שֶׁמָּא מִתּוֹכָם יִלְמְדוּ לְשַׁקֵּר.

---

who were at the meeting. When pressed, he gave descriptions of the people who attended. Whenever his testimony was challenged, he became very defensive, and gave further proof about the allegations. After the hypnotic suggestion was removed, he was unable to recall any of the names or places he had mentioned. The entire conversation had been filmed, and when he saw himself testifying about the details of the people at the meetings, he was totally bewildered. The names and places he had cited were completely unknown to him.

This demonstrates that if a person has an idea which he believes to be true, he can manufacture evidence to support it, and will be adamant in insisting on its veracity.

Let us take a simple example. Shimon asked Reuven for a loan of $1000, which Reuven agreed to give him, but never got around to it. However, Reuven is under the impression that he actually did lend him money, and Shimon denies receiving it. It is perfectly possible for Reuven to argue and present all kinds of evidence for his case, in the belief that he is telling the truth. Even though Reuven would never knowingly swear falsely, he may have no problem in taking a solemn oath, because he believes in the truth of his position.

Because of the possibility that a litigant may be distorting facts and believe his distortions to be true, the mishnah advises judges to utilize a high index of suspicion, and to work on the assumption that both litigants may be "wrong." In this way, the judges will do their utmost to ferret out the truth.

וּכְשֶׁנִּפְטָרִים מִלְּפָנֶיךָ, יִהְיוּ בְעֵינֶיךָ כְּזַכָּאִין
But when they are dismissed from you, consider them both as innocent

Once a verdict has been delivered and the litigants have accepted it, you should think of them both as being fine, upright people.

This is an important concept. It is possible that the party who was the loser may have been exposed as dishonest, in that he had tried to enrich himself unjustly at the expense of his adversary. The mishnah tells us not to think this way, but rather to give the person the benefit of the doubt. As was pointed out earlier, he may have thought he was telling the truth, or may have had other rationalizations whereby he justified his position.

The Talmud states that if a man enters into a marriage contract, stipulating with the woman that the marriage should be binding "provided that I am a *tzaddik*," then even if he is a complete *rasha* (wicked person), the marriage

you, consider them both as innocent, provided they have accepted the judgment.

9. **S**himon ben Shatach says: Interrogate the witnesses extensively; yet be cautious with your words, lest they learn from them to lie.

---

must be considered binding, because he may have had a thought of *teshuvah* (*Kiddushin* 49b). In other words, a brief moment of sincere remorse can convert the person who was an absolute degenerate into a *tzaddik!*

In the case of the *din Torah*, a person may be so blinded by his desire for money that he actually believes that his contentions are true. Once the verdict is delivered, he no longer stands to gain from his rationalizations. He may recognize the truth and actually be remorseful for his having wrongly pressed for money or denied a legitimate claim.

The importance of this concept is that it extends far beyond the courtroom. We should always be ready to give another person the benefit of the doubt. Let us just reflect how many times we may have been in a similar position, and later regretted our behavior. Just as we would wish others to judge us favorably and consider that we have done *teshuvah*, we should accord this courtesy to them as well.

9.

וֶהֱוֵי זָהִיר בִּדְבָרֶיךָ,
שֶׁמָּא מִתּוֹכָם יִלְמְדוּ לְשַׁקֵּר
Yet be cautious with your words,
lest they learn from them to lie.

The regulations for a *din Torah* (rabbinic trial) provided by halachah are far beyond what secular law considers to be adequate. The symbol for justice is often a blindfolded person holding a balance scale. The intended message is that the person administering justice is "blind"; i.e., unaffected by anything but the facts of the case.

Unfortunately, this often is not the case. Halachah is much more stringent. For example, both litigants must dress similarly. If one of the litigants is wealthy and the other is poor, the wealthy person is told, "You must come to court dressed in tattered clothes like your adversary, or you must buy him a suit similar to yours." Not even the slightest hint of favoritism may be shown, even in the most subtle way. Indeed, inasmuch as the judge at a *din Torah* may be wearing a *tallis*, there were those who draped the *tallis* over their eyes, so that any inadvertent facial expression should not be seen by either of the litigants and be interpreted as being favorable or unfavorable to the position he is advocating. Halachah does not permit the tactics and dramatic maneuvers that are standard fare in the American courtroom as a means to manipulate the sympathies of the judge and jury.

[יז] **שְׁמַעְיָה** וְאַבְטַלְיוֹן קִבְּלוּ מֵהֶם. שְׁמַעְיָה אוֹמֵר: אֱהַב אֶת הַמְּלָאכָה, וּשְׂנָא אֶת הָרַבָּנוּת, וְאַל תִּתְוַדַּע לָרָשׁוּת.

This mishnah cautions the judge to weigh his words most carefully, because a remark may be misinterpreted by witnesses. They may then adjust their testimony to what they think will be effective, rather than simply supplying the factual information. Even an inflection of the voice may betray the judge's feeling, and both the witnesses and the litigants may be improperly influenced.

Little wonder that the Torah says that a judge should imagine that there is a sword suspended over him, so great is the responsibility of dispensing justice. The proper administration of justice is so great a virtue that it may merit the hastening of the ultimate Redemption.

The latter part of this mishnah is a lesson in parenting as well as an admonition to judges. Be cautious about how you speak, because others may learn from you how to lie.

Parents certainly wish to teach their children to be truthful. It may happen that a child answers the phone, and because the father does not wish to speak to the caller, he may instruct the child, "Tell him I'm not home yet." The father may not realize that he is setting a pattern for the child to lie when it is expedient to do so. A child should be taught to say, "I'm sorry, but my father is not available now." Indeed, it should be pointed out to him that this is to avoid the lie that father is not home at the time.

Children are not too likely to heed everything parents tell them to do, but they are far more likely to emulate what the parent does. If parents are careful not to tell even "white lies," the children are more likely to be truthful.

10.

אֱהַב אֶת הַמְּלָאכָה, וּשְׂנָא אֶת הָרַבָּנוּת
Love work; despise positions of power

Although this mishnah may also have been primarily intended for judges, it has a broader application.

One of the defense mechanisms which people with feelings of low self-esteem employ is to try and control others. Exercising authority over others seems to soothe their feelings of inadequacy and inferiority.

There is certainly a need for authority, but when it is used as a method to gratify one's needs for mastery, it is fraught with danger for both the one controlling and those who are being controlled. A benign ruler looks out for the

10. Shemayah and Avtalyon received the tradition from them.

Shemayah says: Love work; despise positions of power; and do not become overly familiar with the government.

---

interests of his subjects, whereas a power-crazed despot may crush his subjects in order to feed his pathological ego needs. This is equally true of anyone who is in or places himself in a position of authority, whether parent over child, one spouse over another, doctor over patient, etc. Exercise of authority can be benign or malignant.

The work done by people in positions of authority should indeed bring them gratification, but this should be the satisfaction that one has tried to do the best one can, as for example, the doctor who tries to help the patient. The work itself should be enjoyed, but the gratification should not come from exercising one's superiority.

This is consistent with the latter part of the mishnah. Those people who have a drive for power may seek to ally themselves with the government, so that they can have control over others. The ideal public official is a public servant, eager to do the best for his constituents. The Talmud states that when Rabban Gamliel wished to appoint two scholars to governmental posts, he said, "Do not think I am giving you positions of mastery. Rather, it is servitude that I am giving you" (*Horayos* 10a).

People who are ego driven may think they will find salvation in a position of power. The Talmud's wise words should be taken to heart: "Woe unto (a position of authority) because it buries its holders" (*Pesachim* 87b).

There are countless references in the Talmud that elevate the status of the worker. "Work brings honor to its master" (*Nedarim* 49b). The penalty for the theft and sale of an ox is greater than that of the theft of a sheep because the ox is a beast of burden, hence its theft is considered a greater crime (*Bava Kamma* 79b). "The merit of honest work surpasses even that of ancestral good deeds" (*Tanchuma Vayeitzei*). "A person without a trade is comparable to a vineyard which is without a fence or a pit without a guardrail" (*Tosefta Kiddushin* 1). The Talmud is particularly harsh on a person who shuns work because he considers it beneath his dignity. "It is better for a person to skin hides in the marketplace to earn a living than to say, 'Such things are unbecoming for me'" (*Pesachim* 113a).

It is not uncommon for people to think that there is dignity in holding public office, but not in being a laborer. The mishnah rejects such values. We should be much happier earning a livelihood by the work of our hands than by assuming what people may consider to be a position of prominence.

[יא] **אַבְטַלְיוֹן** אוֹמֵר: חֲכָמִים, הִזָּהֲרוּ בְדִבְרֵיכֶם, שֶׁמָּא תָחוּבוּ חוֹבַת גָּלוּת וְתִגְלוּ לִמְקוֹם מַיִם הָרָעִים, וְיִשְׁתּוּ הַתַּלְמִידִים הַבָּאִים אַחֲרֵיכֶם וְיָמוּתוּ, וְנִמְצָא שֵׁם שָׁמַיִם מִתְחַלֵּל.

The gravity of the responsibility of a person in authority can be grasped from the following story.

The son-in-law of the Chofetz Chaim was despondent when was not selected for a rabbinical position for which he vied. The Chofetz Chaim told this story to his son-in-law after eliciting a promise not to reveal it during his lifetime.

"In my younger days I did serve as a community rabbi, and a local butcher was found to be selling nonkosher meat. He was promptly put under a ban, and he came before me, full of remorse and promising never to allow this to happen again. He expressed his willingness to accept the most stringent supervision. Inasmuch as he had a large family to support and his remorse appeared genuine, I allowed him to return to his business, and provided a responsible supervisor for him. Because of the gravity of his misdeed, I imposed a fine to be used for the upkeep of the synagogue.

"Sometime later the butcher died, and shortly thereafter, I had a dream that three saintly looking men were addressing me. 'R' Yisrael Meir,' they said, 'when you imposed that fine on the butcher, did you intend it as a penalty to deter him from repeating his sin, or was your intention that it be a penance and atonement for his sin?' After a bit of reflection, I responded that I had intended the fine to be a penalty rather than an atonement.

"Not too long thereafter I had a second dream, and this time it was the butcher who complained to me, 'Rabbi, what have you done to me? Because you responded to the heavenly tribunal that the fine was not intended as atonement, I have been condemned to go through purgatory to cleanse myself from my sin. If only you had intended this as an atonement, I would have been spared the suffering!' "

The Chofetz Chaim then said to his son-in-law, "Once I realized the overwhelming responsibility that a community rabbi carries, that his very intention may have such an enormous impact on a person's *neshamah*, I decided that I would never again serve in that capacity. Do not fret about not having received the position you applied for."

All this notwithstanding, we do have a need for authoritative and responsible leaders. Indeed, our history of Torah scholars and leaders is a very proud one. Just several decades ago, R' Zvi Pesach Frank of Jerusalem was a living example of a Torah authority who was a true servant of the people, and never allowed his lofty position to give him a feeling of superiority. Whenever anyone came in with a question, seeking his advice or a halachic decision, he promptly attended to the person, even leaving the dining-room table or family celebra-

11. **A**vtalyon *says: Scholars, be cautious with your words, for you may incur the penalty of exile and be banished to a place of evil waters [heresy]. The disciples who follow you there may drink and die, and consequently the Name of Heaven may be desecrated.*

---

tions. When someone of the family suggested that he tell the person to come back at a later time, R' Frank would say, "Wearing out shoe leather is also an expense. I have no right to inflict an unnecessary expense on someone who wants my help."

R' Frank would respond at the very first opportunity to letters he received asking his advice. There is correspondence from him that is dated on Purim, on Erev Yom Kippur, and even on Tishah B'Av.

As he grew older, his family members asked him to reserve several hours in the afternoon for rest, but he was adamant in insisting that anyone who came to consult him be given prompt admission.

R' Frank was a shining example of authority with self-effacement.

11.

חֲכָמִים, הִזָּהֲרוּ בְדִבְרֵיכֶם
Scholars, be cautious with your words

A number of commentaries believe that this refers to the tragic consequences of the words of Antigonos (mishnah 3). It would seem obvious that Antigonos was not denying the principle of reward and punishment. He was simply pointing out that these should not be the prime motivations for proper behavior. Yet, two of his students distorted his words as meaning that there was neither reward nor punishment, hence there is no reason to deny oneself any pleasures of life.

One must be cautious not to allow humility to result in a sense of diminished responsibility. A person who is a respected authority or a Torah scholar should be aware that his words may be taken very seriously by others, and a remark which would be ignored if said by a person of lesser stature may have grave consequences because it will be given far greater credence if said by a prominent person. Poorly chosen words, when spoken by a person who is highly respected, may result in a *chilul Hashem.*

The Talmud emphasizes the importance of avoiding vulgar language, and advises use of euphemisms (*Pesachim* 3a). Yet, the Talmud states, "A Torah scholar who lacks *daas* (wisdom) is worse than an offensive carcass" (*Vayikra Rabbah* 1:15). Why the use of such a harsh expression, when something softer could have been said? It appears that the sages were unable to restrain their disapproval of a Torah scholar who spoke unwisely, because of the grave consequences of poorly chosen words.

The mishnah states that caution in speech is particularly important "because you may go into exile." When a person is nearby, one can ask him to explain his words, and the danger is not as great. However, if he is unavailable to explain himself, his distortions may have far-reaching consequences. This is particularly true in today's world of instant and mass communications. An unwise remark may be picked up by the airwaves or printed in the media and disseminated to the four corners of the earth. An explanatory retraction is of relatively little help, since it is customary for the media to exploit sensationalism. Consequently, they may give an inflammatory comment prominent exposure on the front page, whereas an explanation giving the accurate facts may not appear until several days later, in small print and in an obscure location.

By the same token, it is the responsibility of people to be aware that there is a tendency of warmongers to create turbulence and distort the words of authorities. We should therefore not jump to conclusions, and make every effort to understand precisely what was said. Remarks taken out of context have scant validity.

Everyone shares in the responsibility of avoiding *chilul Hashem*.

R' Reuven Katz provides an important interpretation to this mishnah.

The Talmud states that when R' Yochanan ben Zakkai was near death, his disciples observed him weeping, and they could not understand why so saintly a person who led an exemplary life appeared to be afraid of death. R' Yochanan explained, "There are two possible paths, and I do not know on which one I will be led" (*Berachos* 28b).

R' Katz explains that the great sage was not in the least worried whether he would be taken to *Gan Eden* or to *Gehinnom*. Rather, he was concerned which path his *disciples* would take.

R' Yochanan lived in a time of great political turbulence and danger. There was an element in Israel which was waging rebellion against the Roman Empire, and as long as R' Yochanan was alive, he was able to exert leadership and a degree of control. However, after he died, he was helpless to influence how his disciples would interpret his wishes and instructions. It was perfectly possible that his words could be given two diametrically opposite interpretations, thus sharpening the divisions in Israel. This is why the sage wept, saying, "I don't know on which path *my disciples* will lead me; i.e., how they will interpret my words after I am gone."

R' Katz's explanation of this mishnah is so timely. When great leaders die, there may be fierce differences of opinion as to what their wishes and positions were. This is why the mishnah exhorts scholars and leaders to be as precise as possible in their teachings, to leave little room for misinterpretation.

12.

With the appearance of Hillel and Shammai on the historical scene, a new era in Torah scholarship begins. The Talmud is replete with differences in opinion between the schools of Hillel and Shammai, but notes that the masters themselves disagreed very few times during their entire careers. Many of the differences of opinion between their students were due to their failure to "attend and serve their masters adequately." Note that the problem was not attributed to a deficiency of scholarship, but rather that they did not "attend" the masters adequately. They had a wealth of theoretical knowledge, but relative paucity in understanding how their teachers had applied theory to practice.

In halachah no less than in medicine, "internship" is crucial. All the book learning in the world will not enable a doctor to treat a patient properly, nor will extensive Torah scholarship enable a person to render a halachic decision. One must serve an internship under the tutelage of a halachic authority to observe how Torah principles are applied to real-life situations.

This is particularly relevant today. We are fortunate in having many young people who have studied in yeshivos and who spent several years of post-graduate study in kollel. They may have extensive knowledge of halachic principles, but it is important to realize that this alone does not qualify one to render halachic decisions. We must defer to the halachic authorities who underwent "internship" with their masters, and who acquired the skill of applying halachah to actual day-to-day situations.

Hillel and Shammai are presented to us as two sharply distinct personalities, both in their characters and in their approach to halachah. It is often falsely assumed that these two sages followed the paths of their innate inclinations. It would seem as though they were at the mercy of their inherent traits: Shammai could not be flexible and lenient, and Hillel could not be strict and rigid. This is far from the truth. Our great Torah personalities understood their mission to provide proper guidance for their people. They carefully analyzed the needs of their generation and rose to the challenge of addressing its particular problems.

It is popular to indulge in historical psychology, and some people have ventured to analyze the lives of our great Torah personalities. This is a grave error because there is a tendency to think of them according to our own standards.

The Talmud states, "If the earlier tzaddikim were angels, then by comparison we are humans. If we think of them as humans, then by comparison we are mules" (Shabbos 112b). The difference between ourselves and the tzaddikim of yore is qualitative rather than quantitative, and we must stand in reverence and awe of them and their teachings.

In the short span of time between Hillel and Shammai and their disciples

הִלֵּל אוֹמֵר: הֱוֵי מִתַּלְמִידָיו שֶׁל אַהֲרֹן, אוֹהֵב שָׁלוֹם וְרוֹדֵף שָׁלוֹם, אוֹהֵב אֶת הַבְּרִיּוֹת וּמְקָרְבָן לַתּוֹרָה.

---

there was already a huge gap. The students, albeit great scholars, did not measure up to the greatness of their masters. They consequently disagreed on issues on which the masters had agreed. With the many generations that have elapsed between the Talmudic sages and ourselves, the deep ravine that separates us from them is beyond measurement. It is for this reason that Torah scholars of all ages have stood in virtual awe of their predecessors, and it is for this reason that we dare not apply our logic to override the dictums of our predecessors.

הֱוֵי מִתַּלְמִידָיו שֶׁל אַהֲרֹן
Be among the disciples of Aaron

An accurate translation of this mishnah is *"become* a disciple of Aaron." This means that it is not sufficient to emulate Aaron's behavior as a student might emulate a teacher, but rather to so interject that behavior into one's character that one is transformed and *becomes* like Aaron.

Behavior that is merely emulated is limited in its influence over others. There is an aphorism, "Words that emanate from the heart of one person enter the heart of another" (a paraphrase of *Berachos* 6b). A sincere and genuine emotion is much more effective than the most eloquent lecture.

Aaron's understanding that Torah is the Divine manual for a person's optimum function and achievement of true happiness was absolute, and his love for others was genuine. His desire to bring others closer to Torah was the result of his intense love for them and his sincere desire to enable them to fulfill their mission in life and achieve true happiness. These feelings were communicated automatically and without much didactic teaching.

R' Yisrael of Salant is reported to have said, "The problem is that most people are concerned about their own physical needs and everyone else's spiritual needs." If we wish to bring people closer to Torah, we must have genuine concern for their physical needs as well. It was because Aaron truly observed "Love your neighbor as you do yourself" (*Leviticus* 19:18) that he was able to draw people closer to Torah. If we wish to bring people closer to Torah, we must not only act like Aaron, but *become* like Aaron.

אוֹהֵב אֶת הַבְּרִיּוֹת וּמְקָרְבָן לַתּוֹרָה
Loving people and bringing them closer to the Torah.

I recall as a child, whenever I did something of which my father disapproved, he would shake his head and say, "*Es pahst nisht*" (that isn't becoming of you). In other words, he told me that what I was doing was beneath my dignity, and that I was too good to be behaving that way.

Hillel says: Be among the disciples of Aaron, loving peace and pursuing peace, loving people and bringing them closer to the Torah.

What a wonderful way to deliver the necessary discipline without giving a child the feeling that he is bad! To the contrary, this method of discipline actually elevates rather than depresses a child's self-esteem.

This was the method that Aaron used. By revealing his intense love for a person, that person would think, "How can I do something like this when Aaron thinks so highly of me?" Whereas others who sought to correct peoples' behavior might deliver words of rebuke, Aaron did not have to say anything. Feeling loved by Aaron was sufficient to deter a person from improper behavior.

For this type of love to act as a deterrent, one must be of such stature that one's love bestows a sense of self-esteem, so that improper behavior is seen as being beneath one's dignity. One must therefore *be* like Aaron in order that one's love be edifying.

This is why the principle, "Correct yourself and you can then correct others," is valid. If you wish to have a salutary effect on others, elevate yourself to a spiritual status where your very relationship to others will be corrective.

In the introduction to this volume, we emphasized the importance of being an integral part of the community and sharing in its burdens. As remote as it may seem, every person should feel a sense of responsibility for everything that happens in the community, and not think that his behavior affects no one but himself. This was again stressed in mishnah 6.

Aaron was the High Priest, and one of the *halachos* pertaining to the High Priest is that if someone accidentally killed a person, he was to go into exile to an *ir miklat,* one of the designated cities of refuge, and remain there *until the death of the High Priest,* after which he could return home.

The Talmud asks: In what way is the High Priest involved in this whole affair? The answer is that he should have prayed more fervently that such a mishap should not happen! In other words, the High Priest is considered somewhat at fault for the accidental killing, because his prayer lacked adequate intensity. If he had been truly devoted in his prayers, the calamity of an accidental death would not have occurred.

The mishnah tells us that Aaron's love for his people was so great that he constantly sought that peace should prevail and that there should not be even an inadvertent disruption of peace.

Perhaps we do not bear the awesome responsibility of the High Priest, but neither can we dismiss all responsibility for what happens in the community. Both with our prayers and our good deeds we can increase peace among us.

A aron was a true leader, one who genuinely cared for and loved his people. Parents who truly love their children must sometimes act in the children's interest in a manner that the children may not appreciate. The devoted mother who dearly loves her infant will have him immunized against diseases, even though the painful injection is often followed by 48 hours of fever and discomfort. She inflicts this suffering on the child because of her love for him. A mother who so loves her child that she cannot get herself to put him through the distress of immunization is exposing the child to life-threatening diseases, and this is a misguided love.

Our leaders, like our parents, must look out for our welfare. Those who think they can make Judaism more palatable to their flock by being permissive with Torah observance are like the mother who will seek to please her child by serving meals consisting of taffy apples, popcorn, chocolate, and ice cream. The child may certainly be pleased and eat his meals with gusto, but the mother is causing him great harm by her failure to provide proper nutrition that will make him healthy. The mother who truly loves her child will prepare nutritious meals, and the child will have to learn to eat the vegetables that he may not prefer.

The mishnah tells us that because of Aaron's profound love for his people, he brought them *closer to Torah*. Had he been like the foolish mother, he might have tried to adapt the Torah to better suit his peoples' fancies.

Our leaders today have the option of adapting people to the Torah, or tampering with Torah to accommodate people's whims. It would be well if they followed in the footsteps of Aaron, who truly loved his people. Because he cared for them, he brought them closer to Torah rather than trying to make the Torah acquiesce to their wishes.

P ursuit of peace can be understood in two ways. One may pursue peace in order to reach it, or one may pursue it as one pursues an enemy, in order to drive it further away.

In his last words to the Israelites, Moses warns against thinking that one can live in peace and tranquillity by rejecting the Torah. One might say, "I will have peace if I simply satisfy all my heart's desires" (*Deuteronomy* 29:18). Moses warns that this attitude will result in grave consequences, and that this person will experience the full wrath of God.

R' Chaim Shmulevitz points out that the punishment for sins is inherent in the sin itself, and does not have to be imposed from without. My clinical experience has proven this to be true. What greater surrender to the gratification of one's desires can there be than a drug addict who satisfies his craving for the "high" of narcotics? Eventually addicts admit that their incessant pursuit of a "high" causes them immeasurable suffering. The consequences of drug

13. **H**e was accustomed to say: He who seeks renown
loses his reputation; he who does not increase

---

addiction are grave even if one does not have to resort to crime to support
one's habit, such as when one becomes addicted to prescription tranquilizers or
narcotics.

Gratification by use of a drug is but the most prominent example of trying to
find tranquillity. True peace can be found only in fulfilling the mission for
which one was created, and not in drugs, money, food, or fame. Those who
say, "I will find my own peace by doing as I wish," are destined to be bitterly
disappointed.

It is this spurious peace that we must pursue as one pursues a mortal foe.

The mishnah tells us that Aaron distinguished between the two types of
peace. He loved the constructive peace and harmony which is brought about
by observance of mitzvos. On the other hand, he relentlessly pursued the
spurious tranquillity which some sought to achieve by gratifying all their earthly
desires.

13.

הוּא הָיָה אוֹמֵר
He was accustomed to say

In this mishnah we find an expression that is
repeated many times in *Ethics Of The Fathers*: "He was accustomed to say." In other
words, it was not just that the sage said this once or even several times, but that
he did so with regularity. However, it would be wrong to assume that Hillel
went around repeating himself constantly. Nothing can be less impressive than
hearing the same sermon again and again.

What the Talmud means to tell us is that "*he,*" i.e., the person himself, the
way he lived and the way he behaved, "*was accustomed to say.*" *The way Hillel
related to everyone in everyday life was the message he delivered.* Rather than
teaching by didactics, Hillel taught by example. Anyone who observed Hillel
could learn the principles whereby Hillel conducted his life, and could then try
to emulate him. Hillel himself *was* the message, and in sharp contrast to a repetitious verbal message, the message of setting an example was most effective.

This is how we should understand the phrase הוּא הָיָה אוֹמֵר, "He was accustomed to say." Our sages taught more by deed than by word.

נְגִיד שְׁמָא אֲבַד שְׁמֵהּ
He who seeks renown
loses his reputation

R' Yaakov Kamenetzky said that if we analyze a
historical incident related by the Talmud (*Pesachim* 66a), this mishnah can be understood as the
logical conclusion of the previous mishnah.

When Hillel returned from Babylon to Eretz Yisrael, the family of Beseira
were the leaders of Jewry. That year, Erev Pesach occurred on Shabbos, and

it was not known whether it was permissible to bring the paschal offering on Shabbos. Hillel pointed out, on the basis of an analysis of Scripture, that it is permissible and indeed obligatory to do so. The Beseiras, recognizing Hillel's superiority, promptly abdicated their position and appointed Hillel as the official leader of the community.

Hillel then sharply reprimanded the Beseira family. "Had you been diligent in studying under the masters, Shemayah and Avtalyon, you would not have been ignorant of this halachah." Shortly after this, Hillel himself overlooked a halachah.

"How is it that the humble, soft-spoken Hillel suddenly delivers such a stinging rebuke to the people who had just suffered the humiliation of losing their status of leadership?" asked R' Kamenetzky. He offers an ingenious explanation.

The difference between Moses and Aaron was not one of innate character traits. Rather, because Moses was the official ruler and leader, he had to exercise the authority of his position, and at various times did so with an iron hand, as in suppressing the rebellion of Korach. Moses could not afford to be the peacemaker, flexible and lenient to all, because this would have resulted in anarchy. Aaron, on the other hand, was at liberty to be kind to all and quick to forgive, setting an example for others to follow in pursuit of peace and harmony.

Once Hillel was appointed to the official leadership, although his character traits remained unchanged, his responsibilities and obligations underwent a radical change. He was therefore duty bound to chastise the family of Beseira for their negligence. He soon, however, felt the distress of being in the position of leadership, where the many pressures can cause an oversight even by the greatest scholar, just as it had happened to him.

These two mishnahs of Hillel can now be understood as a consequence of this incident. Hillel, the scholar and layman, taught that the ideal attitude is that of Aaron, to pursue peace with love and care for all. But when he was thrust into the position of leadership and he felt his new responsibilities and their price, he pointed out the dangers of being in a position of prominence, that it may be self-defeating. Paradoxically, increased fame may even lead to loss of fame, as one is unable to maintain one's level of learning.

Failure to learn diligently, as happened to the family of Beseira, may result in grievous errors. Failure to progress in one's learning, says Hillel, can lead to forgetting what one already knows, as happened to him soon after he assumed the leadership. Finally, Hillel summed it up in a dire warning, that if one exploits his position of leadership for personal glory, one will be utterly destroyed.

ﻉﻍﻉﻰ

Our great Torah personalities, whose positions of leadership required that they be accorded due honor, were often greatly distressed by the acclaim they received.

R' Menachem Mendel of Lubavitch (Tzemach Tzedek) took his young son, Shmuel, along on a trip to visit several communities where his *chassidim* resided. The young boy, who was impressed and thrilled by the throngs of people that came to greet his father and the enormous respect they showed him, wrote home about this. When the Tzemach Tzedek came home and found the letter, he said to his son, "My blood was being spilled like water and you were thrilled by this?"

One of the *tzaddikim* used a parable to explain the distress at being honored. A king who wished to have firsthand observation of the lifestyles of his subjects decided to tour the country incognito. He donned the uniform of an ordinary foot soldier, and with an officer as his guide went among the populace. The people stood up before the officer and greeted him respectfully, totally ignoring the foot soldier who accompanied him. The officer was greatly distressed by this. "If only they knew the true identity of this 'foot soldier,' and realized they were in the presence of the king, they would not pay any attention to me."

God is present everywhere, but too often we are unaware of His presence. When we show due respect to a *tzaddik*, who is always aware of God's presence, this causes him much distress. "If only people knew they were in *God's* presence, they would not pay attention to me."

As distressing as it was to receive honor, there were considerations that overrode this distress.

On the return from a convention attended by the outstanding Torah personalities of the time, throngs of people gathered at each train station to greet their leaders, who came out on the train platform. The Chofetz Chaim, however, refused to join them.

R' Meir Shapiro of Lublin approached the Chofetz Chaim. "Why are you not out there to greet the people who wish to see you?" he asked.

"Why should they wish to see me?" the Chofetz Chaim asked. "Do I look any different than other people? The only reason they wish to see me is because they have the misconception that I am a *tzaddik,* and I do not wish to reinforce that misconception. That would be sheer vanity."

"And so if it is vanity," R' Shapiro said, "what is wrong with that?"

The Chofetz Chaim reacted with surprise. "What is wrong with it? Why, vanity is a grievous sin," he said.

"And so if it is a sin," R' Shapiro continued, "why are you so afraid of a sin?"

"Because for sins we will be punished in *Gehinnom,*" the Chofetz Chaim said.

"And are you not willing to accept some punishment if greeting your fellow Jews will give them some pleasure?" R' Meir said.

The Chofetz Chaim was electrified. Thereafter, whenever the train was about to pull into a station, he was the first one on the platform. Being able to provide pleasure to his people superseded all other considerations.

יָסֵף, וּדְלָא יַלִּיף קְטָלָא חַיָּב, וּדְאִשְׁתַּמַּשׁ בְּתָגָא חֲלָף. א/יד

[יד] **הוּא** הָיָה אוֹמֵר: אִם אֵין אֲנִי לִי, מִי לִי? וּכְשֶׁאֲנִי לְעַצְמִי, מָה אֲנִי? וְאִם לֹא עַכְשָׁו, אֵימָתַי?

וּדְלָא מוֹסִיף יָסֵף
*He who does not increase
[his Torah learning] decreases it*

There are three categories of living beings: animals, angels, and humans. Animals are completely physical beings, and angels are completely spiritual beings. Man is a unique creation, being a synthesis of body and spirit.

Animals grow only in size and strength, but cannot alter themselves in any way. Angels do not grow at all. Man is unique, in that although his physical growth stops at early adulthood, he can continue to grow and advance himself spiritually throughout his entire lifetime.

This uniqueness of man is what defines him and gives him identity as a human being. If a person stops growing spiritually, he fails to exercise that singular trait that is his identity. In that sense, he has lost his uniqueness, he lacks in humanity, and his identity as a full human being has come to an end. This is true regardless of the level at which his growth was arrested. The identifying characteristic of man is upward progress. If he ceases to develop himself when he is at a primitive stage or whether he is highly sophisticated and learned, it is all the same.

Hillel therefore said, "And he who does not increase, i.e., progress, decreases, i.e. comes to an end." How true.

14.

אִם אֵין אֲנִי לִי, מִי לִי
*If I am not for myself,
who will be for me?*

It is not an exaggeration to state that this statement of Hillel is the foundation of optimum mental and emotional health. It warrants some elaboration.

I introduced the book *I Am I* (Mesorah 1993) with the comment by R' Mendel of Kotzk: "If I am I because I am I, and you are you because you are you, then I exist and you exist. However, if I am I because you are you, and you are you because I am I, then I do not exist and you do not exist."

In order for a person to have a meaningful, constructive identity, it should be one which he gives to himself. If a person has no identity other than that given to him by others, he really has no identity at all. He must change like a chameleon, being one thing to his wife, another to his parents, another to his children, another to his employer, another to this friend, and yet another to a different friend.

A person must have a valid awareness of his abilities and character traits. He

[his Torah learning] decreases it; he who refuses to teach [Torah] deserves death; and he who exploits the crown [of Torah] shall fade away.

14. **H**e *was accustomed to say: If I am not for my- self, who will be for me? And if I am for myself, what am I? And if not now, when?*

---

must be aware of his character defects in order to correct them. It is also necessary for him to be cognizant of his character strengths. In this way he can determine which traits need to be developed and reinforced and which tools he should use to do so.

Lack of an accurate self-awareness usually results in feelings of unworthiness and inferiority. In order to compensate for these, a person may try to gain the favor of others by "people-pleasing" techniques. While this may appear to be desirable in that a person may do many favors for others, it is actually a destructive trait. We should indeed do things for others, but the motivation for doing so should be a positive one; i.e., because it is a mitzvah to do so, and not in defense of a delusional inferiority.

Hillel sums this up beautifully in his concise statement, "If I am not for me, then who can be for me?" I.e., if I do not have a personal identity, then who can give me one? If I do have a personal identity, then I am in the position of being able to do acts of kindness for others and be a participating and contribut- ing member of the community. But, "If I then keep only to myself and do not share with others, of what use am I?"

It is a mistake to think that the "people pleasers" who behave this way in order to compensate for feelings of inferiority are healthy people. Hillel teaches us that for our benevolent acts to be praiseworthy, they must emanate from a healthy self-concept.

Hillel's brief statement could be elaborated upon enough to fill two psychol- ogy texts.

אִם אֵין אֲנִי לִי, מִי לִי?
וּכְשֶׁאֲנִי לְעַצְמִי, מָה אֲנִי?

If I am not for myself, who will be for me? And if I am for myself, what am I?

The Baal Shem Tov gave this mishnah a unique interpretation based on the concept that the highest virtue is that of self-effacement. Chas- sidic masters interpreted Moses' statement, "I stood (lit. I stand) between God and you" (at Sinai, *Deuteronomy* 5:5), to mean that it is the "I," the ego, that stands as a barrier between men and God. Once a person is able to divest oneself of personal desires, to nullify himself as an entity and to see himself only and totally as an instrument of doing the Divine will, one can achieve a unity with God that makes him invincible.

Thus, Hillel said, "If I have reached the status where I no longer have an *ani* (ego), then who can harm me? However, if I still own an *ani*, of what worth am I?"

If a person is aware of his ego, he is not in optimum spiritual health. Physically, we are generally not conscious of our eyes, throat, or ears, unless they are diseased and we feel the pain. Similarly, a spiritually healthy person does not go around with a consciousness of himself. Self-consciousness indicates that something is not in order spiritually, just as being conscious of any part of one's body usually means that there is something wrong with it.

Hillel is cited by the Talmud as a paragon of humility, and his statement reflects his essence.

וּכְשֶׁאֲנִי לְעַצְמִי, מָה אֲנִי?
And if I am for myself, what am I?

"*I* want, *I* would like, *I* desire . . ." We may all think we know what we want, but is this always true? Does the real "*I*" want what we think we want?

I have treated thousands of alcoholics and drug addicts, all of whom were bent on self-destruction. At the time they craved alcohol or narcotics they were absolutely certain they knew what they wanted, so much so that they could even kill in order to get their chemical. But is it conceivable that a person could really desire to destroy himself?

Observing the addict makes one wonder whether this person may not be possessed by some kind of demon who has taken over control of the person and drives him to self-destruction. Indeed, the Torah concept is that the *yetzer hara* is a kind of demon, an alien power, as it were, that seeks to destroy its host (*Kiddushin* 30b). This is not the kind of demon that can be exorcised, but is rather the sum total of the desires of the physical-animal component of the human being that seeks gratification at any cost. The antidote to this demon is not exorcism; it is subjugating oneself to Torah. Through Torah one learns how to implement his intellect in the proper way. He can then recognize that man was created with enormous spiritual capacities. He is capable of subduing and harnessing the physical-animal drive.

The addict who says, "I want," is mistaken. The true "I" does not want drugs. It is the *yetzer hara* that deludes the "I" to think it wants drugs.

What is true of the addict is equally true, albeit in a less dramatic form, of the non-addict. When we want something — money, fame, food, conveniences, power, pleasure — we may be absolutely certain that we want it. This may really be very far from the truth. The genuine "I" may not want it at all.

Hillel states, "If I do not have mastery of my *ani*, my 'I,' if I am deluded by the *yetzer hara* to think that I want certain things, who can help me? I am then at the mercy of a force that can delude me to my own destruction."

The key to determining whether a particular drive is that of the real "I" or a machination of the *yetzer hara* is to see whether gratifying this desire is of any value, even remotely, to anyone else. When I eat for health reasons, when I sleep or recreate for health reasons, I am putting myself in a state of optimum functioning, which allows me then to be of service to others, whether family, friends, or in worshipping God. Physical indulgences which do not contribute to optimum health and have no value, even remotely to anyone else, are self-destructive and are not desired by the real "I." This is equally true of alcohol, drugs, nicotine, and even food.

Hillel provides a corollary to his first statement by adding, "If I am but for myself, what is that 'I' worth?" It is a spurious "I" that is only for oneself.

These few words of Hillel can be an excellent guide to living a healthy spiritual and physical life. The two are actually inseparable.

וְאִם לֹא עַכְשָׁו, אֵימָתַי?
And if not now, when?

The evils of procrastination hardly need emphasis. The Talmud states this in relation to studying Torah, where procrastination is progressive. "If you neglect Torah for one day, you will neglect it for two more" (*Jerusalem Talmud, Berachos* 9:8). Procrastination can feed on itself, resulting in a self-defeating vicious cycle. This applies to all other responsibilities as well.

The latter part of Hillel's statement is a logical consequence of the earlier part. A Jew's identity should be that of a Divine servant who is assigned a specific mission in life: that of performing the mitzvos as instructed by the Torah. He is essentially a soldier who must follow the orders of the Commander-in-chief as they are transmitted via the chain of command from generals down to the sergeant. A soldier who is given an order must do so promptly, and does not have the option of delaying it to what he thinks is a more propitious time. The time for performance is now.

This mishnah is also introduced by the expression "He was accustomed to say," which we have interpreted to mean that Hillel's very demeanor spoke for him. Hillel taught that a person has a Divine mission by showing that everything he did was in keeping with this mission.

The Talmud relates that one day, on leaving the academy, the students asked the master where he was going. "To do a mitzvah," Hillel said. "What kind of mitzvah?" the curious students asked. "I am going to the bathhouse."

"In what way is going to the bathhouse a mitzvah?" the students asked. Hillel replied, "Do they not wash the statues of the emperor regularly? If it is proper to keep the emperor's image neat and clean, how much more so must man keep himself clean, since man was created in the image of God."

Hillel demonstrated that the Divine will can be accomplished not only by the study of Torah and performance of manifest mitzvos, but even by going to the bathhouse. Hillel was a faithful soldier in the Divine army. Everything he did conveyed his teachings. Hillel's humility, his identity, his doing for others, and his total devotion to God was consistently evident in his behavior. הוּא הָיָה אוֹמֵר, "He was accustomed to say," not by word, but by deed.

[טו] **שַׁמַּאי** אוֹמֵר: עֲשֵׂה תוֹרָתְךָ קֶבַע, אֱמֹר מְעַט
וַעֲשֵׂה הַרְבֵּה, וֶהֱוֵי מְקַבֵּל אֶת כָּל הָאָדָם
בְּסֵבֶר פָּנִים יָפוֹת.

15.

עֲשֵׂה תוֹרָתְךָ קֶבַע
Make your Torah [study]
a fixed practice

Making the Torah "a fixed practice" is more than just a matter of time. Of course, one should devote as much time as possible to the study of Torah, but there is yet another concept involved.

I met a physician whom I had treated several months earlier for alcoholism, and I asked him whether he was following my recommendations to attend daily meetings of Alcoholics Anonymous. He said, "Yes, I still attend three meetings a day." A bit surprised by this zeal, I asked, "Don't you have office hours?" The doctor answered, "Yes, in between meetings. You see, if I don't attend three meetings a day, I will drink again and I won't have an office at all."

This man understood his priorities. He wanted to stay sober, and nothing else mattered. Doing whatever it took to stay sober came first, and everything else was secondary.

That is how it must be with Torah. The study of Torah must come first, and everything else should fit within that framework. If this priority is observed, one will find more time for Torah study than if one squeezes Torah study into a busy schedule.

A person may do a full day's work, yet be absorbed in Torah, looking for opportunities where he can seize a few moments to study a mishnah or two. It is otherwise with someone who is totally absorbed in his business, and just sets aside some time for Torah study.

A *chassid* who owned a shoe factory visited his Rebbe. After a brief interview the Rebbe said, "I am aware that people put their feet into shoes, but why are you putting your entire head into shoes?"

We believe that how much a person earns is predetermined for him on Rosh Hashanah, and no amount of effort he exerts will allow him to exceed his predetermined amount. On the other hand, whether a person learns Torah and does mitzvos is not predetermined. God leaves this totally to a person's free choice. If we really understood this, we would apply maximum efforts to Torah, since this is within our means to achieve. We might then devote much less to our earnings, since the latter has been predetermined. Regardless of how hard we may try, we cannot exceed our allotment. Is it not absurd that we expend more effort where it does not make a difference?

15. Shammai *says: Make your Torah [study] a fixed practice; say little and do much; and greet everyone with a pleasant countenance.*

אָמֹר מְעַט וְעֲשֵׂה הַרְבֵּה
Say little and do much

R' Moshe Schreiber (*Chasam Sofer*) would spend a considerable amount of time to *daven*. Someone asked him whether it would not be more advantageous for him to spend less time in prayer and use the extra time for more Torah study.

R' Schreiber responded, "The Talmud states that if one prays long, he is rewarded with long life. By adding on years to my life during which I can study Torah, I will more than compensate for the time I devote to prayer."

It is written that each person is given an allotted number of words to speak during his lifetime, and when these are exhausted, his life ends. Hence אָמֹר מְעַט, if we speak less, we will live longer; וְעֲשֵׂה הַרְבֵּה, and we will have greater opportunity to do good deeds. Ergo, speak little, and you will do more.

In stressing the importance of self-esteem, I have tried to distinguish between self-esteem and *gaavah*, (vanity). Self-esteem consists of an awareness of one's strengths and talents, whereas *gaavah* is an attitude of superiority over others.

The Chofetz Chaim's *anivus* (humility) is legendary. Yet this gentle man wrote the epochal *Mishnah Berurah*, establishing himself as the final authority on the *Shulchan Aruch*. How could he assume so exalted a position if he thought so little of himself?

The answer is that the Chofetz Chaim was well aware of his encyclopedic knowledge of Torah. Rather than feel that he was better than others, he was humbled by the thought that with the extraordinary capacities that God had given him, he had not even begun to do enough. It is likely that when he finished the *Mishnah Berurah*, the Chofetz Chaim heaved a sigh and said, "I have done so little. I must use my God-given gifts to do much, much more."

This is what the mishnah tells us. אָמֹר מְעַט, say that you have done very little. That will motivate you to עֲשֵׂה הַרְבֵּה, do much more.

עֲשֵׂה תוֹרָתְךָ . . . וֶהֱוֵי מְקַבֵּל
אֶת כָּל הָאָדָם בְּסֵבֶר פָּנִים יָפוֹת
Make your Torah [study] . . .
and greet everyone with
a pleasant countenance.

It is noteworthy, says R' Meir Auerbach (*Imrei Binah*), that Hillel and Shammai advocate two opposite methodologies. Hillel begins with establishing pleasant interpersonal relationships, which will lead to Torah (mishnah 13), whereas Shammai begins with Torah (עֲשֵׂה תוֹרָתְךָ קֶבַע), and concludes with interpersonal relationships (וֶהֱוֵי מְקַבֵּל אֶת כָּל הָאָדָם). Hillel and Shammai concurred that both Torah and *middos*

[טז] **רַבָּן** גַּמְלִיאֵל הָיָה אוֹמֵר: עֲשֵׂה לְךָ רַב, וְהִסְתַּלֵּק מִן הַסָּפֵק, וְאַל תַּרְבֶּה לְעַשֵּׂר אֲמָדוֹת.

(character traits) are essential, but whereas Hillel proceeds from *middos* to Torah, Shammai proceeds from Torah to *middos*.

The Talmud has established Hillel's opinion as the authoritative halachah, and indeed, R' Yeruchem Levovitz states, "It is an error to think that Torah leads to *middos*. To the contrary, *middos* are a prerequisite for Torah, and that is the truth" (*Daas Chochmah U'mussar*).

The *kaballah* writings state that Shammai's position, too, is valid, but that it is not applicable in the pre-Mashiach world. At this point in history, when so many people are subject to greed, lust, and self-indulgence, we must do as R' Yeruchem says. We must follow the teachings of Hillel to make *middos* the priority, for otherwise we may be subject to distorting Torah to accommodate our self-centered drives.

וֶהֱוֵי מְקַבֵּל אֶת כָּל הָאָדָם בְּסֵבֶר פָּנִים יָפוֹת
And greet everyone with a pleasant countenance.

The literal translation of these words is "Greet everyone with an 'attitude' of a pleasant countenance." The words of the mishnah are carefully measured. Would it not have been enough to say, "Greet everyone with a pleasant countenance?" Why the extra word סֵבֶר, "attitude"?

The Rabbi of Vorki explained, "Sometimes you may not be pleased at meeting someone. In fact, the encounter may even be irritating to you. Nevertheless, try to show an attitude of pleasantness. It is a mitzvah to make people feel good."

R' Yisrael of Salant met a person on the way to *shul* for *Kol Nidrei* prayers on Yom Kippur Eve. R' Yisrael greeted him, but the latter was so absorbed with the solemnity and awesomeness of the Day Of Judgment that he did not return the greeting. R' Yisrael remarked to his disciple, R' Itzele of Petersburg, "Why must I suffer from *his* preoccupation with the Day Of Judgment?"

At any time, regardless of one's mood, the mishnah counsels that a person should be able to present an attitude of pleasantness to everyone.

There are accounts of our Torah personalities who were able to present an attitude of cheerfulness even when they were gravely ill. Those who visited R' Yechiel Gordon, the Dean of the Lomza Yeshivah, during the last months of his life when he was suffering acutely from advanced cancer, related that he would tell stories and try to bring cheer to his visitors. He knew they were saddened to witness his deteriorated state.

External behavior *can* influence one's internal feelings. Acting *as if* one were happy may actually mitigate one's dejection. I once sat across from a psychologist at a convention, and I noticed that periodically he would put his fingers at the corners of his lips and raise them to the configuration of a smile. Noticing

16. R*abban Gamliel was accustomed to say: Make a teacher for yourself, and remove yourself from uncertainty; and do not give excess tithes by estimating [instead of measuring].*

---

my curiosity, he explained that even if there is no feeling of elation, producing an "artificial" smile can elevate a person's mood. Since he did not feel like smiling that day, he was using this gesture to lift his spirits.

Greeting someone cheerfully may elicit a similar response, and one can benefit from the pleasant mood of the other person. Moods can be contagious, and pleasantness begets pleasantness.

16.

עֲשֵׂה לְךָ רַב, וְהִסְתַּלֵּק מִן הַסָּפֵק,
וְאַל תַּרְבֶּה לְעַשֵּׂר אֲמָדוֹת

Make a teacher for yourself, and remove yourself from uncertainty, and do not give excess tithes by estimating

W*hy does Rabban Gamliel repeat "make a teacher for yourself," since this was already stated in mishnah 6? Assuming that he saw fit to say it, why did R' Yehudah HaNasi, who complied the mishnah, see fit to repeat it?

I don't know whether anyone who has not dealt with obsessive-compulsive patients can fully appreciate this mishnah. Rabban Gamliel's three-part statement can apply directly to Obsessive-Compulsive Disorders (OCD).

One of the prominent symptoms of OCD is the inability to accept anything with certainty. Regardless of how many times a person checks something, he remains tormented by doubt. This is why it is sometimes referred to as "the doubting disease." Even reassurance by competent authorities may not resolve the doubt. This inability to satisfy one's doubts can be extremely aggravating and depressing. Severe cases of OCD usually require medical treatment as well. In less severe cases, applying Rabban Gamliel's teaching can help greatly.

Torah observant people who develop OCD are likely to manifest their symptoms in religious practices, such as scrupulousness between meat and milk, far beyond anything required by halachah. One woman with this disorder would scrub her hands until her skin became raw, for fear of transferring contact from milk to meat. She was unable to accept her rabbi's assurance that this was unnecessary, and insisted on doing more than was required by halachah.

When 10 percent of the harvest was given to the Levites, people with OCD probably gave more than the 10 percent for fear that if they gave precisely the right amount they might fall short by a fraction. However, giving more than the required amount is not doing the mitzvah in a better way. To the contrary, it may even result in complications.

א/יז

[יז] **שִׁמְעוֹן** בְּנוֹ אוֹמֵר: כָּל יָמַי גָּדַלְתִּי בֵּין הַחֲכָמִים, וְלֹא מָצָאתִי לַגּוּף טוֹב אֶלָּא שְׁתִיקָה. וְלֹא הַמִּדְרָשׁ הוּא הָעִקָּר, אֶלָּא הַמַּעֲשֶׂה. וְכָל הַמַּרְבֶּה דְבָרִים מֵבִיא חֵטְא.

Rabban Gamliel is not repeating the idea of mishnah 6, which is a general guideline to have a teacher. Rather, he is advising us to have an authority whom we will trust and to whom we will listen. We need to have a *rav* whose ruling we can accept so that we will be able to divest ourselves of doubts. Furthermore, he says to the person plagued with uncertainties, do not try to do more than the halachah requires, because it may actually result in your handling matters the wrong way. Listen to your halachic authority, and do as you are told, and you will be spared the torment of doubt.

17.

וְלֹא מָצָאתִי לַגּוּף טוֹב אֶלָּא שְׁתִיקָה
וְלֹא הַמִּדְרָשׁ הוּא הָעִקָּר, אֶלָּא הַמַּעֲשֶׂה
וְכָל הַמַּרְבֶּה דְבָרִים מֵבִיא חֵטְא

And I found nothing better for the body than silence; it is not the theory that is of primary importance, but the action; and one who talks excessively brings on sin.

Oh, if only we would heed R' Shimon's teachings!

I have had abundant clinical experience in counseling people who have suffered disruptive relationships, whether within the family, socially, or occupationally. The lion's share of distress could have been avoided only if they had heeded their words more carefully. How wise the prophet was in comparing speech to an arrow (*Jeremiah* 9:7), because once a word leaves you it cannot be retrieved, regardless of how deeply you may regret having uttered it.

It is noteworthy that R' Shimon does not say that silence is a boon to the *neshamah*, but rather to the body. We may suffer great physical discomfort and depression because of excessive and unwise speech.

Sometimes harsh words are said in a moment of anger and frustration. They cannot subsequently be withdrawn when one is calmer. An unwise comment made by another person can have devastating effects. Caustic comments may not leave black-and-blue marks, but they can bruise even more than physical blows. Under such conditions, total silence would indeed be golden.

Obviously we must communicate, and speech is the unique trait of human beings. But, R' Shimon tells us, there is a way of communicating that is more effective, and which will permit one to keep speech to the necessary minimum. That method of communication is *action*, which, of course, speaks louder than words. If you wish to convey love for another person, do so by acting in a way which will please him or her. Husbands who assist their wives with the house-

17. Shimon *his son says: All my days I have been raised among the Sages, and I found nothing better for the body than silence; it is not the theory that is of primary importance, but the action; and one who talks excessively brings on sin.*

---

work and the care of the children are showing their affection much more than by just mouthing sweet words. Parents who act in a manner from which their children can learn by example are conveying far more effective teaching than by lecturing them.

The word חֵטְא, which R' Shimon uses, can mean "lack" as well as sin. Superfluous speech often indicates a lack of deeds.

God created the universe with verbal commands. It is the Divine prerogative to create *only* with words. Man does not have this capacity. He must be creative with actions rather than with words. Perhaps this is what Solomon meant with his cryptic statement, "For God is in heaven and you are on earth, so let your words be few" (*Ecclesiastes* 5:1). Our tools should be deeds rather than words.

Yes, if only we heeded R' Shimon's advice, how different life might be!

וְלֹא מָצָאתִי לַגּוּף טוֹב אֶלָּא שְׁתִיקָה
And I found nothing better for the body than silence

Silence can be of definite benefit to the *guf* (body).

The *mussar* tomes of yore prescribe a variety of procedures for *teshuvah* (penance), including fasting and other bodily deprivations. More recent ethicists, realizing that contemporary man cannot tolerate excessive fasting, have advocated "*taanis dibur*" or a withholding of speech rather than of food. The Chofetz Chaim in the *Mishnah Berurah* (571:2) clearly states that keeping silent is a more effective method of *teshuvah* than fasting.

We can thus understand another application of R' Shimon's statement. By keeping silent, we spare the *guf* the distress of food deprivation and other self-flagellation. Silence is thus a great boon to the *guf*.

We generally assume that "silence" refers to a withholding of speech on the part of the speaker. It is more comprehensive, however, because silence can refer to the listener as well. For example, a deaf person lives in a world of silence, regardless of how many people may be talking to him.

We may be negatively affected by what we hear just as we may cause harm by what we say. It is as important to be as selective about our hearing as about our speech.

The chassidic master, R' Yitzchak of Neschiz, at times did not understand what people were saying to him. He once explained to his son, "When people

רַבָּן [יח] שִׁמְעוֹן בֶּן גַּמְלִיאֵל אוֹמֵר: עַל שְׁלֹשָׁה
דְבָרִים הָעוֹלָם קַיָּם – עַל הַדִּין וְעַל הָאֱמֶת
וְעַל הַשָּׁלוֹם, שֶׁנֶּאֱמַר: ,,אֱמֶת וּמִשְׁפַּט שָׁלוֹם שִׁפְטוּ
בְּשַׁעֲרֵיכֶם."

---

speak untruth or other improper talk, I cannot make out any words. All I hear
is noise."

We have an excellent model for this in modern electronics. There are
hearing aids that do not amplify all sounds, but are programmed to amplify
only those sounds that the person does not hear well as determined by hearing
tests. The tiny apparatus can select which sounds it processes, and others to
which it does not react. Many people prefer this newer model. They were
unable to use the older model that amplified all sounds because, they say, they
heard "only noise."

The human brain, with its more than 14 billion cells, can put this tiny
electronic instrument to shame. We can program our hearing so that we
essentially block out that which we should not hear. Granted, this takes a great
deal of effort, dedication, and training, but we can achieve a selectivity in the
silence of the sounds we receive as well as those we emit.

וְלֹא הַמִּדְרָשׁ הוּא הָעִקָּר, אֶלָּא הַמַּעֲשֶׂה
*It is not the theory that is of primary
importance, but the action*

R' Shimon appears to have anticipated the most recent advances in psychology.

Traditional psychotherapy was
based on an understanding of psychodynamics. The patient's symptoms were
considered to have had an origin in some experiences, possibly traumatic, of
his early life, often going back to the childhood years. The psychotherapist
would elicit an exhaustive history, searching for the events that were responsible for development of the symptoms. After these were discovered and the
patient understood how he may have distorted or misinterpreted these events
and the effect they had on his thoughts and emotions, the causative factors
would be eliminated. The symptoms would then disappear.

That was the theory. The problem was that too often it did not bear fruit,
and in spite of much insight and understanding, the patient's symptoms persisted.

During the past few decades, several different schools of behavioral psychology have emerged. While they may vary in methodology, their common
denominator is to work with overcoming the symptoms; i.e., changing the
behavior, and leaving the understanding of its origin for a later time. For
example, the phobic person is encouraged to tackle the phobia head on, and
if he is, say, afraid of crowds, the therapist gives him support to go into
crowds, working with him in the here and now on overcoming the phobia.

18. **R**abban Shimon ben Gamliel says: The world endures on three things — law, truth, and peace, as it
is said: You shall adjudicate the verdict of truth and peace
at your gates (Zechariah 8:16).

The therapist may also provide additional coping skills or relaxation techniques. An understanding of the reasons why the phobia developed in the first
place may be dealt with at a later time.

The traditional approach was based on the theory that insight will change
behavior. The contemporary approach, which is much more effective, is to
change the pathologic behavior first.

This is evident in R' Shimon's statement: "It is not the theory that is of
primary importance, but rather the action."

18.

עַל שְׁלֹשָׁה דְבָרִים הָעוֹלָם קַיָּם –
עַל הַדִּין וְעַל הָאֱמֶת וְעַל הַשָּׁלוֹם

*The world endures on three things —
law, truth and peace*

This mishnah is neither a repetition nor a refutation of mishnah
2. The former is referring to the
virtues and merits which sustain
the world. This mishnah is refer-
ring to the requisites for society to exist and function.

The teachings of this mishnah are of particular significance today, because
we are facing the threat of social disintegration. Crime is rampant. The number of criminals requiring incarceration is increasing at a more rapid rate than
the construction of prisons to contain them. Scandal and corruption per-
vade all levels of government. Our streets are unsafe, and our youth is
being destroyed by drugs. Rabban Shimon ben Gamliel's words are worth
heeding.

"Law, truth, and peace." Yes, we have a legal system and a judiciary, but
it is clearly not providing for an orderly society. Why? Because law cannot
exist if it does not go hand in hand with truth. The prerequisite for law should
be *truth*. I have spoken with criminal lawyers who have said that their job is to
have their clients acquitted, or at least get the most lenient punishment possible. They may know their client is guilty, but they must nevertheless argue that
he is innocent.

We pointed out in the introduction that legislation that is based totally on
human intellect is unreliable. Sodom had a code of laws, one which was
predicated on the desires of the people. That system justified the most inhumane behavior. Nazi Germany legalized the worst atrocities known to
mankind. Even after the exposure of the horrors of Dr. Mengele and other

Nazi criminals, there were countries that sheltered them. When law is not based on unalterable principles, it cannot assure the peace that is necessary to sustain a society.

Truth is not relative. Two plus two has equaled four for thousands of years and will continue to do so unto eternity. Truth must be the basis of law, and law must be based on unchangeable values.

A second fault with our legal system is that it is not in search of truth as a goal. We have a variety of games with two opposing teams: baseball, football, basketball, and hockey. The courtroom is but another arena where the prosecution and defense are involved in a game, with the judge acting as referee. There is no pretense of a search for truth. A lawyer may know that his client is guilty of the most vicious and heinous crime, yet he will move heaven and earth together to have him acquitted and turned loose to prey on society once again.

A homeless woman was brought to our psychiatric hospital and admitted on an emergency involuntary commitment, because she was senile and could not look after herself. Inasmuch as the weather was frigid, she found warmth in the bus depot and would ride the buses back and forth. In the hospital she was cared for properly, but she insisted on leaving.

The law provided that within five days after involuntary admission, the patient must have a hearing before a magistrate to determine whether she could be detained in the hospital. A court-appointed lawyer was provided for her "defense," and he discovered a technical flaw in the application for commitment, which resulted in the case being dismissed.

As we left the hearing room, the lawyer asked me, "What are you going to do with her now?" I replied, "I have no choice but to let her leave." The lawyer protested, "You can't do that. She'll die out there in the cold!" "But *you* were the one who had the case dismissed and got her out!" I said. The lawyer responded, " I was just doing my job."

When a legal system is driven by each side desiring to win, with no concern whether the good of the person or the community is being served, it is but a game. Unfortunately, the vehicle of this game is not a ball or a puck, but human lives.

Rabban Shimon ben Gamliel's words are a stern warning. For there to be peace in a society, there must be a system of laws that is based upon truth.

וְעַל הַשָּׁלוֹם
And peace

Shalom (peace) is without question the most important ingredient for a society's existence. Indeed, the Talmud states that God did not find any suitable receptacle for His blessings other than *shalom* (*Uktzin* 3:12). This notwithstanding, even *shalom* must be qualified. A *shalom* that is without truth and law is not constructive.

A tourist who visited a zoo in Communist Russia was told, "See, we have already reached the Messianic Era," and he showed him that a lion and a lamb shared the same cage. The visitor was duly impressed and expressed his surprise to a local citizen, who whispered in his ear, "Sure, but every day they give the lion a fresh lamb." That is not the kind of peace promised for the Messianic Era.

In abusive families there may be a kind of tense peace prevailing, which is based on everyone's fear of provoking the abuser. This is not *shalom bayis* (a peaceful home).

The Midrash relates that before God created man He took counsel with the angels. The angels of *chesed* (kindness) and *tzedek* (justice) advised that man be created because he would be kind, do good deeds, and give charity. The angels of *shalom* and *emes* (truth) advised against it because man is argumentative and false. God then cast *emes* down to earth and proceeded to create man (*Bereshis Rabbah* 8).

But what about the objection raised by *shalom*? How was this answered? The commentaries say, with *emes* out of the way, it is easy to appease and achieve *shalom*.

The *shalom* that is conducive to the healthy function of society and of the family unit is a *shalom* that is based on truth and law. There are no secrets, no cover-ups, no misinformation. There is a profound respect for the dignity and status of everyone — man, woman, and child. Only this kind of *shalom* is a receptacle for the Divine blessings.

רַבִּי חֲנַנְיָא בֶּן עֲקַשְׁיָא אוֹמֵר: רָצָה הַקָּדוֹשׁ בָּרוּךְ הוּא
לְזַכּוֹת אֶת יִשְׂרָאֵל, לְפִיכָךְ הִרְבָּה לָהֶם תּוֹרָה
וּמִצְוֹת, שֶׁנֶּאֱמַר: „יהוה חָפֵץ לְמַעַן צִדְקוֹ, יַגְדִּיל תּוֹרָה
וְיַאְדִּיר.“

The recitation of each chapter of *Pirkei Avos* is followed by these words
from the mishnah (*Makkos* 26b). רָצָה הַקָּדוֹשׁ בָּרוּךְ הוּא לְזַכּוֹת אֶת יִשְׂרָאֵל, לְפִיכָךְ
הִרְבָּה לָהֶם תּוֹרָה וּמִצְוֹת — God wished to confer merit upon Israel; therefore he
gave them Torah and mitzvos in abundance.

This would appear to contradict the *Maharsha* who states that inasmuch as
there are 365 prohibitions as compared to 248 positive commandments, a
person is more apt to transgress a prohibition than to fulfill a commandment.
How, then, is the abundance of mitzvos to our advantage?

In Chapter 4 mishnah 2 it is stated that one mitzvah attracts another. This is
a law of nature that God has instituted, much the same as the law of gravity or
the phenomenon of magnetism. Just as a magnet attracts iron filings, so
does performance of one mitzvah create an attraction to perform another
mitzvah.

There are a number of mitzvos which would have been observed had they
not been decreed in the Torah. For example, one fulfills a mitzvah when he
avoids eating insects. Had the Torah not prohibited this, we would avoid this
because it is repulsive. However, if we check our vegetables to avoid eating
insects, we are fulfilling a mitzvah. This creates an impetus to do other
mitzvos. Few people have murderous impulses, yet when they refrain from
killing someone they have fulfilled one of the Ten Commandments. Most
people would respect their parents even if this had not been commanded by
the Torah. All that is necessary is that we keep in mind that we are doing these
things or abstaining from things because it is a mitzvah. We then have a
mitzvah to our credit, and this attracts us to do other mitzvos, some of which
may be more difficult to fulfill.

The fact that we have many mitzvos that are relatively easy to observe
facilitates the performance of more difficult mitzvos. This is why the abun-

Rabbi Chanania ben Akashia says: The Holy One, Blessed is He, wished to confer merit upon Israel; therefore He gave them Torah and mitzvos in abundance, as it is said: HASHEM desired, for the sake of its [Israel's] righteousness, that the Torah be made great and glorious (Isaiah 42:21)..

---

dance of mitzvos is to our advantage. The challenge of more difficult mitzvos is lessened by the fact that many things that we would do on our own have the status of mitzvos.

The teachings in *Ethics of the Fathers* are not easily adopted. The development of proper *middos* (character traits) often requires much effort and diligence. One might think that this is asking too much of the average person. Each chapter is therefore followed by the above statement. God has made it easier for us to achieve the spirituality of *Ethics of the Fathers* by giving a number of our natural inclinations the status of mitzvos. Observance of the latter puts the fulfillment of the requirements listed herein within everyone's reach.

This passage may also have another meaning. The Midrash states that the Torah and mitzvos were given to refine our character. "The manner of slaughtering an animal does not affect God. The mitzvos were given to refine man" (*Bereishis Rabbah* 44:1). The Torah is thus the Manufacturer's instruction manual. It enables us to fulfill the purpose of our existence: to become spiritual people.

The word לְזַכּוֹת also means "to purify." The above quote therefore states that the abundance of mitzvos were given to us to enable us to refine and purify ourselves.

The Talmud states that had the Torah not been given, we would have been held responsible to develop proper character traits by observing nature (*Eruvin* 100b). This would have been an awesome responsibility. We could easily have drawn the wrong conclusion with our unaided intellect. God was therefore kind to us in providing us with clear instructions on proper behavior.

Ethics of the Fathers gives us the guidance for refining and purifying ourselves. At the completion of each chapter we therefore express our gratitude to God for having given us precise instructions to fulfill our mission in life.

פרק שני ✍
Chapter Two

כָּל יִשְׂרָאֵל יֵשׁ לָהֶם חֵלֶק לָעוֹלָם הַבָּא, שֶׁנֶּאֱמַר:
„וְעַמֵּךְ כֻּלָּם צַדִּיקִים, לְעוֹלָם יִירְשׁוּ
אָרֶץ, נֵצֶר מַטָּעַי, מַעֲשֵׂה יָדַי לְהִתְפָּאֵר."

All Israel has a share in the World to Come, as it is
said: And your people are all righteous; they shall
inherit the land forever; a branch of My plantings, My
handiwork, in which to take pride (Isaiah 60:21).

פרק שני

[א] **רַבִּי** אוֹמֵר: אֵיזוֹ הִיא דֶרֶךְ יְשָׁרָה שֶׁיָּבֹר לוֹ הָאָדָם? כָּל

Chapter Two

1.

The first mishnah of this chapter is authored by R' Yehudah *HaNasi*, one of the greatest Torah personalities in all Jewish history. In the Talmud, R' Yehudah *HaNasi* is most often mentioned not by name, but by the title "Rebbi", i.e., *the* Rabbi. At other times he is referred to as *Rabbeinu Hakadosh,* our holy teacher, an appellation not given to any of the other great sages of the Talmud.

R' Yehudah *HaNasi* is indeed *the* Rabbi of Judaism, because he edited and organized the entire Mishnah, which is the foundation of the Talmud. The enormity of this achievement can be grasped only by those familiar with the Talmud. This task required not only an encyclopedic knowledge of the many opinions that had been set forth in halachah over the centuries, but also a clarity of thought and the strength of conviction to determine which of the countless opinions should be recorded, which should be established as the halachah, and which minority opinions should be given mention. Furthermore, since tradition had it that the Oral Law was not to be recorded in writing, all of halachah had to be formulated in a most concise text which could be committed to memory. (It was only following R' Yehudah *HaNasi* that writing down the text of the Mishnah was permitted.) The Mishnah, therefore, had to be constructed in a concise form. Its students would then have to essentially reconstitute it and expand it to reveal its full content. This was the monumental achievement of R' Yehudah *HaNasi.*

There is an interesting parallel among the fathers of Judaism. The Patriarch Abraham personified *chesed,* loving-kindness. However, kindness and love in a culture do not have the strength to serve as the foundation of a lasting system. The Patriarch Isaac represented *gevurah,* firmness and discipline, which, standing alone and unmitigated, is too harsh an ideal and too demanding for the average person. It was Jacob (Israel) who was able to synthesize and blend the two qualities, *chesed* and *gevurah,* into *tiferes* (beauty and glory). It was he who became the father of the twelve tribes and the nation which refers to itself as *Bnei Yisrael,* the children of Israel.

R' Yehudah *HaNasi* is a descendant of Hillel. Hillel was the founder of a dynasty of leadership, and is depicted as the pillar of *chesed.* His grandson, the elder Rabban Gamliel, personified *gevurah,* as he established the authority of the *Nasi* (prince). But it was R' Yehudah *HaNasi,* the parallel of Jacob, who became the foundation of Torah for all time. He blended the attributes of his

1. Rabbi *says: Which one of the proper paths should a person choose for himself? Whatever [path]*

---

predecessors, manifesting them in his personal life, and concertizing them in halachah.

Rebbi was a close friend of Antoninus. There is a difference of opinion among historians whether this was the emperor Marcus Aurelius or the Roman governor of Israel. Regardless, Rabbi Yehudah had a close relationship to the ruling powers, and was able to secure lenient conditions for his generation, enabling Torah academies to flourish. His immense wealth notwithstanding, Rebbi swore on his deathbed that he had never derived anything but the most essential benefit from any of his wealth, and that he maintained the regal character of his court solely to earn the deference of the populace to the authority of the prince.

In all the vast Mishnah, Rebbi cites his own opinion only several times, and even then generally defers in halachah to his peers who disagreed with him. His greatness can be seen in his utter self-effacement. Indeed, when Rebbi died, the Talmud states that with his passing "humility disappeared" (*Sotah* 49a).

R' Yehudah *HaNasi,* like the Patriarch Jacob, represents *tiferes,* the beauty of blending *chesed* and *gevurah.* It is therefore only natural and appropriate that he designate the proper path of life as that which results in *tiferes.* As one who dedicated his energies toward combing through mounds of opinions to select those that should be embodied in halachah, he begins his teaching with instructions how to choose or select a lifestyle from among the many that may be ideal for the individual.

How right the Talmud is when it praises the Almighty as "Blessed is He Who has chosen the sages and their teachings" (*Ethics of the Fathers* 6:1). The sages personified the teachings by the very way in which they lived.

אֵיזוֹ הִיא דֶרֶךְ יְשָׁרָה שֶׁיָּבֹר לוֹ הָאָדָם?
Which one of the proper paths should a person choose for himself?

If we look closely at the words of the mishnah, it does not ask, "Which is the proper path a person should choose?" But rather "Which *one of the proper paths* should a person choose?" In other words, there may be any number of proper adjustments to life, but it is not "one size fits all." While there are no two ways insofar as halachah is concerned, there are a variety of ways within the framework of halachah. A person should find which way is the most appropriate for him.

For example, within Torah study there are different approaches, and one should utilize his innate abilities rather than try to imitate another. One *Rosh*

אַ/ב שֶׁהִיא תִפְאֶרֶת לְעֹשֶׂהָ וְתִפְאֶרֶת לוֹ מִן הָאָדָם. וֶהֱוֵי

Yeshivah explained that the admiration for the genius of R' Chaim of Brisk was so great that many of his students tried to follow his brilliant analytic method. Those whose minds were not of analytical bent were unsuccessful in applying this method, and their arguments may appear forced and artificial.

The Talmud states, "Many tried to emulate R' Shimon bar Yochai (who totally separated himself from anything mundane) but they did not succeed" (*Berachos* 35b). Their lack of success resulted because they tried to emulate R' Shimon, whereas they were not at a level to adopt this lifestyle on their own.

Jews from many lands have customs and practices which are part of their culture, a heritage from their ancestors. When they enter a new environment, they may abandon their own customs and adopt those of their neighbors. This is not always wise. The traditions of centuries should not be cast aside lightly.

The Seer of Lublin said that people should choose the path that is proper for *them*. This may require consultation with a competent Torah authority. By the same token, they should respect ways that are different than their own. It is so tragic to see divisiveness between Jews with sundry backgrounds, and even more tragic when such difficulties are allowed to create friction within families.

The words of the mishnah must be studied carefully. There are many proper paths from which a person may chose.

כָּל שֶׁהִיא תִפְאֶרֶת לְעֹשֶׂהָ
וְתִפְאֶרֶת לוֹ מִן הָאָדָם
**Whatever [path] is a credit to himself
and earns him the esteem
of fellow men**

The desirable path in life is one which will not only be respected by others, but one which will also result in self-respect.

There are some people who engage in practices which they would rather not do, but feel compelled to do so by circumstances. They may justify their actions in a variety of ways, often claiming that their obligation to provide for their families' needs necessitates their cutting corners. They may feel pressured by their peer groups, or that circumstances warrant this particular behavior. They may be pressured by compulsions, such as addiction to chemicals or gambling. When asked if they are truly proud of the way they are living, they may initially answer in the affirmative, which is often only a defensive, knee-jerk response. When they give some contemplation to their lifestyle, they often admit that they really wish they could live otherwise.

I once had a patient who had lived a dissolute life for many years. Wishing to finally break away from this, and after several nonvoluntary hospital admissions, she admitted herself voluntarily to a state mental hospital, where she spent an entire year. Upon leaving the hospital she led an exemplary and highly spiritual life. She had not actually been mentally ill, but could no longer

---

tolerate her behavior. The thought "I am too good to be living this way" gave her no peace, and in desperation she took the radical measure of seeking asylum in a mental hospital to escape the destructive pattern which had become her routine, and to initiate a change in her lifestyle.

It is not enough to live in a way that earns the respect of others. It is possible for a person to dissimulate, and to present himself to people in a way that they can respect him, even though his true essence is hardly praiseworthy. A person must be motivated by self-respect, and be at peace with himself.

Of course, an individual may be totally without a conscience, as is characteristic of sociopaths. With this exception, every person has an internal drive to live a better life. This drive cannot be completely suppressed, even when the circumstances may influence a person to behave improperly.

The Talmud tells of Elazar ben Doradia, who lived an immoral and degenerate life, until he was suddenly motivated to take account of himself. He was so heartbroken by the realization of his dissolute behavior and his deplorable lifestyle that he wept brokenheartedly, until he died while still weeping. (*Avodah Zarah* 17a). It is more than likely that even during the time that he was driven by his base desires, Elazar must have had a nagging feeling that his actions were really beneath his dignity.

A good guide to behavior is for us to ask ourselves, "Am I really proud of what I am doing?" and give this question a few moments of serious thought.

וְתִפְאֶרֶת לוֹ מִן הָאָדָם
And earns him the esteem of fellow men

Why should a person behave in a way to evoke praise from others? Is this not being motivated by vanity, by a quest for admiration?

The intent of the mishnah is not that one should elicit glorification from others, but rather that one should act in a manner that will cause people to respect the principles which he represents.

The Talmud states that if a person has studied Torah and lives an honorable life, with honesty, integrity, courtesy, and consideration for others, then people will say, "How fortunate are his father and teacher who taught him Torah, and woe unto those who have not learned Torah. Just see how pleasant and honest his actions are." If, however, he fails to live an honorable life, people will be critical not only of him, but of his parents and teachers, and this will result in disgracing the Torah (*Yoma* 86a). The Talmud clearly demands a higher standard from those who represent Torah observance.

It is therefore not enough for a person to act in a way that he considers proper for himself as an individual. He must realize that he has the capacity to promote *kiddush Hashem*, the sanctification of God, or the reverse, a *chillul Hashem*, a desecration of God. This is the intent of the mishnah when it urges the kind of behavior that will merit admiration from others.

זָהִיר בְּמִצְוָה קַלָּה כְּבַחֲמוּרָה, שֶׁאֵין אַתָּה יוֹדֵעַ מַתַּן שְׂכָרָן שֶׁל מִצְוֹת. וֶהֱוֵי מְחַשֵּׁב הֶפְסֵד מִצְוָה כְּנֶגֶד שְׂכָרָהּ, וּשְׂכַר עֲבֵרָה כְּנֶגֶד הֶפְסֵדָהּ.

וֶהֱוֵי זָהִיר בְּמִצְוָה קַלָּה כְּבַחֲמוּרָה, שֶׁאֵין אַתָּה יוֹדֵעַ מַתַּן שְׂכָרָן שֶׁל מִצְוֹת
Be as scrupulous in performing a "minor" mitzvah as in a "major" one, for you do not know the reward given for the [respective] mitzvos

The implication in this mishnah appears to be that one should be most cautious about "minor" mitzvos only because their reward might be even greater than that of "major" mitzvos. Hence, if one were to know which mitzvos have greater reward, one might do well to choose these. This would be a direct contradiction to the teachings of Antigonos (1:3) who says that anticipation of reward should *not* be the prime motivation behind doing mitzvos.

Perhaps we can better understand this with the teachings of chassidic masters, who emphasize the concept of נַחַת רוּחַ לְהַקָּדוֹשׁ בָּרוּךְ הוּא, that when we do mitzvos, we give God pleasure. They state that like a loving and devoted father, God wishes to bestow His blessings upon His children. However, God conducts the world according to a system of justice, מִדָּה כְּנֶגֶד מִדָּה, (measure for measure), which requires that a person must be deserving of God's bounty in order to be rewarded. Thus, when a person does a mitzvah, he enables God to reward him, and this is the נַחַת רוּחַ, the pleasure that we can give to God.

It follows that if a person is meticulous about observing even minute details, things which others may consider to be unimportant, he gives God even greater reason for rewarding him. A father is extremely pleased when he sees his children doing their utmost to please him, not only by abiding by his explicit wishes, but by trying to maximize his comfort by doing things which he might have indicated as desirable only by inference. Similarly, God is pleased when we do things that might appear insignificant to us, but we do them because they are His will.

It is not the receiving of reward that should be the motivation, as Antigonos said, but rather providing God with the reason for being bountiful. In this respect, obeying the "lesser" mitzvos may even merit greater reward.

This is a lofty concept, and requires a great measure of devotion to God, for one must be able to look away from oneself and one's own gratification, and rather live in a way that will give God נַחַת רוּחַ.

וֶהֱוֵי זָהִיר בְּמִצְוָה קַלָּה
Be scrupulous in performing a "minor" mitzvah

My father told me about a young man in Kiev who was very ambitious. Knowing that in the anti-Semitic climate of czarist Russia he could never achieve any success in business, he denied his Judaism, assiduously avoiding anything that might betray his identity.

2/1 *Be as scrupulous in performing a "minor" mitzvah as in a "major" one, for you do not know the reward given for the [respective] mitzvos. Calculate the cost of a mitzvah against its reward, and the reward of a sin against its cost.*

One day he heard that an unidentified body had been pulled from the river. The victim had been found wearing a *tallis kattan,* and was obviously of the Jewish faith. He was therefore turned over to the Jewish community for burial. The assimilated man reasoned that although it was necessary for him to conceal his Judaism in order to advance himself, he did not wish to be separated from his people forever. He reasoned that if oppression of Jews required him to be considered a gentile during his lifetime, he nevertheless wished to be buried among Jews He therefore began wearing a *tallis kattan.* Concealed under his shirt, no one could detect anything, but when he died, he would be identified as a Jew and given a proper burial.

Shortly after he began wearing the *tallis kattan,* he began avoiding eating pork, fasted on Yom Kippur, and would try to find ways to try to avoid working on Shabbos without tipping his hand. To make a long story short, he eventually became a full *baal teshuvah.* All this began with the clandestine wearing of a *tallis kattan!*

The Talmud says, "The reward of one mitzvah is another mitzvah" (*Ethics of the Fathers* 4:2). This is what this mishnah is telling us. Be cautious to observe even what appears to be a simple, effortless mitzvah, because it may set into motion a series of events that will lead to observance of many more mitzvos. You may think that the reward for mitzvos is only something that you will receive as a bonus. There is also a far greater reward: that performance of any mitzvah will lead to performance of many more mitzvos.

וֶהֱוֵי זָהִיר בְּמִצְוָה קַלָּה כְּבַחֲמוּרָה
Be as scrupulous in performing a "minor" mitzvah as in a "major" one

---

According to R' Yaakov Kamenetzky, this mishnah conveys an important Torah principle.

We have already seen that Antigonos de-emphasized reward as a motivation for performance of mitzvos. External reward is much like a mother promising her child ice cream for dessert if he will eat vegetables. The latter contains the nutrients which are essential to keep him healthy. Since the juvenile mind cannot grasp this, the mother offers him something which he can appreciate: ice cream. So it is with external reward. It is in the World to Come that we will receive it, but now let us set it aside and as mature individuals realize that the mitzvos are our "nutrients." This is what is meant by "the reward of a mitzvah is the mitzvah itself" (*Ethics of the Fathers* 4:2). This is the true reward, which is totally different and separate from the external reward.

Our concept of "easy" or minor mitzvos versus "difficult" or major mitzvos is based on our own experiences. If we hire someone to do extremely hard labor, his payment will be greater than if the task is relatively simple. This is because the work he is doing is for *us* rather than for himself. This is not so with mitzvos, which are not intended to benefit God, as the prophet says, "If you do right, what have you given to God?" (*Job* 35:6-7). God is All-perfect and needs nothing from us. The mitzvos are for our own perfection.

Yes, the Talmud does say, "the reward is commensurate with the effort" (below 5:26), but this refers to the external reward. The inherent reward, the self-perfection, is not dependent on the degree of effort.

For example, says R' Kamenetzky, fasting 26 hours on Tishah B'Av is taxing on a person and is a sacrifice. On the other hand, eating on the day before Yom Kippur does not require any effort at all and is certainly not a sacrifice. Yet, the latter is a Scriptural mitzvah, which outweighs the Rabbinic ordinance of fasting on Tishah B'Av. The external reward for the sacrifice of fasting may be greater, but the self-perfection resulting from fulfilling the mitzvah of eating on Erev Yom Kippur surpasses it.

The mishnah therefore tells us to be most cautious not to judge mitzvos as major or minor by our own standards. How a given mitzvah contributes to our self-perfection is beyond our understanding and known only to God.

שֶׁאֵין אַתָּה יוֹדֵעַ מַתַּן שְׂכָרָן שֶׁל מִצְוֹת
For you do not know the reward given for the [respective] mitzvos

---

A man came to the chassidic master of Apt. He related that he was a merchant who had fallen on hard times, and asked for a blessing from the rabbi, because he had to marry off his daughter. Without a dowry, she had little chance of a good match. He stated that he was completely impoverished, and his entire fortune consisted of a single ruble. The rabbi responded, "You may return home, and the first opportunity you have to make any kind of deal, you should do so, and God will bless you."

The man was bewildered, wondering what kind of deal he could possibly make without money, but his belief in the blessing of the *Tzaddik* was strong and he made his way home.

The man stopped at an inn, and he saw that there were a group of diamond merchants showing their wares to one another.

"What are you looking at?" one of the merchants asked the man. "Perhaps you wish to buy a diamond."

"I certainly do," the man answered. "How much money do you have?" he was asked.

"One ruble," the man answered, whereupon all the merchants burst into laughter. One of the merchants said, "Well, for one ruble I cannot sell you a diamond, but I'll tell you what. I can sell you my portion in Paradise for one ruble."

"Agreed!" the man answered, taking out the ruble and putting it on the table. "But you must write me a bill of sale just as for any other transaction."

All the merchants had a hearty laugh, and the one who suggested the sale wrote on a slip of paper that he sells his portion in Paradise to this man for one ruble.

Shortly thereafter the wife of the diamond merchant, who actually owned the diamonds for they were her inheritance, came in and asked the group what their hilarity was all about. When she heard that her husband had sold his portion in Paradise, she exclaimed, "What! You gave away your portion in Paradise? Why, that's horrible! I will not live with a man who has no portion in Paradise."

The merchant, seeing that his wife was so alarmed, reassured her that it was only a joke, and not to take it seriously. The man who had purchased the share in Paradise said, "No, that is not so. I was absolutely sincere when I paid one ruble for the share in Paradise, and here I have a bill of sale to prove it."

"You did that?" the woman screamed at her husband. "You either retrieve your portion in Paradise promptly, or I will demand a divorce."

The merchant, seeing how upset his wife was, approached the man and said, "My dear man, you see how distraught my wife is. I will return your ruble, and we will void the deal."

"I'm sorry," the man said. "A deal is a deal. I am not going to allow you to renege on a legal transaction."

"Well, then, I will give you 5 rubles," the merchant said.

The man shook his head. "I will take nothing less than 1,000 rubles to return your share in Paradise to you."

"One thousand rubles!" the merchant said. "Are you out of your mind? Just to please my wife, I will give you 10 rubles, and let's finish this affair."

The man was adamant. "I will take nothing less than 1,000 rubles," he said.

The merchant's wife, listening to the dialogue, said to her husband, "If he wants 10,000 rubles, you must give it to him, or our marriage has come to an end. I will simply not live with a man who has given away his share in Paradise."

The merchant tried to bargain with the man, but the latter was insistent, saying, "You think I am a nobody, don't you? I, too, was once a well-to-do merchant, but my business failed. The *Tzaddik* of Apt told me that I would succeed with the first deal I made to acquire the necessary money to marry off my daughter. I will take nothing less than 1,000 rubles."

The merchant, at his wife's insistence, had no choice other than to give the man 1,000 rubles. The merchant's wife then asked the man, "Could you please introduce me to the *Tzaddik* of Apt?"

Upon meeting the *Tzaddik,* the woman asked, "How is it possible that something for which the man paid only one ruble should be sold for 1,000 rubles?"

The *Tzaddik* responded, "My dear woman, when your husband sold his share in Paradise, it was not worth even one ruble. Once he understood how important it is to have a share in Paradise and realized his folly, his share in Paradise grew exceedingly great, and was worth the thousand rubles he paid for it."

Our heavenly reward can indeed fluctuate. Perhaps this is what the mishnah means: that we can never grasp the reward for mitzvos.

הִסְתַּכֵּל בִּשְׁלֹשָׁה דְבָרִים, וְאֵין אַתָּה בָא לִידֵי עֲבֵרָה; דַּע מַה לְמַעְלָה מִמְּךָ – עַיִן רוֹאָה, וְאֹזֶן שׁוֹמַעַת, וְכָל מַעֲשֶׂיךָ בְּסֵפֶר נִכְתָּבִים.

וֶהֱוֵי מְחַשֵּׁב הֶפְסֵד מִצְוָה כְּנֶגֶד שְׂכָרָהּ, וּשְׂכַר עֲבֵרָה כְּנֶגֶד הֶפְסֵדָהּ
Calculate the cost of a mitzvah against its reward, and the reward of a sin against its cost

The concept of calculating gain versus loss in the performance of mitzvos and/or avoidance of sin appears to be in conflict with Antigonos (Chapter 1, mishnah 3) who de-emphasizes reward and punishment as motivating factors. We have already referred to this a bit earlier, but let us take another look at this concept.

In Chapter 1, mishnah 14 we defined the true "self" as being the *neshamah*, whose existence is eternal. The body is but a container, as it were, a vehicle whereby the spiritual *neshamah* can accomplish things. The function of the *neshamah* in this mundane world is to reach a stage of *tikun* or fulfillment, which is achieved by the performance of mitzvos. The *neshamah* is "rewarded" when a person performs mitzvos, and it is negatively affected if he sins.

If we correctly understand the above concept of the *self*, we may see that there is a kind of "selfishness" that is actually praiseworthy; i.e., when a person looks out for the interest of the true self, the *neshamah*. The popular idiom of "look out for number one" is a fallacy, because it considers one's personal gratification as being "number one." When the drug addict injects himself with heroin, he may think he is looking out for number one. However, his transitory euphoria is acquired at a tremendous cost to himself.

When confronted with choice, the mishnah tells us to look at what is the real gain and what is the real loss. Consider the reward that a mitzvah will bring: the perfection of the true self. In the light of this, the temporary inconvenience of the effort required for performance of the mitzvah is minuscule. On the other hand, the ephemeral pleasure of a sin is obscured by the regression it will bring to the *neshamah* and the damage to the true self.

This mishnah in no way conflicts with Antigonos. Indeed, careful attention to the words of Antigonos reveals that he discourages anticipation of פְּרָס, *reward*, something external to the mitzvah itself. Our mishnah is referring to the gain and loss inherent within the mitzvah or the sin.

R' Yehudah *HaNasi* is simply appealing to our better judgment: Choose a path in life that is truly to your own ultimate advantage.

דַּע מַה לְמַעְלָה מִמְּךָ – עַיִן רוֹאָה, וְאֹזֶן שׁוֹמַעַת
Know what is above You — a watchful Eye, an attentive Ear

The trilogy can be better understood in the light of cognitive psychology, which our sages anticipated some 2,000 years ago.

2/1 *Consider three things, and you will not come into the grip of sin: Know what is above you — a watchful Eye, an attentive Ear, and all your deeds are recorded in a Book.*

Cognitive psychology teaches us that most problems in adjustment to life are due to a distortion of perception. A number of people may see the same thing, and each one may give a different version of what he saw. Indeed, some of the descriptions may contradict each other. Similarly, we may hear something and come to a conclusion about what we heard, whereas the actual statement and what we think we heard may be poles apart. In other words, many of the difficulties of coping with reality are due to a misperception of reality.

The tendency to misperceive reality is in great part an occupational hazard of being human, of having inclinations and desires that are a consequence of the animal-like body we inhabit. This is evident in the final words of Moses, who said, "I set before you today life and death, a blessing and a curse, and (I advise you) you shall choose life. . .to harken to the voice of God . . . for He is your life" (*Deuteronomy* 30:19-20). Why is this admonition necessary? Who would be so foolish to choose death and curse above life and blessing? It is only because we are subject to misperception, and we may see good as being bad and vice versa. Our desires can play havoc with our senses.

If you wish to avoid doing wrong, our mishnah tells us, consider the frailty of your perceptions. To see and hear correctly may be above and beyond you, because your perceptions are subject to distortion. Your eyes and ears are not as much under your control as you think. If you wish to do what is right, allow your actions to be guided by what is written in the Torah. The Torah is the Manufacturer's guide to proper and optimal operation of the apparatus He created.

One might ask, "But is it not possible for a person to misunderstand and distort what is written in the Torah?" R' Yehudah *HaNasi* provided for this in Chapter 1, when he quoted his grandfather, Rabban Gamliel, in mishnah 16: "Make a teacher for yourself, and remove yourself from uncertainty," i.e., you will be free of doubt. A competent Torah authority as a mentor will enable you to understand Torah properly and make the correct choices in life.

וְכָל מַעֲשֶׂיךָ בְּסֵפֶר נִכְתָּבִים
And all your deeds are recorded in a Book.

Once it has been stated that none of our actions and words go unseen and unheard and that God sees and hears all that we do, why is it necessary to state that everything is recorded? Surely God's memory retains everything, hence whether something is recorded or not will make no difference when we stand before the Heavenly tribunal for judgment.

Our modern technology has enabled us not only to see and hear from afar, but also to record everything. So think of it this way. On Judgment Day, there

רַבָּן [כ] גַּמְלִיאֵל בְּנוֹ שֶׁל רַבִּי יְהוּדָה הַנָּשִׂיא אוֹמֵר:
יָפֶה תַלְמוּד תּוֹרָה עִם דֶּרֶךְ אֶרֶץ, שֶׁיְּגִיעַת
שְׁנֵיהֶם מַשְׁכַּחַת עָוֹן. וְכָל תּוֹרָה שֶׁאֵין עִמָּהּ מְלָאכָה,

---

may be no need for inflicting any punishment whatever on wrongdoers. The tribunal will simply show a video of one's entire life. Can there be a greater punishment than having to watch a replay of everything one did during one's lifetime? Would one not be consumed with shame? And what if the video will be played before an audience? Can one imagine the pain of the embarrassment?

R' Yehudah *HaNasi* is trying to teach us how to live properly, and he advises us to behave in a way that we will not be embarrassed when a replay of our lives is shown to us and to others.

2.

יָפֶה תַלְמוּד תּוֹרָה עִם דֶּרֶךְ אֶרֶץ
Torah study is acceptable
together with an occupation

When you work and engage in earning a livelihood, said the Baal Shem Tov, be sure that Torah accompanies you. In addition to assuring that all our work and business dealings will comply with Torah, there is yet another benefit to be accrued.

A man once came over to a Rebbe complaining that his business was failing. He had inherited a store, but while his father had done a brisk business, the man's fortunes were not good. Although nothing had changed in the business, there was a dearth of customers.

"Nothing has changed, you say?" asked the Rebbe. "Tell me, what do you do when there is a lull in the store, and there are no customers?"

"I read a newspaper, and catch up on what is happening in the world," the man said. "Aha!" said the Rebbe. "There is your problem. When things were quiet, your father would pick up a *Mishnayos* and learn, or recite *Tehillim* (Psalms). This irritated Satan to no end. In order to distract your father from his Torah study and prayer, Satan would urge people to go to his store. This way, his brisk business would interrupt his study and prayer.

"You, on the other hand, idle away your free time, which is just what Satan wishes. Why should he bother sending customers to distract you?"

שֶׁיְּגִיעַת שְׁנֵיהֶם מַשְׁכַּחַת עָוֹן
For exertion of them both
makes sin forgotten

R' Mendel of Kotzk used to say, "The reason one should not sin is not because it is forbidden, but because one should not have time for sin. When you are not engaged in working for a livelihood you should be studying Torah. You will simply not have the time to sin."

Modern man has been blessed with many time-saving devices: jet planes,

2. **R**abban Gamliel, the son of Rabbi Yehudah HaNasi, says: Torah study is acceptable together with an occupation, for exertion of them both makes sin forgotten. All Torah study that is not joined with work will

---

microwave ovens, fax machines, high-speed computers, and fast foods. Tasks over which our ancestors had to labor for hours, days, and weeks are now accomplished in a fraction of the time. Our generation should have produced an unprecedented knowledge of Torah among lay people. Had they followed the wise advice of the Rabbi of Kotzk, this would indeed have occurred.

Unfortunately the precious gift of time that modern technology has provided us is too often squandered on meaningless pastimes. Such idle time is indeed a fertile ground for many self-defeating behaviors. Furthermore, our children learn from observing their parents. If we set an example that time can be wasted, we can hardly blame them for the partying that has proven to be the breeding grounds for many of young peoples' troubles.

Filling our time with constructive activities is the best deterrent to improper and unhealthy behavior.

יָפֶה תַלְמוּד תּוֹרָה עִם דֶּרֶךְ אֶרֶץ,
שֶׁיְּגִיעַת שְׁנֵיהֶם מַשְׁכַּחַת עָוֹן

Torah study is acceptable together with an occupation, for exertion of them both makes sin forgotten

The *Midrash Shmuel* points out that there are several ways of combining Torah study with earning a livelihood. Some people spend most of their day at work or at business, and have a set time for a *shiur* (study session), perhaps the *daf yomi*. Specifying time for Torah study both in the morning and evening is imperative. One of the questions we will be asked on Judgment Day is "Did you designate time for Torah study?" Complying with the minimum standards is acceptable.

Better yet is one who devotes half of the day to Torah study and suffices with a half day for work. Hence the mishnah refers to the first category as יָפֶה, acceptable, whereas the second category יְגִיעַת שְׁנֵיהֶם, exerting oneself for both, has the advantage in that it will protect a person from sin.

Regardless of which pattern one employs, a person should understand that Torah is the goal. Work is but a means for sustenance, to enable us to sustain ourselves so that we are able to achieve the goal. Realization of what is primary and what is secondary is crucial. If earning money becomes the primary concern and Torah is seen as a mere condiment, the Torah has no lasting quality.

It is related that the Chofetz Chaim kept his store open just long enough to earn for his needs. The remainder of the day was totally devoted to Torah study. Perhaps we do not aspire to the spirituality of the Chofetz Chaim (and

סוֹפָהּ בְּטֵלָה וְגוֹרֶרֶת עָוֹן. וְכָל הָעוֹסְקִים עִם הַצִּבּוּר, יִהְיוּ
עוֹסְקִים עִמָּהֶם לְשֵׁם שָׁמַיִם, שֶׁזְּכוּת אֲבוֹתָם מְסַיַּעְתָּם,
וְצִדְקָתָם עוֹמֶדֶת לָעַד. וְאַתֶּם, מַעֲלֶה אֲנִי עֲלֵיכֶם שָׂכָר
הַרְבֵּה, כְּאִלוּ עֲשִׂיתֶם.

---

why not?), but if we would truly appreciate Torah as the goal in life and work as a necessary means, our allotment of time to each would be more favorable for Torah study.

**וְכָל תּוֹרָה שֶׁאֵין עִמָּהּ מְלָאכָה,
סוֹפָהּ בְּטֵלָה**
*All Torah study that is not joined
with work will cease in the end*

Some people seem to have been endowed with a gift of a highly efficient memory, and they may retain everything they see or hear. Most of us, however, must look for ways to retain what we have learned. Constant review of the material is essential to forestall forgetfulness. R' Moshe Feinstein once confided that he had reviewed the *Shulchan Aruch* 400 times! There seems little doubt that concentration and effort enhance retention. The principle "easy come, easy go" is quite valid. Retention of Torah requires work. Studying a portion of the Torah laboriously — with careful analysis and preferably discussing it with a colleague, raising questions and resolving them — will impress the material on one's memory.

We have been blessed with easy access to Torah. We may listen to Torah over the phone, view it on our computer screen, or listen to a tape as we drive. While these are all laudable, they do not fulfill the criterion of "working in Torah." These methods may indeed enhance our knowledge, but unless we exert ourselves and work toward a better understanding of what we have learned, reinforcing it with review, it may leave us as easily as it came to us.

When we have something important to do and we are afraid that we might forget it, we leave ourselves reminders. If we appreciate the importance of Torah, we will do what is necessary to make certain that we do not forget it.

**וְכָל הָעוֹסְקִים עִם הַצִּבּוּר, יִהְיוּ עוֹסְקִים עִמָּהֶם לְשֵׁם
שָׁמַיִם, שֶׁזְּכוּת אֲבוֹתָם מְסַיַּעְתָּם, וְצִדְקָתָם עוֹמֶדֶת לָעַד.
וְאַתֶּם, מַעֲלֶה אֲנִי עֲלֵיכֶם שָׂכָר הַרְבֵּה, כְּאִלוּ עֲשִׂיתֶם**
*All those who are engaged in public service
should exert themselves for the sake of Heaven,
for then the merit of their ancestors will assist
them, and their righteousness will endure forever.
And you [the public servants] will be fully rewarded
for your efforts, as though you had achieved it.*

This portion of the mishnah is rather cryptic, as many commentaries have pointed out. Why does the mishnah single out that "those who are engaged in public service should exert themselves for the sake of Heaven"? Is this not a requirement for everything one does? And what is meant by "the merit of their ancestors will assist them"?

cease in the end, and lead to sin. All those who are engaged in public service should exert themselves for the sake of Heaven, for then the merit of their ancestors will assist them, and their righteousness will endure forever. And you [the public servants] will be fully rewarded for your efforts, as though you had achieved it.

It would appear that this refers to the ancestors of the public servants. How is this relevant? And finally, what is meant by being rewarded "as though you had achieved *it*"? Achieved what?

Many commentaries struggle with an explanation of this mishnah. I will be bold enough to suggest another interpretation, but you must bear with me for a bit of introduction.

People who deliver human services, whether it be a doctor, teacher, social worker, etc., may be variously motivated in their work. Inasmuch as I am most familiar with the medical field, I will choose doctors as an example.

Let us take two young men, Joe and Ben. Joe is a person who is very bright, but who has had unwarranted feelings of inferiority since childhood. One possible adjustment to escape these distressing feelings is to seek a position of prominence, or to do things which will elicit admiration from others. Joe reasons that becoming a doctor will do both. His emotional well-being is to a great extent dependent on successful outcomes of treatment for which his patients will be grateful.

Ben grew up with a healthy self-esteem. He, too, chose medicine, but he made his choice because he felt there was economic security in being a doctor, and he does not need anything to validate his self-worth. Let us see how a particular patient would fare with each.

Mr. Smith consults Dr. Ben for abdominal pain. Dr. Ben takes a careful history, does a physical exam, and performs some routine laboratory tests. He reassures the patient that there is nothing seriously wrong, and prescribes a diet and antacids. Two weeks later Mr. Smith returns, complaining that he feels worse. Dr. Ben then orders a number of diagnostic studies, all of which are normal. He reassures Smith, telling him that he probably has an "irritable bowel syndrome," for which he prescribes antispasmodics.

Ten days later Smith comes to Dr. Ben's office, doubled up in pain. "You've got to help me, doc," he says. Dr. Ben reviews the case and says, "Mr. Smith, I really cannot find the problem. Let me refer you to a group of gastroenterologists. I will send them the test results, and perhaps they can help you." Dr. Ben wishes that he had been able to help Smith, but he does not see this inability as any reflection on his competence.

Suppose, however, that Smith had consulted Dr. Joe, who manages the first two visits just as Dr. Ben did. However, the third visit is quite different. Dr. Joe sees Smith's persistent complaint as questioning his competence. Remember,

---

Dr. Joe has always felt inadequate, and when he has a poor result in treatment, he interprets this as a threat and a blow to his already low self-esteem. He cannot refer Smith elsewhere, because this would be tantamount to admitting that he is incompetent. Instead, he reacts in one of three ways, all of which I have witnessed.

1. "Hm, Smith, there is something going on here that is not showing up on the diagnostic tests. We must do exploratory surgery to find out just what is wrong." Smith is subjected to unnecessary surgery.

2. "Look here, Smith, all your tests are negative. There is nothing wrong with you. It's all in your head, psychosomatic. I'm going to refer you to a psychiatrist." Essentially, Dr. Joe is angry at Smith for considering him incompetent, and retaliates by calling him neurotic.

3. "Well, I can't let you suffer like this. Here is a prescription for a painkiller, which you may take every four hours." Three years later Smith is admitted to my rehabilitation institute, because he became addicted to narcotics.

Anyone who suffers from unwarranted feelings of inadequacy and inferiority, and needs successful results to vindicate him and raise his self-esteem, may react to unsuccessful results in the way Dr. Joe did. Anyone who provides human services of any type, if he or she has a low self-esteem, is vulnerable to react defensively when unfavorable results occur. Thus, doctors, teachers, therapists, social workers, and public servants are subject to such reactions. While their efforts are directed toward helping others, there is a very strong ego involvement, essentially a selfish drive as well.

This may be the message of this mishnah. Of course, everything one does should be לְשֵׁם שָׁמַיִם, with the intent of fulfilling the Divine will. Public servants should be particularly motivated by the Divine will, and not look upon their service to the public to satisfy their ego needs. If they are not motivated לְשֵׁם שָׁמַיִם, and need positive results to vindicate them, they may, like Dr. Joe, do things that may be detrimental to the public. No one can control the outcome of one's efforts. All one can do is the best one is capable of doing, and with the purest of intentions.

Our ancestor, the Patriarch Abraham, received God's blessing because he taught his children the way of God (*Genesis* 18:19). Unfortunately, Abraham's son Ishmael did not accept his father's teachings. The Patriarch Isaac was totally devoted to God, to the point of being willing to give up his life for God (*Genesis* 22:9). Isaac certainly taught his children to the best of his ability, yet Esau deviated from his father's ways. We have always continued to invoke the merits of the Patriarchs in our prayers. Their righteousness, *that of the Patriarchs,* prevails forever, and has not been diminished in the least by the fact that some of the results of their efforts were unfavorable. They were judged by what they did, and not by what resulted. This is the attitude which public servants must have. If their intentions are proper, an unsuccessful result should not be taken as a reflection of their competence.

We can now see the closing words of the mishnah as following logically from the above, "And you [the public servants] will be fully rewarded for your efforts, *as though you had achieved it.*" As long as your intentions are לְשֵׁם שָׁמַיִם, the outcome is irrelevant as far as your reward is concerned. You cannot control outcome. Just as the Patriarchs were rewarded for their efforts, even though some of the outcome was unfavorable, so will you, the public servants who work לְשֵׁם שָׁמַיִם, be rewarded for your services, which should be with the finest motivation and the purest intentions.

3.

הֱווּ זְהִירִין בָּרָשׁוּת
Beware of rulers

This mishnah hardly requires commentary. The experience of centuries of history has demonstrated its truth. Joseph was the savior of Egypt, and his grandchildren were cruelly enslaved. Abarbanel was the chief finance minister to King Ferdinand of Spain. He was exiled in the expulsion, with his money and belongings being confiscated. We know that office seekers may befriend anyone who they think can help them acquire the coveted position, but the favor is often soon forgotten.

There is, however, a rather interesting interpretation of this mishnah, if we allow ourselves the liberty of changing some vowel sounds. (Remember, the Mishnah was recorded without vowel markings.) The word רָשׁוּת may also be read as רְשׁוּת, which would then be translated as "be watchful about the things that are permissible."

The works of *mussar* and *chassidus* stress the danger of indulging in permissible pleasures. Yielding to cravings for permissible things may erode the resistance to forbidden things. On the other hand, restraining oneself from giving in to permissible pleasures makes it much easier to resist prohibited ones.

It is well known that in military strategy, a preemptive strike is most effective: The best defense is offense. When one must struggle against the *yetzer hara's* incitement to do forbidden things, one is fighting defensively on one's own territory. If we restrain ourselves from some permissible pleasures, we are fighting the *yetzer hara* on *its* territory, a most efficient maneuver. As R' Shneur Zalman said, "That which is forbidden is prohibited, and much of which is permissible is not necessary."

Our ethical works state that permissible things should be used in a way that promotes a person's mission on earth. One cannot fulfill the mitzvos, the Torah obligations, unless one has the physical and emotional capabilities to do so, and optimal health will enable optimal function. Thus, eating, sleeping, judicious relaxation and recreation, and earning a livelihood are all essential for optimal function. These are a person's *needs,* and when directed towards

ב/ד   לְצָרֶךְ עַצְמָן; נִרְאִין כְּאוֹהֲבִין בִּשְׁעַת הֲנָאָתָן, וְאֵין עוֹמְדִין לוֹ לָאָדָם בִּשְׁעַת דָּחֳקוֹ.

[ד] **הוּא** הָיָה אוֹמֵר: עֲשֵׂה רְצוֹנוֹ כִּרְצוֹנֶךָ, כְּדֵי שֶׁיַּעֲשֶׂה רְצוֹנְךָ כִּרְצוֹנוֹ. בַּטֵּל רְצוֹנְךָ מִפְּנֵי רְצוֹנוֹ, כְּדֵי שֶׁיְּבַטֵּל רְצוֹן אֲחֵרִים מִפְּנֵי רְצוֹנֶךָ.

---

mitzvos, they become a mitzvah in themselves. Once the actual needs are met, and one indulges in excesses for sheer pleasure, one is bringing oneself dangerously close to overstepping the boundary into the territory of the forbidden.

One might think that earthly pleasures are one's best friends, since they provide gratification, but their love is treacherous. If we become dependent on them for our gratification, we are setting ourselves up for disappointment.

A young man in treatment for drug addiction wrote a "letter to drugs" in which he said, "You promised me everything. You gave me great pleasure, but you were slyly ensnaring me. Instead of everything you promised, you took everything away from me. I lost my wife, my children, my job, my health, and the respect of my friends." While permissible pleasures may not be as overtly dangerous as drugs, they are nevertheless not without risk. People who become addicted to food or to making money may admit that they have lost control. They may acknowledge that they have suffered harmful consequences from what began as apparent proper behavior, but accelerated beyond their control.

We can thus understand the mishnah, "Be cautious about permissible things." They are brought within one's reach in order to meet one's actual needs. They appear to be friendly, but they will not help a person when he is distressed.

4.

עֲשֵׂה רְצוֹנוֹ . . . בַּטֵּל רְצוֹנְךָ
Treat His will . . . Nullify your will

Why is it necessary for the mishnah to essentially repeat itself? Is there any difference between "Treat His will as if it were your will" and "Nullify your will in the face of His will"? Are they not very similar if not identical? And just what is meant by "He will nullify the will of others in the face of your will"? More precisely, who are these "others" whose will we would desire should be negated before ours?

The answer to the last question should be obvious. First and foremost, we would of course wish our children to accept our authority and to defer to our

their own benefit; they act friendly when it benefits them, but do not stand by someone in his time of need.

4. **H**e *was accustomed to say: Treat His will as if it were your will, so that He will treat your will as if it were His will. Nullify your will in the face of His will, so that He will nullify the will of others in the face of your will.*

---

more mature wisdom as parents. We would hope that they would negate their will before ours. Needless to say, the degree of adolescent turmoil which prevails in our society indicates that we have been less than startlingly successful in this respect. One might think that in Torah-observant families this problem is at a minimum. Unfortunately, even if there is more deference to parents in such families, the incidence of adolescent defiance is anything but negligible.

It is a truism that children learn most by emulating their parents, by our modeling for them, rather than by our lecturing them. The obvious question is then: In what way do parents model deference to a higher authority?

You might say that in a Torah-observant family there is an abundance of deference to a higher authority. Virtually our entire lives are regulated by the dictates of halachah, which we understand to be the will of God. Furthermore, when we have any questions whether something is permissible, we defer to the decision of a *posek* (halachic authority). What greater deference to authority can there be than that of a Torah-observant family?

I believe we are missing a crucial point. Rashi quotes the Talmudic statement that a person should not say, "I detest pork," but rather, "I do like pork, but my heavenly Father has forbidden it (*Leviticus*, 20:26), and this is also true of other prohibitions. This is an example of negating our will before a Higher Authority, i.e., negating our will before that of God.

Let me ask: Just when does a Torah-observant person feel that the reason he abstains from pork is because, while he indeed likes it, it has been forbidden? For the vast majority of Torah Jews, pork is an abomination, and even the thought of eating pork is enough to make one nauseous. When, then, do we observe this teaching of the Talmud?

The prohibition of pork is but one example of our attitude toward things forbidden by the Torah. For example, for a Torah-observant person, the thought of driving to the office to work on Shabbos is simply shocking, and he would no more consider this a possibility than trying to fly by flapping his arms. In such instances, we have indeed been successful in internalizing God's will and making His will our own, but we have thereby complied only with the first part of the mishnah.

When *do* we have a will for something and then negate it in deference to the Divine will? The Talmudic statement is an expression of the second part of the mishnah, where we *do* have a will for something and then negate it in deference to the will of God. Have we been so successful in internalizing the Divine will that by achieving the first part of the mishnah we have eliminated the second?

On the one hand, we have been further deprived of applying this Talmudic teaching, at least insofar as abstinence from nonkosher foods is concerned. As a child, I used to enjoy toasting marshmallows, until we discovered that they were not reliably kosher. I truly loved them, but was unable to eat them, and that did constitute a deference to authority. I actually had to negate my own will. Today's youngsters are deprived of such an experience, because not only are kosher marshmallows available, but there is virtually no food from which they must abstain. We are blessed with an availability of everything at the highest level of kosher supervision.

I must actually make a diligent search for things I would like to do but from which I abstain only because of deference to authority. Because we have varying authorities on certain issues, we may be able to circumvent deference. Often we can find a *heter* (permit) to do what we desire. For example, there is a difference of opinion as to whether a man is permitted to wear a wrist watch on Shabbos. Is it ornamental and can he therefore be considered "wearing," or is it worn for its function of telling time, in which case it is considered as transporting an object from a private to a public domain? My rabbi maintains it is not permissible. However, I might say that "I am not bound by his opinion, since there are other opinions that it is permissible." This is then an example of something we wish to do which is ruled improper by one authority, but rather than defer to that authority, we unjustifiably find another authority that is more to our liking.

Perhaps there are some things which we do indeed deny ourselves because we accept halachah, but many of these are private and do not provide us with the opportunity of modeling for our children.

There are thus not too many things today that lend themselves to our demonstrating deference to authority when the latter restricts something we wish to do. Of course, there is still *lashon hara,* and it would be most beneficial if our children would hear us say, "We can't continue to talk about that because it is *lashon hara.* " Another possibility is to accept the halachah that we may not talk in *shul.* We may let our children know how pleasant it would be to have a conversation with people whom we meet only on Shabbos in *shul,* but because we respect the *kedushah* of the *shul,* we refrain from doing so. This would be a demonstration of deference to authority.

It may be necessary to make a concerted effort to find areas whereby we can demonstrate the Talmudic principle. Teaching deference to authority is of primary importance in modern life, where traditional respect for authority has been so seriously eroded. We would be wise to find ways in which we can accomplish this.

My work in the treatment of alcoholics has given me many insights into ways to overcome self-defeating behaviors other than drinking. I am in good company, because the prophets often chastised people for their errant behavior by comparing them to alcoholics (*Isaiah* 29:9). In fact, if we were to take a text on alcoholism and substitute "sin" for "alcohol," the result would be a fine treatise on *mussar*.

There is value in learning *teshuvah* techniques from the recovering alcoholic, because we can observe the struggle and the results in the concrete rather than discuss them in the abstract. We may better see not only *what* works, but also *why* it works.

Once an alcoholic recognizes the destructive nature of his drinking and decides to overcome it, one of the steps he takes is "to turn my will over to God." Alcoholism has been described as "self-will run riot." The person who wishes to recover recognizes that his own will is unreliable, because it was his yielding to his will that led to his downfall. He must therefore set aside his own will and accept the will of God as that which should guide him in his behavior.

The initial phase of recovery may be very challenging, as the person must struggle against recurring impulses to drink. However, many recovering alcoholics say that after successfully struggling for abstinence, "I awoke one day and found my craving for alcohol was gone. My prayers had been answered, and God relieved me of my craving for alcohol." They feel that God did for them what they could not do for themselves, but only after they had made a maximum effort.

This observation helped me to better understand the mishnah. Our own will is unreliable and may be treacherous. Our judgments may be distorted by our desires for gratification, and we may rationalize in an ingenious manner to justify fulfilling them. The wise Solomon said, "All of a person's ways appear just and proper in his own eyes" (*Proverbs* 16:2). Truly proper behavior can result only if we set our own will aside and accept the Divine will as that which will determine our actions.

Deferring to God's will may not be easy, and may at times be a formidable challenge. However, if we do so, we will find that "one who seeks to purify himself will be helped by God to achieve his goal" (*Shabbos* 104a). He may eventually find that there is no longer a struggle, and that God has removed his cravings for improper things. "Give me an opening like the tip of a needle, and I will broaden it like the portal of a banquet hall" (*Shir HaShirim Rabbah* 5:3), and "God will watch the steps of the righteous" (*I Samuel* 2:9) to deter them from errant ways.

It is only necessary to recognize that our own will is unreliable, and to be wise enough to substitute God's will for our own. We can then be certain that God will do for us what we cannot do for ourselves.

ב/ה **הַלֵּל** [ה] אוֹמֵר: אַל תִּפְרוֹשׁ מִן הַצִּבּוּר, וְאַל תַּאֲמִין
בְּעַצְמְךָ עַד יוֹם מוֹתְךָ, וְאַל תָּדִין אֶת חֲבֵרְךָ
עַד שֶׁתַּגִּיעַ לִמְקוֹמוֹ, וְאַל תֹּאמַר דָּבָר שֶׁאִי אֶפְשָׁר לִשְׁמוֹעַ,

---

5.

אַל תִּפְרוֹשׁ מִן הַצִּבּוּר
*Do not separate yourself
from the community*

In the introduction, we stressed the importance of not separating oneself from the community, and that even if a person is derelict in observance of Torah and does not merit Paradise on his own, he nevertheless may enter Paradise by virtue of his participation with the community. This is further confirmed by Rambam (*Hilchos Teshuvah* 3:11), who states that a person who separates himself from the community loses his portion in Paradise, which undoubtedly refers to that share which he would enjoy as a member of the community.

Separating oneself does not necessarily mean that one rejects the community by relocating geographically or even that one fails to participate in community projects. It can be much more subtle than that, as we can see from an episode in the Talmud (*Pesachim* 70b).

Two scholars left the community because the majority rejected their position on a particular halachah. When Rav suggested to the sages that they try to understand the minority opinion of these two sholars, the response was, "We are not interested in understanding the opinion of separatists."

This is an interesting passage, because the entire Talmud consists of dialogue and discussion of varying opinions, and sometimes the exchanges can be quite sharp. Minority opinions are consistently quoted and discussed. Why then, does the Talmud refuse to analyze this particular minority opinion?

The answer is that we are indeed permitted to differ. In Talmudic times, those who held minority opinions were permitted to follow them, even though the accepted halachah was otherwise. However, we must always keep an open mind and be willing to listen to a different point of view. The two scholars who left the community because of their disagreement had closed their minds and had adopted a dogmatic attitude. Their unwillingness to even consider a differing viewpoint indicated that they were separatists, and the Talmud had no interest in the dogmatic ideas of someone who closes his mind to anything that is not in keeping with his own opinion. This attitude is one of arrogance and vanity, something which is despicable from an ethical standpoint.

We must therefore be careful to avoid the separatism that will result from vanity and arrogance, of insisting that one is right, and not be willing to subject one's position to critical analysis. Truth will stand up under scrutiny. It is only falsehood that must be protected against any challenge that will disprove it.

5. **H**illel says: Do not separate yourself from the community; do not believe in yourself until the day you die; do not judge your fellow until you have reached his place; do not make a statement that cannot be easily understood,

---

וְאַל תַּאֲמִין בְּעַצְמְךָ עַד יוֹם מוֹתְךָ
Do not believe in yourself until the day you die

Again, recourse to the recovering alcoholic demonstrates very clearly the importance of this teaching.

A lengthy abstinence from alcohol may give a person a false sense of security that he has totally overcome his problem, and he may then lower his guard. This is when relapse is likely to occur. The recovering person must see alcohol as his enemy, lurking to destroy him, and searching for a vulnerable spot at which to attack. We can see the truth of the words of Rabbeinu Bachya in bold action: "You may be asleep, but the *yetzer hara* is never asleep. It constantly seeks to ensnare you" (*Duties of the Heart, Shaar Yichud Hamaaseh* 5).

Simply resolving never to sin again is as ineffective as resolving never to drink again. The alcoholic must continue to reinforce his defenses as long as he lives, and that applies equally to anyone who wishes to avoid sin.

One man with 30 years of sobriety referred to himself as "recovering" but not "recovered." "I cannot consider myself cured of this disease, but only that I am keeping it at bay. If I die without having relapsed, I will then have recovered." Indeed, when he died at age 83 after 42 years of sobriety, the announcement of his death was appropriately worded: "John has recovered."

We must forever be on the alert and on guard against the sly maneuvers of the *yetzer hara,* and we must utilize the methods that our great ethicists have provided to protect ourselves.

וְאַל תָּדִין אֶת חֲבֵרְךָ
עַד שֶׁתַּגִּיעַ לִמְקוֹמוֹ
Do not judge your fellow until you have reached his place

A man once asked R' Michel of Zlotchow to prescribe a course of penance for him, because he had inadvertently violated Shabbos. R' Michel reprimanded him sharply, explaining that violation of Shabbos is a grievous sin. An inadvertent violation indicates that one had been negligent in remembering that it was Shabbos. He therefore prescribed a taxing course of penance.

When this man came to the Baal Shem Tov, the latter told him that severe penance was unnecessary, and that it was sufficient that he supply candles for the synagogue service. However, the tallow candles he donated were eaten by a dog who had entered the synagogue via an open door, and the replacement candles blew out as soon as they were kindled. The man took this as a sign that God was rejecting his penance, and reported this to the Baal Shem Tov.

"I believe that R' Michel is behind this," the Baal Shem Tov said, and sent a message to R' Michel that he wished him to come for Shabbos.

R' Michel began the trip on Thursday, with ample time to reach the Baal Shem Tov before Shabbos. However, a strange series of events occurred that caused inordinate delays. First an axle broke, and after that the horse fell dead. When a fresh horse was acquired, a torrential rain turned the dirt road into mud, into which the wagon became mired. The repeated delays resulted in R' Michel's arrival rather late Friday afternoon, and when he entered he saw that the Baal Shem Tov was holding a wine goblet and chanting the *kiddush*. He assumed that it was already Shabbos, and believing that he had violated the sacred Shabbos by traveling, he fainted.

The Baal Shem Tov revived him and said, "It is not yet Shabbos. I happened to have ushered in the Shabbos well before sunset.

"But tell me, R' Michel," the Baal Shem Tov continued, "when you thought you had violated the Shabbos, how did you feel? Were you not grievously distressed when you believed you had sinned? Is not the distress of feeling one has sinned and the sincere remorse sufficient penance? Is there really a need for prescribing rigorous self-deprivations when one is already suffering the pangs of one's conscience? Is this not what the mishnah means, that we should not judge a person until we have placed ourselves in his situation?"

In some cases we cannot identify with a person unless we are indeed subjected to similar conditions. "But," says R' Elya Meir Bloch, "one does not necessarily have to put oneself in the same position in order to empathize. We can identify with another person by seeking to fully understand the other person's circumstances. We must suspend judgment until we have had the opportunity to thoroughly know all the factors that went into a person's behavior. Then and only then can we appreciate another's position, and only then can we render judgment."

This does not mean that empathizing with another person will always result in a favorable judgment. While identifying with him, we must be able to detach and become more objective. But even if the judgment is not favorable, it will be fair, and to judge fairly is all that can be expected of us.

It is with some trepidation that I write these lines, because the concept I am presenting is vulnerable to misinterpretation, and the consequences of such distortion could be very harmful. Nevertheless, since I believe this concept to be valid, I feel it should be presented. My only request is that it be read carefully.

The Rabbi of Kotzk said, "The Torah commands, 'Do not deceive your fellow man' (*Leviticus* 25:14,17). That is the actual *din* (law). What is the *lifnim meshuras hadin* (going beyond the minimal requirements of the law)?

That one should not deceive oneself."

I would like to paraphrase the words of the Rabbi of Kotzk to apply to our mishnah. The law is, "Do not judge another person until you have placed yourself in his circumstances." The extension of this is, "Do not judge *yourself* until you have placed yourself in similar circumstances." Let me explain.

There is a natural law that governs human behavior, which is as inviolable as the physical law of gravity, and may be thought of as "the law of human gravitation." This law states that *a human being will always gravitate toward whatever is most comfortable and least distressful.* There can be great variation in what is considered most comfortable and least distressful, but the principle is universal.

For example, a person who surrenders his life for *kiddush Hashem* (accepting martyrdom to sanctify God), and allows himself to be killed rather than to renounce his faith in God, does so not because he is willing to accept a greater distress, but because his value system is such that denying *Hashem* is actually a greater distress than losing his life. Indeed, the greatness of *kiddush Hashem* is not that it is a sacrifice, but to the contrary — that one has so intense a love for and devotion to *Hashem* that to deny Him would be the greatest distress possible. In choosing martyrdom one has again chosen the most comfortable and least distressing option. One's greatness lies precisely in having developed a value system of this caliber.

We may think back about a sin we committed, or some inappropriate behavior, and we may severely chastise ourselves for it. We may be remorseful and resolve never to repeat that act again. Although this may appear to be adequate *teshuvah,* it is not yet sufficient, *unless we understand how it came about,* because only then will we be in a position to avoid a recurrence.

Unless we understand how a misdeed came about and why we were vulnerable to do it, we are likely to deny it, because there is a tendency to disown something which we consider totally alien and unacceptable to us. The *Sfas Emes* gives us this illuminating insight in his comment on the verses in *Genesis* (18:12-15). The Torah states that when Sarah was told that she would bear a child in her old age, she was in disbelief. When Abraham reprimanded her for doubting God's promise, "Sarah denied, saying 'I did not ridicule,' because she was afraid." The *Sfas Emes* says that Sarah did not lie, but rather that she was *in denial.* Sarah's belief in God and her reverence for God were so great that she could not imagine herself having questioned God's word. "Because she was afraid," means that her degree of *yiras Shamayim* (reverence for God) was so great that it was unthinkable for her that she had even a momentary doubt. When she said, "I did not ridicule," she felt she was telling the truth, as is the case when someone is *in denial.*

Obviously, when a person is in denial and disowns an action, there is no

ב/ה שֶׁסּוֹפוֹ לְהִשָּׁמַע. וְאַל תֹּאמַר לִכְשֶׁאֶפָּנֶה אֶשְׁנֶה, שֶׁמָּא לֹא תִפָּנֶה.

---

possibility of *teshuvah*. One cannot have remorse for something one is not aware of having done. We must therefore be aware of our frailties and vulnerabilities as human beings. We must understand how it came about that we did something we should not have done, and what the circumstances were that caused our thinking to be distorted.

My concern in presenting this is that one might think that to understand how and why something happened is to justify it. This is by no means so. There is no justification for doing wrong, and according to the Torah, even a sin committed inadvertently requires penance and forgiveness. Torah does not accept a defense of "irresistible impulse," because a person is always responsible for his actions. The Talmudic statement that "a person is always liable for any damage he does, whether intentionally or unintentionally, whether asleep or awake" (*Bava Kamma* 26a) applies to all one's actions. The understanding of how and why something happened is an investigation as to "how was it that I acted irresponsibly," and by discovering how and why something happened, we are in a position to take corrective measures so that we do not repeat a mistake.

The extension of the mishnah that we should not judge ourselves until we have placed ourselves in the position of when we did wrong is therefore *not* a justification of the act, but to the contrary, a method to allow us to be aware of what we did. A harsh self-judgment without an understanding of how a mistake came about is likely to result in denial, in which case we are helpless to avoid its repetition.

וְאַל תֹּאמַר דָּבָר שֶׁאִי אֶפְשָׁר לִשְׁמוֹעַ, שֶׁסּוֹפוֹ לְהִשָּׁמַע
Do not make a statement that cannot be easily understood, on the ground that it will be understood eventually

The meaning of this portion of the mishnah is somewhat obscure, and a number of commentaries have offered explanations. There may be another interpretation from a psychological aspect, which appears to account for the exact words of the mishnah.

Not infrequently, people are in *denial* of an issue. Denial is not the same as lying. Lying is a willful distortion of fact, whereas someone who is in denial is unable to recognize some facts about himself or others.

In psychotherapy, when the patient is in denial and is unable to see what the therapist is pointing out, it is fruitless to try and hammer in the insight. When denial is in operation, the internal resistance to recognition is overwhelming. Any attempt by the therapist to break through the denial is likely to

on the ground that it will be understood eventually; and do not say, "When I am free I will study," for perhaps you will not become free.

accomplish nothing other than to irritate the patient and put him into an adversary position. An accomplished therapist will instead turn his attention to other issues, especially to those factors that might be responsible for the denial. Eventually, the resistance and denial may diminish, and the patient is then capable of achieving the insight, often without any further prodding from the therapist.

If I were teaching students of psychology, and wished to convey this concept to them, I would say, "Do not tell the patient anything which he is incapable of hearing. Eventually he will come to hear it himself." These are virtually the exact words of the mishnah.

This teaching is by no means exclusive for psychotherapists. It is equally valid for rabbis, counselors, teachers, and parents, and its truth is crystal clear.

וְאַל תֹּאמַר לִכְשָׁאֶפָּנֶה אֶשְׁנֶה,
שֶׁמָּא לֹא תִפָּנֶה
And do not say, "When I am free I will study," for perhaps you will not become free.

Hillel was keenly aware of the psychology of procrastination. Essentially, the procrastinator does not want to do something, not today, not tomorrow, not ever. However, he is reluctant to admit, even to himself, that he wishes to avoid the task completely, so he deludes himself by saying, "Yes, I do wish to do it, but for various reasons, today is not the proper time, so I will do it tomorrow when it will be more appropriate." People who know they should stop smoking or binging on food regularly resolve to do it at a more propitious time, such as when the semester is over, on vacation, or after the tumult of the Bar Mitzvah is over. One of the classic texts on alcoholism is entitled *I'll Quit Tomorrow*.

R' Mendel of Kotzk pointed out that the Torah forbids deceiving someone else. "It is even worse," he said, "when a person deceives himself." While deceiving someone else is an immoral act, deceiving oneself is simply stupid. The individual becomes the victim of his own wile. If the procrastinator would say to himself, "I don't want to do it, therefore I am not going to do it," such as preparing one's income tax, there is a likelihood that the realization that he *must* do it will lead him to take action. Putting it off until a later time takes away this reality stimulus.

Hillel therefore tells the procrastinator, "Don't fool yourself. If you put off doing it until tomorrow, you may never get around to doing it, because you will again delay tomorrow just as you did today."

הוּא [ו] הָיָה אוֹמֵר: אֵין בּוּר יְרֵא חֵטְא, וְלֹא עַם הָאָרֶץ חָסִיד, וְלֹא הַבַּיְשָׁן לָמֵד, וְלֹא הַקַּפְּדָן מְלַמֵּד, וְלֹא כָל הַמַּרְבֶּה בִסְחוֹרָה מַחְכִּים, וּבְמָקוֹם שֶׁאֵין אֲנָשִׁים, הִשְׁתַּדֵּל לִהְיוֹת אִישׁ.

6.

אֵין בּוּר יְרֵא חֵטְא, וְלֹא עַם הָאָרֶץ חָסִיד
A boor cannot be fearful of sin; an am haaretz cannot be scrupulously pious

The term בּוּר refers to a person who lacks essential Torah knowledge. עַם הָאָרֶץ, am haaretz, is a term which the Talmud uses to refer to a person who may have acquired Torah knowledge, but has not been in close contact with Torah scholars (*Berachos* 47b).

A person lacking essential Torah knowledge is often unable to avoid sin, simply because he may be unaware of what is forbidden. One Shabbos, a very devout woman, who would never have thought of violating the least rabbinical ordinance (*d'rabbanan*) accidentally dropped some food on her dress. She dipped a cloth napkin into water and tried to remove the stain, clearly unaware that what she was doing was a violation of a Scriptural prohibition (*d'oraisa*). Cleaning a stain is equivalent to laundering, which is one of the 39 labors prohibited on Shabbos. The person who is knowledgeable in halachah would not, of course, be subject to such an error, and he may indeed be a *tzaddik*. But to be a *chassid* is a level higher than that of a *tzaddik*. In *The Path of the Just*, Ramchal requires perfection of several levels of piety before one reaches the status of *chassid*.

A *tzaddik* is guided by halachah, and everything he does complies with halachah. Hence, he can easily determine by recourse to the *Shulchan Aruch* what he must do and what he may not do. Not so with the person who wishes to be a *chassid*, and do more than the halachah requires. Here knowledge of Torah is not enough, and a person who uses his own judgment as to what he should do may err. In this case it is necessary to have close ties with a recognized Torah scholar, to be able to consult about what one wishes to do.

For example, a pious person may wish to fast as penance for his sins, which is not required by the *Shulchan Aruch*. This course of action should be followed only after approval by a competent Torah authority. For some people, fasting may be counterproductive, as it may impair one's ability to study Torah and perform mitzvos.

We may read about *middos* (character traits) in ethical works, but all the book learning does not equal observing the *middos* of a Torah personality. As was pointed out earlier (Chapter 1:13), these exceptional individuals teach us by their actions as well as by their words.

6. **H**e was accustomed to say: A boor cannot be fearful of sin; an am haaretz cannot be scrupulously pious; a bashful person cannot learn, and a quick, impatient person cannot teach; anyone excessively occupied in business cannot become a scholar; and in a place where there are no leaders, strive to be a leader.

וְלֹא הַבַּיְשָׁן לָמֵד, וְלֹא הַקַּפְּדָן מְלַמֵּד
A bashful person cannot learn, and a quick, impatient person cannot teach

Every character trait may be constructive when put to good use. It is commendable for a person to be modest, and the kind of boldness that results in "pushiness" or in displaying all one knows constitutes ga-avah (vanity), a most undesirable trait. The type of בּוּשָׁה that constitutes modesty is praiseworthy. However, there may be a בּוּשָׁה that is shyness, and when this is misguided, it may be detrimental. The mishnah states that shyness can interfere with learning. A shy person may remain ignorant of important material.

A person who is too shy to ask an instructor for a clearer explanation or concept may fear that posing a question will betray his ignorance. This is likely to happen in people who have poor self-esteem, who are defensive and are cautious that others should not detect their fantasized inadequacies. Although it is perfectly legitimate for a student to ask for clarification, the person with a fragile ego may hesitate to do so. He may thus remain ignorant of important data, and this ignorance may lead to erroneous choices.

Experience is a most effective teacher, and we learn best by making and correcting mistakes. Indeed, the Talmud states that a person does not fully grasp a halachah until he has erred in its interpretation and is corrected (*Gittin* 43a). While one certainly wishes to avoid failure, we should realize that it is always a possibility, and while failure is unpleasant, it need not be seen as devastating. A person with low self-esteem, however, may see any failure as confirming his sense of inadequacy and unworthiness, and he may not venture to try anything for fear that doing so may result in failure. This attitude results in his being stagnant, never advancing beyond the status quo. This is the undesirable shyness which hampers a person's growth.

The trait of קַפְּדָן may be best described as "irascibility secondary to scrupulos-ity." In other words, the person demands perfection, and is very short with anyone who exhibits any imperfection. If this trait is kept within boundaries, it may be constructive, as when one strives for perfection and is appropriately dissatisfied with defects in himself. Obviously, scrupulosity can be carried to an extreme and is then destructive. When judiciously used, it can enhance a person's growth.

While the intolerance of imperfection in oneself may be salutary if not taken

[ז] אַף הוּא רָאָה גֻּלְגֹּלֶת אַחַת שֶׁצָּפָה עַל פְּנֵי הַמָּיִם. אָמַר לָהּ: "עַל דַּאֲטֵפְתְּ אַטְפוּךְ, וְסוֹף מְטַיְּפַיִךְ יְטוּפוּן".

---

to an extreme, it is harmful when directed toward others, especially in a teacher toward a student. An irascible teacher may stifle the student's desire for clarification, and he will be unable to successfully transmit the required knowledge. It is quite likely that the קַפְּדָן, too, is a manifestation of low self-esteem, because the instructor with a fragile ego may interpret a student's question for clarification of what he said as indicating that he did not explain things adequately the first time around. He may take this as an indication that he is considered incompetent as a teacher. People with poor self-esteem are prone to interpret many things as negative reflections on themselves.

This leads us to the final portion of the mishnah. We occasionally see people who have an insatiable desire for wealth. There are billionaires who would not exhaust their vast wealth if they lived a thousand years, yet they persist in trying to increase their immense wealth as if they did not know where their next meal was coming from. For some reason, society does not see this as abnormal.

There is a story about a man who came to see a psychiatrist. "What is your problem?" the psychiatrist asked.

"I don't have any problems," the man said.

"Then why have you come to consult me?" the psychiatrist asked.

"Well, my family insisted I must come to you," the man answered.

"What does your family think is wrong with you?" the psychiatrist asked.

"They think that there is something wrong with me because I like pancakes," the man said.

"That's absurd," the psychiatrist said. "There's nothing wrong with liking pancakes. I like pancakes myself."

The patient's eyes lit up. "You do! Then you must come to my house. I have crates and crates full of them up in the attic."

Making enough pancakes for a meal is proper, and making a few extra to store in the freezer for another meal is perfectly appropriate. But when one collects crates of pancakes in the attic, one is obviously sick. We really should have the same attitude toward money, accumulating enough for our needs plus putting some away for a rainy day. However, if money becomes an end in itself, and one continues to amass more wealth than one can ever use, it really is as foolish as collecting pancakes.

When food is eaten for nutrition, it is healthy. If one eats excessively, beyond the body's nutritional needs, the food must be serving some other function. Invariably, for the compulsive overeater, food is a kind of drug. Much the same is true of an irrational appetite for money. In all likelihood, money has come to represent security, and just as the compulsive overeater finds security in food, so does the compulsive money hoarder finds security in money, even when it

7. **H**e *also saw a skull floating on the water. He said to it: "Because you drowned others, they drowned you; and eventually those who drowned you will be drowned."*

---

cannot serve any realistic function.

The use of food or money for security betrays a person's profound sense of insecurity, which is generally a consequence of low self-esteem. Since this low self-esteem is not warranted and not reality bound, there is an endless pursuit for more and more food or more and more money.

True, society does not see the desire for excess money as similar to compulsive overeating, but the Talmud sees them as equivalent. The expression כָּל הַמַּרְבֶּה בִסְחוֹרָה refers to someone who *exceeds* the necessary exertion in commerce. He is certainly acting foolishly.

And finally, low self-esteem may not allow a person to assume a position of leadership, except in those cases where one defends himself against feelings of inadequacy by exhibiting grandiosity. In the latter situation the person may strive to place himself above others and even to control them. A truly humble person, whose self-esteem is intact, may balk at assuming leadership, but when it becomes necessary, he will rise to the occasion. This is best exemplified by Moses, who initially resisted the call to become a leader, and then became the paragon of leaders. A person with a healthy ego will swing into action and do his part, while a person with low self-esteem will shirk responsibility. Like the person with misguided shyness, his unwarranted feelings of inadequacy may paralyze him.

Hillel's humility was healthy and his self-esteem was intact. He was therefore able to instruct us on some of the manifestations of low self-esteem.

7.

אַף הוּא רָאָה גֻּלְגֹּלֶת אַחַת
שֶׁצָּפָה עַל פְּנֵי הַמָּיִם
He also saw a skull
floating on the water.

Why does the mishnah say "He *also* saw a skull floating"? What is the antecedent that warrants the "also"?

This mishnah is better understood in context. The Talmudic tractate *Avos D'Rav Nassan* is an expanded version of *Ethics of the Fathers,* and relates an episode where Hillel encountered some wheat merchants and asked them the price of the wheat. "Two *dinars* a *se'ah,*" they answered. A bit later he met a second group of wheat merchants and again asked the price. "Three *dinars* a *se'ah,*" they said. "But just a bit earlier some merchants were selling the same quality wheat for two *dinars,*" Hillel said. The merchants responded, "Foolish Babylonian! Don't you know that the price depends on how much work was expended?" indicating that because they had worked harder to produce the grain, they charged more for it.

It was after this encounter that Hillel made his comment on the floating skull,

[ח] **הוּא** הָיָה אוֹמֵר: מַרְבֶּה בָשָׂר, מַרְבֶּה רִמָּה; מַרְבֶּה
נְכָסִים, מַרְבֶּה דְאָגָה; מַרְבֶּה נָשִׁים, מַרְבֶּה
כְשָׁפִים; מַרְבֶּה שְׁפָחוֹת, מַרְבֶּה זִמָּה; מַרְבֶּה עֲבָדִים, מַרְבֶּה
גָזֵל. מַרְבֶּה תוֹרָה, מַרְבֶּה חַיִּים; מַרְבֶּה יְשִׁיבָה, מַרְבֶּה חָכְמָה;

and the term "also" is used because his comment is a continuation of the principle that "The reward is commensurate with the effort." Objectively, the wheat of both merchants appeared identical. The only reason for the higher price was that a greater expenditure of work went into the one, but this factor was not evident in the wheat. Two people may achieve identical goals, yet one may be rewarded more than the other. An observer may see this as unfair, perhaps due to favoritism. However, since the one expended greater effort, his reward is greater, because reward is commensurate with the effort invested.

Hillel then extended this principle to the appropriateness of punishment. Upon seeing the skull of one who had been drowned, he said that he met his fate because he had drowned someone. "Yet," Hillel said, "those who drowned him were also guilty and will receive their punishment. No one has the right to take the law into his own hands." Even if a criminal deserves death as a punishment, it can only be carried out by a court of law.

Belief in Divine justice is one of the essential principles of Judaism. Both individually and collectively, this principle has faced many challenges. Even Moses was troubled by the suffering of the innocent, and asked God for an explanation, only to be told that the secret of Divine justice cannot be revealed to any living person. Even Moses, who was privy to almost everything in heaven, would have to wait until his soul was free of the physical body before he could understand this (*Berachos* 7a).

Indeed, when after 40 years of devotion and self-sacrifice Moses' heartrending pleas to be permitted to enter the Promised Land were turned down, Moses said, "God's actions are perfect" (*Deuteronomy* 32:4), and he accepted the harsh Divine judgment gracefully.

A problem that defied solution for Moses will never be resolved for us. We can only accept the principle of Divine fairness and justice on faith, since it is beyond the capacity of the human mind to understand it.

This is the point which Hillel wished to stress. The truth of Divine justice can be known only to One Who knows infinite time and infinite space. To anyone else, any incident is as incomprehensible as a single piece of a huge, million-piece jigsaw puzzle. When the piece fits into its proper place, it can be seen as a part of the whole, but in isolation it has no meaning. Only one who knows infinite time and space can grasp the whole picture. Since we can see only a tiny fragment of a vast universe, we are unable to grasp the meaning of any isolated occurrence. Both reward and punishment are *ultimately* fair, but we are not privy to the "ultimate."

8. He was accustomed to say: *The more flesh, the more worms; the more possessions, the more worry; the more wives, the more witchcraft; the more maidservants, the more lewdness; the more manservants, the more thievery. [However,] the more Torah, the more life; the more study, the more wisdom;*

8.

מַרְבֶּה נְכָסִים, מַרְבֶּה דְאָגָה
The more possessions,
the more worry

Sometimes we may think that more is better, only to discover that this mishnah is so right.

When I became director of psychiatry in a large hospital, I found the work quite stressful. I had a small staff, and the demands on my time were great. I was frequently called during the night for various emergency problems. I was therefore thrilled when we were offered a government grant to develop a comprehensive mental health center, which enabled me to hire several psychiatrists, psychologists, and social workers.

My sense of relief was short lived. As chief of the department, I found myself responsible for everything done by any person on the staff. After several months I actually longed for the days when I did everything by myself, and was responsible only for my own actions.

One day I must have appeared very exhausted, and when I met the hospital administrator in the corridor, he noted my weariness and said, "Perhaps you need someone to assist you."

I responded, "One more assistant and I quit."

I have encountered many executives who had worked hard to attain their position, only to find that they had much less stress before they achieved the coveted goal. Just as with personnel, so also with belongings. Few people are satisfied with what they have, and the aspirations of the wealthy far exceed those of people with lesser means, resulting in an endless pursuit of an ever retreating goal. Furthermore, people who own little have little anxiety about possible losses, since they do not have much to lose. Not so with the wealthy, who may fear that unforeseen economic upheavals may deprive them of their wealth. They are terribly anxious that they might not be able to continue to live according to the luxury to which they have become accustomed.

Solomon was so right. "The sleep of the laborer is sweet, but the abundance of the wealthy does not let him sleep [peacefully]" (*Ecclesiastes* 5:11).

מַרְבֶּה עֲבָדִים, מַרְבֶּה גָזֵל. מַרְבֶּה תוֹרָה,
מַרְבֶּה חַיִּים; מַרְבֶּה יְשִׁיבָה, מַרְבֶּה חָכְמָה
The more manservants, the more thievery.
[However] the more Torah, the more life;
the more study, the more wisdom

This mishnah lists a number of things which are harmful in excess, and several things which, to the contrary, are very beneficial even if one exceeds the norm. There are some

מַרְבֶּה עֵצָה, מַרְבֶּה תְבוּנָה; מַרְבֶּה צְדָקָה, מַרְבֶּה שָׁלוֹם. קָנָה שֵׁם טוֹב, קָנָה לְעַצְמוֹ; קָנָה לוֹ דִבְרֵי תוֹרָה, קָנָה לוֹ חַיֵּי הָעוֹלָם הַבָּא.

[ט] **רַבָּן** יוֹחָנָן בֶּן זַכַּאי קִבֵּל מֵהִלֵּל וּמִשַׁמַּאי. הוּא הָיָה

---

things in life which may be harmful to excess which are not listed in the mishnah, and other things which are advantageous in abundance. What are the guidelines to know to which category something belongs?

The human being is a composite of a physical body and a spiritual soul. The body is essentially an animal body, and if we observe nature closely, we will find that animals generally do not indulge in excesses. For example, a lion or tiger will kill its prey for food, but once the body's nutritional needs have been met, they stop eating. Animals in the wild do not become obese. When their natural needs are met, they abstain.

It would be well if the human being attended to his physical needs as animals do, only to the degree that one's physiology and good health requires. An excess of food or drink, beyond the body's physiological needs, is likely to be harmful.

The *neshamah* (soul), on the other hand, is akin to God, and in contrast to the body, its needs may be infinite. Hence, when attending to one's spiritual needs, there may not be precise limitations. There are some things for which halachah does designate an appropriate limit, but for many other spiritual activities — such as helping others or study of Torah — there are no limits.

This is evident in the mishnah. All the things whose excess is harmful can be noted to be related to physical desires. Those whose excess is beneficial are of a spiritual character. The rule is therefore that one should place limits on physical pursuits, but in spiritual pursuits, unless specifically restricted by halachah, the more the better.

9.

The history of the Jewish nation is replete with people of enormous stature, yet few have impacted on our history as much as R' Yochanan ben Zakkai. His greatness was evident to his teacher, Hillel. The Talmud states that Hillel had 80 students, and that R' Yochanan was the youngest of them. One time Hillel was ill, and when his students visited him, R' Yochanan remained outside. Hillel scanned the group and asked, "Where is the youngest among you, who is a father of wisdom and a father of generations to come?" R' Yochanan could not have been more than in his 20s when the master not only praised his great wisdom, but also foresaw his impact on Jewish history. This resulted from R' Yochanan's leadership some 80 years later.

R' Yochanan lived in the era when the Romans laid siege to Jerusalem.

2/9 *the more counsel, the more understanding; the more charity, the more peace. One who has gained a good reputation has gained it for his own benefit; one who has gained himself Torah knowledge has gained himself the life of the World to Come.*

9. **R**abban Yochanan ben Zakkai received the tradition from Hillel and Shammai. He was accustomed to

---

There were zealots who refused to accept the obvious, that they were no match for the might of Rome. Perhaps they wished to emulate the Maccabees, who successfully battled the forces of the Syrian Greeks. R' Yochanan counseled otherwise, and recommended acceptance of allegiance to Rome (*Gittin* 56a).

There was a major difference between the Greeks and the Romans. The Greeks' primary interest was to replace the Torah with Hellenism, which would have essentially meant the demise of Judaism. Rome was at that time not interested in religion or philosophy, and sought only political dominance. To those who put up fierce resistance in Jerusalem, Vespasian said, "You fools! Why are you forcing me to destroy the city and burn the Temple? All I ask is that you accept the sovereignty of Rome, and if you do, I will lift the siege and leave." R' Yochanan — recognizing the futility of resistance and realizing that although they would lose their political independence, the Jewish way of life could be preserved — advised making peace with Rome.

R' Yochanan realized that the zealots would refuse to follow his recommendations and that they would not permit anyone to leave Jerusalem to negotiate with Vespasian. He was convinced that Jerusalem was certain to be razed. He therefore had himself placed in a coffin and carried out of Jerusalem by his trusted disciples. He made his way to Vespasian, who was then a Roman general, and addressed him as "Emperor." "I am but a Roman officer," Vespasian said, but R' Yochanan did not retract. While they were in session, a messenger brought news from Rome that the emperor had died and that the Senate had elected Vespasian to be his successor.

Favorably impressed by R' Yochanan, Vespasian said he would grant him a request. "I asked for the preservation of the academy of Yavneh, the restoration of the leadership to the dynasty of Hillel, and a physician to heal Rabbi Tzadok, who had fasted 40 years in prayer that Jerusalem be spared." These requests were granted. Some of the sages were critical of R' Yochanan for not exploiting the opportunity and asking Vespasian to spare Jerusalem. R' Yochanan knew, however, that this request would not be granted, and since he was certain that this would be refused, he would have lost the opportunity to achieve anything. He therefore resigned himself to the inevitable, and made a request which he felt would benefit Judaism in the long term.

How right Hillel was when, some 80 years earlier, he predicted that the young R' Yochanan would be a "father of generations to come." By preserving the academy of Yavneh, R' Yochanan insured the continuity of Torah, and by restoring the dynasty of Hillel, he reestablished the authority of the *Nasi* (leader of the community). Political liberty was indeed lost, but the liberty of the Jewish spirit remained.

Any thinking person at that time would have predicted that the might of Rome would prevail forever, that the tiny, helpless state of Judah would disappear from the world map into oblivion, and that its inhabitants would be engulfed in exile and would disappear by assimilation.

Shortly after the Yom Kippur War, I visited Israel, and indeed spirits were low. Many families had suffered losses, and the shock of the war had seriously dampened the euphoria that had resulted from the triumph of the Six Day War. I left Israel with profound feelings of sadness.

On the way back from Israel, I stopped off in Rome and visited the ruins of ancient Rome — the Coliseum and the Forum. I walked among the broken columns of once-proud buildings, and I came to the Arch of Titus. On the arch there is the bas relief of the Sack of Jerusalem, with Roman soldiers carrying off the Menorah, and the inscription *Judea Capta,* Judah was taken captive. Under this relief someone had scrawled graffiti in white chalk: עַם יִשְׂרָאֵל חַי, the nation of Israel lives on!

It was difficult to contain my feelings at that moment. How I wished R' Yochanan ben Zakkai was there to see how right he was. The mighty Roman empire had crumbled, but the Jewish nation, due to the preservation of Torah by the academy of Yavneh, continued to exist and overcome enormous challenges to its existence. Except for history students, Vespasian has no significance. Even to them he is but a historical relic. But for Jews, דָּוִד מֶלֶךְ יִשְׂרָאֵל חַי וְקַיָּם, *David the king of Israel lives and continues to reign,* through his *Tehillim* and in our anticipation of the ultimate Redemption by a descendant of David. How different the present is from that moment when R' Yochanan ben Zakkai had to plead with Emperor Vespasian. History has proven that it was R' Yochanan who ultimately triumphed.

This is the R' Yochanan, "father of wisdom and father of generations," that shares with us both his own teachings as well as those which he can convey to us by way of his illustrious students.

אִם לָמַדְתָּ תּוֹרָה הַרְבֵּה,
אַל תַּחֲזִיק טוֹבָה לְעַצְמָךְ, כִּי לְכַךְ נוֹצָרְתָּ
If you have studied much Torah,
do not take credit for yourself, because
that is what you were created to do.

Why should one not think highly of himself if he has studied much Torah?

A prominent physician was given an award for years of outstanding service to the commu-

2/9   *say: If you have studied much Torah, do not take credit for yourself, because that is what you were created to do.*

---

nity. In his response, he wondered why he was given the award. "Am I going to receive an award for brushing my teeth each morning?"

The doctor's comment is well taken. Fulfilling one's obligation should hardly be grounds for an award. There are indeed many fine physicians who are devoted to the community and little reason any one doctor should be singled out.

Similarly, our obligation is to learn Torah. Why, then, should a person feel that he is deserving of praise for doing what he is supposed to do?

Another interpretation of this mishnah is that a singer should not see himself as being worthy of praise for his ability to sing. He happens to be the fortunate recipient of a Divine gift of a beautiful voice, just as an artist is the beneficiary of the ability to draw or sculpt. These are not innate talents that they worked to achieve, but Divine gifts which they should put to good use.

A person who is endowed with a brilliant intellect and can grasp and retain a great deal of Torah should not consider himself superior to others. Some commentaries note that the Torah cites Moses as being the most humble person on earth. How could he have been humble when the Torah testifies that he was the greatest of all prophets? The answer is that Moses recognized his prophetic capabilities as being a Divine gift, and felt that had someone else been given the capabilities, he would have developed them to an even higher degree than he did. Moses saw himself as not having fulfilled the potential with which he was blessed.

We repeatedly encounter the importance of humility in *Ethics Of The Fathers*. This mishnah cautions us not to allow our excellence in any field, even Torah study, to inflate our ego. Indeed, it was our greatest Torah personages who exhibited the most exemplary humility, and we should learn this vital trait from them.

In *Avos D'Rav Nassan*, the wording is, "If you have *done* a great deal of Torah," but the intention is the same as our mishnah, since abstract learning without applying Torah in our lives is hardly meritorious.

The Talmud states that there was an ongoing dispute between the schools of Hillel and Shammai whether it was good for man that he was created or not. The conclusion was that inasmuch as the risk of going astray and harming oneself is so great, we cannot say that it was to man's advantage to be created. However, now that man was created, he must be most careful that he behaves properly.

In *Let Us Make Man*, I pointed out that both angels and animals were created in a state of perfection. Angels never undergo any kind of change, and animals grow only in size and strength, but they do not develop themselves. Even those forms of life that do undergo a change, such as a caterpillar turning into a

ב/י-יא [י] **חֲמִשָּׁה** תַּלְמִידִים הָיוּ לוֹ לְרַבָּן יוֹחָנָן בֶּן זַכַּאי, וְאֵלּוּ
הֵן: רַבִּי אֱלִיעֶזֶר בֶּן הֻרְקָנוֹס, רַבִּי יְהוֹשֻׁעַ
בֶּן חֲנַנְיָא, רַבִּי יוֹסֵי הַכֹּהֵן, רַבִּי שִׁמְעוֹן בֶּן נְתַנְאֵל, וְרַבִּי
אֶלְעָזָר בֶּן עֲרָךְ.

[יא] **הוּא** הָיָה מוֹנֶה שְׁבָחָן: (רַבִּי) אֱלִיעֶזֶר בֶּן הֻרְקָנוֹס,

---

butterfly, do so because this has been programmed into their genes. It is not a voluntary development. A caterpillar has no way of refusing to spin a cocoon and be transformed into a butterfly. The only creature that can *willfully and volitionally* change is the human being.

The Divine concept of man was that he was to be an entity that would be created with potential but would perfect himself and become "man." If God had created man in a state of completion, man would have been either another animal or an angel. Therefore, since God desired a being that would have to work toward perfection, man had to be created in an imperfect state.

The Baal Shem Tov explains that this is why God said, "Let *us* make man." Everything else in Creation was created by God alone, but for creation of "man," God needed man's participation. Hence the "us" refers to man assisting God in his own formation.

Man can achieve perfection only by following the dictates of God. For other peoples, this is the fulfillment of the seven categories of Noahide mitzvos, and for Jews it is the Torah. Fulfilling Torah requirements is hardly an achievement about which one should boast. It is not doing something beyond the call of duty. To the contrary, just as it is natural for animals to eat to exist, so is natural for man to observe the Divine will to achieve his very existence as "man."

This can be seen as the meaning of the mishnah. Perfecting oneself via Torah is not a reason for vanity. It is simply following natural law.

10-11.

חֲמִשָּׁה תַּלְמִידִים הָיוּ לוֹ לְרַבָּן יוֹחָנָן בֶּן זַכַּאי
Rabban Yochanan ben Zakkai had five [primary] disciples.

A careful study of this mishnah reveals an extra word: לוֹ. Literally, this translates: There were five disciples *to him*, to R' Yochanan ben Zakkai. The "לוֹ" could just have well been omitted without changing the manifest meaning of the sentence. Its presence indicates that these disciples had a special relationship "to him." An interpretation of this extra word may answer the question, "Why does the mishnah state that R' Yochanan had five disciples, when we know for a fact that he had many more students?"

In Torah there should be a special relationship between teacher and student.

10. **R**abban Yochanan ben Zakkai had five [primary] dis-
ciples. They were: Rabbi Eliezer ben Hyrkanos,
Rabbi Yehoshua ben Chanania, Rabbi Yose the Kohen,
Rabbi Shimon ben Nesanel, and Rabbi Elazar ben Arach.

11. **H**e used to enumerate their praises: (Rabbi) Eliezer

R' Moshe Schreiber (*Chasam Sofer*) once remarked that he had 13 *"talmidim"* (students). When someone pointed out the obvious, that his yeshivah counted many additional students, R' Schreiber responded, "A true *talmid* is one who is not detached from his master from the moment he wakes up until he goes to sleep. Everything he does, even his thoughts, follow the model of his master. I have only 13 students such as this."

The Talmud relates that R' Eliezer said, "I have never said anything that I did not hear from my master" (*Succah* 28a). R' Chaim Shmulevitz asked, "How can this be? We know that R' Eliezer was an innovator of much Torah knowledge." He answers, "True, but R' Eliezer never said a halachah until he was absolutely certain that this is what his master would have said. His thinking was completely molded after his master's methods of thought, hence all of his innovations could be attributed to his master. That is a true *talmid*" (*Sichos Mussar* 5731:23).

We can understand the mishnah in this light. R' Yochanan had many students, but only these five were לו, *to him*, completely attached to him and true heirs of his method of Torah analysis.

While we have been blessed in recent decades with an unprecedented proliferation of Torah institutions, there seems to have been an unfortunate side effect. I recall, in my younger years, that when a yeshivah student was asked where he was learning, the answer was, "I am a *talmid* of Reb Ahron" (R' Aharon Kotler), or "I am a *talmid* of Reb Shloime (R' Shloime Heiman)," or "I am a *talmid* of Reb Reuvein (R' Reuvein Grozovski)," or "I am a *talmid* of Reb Moshe (R' Moshe Feinstein)."

Today, a student will tell you *where* he learns, but not with whom. "I learn at the Mir," or "I learn at Ponovezh," or "I learn at Tshebin." I no longer hear the name of the person who is the master in Torah, but rather a place.

Although we are fulfilling the dictates of the mishnah (Chapter 1, mishnah 1) to produce many students, we should not sacrifice the precious relationship of student to teacher. The concept of whose *talmid* one is should be restored.

חֲמִשָּׁה תַלְמִידִים הָיוּ לוֹ . . .
הוּא הָיָה מוֹנֶה שִׁבְחָן

[He] had five [primary] disciples . . .
He used to enumerate their praises

How can the mishnah state that R' Yochanan ben Zakkai had five disciples, when we know that he had many more than that?

The Rabbi of Radomsk explains

that these particular five disciples were extremely humble, and were not aware of their own salutary character traits. Indeed R' Yochanan had other disciples. However, these five were so self-effaced that he found it necessary to call attention to their greatness.

This interpretation confirms an important ethical concept: Humility should not be allowed to blind a person to his own virtues. There is a danger that if a person is not aware of his strengths, he may not exercise them when necessary, and the results of such humility may be tragic.

King Saul was most humble (*I Samuel* 10:21-22), and it was precisely his humility that resulted in his losing the monarchy, when, instead of exercising his authority as king, he submitted to the public will. The words of the prophet Samuel indicate this misapplication of humility. "Though you are small in your own eyes, you are the head of the tribes of Israel" (*I Samuel* 15:17). Similarly, the Talmud states, "The humility of R' Zechariah led to the destruction of our Temple" (*Gittin* 57a).

R' Yehudah Leib Chasman said, "It is not humility to be ignorant of one's strengths; rather, it is pure folly." This is reiterated by another ethicist who said, "If a person is unaware of his defects, then he does not know what he must correct. However, it is far worse if he does not know his strengths, for then he cannot utilize the abilities he has to perfect himself."

R' Yochanan feared that because of their profound humility these five disciples might be oblivious of their positive traits. This is why he had to alert them to their own strengths.

**(רַבִּי) אֱלִיעֶזֶר בֶּן הֻרְקָנוֹס
בּוֹר סוּד שֶׁאֵינוֹ מְאַבֵּד טִפָּה**
*(Rabbi) Eliezer ben Hyrkanos is [like]
a cemented cistern that loses not a drop*

In what way is a highly retentive memory a praise? Some people are born with a photographic memory, and their ability to remember everything is not something they developed by their own efforts. Shall we praise someone because he was born with musical or artistic talent?

R' Eliezer was *not* born with a photographic memory. He remembered every word of Torah because it was important to him. We rarely forget things that are vitally important to us. Psychoanalytic theory states that if a person forgets something important, there was some reason, perhaps unconscious, why he did not wish to remember it.

A *chassid* once complained to his Rebbe that his memory was failing him, and that he was unable to recall much of what he had learned. "Is it not strange," the Rebbe asked, "that you have not forgotten to put the fork to your mouth when you eat? If Torah were as important to you as eating, you would

ben Hyrkanos is [like] a cemented cistern that loses not a drop; (Rabbi) Yehoshua ben Chanania, praiseworthy is she who bore him; (Rabbi) Yose the Kohen is a scrupulously pious person; (Rabbi) Shimon ben Nesanel

---

not have forgotten it."

There is no question that things on which we concentrate a great deal make a deeper impression, and that truly important things are usually not forgotten. It may indeed occur that a heart patient may forget a dose of medication, but when he does, he will take action to avoid forgetting again. There is something we can do to retain Torah: review it many times.

The noted Torah scholar, Maharam Shick, lost his eyesight in his old age. He wept bitterly that he was unable to read and study Torah. "If only I had known that I would lose my eyesight, I would have learned Torah differently."

"What would you have done?" asked his friends. "Learned 25 hours a day instead of 24?"

"No, but I would have spent more time reviewing rather than learning new material. In that way I would have remembered much more, and without my eyesight, I would be able to study the Torah I retained."

R' Yochanan knew very well why R' Eliezer remembered everything he learned, and that it was not because he was born with a photographic memory.

(רַבִּי) יְהוֹשֻׁעַ בֶּן חֲנַנְיָא, אַשְׁרֵי יוֹלַדְתּוֹ
[Rabbi] Yehoshua ben Chanania,
praiseworthy is she who bore him

Many commentaries ask, inasmuch as R' Yochanan wished to praise R' Yehoshua, why did he say "Praiseworthy is she who bore him. . ." This is generally taken to refer to the fact that when R' Yehoshua's mother was expecting him, she made the rounds of all the Torah academies so that he might always hear Torah study (*Jerusalem Talmud, Yevamos* 1:6). When he was an infant, she placed his crib adjacent to the yeshivah so that the first sounds that would enter his brain would be the sounds of Torah. R' Yochanan's comment on R' Yehoshua is thus a praise of his mother rather than of him.

R' Yochanan's remark is of great importance and has practical application. For too long, psychologists have been blaming one's parents if one turned out to have emotional or behavioral problems. Too often this exonerates a person, who may fail to take responsibility for his shortcomings. While I do not underestimate that parental actions can impact upon a child, my response to people who wish to blame their parents for their problems is, "Even if you are what your parents made you, if you stay that way, it is your own fault." At any time in our lives we can make changes, even radical changes in ourselves. Our upbringing may be an important factor, but it does not *determine* what we will be.

R' Yochanan wished to stress this point. Precisely because R' Yehoshua's mother's efforts to inculcate her child with Torah were well known, R' Yochanan wished to point out that R' Yehoshua's greatness was not totally of his mother's doing. Thus, while lauding his mother, he pointed out that it was R' Yehoshua who was ultimately responsible for being the outstanding Torah scholar that he became. He, as well as his mother, deserved to be praised. We are at all times responsible for what we are.

(רַבִּי) שִׁמְעוֹן בֶּן נְתַנְאֵל, יְרֵא חֵטְא
(Rabbi) Shimon ben Nesanel fears sin

As was noted, these five disciples of R' Yochanan ben Zakkai were the greatest of the great. It seems a bit unusual that the master praised one of these spiritual giants merely as "someone who fears sin." This is something that would be expected of anyone who is committed to Torah observance, even the simplest person.

There is a great difference in degree, however, among people who fear sin. R' Shneur Zalman states that the *neshamah* has an inherent craving to adhere to its source in God, and the natural state is for the *neshamah* to cling to God much as iron filings cling to a powerful magnet. Any sin, even the minutest deviation from Torah, creates a barrier and causes a separation between the *neshamah* and God. If a person feels deeply that his life-sustaining energy comes from God, he will fear any separation from God much as a person who has suffered from a respiratory arrest fears another attack that would stop his breathing, depriving him of the oxygen necessary for life. The words of the prayer, "For Torah is our life," are taken very literally, and for such a person, the possibility of sin is much more than a concern about doing wrong. It is an actual dread of losing one's spiritual life, and the possibility of sin can cause a panic reaction. This is a kind of "fear" which characterized R' Shimon.

R' Yochanan's approach to fear of sin is of interest. When his students once asked him why the Torah penalizes a thief who steals in stealth more than a bold robber, R' Yochanan replied that the robber boldly commits his crime in broad daylight, showing that he fears neither God nor man. A stealthy thief, however, who operates under the cover of darkness so that he should not be seen, is obviously only concerned about being detected by human beings. He does not care that God sees him. The stealthy thief has a greater fear of people than he has of God, and for this affront to God he is penalized more than a robber (*Bava Kamma* 79b).

When R' Yochanan was near death, his disciples asked him for his blessing. He responded, "May you have as great a fear of God as you do of other people." They were taken aback and said, "Is that what you think of us?" R' Yochanan replied, "I hope you can achieve that" (*Berachos* 28b).

Is it not remarkable that R' Yochanan expected the same thing of his disciples that he did of a common thief? How can one compare the greatest of the great to the lowest of the low?

R' Yochanan's grasp of human nature was profound. The greatness to which every person can rise is virtually limitless. Rambam says, "Every person has the capacity to be as great a tzaddik as Moses" (*Hil. Teshuvah* 5:2). Every person, without exception. Yes, even one who has become so depraved as a thief still has the capacity not only for *teshuvah,* but to rise to dazzling spiritual heights. On the other hand, it is also possible for a person who has achieved the highest level of spirituality to tumble to the lowest depths, as we see from the case of the High Priest who after 80 years of devoted service, became a heretic (*Berachos* 29a).

By giving his disciples both messages, R' Yochanan taught them that even when one has achieved great spirituality, one must always be on guard and not feel that one is beyond error. Conversely, even a person who has degenerated to the sorriest state should never despair. He, too, can elevate himself to spiritual greatness.

וְ(רַבִּי) אֶלְעָזָר בֶּן עֲרָךְ, כְּמַעְיָן הַמִּתְגַּבֵּר
and (Rabbi) Elazar ben Arach is like a spring flowing stronger and stronger.

There are two types of achievers, whose behavior may appear on the surface to be identical, but they are in fact qualitatively different.

A person may be endowed with much talent and may have a great deal to offer to others. He gives of himself and he thoroughly enjoys doing so. He is much like the nursing mother, who may be very uncomfortable when her breasts are engorged with milk, and feels great relief when her infant nurses. After several hours, when the milk is replenished, she again feels discomfort. She has a need to give to her infant, and the relief when the infant takes from her gives her much pleasure. So it is with a teacher who has vast knowledge, who wishes to share it with his students. When he does so, his knowledge actually increases. The Talmud quotes R' Chaninah's statement: "I have learned much from my teachers, but most from my students" (*Taanis* 7a). Although this person has a constant need to give, he has great satisfaction from his teaching.

There is another type of person who always strives to produce, but for an entirely different reason. There are many highly gifted people, who, for reasons known or unknown, may have severe feelings of inferiority, totally out of keeping with their true character. Because they feel inadequate, they may try to overcome these distressful feelings by being productive, in order to prove both to themselves and to the world that they are *not* inadequate. Unfortu-

הוּא [יב] הָיָה אוֹמֵר: אִם יִהְיוּ כָּל חַכְמֵי יִשְׂרָאֵל בְּכַף
מֹאזְנַיִם, וֶאֱלִיעֶזֶר בֶּן הָרְקָנוֹס בְּכַף שְׁנִיָּה,
מַכְרִיעַ אֶת כֻּלָּם. אַבָּא שָׁאוּל אוֹמֵר מִשְּׁמוֹ: אִם יִהְיוּ כָּל
חַכְמֵי יִשְׂרָאֵל בְּכַף מֹאזְנַיִם, וְ(רַבִּי) אֱלִיעֶזֶר בֶּן הָרְקָנוֹס
אַף עִמָּהֶם, וְ(רַבִּי) אֶלְעָזָר בֶּן עֲרָךְ בְּכַף שְׁנִיָּה, מַכְרִיעַ אֶת
כֻּלָּם.

אָמַר [יג] לָהֶם: צְאוּ וּרְאוּ אֵיזוֹ הִיא דֶרֶךְ טוֹבָה
שֶׁיִּדְבַּק בָּהּ הָאָדָם. רַבִּי אֱלִיעֶזֶר אוֹמֵר:

---

nately, since the feeling of inferiority is not based on reality, it cannot be
compensated for by the greatest achievements. It is impossible to compensate
for a defect that does not exist in reality and is essentially a delusion. While this
person may also produce a great deal, he is forever dissatisfied, in sharp
contrast to a person who achieves because he is motivated by the overflowing
of his talents.

The characteristic of a spring is that it may reach a certain level and then
remain stationary, and additional water will come forth only when one fetches
water from the spring. Taking from the spring is the stimulus that results in the
source of the spring releasing more water.

This was the nature of R' Elazar. He was like a spring that constantly renewed
and increased its strength. The more Torah he expounded, the more Torah he
acquired. Little wonder that the master considered him as equal to all his peers
combined.

12.

וְ(רַבִּי) אֶלְעָזָר בֶּן עֲרָךְ . . . מַכְרִיעַ אֶת כֻּלָּם
(Rabbi) Elazar ben Arach . . .
he would outweigh them all

R' Yochanan ben Zakkai testified
to the greatness of R' Elazar ben
Arach. Once, when R' Elazar expounded on the most profound as-
pects of Torah, his master, R' Yochanan, kissed him and said, "How fortunate
is the Patriarch Abraham to have R' Elazar as his descendant." It is clear that
our mishnah wishes to indicate the overwhelming superiority of R' Elazar
ben Arach. However, we may ask, what purpose does this tribute serve
for us?

The Talmud states that R' Elazar ben Arach left the academy of Yavneh and
settled in a place where he felt that the purity of the water and the tranquillity
of the environment would permit him to think more clearly. He expected that
his students would soon follow him, and when they remained in Yavneh, he,

12. **H**e *[Rabban Yochanan ben Zakkai] was accustomed to say: If all of the sages of Israel were on one pan of a balance scale, and Eliezer ben Hyrkanos were on the other, he would outweigh them all. Abba Shaul said in [Rabban Yochanan's] name: If all the sages of Israel with even (Rabbi) Eliezer ben Hyrkanos among them were on one pan of the balance scale, and (Rabbi) Elazar ben Arach were on the other, he would outweigh them all.*

13. **H**e *[Rabban Yochanan ben Zakkai] said to them [the five disciples]: Go out and discern which is the proper path to which a man should cling. Rabbi Eliezer says:*

---

too, wished to return. However, his wife persuaded him otherwise. "It is they who need you, not you who needs them. Let them come here." When they did not come, R' Elazar's seclusion resulted in his forgetting his enormous amount of knowledge. The Talmud states that it was only due to the intense prayers of his colleagues that he regained his vast store of wisdom.

We can therefore understand why R' Elazar said, "Take yourself to a place of Torah study" (*Shabbos* 147b). This episode teaches us that regardless of one's proficiency in Torah, one is in danger of losing it if one is lax in diligently pursuing its study with students and peers, and constantly reviewing it. Not even R' Elazar ben Arach, the greatest of them all, was immune to the consequence of departing from the hub of Torah study. Anyone who thinks that his fund of Torah knowledge is so great that he can ease up on his Torah study should learn from this example.

13.

צְאוּ וּרְאוּ אֵיזוֹ הִיא דֶרֶךְ טוֹבָה שֶׁיִּדְבַּק בָּהּ הָאָדָם
Go out and discern which is the proper path to which a man should cling.

What is meant by "go out" and discern? Where were they to go?

As we have noted, the *neshamah* is akin to God, and hence it is boundless. The body, with its many earthly needs, is finite and restricted. Furthermore, bodily desires may distort a person's judgment, just as the offer of a bribe may distort a judge's capacity to see the truth in the litigation before him. Thus, R' Yochanan ben Zakkai told his disciples that in order to be able to see the true good in life, they must *go out* from themselves, as it were, and take leave of their physical and earthly nature, for this aspect can impair their perception of the true good.

R' Zvi Elimelech of Dinov (*Bnei Yissaschar*) gives a beautiful interpretation

עַיִן טוֹבָה. רַבִּי יְהוֹשֻׁעַ אוֹמֵר: חָבֵר טוֹב. רַבִּי יוֹסֵי אוֹמֵר:
שָׁכֵן טוֹב. רַבִּי שִׁמְעוֹן אוֹמֵר: הָרוֹאֶה אֶת הַנּוֹלָד. רַבִּי
אֶלְעָזָר אוֹמֵר: לֵב טוֹב. אָמַר לָהֶם: רוֹאֶה אֲנִי אֶת דִּבְרֵי
אֶלְעָזָר בֶּן עֲרָךְ מִדִּבְרֵיכֶם, שֶׁבִּכְלַל דְּבָרָיו דִּבְרֵיכֶם.

[יד] **אָמַר** לָהֶם: צְאוּ וּרְאוּ אֵיזוֹ הִיא דֶּרֶךְ רָעָה
שֶׁיִּתְרַחֵק מִמֶּנָּה הָאָדָם. רַבִּי אֱלִיעֶזֶר
אוֹמֵר: עַיִן רָעָה. רַבִּי יְהוֹשֻׁעַ אוֹמֵר: חָבֵר רָע. רַבִּי יוֹסֵי
אוֹמֵר: שָׁכֵן רָע. רַבִּי שִׁמְעוֹן אוֹמֵר: הַלֹּוֶה וְאֵינוֹ מְשַׁלֵּם.

---

to this mishnah. He states that Torah scholars use the Torah as their only source of knowledge. When R' Yochanan told his disciple to look for the true good (*tov*), they knew that the only place to find it was in the Torah, and the first time "*tov*" is mentioned in the Torah is in the account of Creation, "God saw the light that it was *tov* (good)" (*Genesis* 1:4). The disciples sought to understand what it was about the light that warranted it being referred to as "tov."

R' Eliezer states the obvious. Light enables a person to see well. Hence, a beneficent eye, that looks upon everything favorably, is the true good. R' Yehoshua noted that at Creation, light and darkness were intermixed, attached to each other, hence the term "*tov*" refers to companionship. R' Yose pointed out that light was then separated from darkness, and they each had their separate existence, but were always close to one another, with one taking over where the other left off. "Tov" therefore refers to a good neighbor. R' Shimon said that inasmuch as the Midrash states that the light of Creation was so powerful that it enabled a person to see "from one end of the world to the other," which he took to mean in time as well as space, "tov" therefore refers to the ability to foresee the future.

R' Elazar ben Arach noted that the word "tov" is the 33rd word in the Torah. It is preceded by 32 other words. Inasmuch as לב (heart) is the numerical equivalent of 32, the Torah is telling us that a good heart (*lev*) is the true good. R' Yochanan ben Zakkai then said that inasmuch as the first 32 words include *all* the features that the other disciples had mentioned, this indicates that a good heart is comprehensive and all inclusive. R' Elazar ben Arach's value concept of the true good contains all the others.

רַבִּי יְהוֹשֻׁעַ אוֹמֵר: חָבֵר טוֹב
Rabbi Yehoshua says:
A good friend.

When R' Yehoshua said that "a good friend" is the finest path in life, he did not mean to *have* a good friend, but rather to *be* a good friend.

2/14   *A good eye. Rabbi Yehoshua says: A good friend. Rabbi Yose says: A good neighbor. Rabbi Shimon says: One who considers the outcome [of a deed]. R' Elazar says: A good heart. He said to them: I prefer the words of Elazar ben Arach to your words, for your words are included in his words.*

14. **H**e said to them: Go out and discern which is the evil path from which a man should distance himself. *Rabbi Eliezer says: An evil eye. Rabbi Yehoshua says: A wicked friend. Rabbi Yose says: A wicked neighbor. Rabbi Shimon says: One who borrows and does not repay;*

We see billboards that proclaim, "A good friend does not let his friend drive drunk!" A drunken person may put up a fierce struggle if you try to take his car keys from him, but a good friend who wishes to protect him from death or serious injury will nonetheless do just that.

We may see a person doing something that we believe to be self-destructive. Some people are afraid to point this out to him, for fear that he will be offended and the result will be that they may lose a friendly relationship. If he were about to step into a deep ditch, they would certainly caution him. Why should this be any different? If you are a true friend, he will know that your intentions were in his interest. If he is the kind of person who will sever his relationship with you because you tried to help him, you have probably not lost much.

A physician friend of mine relates that he was admitted five times to a hospital because of alcohol intoxication. To "protect" him, he was given various diagnoses other than the true one, lest exposing his problem would jeopardize his career. His untreated alcoholism brought him near death, and he states, "My colleagues almost killed me with their kindness."

The Psalmist states, "When people rise up against me, I listen" (*Psalms* 92:12). David complained that as king, there were few people who would dare to reprimand him. He had to rely on his enemies to become aware of his shortcomings.

By the same token, take care not to be offended when you are corrected or criticized. The one who alerts you that you may be doing something wrong may in truth be your best friend.

Just as "a good friend" means being one rather than having one, Rabbi Yose's statement similarly means to *be* a good neighbor. A person has no control over who moves in next door to him, hence one cannot always *have* good neighbors, but one can always be one.

אֶחָד הַלֹּוֶה מִן הָאָדָם כְּלֹוֶה מִן הַמָּקוֹם, שֶׁנֶּאֱמַר: ,,לֹוֶה
רָשָׁע וְלֹא יְשַׁלֵּם, וְצַדִּיק חוֹנֵן וְנוֹתֵן". רַבִּי אֶלְעָזָר אוֹמֵר:
לֵב רָע. אָמַר לָהֶם: רוֹאֶה אֲנִי אֶת דִּבְרֵי אֶלְעָזָר בֶּן עֲרָךְ
מִדִּבְרֵיכֶם, שֶׁבִּכְלַל דְּבָרָיו דִּבְרֵיכֶם.

[טז] **הֵם** אָמְרוּ שְׁלֹשָׁה דְבָרִים. רַבִּי אֱלִיעֶזֶר אוֹמֵר:

<hr>

14.

רַבִּי שִׁמְעוֹן אוֹמֵר: הַלֹּוֶה וְאֵינוֹ מְשַׁלֵּם.
אֶחָד הַלֹּוֶה מִן הָאָדָם כְּלֹוֶה מִן הַמָּקוֹם
Rabbi Shimon says: One who borrows and
does not repay; one who borrows from man
is like one who borrows from the Omnipresent

The difficulty with this mishnah is obvious. All those who cited which positive trait a person should adopt gave the converse as the negative trait one should avoid; i.e., a bad eye is the opposite of a good eye, a bad friend is the opposite of a good friend, etc. R' Shimon is an exception. He cites the commendable trait as being able to see the consequences of one's behavior. We would expect the bad trait to be not seeing them. Instead, he cites as the bad trait "one who borrows and does not pay back." This seems to be an anomaly in the mishnah.

The simplest interpretation is that R' Shimon is in fact giving the converse of the positive trait. Anyone who does not repay what he borrowed may profit in the short term, but in addition to being dishonest, he is also being self-defeating. The word will quickly spread that he cannot be trusted to pay his debts. Should he be in need of a loan at a later time, he will be unable to find anyone who is willing to lend him any money. He is thus someone who does not think of the consequences of his actions.

R' Shimon states that failure to pay a debt is equally reprehensible whether the lender is a human being or God. In what way is God a lender?

The essence of *teshuvah* is confessing that one has done wrong. Indeed, Rambam cites *confession* rather than *teshuvah* as being the Scriptural mitzvah. It is therefore of interest that the Torah dictates the mitzvah of confession in regard to someone who committed theft (*Numbers* 5:6). Why did the Torah choose this particular sin as the prototype for confession?

The term theft is not restricted to *taking* another person's property. It can also be applied to the unauthorized use of a person's property. Thus, if someone borrows an item and the lender specifies in what way it may be used, the borrower may not put it to any other use. If he does, his actions are equivalent to theft, since he is making use of the belonging without the owner's permission.

one who borrows from man is like one who borrows from the Omnipresent, as it says: The wicked one borrows and does not pay, while the Righteous One is gracious and gives (Psalms 37:21). Rabbi Elazar says: A wicked heart. He [Rabban Yochanan ben Zakkai] said to them: I prefer the words of Elazar ben Arach to your words, for your words are included in his words.

15. **T**hey each said three things. Rabbi Eliezer says:

Our lives are not outright Divine gifts, but rather loans. One day we will return our *neshamos* to God. God gave us all our faculties in order that we may do His will; i.e., fulfill His mitzvos. If we misuse the faculty of vision to look at forbidden things, the faculty of hearing to listen to *lashon hara*, the ability to eat to consume nonkosher foods etc., we are misusing these faculties for things other than those specified by God. This is why the mitzvah of confession is cited in regard to theft. Every sin, every transgression is essentially a theft, a misuse of the abilities and energies we were given to do good.

How does one repay God for having misappropriated the capacities He lent us? By proper *teshuvah*, which He tells us serves as compensation for our misdeeds.

R' Shneur Zalman says that committing a sin results in a rift, distancing man from God. If a person truly understood this, he would be careful to avoid sin. The Talmud states that a person does not sin unless he has taken leave of his senses (*Sotah* 3a). His folly consists of thinking that his relationship to God will not be affected by his sin. The person who sins fails to see the grave consequences of his act. Inasmuch as by "borrowing from God and not repaying" R' Shimon is referring to someone who sins, his statement can indeed be seen as the converse of the positive trait of seeing the consequences of one's behavior.

15.

הֵם אָמְרוּ שְׁלֹשָׁה דְבָרִים
They each said three things.

The mishnah states that R' Eliezer said three things, then it proceeds to list four. R' Ovadia (*Bartenura*) explains that "Let your fellow's honor be as dear to you as your own" and "Do not anger easily" are really one statement. A person who is concerned about protecting the dignity of another will be hesitant to lose his composure, lest he insult the other person in his rage.

We may consider these two statements as one in yet another way. Inasmuch as the emotion of anger is essentially spontaneous, and is virtually a reflex

יְהִי כְבוֹד חֲבֵרְךָ חָבִיב עָלֶיךָ כְּשֶׁלָּךְ, וְאַל תְּהִי נוֹחַ לִכְעוֹס; וְשׁוּב יוֹם אֶחָד לִפְנֵי מִיתָתְךָ; וֶהֱוֵי מִתְחַמֵּם כְּנֶגֶד אוּרָן שֶׁל חֲכָמִים,

---

response to provocation, how can one prevent feelings of anger? Let us consider, however, how many times something we said or did was misunderstood. While our intentions were good, our words or actions were taken as provocative and aroused an angry response. We then try to explain ourselves and clarify what we meant. We should give others the benefit of the doubt when we are provoked, and consider that we may be misunderstanding them. If we would give them the opportunity to explain themselves, we would be less likely to become angry. Thus, says R' Eliezer, if you treat others the way you would wish to be treated, you may indeed avoid becoming angry.

If the criterion for respecting others is one's own self-respect, it follows that a person must respect himself. Most of my books are devoted to elaboration of a single theme: self-esteem. The pivotal role of self-esteem is evident from this mishnah, because if we do not have a sense of dignity and honor, we are unlikely to dignify others.

The chassidic master, R' Shmelke of Nikolsburg, gave this mishnah a unique interpretation. Upon arriving in a town where he was greeted by a throng of admirers, he asked for a few moments of seclusion before he met them. One curious *chassid* put his ear to the door and heard R' Shmelke say, "Shalom, holy Rabbi. Thank you for honoring us with your presence," and such other expressions of homage. He later asked the Rabbi for an explanation.

R' Shmelke said, "I knew what my followers were going to say to me. They would be addressing me with praises and superlatives, and I might just be gullible enough to believe them and become vain. I therefore said these things to myself, and they were so meaningless to me when I said them, that they made no impression on me when others said them. This is what the mishnah means, 'Let fellow's honor be as dear to you as your own.' In other words, do not allow yourself to be moved by the praise of others any more than when you praise yourself."

יְהִי כְבוֹד חֲבֵרְךָ חָבִיב עָלֶיךָ כְּשֶׁלָּךְ
Let your fellow's honor be as dear to you as your own

The Talmud does not compromise in the least on its demand for respecting the dignity of every human being. We see this in the harsh statement in Chapter 3, mishnah 15 on the severity of the sin of humiliating a person in public. Indeed, the Talmud states that human dignity is of such great importance that it may sometimes override even Scriptural prohibitions (*Berachos* 19b). The *Jerusalem Talmud* states that on Judgment Day we will be asked, "Did you relate to God properly?" and also "Did you relate properly to your fellow man?", which indicates that both are given equal importance!

It is important to note that even though the Talmud is very demanding

Let your fellow's honor be as dear to you as your own, and do not anger easily; repent one day before your death; warm yourself by the fire of the sages, but beware

---

of preserving the dignity of another person by making it "as dear to you as your own," it is even *more* demanding of the respect that a husband must accord his wife. In this case the Talmud is not satisfied with the husband's considering the wife's dignity as dear to him as his own, and states, "You should respect your wife even *more* than you expect to be respected yourself" (*Yevamos* 62b). In order to be compliant with Torah, a husband must be most careful how he relates to his wife. Harsh language is undignified and frank insults are intolerable. Some disagreements between husband and wife may be unavoidable, but one must always be careful not to impinge on his wife's dignity. The Torah requires a person to be most respectful when disagreeing with a parent or a scholar. This is equally true when disagreeing with one's spouse.

We are not at liberty to choose to observe some Torah tenets and ignore others. A husband who compromises his wife's dignity by lack of respect is in frank violation of Torah. The more attentive one is in observance of all Torah requirements, such as Shabbos and *kashrus,* the more cautious he should be to observe the Torah requirement of conducting himself with great respect toward everyone, and especially toward his wife.

וְשׁוּב יוֹם אֶחָד לְפְנֵי מִיתָתְךּ
Repent one day before your death

This statement of the mishnah is understood by the question R' Eliezer's students asked, "How is one to know the day one will die?" R' Eliezer responded, "That is exactly what I meant. Since one is never certain that one will not die the next day, one should do *teshuvah* every day."

While *teshuvah* is certainly important, this mishnah may have yet another meaning. Many people spend the lion's share of their waking hours in their business pursuits, and are so absorbed in these efforts that they spend relatively little time with the family. Certainly we wish to increase our earnings so that we can better provide for the family, but we should realize that material things should not take priority. When we absent ourselves from the family we indicate a sense of low self-esteem. If we truly valued ourselves, we would realize that giving *ourselves* to the family surpasses in importance the many other things we wish to give them.

How often have people who realized that their days were numbered said, "I wish I had spent more time with my family." I seriously doubt that anyone approaching death has ever said, "My only regret is that I did not spend more time at the office." Is it not tragic that the moment of true insight as to what should be most important in our lives may not come until it is too late?

Rabbi Eliezer advises us not to postpone grasping what is most important

ב/טו וֶהֱוֵי זָהִיר בְּגַחַלְתָּן שֶׁלֹּא תִכָּוֶה – שֶׁנְּשִׁיכָתָן נְשִׁיכַת שׁוּעָל,
וַעֲקִיצָתָן עֲקִיצַת עַקְרָב, וּלְחִישָׁתָן לְחִישַׁת שָׂרָף, וְכָל
דִּבְרֵיהֶם כְּגַחֲלֵי אֵשׁ.

---

until our last days. We can enrich our lives if we would live them with the values
we appreciate when life is almost over.

וֶהֱוֵי זָהִיר בְּגַחַלְתָּן שֶׁלֹּא תִכָּוֶה
**But beware of their glowing coal
lest you be scorched**

R' Eliezer's warning to beware of offending a scholar can be better understood through a comment by the
ethicist, R' Chaim Shmulevitz. The Tal-
mud relates that on three occasions Moses became angry, and that with each of
these, he subsequently erred in a halachah. R' Shmulevitz points out that
Moses' error was not a punishment for expressing anger, but rather a natural
consequence. When a person puts his hand into a flame he is not "punished"
by being burnt. This is simply a natural consequence, and so is the distortion of
thought that is brought about by anger simply a natural consequence.

Tzaddikim do not wish to punish anyone for any personal grievance. However, if anyone causes pain to a *tzaddik,* he may suffer grave consequences as
a natural phenomenon, similar to R' Schmulevitz's example of sustaining a burn
by contact with fire.

R' Eliezer ben Hyrkanos is one of the outstanding sages in the Talmud, often
being referred to as "the great R' Eliezer." This notwithstanding, R' Eliezer's
involvement in a dispute with his colleagues led to a tragic occurrence.

In a halachic discussion regarding laws of purity and impurity, R' Eliezer
differed with every one of his peers. To prove the accuracy of his position,
R' Eliezer evoked several miraculous incidents. His colleagues were not
convinced, saying that supernatural phenomenon do not determine halachah. R' Eliezer called upon God to testify that he was indeed correct. A voice
rang from heaven: "Why do you dispute with R' Eliezer? His halachic opinion prevails everywhere." The other sages responded, "The Torah states
that the halachah is determined by the majority opinion. It is a tenet of
the Jewish faith that the laws of the Torah will never be abrogated, and that
God will not alter the Torah in any way. The halachah must therefore be
that of the majority opinion, in spite of the heavenly decree to the contrary."

Although vanquished in the dispute, R' Eliezer refused to yield, and the *Nasi,*
Rabban Gamliel, invoked the sharp measure of excommunication for his defying the majority. This extraordinarily great scholar was bereft of his students,
who could not approach him because of the ban.

One time Rabban Gamliel was on a ship when a fierce storm arose and
threatened to shatter the ship. Realizing that this was undoubtedly due to his

*of their glowing coal lest you be scorched — for their bite is
the bite of a fox, their sting is the sting of a scorpion, their
hiss is the hiss of a serpent, and all their words are like fiery
coals.*

---

having offended R' Eliezer, Rabban Gamliel called out, "Master of the universe!
You know that what I did was not for my personal glory, but rather that the
authority of Torah not be jeopardized by divisiveness," whereupon the storm
abated.

R' Eliezer's wife (Rabban Gamliel's sister) tried to mitigate her husband's
suffering which resulted from the excommunication. In particular, she did not
allow him to assume the position of intense supplication during the *tachanun*
prayer, since this was conducive to arousing feelings of anguish. One time she
failed to prevent this, and when she noted that R' Eliezer had lowered his head
in the *tachanun* prayer and that his pain had surfaced, she exclaimed, "I fear
you have killed my brother!" Rabban Gamliel did indeed die at that time, but not
because R' Eliezer had wished him any harm. As R' Schmulevitz pointed out,
this was the natural consequence of having caused a *tzaddik* to suffer, regardless
of how justifiable the action was. Similarly, Moses' anger was indeed justified,
but he suffered the consequences nevertheless.

We can now understand why R' Eliezer issued the warning to be extremely
cautious not to offend a *tzaddik*. Although the latter would certainly forgive and
set aside any personal feelings, this would not eliminate the natural consequences. R' Eliezer's metaphor is most precise: "Beware of their glowing coal,
lest you be scorched." Forgiving someone for putting his hand in a flame will not
prevent the burn, nor will a *tzaddik's* forgiveness mitigate the consequences of
the offense.

שֶׁנְּשִׁיכָתָן נְשִׁיכַת שׁוּעָל,
וַעֲקִיצָתָן עֲקִיצַת עַקְרָב,
וּלְחִישָׁתָן לְחִישַׁת שָׂרָף

*For their bite is the bite of a fox,
their sting is the sting of a scorpion,
their hiss is the hiss of a serpent*

In its warning to beware of offending
Torah scholars, the mishnah uses
three terms: bite, sting, hiss. In Hebrew, the words are נְשִׁיכָה, עֲקִיצָה,
לְחִישָׁה. The first letters of these three
words make up the word נַעַל – נְשִׁיכָה,
עֲקִיצָה, לְחִישָׁה.

When God appeared to Moses in the burning bush, he commanded Moses:
"Remove your shoes from your feet" (*Exodus* 3:5). שַׁל נְעָלֶיךָ מֵעַל רַגְלֶיךָ may also
mean "your habits," and if we understand the word נַעַל to be the mnemonic for
נְשִׁיכָה (bite), עֲקִיצָה (sting), and לְחִישָׁה (hiss), we can understand the Divine
message contained in this sentence. Although someone who offends a scholar
might be punished, a leader must make himself so impervious to criticism that
he is not emotionally affected by negative comments and reactions. He would
then not be a catalyst for others to suffer. God was thus saying to Moses, "In

[טז] **רַבִּי** יְהוֹשֻׁעַ אוֹמֵר: עַיִן הָרָע, וְיֵצֶר הָרָע, וְשִׂנְאַת הַבְּרִיּוֹת מוֹצִיאִין אֶת הָאָדָם מִן הָעוֹלָם.

[יז] **רַבִּי** יוֹסֵי אוֹמֵר: יְהִי מָמוֹן חֲבֵרְךָ חָבִיב עָלֶיךָ כְּשֶׁלָּךְ;

---

order for you to become a leader, you must divest yourself of the נַעַל, the punitive consequences that result when a scholar feels offended."

Indeed, we see how Moses observed this command. In the decades of his stewardship, he repeatedly was provoked by the Israelites. Rather than be offended by them, he cared for them with incomparable love, and set a precedent for subsequent leaders. The lives of our great Torah personalities, which were characterized by extraordinary self-effacement, indicate that they indeed emulated Moses.

16.

רַבִּי יְהוֹשֻׁעַ אוֹמֵר: עַיִן הָרָע, וְיֵצֶר הָרָע, וְשִׂנְאַת הַבְּרִיּוֹת מוֹצִיאִין אֶת הָאָדָם מִן הָעוֹלָם
Rabbi Yehoshua says: An evil eye, the evil inclination, and hatred of other people remove a person from the world.

The expression "removes a person from the world" is a rather unusual way of describing the consequences of doing evil. On the other hand, the Talmud states that when a person does good, it is as though he were a partner to God in the work of Creation (cf. *Shabbos* 10a). Again, this appears a rather unusual way of describing the merits of one who does good.

In *The Way of God* (2:1), RaMCHaL states, "God's purpose in Creation was to bestow of His good to another." Inasmuch as the purpose of Creation was to do good, one who brings good into the world is essentially sharing a purpose with God. On the other hand, one who does evil is, as it were, undoing the purpose of Creation. He therefore "removes himself from the world."

That "truth" and "good" are synonymous is evident from the emphasis on truth in Creation. The commentaries point out that the final letters of the first three words of Genesis spell *emes,* as do the final letters of the last three words of the segment on Creation (*Genesis* 2:3). This is to indicate that truth is the beginning and end of Creation. On the other hand, evil is synonymous with *sheker* (falsehood).

The Baal Shem Tov explains that the treachery of the *yetzer hara* is that it deludes the person into thinking that wrong is right and that evil is good. He thereby explains the verse in the morning blessings, "and compel our *yetzer* to be subservient to You." "What is it that we pray for?" asked the Baal Shem Tov. "Are we asking that the *yetzer hara* should urge us to do mitzvos? After all, it was created to tempt us to sin, and it is our task to resist this temptation. It is

16. **R**abbi Yehoshua says: An evil eye, the evil inclination, and hatred of other people remove a person from the world.

17. **R**abbi Yose says: Let your fellow's belongings be as dear to you as your own; apply yourself to

---

hardly reasonable to ask that the *yetzer hara* encourage us to do God's will."

The Baal Shem Tov explains that the function for which the *yetzer hara* was created was indeed to tempt us to do something we desire even though we may know it to be wrong. This is something we could cope with. The problem is that the *yetzer hara* does not simply tell us to do wrong. Rather, it deludes us into thinking that what is wrong is really right, and that what is in fact bad is really good. We are then essentially defenseless, because we may not even realize that what we are doing is sinful. The *yetzer hara* may even disguise a sin as a mitzvah! Hence we pray, "Compel the *yetzer* (*hara*) to be subservient to You," i.e., to do that which it was intended to do, to incite us to sin. Take away its capacity to deceive and delude us into thinking that evil is good.

We can now understand why R' Yehoshua states that the *yetzer hara* "removes a person from the world." The purpose of the world is truth and good. The wile of the *yetzer hara* in making us misperceive reality and think that evil is good is the ultimate in falsehood. It defeats the purpose of Creation and "removes a person from the world."

17.

יְהִי מָמוֹן חֲבֵרְךָ חָבִיב עָלֶיךָ כְּשֶׁלָּךְ
Let your fellow's belongings be as dear to you as your own

To be as protective of another's property as of your own is not quite enough. You may take risks with your own possessions, even exposing them to damage if you are so inclined. However, you have no right to do so to your neighbor's belongings. This cannot therefore be the intent of the mishnah.

My great uncle, R' Yehoshua Heschel Rabinowitz, therefore interpreted the mishnah to mean: Let that which you *give* to your neighbor (i.e., *tzedakah*) be as dear to you as what you own and retain. This mishnah thus echoes the message of the verse in Scripture, "That which a man gives to the *Kohen* shall be his" (*Numbers* 5:10).

During the Golden Age of Jews in Spain, the minister of finance was the renowned scholar Don Isaac Abarbanel. He enjoyed the unwavering trust of the king. Several anti-Semitic people in the court sought to defame him, and repeatedly told the king that this minister was growing extremely wealthy by embezzling from the royal treasury, and that his estate far exceeded what he could amass from his salary. Although the king tried to ignore these accusa-

ב/יז וְהַתְקֵן עַצְמְךָ לִלְמוֹד תּוֹרָה, שֶׁאֵינָהּ יְרֻשָּׁה לָךְ; וְכָל מַעֲשֶׂיךָ יִהְיוּ לְשֵׁם שָׁמָיִם.

---

tions, their repetition eventually led him to ask his minister to present him with an accurate inventory of all he owned.

Several days later, the minister presented the king with a rather meager account. The king remarked, "This cannot be. You obviously own much more than this."

"Your Majesty," the minister said, "your inquiry as to how much I own could result only from the efforts of my enemies to discredit me. If they can cause Your Majesty to suspect me of embezzlement, they may also prevail on your Majesty to confiscate my belongings. I can hardly consider anything that I can lose at a moment's notice as being truly mine. I therefore made a list of all that I have given to charity, because that can never be taken from me. That is all I can truly claim as my own, and that is the amount I have submitted to Your Majesty."

This is what Scripture means: All that one gives away to the *Kohen*, in fulfillment of the mitzvah of tithing, that is truly his. Regardless of the vicissitudes of the marketplace, that which one has given away can never be lost.

This is also the intent of the mishnah. Let that which you have given to others as *tzedakah* be as dear to you as that which you own. Your *tzedakah* is truly your own. You can never be deprived of it.

יְהִי מָמוֹן חֲבֵרֶךָ חָבִיב . . .
וְהַתְקֵן עַצְמְךָ לִלְמוֹד תּוֹרָה

Let your fellow's belongings be as dear . . .
apply yourself to study the Torah

Why are these two statements juxtaposed?

The Talmud relates that a heathen told Hillel that he would convert to Judaism if Hillel could teach him the entire Torah in as long a time as he could stand on one foot. Hillel responded, "Love your neighbor as yourself; i.e., do not do anything to someone else that you would not want done to you. That is the essence of Torah. As for the rest, you must learn it" (*Shabbos* 31a). While relating to others with decency and consideration is of great importance, it still does not constitute the entirety of Torah. One must *learn* Torah to fulfill it.

There are some people who believe that the humanism in Torah is all that counts. Hillel clearly stated that while it is important, it is not enough. There are many mitzvos that apply between man and God, and these may not be neglected.

Rabbi Yose, who was described by R' Yochanan ben Zakkai as a *chassid*, someone who extends himself beyond the letter of the law to be fair to others, stresses that there is more to Torah observance than proper interpersonal relationships. Even someone who has fulfilled the obligation to be as considerate of another's belongings as of his own must nevertheless, like the heathen

---

who came to Hillel, study Torah to become cognizant of everything else he must do.

וְהַתְקֵן עַצְמְךָ לִלְמוֹד תּוֹרָה,
שֶׁאֵינָה יְרֻשָּׁה לָךְ
Apply yourself to study the Torah,
for it is not yours by inheritance

Does this not contradict Moses' statement, "Moses instructed us in the Torah, it *is an inheritance* to the congregation of Jacob" (*Deuteronomy* 33:4)?

The Rabbi of Gur explained that the antecedent of "it" is not the Torah, but rather "the study." In other words, the mishnah is saying that whereas the Torah itself is an inheritance, the *study* of Torah is not. It is very similar to someone inheriting a large sum of money which is in the bank. It is indeed his, but if he does not put it to use, the mere ownership of the money does nothing for him. This is also true of Torah, which our ancestors received and bequeathed to us. Unless we make the effort to study it, the fact that it is ours is of little value.

The mishnah is also telling us that the study of Torah requires preparation. In a college catalogue, we find courses which cannot be taken unless the prerequisites have been met. For Torah, the prerequisite is *middos*, proper character traits. Without the latter, Torah knowledge is academic at best, and may be harmful at worst (*Yoma* 72b).

The Seer of Lublin would meditate prior to begin his study of Torah. He said that he must do *teshuvah* to cleanse himself of his sins, for otherwise he is subject to the reprimand, "And to the wicked person God says, 'What right do you have to study My law?' " (*Psalms* 50:16). We can only ponder what kind of "sins" this holy man had! He nevertheless felt that he must divest himself of them in order to be able to study Torah properly. This should help us understand the mishnah's requirement of preparation for study of Torah. As in the analogy of one who inherited great wealth, unless he understands how to put it to good use, he may squander it foolishly and even destructively. This can also be said of Torah.

וְכָל מַעֲשֶׂיךָ יִהְיוּ לְשֵׁם שָׁמַיִם
And let all your deeds be
for the sake of Heaven.

This mishnah is usually interpreted to mean that everything one does, even the mundane activities of everyday life, should be done with the intent of serving God. Not only are the manifest mitzvos sacred, but all of a person's life can be sublimated. One should eat in order to have the energy to study Torah and do mitzvos, and sleep in order to be rested so that he can properly execute his Divine mission on earth.

רבי שמעון אוֹמֵר: הֱוֵי זָהִיר בִּקְרִיאַת שְׁמַע [יח]
וּבִתְפִלָּה; וּכְשֶׁאַתָּה מִתְפַּלֵּל, אַל
תַּעַשׂ תְּפִלָּתְךָ קֶבַע, אֶלָּא רַחֲמִים וְתַחֲנוּנִים לִפְנֵי הַמָּקוֹם,

These actions, too, are thereby elevated to a state of sanctity.

When R' Leib Eiger, the son of the great Talmudist R' Shlomo Eiger, became a *chassid* of R' Mendel of Kotzk, his father was deeply grieved. At that
time, *chassidim* were suspected of neglecting the study of Talmud. They were
also criticized for not adhering to the time limits for morning services as
specified in halachah. When R' Leib was to return home, he asked R' Mendel,
"What can I say to my father when he challenges me why we *daven* later than
prescribed by the *Shulchan Aruch*?" Rabbi Mended replied, "Tell him that
Rambam says that if someone hires a worker to chop wood, and the worker
spends time sharpening the ax, he must pay him for sharpening his tools just
as he does for cutting the wood. The only reason we delay praying is because
we prepare ourselves to be able to pray with proper concentration. The
preparation for prayer is essentially part of the prayer itself."

If we eat, drink, rest, and work in order to be able to properly perform the
mitzvos, these mundane acts become part of the mitzvah itself.

R' Mendel adds another interpretation to this mishnah. "Let us not forget
that *all* one's actions, even the things that are done for the sake of Heaven,
must be done for the sake of Heaven."

What R' Mendel meant by this statement is that we must take care that the
Torah and mitzvos we do should not be diluted by personal interests or
improper behavior. R' Yisrael of Salant said that the most difficult contaminant
to eliminate in performance of a mitzvah may be something that a person
considers to be proper and worthy. As an example, if someone is in so great a
hurry to attend a lecture on Torah that he is rude and pushes people out of his
way, his haste to get to the lecture is not at all a virtue. Yet, the person may
think he is doing God's will by hurrying to the Torah lecture. "Be careful," R'
Mendel said, "that when you do a mitzvah, you do it the way God wants it
done."

18.

הֱוֵי זָהִיר בִּקְרִיאַת שְׁמַע . . .
אֶלָּא . . . וְתַחֲנוּנִים לִפְנֵי הַמָּקוֹם
Be meticulous in reading the Shema . . .
rather [your prayer should be . . .]
. . . a supplication before the Omnipresent

There are some concepts in
Judaism that may appear
to be logically contradictory,
yet which must be accepted
on the basis of faith. For example, we believe that God
has infinite foresight, and knows everything that will occur until the end of time.
We also believe that a person is totally free to make moral decisions. Whether

18. **R**abbi Shimon says: Be meticulous in reading the She-ma and in prayer; when you pray, do not make your prayer a set routine, rather [your prayer should be an entreaty for] mercy and a supplication before the Omnipresent,

---

he does right or wrong is not predetermined, but rather his free choice. Jewish philosophers have struggled to reconcile these two tenets of faith. Inasmuch as God knows what I am going to do, how can I be said to be free in deciding what to do? Can I do other than what God knows I will do? Does not Divine foreknowledge constitute predetermination? As we will see a bit later, we must accept these apparently conflicting concepts on the basis of faith, since their coexistence is not compatible with logic.

A somewhat similar dilemma is presented by prayer. We believe that every-thing that God does is for the good, and that God never does anything that is wrong (*Lamentations* 3:38). Even those happenings which appear to us to be dreadful are for an ultimate good.

It is related that during the lifetime of the *Maggid* of Mezeritch there were no harsh decrees against the Jews, but these resurfaced after his death. One of the *Maggid's* disciples wondered, inasmuch as *tzaddikim* are even greater when they are in Heaven than when on earth (*Chullin* 7b), how is it that the *Maggid* has ceased to intervene to ward off harsh anti-Semitic decrees? The *Maggid* appeared to him in a dream and said, "When I was on earth and my percep-tions were based on my human understanding, I intervened to annul what I saw as being harmful. From my perspective in Heaven I can understand the ultimate good that will result from what appears to be harmful. I cannot inter-vene to prevent an ultimate good."

During his lifetime the *Maggid's* faith in the absolute beneficence of God was certainly unshakable. Even during his earthy existence, he knew that every-thing that God did was for an ultimate good. Why did he intervene to prevent these harsh decrees if he believed they were for an ultimate good?

The relevance of this question to our mishnah is because there is an apparent conflict between the *Shema* and the prayers of the *Amidah*. The *Shema* expresses the absolute Divine beneficence. We refer to God as *Hashem*, the written Tetragrammaton, which is indicative of His manifest mercy and kind-ness. We also mention the appellation *Elokim*, which refers to the Divine attribute of rigorous firmness. We then say *Hashem Echad*, that God is abso-lute Oneness. Even that which appears to us to be harsh is in fact kindness and merciful. Once we have declared our faith in God's absolute beneficence, how do we then pray in the *Amidah* for relief from the various distresses we expe-rience? Are not these distresses to our own advantage in ways which we cannot understand?

We may resolve this issue by noting an intriguing passage in the Talmud. Although Moses referred to God as mighty and awesome (*Deuteronomy*

שֶׁנֶּאֱמַר: ,,כִּי חַנּוּן וְרַחוּם הוּא אֶרֶךְ אַפַּיִם וְרַב חֶסֶד וְנִחָם
עַל הָרָעָה"; וְאַל תְּהִי רָשָׁע בִּפְנֵי עַצְמֶךָ.

[יט] **רַבִּי** אֶלְעָזָר אוֹמֵר: הֱוֵי שָׁקוּד לִלְמוֹד תּוֹרָה, וְדַע
מַה שֶׁתָּשִׁיב לְאֶפִּיקוֹרוֹס; וְדַע לִפְנֵי מִי

10:17), the prophet Jeremiah did not refer to God as awesome, because "If heathens can dance in His Sanctuary, where is His awesomeness?" Daniel omitted the term "mighty", saying, "If heathens enslave His children, where is His might?" The Talmud asks: Did these prophets have any doubt about the Divine awesomeness and might? The Talmud answers that indeed their faith was firm. However they knew that the truth is dearest to God. Since they could not perceive His awesomeness and might with their own eyes, they did not wish to assert anything which, to their human senses, appeared not to be true (*Yoma* 69b).

This is an important concept, and it is contained in this mishnah. We indeed assert our faith in the absolute beneficence of God when we recite the *Shema*, yet we are permitted to pray for relief from distress in the *Amidah*. Like the prophets, we may also respect our sense perceptions. Our sense perceptions notwithstanding, we have firm faith in God's beneficence. Our convictions notwithstanding, we may pray for relief of suffering.

וְאַל תְּהִי רָשָׁע בִּפְנֵי עַצְמֶךָ
And do not judge yourself to be a wicked person.

The commentaries call our attention to an apparent conflict. The Talmud says, "Even if the whole world tells you that you are a *tzaddik*, you should consider yourself as a *rasha*" (*Niddah* 30b). This mishnah tells us not to think of ourselves as a *rasha*. R' Shneur Zalman reconciles the two statements by pointing out that the Talmud in *Niddah* says to think of oneself *as if* one were a *rasha*, which is different than having a self-concept that one is *in fact* a *rasha*. Having an identity as a bad person may render one hopeless. What is the purpose of trying to do good if I am bad in essence?

In psychology we distinguish between *guilt* and *shame*. Guilt is a distressful sensation resulting from the awareness that one has done something wrong. Healthy guilt can lead to *teshuvah*, to making amends for the wrong and to take preventive measures to avoid a recurrence. Shame, on the other hand, is a sensation that one *is* somehow bad, even though one may not be able to identify why he should think of himself as being bad. To put in another way, guilt is a statement, "I made a mistake," whereas shame is a statement, "I *am* a mistake." In the latter case, no corrective action can be taken, since one has no idea of what must be corrected.

Shame can lead to despair. In several of my writings I point out the need for

as it is said: For He is gracious and compassionate, slow to anger, abounding in kindness, and relentful of punishment (Joel 2:13); and do not judge yourself to be a wicked person.

19. **R**abbi Elazar says: Be diligent in the study of Torah, and know what to answer a heretic; know before Whom

---

self-esteem. A person should feel that he is inherently good. Regardless of what may have transpired in the past, a person is always capable of doing good, redeeming oneself, and achieving a high level of spirituality.

To think about oneself *as if* one were bad means that one knows that he is indeed good, but that he may have committed some wrongs which need correction. Our mishnah uses the term בִּפְנֵי עַצְמֶךְ, which means that one should not think of one's עֶצֶם, one's very essence, as being bad, because this may lead to despair of doing good.

19.

הֱוֵי שָׁקוּד לִלְמוֹד תּוֹרָה,
וְדַע מַה שֶׁתָּשִׁיב לְאֶפִּיקוֹרוֹס
Be diligent in the study of Torah,
and know what to answer a heretic

The study of secular philosophy has been discouraged by Torah authorities throughout the ages. Various reasons are given why Rambam was well versed in Aristotelian philosophy, and we are warned not to try to emulate Rambam. Whereas the study of physical sciences such as mathematics, physics, medicine, etc. can have practical applications and can enable one to earn a livelihood, philosophy is purely abstract and has no utilitarian value. On the other hand, some philosophic concepts may cause a person to doubt Torah teachings. A person who is not sufficiently strong in his convictions and who may be vulnerable to behaviors that are forbidden by the Torah may exploit philosophy as a rationalization for deviating from Torah and as a sanction for yielding to temptations. Indeed, the Talmud states that although Scripture tells of the Israelites' repeated attraction to idolatry, "they knew that the idols were worthless. They embraced idolatry in order to give sanction to their lustful behavior" (*Sanhedrin* 63b). This is the danger of indulgence in secular philosophy as well. All the necessary philosophic concepts of God and the universe can be found in Torah literature.

One of the arguments that has been presented to justify the study of philosophy is that one must be capable of defending Torah principles from the challenges that are raised by philosophers. Unless one is well versed in secular philosophy, one is unable to refute these arguments.

In mishnah 11, R' Yehoshua is extolled as "praiseworthy is she who bore him." As was noted, this refers to his mother having asked the Torah scholars to pray that the child she was carrying would be a Torah scholar. Furthermore, she placed his crib near the door of the yeshivah, so that the first sounds that would register on the infant's brain would be those of Torah. From intrauterine life through infancy and maturation, R' Yehoshua was totally absorbed in Torah study. Yet, when it was necessary to send someone to Rome to plead Israel's case, who was chosen? R' Yehoshua. When it was necessary to enter into dialogue with the philosophers of Athens, who was chosen? R' Yehoshua.

The emperor Hadrian challenged R' Yehoshua's contention that there was a God Who was in charge of the world. Hadrian said, "If you do not show Him to me, I cannot believe that He exists." R' Yehoshua said, " It is simple to see God. Just look into the sun, and you will see Him."

The emperor tried to look into the sun, but quickly turned away from the painfully blinding light. "How can I look into the sun?" he said. "The light blinds me." R' Yehoshua responded, "Let Your Majesty hear what your mouth is saying. The sun is but a small fragment of God's Creation, and its light is minuscule compared to the light of God. If you cannot look into the sun, how can you expect to look at God?" (*Chullin* 60b).

On another occasion Hadrian boasted, "I am a greater leader than your Moses." R' Yehoshua responded, "Can Your Majesty decree that no one in the kingdom light a fire for three days?"

"Of course," Hadrian said, and promptly issued a decree prohibiting anyone to light a flame for the next three days.

Later that day and the following day, R' Yehoshua accompanied the emperor to the palace roof, and looking over the city, they could see smoke issuing forth from several houses. "It appears that not everyone is abiding by Your Majesty's decree of just yesterday," R' Yehoshua said, "even though Your Majesty has an army that can enforce it. More than a thousand years ago, Moses decreed that no one light a fire on the Sabbath. Let Your Majesty send servants to Jewish homes on the Sabbath, and see if anyone has kindled a flame. Moses is not living and there is no police force to arrest anyone who violates his decree. Who, then, is the more powerful leader?" (*Koheles Rabbah* 9).

It is clear that R' Yehoshua's ability to relate to the secular world did not stem from a familiarity with secular philosophy, but rather from his erudition in Torah. R' Elazar, who knew R' Yehoshua well, therefore states, "Be diligent in the study of Torah. It will provide all that you will need to respond effectively to the challenges of heretics."

וְנֶאֱמָן הוּא בַּעַל מְלַאכְתָּךְ
and [know] that the Master of your work can be relied upon

Let us carefully note the wording of this mishnah: "The Master of your work can be relied upon to pay you the wage for your achievements."

The Talmud states that the physiologic, animalistic drives that are part and parcel of a human being, which we may refer to as the *yetzer hara,* are so powerful that it would be impossible to withstand them without Divine assistance (*Kiddushin* 30b). We might ask: Why then is a person fully rewarded for doing mitzvos, if a major part of the mitzvos can be accomplished only with God's assistance? It would seem that God, rather than the person, should take credit for the achievement. The answer is that this is a benevolence of God. He gives the person a greater reward than he in fact deserves.

We may think of the performance of a mitzvah as being akin to a machine, which will operate only if someone pushes the button to start it. This is essentially what the Talmud says, quoting God: "Give Me an opening the size of the tip of a needle, and I will broaden it to the size of the portal of a huge banquet hall" (*Shir HaShirim Rabbah* 5:3). The Rabbi of Kotzk commented, "Yes, but the opening must be through and through, and not merely a superficial scratch." Just touching the button will not set the machine in motion. You must push it hard and hold it there for awhile. If we begin a mitzvah with sincerity, we will merit God's assistance in bringing it to a successful completion.

We can now better understand the verse "The kindness is Yours, Oh God, for You reward a person according to his deeds" (*Psalms* 62:13). The obvious problem is that rewarding a person according to his deeds is simply being just and fair, and not really an act of kindness. The answer lies in a more accurate translation of the verse, which is "You reward a person *just as if* he had done the deed." In other words, although a person has only initiated a mitzvah, and the lion's share of the mitzvah was carried out by the assistance of God, one is rewarded *as if* he did everything That is indeed an act of Divine benevolence.

This is what our mishnah says, referring to God as "The Master of your work," or in other words, the One who is doing most of the work. God can be relied upon to reward you as if it were *all* accomplished by your own efforts.

This concept has a significant implication. We may sometimes look upon a particular mitzvah as presenting a formidable challenge, something extremely difficult to fulfill. We may even consider it beyond our capacity. We should therefore remember that all we are called upon to do is to make an honest beginning. If we do so with sincerity, God will assist us the rest of the way.

כ] **רַבִּי** טַרְפוֹן אוֹמֵר: הַיּוֹם קָצֵר, וְהַמְּלָאכָה מְרֻבָּה,
וְהַפּוֹעֲלִים עֲצֵלִים, וְהַשָּׂכָר הַרְבֵּה, וּבַעַל
הַבַּיִת דּוֹחֵק.

20.

**הַיּוֹם קָצֵר, וְהַמְּלָאכָה מְרֻבָּה, וְהַפּוֹעֲלִים
עֲצֵלִים, וְהַשָּׂכָר הַרְבֵּה, וּבַעַל הַבַּיִת דּוֹחֵק**
*The day is short, the task is abundant,
the laborers are lazy, the reward is great,
and the Master of the house is insistent.*

R' Tarfon provides us with teachings that are meant to give structure to our lives. There is much to do and relatively little time to get the work done. Although one is not expected to complete the entire task, one has no right to be indolent, and one is obligated to do as much as he can. While there is great reward for being diligent in the work, the full payment is not to be received in one's earthly life.

The Talmud is not a history book. It is Torah, and inasmuch as "Torah" means teaching and guidance, we must understand that everything in the Talmud serves as an instruction for us. We are to learn lessons on how to live not only from the manifest halachah in the Talmud, but also from the various incidents it relates, particularly those about the personal lives of the sages. We may better appreciate the teachings of R' Tarfon if we know something of what the Talmud relates about his personal life.

Firstly, R' Tarfon is described as being very wealthy. His own definition of a wealthy person is "someone who owns 100 vineyards and 100 fields, and has 100 laborers working them" (*Shabbos* 25b). It is easy to see why he understood that just as with management of one's property, in order to succeed in life one must be aware of several things. One must know that there is little time and much work that must be done, that the workers are indolent, and that the owner is very demanding. However, the owner can be trusted to handsomely compensate those who work diligently, even if they do not complete a given assignment.

A healthy Torah attitude toward wealth can be derived from the following incident. R' Akiva asked R' Tarfon whether he might be interested in purchasing several properties. R' Tarfon gave him 4,000 gold dinars, which R' Akiva promptly distributed to needy scholars. When R' Tarfon asked him for a progress report on his investments, R' Akiva took him to the yeshivah, and asked a young child to read the *Psalms* aloud. When he came to the verse, "He distributed alms to the poor, hence his righteousness persists forever" (*Psalms* 112:9), R' Akiva said, "These are your investments." R' Tarfon arose, embraced and kissed R' Akiva and said, "You are my teacher and my master! You are my teacher of knowledge, and my master in showing me how to live

20. R*abbi Tarfon says: The day is short, the task is abundant, the laborers are lazy, the reward is great, and
the Master of the house is insistent.*

---

properly." He promptly gave him additional money to distribute (*Vayikra Rabbah* 34:16).

R' Tarfon's respect for the sanctity of Torah can be seen from the following incident. One time he went into one of his orchards and ate some of the fruit. The watchman did not recognize him, and mistaking him to be a trespasser who was stealing the fruit, he beat him mercilessly, threw him into a sack and was about to drown him in the river. Realizing his life was in peril, R' Tarfon said, "Go to Tarfon's home and tell them he needs his shroud." When the watchman understood this was his master, he fell before his feet and cried, "Forgive me, my master!" R' Tarfon responded, "Believe me, with every blow you gave me, I promptly forgave you." R' Chanania said of R' Tarfon, "I know that he was forever concerned that perhaps his life was spared because he had revealed himself to be a scholar, and he would bemoan himself saying, 'Woe is to me! I exploited the Torah for my personal gain' " (*Jerusalem Talmud, Sheviis* 4).

R' Tarfon's encyclopedic knowledge of Torah and his love for teaching is revealed in the Talmudic assessment, "R' Tarfon can be compared to a huge pile of walnuts, because if you just move one walnut, all the others are moved." If a student asked R' Tarfon a single question, he would respond by citing myriads of sources from Scripture, the mishnah, and the midrash. When the student left he felt 'laden with blessings' " (*Avos D'Rav Nassan* 18).

R' Tarfon's great piety was equaled by his impeccable integrity. One time he issued a ruling concerning the lesion of a cow. He ruled that it was not kosher. When he subsequently learned that the authorities of the academy of Yavneh ruled that it was indeed kosher, he offered to compensate its owner for having caused him a loss (*Bechoros* 28b).

R' Tarfon was as sensitive to people's feelings as to their possessions, saying, "I doubt whether there is anyone in this generation who is qualified to rebuke others. Everyone has defects of their own" (*Arachin* 16b, according to the version of *Shitah Mekubetzes*). He was also opposed to capital punishment, saying, "Had I been a member of the High Court, no one would ever have been executed" (*Makkos* 7a).

Perhaps the most moving insight into this great personage can be seen from the following episode. One Shabbos, R' Tarfon's mother lost a sandal. It is forbidden to carry a pair of sandals from the house to the street on Shabbos and R' Tarfon did not wish her to walk barefoot for fear she might sustain a bruise. He therefore prostrated himself on the ground, and put the palms of his hands under her feet, moving along with her as she walked. She could step on his palms rather than on the rough ground (*Jerusalem Talmud, Peah* 1:1).

[כא] **הוּא** הָיָה אוֹמֵר: לֹא עָלֶיךָ הַמְּלָאכָה לִגְמוֹר, וְלֹא אַתָּה בֶן חוֹרִין לְהִבָּטֵל מִמֶּנָּה. אִם לָמַדְתָּ תּוֹרָה הַרְבֵּה, נוֹתְנִים לְךָ שָׂכָר הַרְבֵּה; וְנֶאֱמָן הוּא בַּעַל מְלַאכְתֶּךָ, שֶׁיְּשַׁלֶּם לְךָ שְׂכַר פְּעֻלָּתֶךָ. וְדַע שֶׁמַּתַּן שְׂכָרָן שֶׁל צַדִּיקִים לֶעָתִיד לָבֹא.

❧ ❧ ❧

רַבִּי חֲנַנְיָא בֶּן עֲקַשְׁיָא אוֹמֵר: רָצָה הַקָּדוֹשׁ בָּרוּךְ הוּא לְזַכּוֹת אֶת יִשְׂרָאֵל, לְפִיכָךְ הִרְבָּה לָהֶם תּוֹרָה וּמִצְוֹת, שֶׁנֶּאֱמַר: ,,יהוה חָפֵץ לְמַעַן צִדְקוֹ, יַגְדִּיל תּוֹרָה וְיַאְדִּיר׳׳.

As we noted earlier, the expression הוּא הָיָה אוֹמֵר means that he conveyed his teachings by his behavior, by his demeanor, and by his very essence. R' Tarfon indeed lived by his words that conclude this chapter, that the reward of the righteous will be in the Eternal World, and not during one's sojourn on earth. All his children predeceased him. His only surviving descendant was a grandson, from whom he had little *nachas* (*Bava Metzia* 88a). Lest those who observed the tragedies that this great *tzaddik* suffered question the Divine justice, he reassured them that God can be trusted to reward one who lives his life properly.

This, then, is the person who instructs us on giving structure to our lives. Secularists may claim that they, too, have authoritative ethicists. I doubt that we would find the equal of R' Tarfon among them.

21.

וְדַע שֶׁמַּתַּן שְׂכָרָן שֶׁל צַדִּיקִים לֶעָתִיד לָבֹא
And know that the reward of the righteous will be given in the World to Come.

---

*T*zaddikim, following the teachings of Antigonos (*Ethics of the Fathers* 1:3), are not motivated by nor are they interested in personal reward, whether in this world or the next. Their sole interest is *kevod Shamayim* (the honor of God), as the psalmist says, "It is not for ourselves that we seek honor, but for Your Name" (*Psalms* 115:1). Rabbi

21. **H**e [R' Tarfon] was accustomed to say: You are not required to complete the task, yet you are not free to withdraw from it. If you have studied much Torah, they give you great reward; and the Master of your work can be relied upon to pay you the wage of your labor, and know that the reward of the righteous will be given in the World to Come.

❧ ❧ ❧

Rabbi Chanania ben Akashia says: The Holy One, Blessed is He, wished to confer merit upon Israel; therefore He gave them Torah and mitzvos in abundance, as it is said: "HASHEM desired, for the sake of its [Israel's] righteousness, that the Torah be made great and glorious" (Isaiah 42:21).

Levi Yitzchak of Berditchev is known to have chanted, "The Russian people say that their king is a king. The German people say that their king is a king. The Polish people say that their king is a king. But I, Levi Yitzchak the son of Sarah from Berditchev, say that You are the only King, *Yisgadal Veyiskadash Shmei Rabbah* (May the Name of the Great One be glorified and sanctified)."

The way the world is now, the presence of God is concealed. The chassidic master, R' Mendel of Rimanov, was once walking with several of his *chassidim,* when they came upon a child who was crying. The Rebbe asked the child what the trouble was, and the child said, "I am playing hide and seek with my friends. I hid myself, but no one is coming to look for me." The Rebbe turned to his *chassidim* and said, "The Almighty has concealed Himself in His works in the world. How distressed He must be that no one is looking for Him!"

At the close of our daily prayers, we say in *Aleinu* that we hope for the day when the glory of God will be manifest and be seen by all living things. "On that day, God will be One and His Name will be One," meaning that everyone will acknowledge the sovereignty of God.

This is what *tzaddikim* long for, says R' Shlomo of Radomsk, and this is what R' Tarfon says in our mishnah. "Know that the reward of *tzaddikim* is what will transpire in the World to Come, when the majesty and sovereignty of God will be universally recognized."

פרק שלישי §

Chapter Three

כָּל יִשְׂרָאֵל יֵשׁ לָהֶם חֵלֶק לָעוֹלָם הַבָּא, שֶׁנֶּאֱמַר:
„וְעַמֵּךְ כֻּלָּם צַדִּיקִים, לְעוֹלָם יִירְשׁוּ
אָרֶץ, נֵצֶר מַטָּעַי, מַעֲשֵׂה יָדַי לְהִתְפָּאֵר.‟

All Israel has a share in the World to Come, as it is
said: And your people are all righteous; they shall
inherit the land forever; a branch of My plantings, My
handiwork, in which to take pride (Isaiah 60:21).

[א] **עֲקַבְיָא** בֶּן מַהֲלַלְאֵל אוֹמֵר: הִסְתַּכֵּל בִּשְׁלשָׁה דְבָרִים

Chapter Three

1.

עֲקַבְיָא בֶּן מַהֲלַלְאֵל אוֹמֵר
Akavia ben Mahalalel says

It is worthwhile to learn something about the author of this mishnah, Akavia ben Mahalalel. We know that he stood head and shoulders above all his peers, who wished to appoint him as the Head of the Sanhedrin. However, Akavia differed with his colleagues on four *halachos*, and he was told that if he would retract his position on these four issues, the distinguished position would be his. Akavia stated that inasmuch as he was espousing the opinion of his teachers, he felt that this was the prevailing opinion of the authorities of the previous generation. He was therefore not at liberty to retract. Furthermore, he argued, if he did yield to his colleagues who now constituted a majority of the Torah scholars, he might be accused of having changed his mind because he could not resist the lure of the lofty position as Head of the Sanhedrin. "I may be considered a fool for not yielding and thereby forfeiting this singular honor, but I would be considered unscrupulous if I did yield. I would rather people think of me as foolish than as corrupt" (*Eduyos* 5:6-7).

According to one source in the Talmud, the great Akavia was excommunicated — the harshest disciplinary action that could be administered. This was not because he was intransigent — disagreement among the Talmudic sages was not unusual. Rather, it was because it was assumed, correctly or incorrectly, that he had offended the dignity of the leaders of the previous generation.

One of the subjects of dispute between Akavia and his colleagues was whether the *sotah* ritual prescribed in the Torah for a woman suspected of adultery (*Numbers* 5:11-31) applied to converts as well as to those who were born into the Jewish faith. Akavia contended that it did not. When he was told that the great sages Shemayah and Avtalyon (*Ethics of the Fathers* 1:10) did perform the ritual for a convert, Akavia made a remark which was interpreted as "they did so because they, too, were converts, and they wished to validate themselves." This was considered an intolerable insult, which warranted the harshest discipline.

Why does the Talmud relate this to us? To show that there was no favoritism. Even the greatest scholar was held accountable for a comment which might have been interpreted as disrespectful of the accepted authorities.

Chapter Three

1. **A**kavia ben Mahalalel says: Consider three things

Although Akavia held firm to his opinion, he can hardly be considered intransigent. On his deathbed he instructed his son to abide by the majority opinion in the *halachos* that were in dispute. "But you disagreed with them," his son said. "Yes," Akavia replied. "I disagreed because my position was based on the majority of *my* generation. You must abide by the opinion of the majority of *your* generation."

The son then made a request of the dying father. "Ask your colleagues to treat me with consideration." Akavia refused this request, and with virtually his last breath, he uttered words which should be engraved on the minds of everyone: "Your own actions will determine how you are received. It is your actions that will determine whether you are accepted or rejected." At his moment of parting from his child, Akavia did not allow his paternal compassion to override his sense of justice. Nepotism may be a distortion of truth, and to this great sage, truth was not negotiable.

Knowing this about Akavia ben Mahalalel, we might listen to his teachings a bit more attentively.

הִסְתַּכֵּל בִּשְׁלֹשָׁה דְבָרִים . . .
Consider three things . . .

When one of the Baal Shem Tov's disciples left to spend a Shabbos in a different city, the Baal Shem Tov said to him, "Be sure to review the mishnah of Akavia ben Mahalalel." The disciple did not understand the reason for this, but did as the master said.

On Shabbos, several of the "enlightened" young men in the community thought they would be able to show up the visitor as being an impostor who feigned to be a Torah scholar. They challenged him to explain a cryptic midrash. "The midrash states that the reason that Adam sinned was because he only saw two, and had he seen three, he would not have sinned. What can that possibly mean?"

The disciple now understood the Baal Shem Tov's instruction. "This is very elementary," he said. "The mishnah says that in order to avoid sin, a person must concentrate on three things: his humble beginning from a putrid drop, his ultimate end in the grave, and that he will stand before God to be judged. Adam could only see two of these three things. He did not have a humble origin from a putrid drop. To the contrary, he had a glorious origin, being the handiwork of the Creator Himself. Inasmuch as Akavia said that one must see all three items in order to avoid sin, and Adam could only see two of the three, he was vulnerable to sin."

The *chutzpah* of the young men backfired, and they walked away in embarrassment, having considered something so elementary as insoluble.

ג/א וְאֵין אַתָּה בָא לִידֵי עֲבֵרָה: דַּע מֵאַיִן בָּאתָ, וּלְאָן אַתָּה הוֹלֵךְ,
וְלִפְנֵי מִי אַתָּה עָתִיד לִתֵּן דִּין וְחֶשְׁבּוֹן. מֵאַיִן בָּאתָ?

הִסְתַּכֵּל בִּשְׁלֹשָׁה דְבָרִים
וְאֵין אַתָּה בָא לִידֵי עֲבֵרָה
Consider three things and you
will not come into the hands of sin

One of the commentaries notes that there seems to be a conspicuous omission: Akavia does not mention Torah observance as a deterrent to sin! He explains that the Talmud states, "I created a *yetzer hara,* and I created the Torah as its remedy" (*Kiddushin* 30b). This implies that the Torah is a "treatment" or remedy for someone who has already yielded to the *yetzer hara,* whereas Akavia is listing those things that will *prevent* one from sinning in the first place. Hence Akavia states that the three things he mentions will prevent someone from "coming to sin." We are thus concerned with prevention rather than cure.

It is also noteworthy that Akavia uses the expression "into the hands of sin" which implies that a person may lose control if he falls "into the hands of sin," and be at its mercy, as it were.

These two observations on Akavia's statement struck a familiar cord with me. In my work with addictive conditions, I encounter both the need to treat an existing problem, and also the need to prevent its occurrence. Indeed, if one fails to prevent addiction, one "falls into its hands," and loses self-control. It is much the same with sin. The Talmud states that if a person repeats a sin, he no longer sees that it is wrong and is therefore likely to continue it (*Yoma* 86b).

It follows that the methodology for preventing sin may be very similar to that for preventing addiction. An insight into the latter came to me when the slogan "Just Say No To Drugs" was first popularized. Researchers who asked young people for their reaction to this slogan often encountered a response, "Why should we say no to drugs? What else is there?" It became apparent to me that recourse to drugs is likely to occur when a person has no other aspirations. Perhaps sinful behavior is similarly a consequence of a lack of awareness that there is indeed "something else" to life.

Why should a person feel that life is so devoid of anything gratifying that one is willing to subject oneself to the real dangers of toxic drugs? It may well be because a person fails to see any goal in life other than having pleasure, and since pleasure is so often elusive, one may turn to chemicals that affect the brain in a way to produce a pleasurable sensation.

Pleasure-seeking behavior carries a high risk of frustration. Some people who are deprived of worldly possessions simply despair of achieving pleasure. On the other hand, people who are affluent and have the means for many pleasurable activities may find that earthly pleasures are ephemeral. The gustatory joy of a tasty meal is hardly a memory several hours later, and the constant pursuit of more pleasurable activities may result in disillusionment. I have had drug

and you will not come into the hands of sin: Know whence you came, whither you go, and before Whom you will give a judgment and an accounting. "Whence you came?"

---

addicts from both segments of the population, those who were discouraged of ever achieving pleasure in life, and those for whom all available pleasures were ultimately disappointing.

Sinful behavior is nothing other than yielding to temptation for pleasurable gratifications of various kinds. As with addiction, such behavior can be avoided if one believes there is "something else." In other words, there is something more to life than pleasurable indulgences. The realization that one was created for a purpose, that the physical body one wishes to satisfy is nothing but a handful of dust, and that one will be held accountable for what one achieved during one's lifetime will result in a concept of "something else." Rather than being a pleasure-seeking animal, the human being has a mission, and how much pleasure a person experiences in life is totally irrelevant to his true and ultimate goal. Akavia states that to achieve this conviction one must give close scrutiny to one's life. הִסְתַּכֵּל means more than just "look and see." It means to carefully observe and consider. Just a bit of serious reflection will enable one to realize that if the purpose of existence were nothing more than to experience pleasure, the brilliant intellect which the human being has is totally superfluous. Animals are far more likely to achieve contentment than are humans, who are so prone to stress and suffering. The wise Solomon stated, "To increase knowledge is to increase suffering" (*Ecclesiastes* 1:18).

And so we have the formula for avoiding sin. הִסְתַּכֵּל, observe closely and intensely. Consider the three factors which indicate a supernal purpose in life. You will then realize there is indeed "something else," something which befits the dignity of intelligent man and elevates him above the level of all other creatures.

וְלִפְנֵי מִי אַתָּה עָתִיד
לִתֵּן דִּין וְחֶשְׁבּוֹן
And before Whom
you will give a judgment
and an accounting

Many commentaries note that the text of the mishnah, *din vecheshbon* (a judgment and an accounting), appears to be in reverse order. The sequence of events in a trial is that the judgment or verdict comes *after* the account, not before. Various explanations are given for this.

The *Gaon* of Vilna states that "judgment" refers to that of the sin one committed, whereas "accounting" refers to the dereliction of wasting time on sin, time that could have been utilized to perform mitzvos. In other words, there are two punishments for sin: one for the actual sin, and the other for not having utilized the time spent on sin for doing mitzvos.

R' Moshe of Uhel (*Yismach Moshe*) points out that whereas a person might offer a defense for having sinned that he was unable to withstand the

מִטָּפָה סְרוּחָה. וּלְאָן אַתָּה הוֹלֵךְ? לִמְקוֹם עָפָר, רִמָּה
וְתוֹלֵעָה. וְלִפְנֵי מִי אַתָּה עָתִיד לְתֵן דִּין וְחֶשְׁבּוֹן? לִפְנֵי מֶלֶךְ
מַלְכֵי הַמְּלָכִים, הַקָּדוֹשׁ בָּרוּךְ הוּא.

[ב] **רבי** חֲנִינָא סְגַן הַכֹּהֲנִים אוֹמֵר: הֱוֵי מִתְפַּלֵּל
בִּשְׁלוֹמָהּ שֶׁל מַלְכוּת, שֶׁאִלְמָלֵא מוֹרָאָהּ, אִישׁ
אֶת רֵעֵהוּ חַיִּים בְּלָעוֹ.

---

overwhelming force of temptation, he cannot use this defense for not having done *teshuvah* for his sin. After he committed the sin, the temptation was over and the desire had already been gratified. Why did he now not repent having sinned? The failure to do *teshuvah* may therefore be an even greater offense than the sin itself. The "judgment" refers to the sin, and the "accounting" refers to the failure to do *teshuvah*. The two are thus in proper order.

Another explanation is based on the Talmudic statement that a person should always think of himself as having an equal number of mitzvos and sins, and that the world is comprised of an equal number of sinful and virtuous ones people. If a person commits a single sin, he upsets his own balance, since his sins are now in the majority, and he is judged sinful. This now upsets the balance of the world, because there are now more sinful people than virtuous (*Ethics of the Fathers* 1:6). "Judgment" refers to one's sin, and "accounting" refers to the impact the sin had on the rest of the world, which was consequently considered as having a majority of sinful people.

Perhaps this mishnah can be understood according to the principle that "the kingdom of Heaven is conducted similar to earthly kingdoms" (*Berachos* 58a). In secular courts, a verdict is rendered, and then there is a pre-sentence investigation which may influence the sentence. Thus, if the defendant is found to have generally been a person of good character he may be given a less severe sentence. "Accounting" refers to the pre-sentence investigation that follows the verdict.

The Rebbe of Lubavitch provides yet another interpretation. The Baal Shem Tov said that God relates to a person just as a shadow mimics the object, and that He deals with a person in the same way that a person deals with others. Thus, after a person has been judged and a verdict has been rendered, the Heavenly Tribunal considers how this person reacted to others who committed offenses against him. If he was forgiving toward others, then his sentence will be lenient. If he was harsh and unforgiving, he would be shown little mercy. "Accounting" refers to a scrutiny of how one treated others. This accounting follows the verdict.

— from a putrid drop; "whither you go?" — to a place of dust, worms, and maggots; "and before Whom will you give a judgment and an accounting?" — before the King Who reigns over kings, the Holy One, Blessed is He.

2. **R**abbi Chanina, the deputy Kohen Gadol, says: Pray for the welfare of the government, because if people did not fear it, a person would swallow his fellow alive.

2.

הֱוֵי מִתְפַּלֵל בִּשְׁלוֹמָהּ
שֶׁל מַלְכוּת

**Pray for the welfare
of the government**

R' Chanina's statement is a sad reflection on human nature. If there were no fear of discipline and punishment by the temporal power, people might ruthlessly destroy one another. Not only might they injure or kill, but they might devour each other alive. Not only might they behave cold-bloodedly against an enemy, but might even turn mercilessly against a friend. Even the worst despotism is better than anarchy.

But what about people who have a religious commitment? Certainly the dictates of the religion to which they ascribe would be a sufficient deterrent of such inhumane behavior.

R' Chanina knew better. As a deputy to the High Priest, he was aware of the depravity that prevailed during the latter days of the Second Temple, a time during which Torah observance was often stripped of its beautiful spirituality, and deteriorated into religiosity. The Talmud tells us about this so that we should be on guard against distortion of Torah observance.

Two young *Kohanim* were competing for the privilege of bringing the daily offering to the altar. When one saw that the other would succeed, he fatally stabbed him (*Yoma* 23a). And this in the Name of God! The Talmud goes on to say that it was not that the service of the Temple ranked so high in people's values, which would never justify such horrible behavior. Rather, the value of life had become so cheap that there was little deterrent to murder.

R' Yisrael of Salant warns us against distorting Torah, and that indecent behavior can never be justified for the sake of Torah. He cites the hypocrisy of someone forcing his way to the front row, rudely pushing others aside in order to better hear a lecture on *mussar* (ethics).

Earlier we noted that Rabban Yochanan ben Zakkai, in his parting words to his disciples, told them that they should have at least as much fear of God as they do of people. R' Chanina echoes this. Our sages were well aware of the spiritual heights to which a human being may rise, but they were also aware of the depths to which a person may descend. The *yetzer hara* is always at work, and is particularly challenging to people who, because they have achieved an

[ג] **רַבִּי** חֲנִינָא בֶּן תְּרַדְיוֹן אוֹמֵר: שְׁנַיִם שֶׁיּוֹשְׁבִין וְאֵין
בֵּינֵיהֶם דִּבְרֵי תוֹרָה, הֲרֵי זֶה מוֹשַׁב לֵצִים,
שֶׁנֶּאֱמַר: ,,וּבְמוֹשַׁב לֵצִים לֹא יָשָׁב". אֲבָל שְׁנַיִם שֶׁיּוֹשְׁבִין

---

element of greatness, may be more vulnerable to a precipitous decline (*Succah* 52a).

R' Mendel of Kotzk gave this mishnah a unique interpretation, reading it not as "pray for the peace (welfare) of the government" but rather "pray when the government is at peace." R' Mendel was reflecting on the history of our people, who sometimes suffered the worst persecutions when the country they lived in was at peace. If the country was at war, it may have been distracted by other concerns, and not have time to bother with the Jews. But if there was nothing to distract them, this was ironically the time that the worst anti-Semitic oppressions occurred.

It seems part and parcel of human nature to seek out a scapegoat. People are not prone to look within themselves for the cause of their discontent, because this would require them to make changes in themselves. It is so much easier to blame others, because one can thus exempt himself from the need to change. This is certainly true of individuals, and R' Mendel tells us that it is equally true of populations as a whole.

There is always an element of discontent. Few people are satisfied with what they have. If there is turmoil in the country, it is possible that people will focus upon this as the cause for their discontent, and leave the Jews alone. When there is peace and nothing else to blame, there is greater risk that "the Jewish problem" will come to the fore. Hence, "Pray with great intensity when the country is at peace. This may be a most dangerous period."

3.

שְׁנַיִם שֶׁיּוֹשְׁבִין וְאֵין בֵּינֵיהֶם
דִּבְרֵי תוֹרָה, הֲרֵי זֶה מוֹשַׁב לֵצִים
If two sit together and there are
no words of Torah between them,
it is a session of scorners

If two people are sitting together and are not involved in the study of Torah, why are they assumed to be scorners? They might be engaged in a discussion of business, or in something pertaining to community affairs. Is it not too harsh a judgment that any session that does not deal in Torah is one of scorners?

In our morning prayers we recite a *berachah* that we have been Divinely commanded "to be engaged in the words of Torah." Note that the term is "to be engaged" rather than "to study." It is only natural that people must have other essential activities, which include work and commerce. However, every-

3. Rabbi Chanina ben Tradyon says: If two sit together and there are no words of Torah between them, it is a session of scorners, as it is said: In the session of scorners he does not sit (Psalms 1:1). But if two sit together

---

thing we do must be goal directed, and our ultimate goal is to abide by the Torah. In order to do so, we must eat, sleep, and earn a livelihood, because unless we have the essentials of life we cannot fulfill the mitzvos. Even rest and entertainment, when done in a measure that promotes optimum health and functioning, can be considered in the service of Torah observance. It is only when one's actions are aimless, without a goal, that one may be considered to be a scorner. The Hebrew word *leitz*, meaning a scorner or scoffer, refers to a person who does not see life as a serious mission, and who dismisses the concept of an ultimate goal, viewing it as an absurdity.

It is of interest that there is no Hebrew equivalent for the word "fun." There are words for enjoyment and amusement, but not for "fun." Why? Because "fun" refers to activities which are not goal directed, as is evident in the expression of doing something "just for the fun of it." The attitude that one can indulge in actions that are purposeless is considered scorning or scoffing at life.

Thus, if two people are engaged in a discussion of business, community affairs, or anything else that is constructive and conducive to purposeful living, they are indeed engaged in "divrei Torah" and are not considered to be *leitzim*.

It is indeed appropriate that R' Chanina ben Tradyon is the author of the mishnah that focuses on the purpose of life as being goal directed with Torah as the ultimate goal. R' Chanina is virtually without peer in his dedication to Torah.

The Talmud (*Avodah Zarah* 18a) relates that R' Yose said to R' Chanina, "My dear brother, are you not aware that God has empowered the Roman empire to wreak His wrath upon us, to destroy His Temple and kill His pious servants, yet you defiantly expound Torah publicly, exposing yourself to danger?"

R' Chanina replied, "I will continue to do so, and rely on God's mercy."

"How dare you expose yourself to danger and expect miracles!" R' Yose said. "Both you and the Torah are apt to be put to the stake."

Shortly after R' Yose's death, R' Chanina was arrested for teaching Torah in defiance of the Roman government's prohibition, answering the prosecutor's charge with, "I only did what God commanded me." Both R' Chanina and his wife were condemned to death.

R' Chanina was wrapped in a Torah scroll and was set afire. To prolong his torture, the Romans applied wet cloths to his chest. His daughter wept, "Father, is this the reward for studying Torah?" and R' Chanina replied, "If only I was being burned, it might be difficult for me, but since I am being burned together with the Torah, whoever will avenge the Torah will avenge me as well."

וְיֵשׁ בֵּינֵיהֶם דִּבְרֵי תוֹרָה, שְׁכִינָה שְׁרוּיָה בֵּינֵיהֶם, שֶׁנֶּאֱמַר: „אָז נִדְבְּרוּ יִרְאֵי יהוה אִישׁ אֶל רֵעֵהוּ, וַיַּקְשֵׁב יהוה וַיִּשְׁמָע, וַיִּכָּתֵב סֵפֶר זִכָּרוֹן לְפָנָיו, לְיִרְאֵי יהוה וּלְחֹשְׁבֵי שְׁמוֹ." אֵין לִי אֶלָּא שְׁנַיִם; מִנַּיִן שֶׁאֲפִילוּ אֶחָד שֶׁיּוֹשֵׁב וְעוֹסֵק בַּתּוֹרָה, שֶׁהַקָּדוֹשׁ בָּרוּךְ הוּא קוֹבֵעַ לוֹ שָׂכָר? שֶׁנֶּאֱמַר: „יֵשֵׁב בָּדָד וְיִדֹּם, כִּי נָטַל עָלָיו."

[ד] רַבִּי שִׁמְעוֹן אוֹמֵר: שְׁלֹשָׁה שֶׁאָכְלוּ עַל שֻׁלְחָן אֶחָד וְלֹא אָמְרוּ עָלָיו דִּבְרֵי תוֹרָה, כְּאִלּוּ אָכְלוּ מִזִּבְחֵי מֵתִים, שֶׁנֶּאֱמַר: „כִּי כָּל שֻׁלְחָנוֹת מָלְאוּ קִיא צֹאָה,

R' Chanina's disciples, noting the master staring intently, asked, "What is it that you see?" R' Chanina answered in prophetic words that have unfortunately been a repetitive theme throughout Jewish history: "I see a parchment burning, but the letters take wing through the air." Many times our citadels of Torah study have been destroyed, but whereas the enemy may destroy buildings and scholars, the words of Torah have always sprouted wings, and have always taken root elsewhere.

Even the executioner was moved by the composure of this saintly man in his moments of agony. "Master," he said, "if I hasten your death and relieve your suffering by removing the wet cloths and adding wood to the fire, will I merit Paradise?"

"Indeed so," R' Chanina said.

The executioner did so. And as R' Chanina breathed his last, the executioner leaped into the flames and died along with him, whereupon a heavenly voice thundered, "R' Chanina and the executioner shall both enter Paradise." When R' Yehudah *HaNasi* learned of this, he wept. "Some may earn Paradise through a lifetime of devotion, and others may earn it in just a brief moment" (*Avodah Zarah* 18a).

We can now understand why R' Chanina said that anyone whose life is not goal directed toward Torah is a scoffer. He lived by his teachings: A life that is devoid of Torah is not worth living.

4.

שְׁלֹשָׁה שֶׁאָכְלוּ עַל שֻׁלְחָן אֶחָד
*If three have eaten
at the same table*

The Jewish nation is classified into three categories: *Kohanim, Leviim,* and *Yisraelim* (Priests, Levites and Israelites).

During the time of the Temple, these three could not eat together, because *terumah,* the tithe given to the *Kohanim,* could not be eaten by the others. However, all could partake of sanctified food, for the Levites

and words of Torah are between them, the Divine Presence rests between them, as it is said: Then those who fear HASHEM spoke to one another, and HASHEM listened and heard, and a book of remembrance was written before Him for those who fear HASHEM and give thought to His Name (Malachi 3:16). From this verse we would know this only about two people; how do we know that if even one person sits and occupies himself with Torah, the Holy One, Blessed is He, determines a reward for him? For it is said: Let one sit in solitude and be still, for he will have received [a reward] for it (Lamentations 3:28).

4. **R**abbi Shimon says: If three have eaten at the same table and have not spoken words of Torah there, it is as if they have eaten of offerings to the dead idols, as it is said: For all tables are full of vomit and filth,

---

also received a tithe, and the remainder had a status of sanctity for the Israelites, since it had been appropriately tithed. The "three eating together" is an expression indicating a condition that prevails after the loss of the Temple, when the method of sanctifying food by tithing is no longer available to us. We may nevertheless sanctify our food by sharing words of Torah at every meal. As pointed out earlier, when we engage in mundane activities in order to enable us to properly fulfill Torah objectives, these are elevated to a level of spirituality and sanctity.

Just as one's table can become an altar, so can one's home become a sanctuary. The *Alter* of Slobodka cited the midrash that relates that R' Yochanan would never enter his home without first knocking on the door, because the Torah informs us that the High Priest had bells on his vestments, so that the sound would announce his entry into the Sanctuary (*Vayikra Rabbah* 21).

"How did R' Yochanan derive the practice of announcing his entry into his home from the High Priest's entry into the sanctuary?" asked the Alter. "It must be because every Jewish home should be a sanctuary, a place that is totally dedicated to serving God."

וְלֹא אָמְרוּ עָלָיו דִּבְרֵי תוֹרָה,
כְּאִלּוּ אָכְלוּ מִזִּבְחֵי מֵתִים
And have not spoken words of Torah there, it is as if they have eaten of offerings to the dead idols

Chassidic writings raise the question: Inasmuch as the foods we eat provide only physical nutrients, where does the *neshamah* get its nutrients? They answer that in every physical object there is a spark, a nucleus of *kedushah* and Godliness, which enables the object to exist. This is true of food as well. This nucleus of divinity that is within the food is the nutrition

ג/ה בְּלִי מָקוֹם"; אֲבָל שְׁלשָׁה שֶׁאָכְלוּ עַל שֻׁלְחָן אֶחָד וְאָמְרוּ
עָלָיו דִּבְרֵי תוֹרָה, כְּאִלּוּ אָכְלוּ מִשֻׁלְחָנוֹ שֶׁל מָקוֹם, שֶׁנֶּאֱמַר:
„וַיְדַבֵּר אֵלַי, זֶה הַשֻׁלְחָן אֲשֶׁר לִפְנֵי יהוה."

[ה] רַבִּי חֲנִינָא בֶּן חֲכִינַאי אוֹמֵר: הַנֵּעוֹר בַּלַּיְלָה,
וְהַמְהַלֵּךְ בַּדֶּרֶךְ יְחִידִי, וּמְפַנֶּה לִבּוֹ לְבַטָּלָה —
הֲרֵי זֶה מִתְחַיֵּב בְּנַפְשׁוֹ.

of the *neshamah.*

Just as physical digestion is dependent on the presence of certain enzymes that convert the food into the body's necessary building blocks, so is the absorption of the nucleus of *kedushah* that is within the food dependent on the spiritual "enzymes." These are the *berachos* that proceed consumption of food, whereby one invokes the Name of God as one thanks Him for the food. Similarly, sharing words of Torah at the table enables the *neshamah* to extract the spark of *kedushah* in the food and absorb it.

If one eats without reciting the appropriate *berachos* or sharing words of Torah, the body indeed absorbs the minerals, proteins, fats, and carbohydrates which give it life. However, insofar as the *neshamah* is concerned, the nucleus of Godliness that was in the food is not extracted. The *neshamah* does not get its life-sustaining nutrition. What could have been considered equivalent to eating the meat of an offering is instead *zivchei meisim,* literally, a lifeless offering.

We have already noted that everything a person does, even the most mundane acts, can be directed toward the service of God. Eating in a manner that nourishes the *neshamah* is indeed fulfilling the Divine wish.

Chassidus teaches that retrieving the sparks of Godliness that are dispersed within the physical world hastens the ultimate Redemption of Israel. Think of it! A person has the extraordinary power of hastening the Redemption by eating properly! All that is necessary is that we elevate ourselves above the animal level. Instead of eating simply to satiate our hunger, which is essentially an animal trait, we should exercise our unique human capacity and make our eating purposeful.

5.

הַנֵּעוֹר בַּלַּיְלָה . . . הֲרֵי זֶה מִתְחַיֵּב בְּנַפְשׁוֹ
One who stays awake at night . . . indeed, he bears guilt for his soul.

While there is no justification for not utilizing time for the study of Torah, there may nevertheless be mitigating circumstances that might be pleaded in one's defense. A person may be under stress or be so distracted by things in his environment that he may not be able to concentrate on Torah. But when there are no mitigating circumstances, a person is defenseless. This is

without the Omnipresent (Isaiah 28:8). But if three have eaten at the same table and have spoken words of Torah there, it is as if they have eaten from the table of the Omnipresent, as it is said: And he said to me, "This is the table that is before HASHEM" (Ezekiel 41:22).

5. **R**abbi Chanina ben Chachinai says: One who stays awake at night or who travels alone on the road, but turns his heart to idleness – indeed, he bears guilt for his soul.

---

equally true of all transgressions.

The chassidic master, R' Baruch of Mezhiboz, was openly critical of R' Levi Yitzchak of Berditchev, which perplexed many *chassidim*, who knew that R' Levi Yitzchak was held in the highest regard by everyone.

One time two merchants went to the market in Berditchev, and went to visit R' Levi Yitzchak. They happened to come in when the rabbi was praying. To their great surprise he ran to one of the merchants, seized him by the lapels and screamed, "What will the angel Michael say in your behalf?"

When they returned to Mezhiboz they felt that they had a juicy piece of gossip to tell R' Baruch, who would certainly welcome hearing the irrational behavior of R' Levi Yitzchak. Upon hearing the tale, R' Baruch shouted at the one merchant, "You thief! You must promptly return the money you stole from your friend!"

R' Baruch explained, "Although there can never be any justification for thievery, the angel Michael, who seeks to defend the sinful, may plead for lenience for the *ganiff*. He may claim that the thief was driven to steal because he could not witness the hunger and poverty of his family, and his emotions overwhelmed his judgment.

"But you, who are well to do, what defense can the angel Michael plead for you?"

"This is what R' Levi Yitzchak meant," R' Baruch said. "Yes, he is a great *tzaddik*, with prophetic vision. Why then do I criticize him? Because his service to God is so pure and intense that the angels say, 'What need is there for a Temple and a High Priest? No one could do better than Levi Yitzchak!' I wish to declare that I am not willing to accept R' Levi Yitzchak in lieu of the High Priest, and I insist on our Redemption and the rebuilding of the Temple."

There are times when we may have valid reasons as to why we did not study Torah. But if we are awake at night, or are alone on our travels, with no one distracting us, what defense can there be for not studying Torah then?

It is true that there are many demands on our time. We are busy earning a living, helping with the children, and doing various chores. We may be able to explain to the Heavenly tribunal why we did not spend more time studying Torah.

[ו] רַבִּי נְחוּנְיָא בֶּן הַקָּנָה אוֹמֵר: כָּל הַמְּקַבֵּל עָלָיו עֹל
תּוֹרָה, מַעֲבִירִין מִמֶּנּוּ עֹל מַלְכוּת וְעֹל דֶּרֶךְ
אֶרֶץ; וְכָל הַפּוֹרֵק מִמֶּנּוּ עֹל תּוֹרָה, נוֹתְנִין עָלָיו עֹל מַלְכוּת
וְעֹל דֶּרֶךְ אֶרֶץ.

[ז] רַבִּי חֲלַפְתָּא בֶּן דּוֹסָא אִישׁ כְּפַר חֲנַנְיָא אוֹמֵר:
עֲשָׂרָה שֶׁיּוֹשְׁבִין וְעוֹסְקִין בַּתּוֹרָה, שְׁכִינָה
שְׁרוּיָה בֵּינֵיהֶם, שֶׁנֶּאֱמַר: ,,אֱלֹהִים נִצָּב בַּעֲדַת אֵל.‏"
וּמִנַּיִן אֲפִילוּ חֲמִשָּׁה? שֶׁנֶּאֱמַר: ,,וַאֲגֻדָּתוֹ עַל אֶרֶץ יְסָדָהּ.‏"
וּמִנַּיִן אֲפִילוּ שְׁלֹשָׁה? שֶׁנֶּאֱמַר: ,,בְּקֶרֶב אֱלֹהִים יִשְׁפֹּט.‏"
וּמִנַּיִן אֲפִילוּ שְׁנַיִם? שֶׁנֶּאֱמַר: ,,אָז נִדְבְּרוּ יִרְאֵי יהוה אִישׁ אֶל
רֵעֵהוּ וַיַּקְשֵׁב יהוה וַיִּשְׁמָע.‏" וּמִנַּיִן אֲפִילוּ אֶחָד? שֶׁנֶּאֱמַר:

But what about the time that we have available that we do not utilize in Torah study, such as traveling in the car, when we could be listening to the many Torah tapes that are available? Perhaps we might say that we did not wish to be distracted from driving. But what if we use our cellular phones while driving, even to conduct business? We can hardly claim that listening to Torah tapes would be more distracting.

Let us take the words of the mishnah to heart. Let us search out those moments that are available to us and use them for Torah study.

6.

כָּל הַמְּקַבֵּל עָלָיו עֹל תּוֹרָה
If someone accepts upon himself the yoke of Torah

It is noteworthy that R' Nechunia does not talk about someone who *learns* Torah, or someone who *observes* Torah, but about someone who *accepts the yoke of Torah* upon himself. The term *kabbalas ol* (acceptance of the yoke) is regularly used to describe the desirable attitude of servitude toward God.

The concept of a yoke is that just as the animal that plows under a yoke is doing the will of its master rather than seeking its own pleasure, so must one consider one's mission on earth as fulfilling the Divine will rather than seeking gratification of one's desires. Furthermore, just as the animal under a yoke does not deviate to the left or the right from the course it must follow, so must a person adhere to the prescribed course and not be distracted by anything else. Self-centered desires have no place when one is under a yoke.

R' Nechunia was totally devoid of self-centered motives. When he entered the academy, it was noted that he uttered a brief silent prayer. When he was asked what the content of his prayer was, he said, "I pray that I do not make a

3/6-7 **6.** R*abbi Nechunia ben Hakanah says: If someone accepts upon himself the yoke of Torah — the yoke of government and the yoke of worldly responsibilities are removed from him. But if someone throws off the yoke of Torah from himself — the yoke of government and the yoke of worldly responsibilities are placed upon him.*

7. R*abbi Chalafta ben Dosa of Kfar Chanania says: If ten people sit together and engage in Torah study, the Divine Presence is present among them, as it is said: God stands in the assembly of God (Psalms 82:1). How do we know this [is true] even of five? For it is said: He has established His bundle upon earth (Amos 9:6). How do we know this [is true] even of three? For it is said: In the midst of judges He shall judge (Psalms 82:1). How do we know this [is true] even of two? For it is said: Then those who fear HASHEM spoke to one another, and HASHEM listened and heard (Malachi 3:16). How do we know this [is true] even of one?*

---

mistake which will cause other students to jeer at me, for then I will have been the cause of their rudeness." R' Nechunia was not concerned that he might be embarrassed, but rather that he might cause others to sin. When asked to what he attributed his longevity, he replied, "I never took pride in someone else's mistakes." R' Nechunia's self-effacement was total, and he was therefore able to speak of servitude to God as being under a yoke.

But what about his assertion that one who accepts the yoke of Torah is freed of the yoke of government and the yoke of worldly responsibilities? Do we not see many Torah scholars who bear both?

"No," says R' Nechunia. "They may indeed have various other duties to perform and work to do, but these do not have the characteristics of a yoke. In these spheres a person has some leeway. These activities may even be self-serving. It is only the servitude to God which constitutes a yoke, because here one must divest himself of any ego-centered motivation."

7.

עֲשָׂרָה שֶׁיּוֹשְׁבִין . . . וּמִנַּיִן אֲפִילוּ אֶחָד
If ten people sit together . . . How do we know this [is true] even of one?

This mishnah tells us that there is a greater significance when a larger number of people learn Torah together. We find something similar in regard to the blessing after meals, where one opinion in the mishnah (*Berachos*

ג/ח „בְּכָל הַמָּקוֹם אֲשֶׁר אַזְכִּיר אֶת שְׁמִי, אָבוֹא אֵלֶיךָ וּבֵרַכְתִּיךָ."

[ח] **רַבִּי** אֶלְעָזָר אִישׁ בַּרְתּוֹתָא אוֹמֵר: תֶּן לוֹ מִשֶּׁלּוֹ, שֶׁאַתָּה וְשֶׁלְּךָ שֶׁלּוֹ; וְכֵן בְּדָוִד הוּא אוֹמֵר: „כִּי מִמְּךָ הַכֹּל, וּמִיָּדְךָ נָתַנּוּ לָךְ."

49b) holds that the expression of praise for God is greater according to the number of people who have dined together. Why should the number of people make a difference?

We may gain an insight into this from a question the Talmud raises in discussing our mishnah. Inasmuch as the Divine blessing is bestowed even on a person who studies Torah alone, why does the mishnah have to state that this is true for two or more? The Talmud answers that although a single individual is indeed blessed for studying Torah, "his mitzvah is not recorded in the book of remembrances" as it is for two or more people (*Berachos* 6a).

This answer leaves something to be desired. What difference does it make whether it is recorded in the book of remembrances or not? Furthermore, just what is meant by a "book of remembrances"? God's memory is neither limited nor fallible, and He retains everything whether or not it is recorded.

The chassidic master, R' Zvi Elimelech of Dinov, explains that the Divine memory needs no reminders. If there is a need for a memory aid, it is intended for humans, not for God. A person may indeed learn Torah on his own, but while he may achieve personal growth thereby, it does not make an impact on others. In particular, future generations may not benefit much from an individual's spirituality if it was not conveyed and shared with others. When Torah is studied together with others, there is not only a greater exchange of ideas and a better quality of understanding, but it is more likely to have an impact on future generations. The experience of a multitude leaves a greater impression, and the more people that participate in the study of Torah, the greater is the likelihood that the love of Torah will be passed on to their descendants.

There is a natural tendency to revere one's ancestors, and the values that were cherished by grandparents do have an impact on future generations, even when the latter tend to drift away from Torah observance. I recall an incident where a synagogue in our community wished to modify its status and drift away from the traditions of its founders. My father attended a meeting of the membership and asked to speak. He then took a volume of the Talmud from the bookcase, and turned its pages. At several places, he found hairs of beards that had been deposited in the pages of the volume, according to the tradition that when a hair of one's beard comes loose, it is placed in a Torah volume. Turning to the younger generation in attendance he said, " You seem to think that your ancestors who founded this synagogue are no longer with us.

3/8 *For it is said: In every place where I cause My Name to be mentioned, I will come to you and bless you (Exodus 20:21).*

8. R*abbi Elazar of Bartosa says: Give Him from His Own, for you and your possessions are His. And so has David said: For everything is from You, and from Your Own Hand we have given You (I Chronicles 29:14).*

Indeed, they have passed on, but they left something of themselves behind, perhaps to remind you that they wish to remain with us, in spirit if not in body. You remember the saintly countenances of your *zeides,* and how you sat on their laps, perhaps stroking their flowing white beards, and feeling a closeness not only to them, but to their *zeides* as well. These hairs of their beards which came loose as they stroked their beards when they studied Torah are here as reminders of who they were and in whose footsteps you are to follow."

God does not need a book of remembrances, but we do. The more people that join together to learn Torah, the greater an impression they leave on the future. This is true in the study of Torah as well as in prayer, and it is our obligation not only to study Torah, but to preserve it and transmit it to our children, and this is strengthened when we do so together.

8.

תֶּן לוֹ מִשֶּׁלּוֹ שֶׁאַתָּה וְשֶׁלְּךָ שֶׁלּוֹ
Give Him from His Own, for you and your possessions are His.

This mishnah is generally understood to mean that a person should not begrudge giving *tzedakah,* because one is merely giving the poor person that which is rightfully his, and had been provided by God to the donor in safekeeping until a needy individual would ask for it.

This mishnah was not a new concept to me. As a child I would hear of the manner in which my ancestors gave *tzedakah.* My great-grandfather, the Rebbe of Hornostipol, had a large income from the donations given him by his *chassidim.* There was never enough money for the household expenses, limited as they were, because he would give *all* the money away to the needy. We must remember that in Europe there was no welfare system, and the poor were totally dependent upon *tzedakah* for survival.

One time my great-grandmother came into *Zeide's* study, shortly after he had been visited by a wealthy *chassid* from Kiev, and asked for some money for the household needs. "I don't have any money," *Zeide* said.

"That cannot be," *Bubby* said. "I just saw that *chassid* from Kiev leave, and I am sure he gave you a handsome amount."

"Yes, he did," *Zeide* said. Then he pointed to his two vest pockets. "You

[ט] **רַבִּי** יַעֲקֹב אוֹמֵר: הַמְהַלֵּךְ בַּדֶּרֶךְ וְשׁוֹנֶה, וּמַפְסִיק
מִמִּשְׁנָתוֹ, וְאוֹמֵר: ,,מַה נָּאֶה אִילָן זֶה! וּמַה נָּאֶה
נִיר זֶה!" – מַעֲלֶה עָלָיו הַכָּתוּב כְּאִלּוּ מִתְחַיֵּב בְּנַפְשׁוֹ.

---

see, this pocket is where I put the money for myself, and this other pocket is
where I put money for *tzedakah*. Today's *tzedakah* money is for a man who
has no money to marry off his daughter. The money I was just given went into
the *tzedakah* pocket for *hachnasas kallah,* and it doesn't belong to me. So
when I told you I have no money, I was telling the truth.

When *Zeide* saw that *Bubby* was not too happy with his answer he said,
"Look, it is obvious that God has given some people more and others less, and
He has appointed people like myself as agents to make a more equitable
distribution. For performing this service, I am entitled to a wage. If I take more
than what I have coming to me, that would be embezzlement, and I would be
dismissed from my position, in which case we would have nothing at all to live
on."

The Torah tells us that when we give to the poor, we should not do so with
any resentment that we are giving away our hard-earned money (*Deuteronomy* 15:10). The proper attitude can be achieved with the message of this
mishnah. We are really not giving away anything that was truly our own in the
first place.

9.

הַמְהַלֵּךְ בַּדֶּרֶךְ וְשׁוֹנֶה,
וּמַפְסִיק מִמִּשְׁנָתוֹ...
One who walks on the road
while reviewing [a Torah lesson]
and interrupts his review . . .

Virtually all the commentaries raise the
question on this mishnah: Granted
that it is improper to interrupt one's
study of Torah to observe the beauty of
nature, but does this really justify so
harsh a judgment, to consider it the
equivalent of a capital crime?

In order to understand this mishnah, let us first look at Psalm 19.

> *A song of David.*
> *The heavens declare the glory of God,*
> *and the expanse of the sky tells of His handiwork.*
> *Day following day brings expression of praise,*
> *and night following night bespeaks wisdom.*
> *There is no speech and there are no words;*
> *their sound is unheard.*
> *Their line goes forth throughout the earth,*
> *and their words reach the farthest ends of the land.*
> *In their midst He has set up a tent for the sun.*

9. **R**abbi Yaakov says: One who walks on the road while reviewing [a Torah lesson] and interrupts his review, and exclaims: "How beautiful is this tree! How beautiful is this plowed furrow!" — Scripture considers it as if he bears guilt for his soul.

The sun is like a groom coming forth from his bridal chamber,
rejoicing like a warrior to run the course.
The end of the heavens is its source,
and its circuit is to their [other] end;
nothing is hidden from its heat.

We have here an illustrious ode, a praise to God and an appreciation of Him through the grandeur of nature. But let us look at what immediately follows:

The Torah of God is perfect, it restores the soul.
The testimony of God is trustworthy, making the simple one wise.

There seems to be no transitional sentence, but rather an abrupt change from a description of the beauty of nature to the value of Torah. How are we to understand this?

The receiving of the Torah at Sinai was *the* turning point, not only in the history of the Jewish people, but in the very way that we are to lead our lives and direct our thoughts. The Patriarch Abraham arrived at his belief in God through his philosophic speculation, following which God revealed Himself to him. After Sinai we no longer reach a relationship with God via philosophic reasoning, but rather through Torah observance. The Talmud states that had the Torah not been given, we would have been expected to learn proper behavior by observation of nature, to have learned respect for private property by observing ants, modesty from observing cats, and fidelity from observing doves (*Eruvin* 100b). But that is if the Torah had *not* been given. Once we were given the Torah, we are not to learn *middos* from nature alone, but also and primarily from Torah teachings.

Yes, it is possible to look at the grandeur of nature and come to an awareness of the existence and the greatness of God, Who designed and created so marvelous a universe. One can look at the vastness of the universe through a telescope and begin to appreciate the infinity of God. One can look at a leaf through a microscope and have a breathtaking experience in noting its exquisite structure and metabolism. However, now that we have the Torah we are supposed to look both at the macrocosm and the microcosm *through the perspective of Torah* rather than with our unaided intellect.

This is the message of Psalm 19. The signature of God is indeed in the star-studded heavens, but we are to find Him through Torah, and even to look

ג/י [יי] **רַבִּי** דוֹסְתַּאי בַּר יַנַּאי מִשּׁוּם רַבִּי מֵאִיר אוֹמֵר: כָּל
הַשּׁוֹכֵחַ דָּבָר אֶחָד מִמִּשְׁנָתוֹ, מַעֲלֶה עָלָיו
הַכָּתוּב כְּאִלּוּ מִתְחַיֵּב בְּנַפְשׁוֹ, שֶׁנֶּאֱמַר: ,,רַק הִשָּׁמֶר לְךָ,
וּשְׁמֹר נַפְשְׁךָ מְאֹד, פֶּן תִּשְׁכַּח אֶת הַדְּבָרִים אֲשֶׁר רָאוּ עֵינֶיךָ.''

---

at the heavens with a Torah attitude. Thus, when we observe the grandiosity
of nature, whether a snow-capped mountain peak, the vastness of the ocean,
or a comet streaking across the sky, we recite the blessing, "Who does the work
of Creation," reminding us of the account in Genesis. We express our belief
that God constantly renews the work of Creation.

The message of the psalm is also the message of the mishnah. One who
observes the beauty of a tree, but does so *with an interruption of Torah*,
meaning that he does not look at nature through a Torah perspective but
independently with his unaided intellect, is מִתְחַיֵּב בְּנַפְשׁוֹ, he bears guilt for his
soul.

Why is this so? Take the example of a blind person, who develops an acute
sense of hearing to compensate for his loss of vision. This enables him to detect
the sound of automobile engines. He also knows how to ambulate with the
help of a moving cane, and he can detect where the sidewalk ends and the
street begins. Since these are the only tools he has, he must use them to get
around, hopefully avoiding danger. But what would we think of a sighted
person who blindfolds himself and walks the streets with the help of a cane,
trying to determine when it is safe to cross the street by listening to the sound
of oncoming traffic? We would certainly think of such a person as being foolish,
taking unnecessary risks and exposing himself to danger, when he could utilize
his sight to see where he was going.

So it is with our perspective of the world and our lives in it. Without Torah,
we had to use whatever tools we had, like the person without eyesight. Once
we were given the Torah, it provides the vision and perspective whereby we
adjust to reality. Failure to use this gift of vision, and to try and function
with our unaided intellect, is indeed מִתְחַיֵּב בְּנַפְשׁוֹ, putting our very lives at great
risk.

The human intellect is indeed marvelous, but it is nevertheless subject to the
influence of emotion. Our judgment processes can be impacted upon by our
desires. The Talmud states that although Scripture relates that the Israelites
deviated to idol worship, "they never thought that there was any substance to
the idols, but were only looking for something to give sanction to their lust"
(*Sanhedrin* 63b). Thus, there was never any intellectual belief in idols, but
because they had strong desires which were forbidden by the Torah, they
sought to establish another authority which would allow them to pursue their
desires.

We cannot therefore rely on our unaided intellect to reach the truth, because

10. **R**abbi Dostai bar Yannai says in the name of Rabbi Meir: Whoever forgets anything of his Torah learning, Scripture considers it as if he bears guilt for his soul, as it says: But beware and guard your soul exceedingly, lest you forget the things your eyes have seen

---

our emotions may distort our thinking. Yes, our intellect may indeed enable us to realize that there is a God, but this realization may not be able to withstand intense emotional stress. This is why we must make our intellect subject to the truth of Torah.

The message of Psalm 19 and of our mishnah is also conveyed in our prayers. In the blessings of the *Shema* which precede the *Amidah*, the first speaks of the grandeur of nature: "How great are Your works, O God, You made them all with wisdom; the world is full of Your possessions." In the context of this *berachah* we have the declaration of the angels, "Holy, holy, holy, God Master of Legions, the whole world is full of His glory." In the second *berachah* we refer to our possession of the Torah, and we ask, "Enlighten our eyes with Your Torah," and this leads to *Shema Yisrael*, our declaration of our belief in God. The angels, who are free of desires and temptation, can declare their adoration of God through their awareness of His glory in the world. For us humans, this is not enough, because we are too vulnerable to distortion of thought and judgment by powerful emotions. The martyrs of Jewish history, who surrendered their lives rather than deny God, might not have been motivated to this heroism had they been aware of God only through nature. It was the strength of their belief through Torah that enabled them to overcome even the strongest emotion, that of self-survival.

Once our belief in God is firm, our appreciation of His glory can indeed be strengthened by observation of nature, but our belief must have a firm and unshakable foundation.

10.

כָּל הַשּׁוֹכֵחַ דָּבָר אֶחָד מִמִּשְׁנָתוֹ,
מַעֲלֶה עָלָיו הַכָּתוּב כְּאִלּוּ מִתְחַיֵּב בְּנַפְשׁוֹ
Whoever forgets anything of his Torah learning, Scripture considers it as if he bears guilt for his soul

As with the previous mishnah, we may wonder why so harsh a treatment is accorded someone who has forgotten "one item" of his learning.

Several of the chassidic masters interpret the words of this mishnah, not as "forgetting one item," but rather as forgetting "the One," i.e., God, Whom we always refer to as *Echad* (the One). *Dovor Echad* may also be understood as "the single statement," in which case it refers to the midrash that

ג/יא יָכוֹל אֲפִילוּ תָּקְפָה עָלָיו מִשְׁנָתוֹ? תַּלְמוּד לוֹמַר: ,,וּפֶן יָסוּרוּ מִלְּבָבְךָ כֹּל יְמֵי חַיֶּיךָ", הָא אֵינוֹ מִתְחַיֵּב בְּנַפְשׁוֹ עַד שֶׁיֵּשֵׁב וִיסִירֵם מִלִּבּוֹ.

[יא] **רַבִּי** חֲנִינָא בֶּן דּוֹסָא אוֹמֵר: כֹּל שֶׁיִּרְאַת חֶטְאוֹ קוֹדֶמֶת לְחָכְמָתוֹ, חָכְמָתוֹ מִתְקַיֶּמֶת; וְכֹל שֶׁחָכְמָתוֹ קוֹדֶמֶת לְיִרְאַת חֶטְאוֹ, אֵין חָכְמָתוֹ מִתְקַיֶּמֶת.

---

the first two of the Ten Commandments were said with *dibur echad*, two statements in one, and it is this *dibur echad* that one dare not forget. Also, the chassidic classics teach that "Israel, the Torah, and God are one." It is these references to "one" that a person may not forget, because forgetting that God is the origin of Torah and that the purpose of learning Torah is to bring a person into a close relationship with God strips Torah of its true function and meaning.

A Torah that is devoid of God becomes nothing more than another body of knowledge. However, whereas worldly knowledge, such as science and mathematics, can have valuable practical applications, a Torah which is devoid of God is destructive. The Talmud says that Torah can be life-sustaining when it is studied properly, but may become a destructive force when it is not (*Yoma* 72b).

The Seer of Lublin said to his disciple, R' Bunim of P'shische, "If you ever see me so engrossed in the study of Torah that I appear to have even momentarily lost sight of the Immanent Presence of God, please bring it to my attention." One time R' Bunim noted the Seer to be in profound thought about a difficult passage in the Talmud. He was about to remind the master as he had been instructed, when the Seer said, "I remember, my child."

The Talmud states that no one could explain why the Israelites were driven from their homeland, until God explained, "Because they did not recite the proper *berachah* before studying the Torah" (*Bava Metzia* 85b). Although there was great Torah scholarship, the failure to appreciate the Torah as God given warranted the harshest consequences.

This, then, is the reason for the severe judgment of this mishnah. It refers to one who separates Torah from God, and forgets that the essence of Torah is the "*Echad.*"

11.

כָּל שֶׁיִּרְאַת חֶטְאוֹ קוֹדֶמֶת לְחָכְמָתוֹ
Anyone whose fear of sin takes precedence over his wisdom

Careful attention to the words of the mishnah reveals the use of the possessive: "*whose* fear of sin takes precedence over *his* wisdom." This means that there

(Deuteronomy 4:9). Does this apply even if [he forgot because] his studies were too difficult for him? [This is not so, for] Scripture says: And lest they be removed from your heart all the days of your life (ibid.); thus, one bears no guilt for his soul unless he sits [idly] and [through lack of concentration and review] removes them from his consciousness.

11. **R**abbi Chanina ben Dosa says: Anyone whose fear of sin takes precedence over his wisdom, his wisdom will endure; but anyone whose wisdom takes precedence over his fear of sin, his wisdom will not endure.

---

should be a correlation between one's wisdom and one's fear of sin. The fear of sin of a scholar must surpass that of an unlearned person. A level of fear of sin that would be adequate for the latter would be insufficient for the former.

The chassidic master, R' Elimelech of Lizhensk, was once castigating himself in the harshest manner, referring to himself as an incorrigible sinner. One of his disciples could not tolerate the master's self-flagellation and asked, "How can you say these terrible things about yourself when you know they are not true?"

R' Elimelech answered, "There was once a king who wished to redesign his palace and all the royal trappings. One of the laborers who worked at construction of the new palace bore a grudge against the king, and intentionally dug the foundation 10 meters off course. When this was detected, he was soundly whipped, and made to fill up the ditch.

"The jeweler who was assigned the task of preparing the diamond that was to be the centerpiece of the crown was negligent, and deviated a fraction of a millimeter in cutting the diamond. The beauty of the gem was ruined, and he was given a lengthy prison sentence for his negligence.

"How is it that the jeweler, whose error was but a mere fraction of a millimeter, a deviation that is infinitesimal compared to the laborer's deviation of 10 meters, was given so severe a penalty, whereas the laborer was less severely punished and sent back to work? It is because someone who works with the crown jewels has a far greater responsibility than one who digs the foundation. Even the minutest deviation is considered a serious offense.

"So it is with sin. For a person of limited spiritual resources, a sin consists of a gross violation. For a person whose spirituality should be of the highest order, the expectations are much greater, and for him the most infinitesimal dereliction is considered a serious offense.

"With the kind of teachers I have had, and with the knowledge I have of what I should be, I am falling far short of the mark."

It was R' Elimelech who said, "I am confident that I will be admitted to *Gan Eden* (Paradise). The Heavenly tribunal will ask me, 'Melech, did you learn Torah as you should have?' and I will say 'No.' Then they will ask, 'Melech, did you do the mitzvos the way you should have?' and I will say 'No.' Then they will say, 'Melech speaks the truth, and for telling the truth he deserves *Gan Eden*.'"

It is of interest that our great *tzaddikim* were extremely humble at the very time that they were aware of their enormous spirituality. Like Moses, who was the only human being to ever speak to God "face to face" (*Deuteronomy* 34:10), yet is described by the Torah as being the most humble of all human beings (*Numbers* 12:3), our *tzaddikim* knew of their achievements They were aware both of the infinite greatness of God and the unlimited potential of their Divine *neshamah,* and they always felt they were derelict in their service to God. There is much that we must learn from them.

Wisdom is a Divine gift. Although a person must seek to acquire wisdom by learning and experience, it is much like acquiring a skill to play a musical instrument. If a person is tone deaf or is otherwise not musically inclined, all the lessons in the world cannot make him into a musician. One must have a natural proclivity for music, which one can then cultivate to various degree of perfection.

So it is with wisdom. A person cannot become wise if he lacks the substrate of wisdom, and the latter is a gift from God. The prophet Daniel said, "God gives wisdom to the wise" (*Daniel* 2:21).

But we appear to have a bit of a problem here. If God gives the substrate of wisdom to those who are already wise, from where did they get their initial wisdom? The answer is that the initial wisdom is *yiras Shamayim,* reverence for God, and this is within everyone's grasp.

Indeed, *yiras Shamayim* is the only thing which God does not give anyone, and which one must achieve on his own. Moses said, 'What does your God ask of you but to revere Him?" (*Deuteronomy* 10:12). *Yiras Shamayim* is the only thing which God must ask of man, because it is the basis of free will, with which God does not intervene.

Scripture says, "Behold, fear of God is wisdom" (*Job* 28:28). Thus, if one begins with *yiras Shamayim,* then one has the prerequisite, the rudiments of wisdom, the soil in which wisdom can take root and grow. One can then merit the Divine gift, of "wisdom to the wise." If one does not have *yiras Shamayim*, then whatever wisdom he thinks he may have is not truly wisdom, but some imitation thereof, which cannot have any permanence. Indeed, the Talmud says that if one studies Torah without *yiras Shamayim* it would be preferable had he remained ignorant of Torah (*Yoma* 72b)!

Many commentaries point out that this mishnah seems to contradict an earlier mishnah (2:5) which states that an ignorant person cannot have proper fear of sin. This implies that knowledge of Torah is a prerequisite to the development of *yiras Shamayim* rather than the converse. Perhaps my clinical experience may shed some light on this.

In working with young people who are involved with drug use, I regularly find that although they certainly wish to live and are fearful of being injured, they nevertheless risk their health and very lives by using dangerous drugs. Why? Because they have a delusion of immunity: "It won't happen to me." Even if they see a friend die from the use of drugs, this does not discourage their own use. They rationalize, "He did not know how to use the drug." In other words, they do not see the danger of drugs as pertaining to them. It is the challenge of drug prevention programs to overcome this delusion of immunity, so that these youngsters should realize that they are at great risk of harm.

So it is with sin. The wise person understands that God has no personal needs. The Talmud says, He does not stand to gain whether a person observes the Torah or not (*Tanchuma Shemini* 12). The mitzvos are given for our welfare, and if we transgress them we only injure ourselves. The Talmud also states that a person does not sin unless he has taken leave of his senses (*Sotah* 3a). Thus, even if a person is fearful of suffering harm, he may expose himself to danger if he does not realize that what he is doing is in fact harmful. There are, of course, some people who are reckless and seem to have no instinct of self-preservation. They may do things which they know are fraught with great danger. There are also some people who may see no purpose in life.

We thus have two ingredients that are essential for avoidance of sin. Firstly, one must have a fear of self-harm, and secondly, one must have a realization that certain acts are in fact harmful, and not have a delusion of immunity.

Our mishnah states that one must begin with a basic fear of harming oneself, because otherwise, even the knowledge that certain acts are dangerous will not deter one from doing them. If this fear is present, one must then have an awareness of what it is that is harmful, and not have a delusion of immunity. This is the point of the earlier mishnah, that a person who is ignorant cannot have *yiras Shamayim*. Although he may wish to avoid harm, he is unaware that transgressing Torah is harmful to him. The two mishnahs are thus in no way conflicting.

ג/יב-יג **הוא** הָיָה אוֹמֵר: כֹּל שֶׁמַּעֲשָׂיו מְרֻבִּין מֵחָכְמָתוֹ, חָכְמָתוֹ מִתְקַיֶּמֶת; וְכֹל שֶׁחָכְמָתוֹ מְרֻבָּה מִמַּעֲשָׂיו, אֵין חָכְמָתוֹ מִתְקַיֶּמֶת. [יב]

[יג] **הוא** הָיָה אוֹמֵר: כֹּל שֶׁרוּחַ הַבְּרִיּוֹת נוֹחָה הֵימֶנּוּ, רוּחַ הַמָּקוֹם נוֹחָה הֵימֶנּוּ; וְכֹל

12.

וְכֹל שֶׁחָכְמָתוֹ מְרֻבָּה מִמַּעֲשָׂיו,
אֵין חָכְמָתוֹ מִתְקַיֶּמֶת
But anyone whose wisdom
exceeds his good deeds,
his wisdom will not endure

This mishnah helped me understand an interesting phenomenon. During my travels, I have at times visited a "university city"; i.e., a community which is essentially comprised of colleges, and whose economy is centered about the educational institutes. I have always felt that these communities were somehow different than other cities I visited, and I even felt a bit ill at ease there, but I was unable to identify the feeling or why it was somewhat unpleasant. When I came to this mishnah, I realized that what was bothering me was that these communities may indeed be citadels of knowledge, but it is knowledge that remains unapplied. Perhaps when the students disperse they may then apply what they have learned, but within the community itself there is a preponderance of knowledge over deeds. The mishnah says that this state of affairs makes the knowledge of questionable value. The denizens of the ivory towers are not always completely in touch with reality.

Our mishnah is critical even of Torah knowledge when it remains an academic exercise and is not translated into action. The Baal Shem Tov stressed the importance of this mishnah. "If one learns the *halachos* of commerce in the Talmud, one has a great mitzvah. How much more so when one applies these *halachos* in his daily life, transacting business according to Torah principles." If this is so regarding Torah learning, how much more so is this true of general knowledge, which has little value if it is not applied constructively.

It is related that the great Talmudist, R' Pinchas Horowitz, author of the monumental Talmudic commentary, *Haflaah*, heard of the chassidic master, the *Maggid* of Mezeritch, and was curious to investigate *Chassidus*. He visited the *Maggid*, and was unimpressed by what he observed. When he took leave of the *Maggid*, the latter suggested that he engage R' Zusia in a scholarly discussion.

R' Zusia kept his erudition a secret. No one ever saw him studying. Rather, he was sweeping the floor or stoking the fire, or otherwise tending to the needs of the house of study. When R' Pinchas approached him, R' Zusia said, "There must be some mistake. I am not a scholar and there is nothing you can discuss with me." At R' Pinchas' insistence, R' Zusia said, "I can only tell you something I overheard the others say.

"I heard the students reading a portion of the Talmud where R' Huna says,

3/12-13 **12.** **H**e *was accustomed to say: Anyone whose good deeds exceed his wisdom, his wisdom will endure; but anyone whose wisdom exceeds his good deeds, his wisdom will not endure.*

13. **H**e *was accustomed to say: If the spirit of one's fellows is pleased with him, the spirit of the Omnipresent is*

'Nine men and the *aron kodesh* (the ark containing the Torah) can constitute a *minyan.'* R' Nachman challenges this, saying, 'Is then the ark a person?' (*Berachos* 47b). Now what kind of a question is that? R' Huna knew full well that the ark is not a person, yet he felt that it could be counted toward the *minyan.* If R' Nachman wished to disagree with him, he should have simply said so. To ask, 'Is the ark a person?' makes no sense. R' Huna made his statement even though he knew very well that the ark was not a person. Perhaps you can explain that to me," R' Zusia said.

R' Pinchas was taken aback. In spite of his enormous erudition, he had no answer to so obvious a question.

R' Zusia shrugged his shoulders. "Maybe the Talmud meant it this way," he said. "R' Huna was of the opinion that since the ark was full of Torah, it could contribute to a *minyan.* R' Nachman's challenge was, 'Granted the ark is full of Torah, but you can be full of Torah and still not be a *mentsch.'* "

R' Pinchas was electrified. R' Zusia's words penetrated to his very core. He realized that his enormous erudition should have elevated him to a much higher level of spirituality. He remained with the *Maggid* and became one of his foremost disciples.

It is related that a scholar once boasted about his learning. "I have done the entire Talmud," he said. "Is that so?" someone remarked. "You may have done the entire Talmud, but what has the Talmud done for you?"

The previous mishnah states that an attitude of reverence for God is a prerequisite for Torah. This mishnah takes us one step further. The *yiras Shamayim* must be translated into deeds. Had the Torah been intended to be only an intellectual exercise, it would have remained with the heavenly angels. It was given to man because it was meant to elevate man to fulfillment of his enormous spiritual potential. Failure to use Torah in this way is a gross dereliction.

13.

כֹּל שֶׁרוּחַ הַבְּרִיּוֹת נוֹחָה הֵימֶנּוּ,
רוּחַ הַמָּקוֹם נוֹחָה הֵימֶנּוּ
If the spirit of one's fellows is pleased with him, the spirit of the Omnipresent is pleased with him

This appears to be a rather bold statement, and gives rise to some question. For example, there are some people who have feelings of inferiority which cause them to think that others will not like them. In order to gain

ג/יד שֶׁאֵין רוּחַ הַבְּרִיּוֹת נוֹחָה הֵימֶנּוּ, אֵין רוּחַ הַמָּקוֹם נוֹחָה הֵימֶנּוּ.

[יד] **רַבִּי** דוֹסָא בֶּן הָרְכִּינַס אוֹמֵר: שֵׁנָה שֶׁל שַׁחֲרִית, וְיַיִן שֶׁל צָהֳרַיִם, וְשִׂיחַת הַיְלָדִים, וִישִׁיבַת בָּתֵּי כְנֵסִיּוֹת שֶׁל עַמֵּי הָאָרֶץ מוֹצִיאִין אֶת הָאָדָם מִן הָעוֹלָם.

---

friendship, they go out of their way to do things for people, in the hope that this will make them more acceptable. These "people pleasers" may indeed be well liked by others, but this hardly seems to warrant an assurance that God is particularly happy with them. They may be doing some things which are quite displeasing to God. It would appear to be an overstatement that *everyone* who is well liked by others is also liked by God.

The resolution to this difficulty may lie in a more precise translation of the word כל. Instead of reading it as "*Everyone* who is pleasing to his fellows," it should be read as "One who is *always* pleasing to his fellows." A "people pleaser" may indeed be well liked by many people for a while, but this defensive maneuver cannot stand the test of time.

There is a fable about a man who had a pet cat whom he had so domesticated that it virtually behaved like a human being. He boasted about his achievement to his friends. One day they were sitting at a party, and he had the cat dressed in a tuxedo, sitting at the table and looking very distinguished. One of the friends then let a mouse loose, whereupon the cat, with formal clothes and all, jumped onto the table in pursuit of the mouse, upsetting all the bowls and pitchers and causing quite a havoc. In spite of all the grooming, the cat remained very catlike at the core and, when put to the test, behaved accordingly.

The human being, by his innate nature, is very self-centered. His natural instinct is to do those things which gratify his desires. He may indeed undergo transformation into a spiritual being, a person who lives by the Torah precept of "Love your fellow man as [you do] yourself," but this transformation requires a great deal of character development. It is contingent upon a surrender of his own will and adopting the will of God as his motivating drive, as is stated in Chapter 2 mishnah 4. Anything short of this is superficial, and when the individual is put to the test, his innate egocentric drives will dominate. The "people pleaser" may behave in a manner that may endear him to others, but like the domesticated cat whose instinct to catch the mouse overcame all his training, the "people pleaser's" underlying personality will eventually emerge. This person's superficial adaptation as a benefactor to mankind cannot withstand the test of *mesiras nefesh*.

The person who will not relapse into egocentricity and who will *always* be pleasing to his fellow man is someone who has achieved a level of spirituality

pleased with him; but if the spirit of one's fellows is not pleased with him, the spirit of the Omnipresent is not pleased with him.

14. **R**abbi Dosa ben Harkinas was accustomed to say: *Morning sleep, midday wine, children's chatter, and sitting at gatherings of the ignorant remove a man from the world.*

---

that can be acquired only by being the kind of person who does only that which meets with God's approval. This is what the mishnah means by כֹּל שֶׁרוּחַ הַבְּרִיּוֹת נוֹחָה הֵימֶנּוּ, someone who will *always* be pleasing to others is indeed someone who is beloved by God.

14.

שֵׁנָה שֶׁל שַׁחֲרִית . . .
מוֹצִיאִין אֶת הָאָדָם מִן הָעוֹלָם
*Morning sleep . . . remove
a man from the world.*

The "morning hours" may also be understood as the early years of a person's life, which are all too often "slept away." On several occasions the Talmud states that R' Yehudah *HaNasi* wept, saying, "It is possible for a person to achieve his entire world in one brief moment" (*Avodah Zarah* 10b). He would say this when he noticed a person redeem himself after wasting away an entire lifetime. Why would such an observation cause sadness and move him to tears? Because even though a person did redeem himself in one moment, a wasted lifetime is a terrible tragedy. Just think of what that person could have accomplished had he lived properly all his life!

This is a particularly important issue in these days, when so many young people go astray, whether into drugs or other self-destructive behavior. They may come to their senses when they are well into their adult years, but the years of their youth, when they were at their highest learning capacity, can never be regained. This is indeed tragic. Obviously, if there were any way to help young people preserve these precious years and avoid squandering them foolishly, this would be an invaluable contribution to them and to mankind as a whole,

Children often mimic the behavior of adults. If the values of the mature culture are defective, it is only natural that young people will be apt to adopt them.

The term "mature culture" may not be accurate. Yes, there is an adult culture, consisting of people from age 20 to 80 plus, but age does not necessary make for maturity. Perhaps the most distinctive feature of the juvenile is "I want what I want and I want it now!" A truly mature person gives greater consideration to the appropriateness of his desires, and if their gratification may have negative consequences, he will forego them. Furthermore, a mature person is able to delay gratification, whereas the child typically wails, "But I want it right now."

A 45-year-old executive, who has a graduate degree and functions effectively in operating a large corporation, may indeed be thought of as mature. However, if he lights up a cigarette, and gratifies his desire for nicotine in spite of his knowledge that this may seriously impair his health and endanger his very life, he is exhibiting immature behavior. A group of people whose lust for money results in their polluting the air and water and in upsetting the ecology cannot be thought of as truly mature. An analysis of what the adult culture is doing reveals much juvenile behavior. When it sacrifices decency and morality by exploiting indecency and violence on television in order to bring in lucrative advertisements, it is anything but mature.

The mishnah lists four examples of adult behavior that cannot be thought of as mature. When the adult culture tolerates, condones, and even promotes these, it is adopting a lifestyle which young people are likely to mimic. Some of these young people will be ruined for life by following a juvenile lifestyle, while others may pull out of the nose dive at a later age, but like R' Yehudah, we may cry for those who redeem themselves at a later age. They have allowed the most productive years of their lives to be wasted. If we wish to do the utmost for our children, let us avoid the types of behavior characterized by the examples of this mishnah. Let us set an example of true maturity for them.

מוֹצִיאִין אֶת הָאָדָם מִן הָעוֹלָם
Remove a man from the world.

The expression "remove a man from the world" is a rather unusual term for the Talmud to express its disapproval of something. When we find such expressions, we should investigate whether it may have some special meaning.

When I first began treating addictive diseases, I used to speak about "alcoholism." It soon became apparent to me that this was too narrow a term. Many people were abusing other chemical substances that had essentially the same actions as alcohol, such as sleeping pills, tranquilizers, and painkillers. I therefore began using the term "sedatavism" rather than alcoholism. When I realized that chemicals such as cocaine and "speed" have no sedative effect but, to the contrary, are stimulants, I began talking about "chemicalism."

I soon discovered that this term, too, was restrictive. There were other conditions which did not involve use of chemicals, but were nevertheless quite similar to alcoholism. Since then I have been using the term "escapism" to refer to any of the many ways which people may employ to avoid coping with reality.

Escapism has deleterious consequences, because when reality problems arise and are not dealt with appropriately, they invariably get worse. Reality poses many challenges for most people. The only way these can be managed constructively is to face them and deal with them. Running away from these challenges leaves them unattended, and they then result in more complicated difficulties. This is equally true whether one tries to escape reality by rendering oneself oblivious to it by means of mind-altering chemicals, by daydreaming, by indolence, or by any other behavior that does not deal effectively with the problem at hand. These behaviors virtually "remove a person from the world." The Talmud could not have found a more accurate description.

A person may dream at night, or daydream during waking hours. Neither dream changes reality. There are indeed dreams that do change reality, but they are not of an escapist nature. When R' Yosef Kahaneman, the Rosh Yeshivah of Ponovezh, arrived in Eretz Yisrael after surviving the Holocaust, he came with nothing but the clothes he wore. When he announced in Bnai Brak, "Here we will establish a great yeshivah," some people discouraged him, saying, "Rabbi, you are a dreamer." R' Kahaneman replied, "You are right. I am dreaming — but I am not asleep." Indeed, the Rabbi of Ponovezh was wide awake, and he was able to change reality single-handedly, establishing what is perhaps the greatest yeshivah of our generation.

Some people avoid reality simply by not arising early in the morning, as if the world will become an easier place in the extra few hours they remain in bed. Those who have recourse to alcohol during the day will find that the same problems and usually more difficult ones will confront them when they emerge from their chemical oblivion. Similarly, engaging in juvenile behavior or spending hours at the racetrack or in other pastimes do indeed distract one from reality and remove him from the world in which he was intended to achieve something. The colloquial expression that refers to pastimes as "killing time" is most appropriate. We would be wise to think of the significance of this term. Time is the one commodity which is irreplaceable, and to "kill" it is the height of folly. It has been wisely said that killing time is not murder, but suicide, and such behavior indeed "removes one from the world."

Some people may think that sleeping long hours gives the body the rest it needs and is conducive to long life. The author of this mishnah, R' Dosa, enjoyed longevity (*Yevamos* 17a), and it is he who warns against lingering too long in bed.

I was impressed with the autobiography of the Nobel laureate, S.Y. Agnon, who related that his father had to open his store early. He wished to teach his son Torah, and he would wake the child before dawn so that he could learn with him before attending early morning services. Agnon's mother, who was protective of her child, would plead with the father, "Let the child sleep! He is young and needs to grow." The father responded, "What! You want him to grow up to be a *goy*?" One might think that the child would have grown up with marginal health and with a negative attitude toward Torah. After all, he was pulled out of bed on cold winter mornings to study Torah. But this child who was aroused out of his sleep while it was still dark lived to a ripe old age, remained loyal to Torah study and observance throughout his long life, and

[טו] **רַבִּי** אֶלְעָזָר הַמּוֹדָעִי אוֹמֵר: הַמְחַלֵּל אֶת הַקָּדָשִׁים,
וְהַמְבַזֶּה אֶת הַמּוֹעֲדוֹת, וְהַמַּלְבִּין פְּנֵי חֲבֵרוֹ
בָּרַבִּים, וְהַמֵּפֵר בְּרִיתוֹ שֶׁל אַבְרָהָם אָבִינוּ, וְהַמְגַלֶּה פָנִים
בַּתּוֹרָה שֶׁלֹּא כַהֲלָכָה, אַף עַל פִּי שֶׁיֵּשׁ בְּיָדוֹ תּוֹרָה וּמַעֲשִׂים
טוֹבִים – אֵין לוֹ חֵלֶק לָעוֹלָם הַבָּא.

---

brought great pride to his people by his contributions to world literature.

Our sages knew what keeps a person within the world and what removes him from it.

15.

המְחַלֵּל אֶת הַקָּדָשִׁים . . .
אֵין לוֹ חֵלֶק לָעוֹלָם הַבָּא

One who desecrates sacred things . . .
he has no share in the World to Come.

This mishnah is nothing less than startling. The Talmud states that a sin does not extinguish Torah (*Sotah* 21a). If someone who learned Torah erred and committed a grievous sin, even if it involved a Scriptural prohibition, it would not negate the merits of his Torah study. Yet, if he did any of the things listed in this mishnah, he not only loses the merits of his Torah study and mitzvos, but also forfeits his share in *Gan Eden* (Paradise)! Think of it. A person who was dedicated to the study and observance of Torah for 85 years, not overlooking a single mitzvah and not letting a moment go by being idle of Torah, makes a remark that causes another person to be humiliated in public. If he does not apologize, he loses all the merits of 85 years of devotion to Torah and mitzvos. This would not have resulted even had he eaten *tereifah*! How are we to understand this?

This mishnah underscores a concept to which we have already alluded: the overriding importance of *attitude*. This is evident in the Talmudic statement that *derech eretz* (decency or respect) is a prerequisite for Torah (*Vayikra Rabbah* 9:3), and in the statement that although there was Torah scholarship, Jerusalem was destroyed "because they did not recite the proper blessing prior to studying Torah" (*Bava Metzia* 85b). And, "Torah can be either life sustaining or a deadly poison, depending on one's attitude" (*Yoma* 72b).

The items listed in this mishnah, although they are not Scriptural prohibitions (except for circumcision) are an indication of attitude. A person who does not show proper reverence for items of holiness or who dismisses the intermediate days of Yom Tov with disdain betrays an attitude of arrogance. To publicly humiliate someone is at one and the same time an act of arrogance, vanity, and lack of consideration. The Talmud states that on Judgment Day one will be asked, "Did you relate with due respect toward God, and did you relate with due respect to your fellow man?" The two are accorded equal weight.

15. Rabbi *Elazar the Moda'ite used to say: One who desecrates sacred things, who disgraces the festivals, who humiliates his fellow in public, who nullifies the covenant of our forefather Abraham, or who perverts the meaning of the Torah contrary to halachah — though he may have Torah and good deeds, he has no share in the World to Come.*

There is a profound psychological concept in this mishnah. Granted, a person may have erred seriously in not showing proper respect toward items of holiness or in making an insulting remark about another person. But should he do so at age 85, why does this negate all those decades of Torah study and mitzvos which may have indeed been done with proper attitude?

Perhaps we may understand this with an interpretation that I heard from my brother, Professor Aaron Twerski, in regard to Job. The Scripture describes Job as a person who was so meticulous in observance of Torah that he would bring offerings on behalf of each of his children *every week* to ask forgiveness for them, *"lest my children might have sinned and blasphemed God in their hearts.* This is what Job did all his days" (*Job* 1:5).

Let us reflect a moment. All Job's children were well to do, and all the siblings would celebrate together. They had nothing to complain of. Why in the world should anyone even think of something so absurd that they "might have sinned and blasphemed God"? Blasphemy is undoubtedly a most unusual occurrence. It is likely to occur only in someone who is suffering so severely that he feels an intense anger toward God. For Job to have thought that his children, who were happy and celebrating life together, might have blasphemed God is so far-fetched, so unrealistic, that it is the height of absurdity!

"The reason for this," said Professor Twerski, "is that Job was 'a professional *tzaddik.'* Job made a long list of all possible transgressions in the Torah, all 365 of them. In an obsessive manner he went down the list, checking each one off, and asking forgiveness even for sins that could not have possibly occurred. Yes, Job's observance of Torah was indeed perfect, but it was the perfection of a computer, not a sentient, thinking human being. There was no spontaneity in Job's mitzvos, no sense of devotion or closeness to God, only a series of rigid, mechanical actions. Mitzvos like this do not have the merit to protect anyone from harm."

Yes, it is possible to be scrupulous in following every letter of the Torah and still be distant from God. The purpose of Torah and mitzvos is to refine a person's character. This does not occur when they are done in a mechanical, obsessive manner.

If a person studied Torah and did mitzvos all his life, and at age 85 publicly humiliates someone and does not apologize for it, this indicates that his

[טז] **רַבִּי** יִשְׁמָעֵאל אוֹמֵר: הֱוֵי קַל לְרֹאשׁ, וְנוֹחַ
לְתִשְׁחֹרֶת, וֶהֱוֵי מְקַבֵּל אֶת כָּל הָאָדָם
בְּשִׂמְחָה.

[יז] **רַבִּי** עֲקִיבָא אוֹמֵר: שְׂחוֹק וְקַלּוּת רֹאשׁ מַרְגִּילִין
אֶת הָאָדָם לְעֶרְוָה. מָסֹרֶת סְיָג לַתּוֹרָה;

---

study of Torah and his performance of mitzvos had made no impression on him. They did not change his character one bit. As we noted earlier (3:12), it is possible for a person to have learned the entire Talmud, but in a way that it did not affect him. This kind of sterile Torah study and rote performance of mitzvos is of little value.

It is of particular interest to note the wording of the mishnah. It does not say that anyone who commits any of the listed transgressions *loses* his portion in the World to Come, but rather that he does not *have* a portion. Anyone whose attitude is such that committing any of these transgressions does not bother him enough to make amends does not earn a share in the World to Come.

16.

הֱוֵי קַל לְרֹאשׁ, וְנוֹחַ לְתִשְׁחֹרֶת
Be yielding to a superior, pleasant to the young

This mishnah is most unique. The words of R' Yishmael are so cryptic that not only has the mishnah been given various and sundry interpretations, but even the very words of the mishnah have been translated in more ways than any other mishnah in *Ethics of the Fathers*. The translation given above is that of *Midrash Shmuel.* R' Moshe Alashkar translates the word "rosh" to refer to God, and the word "tishchores" to refer to prophets and Torah scholars. According to this interpretation the mishnah reads, "Be yielding in your service to God, and be pleasant to Torah scholars."

Another translation and interpretation is that of Rabbeinu Yonah, according to which the mishnah says, "Humble yourself before the ruler, and be submissive to other authorities." According to Meiri, "tishchores" means immature people, and the mishnah is telling us that although we should bow to the wishes of superiors, we should use calmness and diplomacy to reject the unwise opinions of the immature. Ritva interprets "tishchores" to refer to those who exhaust themselves in the study of Torah, while Rashbam takes "rosh" as meaning one's head, and "tishchores" as referring to a reed, in which case the mishnah says, "Unburden your head and be as flexible as a reed." Bartenura has "tishchores" as meaning the early years of one's life, while Rashi translates it to mean one's old age. Yet others translate "tishchores" from the root word meaning to plead, and still others relate it to the root word "to become free."

16. **R**abbi Yishmael says: Be yielding to a superior, pleasant to the young, and receive every person cheerfully.

17. **R**abbi Akiva says: Mockery and levity accustom a man to immorality. The transmitted Oral Torah is a

---

It is of interest that very few commentaries associate the latter part of the mishnah, "to receive every person cheerfully," to the first part.

There is an axiom in Torah that when scholars differ, all opinions are valid, even if they may be polar opposites (*Eruvin* 13b). Let us therefore assume that *all* the interpretations are true, and approach the mishnah by trying to understand the latter half. Is it not a bit much to expect one to receive *every* person cheerfully? In Chapter 1 mishnah 15 Shammai states that we must *greet* everyone with a pleasant countenance. This is quite feasible, but how are we to receive every person cheerfully? Courtesy is a behavior, whereas cheerfulness is a feeling. There are some people whose presence is not particularly desirable, and yet others whom we would totally wish to avoid. How can one be asked to be cheerful with their presence?

We might better understand this mishnah if we consider the Talmudic statement that "A person is required to praise God even for unpleasant happenings" (*Berachos* 54a). The Talmud explains that this must be done with *simchah*. Again we might ask: Granted that a person must accept even harsh Divine judgments with acknowledgments of God's absolute justice, but how can one be expected to do so with joy when he is in distress? The answer to this lies in Rashi's interpretation (ibid.60b) that the word *simchah* in this context does not mean "joy" but rather "with a complete heart," i.e., with equanimity. We may apply Rashi's translation of *simchah* to our mishnah as well, in which case it does not require that we receive everyone cheerfully, but that we do so with *equanimity*. That is certainly within our capacity.

If we understand the intent of the mishnah as requiring us to receive everyone with equanimity, i.e., not to be overwhelmed by people in positions of superiority, nor be arrogant to those who are of lower status, then all of the various interpretations of the commentaries listed above are appropriate. They all dictate that we relate to various people in a manner appropriate to the circumstances. It is important that we always maintain our composure regardless of who confronts us. Understanding *simchah* in this way, this many-faceted mishnah becomes a valuable lesson in interpersonal relations.

17.

שְׂחוֹק וְקַלּוּת רֹאשׁ מַרְגִּילִין אֶת הָאָדָם לְעֶרְוָה
***Mockery and levity accustom
a man to immorality.***

This mishnah lists a number of behaviors that function as "fences" or protections for other items; however, there seems to be an in-

גּ/יח מַעְשְׂרוֹת סְיָג לָעֹשֶׁר; נְדָרִים סְיָג לַפְּרִישׁוּת; סְיָג לַחָכְמָה שְׁתִיקָה.

[יח] **הוּא** הָיָה אוֹמֵר: חָבִיב אָדָם שֶׁנִּבְרָא בְצֶלֶם; חִבָּה יְתֵרָה נוֹדַעַת לוֹ שֶׁנִּבְרָא בְצֶלֶם, שֶׁנֶּאֱמַר: ‚‚כִּי

---

consistency. In regard to immorality the mishnah does not state what would serve as a deterrent or a "fence" to protect one from immorality. Rather, the mishnah lists risk factors for immorality. This cannot be coincidental. Why does the mishnah state what the factors are that may lead to immorality, rather than what kinds of things would be deterrents to immorality?

It is tempting to say that this mishnah was prophetic. In our modern world, immorality is accepted virtually as a norm. People who should serve as paragons of virtue act immorally, yet these breaches of trust are not taken seriously. Those who seek to spread depravity and introduce obscenity to our neighborhoods and our homes wrap themselves in the First Amendment. More recently, the Internet has enabled people to access such material in utmost privacy. How did we reach a stage of such moral decadence?

Many years ago we had entertainment on the radio, which was generally clean and fairly innocent humor. Even then, the need for comedians to bring mirth and laughter to people should have been a warning, an indication that there is something wrong with the way we are living. Why must we have recourse to professional comedians to make us smile? Perhaps if we had lived truly spiritual lives, we would have provided our spirits with the kind of nourishment that would make a person healthy both spiritually as well as physically. We might not have had as great a need for jesters to produce smiles on our faces or give us reasons for laughter. But let us set that aside, and accept the fact that perhaps we were not at that level of spirituality. We may have found life to be somewhat depressing, and we had recourse to comedians just as kings had need for court jesters.

In the middle of the 20th century, the phenomenon of television was introduced to western civilization. In its early days, many halachic authorities strongly discouraged and even prohibited access to television. At that time, many people felt that this was an overreaction — an alarmist, extremist attitude. Some 50 years later, we can see the correctness of their position. What initially began as innocent entertainment, with the antics of talented comedians and comedy shows, gradually deteriorated into frank immorality, exhibitionism, explicit sensuousness, and graphic violence. Most students of human behavior concur that these have resulted in an increase in violent behavior and immorality, especially among our youth. This all began in a rather innocent fashion with a desire for levity and frivolity. Although the origin appeared to be harmless in the 1940s, we can see the consequences in the 1990s.

*[protective] fence around the Torah; tithes are a [protec-
tive] fence for wealth; vows are a [protective] fence for
abstinence; a [protective] fence for wisdom is silence.*

18. He *[R' Akiva] was accustomed to say: Beloved is
man, for he was created in [God's] image; it is indicative of a greater love that it was made known to him
that he was created in [God's] image, as it is said: For in the*

The words of the mishnah are thus prophetic. If you condone frivolity and
levity, it will eventually lead to immorality. Many of us believed that there was
nothing wrong with "Father Knows Best" and other rather innocent programs.
Time has proven that our sages knew better.

Frivolity and levity should not be confused with *simchah*. To the contrary,
simchah is a highly prized quality, but should be thought of as *simchah shel
mitzvah*. There should be joy not only in the performance of actual mitzvos, but
also when a person leads the kind of life that is required by Torah. Much of
what he does is then a mitzvah, and even many of the usual activities of daily
lives, when properly goal oriented, can be considered to be a mitzvah. There
is also much uplifting humor, examples of which I provided in my book *Smiling
Each Day*. A true Torah life should enable a person to have joy without having
to rely on paid professionals.

18.

חָבִיב אָדָם שֶׁנִּבְרָא בְּצֶלֶם . . .
*Beloved is man, for he was
created in [God's] image. . .*

This mishnah lends itself to various interpretations. In many of my writings I have repeatedly stressed the pivotal role of self-
esteem in making a proper adjustment to life.
One can only have a healthy adjustment to life if one perceives reality correctly.
A misperception of reality will inevitably result in one or more maladjustments.
If a person has character assets and is unaware of them, and thinks less of
himself than he actually is, this is a misperception of reality. It is a fact that man
was created in the Divine image. This imbues him with many important assets.
To be unaware of this is a serious misperception of one's reality. As an example, think of a person who is impoverished, and is unaware that a relative left
him a huge inheritance. He may struggle through life with much distress,
whereas he could be living in great comfort if he only knew what he had.

Man was not only created in the Divine image, but was told this, and his
failure to be aware of this is tragic.

What does it mean to be created in the "Divine image"? Inasmuch as we
know that God has no shape or form, it obviously cannot refer to man's

physical being. Rather, if we read *Genesis* carefully, we note that man was created after all other living things. God said to the angels, "Let us make man in Our image," which clearly means that in contrast to other forms of life which have only a physical component, man was to be unique in that he would have a *spirit*. The spirit is a component which he shares with God and with the angels.

Man's spirit is comprised of a number of capacities, among which are: the ability to acquire and transmit knowledge, to reflect on the purpose of existence, to think of the past and to contemplate the future, to make salutary changes in himself, to sacrifice his own comfort and even his very being for his beliefs or for the welfare of others, and to be totally free to make decisions and to act upon them, even in defiance of bodily urges. These are impossible for other living things. Man's greatness does not lie in his physical prowess, but in his exercising the many components of his spirit.

That man was given the precious gift of a spirit indicates that he is beloved by God. The awareness that he has this spirit can make him beloved by others as well.

My first literary effort was a book entitled *Like Yourself, and Others Will Too*, in which I pointed out that a person can be loved and respected by others only to the extent that he loves and respects himself. People with low self-esteem are apt to isolate themselves and avoid meaningful relationships. They may behave in a number of ways that will prevent them from acquiring the affection of others. The awareness that one has a Divine spirit can give one a sense of worth and enable a development of oneself that will result in self-esteem and cause one to be beloved by others.

Furthermore, true love is reciprocal, as Scripture states, "As water reflects a face back to a face, so one's heart is reflected back to him by another" (*Proverbs* 27:19). The Torah also states, "Love your fellow as [you do] yourself" (*Leviticus* 19:18). It follows that if one does not love oneself, one cannot love another, and if one does not love others, one cannot be loved by others.

A healthy self-image is thus essential for emotional and psychological well-being, and the knowledge that we were created in the Divine image should be ample reason why our self-image should be positive.

חֲבִיבִין יִשְׂרָאֵל, שֶׁנִּקְרְאוּ בָנִים לַמָּקוֹם;
חִבָּה יְתֵרָה נוֹדַעַת לָהֶם שֶׁנִּקְרְאוּ בָנִים לַמָּקוֹם

Beloved are the people of Israel, for they are described as children of the Omnipresent; it is indicative of a greater love that it was made known to them that they are described as children of the Omnipresent

Together with the knowledge that one has a Divine spirit, the awareness that one is a child of God can greatly impact a person's behavior.

I recall that as a child, when my father disapproved of something I had done, he did not scold me or discipline me harshly, but rather remarked, *"Es pahst nisht"* (That is not befitting of you). I was not told that I was bad for doing something wrong, but rather that I was too good to be doing something that was beneath my dignity. This is an ingenious way of disciplining children without causing them to feel bad about themselves. A person who wears a fine silk garment will take great caution not to let it be stained. Someone who wears soiled jeans may care little about their getting stained.

In my work with people who are addicted to drugs or alcohol, I ask them how they would care for a brand-new luxury automobile. Of course, they tell me that they would wax and polish it and be most careful not to let it sustain a dent or scratch. I then ask them if they had been aware that the substances they were using were harmful to themselves, and they reply in the affirmative. "If you are instinctively protective of a new automobile to avoid it being damaged, why did this same instinct not prevail to prevent you from doing damage to yourself?" Inevitably it turns out that whereas they felt that the automobile was beautiful and valuable, this is not how they felt about themselves. Lasting recovery from addictive diseases requires that a person develop a healthy self-esteem. A true sense of self-worth will militate against a person doing anything that can be damaging to himself.

Addicts are not the only people who lack self-esteem. To some degree, this is true of everyone, and to whatever degree it exists, to that degree it inhibits a person from exercising his full potential. My great-grandfather, the *Tzaddik* of Sanz, used to tell the following parable before Rosh Hashanah.

A prince once committed a severe offense, which resulted in his being exiled to a very distant corner of the kingdom. In order to sustain himself, he tried to do all kinds of work. However, inasmuch as he had grown up in a palatial environment, he had never learned any manual skills, and consequently was unable to earn a living. He therefore decided to become a shepherd, because this required no particular skill.

The prince often suffered intense discomfort in the fields where he was exposed to the blazing sun for hours. He noted that other shepherds built themselves little huts out of straw and branches, which provided them the comfort of shade. Try as he might, he could never put together a hut that could last, and he was very frustrated.

One day he heard that his father, the king, was coming to a nearby city for a royal visit. There was a custom that during the royal parade, people would write requests on slips of paper and throw it at the king's coach. Whoever was fortu-

שֶׁנֶּאֱמַר: "בָּנִים אַתֶּם לַיהוה אֱלֹהֵיכֶם." חֲבִיבִין יִשְׂרָאֵל,
שֶׁנִּתַּן לָהֶם כְּלִי חֶמְדָּה; חִבָּה יְתֵרָה נוֹדַעַת לָהֶם, שֶׁנִּתַּן
לָהֶם כְּלִי חֶמְדָּה, שֶׁנֶּאֱמַר: "כִּי לֶקַח טוֹב נָתַתִּי לָכֶם, תּוֹרָתִי
אַל תַּעֲזֹבוּ."

nate enough that his petition landed in the coach would have his wish granted.

On the day of the parade the prince went into the city, and when the royal coach passed by he threw in his slip of paper, on which he had requested that he be provided with a hut that would protect him from the sun. This piece of paper landed in the coach, and when the king opened it, he recognized his son's handwriting. He began to weep. "How terribly low my son has sunk, that he no longer remembers that he is a prince. His request should have been to be taken back to the palace, where he could have all the privileges and comforts of his position. Instead, he has resigned himself to being a mere shepherd. All he can aspire to is to have a straw hut."

As the *Tzaddik* related this parable, he wept along with the king. "We will soon be standing in the Immanent Presence of God on Rosh Hashanah, a time which is especially propitious for our prayers to be answered. What do we ask for? More money, success in our ventures, perhaps a more spacious home, and other mundane things. We seem to forget that we are princes, and that we should ask to be returned to our royal home in Jerusalem. With the Redemption we will have everything, yet we have resigned ourselves to being in exile. All we aspire to is to have some greater comforts in exile. Like the foolish prince, we ask for the equivalent of a straw hut, whereas we should be asking to be restored to our princely state."

If we examine our prayers and consider our aspirations, we will see that we are all lacking in self-esteem.

The status of being considered children of God has additional implications, as was pointed out by the chassidic master, the *Maggid* of Mezeritch.

The Midrash states that when the children of Israel do the will of God, they are considered His children. When they do not do the will of God, they are considered to be only His servants (*Shemos Rabbah* 24:1). "But how can someone be considered a servant if he does not obey his master's instructions?" asked the *Maggid*.

The *Maggid* therefore explained that the words of the midrash are misunderstood.

The Talmud states that a *tzaddik* has the capacity to veto a Divine decree (*Moed Katan* 16b), and the corollary to this is that a *tzaddik* can decree something and God will fulfill the *tzaddik's* wish (cf. *Shabbos* 59b). There are many instances in the Talmud where *tzaddikim* decreed and their wishes were carried out.

"For someone to have this capacity, he must be so devoted to God that he

3/18   *as it is said: You are children of HASHEM, your God (Deut-eronomy 14:1). Beloved are the people of Israel, for a cherished utensil was given to them; it is indicative of a greater love that it was made known to them that they were given a cherished utensil, as it is said: For I have given you a good teaching; do not forsake My Torah (Proverbs 4:2).*

---

is truly like His child," the *Maggid* said. "It is only normal for a father who loves his child to fulfill his requests. If the father sees that his child desires something intensely, he will set aside his own will in favor of that of his child. In other words, the father now wants what the child wants, and the child has, as it were, fashioned the father's will.

"This degree of total devotion is not attained even by those who are observant of Torah. This is a degree of self-effacement before God and intense adherence to Him that is achieved only by *tzaddikim*. We must read the words of the Midrash not as '*do* the will of God' because servants of God also do his will. The children of God are those who '*fashion* the will of God.' Rabban Yochanan ben Zakkai said of R' Chanina ben Dosa, 'I am like an officer before the king, whereas R' Chanina is like the king's servant.' I may have greater knowledge of Torah, but R' Chanina has easier access to God and can have his requests fulfilled more readily than I.' "

We are beloved by God because we are described as His children. To truly be a child of God, however, we must strive for the self-effacement and total devotion that far exceeds even that of a loyal servant.

חֲבִיבִין יִשְׂרָאֵל, שֶׁנִּתַּן לָהֶם כְּלִי חֶמְדָּה
Beloved are the people of Israel, for a cherished utensil was given to them

Today there is a great proliferation of Torah teaching, and much Torah study is readily available. Some have questioned the wisdom of this, because Torah teaching may fall into the wrong hands. This is a controversy that goes all the way back to Talmudic days, when Rabban Gamliel wished to teach Torah only to those whom he considered deserving of it, while R' Elazar ben Azariah opened the doors of the academy to all.

A similar controversy arose among the disciples of the *Maggid* of Mezeritch in regard to the teachings of *Chassidus*. R' Shneur Zalman favored wide dissemination, whereas others felt that the general public might not value and respect these teachings adequately.

One time R' Pinchas of Koretz visited the *Maggid*, and found a page of chassidic writings on the floor. He protested that these writings should not be given widespread distribution, pointing out that they had been treated with disrespect.

ג/יט ‏[יט]‏ **הַכֹּל** צָפוּי, וְהָרְשׁוּת נְתוּנָה. וּבְטוֹב הָעוֹלָם נָדוֹן,
וְהַכֹּל לְפִי רֹב הַמַּעֲשֶׂה.

R' Shneur Zalman told R' Pinchas a parable. A king's child took ill, and his condition progressively deteriorated. The doctors were unable to find a remedy for the child. The king sent out messages throughout his kingdom that anyone who could cure the prince would be richly rewarded.

One day a man came and stated that he had found an old medical manuscript which stated that this disease could be cured by administering a precious gem. The gem was to be crushed, mixed into a liquid, and drunk. The king promptly sent messengers to find this particular gem. They returned empty-handed, but one of them remarked, "We need not seek the gem elsewhere. It is the centerpiece of the royal crown."

"Then what are you waiting for?" the king demanded. "Remove it immediately and crush it!"

In the meantime the prince's condition worsened so that he was unable to swallow anything. "Perhaps we should not destroy the gem," the king's advisors said. "It does not appear the prince will be able to swallow it."

The king became irate. "Crush it and dissolve the gem!" he said. "We will open the child's mouth and put in a few drops. Even if the rest spills to the ground, perhaps these few drops will be enough to save his life."

"I will concede," R' Shneur Zalman said, "that if we disseminate *Chassidus* widely, much of it may fall to the ground. But if even only a few drops enter into a person's heart and mind, it can be spiritually life-saving."

The children of Israel are beloved to God, and that is why he gave them something so valuable and cherished as the Torah. Is it possible that if it is widely disseminated some may "fall to the ground"? Yes, but if only a few drops of Torah enter the mouths of any of God's children, He is pleased thereby.

שֶׁנִּתַּן לָהֶם כְּלִי חֶמְדָּה
For a cherished utensil was given to them

The words *kli chemdah* can also be translated "a utensil for desire."

We have noted earlier that man was created with many emotional drives, and it is his responsibility to channel them properly. Hate is indeed a despicable emotion, yet one may hate injustice, and this may lead him to take measures to right the wrongs. Pride may be sinful, but one may be too proud to behave improperly because it is beneath his dignity. Love may deteriorate into lust, but it can be channeled constructively to love of God, love of Torah, and love of mitzvos.

When liquid is poured into a utensil, it takes the shape of that utensil. When emotions are processed through Torah, they take its shape. Torah is the "utensil" which should be used to contain and hence shape man's desires.

When R' Yosef Yitzchak of Lubavitch was a child, he was very beautiful. His father, R' Sholom Dov, loved him with great passion. One time the child fell

19. **E**verything is foreseen, yet the freedom of choice is given. The world is judged with goodness, and everything depends on the abundance of good deeds.

---

asleep in his father's study, and when R' Sholom Dov carried him to bed, he was overcome by an intense urge to kiss him. However, he restrained himself, and used the emotional energy to write an essay on *Chassidus*. Many years later, R' Sholom Dov gave his son this essay, and said, "Here you have a chassidic kiss."

There is certainly nothing wrong with kissing one's child. Had the child been awake, the father might have felt that his demonstration of affection would be of benefit to the child. However, inasmuch as the child was asleep, the kiss would have been purely a gratification of his desire. Rather than yield to this, he channeled this intense love to a closer relationship with God, upon which he expounded in his essay.

Earlier we noted that when the Patriarch Jacob and his son Joseph met after 22 years of separation, they embraced and Joseph wept. Rashi says that Jacob did not cry, because he was reciting the *Shema*. Why did Jacob recite the *Shema* just at the moment of this emotional reunion? Because Jacob felt that so intense a feeling as that which he was experiencing should be directed to the highest goal possible, to love of God.

Granted, we are not in the same league as these great *tzaddikim*. Yet, there is much that we can do with our feelings to channel them to spiritual goals. To do so, we must process them through the *kli chemdah*, the utensil for desires, the Torah.

19.

הַכֹּל צָפוּי, וְהָרְשׁוּת נְתוּנָה
Everything is foreseen, yet the freedom of choice is given

This mishnah addresses one of the most difficult issues in Torah philosophy; namely, the apparent conflict of two principles of Judaism. We believe that God has Omniscient knowledge, and knows everything that was, that is, and that will ever be. We also believe that man has total freedom of will in ethical and moral matters, and at any moment he is absolutely free to choose whether to do right or wrong. The obvious difficulty is that if God knows what I am going to do tomorrow, how can it be that I will have the freedom tomorrow to make a choice? If I do other than what God knows, then His knowledge is not perfect, which is impossible. On the other hand, if I must do what He knows I will do, then I do not have the freedom to do otherwise.

This dilemma has plagued theologians throughout the ages. Reams have been written to try and resolve this conflict. One of the best known explanations is that given by Rambam. If one looks closely, Rambam does not explain it in

[כ] **הוּא** הָיָה אוֹמֵר: הַכֹּל נָתוּן בָּעֵרָבוֹן, וּמְצוּדָה
פְרוּסָה עַל כָּל הַחַיִּים. הֶחָנוּת פְּתוּחָה,
וְהֶחֶנְוָנִי מַקִּיף, וְהַפִּנְקָס פָּתוּחַ, וְהַיָּד כּוֹתֶבֶת, וְכָל הָרוֹצֶה
לִלְווֹת יָבֹא וְיִלְוֶה. וְהַגַּבָּאִים מַחֲזִירִין תָּדִיר בְּכָל יוֹם

---

a way that enables us to reconcile the two principles, but rather explains why it is beyond our understanding.

Rambam states that God is so far removed from anything we have come in contact with that we cannot possibly understand Him. We may speak of "eternity" and "infinity," but these are just words. We cannot have a grasp of anything that did not have a beginning or that has no limits. Just as God is beyond our comprehension, so are what we refer to as His attributes beyond our comprehension. Thus, when we refer to God's knowledge, we have no inkling what that knowledge is like. While our concept of knowledge is such that foreknowledge is incompatible with free choice, God's knowledge does not conflict with free choice. What, then, is God's knowledge like? That is something we cannot possibly understand, any more than we can understand God Himself. It is clear that Rambam does not reconcile the two principles to comply with our understanding. Rather he tells us why we cannot understand.

This may be unsatisfactory to people who wish to understand everything, but as for myself, if Rambam was satisfied with something beyond his understanding, I can hardly ask for more.

R' Zvi Elimelech of Dinov states that inasmuch as God's benevolence is boundless, if it were to our advantage to understand how foreknowledge and free-will can coexist, God would not have concealed it from us. We must defer to His superior wisdom, and recognize that the irresolution of these two principles is somehow for our own good. Perhaps this is what R' Akiva meant by the statement that follows his citing the two conflicting principles: "The world is judged with goodness." Wiser people than myself were able to accept this on the basis of faith, and I do not have to improve on that.

וְהַכֹּל לְפִי רֹב הַמַּעֲשֶׂה
And everything depends on the abundance of good deeds

The final words of this mishnah can also be read as "everything depends on the many results of one's deeds," in which case it is an extension of the preceding statement, that "the world is judged with goodness."

As we have pointed out earlier, there is a system of Divine justice, and God, as it were, is bound by His own system. He can indeed forgive when forgiveness is merited, but He does not step out of His system. Hence the Talmud states that one may not say, "God will overlook this transgression" (*Bava Kamma* 50a). Nothing is overlooked, and a person is held accountable for

20. **H**e was accustomed to say: Everything is given on collateral, and a net is spread over all the living. The store is open; the Merchant extends credit; the ledger is open; the hand writes; and whoever wishes to borrow, let him come and borrow. The collectors make their rounds constantly, every day,

---

everything. While forgiveness as a result of proper *teshuvah* is within Divine justice, to overlook something would be a breach of justice.

The Talmud states that the measure of reward for a good deed is far greater than the measure of punishment for a sin (*Sotah* 11a). How does this comply with Divine justice?

One of the commentaries provides the answer. A person may give *tzedakah* to a needy family, as a result of which the children can be fed, clothed, and cared for properly. They then grow and develop and are able to do mitzvos. It is only fair that the donor be rewarded for the good he enabled to happen with his single act of *tzedakah*. If you were to ask him, "Would you wish that your *tzedakah* should lead to all these desirable results?" he would certainly say, "Of course." However, suppose he had stolen some money, as a result of which the victim was unable to get the necessities of life and consequently was unable to provide adequately for his family. Had you asked the thief, "Did you want all these tragic consequences to occur?" he would certainly say, "No! Never did I want this to happen. I stole because I did not have money for my needs, but I would certainly have wished that no one suffer."

The intention behind an act warrants an appropriate response. The benefactor's intentions are that everyone should benefit from his act. A sinful person, who was not strong enough to resist temptation and did indeed do wrong, was only interested in satisfying his desire, but did not wish anyone to be harmed thereby. A good deed is therefore rewarded many times over, whereas the punishment for a sin is limited to the act itself.

This concept is contained in our mishnah. The world is judged according to the abundance of the act, but only when it is an act for good, but not one of sin.

20.

הֶחָנוּת פְּתוּחָה, וְהַחֶנְוָנִי מַקִּיף

The store is open;
the Merchant extends credit

The use of parable has been a most effective tool in Jewish literature. Sometimes we are unable to grasp a particular concept, and when it is described in terms we understand better, such as metaphors, we can then go back and understand the more difficult concept. However, we must remember that a parable is only an illustration, and we must not take it literally.

This mishnah uses the analogy of a business enterprise to clarify and emphasize a person's responsibilities and the consequences of his delinquency in

וְנִפְרָעִין מִן הָאָדָם, מִדַּעְתּוֹ וְשֶׁלֹּא מִדַּעְתּוֹ, וְיֵשׁ לָהֶם עַל מַה
שֶׁיִּסְמֹכוּ. וְהַדִּין דִּין אֱמֶת, וְהַכֹּל מְתֻקָּן לִסְעוּדָה.

[כא] **רַבִּי** אֶלְעָזָר בֶּן עֲזַרְיָה אוֹמֵר: אִם אֵין תּוֹרָה,
אֵין דֶּרֶךְ אֶרֶץ; אִם אֵין דֶּרֶךְ אֶרֶץ, אֵין

---

fulfilling them. We must be cautious, however, that we do not take this analogy literally, and conduct our personal and spiritual life as if it were in fact a business enterprise.

Western civilization has become very business minded, probably more than in the past. Many more people are invested in the market, and many more people are tuned in to the economy. This preoccupation with economic issues seems to have had a deleterious impact on our personal lives.

The rules of economics are based primarily on profit or loss. Thus, if a person goes into a business venture with reckless abandon and takes great risks, and happens to hit it rich and make a windfall profit, he is not thought of as irresponsible. Rather, he is hailed as an economic wizard. On the other hand, if someone takes great caution, assiduously adhering to the rules of economics and seeking advice from the best sources, but his business venture turns out to be a total failure, he is considered a *schlimazel*. People will flock to the former for advice, and will shun the latter. Why? Because economic "good and bad" are determined by success or failure: Profit is good, loss is bad. How one came to make the decisions that resulted in success or failure is irrelevant. Good and bad are dependent on outcome, not on intentions. That is the way economics operate, and indeed, that is how economics should operate.

Morality and ethics, however, are just the reverse. Good moral and ethical behavior is determined by intentions rather than outcome. For example, if a doctor does not believe his patient needs surgery, but tells him that he must undergo an operation because he is money hungry and wishes to collect an exorbitant fee, he is an unscrupulous, unethical doctor. It may happen that when he performs the unnecessary surgery, he may discover a tiny cancerous tumor which had as yet not shown any symptoms. He removes it in its early stages, and he saves the patient's life. Is he a hero? No, he is a scoundrel, and one should avoid this kind of a doctor. The fact that he happened to save the patient's life by accidentally discovering an early cancer does not make him a good doctor, even if this patient is eternally grateful to him.

On the other hand, a doctor may have a patient about whom he is very concerned. Without surgery, there is a 75 percent likelihood that the patient will not live a year, and successful surgery can prolong his life. However, the operation is a risky one, and there is a 50 percent chance that the patient will not survive the surgery. The doctor agonizes over this decision, and calls in several consultants for their opinion. After taking all the factors into account and giving it a great amount of thought, he concludes that it would be best to

and collect payment from the person, whether he realizes it or not. They have proof to rely upon; the judgment is a truthful judgment; and everything is prepared for the [final festive] banquet.

21. **R***abbi Elazar ben Azariah says: If there is no Torah, there is no proper ethical conduct; if there is no proper ethical*

---

operate. Unfortunately, the patient does not survive the surgery. Is he a bad doctor? No, he is a highly ethical doctor, and one would be wise to be his patient.

In these cases, the one who had the successful outcome is bad, while the one who had the failure is good. This is because moral and ethical issues are not dependent on outcome. No one has prophecy to foresee what will happen, and there are many things that are beyond our control. All we can do is the best we can do, setting aside our own desires and trying to do what is best for others. When we behave in this way, we are good, regardless of the outcome.

Clinically, I have come across people who harbor guilt for things that happened, even though they tried to do their best. I have encountered parents whose child has gone astray, either to the use of drugs or other destructive behavior, although they tried their utmost to be responsible and caring parents. The tragic outcome occurred in spite of their best efforts. Yet, they are consumed with guilt. On the other hand, there are instances where parents were selfish and negligent, yet the child turned out to be an excellent scholar who achieved high honors. These are the parents who should have felt guilty for their dereliction, even though their child happened to succeed.

In these examples, as in all other phases of ethics and morality, we must not allow the rules of economics to determine our behavior or feelings. One does not play football according to the rules of baseball, and one should not run one's spiritual and personal life according to the rules of economics.

The problem is that when we are totally absorbed in economics, we might not even realize that there is another set of rules. We must be able to disengage ourselves from economic concepts and adopt the rules of ethics and morality that are appropriate to our personal and spiritual lives. Let us therefore use this mishnah as a valuable analogy, but we must remember that our lives are not business enterprises.

21.

אִם אֵין תּוֹרָה, אֵין דֶּרֶךְ אֶרֶץ
If there is no Torah, there is no proper ethical conduct

Various commentaries translate *derech eretz* as "proper ethical conduct" in which case the mishnah is saying that Torah and proper conduct are interrelated. The way the mishnah words it, however, is a bit problematic, since on the one hand it states

---

that *derech eretz* is a prerequisite for Torah, and on the other hand, that Torah is a prerequisite for *derech eretz*. Where should one begin?

It is clear that the mishnah is referring to two levels of *derech eretz*, one which is a prerequisite for Torah (*Vayikra Rabbah* 9), and another which can be reached only through Torah.

R' Moshe of Kosov said that the Torah was indeed given to refine and elevate the *mentsch*. "But first," he said, "one must be a *mentsch*." (The Yiddish word, *mentsch*, literally means " a person," but colloquially "mentsch" means a *decent* person. E.g., "He is a real *mentsch*.") There must be a foundation, upon which Torah can rest, a fertile soil in which it can take root, and this is the basic *derech eretz*.

Whence can this primary *derech eretz* be derived? We noted earlier (3:9) that the Talmud states that had the Torah not been given, we would have been expected to learn laws of decent conduct from observing nature; i.e., respect of private property from ants, fidelity from doves, etc. We might ask, however, without Torah how would we have known which are the desirable animal traits to emulate? Perhaps we would have learned rapaciousness from tigers and promiscuity from dogs. What would have guided us to the proper observations?

R' Yechezkel Levenstein provides the answer (*Kovetz Sichos* 62). Man is held responsible to use his intellect to understand that he was not given his enormous mental capacity and intelligence merely to satisfy his physical desires. If the latter were the purpose of his being, he would have been far better off without his intelligence. Certainly cows in the pasture have greater contentment than people, and Solomon states this emphatically when he says, "For with much wisdom comes much grief, and he who increases knowledge increases pain" (*Ecclesiastes* 1:18) The Steipler *Gaon* says that if you saw a child who was wearing trousers that were dragging behind him, a jacket whose sleeves extended far beyond his arms, and a hat which was down to his nose, you would promptly conclude that the child had put on his father's clothes, because these were certainly not designed for him. Similarly, man's vast intelligence should make it evident to him that the purpose of his creation was not merely to get pleasure out of life. He hardly needed his enormous mental capacities to achieve that.

"For God has made man simple, but they sought many intrigues" (*Ecclesiastes* 7:29). Man should have understood that he was created for a higher purpose, but he made "many intrigues," i.e., many rationalizations, even ingenious rationalizations, to permit him to follow a course of seeking primarily pleasure in life, something which is actually beneath his dignity.

Even without Torah, man's primordial intelligence should have directed him to the elementary principles of morality and decency. Without these, man sinks to an animal level, and Torah cannot be given to animals. Man must first be a *mentsch* in order to be able to receive the Torah.

Obviously, elementary rules of morality and decency do not suffice, any more than learning simple addition and subtraction in grade school is an adequate knowledge of mathematics. Building upon basic arithmetic, a person can receive the teaching that will promote him to the more advanced levels of higher mathematics. Similarly, once the basic principles of morality and decency are in place, which elevate man to a status above brute beasts, man can then be given the Torah which can elevate him to the highest levels of spirituality.

We thus have the two levels of *derech eretz*, says R' Levenstein. The first is based upon a person's intelligence, which should make him aware that he must rise above his physical desires and that he has a goal in life. This must precede Torah. The second level can come only from Torah, which enables a person to discover the nature of that goal and how he is to achieve it.

אִם אֵין יִרְאָה, אֵין חָכְמָה
If there is no fear of God, there is no wisdom.

Is this statement not a contradiction of "If you are told there is wisdom among other nations, you should believe it. If you are told there is Torah among other nations, you should not believe it!" (*Eichah Rabbah* 2:17)? Clearly, there is wisdom and intelligence even among those who do not have a fear of God.

Yes, there is a kind of wisdom among people who do not fear God. It is the kind of wisdom of which Meiri remarks that "Wisdom without *mussar* is like a tent without stakes" (*Commentary to Proverbs* 1:2). Of what use is a tent if it is not tethered to the ground? It obviously cannot provide any shelter.

The apparent contradiction is due to the dual meanings of *chochmah*, which can mean "wisdom" or can mean "intelligence."

We are sadly aware that human intelligence is not synonymous with wisdom. The genius of the human mind has unlocked the power within the atom, a power which can be used to create undreamed-of sources of energy, or which can destroy an entire population within seconds. We live in constant fear of a nuclear holocaust which might result if this power were to fall into the hands of terrorists. The miracle of electronics which has given us access to instantaneous unprecedented information, storage, and retrieval has also given us the television. Unfortunately, this has brought immorality and violence into the living room to corrupt the minds of young and old alike. I attended a parent-teacher meeting of a prominent secular middle school, and heard the headmaster say, "If you wish to save your children, get rid of your television sets."

Yes, there can be the "intelligence" variety of *chochmah* even among those who are not God fearing, but true wisdom can be only with those whose fear of God will channel their intelligence constructively, to enable man to reach his

ג/כא   אִם אֵין דַּעַת, אֵין בִּינָה, אִם אֵין בִּינָה, אֵין דַּעַת. אִם אֵין
קֶמַח, אֵין תּוֹרָה; אִם אֵין תּוֹרָה, אֵין קֶמַח.

---

full potential, to be the spiritual being he was designed to be. If Torah wisdom which is not preceded by fear of God can be destructive (mishnah 11), how much more so secular knowledge.

As with *derech eretz*, which must be understood in this mishnah as existing at two levels, so it is with *yirah*, fear of God. A small child who is punished for running into the street avoids doing so again for fear of being spanked, but as he matures and understands the danger of wandering into oncoming traffic, he is no longer deterred by fear of punishment but by fear of being injured. This is also true of *yirah*. When we are spiritually immature, we are deterred from doing wrong by fear of punishment, but as we grow spiritually we understand that God instructed us on how we must behave, not for His benefit, but that we should not injure ourselves, both physically and spiritually. The initial *yirah* enables us to channel *chochmah* properly, and as we do so, we arrive at a mature concept of *yirah*.

In mishnah 18 we noted the lofty status which God has given us. It should be beneath our dignity to do anything that is not fitting for this status.

Fear of punishment is not a uniquely human trait, and is present in lower forms of life as well. For example, a hungry jackal who is foraging for food and sees a carcass which he craves, but which is being fed on by a ferocious tiger, will not make the slightest attempt to satisfy his hunger by partaking of the carcass. The jackal knows that to impinge on the territory of the tiger will result in his being killed. He forgoes the satisfaction of his appetite and continues to suffer hunger to avoid being killed. The jackal is not in the least restrained by an ethical consideration not to impose upon the rightful property of the tiger.

Suppose that a person is employed in a large financial firm which turns over millions of dollars each day, and he knows how to manipulate the computers to divert money to his personal account. He is very greedy, and lusts for the riches that are within his reach. However, he reflects that the auditing team will undoubtedly have someone who is highly skilled in detecting computer crime. If his embezzlement is detected, he will not only forfeit his ill-begotten money, but will also be severely penalized by a huge fine and a long prison sentence. Since he does not wish to take this risk, he restrains his greed and does not transfer the money, not because it is wrong, but because the possible consequences are prohibitive. This person is really no different than the jackal, who denies his cravings for fear of the painful consequences.

A person may impose self-limits in a situation where he wishes to gratify his desires by doing something which is wrong, but which he knows cannot be detected by others and carries no possibility of punishment. If he restrains himself because he believes this behavior to be morally wrong, he is then

3/21   *If there is no daas, there is no binah; if there is no binah, there is no daas. If there is no flour, there is no Torah; if there is no Torah, there is no flour.*

exercising his unique human trait of ethical behavior.

True *chochmah* does not mean merely cunning or shrewdness, because the latter can lead to corrupt behavior. True *chochmah* can exist only within the framework of *yirah*, which then elevates man to the status of being truly free. A person whose behavior is determined by physical drives and is unable to control his actions unless deterred by the threat of punishment cannot be said to be truly free. Only a person who is not under the compulsion of physical drives and who can make moral and ethical choices can be considered truly free. When man is like this, he is indeed akin to God, and this is what is meant in mishnah 18, that man is fortunate in having been created "in the Divine image."

אִם אֵין דַּעַת, אֵין בִּינָה
If there is no daas, there is no binah

*D*aas is usually translated as "knowledge." In chassidic literature, especially in *Tanya*, *daas* is given another meaning.

The three intellectual human *middos* (traits) are *chochmah, binah, and daas*. The first two refer to man's acquisition of knowledge and his understanding and formulating this knowledge into concepts. At this point, knowledge is still an intellectual entity, unrelated to behavior.

Man also has a variety of other traits, which are referred to as the emotional *middos,* and it is the energy of these emotions which is the driving force behind behavior. Emotions can express themselves in either proper or improper behavior, and behavior is proper only when it is guided by true wisdom, by *chochmah* as defined in this mishnah, and by *binah*, which is the formulation of the raw material of *chochmah* into usable concepts. However, unless there is a bonding of the intellectual capacities to the emotions, the former may remain abstractions which do not govern behavior. It is not all that unusual to find people of great intellect whose behavior as refined human beings leaves much to be desired. *Daas is the bridge that binds man's intellect to his emotions*, so that his behavior is governed by the intellect. Chassidic writings note that the Torah uses the term *daas* to refer to relationship, to a bonding (*Genesis* 4:1). This mishnah states that *binah* and *daas,* understanding or concept formation and the bonding of the intellect to emotions, are interdependent.

Pure concept formation that is not translated into action is sterile. Concepts that are not implemented may remain rather useless abstractions. If they do not affect behavior they are subject to distortion, because they can never be put to

[כב] **הוּא** הָיָה אוֹמֵר: כֹּל שֶׁחָכְמָתוֹ מְרֻבָּה מִמַּעֲשָׂיו,
לְמָה הוּא דוֹמֶה? לְאִילָן שֶׁעֲנָפָיו מְרֻבִּין
וְשָׁרָשָׁיו מוּעָטִין, וְהָרוּחַ בָּאָה וְעוֹקַרְתּוֹ וְהוֹפַכְתּוֹ עַל פָּנָיו,
שֶׁנֶּאֱמַר: "וְהָיָה כְּעַרְעָר בָּעֲרָבָה, וְלֹא יִרְאֶה כִּי יָבוֹא טוֹב,
וְשָׁכַן חֲרֵרִים בַּמִּדְבָּר, אֶרֶץ מְלֵחָה וְלֹא תֵשֵׁב." אֲבָל כֹּל
שֶׁמַּעֲשָׂיו מְרֻבִּין מֵחָכְמָתוֹ, לְמָה הוּא דוֹמֶה? לְאִילָן שֶׁעֲנָפָיו
מוּעָטִין וְשָׁרָשָׁיו מְרֻבִּין, שֶׁאֲפִילוּ כָּל הָרוּחוֹת שֶׁבָּעוֹלָם
בָּאוֹת וְנוֹשְׁבוֹת בּוֹ, אֵין מְזִיזִין אוֹתוֹ מִמְּקוֹמוֹ, שֶׁנֶּאֱמַר: "וְהָיָה
כְּעֵץ שָׁתוּל עַל מַיִם, וְעַל יוּבַל יְשַׁלַּח שָׁרָשָׁיו, וְלֹא יִרְאֶה כִּי
יָבֹא חֹם, וְהָיָה עָלֵהוּ רַעֲנָן, וּבִשְׁנַת בַּצֹּרֶת לֹא יִדְאָג, וְלֹא
יָמִישׁ מֵעֲשׂוֹת פֶּרִי."

---

the test. The theory that the earth is flat persisted for centuries and was assumed to be true, and was disproven only when it was put to the test. It is only
when concepts, driven by the emotional *middos,* affect our lives in some way,
that they are clarified and tested.

Needless to say, implementing emotions without the input of *binah* is disastrous. Energy that is not properly channeled can be grossly destructive, as
became evident when containing the nuclear energy in Chernobyl failed. The
energy of the emotional *middos* must be guided by the intellect.

It is more than coincidental that the Torah use of *daas* in *Genesis* refers to
a bonding that was productive and procreative. This indicates that the function
of *daas* is indeed to harness the energy of the emotional *middos* to bring *binah*
to fruition.

22.

לְמָה הוּא דוֹמֶה? לְאִילָן
To what is he likened? — to a tree

The tree is frequently used in Torah
literature to represent Torah, as in
"It (Torah) is a tree of life" (*Proverbs*
3:18), and also to represent man, based on *Deuteronomy* 20:19.

Chassidic writings teach that the function of man is to transform the earthly
world into a spiritual world. The Rabbi of Kotzk, referring to the phrase (*Psalms*
115:16) "The heaven, the heaven is to God, and the earth He gave to man,"
said that God made the heaven into heaven, and gave the earth to man so that
he should transform *it* into heaven. When a person uses earthly objects in the
performance of mitzvos, they become spiritual objects. The hide of an animal

22. **H**e [R' Elazar ben Azariah] was accustomed to say: Anyone whose wisdom exceeds his good deeds, to what is he likened? — to a tree whose branches are numerous but whose roots are few; then the wind comes and uproots it and turns it upside down, as it is said: And he shall be like an isolated tree in an arid land and shall not see when good comes; he shall dwell on parched soil in the wilderness, on a salted and uninhabited land (Jeremiah 17:6). But one whose good deeds exceed his wisdom, to what is he likened? — to a tree whose branches are few but whose roots are numerous; even if all the winds in the world were to come and blow against it, they could not budge it from its place, as it says: And he shall be like a tree planted by waters, spreading its roots toward the stream, and it shall not notice the heat's arrival, and its foliage shall be fresh; in the year of drought it shall not worry, nor shall it cease from yielding fruit (Jeremiah 17:8).

---

can become sacred when it is used to make *tefillin* or when it is made into parchment for *mezuzos*. The produce of the earth receives a spiritual value when a person uses the energy provided by food to perform mitzvos. It is by observing the ordinances of Torah and living according to Torah teachings that man accomplishes this mission.

The tree is symbolic of this function. It too takes the elements of the earth, water, and the oxygen of the air, and with the energy provided by sunlight miraculously synthesizes wood, leaves, and fruit. These provide both shade and food for all living things, as well as being a home for various creatures. If we did not witness this with our own eyes we would not believe that minerals and water can be combined in such a manner as to bring beautiful and delicious fruit into existence. It is indeed a miracle, and we fail to recognize it as such only because it is so commonplace that we take it for granted.

Just as elements can be combined and transformed into fruit, so can all earthly objects be transformed into *kedushah* (holiness). The Midrash (*Shir HaShirim Rabbah* 1:2) states that after R' Eliezer's death, R' Yehoshua wept and kissed the stone upon which R' Eliezer sat when he taught Torah, saying, "This stone is like the Holy Ark."

As we go about our daily activities, we would do well to think of our being compared to a tree, so that we may conduct ourselves in a manner that, as the Rabbi of Kotzk said, will enable us to convert the earth into heaven.

[כג] **רַבִּי** אֶלְעָזָר בֶּן חִסְמָא אוֹמֵר: קִנִּין וּפִתְחֵי נִדָּה הֵן הֵן גּוּפֵי הֲלָכוֹת; תְּקוּפוֹת וְגִמַטְרִיָאוֹת — פַּרְפְּרָאוֹת לַחָכְמָה.

❧ ❧ ❧

רַבִּי חֲנַנְיָא בֶּן עֲקַשְׁיָא אוֹמֵר: רָצָה הַקָּדוֹשׁ בָּרוּךְ הוּא לְזַכּוֹת אֶת יִשְׂרָאֵל, לְפִיכָךְ הִרְבָּה לָהֶם תּוֹרָה וּמִצְוֹת, שֶׁנֶּאֱמַר: "יהוה חָפֵץ לְמַעַן צִדְקוֹ, יַגְדִּיל תּוֹרָה וְיַאְדִּיר."

23.

תְּקוּפוֹת וְגִמַטְרִיָאוֹת – פַּרְפְּרָאוֹת לַחָכְמָה
Astronomy and mathematics are like seasonings to wisdom.

Solomon says, "It is better to hear the rebuke of a wise man than one who hears (מֵאִישׁ שֹׁמֵעַ) the song of fools" (Ecclesiastes 7:5). R' Bunim of P'shische noted that it would have been more appropriate to say, "It is better to hear the rebuke of a wise man *than to* listen to the songs of fools." He therefore explains that the Hebrew verse can also be read as "It is better to hear the rebuke of a wise man — מֵאִישׁ שֹׁמֵעַ — *from someone who has listened to* the song of fools." Why? Because if the wise man is a scholar who has spent all his days studying Torah, someone might dismiss his rebuke with, "What does he know? Had he been exposed to the enjoyable pastimes of life, he would not condemn them." However, if someone who has tasted these pleasures of life tells us how worthless they are and that the true value lies in the study of Torah, his words will be given greater weight. Having experienced both, he is capable of judging the value of both.

23. Rabbi Elazar ben Chisma says: The laws of bird offerings, and the laws regarding the beginning of men-
strual periods— these are essential laws; astronomy and
mathematics are like seasonings to wisdom.

🐝　🐝　🐝

Rabbi Chanania ben Akashia says: The Holy One,
Blessed is He, wished to confer merit upon Israel; therefore He gave them Torah and mitzvos in abundance, as it is
said: HASHEM desired, for the sake of its [Israel's] righteousness, that the Torah be made great and glorious (Isaiah
42:21).

There is no question that the physical sciences have value, yet they pale in
comparison with Torah. Ibn Ezra was an accomplished mathematician, but he
is known to us for his commentary on Torah. The Vilna *Gaon* wrote a text on
geometry, but this is not what has preserved him for posterity. Many of our great
Torah scholars were brilliant in the physical sciences and philosophy, but what
they held most important was their study of Torah.

R' Elazar ben Chisma was a great mathematician, of whom the Talmud states
that "he could calculate how many drops of water there are in the sea" (*Horayos*
10). This notwithstanding, he says that mathematics compared to the essential
laws of Torah are like the condiments of a meal. They indeed have a place, but
one must realize their status relative to Torah. A meal without condiments is
nutritional, although it may be enhanced by relishes, but no one makes a meal
of only relish.

It is precisely because R' Eliezer was so proficient in mathematics that he
speaks with authority when he tells us that knowledge of the essential laws of
Torah is of primary importance, and that mathematics have a status of "condiments." In an era where there has been great progress in the physical sciences,
it is important that we not lose sight of what is truly fundamental to our lives.

פרק רביעי ﯓ
Chapter Four

כָּל יִשְׂרָאֵל יֵשׁ לָהֶם חֵלֶק לָעוֹלָם הַבָּא, שֶׁנֶּאֱמַר:
„וְעַמֵּךְ כֻּלָּם צַדִּיקִים, לְעוֹלָם יִירְשׁוּ
אֶרֶץ, נֵצֶר מַטָּעַי, מַעֲשֵׂה יָדַי לְהִתְפָּאֵר."

All Israel has a share in the World to Come, as it is
said: And your people are all righteous; they shall
inherit the land forever; a branch of My plantings, My
handiwork, in which to take pride (Isaiah 60:21).

פֶּרֶק רְבִיעִי

[א] **בֶּן זוֹמָא** אוֹמֵר: אֵיזֶהוּ חָכָם? הַלּוֹמֵד מִכָּל אָדָם,
שֶׁנֶּאֱמַר: ,,מִכָּל מְלַמְּדַי הִשְׂכַּלְתִּי.''

Chapter Four

1.

How different Torah values are from secular values. If you asked the average person whom he considered to be the wisest people in the world, he would probably cite the Nobel prizewinners, heads of departments of the great colleges, or authors of major works in philosophy or the sciences. These are people who essentially function as dispensers of knowledge to the world. If he were asked to list the mightiest people, he would probably name those who rule over large populations and have powerful armies, or perhaps the heads of corporations who control large segments of industry and can affect the lives of millions. If he were asked to name the wealthiest people in the world, he would refer to the list published annually in *Fortune* magazine, and if he were asked who are the most respectable people, he would cite those who received prominent recognition and awards, or who were given honorary degrees by prestigious universities.

Torah values are much different. The wise person is not the one who dispenses knowledge, but the one who seeks to acquire knowledge. The mighty person is not one who is master over others, but is master over his own impulses The wealthy person is not one who owns the most, but who is content with whatever he has; and the respectable person is not the one who receives honors, but one who respects and honors others.

What a different world it would be if people abided by Torah values! How much happier would we be if our aspirations were those of this mishnah rather than those that prevail in society.

אֵיזֶהוּ חָכָם? הַלּוֹמֵד מִכָּל אָדָם
Who is wise?
He who learns from every person

Let us look a bit at the attribute of learning from everyone. "Every person" includes people who may be far less educated than we are. In some ways, there are things we can learn even from wrongdoers. The *Maggid* of Mezeritch said that there are some things we can learn from a thief. For example, a thief does his work at night, when no one can see him. We can learn from that to conceal the degree of our learning, *tzedakah,* and intense service of God, so that we should not seek to impress others with our piety. Or, just as a thief will try again and again if he does not succeed on his first attempt, so we should not give up if we initially fail at something. The *Maggid* also said that there are three things to learn from an infant: 1) Never be idle; 2) always

1. Ben Zoma says: Who is wise? He who learns from every
     person, as it is said: From all my teachers I grew wise

---

smile; and 3) when you want something, cry for it, meaning that when we pray
to God our pleas should be accompanied by tears.

Some people have a problem in accepting teaching from anyone inferior to
them, because they see this as demeaning. These are invariably people with a
fragile ego, who fear that this would mean that the other person is superior to
them. People with a healthy ego are the ones who can learn from everyone.

As I told you earlier, when I was several months into my psychiatric training,
a relative called asking me to refer her to someone who could help her depression.

Several days later an internationally acclaimed psychiatrist called, to consult
with me. I said, "You have the wrong impression. I am not a psychiatrist. I have
just begun my training, and all I know about depression is what I am learning
from your book."

"Oh, yes," he said, "I know depression very well, but you know this patient
better than I do, and you can help me decide on the most effective treatment
regimen." When my instructor heard who had called me for consultation, he
smiled and said, "The only person who would call a first-year resident for
advice is the man who wrote the book. He does not feel threatened that doing
so would hurt his reputation."

I have gathered much valuable knowledge from my alcoholic patients. These
are people who used to suppress their anxiety with alcohol. When they
stopped drinking, they had to find alternative ways of handling stress. Every
recovering alcoholic can therefore provide some techniques for coping with
stress, and this can be helpful to everyone.

For example, one recovering alcoholic said, "I am a football fan, and I would
never miss watching my team play. One week I had to leave town, and I asked
a friend to record the game for me on a videotape. When my friend later gave
me the tape, he said, 'Oh, by the way, the Jets (my team) won.'

"I started watching the game on the video, and my team was losing badly.
At half time they were 20 points behind. At other times I would have been very
upset, but this time I was perfectly calm, because I knew that they were going
to win."

Then the man said, "Ever since I turned my life over to God, I no longer get
upset when things go badly for me, because I know that even if I am '20 points
behind at half time' in my life, things will ultimately turn out good."

I learned something very valuable from this man.

❧

R' Yehudah *HaNasi* says, "Who is a wise man? One who can foresee the future?" (*Tamid* 28a). If we analyze carefully, we will see that R' Yehudah *HaNasi* and Ben Zoma do not disagree.

I must again refer to my work in treating alcoholics to help clarify this. Parents of a youngster who is abusing chemicals or the spouse of an addicted person often consult me, stating that the child or spouse refuses to recognize the problem and seek help. What can they do? I advise them to join in a support group of family members who have gone through a similar problem with a child or spouse, because they can learn much from the experience of others. The course of these conditions are quite similar even among diverse people. By listening to the experiences of others who have dealt with the problem, they can learn what to expect, and to act toward that person in a way that is conducive to recovery.

Sometimes people reject my advice, and insist that they can accept guidance only from a professional counselor. While this may be helpful, it is not as effective as the experience of those who have been there.

Let us go back to the words of R' Yehudah *HaNasi*. Just what does he mean that the wise man is one who can foresee the future? Wise men are not prophets.

The phrase to "foresee the future" uses the word *nolad,* which, while meaning "that which will come to be," can also mean "that which *came* to be." I.e., it can refer both to the past as well as the future. Indeed, if we have a clear knowledge of the past, we can predict the future quite accurately. It has been correctly said that "insanity consists of doing the same thing and expecting different results." If we can find out what kind of actions produce certain results, we are then in a position to know what to do to achieve the desired results and what to do to avoid the undesired results. We can learn this better from people who have gone through similar experiences than from a professional counselor, who may perhaps be more educated, but lacks this particular experience.

In this case, the person who is willing to learn from everyone can benefit from the knowledge that comes from experience. In this way one can predict what is likely to occur and what will be the effects of his actions. The wise person is therefore one who can foresee the future precisely because he is willing to learn from everyone. R' Yehudah *HaNasi* and Ben Zoma are expressing the same concept in different terms.

This principle is certainly not restricted to alcohol problems. In any phase of life, we may learn what to expect from our actions if we allow ourselves to learn from everyone. How foolish we would be to insist on learning from our own mistakes instead of profiting from the mistakes of others, so that we do not repeat them! The truly wise person is one who does not commit this folly.

We should also note that Ben Zoma says that the wise person is one who *learns* from everyone, rather than one who *has learned*; i.e., wisdom is a process of continuous learning. One who may have learned much in the past but fails to keep up his learning may lose some of his wisdom, and the ongoing learning must also be with a willingness to learn from everyone.

אֵיזֶהוּ גִבּוֹר? הַכּוֹבֵשׁ אֶת יִצְרוֹ
Who is strong?
He who subdues his
personal inclination

The popular concept that people who are in control of others in one way or another, whether it be chiefs of state or heads of large companies, are mighty is erroneous. Ironically, the truth is just the converse.

In *Life's Too Short* (St. Martin's Press) I developed the theme of low self-esteem and pointed out a number of behavior patterns that people may employ in order to escape the distressing feeling that they are unworthy or inadequate. One of these mechanisms is to seek control over others, which may give the person an illusion of strength. This defense against feelings of unworth and inferiority cannot and does not eliminate those feelings, which continue to eat away at the person. He must therefore continually extend his control in order to placate them. This explains why conquerors are never satisfied with their conquest, and continue in their efforts to extend their borders to bring more and more people under their control. This is why a person who owns a large company or much property, and has more money than he could consume in three lifetimes, nevertheless pursues further expansion. This may also explain why an abusive husband tries to crush his wife and render her totally helpless. What appears to be a manifestation of strength is in fact a defensive maneuver which betrays an inner weakness.

A person with good self-esteem has no need to dominate others. Some of the world's greatest leaders were actually reluctant to assume a position of authority, and were essentially coerced to do so. Two outstanding examples in the Torah are Moses and King Saul. The indicator of good self-esteem is not a position of dominance, but to the contrary, an attitude of humility.

In *Let Us Make Man* (CIS Publications), I explained that self-esteem and humility are not only fully compatible, but that indeed, humility is *essential* for self-esteem. Humility means that a person is aware of his talents and strengths, but realizes that they are gifts from God. He has no reason to consider himself superior to other people any more than someone would feel superior to his neighbors because he had fine china and silverware which he had borrowed.

A truly humble person is always interested in self-improvement, and particularly in increasing his spirituality. He is not preoccupied with wielding control over others, and can therefore dedicate his efforts to greater self-mastery.

The Talmud states that the struggle with the *yetzer hara* is never over. Indeed, the more a person develops himself spiritually, the more force the *yetzer*

מִגִּבּוֹר, וּמֹשֵׁל בְּרוּחוֹ מִלֹּכֵד עִיר." אֵיזֶהוּ עָשִׁיר? הַשָּׂמֵחַ בְּחֶלְקוֹ, שֶׁנֶּאֱמַר: "יְגִיעַ כַּפֶּיךָ כִּי תֹאכֵל אַשְׁרֶיךָ וְטוֹב לָךְ." "אַשְׁרֶיךָ" – בָּעוֹלָם הַזֶּה, "וְטוֹב לָךְ" – לָעוֹלָם הַבָּא.

---

hara exerts to seduce him to sin. The battle for self-mastery is an ongoing one, and requires progressively greater energies. The person who grows spiritually and does achieve mastery over the *yetzer hara* has demonstrated much greater strength than someone who seeks conquest because he has a need to dominate over others.

The teachings of this mishnah are not only ethical, but also have a firm basis in psychology.

אֵיזֶהוּ עָשִׁיר? הַשָּׂמֵחַ בְּחֶלְקוֹ
Who is rich?
He who is happy with his lot

R' Moshe Schreiber (*Chasam Sofer*) gives this mishnah a novel interpretation. Rather than translating שָׂמֵחַ בְּחֶלְקוֹ as "happy with his lot," he translates it as "happy with his *portion.*"

The Chasam Sofer gives the example of a wealthy father who left a huge inheritance in trust for his young son. The trustees give the young man a *portion* of the money, as they deem it appropriate to meet his legitimate needs. To give him all the money or even just slightly more than his needs would be foolish, because given his immaturity and limited knowledge, the young man would squander it wastefully and possibly even dangerously. (How many young people have I seen who had access to a great deal of money, and it resulted in their ruination as they failed to take life seriously, neglecting a career or indulging in drugs!) Even if the young man asks for more money, the trustees exercise their discretion responsibly, and give him only what they know will be beneficial for him.

We believe in *hashgachah* (Divine providence), that God keeps a watchful eye on us. We may be deserving of much reward, but to give it to us in quantities that we might squander foolishly or that might negatively affect our character would not be to our advantage. God therefore gives us a *portion* that is appropriate for our particular needs, and retains the remainder which will be given to us at the proper time, perhaps in *Gan Eden*.

We must understand that just as a young man who is immature might not know how to use money properly, we may be in a sense "immature" even when we are fully grown and well educated. Our understanding of the world as a whole is limited, and we do not have full knowledge of what is our particular mission in Creation. Only God, whose wisdom and benevolence are infinite, can know what is truly good for us.

R' Zusia of Hanipole lived in abject poverty. Someone who saw his tattered clothes and torn shoes asked him, "How can you recite the daily *berachah*, 'Blessed are You, O God, Who has given me all my needs,' when you are so

4/1 *better than a strong man, and a master of his passions is better than a conqueror of a city (Proverbs 16:32). Who is rich? He who is happy with his lot, as it is said: When you eat of the labor of your hands, you are praiseworthy and all is well with you (Psalms 128:2). You are praiseworthy — in this world; and all is well with you — in the World to Come.*

---

grossly lacking even the basic amenities?" R' Zusia replied, "God knows what my needs are better than I do. If He has determined that one of my needs is poverty, I am happy to accept His infallible judgment."

"This is what the mishnah means," said the Chasam Sofer. "A person who has trust in God will accept the *portion* of what is his, knowing that God holds the remainder in safekeeping, to be given to him when it is to his advantage to have it. A person who has true faith can therefore be happy with the *portion* he is given."

When I wrote *Not Just Stories*, I advocated the use of stories as a most effective teaching tool. I am pleased that my opinion has been confirmed by parents and teachers who have found storytelling to be valuable in conveying certain concepts to young children.

I remember that as a child my mother told me a story about a beggar who was given a magic purse which contained a dollar, and when he removed the dollar, another dollar would take its place. Three days later the beggar was found dead, lying on a huge heap of dollars.

This story has accompanied me throughout my life. It is a simple statement that unless a person is content with what he has, there is never any such thing as "enough." Greed can result in a person forfeiting his very life in the pursuit of an elusive goal which can never be reached.

אֵיזֶהוּ גִבּוֹר? . . . אֵיזֶהוּ עָשִׁיר?
Who is strong? . . . Who is rich?

In *Mussar HaMishnah* R' Ginsburg raises an interesting question: Rambam states that God does not predetermine whether a person will be righteous or wicked, good or bad. These are areas of free will, and moral and ethical behavior are left entirely to a person's choice. Indeed, every person has the capacity to be as great as Moses (*Hilchos Teshuvah* 5:2). Yet, the Talmud states that God does not make His spirit rest on a person unless one is "humble, strong, and wealthy" (*Nedarim* 38a). Inasmuch as whether a person is to be strong or weak, wealthy or poor, *is* predetermined, then one is not really free to become as great as Moses, because if it were decreed before his birth that he would be weak and/or poor, then he would lack one or two of the necessary factors that characterized Moses and that are

ד/ב
אֵיזֶהוּ מְכֻבָּד? הַמְכַבֵּד אֶת הַבְּרִיּוֹת, שֶׁנֶּאֱמַר: „כִּי מְכַבְּדַי
אֲכַבֵּד, וּבֹזַי יֵקָלוּ.״

[ג] **בֶּן עַזַּאי** אוֹמֵר: הֱוֵי רָץ לְמִצְוָה קַלָּה, וּבוֹרֵחַ מִן
הָעֲבֵרָה; שֶׁמִּצְוָה גּוֹרֶרֶת מִצְוָה, וַעֲבֵרָה
גּוֹרֶרֶת עֲבֵרָה, שֶׁשְּׂכַר מִצְוָה מִצְוָה, וּשְׂכַר עֲבֵרָה עֲבֵרָה.

---

requisites for attaining the presence of the Divine spirit.

R' Ginsburg resolves this problem by pointing to our mishnah, which defines strength not as physical prowess, but as attaining mastery over one's *yetzer hara*. Wealth is not having a great deal of money, but being content with whatever one has. Given these definitions, this kind of strength and wealth are not predetermined since they are of a moral and ethical nature, and hence totally subject to a person's free will.

אֵיזֶהוּ מְכֻבָּד? הַמְכַבֵּד אֶת הַבְּרִיּוֹת
Who is honored?
He who honors others

I have frequently discussed the various maneuvers that may be employed by a person who lacks self-esteem. One of them is to belittle others, whereby one may then feel that he is superior to them. This is obviously a desperate defense mechanism, and it is clear that someone who utilizes this must be so lacking in self-respect that he must resort to this.

Another mechanism employed by people with low self-esteem is to pursue acclaim from others. This may lead them to do worthwhile things, but does little to enhance their self-esteem. I was consulted by a patient whose drive to receive recognition resulted in his overtaxing himself. He was the chairman of various community activities in addition to being a busy executive. He said, "I have an entire wall in my home covered with testimonials, trophies, and awards, but they mean nothing to me." Trying to overcome self-esteem by receiving acclaim may provide only temporary relief.

A person who has good self-respect is not dependent on others to honor him. In fact, he is very comfortable in honoring others, and this does not pose any threat to his self-esteem.

You may be sure that a person who speaks *lashon hara* is a person with low self-esteem, else he would not have any need of belittling others.

2.

הֱוֵי רָץ לְמִצְוָה קַלָּה . . .
Run to [perform even]
a "minor" mitzvah. . .

The *Maggid* of Kozhnitz once arose from the Shabbos table and inadvertently nudged it, causing a candle to fall from its holder and be extinguished. The *Maggid* wept uncontrollably, and his son tried

4/2   *Who is honored? He who honors others, as it is said: For those who honor Me I will honor, and those who scorn Me shall be degraded (I Samuel 2:30).*

2. **B**en Azzai says: Run to [perform even] a "minor" mitzvah, and flee from sin; for one mitzvah leads to another mitzvah, and one sin leads to another sin; for the reward of a mitzvah is a mitzvah, and the reward of a sin is a sin.

---

to console him. He pointed out that this was a wholly accidental happening for which he had no liability. The *Maggid* replied, "It is not this that I am crying about. I am worried about what sin this may bring in its wake."

The *Maggid* understood the mishnah correctly. Just as it is a law of nature that a magnet will attract iron, so it is a law of nature that one sin attracts another and that one mitzvah attracts another. Even if he were not liable for the candle going out, he nevertheless feared that it might result in his being confronted with the challenge of struggling with a more serious sin. If we understood the mishnah the way the *Maggid* did, it would have great impact on our behavior. We may sometimes dismiss something as being insignificant, but we must realize that there is no such thing as an insignificant act.

All human behavior can be divided into two categories. There are actions which contribute toward the fulfillment of our purpose on earth, hence they are mitzvos. If one eats and sleeps in order to maintain one's health to be able to do mitzvos, the eating and sleeping are accessories to mitzvos and become mitzvos themselves. If one indulges in things purely for the pleasure they provide, this is misusing the faculties we were given in order to fulfill our mission. Such misuse constitutes a transgression even if it is not a frank violation of Torah. In other words, there is no such thing as a "neutral" action which is neither mitzvah nor sin. Everything we do falls into one of the two categories. Every action we do, even if it is something permissible, may lead us to performance of mitzvos or sin, depending on our intention for the act.

This is why the mishnah advises us to take advantage of "minor" mitzvos and to avoid any and all sin, because each may lead to performance of others in the same category.

שֶׁשְּׂכַר מִצְוָה מִצְוָה
For the reward of a mitzvah is a mitzvah

We usually understand this mishnah to mean that the reward for a mitzvah is that it will result in the opportunity to do another mitzvah. There is also another meaning. We noted earlier that God directs the world completely within His system of justice. Like a father who loves his child, God wishes to bestow abundant goods upon all of His children. However, He

[ג] **הוּא** הָיָה אוֹמֵר: אַל תְּהִי בָז לְכָל אָדָם, וְאַל תְּהִי
מַפְלִיג לְכָל דָּבָר, שֶׁאֵין לְךָ אָדָם שֶׁאֵין לוֹ
שָׁעָה, וְאֵין לְךָ דָּבָר שֶׁאֵין לוֹ מָקוֹם.

---

does not give unearned reward, because this would be contrary to His laws of justice. Hence, God wants us to do mitzvos so that He can give us the good He wishes. Therefore when we do a mitzvah, not only have we done His will, but we have made it possible for Him to reward us. Inasmuch as this gives God pleasure, we now have another mitzvah of providing God with נַחַת רוּחַ. This is itself a mitzvah which deserves to be rewarded, hence an infinite reward can be achieved by the performance of a single mitzvah. This is included in the mishnah's words, that earning the reward for a mitzvah is a mitzvah in its own right.

3.

אַל תְּהִי בָז לְכָל אָדָם
Do not be scornful of any person

Rabbi Shalom Dov of Lubavitch showed great affection for the simple folk. One time, a *chassid* who was a diamond merchant asked the rabbi what virtues he saw in these unlearned people.

The rabbi asked the *chassid* whether he happened to have any of his merchandise with him, whereupon he showed the rabbi a packet of diamonds. The rabbi pointed to a rather large gem and said, "That is indeed a beautiful diamond."

The *chassid* smiled. "No, rabbi," he said, "it happens to be full of defects."

"But it is more beautiful than the other stones," the rabbi said.

The *chassid* explained, "It happens to be larger than the other stones, but because it has defects which can be seen with a magnifying glass, its value is much less. Now here," he said, "is a smaller stone that may not appear as brilliant as the larger one, but it is a perfect stone, and is very valuable. You see, rabbi, to know the value of diamonds one must have expertise."

"I understand," Rabbi Shalom Dov said, "but the same thing is true of knowing the value of people, where one must also have great expertise."

Several years ago, I fully appreciated the truth of the rabbi's words. I had begun a project in Israel to rehabilitate ex-convicts who had run afoul of the law because of their need to support their drug habits. In meeting with the first group, I tried to point out that people who have a good sense of self-worth are unlikely to do things that would cause them harm, just as someone who owns a beautiful new automobile would take caution that it not be scratched and marred.

At this point one of the clients interrupted me, exclaiming, "You expect me to have a sense of self-worth? I am 34, and I have spent 16 years of my life in prison, having been convicted eight times. When I get out of jail, no one wants to hire me because of my prison record, and I can't get a job to support myself. When my family is informed that I will be released from prison they become

3. **H**e was accustomed to say: Do not be scornful of any person, and do not be disdainful of anything, for you have no person without his hour, and you have no thing without its place.

---

terribly upset. I am a burden and an embarrassment to them. I am sure they would rather have me dead! How could I possibly have a feeling of self-worth when everybody in the world considers me worthless and nothing but excess baggage which they would like to be rid of?"

I was taken aback by both this man's desperation and the apparent validity of his words, but I said, "Avi, have you ever seen a display in a jeweler's window? There are dazzling diamonds worth many thousands of dollars. Do you know what those diamonds looked like when they were first extracted from the mine? They looked like dirty, ugly, worthless pieces of glass. Anyone who would judge by their appearance would throw them away. However, there is a *meivin* (expert) who scans the ore, and he may pick up one of these 'worthless' rocks and say, 'Wow! I bet there is a million-dollar gem in this one!'

"An onlooker would say, 'Throw that piece of junk away and wash your hands from the dirt.' But the *meivin* says, 'Just wait and see what's in here.' He then sends the dirty rock to the processing plant, and eventually it yields a dazzling 15-carat diamond, which can blind a person with its brilliance. Of course, there is no way anyone can *put* such beauty into a 'dirty rock.' What the processing plant did was to cut away the layers that covered over the beauty. It only exposed the beauty that had been concealed.

"Avi," I said, "you are telling me that you are worthless. I am the *meivin* who can see the precious diamond within you. If you stay with us, we will help you reveal it."

Avi remained in treatment for three months, then went to a "halfway house," got a job, and continued to work on his recovery. Eventually he moved to independent living.

One day Annette, who was the administrator of the halfway house, received a call from a family whose elderly mother had died and had left an apartment full of furniture for which they had no use. They wished to donate the furniture to the halfway house. Annette called Avi to see whether he could find a way to move the furniture, and Avi assured her he could get a truck and take care of it.

Two days later Avi called to state that he was at the apartment with a truck, but that the furniture was old and dilapidated and could not be used. Annette told him that she did not wish to refuse a donation, and to bring the furniture anyway.

Avi loaded the truck, and at the halfway house was dragging an old, broken sofa up the stairs when an envelope containing 5,000 *shekels* (about $1800) fell from underneath the cushions. In the past, Avi had stolen purses and had broken into homes for as little as *10 shekels*. Here he had *5,000 shekels* of whose existence no one else knew. The rule of "finders-keepers" could easily

ד/ד ‏[ד] **רַבִּי** לְוִיטַס אִישׁ יַבְנֶה אוֹמֵר: מְאֹד מְאֹד הֱוֵי שְׁפַל
רוּחַ, שֶׁתִּקְוַת אֱנוֹשׁ רִמָּה.

---

have been applied, and there would have been no crime in his keeping the money.

Avi called the family to report his find. They thanked him, and suggested he give the money as a donation to the halfway house.

I subsequently met Avi and said, "Didn't I tell you that there was a beautiful diamond within you? How many otherwise honest people would simply have pocketed the money and not said a word about it? Your diamond is brilliant, Avi."

On a subsequent trip to Israel, Annette showed me a plaque that Avi had affixed to the door of the halfway house. It reads: DIAMOND PROCESSING CENTER.

Rabbi Shalom Dov understood the mishnah well. There is no person who should be scorned. You just have to be a *meivin*.

4.

מְאֹד מְאֹד הֱוֵי שְׁפַל רוּחַ
Be exceedingly humble in spirit

There is general agreement that humility is the foundation upon which all other desirable traits can be built. It is of interest, therefore, that Ramban, in the famous letter to his son, begins with instructing him to control his anger, stating that this will lead to humility, "which is the finest of all traits." If, indeed, humility is the finest of all traits, why not begin with it? Why begin with control of anger which will eventually result in humility?

I believe that Ramban is conveying an important concept which has only relatively recently begun to be accepted in psychology. It is probably true that inappropriate or unhealthy behavior may have its roots in some emotional trauma or other previous life experience which gave rise to the particular symptom. Conventional wisdom had been that gaining insight into the origin of the problem and understanding the misperception which gave rise to the problem would result in its alleviation. In many cases this did not happen. Many patients did indeed gain insight into and understanding of the origins of their problem, but this did not afford them any relief.

More recently, behavioral schools of psychology have come to the fore, whose emphasis is primarily on changing the pathologic behavior, leaving insight to a later date. There is reason to believe that this approach is more effective. For example, in treatment of alcoholism, insight into the origins of the problem are notoriously ineffective. The approach of Alcoholics Anonymous, "Don't pick up the first drink and come to AA meetings," has resulted in successful sobriety where traditional psychotherapy has failed.

Humility is a feeling or attitude, and as such may be difficult to acquire. *Behavior* that is associated with humility is easier to identify and implement. Rather than begin with abstract humility, Ramban begins with control of expression of

4. Rabbi Levitas of Yavneh says: Be exceedingly humble in spirit, for the anticipated end of mortal man is worms.

---

anger, since this is a behavior that is more amenable to control than is a feeling.

Ramban goes on to describe behavior that is conducive to humility: the way a person should walk, how one should talk, etc., because these are actions one can take. If one adopts these behaviors, it is likely that they will impact on him so that he indeed begins to *feel* humble.

Let us therefore try to implement the teaching of this mishnah by behaving the way a truly humble person would behave. We may not yet be humble, but if our *actions* will be those of a humble person, an attitude of humility is likely to follow.

מְאֹד מְאֹד הֱוֵי שְׁפַל רוּחַ, שֶׁתִּקְוַת אֱנוֹשׁ רִמָּה
Be exceedingly humble in spirit, for the anticipated end of mortal man is worms.

The wording of this mishnah requires careful analysis. The emphasis on being "exceedingly humble" is certainly understandable, because vanity is considered the worst trait a person can have. Whereas the Torah states that the Divine presence does not leave Israel even when they are in a state of sin (*Exodus* 25:8), this is not so with vanity, in which case God says that "I and a vain person cannot dwell together" (*Sotah* 5a). This notwithstanding, we find that humility can be misapplied, and that there are times when a person must assert himself and take a firm stand. King Saul was noted for his extreme humility which was certainly a virtue (*I Samuel* 9:21), yet the prophet sharply rebuked him for yielding to the wishes of the populace instead of asserting his authority as king. "Though you may be humble in your own eyes, I have set you at the head of the tribes of Israel" (*I Samuel* 15:17). When Moses sent the 12 spies to scout the land of Canaan, he offered a special prayer for Joshua, since he was concerned that because of his profound humility, Joshua might defer to the opinion of the majority (*Targum Yonasan, Numbers* 13:16). And again, "The humility of Zechariah resulted in the destruction of the Temple and the exile of our people" (*Gittin* 56a). It is evident that there can be misguided humility. Why then does the mishnah state categorically that one must be "very, very humble," which implies that there are no exceptions to this?

The answer may lie in the final words of the mishnah, "for the anticipated end of mortal man is worms." The Hebrew word the mishnah uses for "man" is *enosh*. The Talmud states that there are three terms for "man": *adam, ish, enosh*. These are not synonymous, but rather represent three levels of man. *Adam* refers to spiritual man, *ish* to one of lesser spirituality, and *enosh* to one devoid of spirituality.

Man is a composite creature, comprised of a physical body and a Divine soul. Spirituality and vanity are mutually exclusive, and the vain person is therefore one who takes pride in his earthly achievements. Earthly man, or *enosh*, is a person who knows nothing other than indulging in ephemeral physical pleasures. An *enosh* does not look forward to anything beyond his brief sojourn on earth, following which his physical body returns to its elements. It is the *enosh* component of our being that must be kept "exceedingly" humble, because this is where the ego resides. Insofar as *adam* is concerned, this is the spiritual person who is aware that he possesses a Divine soul, and there is no fear that the *neshamah* will be vain. The *neshamah* must maintain an attitude of pride, and not allow itself to be defiled by being lowered to a status beneath its dignity. The *neshamah's* awareness of its being one with God assures that it will never be vain.

The anticipated end of *enosh* is indeed nothing but worms, but this is not so with *adam*, who aspires to being in the Immanent Presence of the glory of God.

מְאֹד מְאֹד הֱוֵי שְׁפַל רוּחַ
Be exceedingly humble in spirit

There are many anecdotes that attest to the humility of our great Torah personalities. Let us cite just a few.

R' Yitzchak Blazer (Reb Itzele of Petersburg) was reputed to be a great Torah scholar. One time he was in attendance at a conference of the leading rabbis of eastern Europe, among whom was R' Yosef Dov Soloveitchik, father of R' Chaim of Brisk. R' Yosef Dov posed a complex Talmudic problem raised by his brilliant son, Reb Chaim, to the group. The attendees promptly entered into a highly sophisticated discussion to resolve the problem, whereby their broad and profound grasp of the Talmud was evident. However, in spite of their enormous erudition, they could not resolve the problem.

During the entire discussion, Reb Itzele sat quietly to one side, and did not participate in the deliberations. R' Yosef Dov wondered, "Is this the person who is reputed to be so knowledgeable in Talmud? Why, he has not offered a single idea!" R' Yosef Dov then proceeded to provide two brilliant solutions to the thorny issue, one which was his own, and a second which Reb Chaim had proposed.

Upon returning home, R' Yosef Dov asked for a copy of Reb Itzele's book, *Pri Yitzchak*, to see just how much of a Talmudist Reb Itzele indeed was. To his astonishment, he found that Reb Itzele has raised the problem posed by Reb Chaim, and had provided both of the suggested solutions! R' Yosef Dov was overcome with admiration of Reb Itzele's humility. He had been silent throughout the entire discussion, although he had mastered the issue and knew the correct answers! To restrain oneself and not demonstrate one's knowledge was virtually superhuman.

The Chida relates that the great Talmudist R' Shlomo Luria (*Maharshal*) had his study above a vegetable store, which was operated by a simple Jew, Reb

Avraham, who also resided there. One night the Maharshal remained in his study far into the night, and heard the voice of Reb Avraham, as he was studying the Talmud and elaborating upon it with the most profound insights. The Maharshal realized that Reb Avraham was a great scholar who had managed to conceal his erudition, and tried to enter into a discussion with him, whereupon Reb Avraham feigned ignorance. The Maharshal persisted, until Reb Avraham dropped his masquerade, but pleaded with the Maharshal not to expose him. He exacted a promise from him to that effect.

The Maharshal felt that the promise was binding only during his lifetime, and in his will he revealed that the humble proprietor of the vegetable store was in fact a Torah scholar without peer, and urged that the city of Lublin appoint Reb Avraham as his successor. Only with much pleading and prodding, and only in deference to the wishes of the Maharshal, did Reb Avraham consent to assume the position as rabbi of Lublin.

The chassidic master, the holy Yehudi of P'shische, once noted that his disciple, R' Bunim, appeared dejected. Upon inquiry as to the cause of his sadness, R' Bunim revealed that he had been sharply berated and humiliated. The master was enraged and said, "How did you respond to this insolent person?" R' Bunim said, "I hugged and kissed him." R' Bunim then took out the noted volume *Shevet Mussar,* saying that the author had rebuked him for his laxity in study of Torah and proper performance of mitzvos. "He pointed out to me that I had been deceiving myself and how distant I was from true devotion to God. What could I do? I embraced the book and kissed it."

R' Bunim said, "The reason a Jew is called a 'yud' is because the letter 'yud' is one tiny dot. If it is expanded vertically it becomes a 'vav,' and if it is broadened, it becomes a 'daled.' It remains a 'yud' only if it retains its diminutive shape. That is how a Jew must be. If he loses his humility and allows his self-concept to expand to grandiosity, he loses his identity as a true 'yud.' "

In our own generation, our great Torah personalities were also paragons of humility. The enormous erudition of R' Moshe Feinstein and R' Yaakov Kamenetzky were equaled only by their self-effacement.

In my correspondence with the Steipler *Gaon,* I addressed him as was proper to the Torah giant of our time. He pleaded that I refrain from using terms of praise "which are not fitting for me. The Talmud says, 'Woe unto the person who is thought to be greater than he is in fact.' "

When my teacher, R' Kreiswirth, invited the Steipler *Gaon* to his child's wedding, the *Gaon* responded that he was reluctant to leave the Holy Land. "Furthermore," he wrote, "I am afraid that I might cause an embarrassment to Torah. I have written some commentaries on the Talmud, which have, *Baruch Hashem*, been accepted in many yeshivos. As a result, some people have come to the erroneous conclusion that I am a great Torah personality. How-

[ה] **רַבִּי** יוֹחָנָן בֶּן בְּרוֹקָא אוֹמֵר: כָּל הַמְּחַלֵּל שֵׁם שָׁמַיִם
בְּסֵתֶר, נִפְרָעִין מִמֶּנּוּ בְּגָלוּי. אֶחָד שׁוֹגֵג וְאֶחָד
מֵזִיד בְּחִלּוּל הַשֵּׁם.

---

ever, I know the truth about myself, and just how distant I am from what a Torah personality should be.

"Therefore," the *Gaon* continued, "if I come to a place where this mistaken concept about me is assumed to be true, some people will come to see me in order to observe the one who has so great a reputation. When they discover the truth about me, they may say, 'Is this what a Torah personality is?' and in that way I will have brought much shame to the Torah, which is an unforgivable sin."

This is how a person whose entire life was devoted to Torah, and whose every move was dictated by halachah, thought about himself.

The midrash states that God boasted to the heavenly angels, "Look what a masterful being I have created." The lives of our great Torah personalities justify this Divine pride.

שֶׁתִּקְוַת אֱנוֹשׁ רִמָּה
For the anticipated end of mortal man is worms.

R' Yonasan Eibeschitz notes that the Hebrew word *tikvah* generally connotes positive anticipation and hope. It is therefore a bit unusual that this term is used in our mishnah. One would hardly say that the "hope" of a person is to end up with worms.

Perhaps the mishnah wishes to convey a reason why humility is so desirable a trait. King David says, "I am but a worm and not a man" (*Psalms 22:7*), and this expression of humility may be intended to elicit Divine mercy.

When the chassidic master, R' Levi Yitzchak of Berditchev, recited the Yom Kippur prayer for forgiveness, "We are full of sin, but You are full of compassion," he would say, "Master of the Universe, even if I am *full* of sin, how big is Levi Yitzchak altogether? How much sin can so small a person contain? But You, Master of the Universe, You are infinite, and since You are *full* of compassion, Your mercy is infinite! Certainly Your infinite mercy can forgive my finite sinfulness."

A person is judged according to his self-concept. If a person is grandiose and thinks himself to be great, his sins will be considered great. If he is humble, his sins will be lesser by proportion. This is why David pleads, "I am but a worm." As R' Levi Yitzchak argued, so small a creature cannot contain much sin, especially in comparison to God's endless compassion.

Perhaps this is the intention of the mishnah. It is to one's advantage to be exceedingly humble, because the *hope* of man is that he be considered a worm, a minuscule creature whose sins may be forgiven by the overwhelmingly greater Divine mercy.

R' Moshe Schreiber (*Chasam Sofer*) states that this may indeed be the defense a person will plead on Judgment Day. The Heavenly tribunal will then

5. **R**abbi Yochanan ben Beroka says: Whoever dese-crates the Name of Heaven in secret, they will exact punishment from him in public; unintentional and inten-tional, both are alike regarding desecration of the Name.

---

say, "Let us see how you conducted yourself during your lifetime." If it is found that the person was indeed humble, did not seek acclaim, was not arrogant, and did not respond in anger when he was slighted, his plea for a merciful judgment will be accepted. If, however, it turns out that one was vain, and was easily offended if he did not receive the respect he felt was his due, his defense will be rejected.

It is related that a *tzaddik* once visited a cemetery, and when he passed a particular tombstone, he asked to be given a chisel. To everyone's amazement he proceeded to chip away some of the lavish appellations that were inscribed on the monument about the deceased. He then said to the onlookers, "I have done this person a huge favor. The Heavenly tribunal was judging him accord-ing to the immense stature ascribed to him, and that would have been much to his detriment. He will now be judged more benevolently."

Only if one is exceedingly humble can one hope for a favorable verdict on Judgment Day.

5.

כָּל הַמְחַלֵּל שֵׁם שָׁמַיִם בְּסֵתֶר,
נִפְרָעִין מִמֶּנּוּ בְּגָלוּי

Whoever desecrates the Name of Heaven in secret, they will exact punishment from him in public

The term used in this mishnah re-quires some explanation. *Chilul Hashem,* desecrating the Divine Name, generally refers to an improper or inde-cent act that will cause others to lose respect for God and the Torah. Such an act done in privacy, unobserved by any other human being, may indeed be sinful, but by definition, it cannot be considered a *chilul Hashem,* since it did not impact on anyone else.

The mishnah may be conveying a most important teaching, something which has become increasingly evident. *There is no way that an improper act can be concealed.* We have seen that even with the ultimate of power, cover-ups have been unsuccessful.

Chilul Hashem is one of the gravest sins, for which there is no mercy. A person should therefore realize that although he may think he can conceal his misdeeds, *every improper act is a potential chilul Hashem.* Exposure is a virtual certainty, which will then be dealt with harshly. Furthermore, inasmuch as *chilul Hashem* may impact upon others and cause them to deter from righteousness, doing so inadvertently is still a grave sin, because the person who observes the behavior may emulate the wrongful act. He is not in the

ד/ו [ו] רַבִּי יִשְׁמָעֵאל בַּר רַבִּי יוֹסֵי אוֹמֵר: הַלּוֹמֵד עַל מְנָת
לְלַמֵּד, מַסְפִּיקִין בְּיָדוֹ לִלְמוֹד וּלְלַמֵּד; וְהַלּוֹמֵד
עַל מְנָת לַעֲשׂוֹת, מַסְפִּיקִין בְּיָדוֹ לִלְמוֹד וּלְלַמֵּד, לִשְׁמוֹר
וְלַעֲשׂוֹת.

---

position to know that it was inadvertent. When a misdeed becomes public knowledge, it is essential that the punishment be public as well, in order to prevent others from following suit.

Yes, we bear a heavy responsibility. As the nation that was chosen to bring Godliness to the world, we must be most watchful that our behavior bring only admiration of God and the Torah, and never the converse.

אֶחָד שׁוֹגֵג וְאֶחָד מֵזִיד בְּחִלּוּל הַשֵּׁם
Unintentional and intentional, both are alike regarding desecration of the Name.

Although desecration of the Divine Name is a grievous sin, why is it dealt with so harshly that an unintentional act is considered as severe a transgression as an intentional act?

There is a concept in halachah: *P'sik reisha v'lo yamus?* Is it possible to cut off a chicken's head and it should not die? This concept is applied when the consequences of an act are inevitable, in which case the perpetrator cannot claim, "I did not know that would happen," any more than one who cut off a chicken's head could say that he did not know it would die. If the consequences of an act are certain to occur, one cannot use a defense of "I didn't think that would happen." In such cases, unintentional acts are considered as though they were intentional.

The Talmud says that if a person who studied Torah behaves improperly, observers will say, "Woe unto the parents and teachers who taught him Torah." They may ascribe his misbehavior to Torah, assuming that Torah teaches people to behave improperly. There can be no greater desecration of the Divine Name than this. Furthermore, an onlooker has no way of knowing whether this person's behavior was unintentional or intentional. Inasmuch as we generally assume that a person knows what he is doing, it will be assumed that he is willfully behaving in this manner.

There are some sins for which there cannot be total forgiveness, even if a person has done proper *teshuvah*. The Talmud gives as an example someone who had an adulterous relationship which resulted in the birth of an illegitimate child. The consequences of his sin persist even if he genuinely regrets his behavior. The consequences of a Torah scholar misbehaving may lead to people losing respect for Torah, and may discourage them from observance of mitzvos. This is a consequence that cannot be undone.

Although the Torah considers an unintentional transgression to be a lesser sin than if it were committed intentionally, there is an exception to this. "Lack

6. R*abbi Yishmael bar Rabbi Yose says: One who studies [Torah] in order to teach is given the means to study and to teach; and one who studies [Torah] in order to practice is given the means to study and to teach, to observe and to practice.*

---

of intent due to ignorance of halachah for a person who should have known better is tantamount to intent" (*Ethics of the Fathers* 4:13). A Torah scholar may not claim ignorance of halachah as a defense.

The expectations Torah has of a person correspond to his status. R' Yehudah *HaNasi* said, "If I buy meat and do not pay my bill promptly, that constitutes a *chilul Hashem*" (*Yoma* 86a). This would not be so for a person of lesser stature. Each person is held to a standard appropriate for him, and acts which would be a *chilul Hashem* for a scholar would not be considered such for a person of lesser learning. However, there are kinds of behavior which would constitute a *chilul Hashem* for anyone, and in such cases, one cannot claim ignorance as a defense.

Because the consequences of *chilul Hashem* may be irrevocable, whatever constitutes a *chilul Hashem* for any given person will thus be dealt with most harshly.

6.

הַלּוֹמֵד עַל מְנָת לְלַמֵּד . . .
וְהַלּוֹמֵד עַל מְנָת לַעֲשׂוֹת
*One who studies [Torah]
in order to teach . . .
and one who studies [Torah]
in order to practice*

Many commentaries have difficulty with this mishnah. It appears that the person who learns Torah in order to practice it is given a much greater reward than one who learns in order to teach. Granted that practice of mitzvos is exceedingly great, but why does it outrank teaching of Torah, which is of overriding importance?

The author of *Benayos Baramah* provides a unique interpretation of the mishnah. It does not mean that one is "given the means" by God, but rather *should be given the means, i.e., by the community.*

There may be two types of Torah scholars. One type is the pure academic, the "ivory tower" scholar, as it were, whose ambition it is to teach Torah in educational institutions. We have great need for such scholars, and the community has a responsibility to see that they are adequately supported so that they can continue their study.

There is also another type of Torah scholar, who wishes not only to teach those students who come to him, but also wishes to do outreach, to go out to the community and convey Torah teaching to people who are not seeking it on their own, and bring them closer to Torah awareness and Torah living. This

ד/ז   [ז]   **רַבִּי** צָדוֹק אוֹמֵר: אַל תִּפְרוֹשׁ מִן הַצִּבּוּר; וְאַל תַּעַשׂ
עַצְמְךָ כְּעוֹרְכֵי הַדַּיָּנִין; וְאַל תַּעֲשֶׂהָ עֲטָרָה

person is following in the footsteps of the Patriarch Abraham, of whom the Torah says that he and his wife Sarah brought people to the belief in the true God, and uses the expression (*Genesis* 12:5), הַנֶּפֶשׁ אֲשֶׁר עָשׂוּ בְחָרָן, "the souls they *made*," i.e., fashioned them into believers. Similarly, R' Yishmael's use of the term עַל מְנָת לַעֲשׂוֹת means in order to fashion people, to provide them with Torah knowledge. This person must be supported adequately by the community, and be given the means to carry out his mission, so that he can indeed reach out to those who would otherwise remain bereft of Torah. He must be provided with adequate support not only to further his own study, but to be able to carry on with his outreach work.

We need both types of scholars, just as we need research scientists who will spend their days in the laboratory, and physicians who will implement the medical discoveries. Both are essential for saving physical lives, and both types of Torah scholars are essential for saving spiritual lives.

7.

אַל תִּפְרוֹשׁ מִן הַצִּבּוּר
Do not separate yourself from the community

In Chapter 6, the Talmud cites as one of the prerequisites for the acquisition of Torah נוֹשֵׂא בְּעֹל עִם חֲבֵרוֹ "to share his fellow's yoke" (6:6). This goes beyond the requirement of *ahavas Yisrael* (love of one's fellow man). Perhaps we may see this as a definition of *ahavas Yisrael;* i.e., it is not considered true love for another unless one is willing to share in his suffering.

R' Yerucham Levovitz elaborates on this concept. He states that it is not sufficient if we have a shallow commiseration with a person in distress. Our love for another person should be of a quality that his pain becomes our pain, because only then are we apt to adequately provide the help he needs. R' Yerucham points out that when the Torah relates that Moses left the palace of Pharaoh and saw how the Israelites were enslaved, "he gave his heart to feel their distress" (*Rashi, Exodus* 2:12), The Midrash states that he put his shoulder under the heavy loads they carried. Why? Because Moses knew that merely by observing their distress he would not be able to identify with them. He knew that it was necessary to personally experience their anguish in order to feel it.

The Talmud states that R' Nechunia was asked to what he attributed his longevity, and he responded, "I never gained honor through another's misery" (*Megillah* 28a). The commentaries note that this is hardly a highly spiritual trait. It would be simply inhumane to take pleasure in someone else's distress. They

7. **R**abbi Tzadok says: Do not separate yourself from the community; [when serving as a judge] do not act as a lawyer; do not make the Torah a crown for

---

therefore explain that R' Nechunia meant that he was never able to fully enjoy his own happy occasions when he knew that others were in distress. R' Nechunia's love and feeling for others was so profound that their suffering dampened the joy he could experience on happy occasions.

There are times when the community suffers, yet an individual may have the ability to extricate himself from the community's plight and be comfortable. This is a violation of the requirement to share in the burden of others.

A *chassid* who lived in abject poverty was told by his wife to ask his Rebbe for a blessing that he prosper. The *chassid*, who was interested primarily in advancing himself spiritually and looked to the Rebbe for spiritual guidance, was hesitant to bother him with mundane problems. However, his wife made him promise that he would tell the Rebbe of his troubles.

The Rebbe listened intently, then gave the *chassid* some money and said, "You must follow my instructions to the letter. You are to go home and use this money to buy the finest foods and delicacies, of which only you may partake. Under no circumstances are you to give your wife and children any of this food. When you have done so, come back and I will attend to your needs."

The *chassid*, always faithful to his Rebbe's instructions, did as he was told. When his wife and children saw him eating delicious food, their mouths watered and their hunger pangs intensified. The man had to sit there and refuse them the food, and each bite he took was torture. The anguish at eating while his family was hungry was unbearable, and each swallow felt like he was eating rocks.

The *chassid* later returned to the Rebbe who said, "If I were to bless you with prosperity, could you really enjoy it when you know that others have so little? Will your anguish not be greater than that of poverty?

"Nevertheless," the Rebbe said, "I will give you a blessing to prosper, but you should know how to put your fortune to good use."

The *chassid* did indeed prosper, but never again ate his meals at home. Instead, he would take food to the *hekdesh* (the community hostel for poor wayfarers), and share his food with the people there.

In the Book of *Ruth* we read that the two sons of Naomi died prematurely because they left their community when it was suffering famine. Although they did have the opportunity to relocate to a land where food was more plentiful, their desertion of their people at a time of distress was considered a grave sin.

The teaching of this mishnah is that we must not isolate ourselves when the community is under stress. We must participate with the community even when we have the means to live in greater comfort.

ד/ח לְהִתְגַּדֵּל בָּהּ, וְלֹא קַרְדֹּם לַחְפָּר בָּהּ. וְכָךְ הָיָה הִלֵּל אוֹמֵר: וְדְאִשְׁתַּמֵּשׁ בְּתָגָא חֳלָף. הָא לָמַדְתָּ: כָּל הַנֶּהֱנֶה מִדִּבְרֵי תוֹרָה, נוֹטֵל חַיָּיו מִן הָעוֹלָם.

[ח] **רַבִּי** יוֹסֵי אוֹמֵר: כָּל הַמְכַבֵּד אֶת הַתּוֹרָה, גּוּפוֹ מְכֻבָּד עַל הַבְּרִיּוֹת; וְכָל הַמְחַלֵּל אֶת

וְלֹא קַרְדֹּם לַחְפָּר בָּהּ
Nor a spade with which to dig.

This statement has elicited a variety of explanations, because it implies that one may not earn one's livelihood by means of one's Torah knowledge. Yet, Torah teachers and rabbis are paid a salary, as they must be, for teaching Torah or rendering halachic decisions. In the face of R' Tzadok's statement, how is this permissible?

One may consult the commentaries for their explanations. However, I have come across a unique interpretation in an anthology which gives no source for it, but it is as striking as it is novel.

This authority says that translating the Hebrew word *kardom* as "spade" is an error. The error occurred because it is used in relation to the verb "to dig." Nowhere in Scripture does *kardom* mean "spade." The word *kardom* appears in Scripture 5 times: *I Samuel* 13:20, 21; *Psalms* 74:5; *Judges* 9:48, and *Jeremiah* 46:22. In all these cases it is clear from the context that *kardom* is an "axe," not a spade. With this insight, R' Tzadok's statement takes on a new light, and immediately does away with the bothersome question.

An axe is not an instrument for digging, and to dig with an axe is inappropriate. If one has the proper competence to be a teacher of Torah or a rabbi, he is indeed appropriate for the job and therefore may use Torah to earn a livelihood. He is putting Torah to proper use, applying it to teaching, to conducting religious rituals, or to rendering halachic decisions. If a person lacks the necessary competence, yet tries to use Torah to earn a living even though he is not qualified for the position, then he is *digging with an axe,* which is an inappropriate tool for the job.

This is an exciting interpretation. All our great personalities who were teachers of Torah or community rabbis were qualified for their positions, and they were therefore not digging with a *kardom* (axe), but rather with a spade. They were in full compliance with R' Tzadok's teaching.

הָא לָמַדְתָּ: כָּל הַנֶּהֱנֶה מִדִּבְרֵי תוֹרָה, נוֹטֵל חַיָּיו מִן הָעוֹלָם
From this you derive that whoever seeks personal benefit from the words of the Torah removes his life from the world.

The Rabbi of Slonim raises some questions on this standard translation. First of all, this is essentially an exact repetition of what Hillel said, and is therefore superfluous. Secondly,

4/8   *self-glorification, nor a spade with which to dig. So too, Hillel used to say: He who exploits the crown [of Torah for personal benefit] shall fade away. From this you derive that whoever seeks personal benefit from the words of Torah removes his life from the world.*

8. **R**abbi Yose says: Whoever honors the Torah is himself honored by people; and whoever disgraces the

---

since it is a restatement of Hillel's teaching, it is hardly a "derivation." Finally, the expression "removes his life from the world" is rather strange. Elsewhere in this volume (3:10), the thought that one may forfeit his life by improper behavior is מִתְחַיֵּב בְּנַפְשׁוֹ, "bears guilt for his soul."

The Rabbi of Slonim therefore suggests a different interpretation of נוֹטֵל חַיָּיו מִן הָעוֹלָם. Inasmuch as Hillel said that one who violates the crown of Torah by improperly exploiting it is punished by a loss of life, it stands to reason that the converse is also true. I.e., if one appreciates Torah, he will *gain* life. Hence, it can be *derived* that if one enjoys Torah, נוֹטֵל חַיָּיו he will get a great deal out of life. This is hardly an exploitation of Torah, but rather an appreciation that studying Torah is the only worthwhile pleasure in the world, since all other pleasures are transitory at best. This interpretation fits well with the wording of the mishnah, and does away with all the difficulties of the standard translation.

8.

כָּל הַמְכַבֵּד אֶת הַתּוֹרָה,
גּוּפוֹ מְכֻבָּד עַל הַבְּרִיּוֹת
Whoever honors the Torah is himself honored by people

The chassidic master, R' Chaim of Kosov, gave the following interpretation of this mishnah.

If a person truly desires and values something, he will go to all lengths to get it, and will not consider anything as being beneath his dignity. If he knew that there is a precious diamond in the dust, he would not hesitate to bend down and search in the dust to find it. Similarly, if one truly values Torah, he will humble himself to gain whatever knowledge he can, even if it means learning from someone who is beneath his status. This type of humbling oneself does not at all compromise a person's dignity. To the contrary, it testifies to his greatness. One who shows his appreciation of Torah by willingness to learn from persons of lesser stature will gain the respect of others rather than lose it.

I have found this to be very true in medicine. Some doctors may be offended when they are asked to bring in a consultant, and will agree to seek an opinion only from someone who has great prominence. They seem to consider asking advice from anyone of lesser stature to be an insult. The test of a person's

[ט] **רַבִּי** יִשְׁמָעֵאל בְּנוֹ אוֹמֵר: הַחוֹשֵׂךְ עַצְמוֹ מִן הַדִּין, פּוֹרֵק מִמֶּנּוּ אֵיבָה וְגָזֵל וּשְׁבוּעַת שָׁוְא. וְהַגַּס לִבּוֹ

---

greatness is his willingness to humble himself to learn from everyone.

I can clearly see the validity of the interpretation of the Rabbi of Kosov. One who truly respects and values Torah will be willing to learn from anyone, and far from impinging on his dignity, it makes him even more honorable.

גּוּפוֹ מְכֻבָּד . . .
גּוּפוֹ מְחֻלָּל עַל הַבְּרִיּוֹת
Is himself honored . . . is himself disgraced by people.

If one reads this mishnah carefully, it does not say that "he will be honored" or that "he will be disgraced," but rather that "his body will be honored or disgraced." Just what does this mean?

The Talmud says that man was created on the last day of Creation. If he develops himself spiritually, he will be told that he was created last because he was the ultimate goal of all Creation. If he fails to live spiritually, he will be told, "even insects were created before you" (*Sanhedrin* 38a). Man can thus be extremely great or infinitesimally small.

Man can hardly be considered great by virtue of his body. Many animals in the wild have bodies that are far superior to that of man. The human body is essentially a receptacle for the Divine spirit, and its value then depends on the quality of that spirit. A cheap earthenware cup full of gold dust has great value for what it contains, but if it is full of sand it has very little value. Man's body is nothing but an earthenware vessel for the spirit.

The midrash states that Hillel told his disciples that he was on his way to do a mitzvah. "What kind of mitzvah?" they asked. "I am going to the bathhouse," Hillel answered. "Why is that a mitzvah?" his students asked. "Because man was created in the image of God, and to keep the image of God clean is a mitzvah," Hillel said (*Vayikra Rabbah* 34).

Man being created in the image of God does not refer to man's physical body, because God does not have a physical body. Rather, it is because the Torah and God are identical, as we are taught, "It (Torah) and He (Hashem) are one" (*Tikkunei Zohar* 64b). It is living a Torah life that makes man's physical body the vehicle whereby he becomes the image of God.

If a person honors Torah by living according to the principles of Torah, thereby developing his spirit, his body is respected for what it contains. If he abandons spirituality and strives only for the pleasures the body seeks, his body as such commands little respect.

9. **R**abbi Yishmael [R' Yose bar Chalafta's] son says:
One who withdraws from judgment removes from
himself hatred, robbery, and [the responsibility for] an
unnecessary oath, but one who is too self-confident

9.

הַחוֹשֵׂךְ עַצְמוֹ מִן הַדִּין
One who withdraws from judgment

One of the explanations offered by Rashi is that a judge should attempt to bring about a compromise rather than apply the letter of the law. Some have questioned why the mishnah would recommend compromise, inasmuch as the Talmud cites Moses as having disagreed with his brother. Aaron sought a peaceful settlement, whereas Moses insisted on strict application of the law (*Sanhedrin* 6b). It would seem preferable that we follow the teachings of Moses.

The commentaries explain that Moses was in a unique position, because inasmuch as he received the halachah from God Himself, he was assured of not erring, whereas a judge may think he is applying the letter of the law, although his understanding of the law may actually be flawed. In this case he would be guilty of giving one of the litigants wrongful possession of the disputed item. Hence it is better to seek a compromise, because when the litigants agree to a settlement, they essentially relinquish claims to more than they received.

It is of interest that Moses once withdrew himself from a case, in keeping with another interpretation of the first portion of the mishnah, which is that a judge should withdraw עַצְמוֹ, i.e., his personal interest from a case. If he cannot divest himself of that, he should disqualify himself as a judge.

The Torah relates that the daughters of Tzelafchad requested that they be declared the rightful heirs to the portion of the land that would have been allotted to their deceased father. They added that he died as a result of a personal sin, and he did not join the Korach rebellion against Moses. Moses then brought their case before God (*Numbers* 27:1-5).

The commentaries said that Moses did not wish to rule on the case, because the daughters of Tzelafchad had said that their father had remained loyal to Moses in the Korach rebellion. Moses felt that he therefore might be biased in favor of the daughters.

How careful one must be to avoid bias by personal interest can be seen from an incident involving the chassidic Rabbi of Apt, who sat as a judge on a *beis din* (rabbinical court). On the third day of the proceedings, the Rabbi of Apt abruptly withdrew from the case without giving any reason. The following Friday night, when he put on his Shabbos kaftan, he found in his pocket an

בְּהוֹרָאָה, שׁוֹטֶה, רָשָׁע, וְגַס רוּחַ. ד/י

יז] **הוּא** הָיָה אוֹמֵר: אַל תְּהִי דָן יְחִידִי, שֶׁאֵין דָּן יְחִידִי
אֶלָּא אֶחָד. וְאַל תֹּאמַר: ״קַבְּלוּ דַעְתִּי!״ שֶׁהֵן
רַשָּׁאִין וְלֹא אָתָּה.

---

envelope with money which one of the litigants had placed there as a bribe, assuming that the rabbi would promptly find the money.

The rabbi then explained, "During the first two days of the proceedings, I was totally objective. On the third day, I felt myself drawn to favor one of the litigants. I had no idea why, but having lost my objectivity, I withdrew from the case. It was only later that I discovered I had been offered a bribe." The rabbi pointed out, "One can see how powerful the influence of a bribe can be. It had affected my objectivity even though I was not consciously aware of it."

This is why the mishnah stresses, according to this interpretation, that a judge must be most cautious to eliminate the עַצְמוֹ, any personal interest from the case at hand.

וְהַגַּס לִבּוֹ בְּהוֹרָאָה, שׁוֹטֶה, רָשָׁע, וְגַס רוּחַ
But one who is too self-confident in issuing legal decisions is a fool, wicked, and arrogant of spirit

How the virtues of being humble and wise can assure a correct halachic judgment can be seen from an incident involving R' Moses Feinstein, whose humility and wisdom are legendary.

A couple came to R' Feinstein to execute a *get* (halachic divorce). They brought their pet dog with them, and the dog was put into a separate room. The scribe then proceeded to write the *get,* which was signed by two witnesses and duly delivered. When the couple was about to leave, the door to the room where the dog had been placed was opened, and the dog promptly ran to the husband, joyously jumping at his master as devoted dogs will do. R' Feinstein called the couple back, tore up the *get* and demanded, "I beswear you to tell the truth! This woman is not your wife, is she?" The stunned husband reluctantly admitted that his wife had objected to the divorce, and he therefore brought another woman to pose as his wife.

Rabbi Feinstein explained to the onlookers, "This was no clairvoyance on my part. When the door was opened, the dog promptly ran to the husband, and did not acknowledge the woman. Had this been the wife, the dog would have run from one to the other."

Scripture says, "Wisdom derives from nothingness" (*Job* 28:12). The commentaries remark that true wisdom can be found only in one who is self-effaced, who considers himself to be "nothing." It was R' Feinstein's profound humility which gave rise to his wisdom. How true are the words of our sages, "A wise person surpasses even a prophet" (*Bava Basra* 12a).

in issuing legal decisions is a fool, wicked, and arrogant of spirit.

10. **H**e was accustomed to say: Do not act as a judge alone, for none judges alone except One; and do not say, "Accept my view," for they are permitted to, but not you.

10.

אַל תְּהִי דָן יְחִידִי
Do not act as a judge alone

In addition to the obvious meaning that one should convene a tribunal of at least three judges to hear a case, there is also another message in this mishnah, which is a continuation of the previous mishnah by the same author. Therein he said that one should not be arrogant in judgment.

The Talmud states that when a Rabbinic tribunal sits in judgment, the Divine Presence rests upon them, as it is written: "God stands in the Divine Assembly, in the midst of judges shall He judge" (*Psalms* 82:1). The Divine Presence assures that the verdict will be just. The Talmud also states that although the Divine Presence does not abandon even a sinful person, it cannot condone any vanity. Of the vain person it is said, "He and I cannot dwell together" (*Arachin* 15b). And again, "Whoever walks with an overbearing attitude, it is as though he pushes God's feet" (*Berachos* 43b).

If a judge is that vain that he believes he is so competent that he can be a lone judge without convening a tribunal, his vanity causes the Divine Presence to absent itself. He is left to judge *alone*, without the spirit of God to assure that justice is done.

The function of the Divine Presence is illustrated in an incident involving Rabbi Yechezkel Landau (*Noda BeYehudah*), whose students posed a question to him about whether a certain lesion in the lungs of an animal is kosher or *tereifah*. When the *Noda BeYehudah* responded that it was kosher, one of the students showed him an authoritative ruling to the contrary. The *Noda BeYehudah* acknowledged his mistake and said, "If this question had been an actual one, and the lungs of the animal had been brought before me for a ruling, I would not have made this error. When a *posek* delivers a halachic decision on a practical question, the Presence of God assures that he does not err. Inasmuch as this was a theoretical rather than a practical question, the Divine Presence was not with me, and with my unaided reason I can err."

It is this humility that invites the Presence of God to guide halachic authorities to the correct decision.

שֶׁאֵין דָן יְחִידִי אֶלָּא אֶחָד
For none judges alone except One

There is an interesting, novel interpretation to this mishnah.

As we have noted earlier, the in-

ד/יא ‏[יא]‏ **רַבִּי** יוֹנָתָן אוֹמֵר: כָּל הַמְקַיֵּם אֶת הַתּוֹרָה מֵעֹנִי,
סוֹפוֹ לְקַיְּמָהּ מֵעֹשֶׁר; וְכָל הַמְבַטֵּל אֶת הַתּוֹרָה
מֵעֹשֶׁר, סוֹפוֹ לְבַטְּלָהּ מֵעֹנִי.

structions and advice that *Ethics of the Fathers* gives to judges are not restricted to jurists. Every person acts as a judge in his own life, deliberating over and making many judgments. Many of these involve a difference of opinion with others. If a person thinks he is right, should he hold to his opinion even if outnumbered by those who oppose it?

While there may not be a hard and fast rule to go by, it is fairly safe to say that if you are the *only one* to hold that opinion, and everyone else is of another mind, they are probably right. It is very unusual for a person who is right to not have at least several people who concur with him.

There is a Yiddish proverb, "If three people say that you are drunk, go sleep it off." We apply this principle in psychiatry as well. If a number of people in a room hear a loud voice but they do not see a speaker, it is likely an announcement coming over the public-address system. If only *one* person hears a voice and all the others hear nothing, it is undoubtedly a hallucination. This has led to the dictum that "insanity is a minority of one."

There is a single incident in history where this was not the case. The Patriarch Abraham had come to the true realization that there was but one Supreme Being, at a time when *everyone*, including his father and brothers, worshipped pagan idols. Abraham stood his ground and did not yield, even though he was a minority of one. In this case Abraham was right and all the others were wrong.

There was no repetition of such a happening, and one should not think that just as Abraham was right even though everyone in the world was wrong, therefore he can claim that privilege for himself. If not a *single person* agrees with you, it is absurd to think that you are the sole possessor of the truth.

This may be the message of the mishnah. If you are a יָחִיד, totally alone in your judgment, do not be obstinate. There was only one אֶחָד who was correct in defying the entire world, and that was *the* אֶחָד, i.e., the one whom Scripture refers to as אֶחָד הָיָה אַבְרָהָם (*Ezekiel* 33:24). For the rest of us, we should not say, "You should accept my opinion," because if you are a יְחִידִי, then the multitude is right rather than you.

11.

כָּל הַמְקַיֵּם אֶת הַתּוֹרָה מֵעֹנִי,
סוֹפוֹ לְקַיְּמָהּ מֵעֹשֶׁר
Whoever fulfills the Torah despite
poverty will ultimately fulfill it in wealth

Several commentaries challenge this interpretation of the mishnah, because it is evident that many devoted Torah scholars and people who were meticulous in observance of Torah lived in poverty all their lives. Where then is the

11. **R**abbi *Yonasan says: Whoever fulfills the Torah despite poverty will ultimately fulfill it in wealth; but whoever neglects the Torah because of wealth will ultimately neglect it in poverty.*

---

fulfillment of the mishnah's promise? They therefore say that the mishnah is not making a promise. Rather, it is making a statement, that if a person observed Torah when he was in poverty, he will likely continue to observe Torah if his fortune changes and he becomes wealthy. However, if someone was not observant of Torah when he was wealthy, he is unlikely to observe Torah if he falls into poverty.

This interpretation of the mishnah conveys an important psychological concept. One of the most thorny issues we confront in psychology is that of *control*. Many people have great difficulty in relinquishing control — or better yet, in acknowledging that they are in fact *not* in control of many of the things they imagine they are in control of. The illusion of control can result in very serious adjustment problems in life simply because an illusion is a distortion of reality. Conducting one's life on a misperception of reality cannot but result in trouble.

The control issue has undoubtedly become a greater problem in recent years, because in the past there were not too many things that were under our control. As science and technology progressively give us more and more things that we can control, the illusion of control of everything becomes stronger.

In the days of the horse and buggy, a driver who wanted the horse to turn to the right would pull on the rein, which caused the horse discomfort as the pressure of the bit increased. To eliminate the discomfort, the horse turned to the right. The driver did not actually *control* the horse, but rather made it an offer that was difficult to refuse. It is possible that if the horse was starved and saw a pile of hay to the left, it might ignore the pull to the right and go to the left. This changed radically with the introduction of the automobile, because now the driver *controls* the direction of the car, and it cannot possibly disobey him.

When I was a child I had a little toy truck which I pushed along the floor. Recently I saw a 3-year-old child sitting with a control panel, gleefully *controlling* every movement of a little vehicle all the way across the room. It is certain that this child will grow up with a greater sense of control than his grandparents had.

A person about to leave the office may dial home and by pushing a few numbers activate the air-conditioning and turn on the washing machine and the oven, so that everything will be ready by the time he comes home. The epitome of remote control was when the spaceship, Explorer II, was beyond the solar system, yet responded to a command from the space center control room some *two billion miles away*. All these wonderful technological advances have had a side-effect of intensifying our illusion of control.

ד/יב   [יב] **רַבִּי** מֵאִיר אוֹמֵר: הֱוֵי מְמַעֵט בְּעֵסֶק, וַעֲסֹק בַּתּוֹרָה;
וֶהֱוֵי שְׁפַל רוּחַ בִּפְנֵי כָל אָדָם; וְאִם בָּטַלְתָּ מִן

Many parents think they can control their children, and some husbands and wives think they can control their spouse, neither of which is healthy or true. People with a need to dominate seek control over others. One of the most striking negative consequences of the need to feel in control is that seen in the alcoholic, whose life may be disintegrating right before his eyes, yet he is adamant in insisting that he can control his drinking and that he has *every* facet of his life under perfect control.

A person who lives in poverty is not likely to have much of an illusion of control. The simple fact that he cannot have many of the things he would like to have proves to him that he does not have control. It is much different with a person who has been successful and is wealthy, who is likely to believe that his shrewd grasp of economics enabled him to amass wealth. Because he can gratify many of his desires, he is apt to believe that he is in control of his destiny.

What happens when a poor person strike it rich? There is always a risk that he may fall into the trap of thinking himself in control, but if he will remember the days when he was destitute and had very little control of things, he may avoid this pitfall. We find this in Moses' message to the Israelites as they were about to enter Canaan. Moses told them that when they prosper they may think that their good fortune is a result of their own efforts and that they are in control, and may consequently falter in their trust in God. He therefore reminded them that they had been helpless slaves, and that it was God Who delivered them from slavery. He told them to remember their 40 years of wandering in the desert when they were totally dependent on God providing them with food and water in the barren wilderness. They should never forget, even when they live in luxury, that they are totally dependent on God (*Deuteronomy* 8:11-18). Indeed, we are taught that except for the freedom of choosing between moral right or wrong, every facet of our lives is under Divine control (*Berachos* 33b).

However, if a person was well to do and was under the illusion of control, he may well retain that illusion even when things go badly for him. Just as the alcoholic is obstinate in relinquishing the illusion of control, so is the person who loses his wealth apt to continue to think he is in control. In fact, the very fact that he lost his wealth may be such a blow to his ego that he defensively *intensifies* his illusion.

I recall the case of a steel magnate who lost everything — family, fortune, social status — as a result of his drinking, and when he completed his in-patient treatment and arrangements were initiated for his going to a halfway house, he was obstinately opposed to this, in spite of the fact that *he had no place to go.* Even at the halfway house he continued to act the role of a powerful steel

12. **R**abbi *Meir said: Limit your business activities and engage in Torah study. Be of humble spirit before every person. If you should neglect the [study of]*

---

magnate! The moment of truth came when, "One day I was standing in front of the halfway house with my hands in my pockets, when it suddenly occurred to me that *I had no keys.* I did not have anything to lock up." Then he went on to say, "After six years of sobriety, I can now show you the keys to my apartment, my office, and my car. Whenever I look at these keys I am reminded of when I had none, and that if I should ever again think that I can control alcohol, I will likely have no keys again."

This important concept is conveyed by this mishnah. Torah observance requires trust in God. A person who observed Torah while he was poor very likely realized the limitations of his own powers, and came to trust in God. If he becomes wealthy and remembers his earlier days, he will retain his trust in God. However, a person whose wealth resulted in his thinking himself as all-powerful may very likely not develop trust in God and may retain the illusion of omnipotence even when stark reality tells him otherwise.

It would therefore be wise if we pay attention to what we say in our prayers and in the *bentching* (blessing after meals), and remember our dependence on God.

12.

הֱוֵי מְמַעֵט בְּעֵסֶק, וַעֲסֹק בַּתּוֹרָה
Limit your business activities and engage in Torah study.

A more precise translation of this mishnah would be, "limit your *engagement* in business activities." This can be understood by a remark made by one of the chassidic masters, who received a *chassid* who owned a shoe factory. The *chassid* proceeded to describe his business in great detail, and it was evident that he was totally immersed in it.

The Rebbe could not resist quipping, "I have seen people put their feet into shoes, but this is the first time I have ever seen anyone put his entire head into shoes!"

The Rabbi of Kotzk echoed this opinion when he referred to the verse (*Psalms* 128:2) which reads, "You will be fortunate if you eat the labor of your hands." "Certainly," said the Rabbi, "but let it be *your hands* that are involved in labor and not your head." In other words, we should indeed work to earn a livelihood, but our minds should not be totally saturated with our work. Although we must work, our thoughts should not forsake Torah.

You may ask: Is it realistic to expect a person to engage in business or concentrate on his work yet be thinking of Torah? Let us take the example of a mother who has an infant child. She puts the child to sleep in the crib and goes about doing her housework — cooking, cleaning, laundry — or perhaps engages in a business that she is operating out of her home. At the slightest, almost inaudible whimper she drops whatever she is doing and runs in to the child. Even though she is busy with whatever she is doing, the baby never leaves her mind completely. At the slightest sound, the baby totally occupies her mind. That is how it should be with Torah. Although we may engage in work or business, we should not be totally distracted from Torah.

Furthermore, being engaged in work or business should not have to distract us from Torah at all. When we work and transact business according to the teachings of Torah and with the *kavannah* that we are doing so, we are indeed engaged in Torah.

One of the chassidic masters lodged at an inn, and in the morning he saw the innkeeper put on his *tallis* and *tefillin*. Just then a customer came in and asked to buy a quart of ale. The innkeeper filled the quart and handed it to the customer, who then asked him to lower the price. The innkeeper turned back, poured the ale back into the barrel and began his *davening*.

The Rebbe later asked him to explain his behavior. "It is very simple," the innkeeper said. "When the customer asked for a quart of ale, I had the opportunity to fulfill the mitzvah in the Torah to give honest weights and measures (*Deuteronomy* 25:15), and I may do a mitzvah before *davening*. When he began to haggle about the price, that was engaging in business, and I do not engage in business before *davening*." This simple, pious person was thinking about the Torah while he was serving a customer.

Perhaps the mishnah is telling us to minimize our engaging in "business." Consciously applying Torah teachings while working or transacting *is* engaging in Torah rather than in business.

The Chofetz Chaim sold the books he wrote, and would leaf through each volume to make certain that all the pages were there, lest he sell a defective product. Think of how much he could have learned during the time he spent checking the books! It is related that while he did the checking he was overheard to be reciting this mishnah, to *engage* in Torah. To make certain that he was not selling a defective product constituted engaging in Torah.

I once entered a small shop in Jerusalem, and found the proprietor studying *Mishnayos*. I asked him whether he had the item I was looking for. He looked up, smiled, and said, "Everything I have is displayed on the shelves. If you see anything you like, I will be glad to sell it to you," and promptly returned to his studying.

I did find something which I bought, and after he handed me the wrapped item he said, "I am a *Kohen*. Let me give you a *berachah*." I left the store having acquired the item I bought, a precious *berachah*, and something even more valuable: an interpretation of this mishnah.

הֱוֵי מְמַעֵט בְּעֵסֶק
Limit your business activities

The Chofetz Chaim journeyed to Warsaw. One man went to the train station early to take a place where he would be the first to greet the *tzaddik*. He did so, and invited the Chofetz Chaim to stay at his home, an invitation which the *tzaddik* accepted.

Riding in the carriage, the Chofetz Chaim asked his host whether he was setting aside specific hours for Torah study. His host began to apologize and defend himself, explaining that his business is so terribly time consuming that he just cannot tear himself away for scheduled hours of Torah study.

"You are in error, my dear friend," the Chofetz Chaim said. "One time a villager took the train into the city to meet with some official, and because the train was going rather slow, he feared he might be late for his appointment. He arose and began pushing on the wall of the coach. 'What are you doing?' someone asked him.

'I'm trying to get the train into the city faster,' the villager said.

"The other passengers laughed, saying, 'You are so foolish. It is the engine that is pulling the train, and your pushing against the wall is not going to make it go faster.'

"It is much the same with you, my dear friend," the Chofetz Chaim said. "God is providing for you, and your exerting extra effort is not going to get you any more than He has determined to give you. I assure you that you will not earn less if you devote more time to Torah study."

A similar thought was voiced by R' Yosef Ber of Brisk, who asked a man what he was doing.

"I have a business," the man answered, and proceeded to describe the nature of his business to the rabbi.

"Yes," R' Yosef Ber said, "but what are you doing?"

The man was a bit bewildered that the rabbi had not understood him, and again described what he was doing.

Again R' Yosef Ber asked, "But what are you doing?"

"I have already explained to you twice what I do for a living. Just what is it that is not clear?" the man asked.

R' Yosef Ber said, "Providing you with a living is what *God* is doing. I asked you what it is that *you* are doing."

It is related that R' Levi Yitzchak of Berditchev once saw a man running in the street. "Where are you running to?" the Rabbi asked.

"I have no time to talk with you now, Rabbi," the man said. "I am hurrying to make my *parnassah* (livelihood)."

"How do you know that your *parnassah* is in the direction you are heading? Perhaps it is in the other direction and you may be running away from it."

If we have proper faith and trust in God, and take to heart the lesson our ancestors learned from the *manna* in the desert — that God will provide for our needs as long as we act properly — we will be able to implement the teaching of this mishnah.

ד/יג הַתּוֹרָה, יֵשׁ לְךָ בְּטֵלִים הַרְבֵּה כְּנֶגְדֶּךָ; וְאִם עָמַלְתָּ בַּתּוֹרָה,
יֵשׁ לוֹ שָׂכָר הַרְבֵּה לִתֶּן לָךְ.

[יג] **רַבִּי** אֱלִיעֶזֶר בֶּן יַעֲקֹב אוֹמֵר: הָעוֹשֶׂה מִצְוָה אַחַת
קוֹנֶה לוֹ פְּרַקְלִיט אֶחָד; וְהָעוֹבֵר עֲבֵרָה אַחַת
קוֹנֶה לוֹ קַטֵּיגוֹר אֶחָד. תְּשׁוּבָה וּמַעֲשִׂים טוֹבִים כִּתְרִיס
בִּפְנֵי הַפֻּרְעָנוּת.

וְאִם בָּטַלְתָּ מִן הַתּוֹרָה, יֵשׁ לְךָ בְּטֵלִים
הַרְבֵּה כְּנֶגְדֶּךָ; וְאִם עָמַלְתָּ בַּתּוֹרָה,
יֵשׁ לוֹ שָׂכָר הַרְבֵּה לִתֶּן לָךְ

If you should neglect the [study of] Torah,
you will have many excuses to neglect it;
but if you labor in the Torah, He has
ample reward to give you.

T he standard translation leaves something to be desired, because the two statements should have paradoxical (i.e., opposite) conclusions. To say that if you neglect Torah you will find many excuses, and (if you do the opposite) and labor in Torah you will receive much reward is not the logical pair of opposites. A more accurate translation might be, "If you are idle of Torah, you will have much idleness, whereas if you study Torah, you will have much gain." This version lends itself to the following explanation.

We noted earlier that all of a person's activities can become part of Torah. Inasmuch as one must be in optimal physical and emotional health to devote himself to Torah study, anything that promotes health and is conducive to Torah study is considered part of Torah study. If a person eats with the intention that the energy he obtains from the food will enable him to study Torah, then his eating contributes to the mitzvah of studying Torah. If he rests because proper rest will make his mind more receptive to what he learns, then rest becomes part of the mitzvah. If he works to earn a livelihood so that he may be able to learn Torah, then work becomes part of the mitzvah. With sincere intent, a person can convert *all* of his daily activities into the mitzvah of Torah study. He can consequently receive reward for doing a mitzvah for his eating, sleeping, working, etc. The cumulative reward will certainly be very great.

On the other hand, if one is idle from Torah, then toward what goal are his daily activities directed? Very often not to any goal at all, and one enters the vicious cycle of eating to live and living to eat. Everything one does is then essentially idle.

The mishnah is now very coherent. Idleness from Torah renders everything futile, whereas if one labors in Torah, everything becomes part of the Torah-study mitzvah and one is handsomely rewarded.

4/13   *Torah, you will have many excuses to neglect it; but if you labor in the Torah, He has ample reward to give you.*

13. **R**abbi Eliezer ben Yaakov says: He who fulfills even a single mitzvah gains himself a single advocate; and he who commits even a single transgression gains himself a single accuser. Repentance and good deeds are like a shield against retribution.

13.

הָעוֹשֶׂה מִצְוָה אַחַת קוֹנֶה לוֹ פְּרַקְלִיט אֶחָד;
וְהָעוֹבֵר עֲבֵרָה אַחַת קוֹנֶה לוֹ קַטֵּיגוֹר אֶחָד

He who fulfills even a single mitzvah gains himself a single advocate; and he who commits even a single transgression gains himself a single accuser.

We know that there are no superfluous words in the mishnah. Therefore we must take note that the mishnah states " a *single* mitzvah, a *single* advocate, a *single* transgression, a *single* accuser." R' Shlomo Kluger points out that the mishnah would have read just as well if the word "single" were omitted. He therefore suggests translating *achas* and *echod* as meaning "the one" rather than "single," and he then gives the following interpretation.

It is indeed true that for each mitzvah a person does he acquires an advocate and that for each transgression he acquires an accuser. These are thought of as "benign angels" or "hostile angels" who defend or accuse a person who is being judged by the heavenly tribunal. However, there are times when God Himself testifies against a sinful person, as is stated in *Malachi* (3:5), that for sins that result from the denial of God, the Almighty Himself acts as a witness. Certainly, R' Shlomo Kluger states, Divine mercy is far greater than Divine harshness, and if God testifies against someone who denies Him, He certainly testifies favorably for those who believe in Him.

Therefore, if a person does "*the* one mitzvah," i.e., the one mitzvah which is the basis of all of Torah, the belief in God, then "*the* One," i.e., God Himself is his advocate and pleads his cause. If a person does "*the* one transgression," i.e., denial of God, which is the root of all transgressions, then "*the* One," God Himself, will bear witness against him.

How awesome it is to realize that a person can invoke God Himself as a witness when he is being judged!

ד/יד   **[יד] רַבִּי** יוֹחָנָן הַסַּנְדְּלָר אוֹמֵר: כָּל כְּנֵסְיָה שֶׁהִיא לְשֵׁם
שָׁמַיִם, סוֹפָהּ לְהִתְקַיֵּם; וְשֶׁאֵינָהּ לְשֵׁם שָׁמַיִם,
אֵין סוֹפָהּ לְהִתְקַיֵּם.

14.

כָּל כְּנֵסְיָה שֶׁהִיא לְשֵׁם שָׁמַיִם, סוֹפָהּ לְהִתְקַיֵּם
Every assembly that is dedicated to the
sake of Heaven will have an enduring effect

The author of *Benayos Baramah* gives this mish-nah a unique interpretation, which conveys an important psychological insight.

The standard translation of לְשֵׁם שָׁמַיִם is "for the sake of Heaven." The literal meaning of the words is "for the name of the sky." In the account of Creation, the Torah says that God created the firmament, רָקִיעַ, and called it שָׁמַיִם, upon which Rashi comments that the word שָׁמַיִם is a composite of the two words אֵשׁ (fire) and מַיִם (water). The word שָׁמַיִם means that God combined fire and water to form the sky or heaven.

Of course, fire and water are the prototypes of polar opposites that cannot coexist. Either the water extinguishes the fire, or the fire vaporizes the water. The miracle of Creation was that God caused these two incompatible entities to join together to form the sky or heaven (*Genesis* 1:8). Thus, the original word for sky was רָקִיעַ, but God gave it the name שָׁמַיִם to teach us that it is possible for polar opposites to not only coexist, but even to cooperate to form the heavens.

One of the prevailing concepts in our culture is that conflicts must be resolved. One of the goals of psychotherapy is to help people overcome and resolve conflicts, as though living with conflict is intolerable. This concept has also led to the attempt to resolve differences among religions, so that some clerics advocate dialogues between representatives of different faiths. They may also promote "rotation" of clerics, inviting rabbis to conduct services in churches, and priests or ministers to conduct services in synagogues. This is not a new phenomenon. Such dialogues have occurred since the Middle Ages, and history has demonstrated that they do nothing to eliminate hostility between advocates of different faiths.

It would be well if we understood that it is not always necessary to resolve conflicts. Different faiths can coexist without compromise, a person can maintain good mental health even if he harbors some conflicts, and it certainly would enhance family unity if various members of the family could agree to disagree, and maintain love and cooperation even though they may differ in their ideas.

This is equally true of any group that convenes to achieve something. It is virtually impossible to have unanimity of opinion in a large group. If there is a divergence of opinion, the group may be paralyzed into inaction. How much

14. **R**abbi Yochanan the Sandler says: Every assembly that is dedicated to the sake of Heaven will have an enduring effect; but one that is not for the sake of Heaven will not have an enduring effect.

more could be accomplished if people agreed to disagree civilly instead of trying to force a compromise which leaves everyone dissatisfied!

The Talmud tells us that although the schools of Hillel and Shammai were often in sharp disagreement about certain rulings, they nevertheless lived in harmony. In fact, although according to the school of Hillel the children of some relationships that the school of Shammai sanctioned were illegitimate, the followers of the two schools nevertheless intermarried. One would tell the other, "This particular *shidduch* is not for you, because according to your school, this person is illegitimate" (see *Yevamos* 13a). If people are sincere and tolerant, harmony can exist without conformity.

This is what the mishnah is telling us. שָׁמַיִם should be taken literally; i.e., the name which God gave the heaven when He created it, and called it שָׁמַיִם, a composite of fire and water, two polar opposites that tolerated one another and united in harmony to form the heaven.

We may apply this interpretation to a comment of the Rabbi of Kotzk, who cited the verse (*Psalms* 115:16), "The heaven, the heaven is Hashem's but the earth He has given to man," and remarked, "God made the heaven שָׁמַיִם, and He gave the earth to man that man should make *it* into שָׁמַיִם, heaven.

We may understand this to mean that God made the harmony of opposites in heaven, and we are to accomplish this on earth. The Torah says that we are to follow in God's ways, which Rashi interprets as meaning that we are to emulate the Divine attributes (*Deuteronomy* 13:5). In keeping with this, we should make the effort to establish harmony even when there is diversity.

It is unfortunate that in our holy land there is so much factionalism and intolerance. When we were attacked by enemies, all differences disappeared, and everyone united to protect our land and its inhabitants. Can we not achieve the same harmony when we are at peace? Can we not realize that even when there is apparent peace we are still the target of hostility, and that our secret weapon is unity? The Talmud states that in the time of King Ahab, many Jews were guilty of the worst sin — idolatry — yet they triumphed because there was unity among them (*Vayikra Rabbah* 26:2).

The Torah states, "I will give peace in the land . . . and a sword will not cross your land" (*Leviticus* 26:6). This is a true blessing, to have peace even when not under attack from enemies.

The mishnah therefore says that any assembly that can be in harmony, like שָׁמַיִם, will indeed produce long-term results.

[טו] **רַבִּי** אֶלְעָזָר בֶּן שַׁמּוּעַ אוֹמֵר: יְהִי כְבוֹד תַּלְמִידְךָ
חָבִיב עָלֶיךָ כְּשֶׁלָּךְ; וּכְבוֹד חֲבֵרְךָ כְּמוֹרָא
רַבָּךְ; וּמוֹרָא רַבָּךְ כְּמוֹרָא שָׁמָיִם.

15.

יְהִי כְבוֹד תַּלְמִידְךָ חָבִיב עָלֶיךָ כְּשֶׁלָּךְ
Let the honor of your student be as dear to you as your own

This mishnah, which describes the ideal teacher/student relationship, may raise the concern of those who remember the educational climate several decades ago.

As we mentioned earlier, students of the Lakewood yeshivah, for example, when asked where they learned would respond "I learn by Reb Ahron," referring to R' Ahron Kotler. Today, however, when asked where he learns, the answer is "at Mir," or "at Ponovezh," or "at Tshebin," or "at Brisk." I no longer hear the name of a *person*, but rather of a *place*. I cannot but conclude that something has happened to the teacher/student relationship, and that the warm, personal relationship that was once the norm has been attenuated.

Perhaps this is merely a reflection of the fact that today there are, *Baruch Hashem*, many more students in yeshivos than in previous days. It may be simply impossible to have as intimate a contact with students as in the past. It may, however, be a casualty of the times we live in, where relatively few relationships have the strength they once did.

You may consider it insignificant, but I believe that how we live can have a definite albeit imperceptible impact on our emotions. Let me give you an example. For my Bar Mitzvah, I received a Sheaffer fountain pen, which remained my trusted writing instrument for 20 years, and when it was lost I actually grieved over it. Whenever anyone wished to borrow my pen, I kept its cap, to make certain the person would not inadvertently put it in his pocket. I actually had a relationship with an *object*. Today, most of the ball-point pens I use were given to me as promotional items, or perhaps by the motels in which I lodged. They are very inexpensive, and if someone borrows one, I am not in the least interested in its being returned. This object relationship no longer exists.

As a child, I remember taking a radio to the repair shop. Today no one even knows how to fix a radio, and if they did, the repair would cost more than a new one. If your radio doesn't work, simply throw it away and buy a new one. Even automobiles may be traded in every three years, regardless of the fact that they may be in perfect condition.

If we look about our homes, we will see many disposable items. "Use and discard" has become the practical motto in modern life. Regrettably, this attitude may have carried over to what were once upon a time very stable and durable relationships.

I have a plain earthenware dish which has absolutely no market value at all, but for me it is priceless. I remember it on my parents' *seder* table when I was 5,

15. **R'** *Elazar ben Shamua says: Let the honor of your student be as dear to you as your own; the honor of your colleague as the reverence for your teacher; and the reverence for your teacher as the reverence for Heaven.*

---

and it has been on our *seder* table for the past 63 years. I do not use it in any way, and its function is just being there.

Disposable dishes are being made more and more decorative. It is conceivable that a busy housewife may say, "Why bother *shlepping* the dishes up and down and having to wash them, when it is so much more convenient to use disposables, and they are available in such attractive designs."

I had a teacher of Talmud who would listen to a student's argument and say, "You are 100 percent right. Now I going to show you where you wrong." This is not self-contradictory. The student's reasoning may be correct, but he is overlooking something which invalidates his argument.

The housewife who will opt for saving her energy by using disposables may be 100 percent right, yet be wrong. Her children and grandchildren may lack something to stimulate recollection of past Passovers.

Let us assume that there are various factors that may weaken the teacher/student relationship. Is this situation correctable? Of course, but not unless we recognize it and make the effort to correct it. Let us not allow ourselves to be influenced by our environment. The teacher/student, parent/child, sibling, and friend relationships are far too important to fall victim to the detachment which is so prevalent in modern life.

יְהִי כְבוֹד תַּלְמִידְךָ . . . כְּמוֹרָא שָׁמָיִם
Let the honor of your student be . . .
as the reverence for Heaven.

Rabbeinu Yonah has a somewhat different version of this mishnah: "Let the honor of your student be as dear to you as that of your colleague, and the honor of your colleague as dear as the reverence of your teacher, and the reverence of your teacher as the reverence of God." If we take the mishnah at its face value and apply the mathematical axiom that quantities that are equal to the same or equal quantities are equal to each other (if a = b and b = c, then a = c), then we have "the honor of the student = the honor of colleague = reverence for teacher = reverence for God," which then contracts to "honor of student = reverence for God." If that is what the mishnah meant, then why does it include two intermediates? Why not simply say, "Let the honor of your student be as dear to you as your reverence for God?"

Let us first note that the latter statement is not as absurd as it may appear. The mishnah does not say to honor or revere your student as you honor or revere God, but rather that the honor of your student *should be as dear to you* as your reverence for God. We have already noted that we do not assign degrees of value to mitzvos (2:1), hence each mitzvah should be as dear to us as any other.

Inasmuch as it is a mitzvah to respect another person, this should be as dear to us as reverence for God, even though the two may be far apart. But the question about the mathematical equation still remains. The mishnah could simply have stated, "Let the honor of the student be as dear to you as your reverence for God." Why the intermediate steps?

The answer may be found in an essay by R' Chaim Shmulevitz. He cites a passage in the Talmud where R' Yehudah *HaNasi* was conducting a class, and was offended by a pungent odor emanating from someone who had eaten garlic. R' Yehudah *HaNasi* requested that whoever it was that had eaten the garlic should please leave, whereupon R' Chiya arose and left. The following day, R' Shimon, the son of R' Yehudah *HaNasi*, rebuked R' Chiya for his insensitivity. R' Chiya responded, "It was not I who had eaten the garlic. I just wished to protect the person who did, whose leaving the room after me would not expose him as the real offender."

The Talmud then asks, "Where did R' Chiya learn to do this noble deed?" and goes on to cite a similar behavior by R' Meir. From where did R' Meir learn this? Because he emulated Shmuel *HaKattan*. And Shmuel *HaKattan* had emulated Shechaniah ben Yechiel who in turn emulated Joshua (*Sanhedrin* 11a).

R' Shmulevitz points out two important teachings. Firstly, he asks, since it is self-evident that protecting someone from humiliation is highly commendable, why does the Talmud ask whence R' Chiya and the others derived this and in whose footsteps they followed? Perhaps R' Chiya had come to the conclusion on his own that this was a proper thing to do.

R' Shmulevitz answers that we cannot always rely on our own judgment as to what is or is not proper. People may be misled by their personal needs and emotions to consider some improper things as being proper. Even gross injustices may be considered to be just. In recent years we have seen how physician-assisted suicide initially evoked a response of horror, but within several years, some legislatures have legitimized it. It is perfectly possible for courts and legislatures to legitimize things that had previously been considered to be abominations. The most striking example of this is the acceptance by Nazi Germany that the extermination of Jews is a virtue.

It is therefore essential, R' Shmulevitz says, that we look to our teachers and Torah personalities to serve as models for us as to what is or is not proper behavior. They, in turn, would have received proper teaching on what is commendable behavior from their teachers, and so on all the way back to Moses.

But then, R' Shmulevitz asked, why could the Talmud not have said that R' Chiya followed in the footsteps of Joshua, the first one known to have acted this way? He answers that the Talmud is telling us that we must try to emulate the Torah personalities nearer to our own generation, with whom we may identify. We may be so far removed from the *tzaddikim* of earlier generations that we cannot conclude that what was right for them is necessarily right for us. R' Chiya had to learn from R' Meir, and R' Meir from Shmuel *HaKattan*, and so on. For R' Chiya to have learned from Joshua was too great a leap.

This is the reason why the mishnah requires intermediates. While it may indeed be true that all mitzvos may have equal value, and that indeed, the honor of your student should be as dear to you as your reverence for God, this is too great a gap to be bridged. We must take things in gradation, even spiritual development. We will do very well if we try to emulate the *tzaddikim* nearer to our own time, but if we reach too far, we may not be able to accomplish anything. Beginning with comparing anything to our relationship to God may be a quantum leap, beyond our capacity to absorb. It is only after we have taken several smaller steps that we can then approach something as great as our relationship to God.

יְהִי כְבוֹד תַּלְמִידְךָ חָבִיב עָלֶיךָ כְּשֶׁלָּךְ
Let the honor of your student
be as dear to you as your own

This verse of the mishnah should be written in bright, flashing neon lights and displayed in every school. It is possible that a teacher may humiliate a student in front of the class, either by applying discipline inappropriately or by commenting something like, "That is a stupid question." A single remark of this type may leave its mark on a student for life.

It is, of course, essential that there be proper decorum in a classroom, and it may be necessary to discipline a student. However, this must be done with great sensitivity, to avoid embarrassing a child. Sometimes a child may behave in a manner that requires that he be reprimanded in front of the class so that other students will realize that such behavior is unacceptable. Even then, the teacher should consider how he would wish to be treated if it were necessary for him to receive a public reprimand.

A follower of the Rabbi of Satmar related that he was present when the rabbi said that humiliating a child is a grievous sin. "Just think," the rabbi said, "what our reaction would be if a *shochet* allowed a *tereifah* chicken to pass for kosher. This would certainly result in the *shochet* being severely penalized or even dismissed from his position. Yet, as grievous a sin as eating *tereifah* may be, it is a sin of brief duration and for which there can be *teshuvah*. However, if a teacher humiliates a child in front of the class, he may inflict lifelong damage to the child's personality and learning ability, for which there may be no *teshuvah*."

This holds true for all teachers, but is of special importance for an instructor who teaches Torah, because the teacher's attitude toward the student may affect the student's attitude toward Torah and God. This is stated by our mishnah: "Let your reverence for your teacher equal your reverence for God." The Talmud states that there are three partners in a person: father, mother, and God. The teacher who conveys Torah to a child represents God, and if a student who is humiliated by a teacher develops a resentment and lack of respect for the teacher, this may result in similar feelings toward God. It is unfortunate that some young people who have turned away from Torah may have done so because they had not been treated properly by their teachers.

[טז] **רַבִּי** יְהוּדָה אוֹמֵר: הֱוֵי זָהִיר בְּתַלְמוּד, שֶׁשִּׁגְגַת תַּלְמוּד עוֹלָה זָדוֹן.

"Let your student's honor be as dear to you as your own" should be the basis of all pedagogy.

וּמוֹרָא רַבָּךְ כְּמוֹרָא שָׁמָיִם
And the reverence for your teacher as the reverence for Heaven.

When Rabban Yochanan ben Zakkai was nearing death, his disciples asked for his blessing. The sage responded, "May your fear of God be as great as your fear of humans." To the surprised students he explained, "A person may refrain from doing something improper because he is afraid that someone might see him, but the fear that God sees him may not be enough of a deterrent." Although Rabban Yochanan was speaking to people of enormous spirituality, he realized that their greatness notwithstanding, human nature cannot be dismissed. We may all begin initially with a greater fear of being detected by others rather than by God. What the spiritual person must do is advance from this position by reasoning, "If I am so concerned about being seen by other people, how much more should I be concerned about being seen by God."

Whenever the chassidic master, R' Nachum of Chernobel, visited a community, he would ask the local *shochet* (ritual slaughterer of animals) to allow him to inspect his knife, to be sure that it met with the highest degree of perfection.

In one such instance, the *shochet*, prior to showing the knife to R' Nachum for inspection, thought that he would polish it just a bit more, to bring it to a higher state of smoothness. But he promptly decided against this, reasoning that if he had been called to perform a ritual slaughter with the knife as it was, he would have done so. "If I feel this knife was smooth enough to satisfy the criterion of the Torah, I should not give the Rabbi any greater importance." He then showed the knife to the Rabbi as it was.

R' Nachum looked at the knife, and without inspecting it, returned it to the *shochet*. "If it is good enough for God, it is certainly good enough for me."

This was the reason for Rabban Yochanan's statement. Human nature may make someone more concerned about the opinions of others than that of God. A person lacking in spirituality may remain at this state, whereas the spiritual person rises above his natural inclination, and moves on to greater reverence of God.

16.

הֱוֵי זָהִיר בְּתַלְמוּד
Be meticulous in study

In the ritual of *vidui* (confession of sins), we cite a number of wrongdoings to which a human being is vulnerable. Among these is *yo'atznu ra*, "We have given bad advice." It is understandable that a person, in a moment of

16. **R**abbi Yehudah says: Be meticulous in study, for a careless misinterpretation is considered tantamount to willful transgression.

---

weakness, may not be able to withstand temptation and may commit any of the sins which bring him pleasure. Why on earth would a person commit the sin of giving someone bad advice? Since this does not result in any pleasurable sensation, no one would do this unless he were frankly malicious, and this is hardly an occurrence of sufficient frequency to warrant yo'atznu ra being included in the vidui which we may recite every day.

The answer is that no one is really suspected of being malicious and deliberately misleading another person. However, it is possible that a person may give others what he feels to be good, sound advice, but is unaware that the advice is in fact bad. This may indeed occur with some frequency.

If a physician has not had adequate experience in treating a particular disease, yet applies a treatment which results in harm to his patient, he is guilty of malpractice. We expect that a physician will practice only in his areas of competence. This standard should apply to everyone. If a person who consults you is likely to accept your advice, then you may give it only if you have sufficient expertise that makes your advice sound.

Even much book-learning and erudition may not be sufficient. Many learned rabbis will not rule on certain halachic issues in which they did not have shimush (practical training) under an authoritative teacher. Unless one has dealt with actual cases under competent supervision, one should refrain from giving direction.

People may accept advice from friends on how to manage their children. What gives these friends the authority to make any recommendations? Parents, with every good intention, may send a daughter back to an abusive husband on the basis of his promise never to harm her again, because they believe his promises have merit. This is bad advice which they give because of their lack of knowledge of the patterns of abuse. The results of such incompetent advice can be most tragic.

Yo'atznu ra does not refer to a deliberate sin, but rather to inadvertently giving improper advice. Yet it is on a par with all the other sins in the vidui, and one is as culpable for this as for the others. Insufficient knowledge is not a defense, because if one did not know, then one *should have known* before giving advice to others. If we do not recognize our limitations, then we ought not to give advice on issues in which we lack sufficient expertise.

"Be meticulous in study, for a careless misinterpretation is considered tantamount to willful transgression." This is also true of advice.

[יז] **רַבִּי** שִׁמְעוֹן אוֹמֵר: שְׁלשָׁה כְתָרִים הֵם: כֶּתֶר תּוֹרָה,
וְכֶתֶר כְּהֻנָּה, וְכֶתֶר מַלְכוּת; וְכֶתֶר שֵׁם טוֹב
עוֹלֶה עַל גַּבֵּיהֶן.

17.

שְׁלשָׁה כְתָרִים הֵם . . .
וְכֶתֶר שֵׁם טוֹב עוֹלֶה עַל גַּבֵּיהֶן
*There are three crowns . . .
but the crown of a good name
surpasses all of them.*

The mishnah refers to three crowns, yet lists four! Perhaps what the mishnah means by this is that there are three crowns that are generally recognized as such, but that there is one more that is not often appreciated as in fact being a crown.

What is a crown? It is a symbol of authority and/or superiority. The crown of royalty indicates the sovereignty of the king, the crown of priesthood indicates the authority of the *Kohen,* and the crown of Torah indicates the position of superiority of the Torah scholar. Each of these three crowns not only indicates the special privileges of the bearer, but also places upon him the awesome responsibility of serving as a model for the general population.

Unfortunately, our history shows that the bearers of these three crowns have not always been models of virtue. Scripture describes a number of kings whose behavior deviated from Torah. During the period of the Second Temple, few of the High Priests were worthy of their position. The Talmud tells us that two of King David's mentors, Doeg and Achitophel, were great Torah scholars, as was R' Meir's teacher, Elisha ben Avuyah. Yet, their characters undermined their Torah knowledge. Hence, while these three crowns should have represented virtue as well as authority and superiority, this was not always the case. We have come to realize that we cannot blindly emulate those who occupy these positions.

However, if a person establishes a reputation as a highly ethical and moral person, his responsibility is extremely great, because he is the one to whom people will look as a beacon of light to show them the proper way of life. Our sages were extremely cautious to make certain that they did not deviate in the least from propriety, lest others be misled by possible misinterpretations of their behavior. R' Yehudah *HaNasi* said, "What constitutes a *chilul Hashem* (desecration of the Divine Name)? For me, it is buying meat and not paying the butcher promptly" (*Yoma* 86a). Although buying on credit is certainly not a sin, R' Yehudah *HaNasi* felt that people might misinterpret his buying on credit as a dereliction in paying his bills. The Talmud says that R' Shimon ben Lakish was extremely cautious with whom he conversed, because anyone to whom he spoke was assumed to be extremely trustworthy, and people would lend this person money without witnesses. They assumed that if R' Shimon ben Lakish conversed with him, he must be a person of impeccable honesty (*Yoma* 9a).

17. **R**abbi Shimon says: There are three crowns — the crown of Torah, the crown of priesthood, and the crown of kingship; but the crown of a good name surpasses all of them.

Because a person of noble *middos* is also likely to be most humble, it is possible that he may be unaware that he bears the crown of exemplary behavior. Thus, a person with a *shem tov,* good name, a reputation of being a decent and honest person, should be aware that he, too, bears a crown. Furthermore, precisely because he is considered to be the ideal person, his impact upon others may be even greater than those who bear any of the other crowns. In this sense, the crown of a *shem tov* is unique in that it is superior to others, yet it may not even be recognized as being a crown.

The Maharal addressed the question of why the mishnah states there are three crowns and then lists four. The Maharal's brilliant answer may be better understood with a brief introduction.

In the entire process of Creation as related in the first chapter of *Genesis,* God brings everything into being on His own. However, when it comes to the creation of man, God says, "Let *us* make man." The obvious question is: To whom was God referring with the word "us." This issue is dealt with by several commentaries and I have mentioned it before.

All living things, said the Baal Shem Tov, are created in a state of completion, and all they need to do is to grow in size. Little bears become big bears, and baby alligators become mature alligators, but no animals transform themselves into something other than what they were created. Even the caterpillar that changes into a beautiful butterfly is no exception to this rule. The caterpillar does not voluntarily choose to become a butterfly. In the caterpillar's genes is a code that will cause it, at a certain stage in its life cycle, to spin a cocoon and emerge as a butterfly. Hence, the caterpillar-butterfly was also created in a completed form.

Angels, as far as we know, do not undergo any growth nor maturation, and thousands of years later, they are the same as when they were created.

God's concept of man was that he was to be a creature that is created in a state of imperfection, and by *his own efforts,* man must bring about his state of completion, which is *to become a spiritual being.* God certainly could have created man in a stage of spiritual perfection, but then man would have essentially been angelic in nature, and not the being that God intended man to be.

Man was created with a physical body similar to that of other living things. Whereas other living things are completely driven by their physical drives, man is supposed to become master over his behavior, and was given the capacity of free will and freedom of choice, so that he may determine his actions. Using

ד/יח   [יח] **רַבִּי** נְהוֹרָאִי אוֹמֵר: הֱוֵי גוֹלֶה לִמְקוֹם תּוֹרָה,
וְאַל תֹּאמַר שֶׁהִיא תָבוֹא אַחֲרֶיךָ, שֶׁחֲבֵרֶיךָ
יְקַיְּמוּהָ בְּיָדֶךָ. וְאֶל בִּינָתְךָ אַל תִּשָּׁעֵן.

---

this capacity, man was to elevate himself far above his physical nature, and by doing so, he would become the spiritual being that God intended.

At the time of Creation, man was not yet the ideal man, but rather only a *potential* of the ideal man. Therefore, God needed the cooperation of *man himself* in bringing about the final product that He desired. God therefore addresses man and says, "Let *us,* you and I, make the ideal man. I am creating you with the potential to become that ideal man, and you must do your share in bringing about the completed being."

It is of interest that on several occasions the Talmud refers to a person who implements various Divine teachings as "a partner to God in the work of Creation." According to the Baal Shem Tov's explanation, this term is most accurate. When man exercises his capacity to become the spiritual person he was intended to become, he is indeed a true partner to God in the work of creation; i.e., his *own* creation.

Let us now turn to the Maharal, who says that the human being is tripartite, composed of a physical body, an intellect, and a spirit which gives him the capacity to use the first two. The three crowns correspond to these three components: priesthood corresponds to the body, since it is paternally linked, and an infant is born a *Kohen;* Torah corresponds to the intellect; and the spirit corresponds to kingship, in that, like a king, the spirit can rule over the person. These three components, says the Maharal, are given to man by God, and these comprise the *potential* of man. The *shem tov,* the good name which man acquires by developing his *middos* that make him into the final product, the ideal man that God wished to create, this *shem tov* represents the very essence of man rather than being just a component.

This is consistent with the Baal Shem Tov's explanation, that the essence of man which distinguishes him from other living beings is the capacity to transform himself. Hence, the crown of *shem tov* is qualitatively different from the other three crowns. They could therefore not be grouped together, since the three are the *components* given to man and constitute the Divine contributions to man, whereas the *shem tov* is not given to man by God, but is man's share in his own creation.

But why use the term *shem tov* to refer to the essence of man? Perhaps it is because the Torah states that God gave man the name "Adam," which has two connotations. "Adam" refers to אֲדָמָה, *adamah,* the earth from which man was formed. "Adam" also refers to אַדְמֶה, *adameh,* or אֲדַמֶּה לְעֶלְיוֹן, *adameh l'Elyon,* to be similar to God. The Torah states that man was indeed created in the image of God, meaning that he has a *neshamah* which is Godlike. The

18. Rabbi Nehorai says: Exile yourself to a place of Torah — and do not assume that it will come after you — for it is your colleagues who will cause it to remain with you; and do not rely on your own understanding (Proverbs 3:5).

---

word "Adam" therefore represents Godliness, the transformation of the physical into the spiritual, which is the essence of man.

Although we usually think of Torah as an end in itself, the midrash states that the Torah was given to man in order to refine him (*Bereishis Rabbah* 44:1). Thus, the Torah is not yet the final goal of man, until he implements it to transform himself into the image of God which he was meant to be.

The crown of *shem tov* therefore stands alone, since it represents man's share in his own creation, in contrast to the other three crowns which are given to man by God. We can also understand why the crown of *shem tov* is considered superior to the others, since all three are essentially instruments whereby the human being is to arrive at the *shem tov*, the conversion of *adamah* to *adameh l'Elyon*, which is the ultimate goal.

18.

הֱוֵי גוֹלֶה לִמְקוֹם תּוֹרָה
Exile yourself to a place of Torah

Before citing a provocative interpretation of this mishnah, a word of introduction is in order.

There are many historical novels, in which the author takes a real-life character about whom a few facts are known, and builds a story around these which is the product of his imagination, or in other words, purely fictional. These may make interesting reading, but one should recognize them for what they are: pure fiction.

This may be quite innocent when applied to a variety of historical figures, but can be very dangerous when the subject of the book is an outstanding Torah personality. The reason for this is simple. We do not mold our lives around Aristotle or try to emulate Benjamin Franklin. If they made any ethical or moral pronouncements, we are not bound by them. In general, whatever contributions they may have made stand on their own merits and are not affected by their personal lives.

It is totally different with Torah personalities, whose teachings are inseparable from their lives. It is an axiom in the Torah world that any comments on Torah made by a person who is not himself thoroughly observant of Torah are rejected. The great Talmudic sage, R' Meir, was criticized for having accepted Torah teachings from Elisha ben Avuyah, an outstanding scholar who had defected from Torah observance. In defense of R' Meir, the Talmud says, "R' Meir found a pomegranate, eating the fruit while discarding the peel" (*Chagigah* 15b). Nevertheless, it was only someone of the stature of R' Meir who was capable of discriminating what he may accept from Elisha and what he must reject. For all others, the rule applies that we do not accept Torah teachings from any scholar whose dedication to Torah observance is incomplete. Our Torah scholars teach us by example, and we learn as much by studying their behavior as by reading their works.

For this reason, we may not "fictionalize" our historical Torah personalities any more than we may take liberties with their teachings. Both are essentially a distortion of Torah.

We must extend this a bit further. There are contemporary Torah personalities of whose erudition and saintliness we stand in awe. We have been afforded the opportunity to learn about the enormous scholarship and encyclopedic knowledge of R' Shlomo Zalman Auerbach, a great scholar and *tzaddik* who died in 1997 and whom we were privileged to see with our own eyes. R' Shlomo Zalman totally effaced himself before the Chofetz Chaim, who lived but one generation earlier. The Chofetz Chaim, in turn, stood in total awe of the *Gaon* of Vilna. It is said that when one of the *Gaon's* students, overwhelmed by the *Gaon's* incomparable grasp of the entire Torah wished to compare him to the Rambam, the *Gaon* shuddered. How dare anyone compare anyone of his generation with the Rambam! We continue this chain of self-effacement back through history. The Rambam effaced himself before the later authors of the Talmud, who stood in awe of their predecessors. When we follow this back to the personalities in Scripture, we realize that in relationship to the *tzaddikim* of earlier times, we are not even like a drop of water compared to the Pacific Ocean, because as vast as that difference is, it is nevertheless *quantitative*, i.e., water to water. The difference between ourselves and the Torah personalities of the past is *qualitative* rather than quantitative. The Talmud aptly states, "If the earlier generations were angels, then by comparison we are humans, but if the earlier generations were humans, then we are donkeys" (*Shabbos* 112b). We may have no greater grasp of their essence than we do of a fourth dimension. Inasmuch as we do consider ourselves to be humans rather than donkeys, it is foolish to for us to take the measure of angels. It is therefore absurd to try to analyze the *tzaddikim* of yore, and certainly to make them characters in historical novels.

When we read that the *tzaddikim* of earlier times "sinned," we should be aware that we really have no understanding of what actually transpired. The Midrash tells us that there were Divine angels who "sinned." How can an angel possibly sin, since an angel is pure spirit and has no *yetzer hara*? The "sins" of angels, as well as what are described as the "sins" of *tzaddikim*, are beyond our comprehension.

Earlier (3:11), we gave a parable told by R' Elimelech of Lizhensk. This parable can likewise be applied here. The deviation of the peasant was thousands of times greater than the fraction of a millimeter deviation of the jeweler, and furthermore, it was an act of intentional defiance. Yet, the punishment of the jeweler, which was minuscule by comparison and not intentional, resulted in a more severe punishment. Why? Because when you are dealing with the centerpiece of the crown, there is no tolerance for error.

R' Elimelech, for all his humility, knew that at his level of spirituality he was dealing with the equivalent of the diamond centerpiece of the crown, and a deviation which would not even be detectable otherwise, such as if the peasant had dug a fraction of a millimeter off course, must be considered a serious transgression. It is for this reason that the Talmud cautions us not to think of the "sins" of biblical figures, e.g., Reuven, Yehudah, and David, according to the superficial meaning of the text. We may not be able to understand exactly what happened, but their "sins" were like those of the jeweler rather than the peasant.

Yet, the Torah presents these accounts as though they were the "peasant" kind of sins. The reason for this is so that we may learn from these episodes that (1) even *tzaddikim* are vulnerable to sin, albeit a qualitatively different type of sin than we are familiar with; and (2) that *teshuvah* merits forgiveness for even serious transgressions (*Jerusalem Talmud, Peah* 1:1). Had the Torah presented these "sins" in terms of deviations of fractions of millimeters, they would have no relevance or application to us.

With this background we can approach an interpretation of this mishnah given by R' Moshe Alashkar.

The Talmud tells us that the author of this mishnah, R' Nehorai, is none other than R' Elazar ben Arach (*Eruvin* 13b), of whom it was said in Chapter 2 mishnah 12 that he was a greater scholar than all the sages combined. As was noted there, when he separated himself from his colleagues, he suffered the loss of his knowledge and even the ability to correctly pronounce the words of the Torah. When he later tried to read a verse in the Torah, he mispronounced every word. His colleagues interceded in prayer for him, and he regained his enormous knowledge (*Shabbos* 147b).

It is impossible to understand this account at its face value. We know people whose last contact with a Hebrew book was in *cheder* in their childhood. After not reading a Hebrew word for 60 years, they can pick up a *siddur* and read it fluently, albeit slowly. Are we to believe that this extraordinarily learned sage could not even read Hebrew because he had not studied Torah with his previous intensity?

We may never know what really happened, but the reason the Talmud presents the account in this manner is to make a point. Although a person may have acquired vast Torah knowledge, one should not rely on that knowledge as being adequate, and one should always continue Torah study. Failure to constantly review and progress in Torah study will result in its erosion. Furthermore, solitary study is inadequate. One must relate to peers and/or to students to achieve clarity in Torah study.

We can therefore understand this mishnah as R' Nehorai, i.e., R' Elazar ben Arach, speaking from his personal experience. "Always be in a place of Torah study, do not separate and expect other scholars to seek you out, and do not rely on your fund of knowledge, regardless how vast it may be."

ד/יט   [יט] **רַבִּי** יַנַּאי אוֹמֵר: אֵין בְּיָדֵינוּ לֹא מִשַּׁלְוַת הָרְשָׁעִים
וְאַף לֹא מִיִּסּוּרֵי הַצַּדִּיקִים.

19.

אֵין בְּיָדֵינוּ
It is not in our
power to explain

The message of this mishnah may be better understood by analyzing another statement by its author, and by considering its approximation to the previous mishnah, which concludes with "do not rely on your understanding."

With all due respect to human intellect, we must appreciate its limitations. True, man's genius has broken the secret of the atom and invented super-computers that can do *trillions* of calculations in a split second. We can send a person deep into the solar system and bring him back, and we can replace failing hearts. Yet, that does not mean we can fathom everything. The Talmud says that Solomon was the wisest of all men, yet he admitted that he was unable to understand the mitzvah of the red heifer (*Yoma* 13a). The reason for this mitzvah was revealed only to Moses, who gleaned this knowledge only by Divine revelation, and not by his own cunning. Even great wisdom has its limitations. Furthermore, even Moses, who understood what was beyond Solomon's grasp, did not understand the mystery of why bad things happen to good people. Moses asked God for a revelation of this secret as well, and this was denied him (*Berachos* 7a). One Talmudic opinion is that Moses wrote the Book of *Job*, where all arguments to explain why the innocent may suffer are presented, only to be refuted.

We may understand why people nevertheless pursue the solution of this mystery, but we should resign ourselves to the fact that we are not going to grasp something which Moses was unable to understand. We cannot possibly grasp this as long as our intellect is limited by residing within a physical body.

A popular book that addresses this question wrongly concludes that the innocent may suffer because God does not control everything in the world, hence the suffering of the innocent is not a violation of Divine justice. We did not have to wait for the latter half of the 20th century to hit upon this as a solution. The Talmud states that several thousands years ago, people believed that after creating the universe, God abandoned it to the physical laws of nature. Torah ideology teaches that God is in total control of everything in the universe, from supergalaxies to microscopic cells. Furthermore, God is absolute goodness and perfect justice. Then why do bad things happen to good people? We do not know and cannot know. This is one area where we must have perfect trust in God.

When we recite the Thirteen Principles of Faith, we say, "I believe with *perfect* faith." In other words, faith that is not limited by the imperfect human mind. In Torah philosophy there is a concept of *emunah peshutah,* or simple faith, which is not subject to human analysis. While it is rather easy for children

19. **R**abbi *Yannai says: It is not in our power to explain either the tranquility of the wicked or the
suffering of the righteous.*

---

to have simple faith, the mature mind may find it difficult to surrender its
analytic capacities and accept things on simple faith.

The Midrash relates an interesting incident involving R' Yannai, the author of
this mishnah. R' Yannai once heard a peddler exclaiming, "Who wants an elixir
of life?" R' Yannai, who was engaged in the study of manifest Torah, asked the
peddler for this magic elixir. "I did not intend this for you or anyone like you,"
the peddler said. When R' Yannai persisted, the peddler drew out the Book of
Psalms, and pointed to the verse, "Who is it that desires life? . . . Restrain your
tongue from evil, and your lips from speaking falsehood" (*Psalms* 34:13-14).
R' Yannai remarked, "All my life I have been reading this verse, and I never
understood it until this peddler made me cognizant of its true meaning"
(*Vayikra Rabbah* 16).

This midrash is baffling. Just what was it that R' Yannai learned from the
peddler that had eluded him during the many years that he had read and
recited this phrase?

Torah is both profound and infinite. Like a perfect diamond that scintillates
with many colors and may present various configurations from different angles,
all of which are true to the diamond, so can the Torah have kaleidoscopic
interpretations, all of which are true. Furthermore, it has been pointed out that
just as the true treasures of the earth lie beneath its surface — the nourishing soil
in which plants grow, diamonds, gold, silver, oil, etc. — so do the rich meanings of the Torah lie beneath the superficial text. Indeed there are four categories in which the Torah may be interpreted: the manifest meaning, the
symbolic meaning, the homiletic, and the concealed secret; and in each category there may be countless versions. Torah scholars may literally lose themselves in the breadth and depth of Torah.

Yet, it is the surface of the earth on which we can walk. The many hidden
riches beneath the soil notwithstanding, we cannot walk on them, and it is the
earth's surface which provides us with a place to live. So it is with Torah. There
are many hidden treasures beneath its surface, but our immediate contact must
be with the text itself.

Some Torah scholars were concerned that in the search for the concealed
treasures, we may lose sight of the manifest meaning. The great Talmudist, R'
Shlomo Luria (Maharshal), who was certainly privy to all the categories of
Torah interpretation, stated that when he recited the *Shema,* he did so with the
simplicity and naiveté of a child, setting aside the various symbolic, homiletic,
and kabbalistic *kavannos* (intentions).

If we pay close attention to the text of the Midrash, it states that at the time R'
Yannai heard the cry of the peddler, he was engaged in the study of the *pshat*

כ] **רַבִּי** מַתְיָא בֶּן חָרָשׁ אוֹמֵר: הֱוֵי מַקְדִּים בִּשְׁלוֹם כָּל אָדָם, וֶהֱוֵי זָנָב לָאֲרָיוֹת, וְאַל תְּהִי רֹאשׁ לְשׁוּעָלִים.

(manifest meaning) of the Torah. He knew the verse of *Psalms* very well, and that when Torah refers to "life" it often means *spiritual* life, as when the Talmud interprets the reward of longevity as referring to the Eternal World rather than this mundane existence. But the peddler, who was most probably a person who knew only the manifest meaning of the verse, was addressing the common folk, many of whom were no more erudite than he. He was pointing out that a person who wishes to live a long and happy life can achieve this by avoiding evil talk and falsehood. As we read earlier in *Ethics of the Fathers*, silence is beneficial to the body as well as to the soul (1:17), and the Talmud tells of a community that enjoyed longevity because no one deviated from the truth (*Sanhedrin* 97a). The "elixir of life" as the peddler understood it refers to a long and happy life on earth. R' Yannai therefore remarked that he was grateful to the peddler for pointing out to him that the verse in *Psalms* should be taken literally. "I did not pay attention to the *manifest* meaning of this verse until the peddler made me cognizant of it."

Following the teaching of the previous mishnah, that we are not to rely on our understanding, R' Yannai points out that there is one mystery of life that we should not try to understand, but to accept it with simplicity and naiveté because it is beyond the grasp of human intellect. We may never fully understand why the wicked may prosper while the righteous may suffer. We must have complete faith and trust in God, that His justice is perfect. Any attempt to solve insoluble mysteries can lead us into error and distortion. It is at times when our intellect is challenged by what appear to us to be injustice that, like the Maharshal, we must close our eyes as we do when we recite the *Shema*, indicating that our human perception can be faulty, and accept the sovereignty of God without any reservations whatever.

20.

הֱוֵי מַקְדִּים בִּשְׁלוֹם כָּל אָדָם
Initiate a greeting to every person

The text of this mishnah lends itself to another interpretation, which was given by R' Jacob Joseph of Pulna. "Initiate peace with everyone." I.e., if you have been involved in a dispute with someone, do not wait for the other party to make overtures of reconciliation, but rather be the first to seek peace.

Initiating peace may come at the price of swallowing one's pride, particularly since it may be interpreted as conceding that one was wrong in the dispute. This should not be permitted to restrain one from initiating the process.

Our heritage is replete with anecdotes of our Torah personalities who sought

20. **R**abbi Masya ben Charash says: Initiate a greeting to every person; and be a tail to lions, rather than a head to foxes.

---

peace at virtually any price, and they gave no consideration whatever to their ego. The wife of R' Yom Tov Lipman was publicly humiliated by another woman, and the outraged leaders of the community wished to penalize the latter for her arrogance. However, no such action could be taken without the rabbi's approval. Knowing that the rabbi would not pay any heed to them, they asked the rabbi's wife to tell him how she was offended, and to take some kind of action of chastisement.

The rabbi's wife waited for a propitious time, and several days later, when she felt her husband might be receptive, she told him about the incident. The rabbi responded, "And you have been harboring a grudge against her for several days? You know that in our prayer before retiring we are to forgive anyone who may have offended us. How could you have retained this resentment so long? You must now go and ask this woman's forgiveness for having held a resentment toward her."

The rabbi's wife did as he suggested, and when she apologized to the woman for harboring a resentment, the latter broke into tears and said, "You do not need to be forgiven. I am the one who must ask your forgiveness for my rudeness toward you."

We could easily have justified the rabbi's wife waiting for the other woman to recognize her errant behavior and apologize, but by taking the initiative, peace was quickly restored.

In the city of Slonim there was a man who brazenly violated Shabbos publicly. The local *rav*, R' Mordechai Rosenblatt, repeatedly warned the man to desist from publicly desecrating Shabbos, and when the latter continued his defiance, the rabbi excommunicated him. In anger, the man came to the rabbi's house and threatened him with a revolver. The members of the household subdued him and called the police, who arrested him. When the man came to trial, R' Mordechai came to court to plead for clemency, and the man was released.

For our Torah personalities, who were as humble as they were great, it was hardly a sacrifice to set aside their ego. They sought to appease anyone who offended them. The Talmud relates that R' Meir enthralled his audience with his expositions on Torah. One time, a woman tarried in the House of Study to listen to R' Meir. This caused her to delay her husband's supper, and the latter was furious. "I will not allow you to set foot in this house until you spit in R' Meir's face," the enraged husband said. The distraught woman left her home. Several weeks had passed when R' Meir learned of this. He sought out the woman and said, "I have been affected by an *ayin hara* (the spell of an evil eye). This can be removed only if someone will spit at me seven times. Could you do me this favor?" When the woman complied, R' Meir said, "Go tell your

[כא] **רַבִּי** יַעֲקֹב אוֹמֵר: הָעוֹלָם הַזֶּה דּוֹמֶה לִפְרוֹזְדּוֹר
בִּפְנֵי הָעוֹלָם הַבָּא, הַתְקֵן עַצְמְךָ בַּפְּרוֹזְדּוֹר,
כְּדֵי שֶׁתִּכָּנֵס לַטְּרַקְלִין.

---

husband that you did even more than he demanded. He asked you to spit at me once, and you did it seven times!"

R' Meir's students asked whether he was not diminishing respect for the Torah by such total self-effacement, and he responded that in the ritual for the woman who was accused of being unfaithful, the *Kohen* writes a portion of the Torah and then erases it (*Numbers* 5:11-21), even though erasing the Divine Name constitutes a sinful desecration of holiness. "God prefers that His Name be erased in order to restore harmony between man and wife. If God is willing to efface Himself for the sake of peace," R' Meir said, "shall I be different?" (*Jerusalem Talmud, Sotah* 1:4).

We begin each day with the introductory prayers, in which we recite a portion of the Talmud that lists those mitzvos for which one is rewarded during his lifetime as well as in heaven. Among these is "restoring peace between man and wife and between man and fellow man."

The author of this mishnah, R' Masya, emphasized the halachic principle that one must violate the sacred Shabbos in order to save a life (*Yoma* 84a). In this mishnah, his concern with restoring peace at all costs, as R' Meir said, is consistent with his concept of the incomparable value of a human being.

וֶהֱוֵי זָנָב לַאֲרָיוֹת,
וְאַל תְּהִי רֹאשׁ לְשׁוּעָלִים
*And be a tail to lions,
rather than a head to foxes.*

In Torah literature, the lion symbolizes not raw might, but rather the strength of being master of oneself, as we see in the mishnah in the next chapter (5:23), "Be as strong as a lion to do the will of your heavenly Father." In Talmudic parables, the fox is always sly and cunning. The teaching of this mishnah is thus that one should associate with people who are masters of themselves and who subdue their physical desires rather than with those who use their cunning to circumvent Torah.

The latter half of this mishnah can be seen as an extension of R' Masya's first statement. The reference to being a tail rather than a head, i.e., leader, is an instruction to those who may seek to bolster a sagging self-esteem by assuming a position of domination over their inferiors. There is a Yiddish folk saying, "What makes a little child happy? Seeing another child who is smaller than himself." As with so many other folk sayings, this contains an important psychological insight. The child who feels dwarfed by all the giant adults in his environment is delighted when he can feel himself taller than someone else. Similarly, people who think poorly of themselves may seek to associate with others to whom they can feel superior.

21. **R**abbi Yaakov says: This world is like an antechamber before the World to Come; prepare yourself in the antechamber so that you may enter the banquet hall.

But what can a person do if he cannot find anyone whom he can consider inferior to himself? Why, he can degrade and belittle others, and think himself to be better than them! There are various mechanisms that people may utilize to bolster a sagging self-esteem, and among these is debasing others. In addition to being a grievous sin, *lashon hara* (slander) indicates that one has a poor self-concept.

In the first portion of the mishnah, R' Masya advocates self-effacement for the sake of peace. People with low self-esteem cannot afford to efface themselves, because this is too threatening to their fragile ego. Self-effacement therefore requires a healthy self concept. Consistent with this, he suggests associating with those wiser than oneself rather than seeking positions of superiority over inferiors. A healthy self-esteem will enable one to implement both of R' Masya's teachings.

21.

הַתְקֵן עַצְמְךָ בַּפְּרוֹזְדוֹר, כְּדֵי שֶׁתִּכָּנֵס לַטְּרַקְלִין
Prepare yourself in the antechamber so that you may enter the banquet hall.

In his epochal *Path of the Just,* which is mandatory reading for anyone who aspires to spirituality, R' Moshe Chaim Luzzatto begins with a discussion of man's duty in this world. Both in this work and in *The Way of God,* Ramchal posits the concept that the goal of life is not to maximize mundane gratification, but to achieve a closeness with God in the Eternal World. He points out that a person who believes in Creation cannot logically maintain that the goal of human life is earthly bliss. If this were so, then the world would be a cruel hoax, since for the overwhelming majority of people life is a struggle, replete with stresses of various types. Life may be anything but blissful, and to attribute this to the Creator would be accusing Him of malicious sadism. The Steipler *Gaon* further points out that if anyone were to see a child dressed in a jacket which reaches his ankle, trousers that drag behind him, and a hat that covers his nose, he would immediately conclude that the child had put on his father's garments, since these outsize garments are obviously not appropriate for the child. Similarly, the enormous capacity of the human intellect is an undeniable indication that man is designed for something far beyond contentment. Cows in the pasture are far more content than humans can possibly be. Minds that can produce masterworks were intended to reach goals that require superior intellect.

In *The Way of God* Ramchal explains the reason for this design. God, Who is the ultimate in benevolence, wishes to give of His infinite goodness to

[כב] **הוּא** הָיָה אוֹמֵר: יָפָה שָׁעָה אַחַת בִּתְשׁוּבָה
וּמַעֲשִׂים טוֹבִים בָּעוֹלָם הַזֶּה מִכֹּל חַיֵּי
הָעוֹלָם הַבָּא; וְיָפָה שָׁעָה אַחַת שֶׁל קוֹרַת רוּחַ בָּעוֹלָם הַבָּא
מִכֹּל חַיֵּי הָעוֹלָם הַזֶּה.

---

man. However, receiving something which one has not earned leaves much
to be desired, and even carries with it a sense of humiliation, just as a beggar
of alms feels dejection when he must rely on the charitableness of others.
Indeed, the *Zohar* refers to unearned reward as "bread of humiliation." God
therefore designed this world, where man must overcome various challenges
and obstacles in order to fulfill the Divine will, and by doing so, he earns his
reward.

Rashi states that when the Patriarch Jacob returned to his homeland after
suffering years of torment, he wished to live in tranquility. God said, "Is it
not enough for the righteous that they will have bliss in the Eternal World,
that they also seek tranquility in their earthly existence?" Jacob subsequently
suffered the ordeal of Joseph's disappearance, and he grieved bitterly for 22
years for his beloved son whom he assumed to be dead (*Genesis* 37:1).

We may not be able to understand why the pious Jacob could not be allowed
to live in peace, but we believe that the goodness of God far surpasses the
greatest benevolence than man can muster. Jacob was to receive great reward in
the Eternal World, and living a tranquil life would have diminished this.

Our lifestyle would be much different if we truly realized that our earthly
existence is merely a means to a greater end. We accept the reality that a person
may have to put in a hard day's work, and except for brief interludes during
the workday, he cannot relax until he comes home in the evening. Our earthly existence is our "workday," and except for brief periods of rest and tranquility,
we are to engage in our work until we return to our true home in the Eternal
World.

Our *tzaddikim* demonstrated this by the way they lived, often surviving on
the bare essentials of life. It is related that a visitor was shocked by the sparse
dwelling of the Chofetz Chaim. "And what type of dwelling do you have?" the
Chofetz Chaim asked. The visitor described his spacious, well-furnished home.
"Do you have similar comforts when you travel?" the Chofetz Chaim asked.
The visitor responded that when he was *en route* he lodged at an inn, where he
usually had a single, small room. "So it is with me," the sage said. "In my
eternal home, I have a lavish dwelling. Here I am but *en route*, and as with you,
a single, simply furnished room is enough."

How different our lives would be if we understood the purpose of our earthly
existence the way the Chofetz Chaim did. This great sage supported himself by
operating a small store, and as soon as he had earned enough to support
himself for that day, he closed the store and devoted himself to the study of

22. **H**e was accustomed to say: Better one hour of repentance and good deeds in this world than the entire
life of the World to Come; and better is one hour of spiritual
bliss in the World to Come than the entire life of this world.

Torah. With this sparse existence, he lived to be almost 100, and by virtue of his epochal *Mishnah Berurah,* there is not a single Torah-observant home in which he does not have a presence. I dare say that the Chofetz Chaim had a more contented life than many people who enjoy the comforts and luxuries of this world.

Most of us do not think of ourselves as being addicted. However, addiction can be defined as being under compulsion to do that which we know is detrimental to us, but are essentially powerless to resist the particular drive. This is equally true whether the compulsion is for alcohol, drugs, cigarettes, etc. Yet, although we profess to believe in the ideology of the Torah, which, as stated in this mishnah, is that this world is but preparatory for the Eternal World, we generally behave as though this world is all there is. Our behavior thus contradicts what we believe, yet we are driven to acquire more money so that we can increase our enjoyment of this world, rather than — like the Chofetz Chaim — devote ourselves to spiritual growth. How different is this really from the person who pursues the ephemeral pleasure of drugs, even though he realizes that they are harmful to him?

We may well consider this mishnah as being pivotal. Everything else in *Ethics of the Fathers* would easily fall into place if we implemented our belief that this world is but a "lobby" or antechamber, in which we have the opportunity to earn our admission to the opulent "banquet hall."

22.

יָפָה שָׁעָה אַחַת בִּתְשׁוּבָה וּמַעֲשִׂים טוֹבִים
**Better one hour of
repentance and good deeds**

The Rambam in *Guide to the Per-plexed* points out that comparison of qualities can be made only among like items, but not among unlike items. One can say that "A" is a better musician than "B," since both are musicians, or that one piece of silk is better than another. It makes no sense, however to say that "A" who is a musician, is of a higher quality than "B," who is a carpenter," or that this piece of silk is of finer quality than that book, since the two are different in character. How, then, can the mishnah say that anything in this earthly world is better than something in the Eternal World, or vice versa, since this world and heaven are totally different in character?

Properly understood, this mishnah is a continuation of R' Yaakov's first statement and reinforces it. R' Yaakov stated that the ultimate purpose of Creation is to bask in the revealed glory of God in *Gan Eden.* One might ask:

Inasmuch as the Talmud tells us that all *neshamos* are taken from beneath the Divine throne, i.e., from a place in heaven where they are in the Immanent Presence of God, what does the *neshamah* stand to gain by coming down to the physical world, where it is subjected to so many challenges to its pristine state? The answer is as mentioned in the discussion of the previous mishnah, that the bliss of being in the Divine Presence is lacking if it is undeserved. It is to the advantage of the *neshamah* to receive its reward after earning it by overcoming the challenges in this world. So much so, that one moment *of heavenly bliss* that is *earned* in this world surpasses all the bliss of the *neshamah* that it received gratis prior to its descent to an earthly existence. The comparison is thus not between this world and heaven, but between two types of heavenly bliss. R' Yaakov states that a fragment of earned reward outweighs a great deal of bliss that was unearned.

There is yet another important concept contained in R' Yaakov's statement. The Torah states, "You shall seek God from there and you will find Him" (*Deuteronomy* 4:29), upon which the Rabbi of Kotzk commented, "The seeking *is* the finding." This brief statement encapsulates profound Torah ideology.

In the ritual recited upon the completion of a volume of Talmud, we say that the work in the study of Torah is different than any other type of work, because the work of Torah study is rewarded, whereas other work is not rewarded. The Chofetz Chaim asked the obvious question, "How can we say that other types of work go unrewarded? Does not the laborer or artisan receive compensation for his work?" The Chofetz Chaim answers that all other types of work are compensated because they lead to some useful product or service. It is therefore the end product which gives the work its value. For example, if a tailor spent all day stitching a piece of cloth that could not be put to any use whatsoever, not even as a patch, no one would compensate him for his many hours of work. The tailor is compensated when his work results in the formation or repair of a garment, and it is the garment that makes the tailor's work compensable.

Torah study is different. Although there are many ways in which Torah study can be applied to virtually every facet of life, Torah study has intrinsic value, even though it may not have application. For example, we study the laws relating to the *ben sorer umoreh* (the rebellious and defiant son), even though the Talmud states that these laws have never been applied and will never be applied. This is also true of the laws regarding *ir hanidachas* (a community which adopted idolatry). If these laws are never applied, why study them, the Talmud asks. The answer is because there is a mitzvah to study Torah, and this mitzvah applies even to portions of Torah that will never be implemented. This, says the Chofetz Chaim, is the distinction between the work in Torah study and other types of work. Torah study is valuable and is rewarded even if it does not result in its actually being applied.

The point of this is that both Torah study and performance of mitzvos are a *process*. In contradistinction to all other actions we are familiar with, where the process leads to the desired goal, with Torah and mitzvos, *the process* **is** *the goal*. When you put a kettle of water on the stove, it is because there is something you want to do with the hot water. It would be absurd to heat up a kettle of water for no purpose at all. With Torah study and performance of mitzvos, there does not have to be a palpable, identifiable goal. The fact that one is doing what God instructed is enough of a goal.

This is the reason why we are discouraged from searching for logical reasons behind mitzvos, because doing so indicates that we consider mitzvos as a means toward something rather than as a goal. It is true that we can see ways in which some mitzvos are of benefit to us, but these must be considered to be secondary. The Torah prefaces the mitzvah of the red heifer with the phrase, "This is the law of the Torah" (*Numbers* 19:2). Just as the mitzvah of the red heifer is refractory to logical understanding, so must we approach all of Torah as primarily beyond our comprehension, and that which we do understand must be considered secondary.

We often think of the goal of mitzvos as being the heavenly rewards we will receive. Indeed, we pointed out earlier that the reason for Creation was so that our reward would be earned rather than gratis. However, earlier (1:3) we are told that our motivation for mitzvos should not be the reward, but rather only to carry out God's will. This is repeated in 2:4. The word "mitzvah," in addition to meaning "commandment," also means "to bind," and it is the process of doing the Divine will that binds us to God. It is related that someone came upon R' Shneur Zalman when he was in profound prayer and heard him crying, "I do not want Your *Gan Eden,* and I do not want Your *Olam Haba* (World to Come). I want only You."

This is what the Rabbi of Kotzk meant with his terse comment, "The seeking *is* the finding." The value of seeking God is in the process itself.

This is a subtle yet profound concept, but if we understand the prayer of R' Shneur Zalman, we can better understand R' Yaakov's statement in our mishnah. The bliss of *Gan Eden* is indeed incalculable, beyond the greatest ecstasy the human mind can possibly imagine, yet it pales in comparison to even one brief period of *teshuvah* and performance of mitzvos, because the latter is *the process,* which *is* the will of God.

People unfamiliar with this concept may ask, "Of what good is Torah study? Why should we send our children to yeshivos where they may spend years studying something which they cannot put to any tangible use?" Some may console themselves with, "The study of Torah sharpens their intellect. Learning Talmud will make them into more efficient lawyers, mathematicians, or physicists." Perhaps it may, but that is not the reason why we study Torah. The more we realize that the *process* of Torah study and performance of mitzvos is in itself the goal, the closer we come to a true grasp of Judaism.

ד/כג

[כג] **רַבִּי** שִׁמְעוֹן בֶּן אֶלְעָזָר אוֹמֵר: אַל תְּרַצֶּה אֶת
חֲבֵרְךָ בִּשְׁעַת כַּעֲסוֹ, וְאַל תְּנַחֲמֵהוּ בְּשָׁעָה
שֶׁמֵּתוֹ מֻטָּל לְפָנָיו, וְאַל תִּשְׁאַל לוֹ בִּשְׁעַת נִדְרוֹ, וְאַל
תִּשְׁתַּדֵּל לִרְאוֹתוֹ בִּשְׁעַת קַלְקָלָתוֹ.

23.

אַל תְּרַצֶּה אֶת חֲבֵרְךָ בִּשְׁעַת כַּעֲסוֹ
*Do not appease your fellow
at the time of his anger*

The truths of this mishnah are so self-evident that they do not require any commentary. To embellish this mishnah with interpretations is gilding the lily. Indeed, the wisest of all men states, "There is a time for everything," and proceeds to list a number of behaviors which require appropriate timing (*Ecclesiastes* 1:9). The very same action that can be beneficial at the proper time may be detrimental at another time, and one must use astute judgment to know when and when not. The best method to avoid saying something at the wrong time is to follow the recommendation of the Ramban in the letter to his son, where he instructs him, "Think about what you are going to say before you say it."

Even if we do think about what we wish to say, it may sometimes be difficult to decide whether it is appropriate or not. A good rule of thumb is to think, "If I were in that person's position, how would I feel if someone said that to me?" This is not foolproof, but it is a good way to begin the deliberation. This is another example of how important it is to empathize with another person. It indicates the wisdom of Hillel's remark to the proselyte that the essence of Torah is "Love your neighbor like yourself" (*Leviticus* 19:18), which he interpreted to mean, "Do not do anything to another person that you would not wish done to you" (*Shabbos* 31a).

Whereas interpretations of this mishnah may be superfluous, there are some practical applications that we should note. The admonition to not look at another person at the time of his degradation often goes unheeded. It is a common occurrence that when an ambulance pulls up, curious neighbors and passersby gather around to see what is happening, and just who is going to be brought out on a stretcher. Certainly these onlookers mean no harm, but they may not be aware that both the patient and the family may wish to keep their privacy, and may be quite irritated by the curiosity of the people assembled. Again, the rule of empathy should be applied. If, God forbid, this happened to you or to someone in your family, would you wish to have a group of spectators? We must always be sensitive to others' feelings.

The Chazon Ish was once walking with a student, and as they approached a house from which the loud exchange of a domestic dispute could be heard,

23. R' *Shimon ben Elazar says: Do not appease your fellow at the time of his anger; do not console him while his dead lies before him; do not question him about his vow at the time he makes it; nor attempt to see him at the time of his degradation.*

---

the Chazon Ish took the student by the hand and made a sharp turn away from the house. He explained, "I know the people who live in that house, and if they saw me passing by and hearing their arguing, they would be embarrassed."

There is another reason not to look at someone who is doing something wrong. The Talmud says that the reason the Torah approximates the laws of the Nazirite to the ritual of the woman suspected of being unfaithful is to impress upon us when we see the ritual which the woman undergoes that we should abstain from wine. Alcohol may result in the weakening of our inhibitions, and we may become more vulnerable to doing something immoral (*Sotah* 2a). The obvious question is that seeing the humiliation resulting from immoral behavior should serve as a deterrent to similar acts. Why must a person reinforce his inhibitions at this point? The answer is that the unpleasant consequences notwithstanding, witnessing improper behavior *may decrease* our resistance to such acts. Contrary to our logical reasoning, this is a time when we must reinforce rather than relax our defenses.

It is also important to know how to *react* when you see someone behaving improperly. Rather than having a knee-jerk response, we should consider whether saying something at this time would really deter him from what he is doing. If it would not, we should delay any criticism to a time when he may be more receptive. Again, the wise teaching of the Ramban should govern everything we say: *Think before you speak.*

A man who was a guest at his friend's home on Shabbos awoke Friday night and was astonished to see his host walking holding a candle. "*Gevalt!*" he shouted. "It's Shabbos." His host turned to him and said, "Oh yes, so it is," and gently set the candle on the table. He then turned to his guest and said, "I awoke in the middle of the night and did not remember it was Shabbos. When you screamed at me, my first impulse was to drop the candle. But then it would have gone out and I would have transgressed the prohibition of extinguishing a flame. This way, I set the candle down safely." In this case, a bit of reflection would have told the guest that his host, who was most observant of Shabbos, would not intentionally take a candle unless, upon awakening from a deep sleep, he would have forgotten that it was Shabbos. The loud shout was most inappropriate, and could have resulted in a more severe transgression.

The teaching of this mishnah is that one should always apply *sechel* (common sense) in relating to others.

ד/כד **[כד] שְׁמוּאֵל** הַקָּטָן אוֹמֵר: ,,בִּנְפֹל אוֹיִבְךָ אַל
תִּשְׂמָח, וּבִכָּשְׁלוֹ אַל יָגֵל לִבֶּךָ. פֶּן יִרְאֶה
יהוה וְרַע בְּעֵינָיו, וְהֵשִׁיב מֵעָלָיו אַפּוֹ.''

24.

בִּנְפֹל אוֹיִבְךָ אַל תִּשְׂמָח
When your enemy falls do not be glad

The Torah is a Torah of reality, given by the Creator of man Whose knowledge of the nature of man is perfect. God knows what is within the reach of a human being. He does not ask of us to do something that is beyond our capability. By the same token, we should realize that anything that God *does* ask of us is something that we can do.

As we said in the previous mishnah, the Torah says, "Love your neighbor as yourself" (*Leviticus* 19:18), which Hillel interpreted to mean "Do not do anything to another person that you would not wish done to you." Why does Hillel take a positive commandment, "Love your neighbor," and turn it into a negative one, "Do *not* do to your neighbor"? This is because Hillel knew that it is impossible for a person to love his enemies, hence God would not ask this of us. We are asked to control our actions and to refrain from doing things that we consider objectionable to others. Even this is a tall order, but it is within our means. To actually love our enemies is beyond the capacity of the average human being.

The Torah tells us not to take revenge and not to harbor resentments (*Leviticus* 19:18). As Ramchal says in *Path of the Just*, taking revenge is extremely sweet, and it requires much effort to restrain oneself. Yet, the Torah demands such restraint. In the above verse from *Proverbs* which Shmuel HaKattan used to quote frequently, we are required to suppress any satisfaction at the downfall of an enemy, but we are not required to love him.

There is a principle in Judaism that we are to emulate the Divine attributes (*Rashi, Deuteronomy* 13:5). The Midrash tells us that when the Egyptians were drowned in the Red Sea, and the heavenly angels wished to sing their daily praises to God, He silenced them, saying, "The works of My hands are drowning in the sea. Now is not the time to sing adulation." Although the Egyptians had been indescribably cruel and murderous toward the Israelites and deserved their punishment, God nevertheless grieved that it had to come to this. God observed the dictum, "Do not rejoice at the downfall of your enemy," and we are required to emulate Him.

But what about the *Shiras HaYam* (the song of the miraculous dividing of the sea; *Exodus* 15:1-19)? Is that not a song of triumph upon the destruction of the Egyptian army? Yes, but the essence of the song is not the personal

24. **S**hmuel HaKattan says: When your enemy falls do not be glad, and when he stumbles let your heart not be joyous, lest HASHEM see and it displease Him, and He turn His wrath from him [to you] (Proverbs 24:17-18).

---

triumph of the Israelites, but rather the glory of God which was revealed in this miracle. It declares the greatness of God to the world. The joy in this revelation overrides the requirement of restraint upon the downfall of a personal enemy. "I shall sing unto God for He is exalted above the arrogant." The angels were not permitted to sing the praise of God because their adulation would not be heard by humans and hence would not enhance the glory of God in this world. Similarly, the prophetess Deborah's song of triumph states, "I will sing unto God" and closes with "So shall all Your enemies perish" (*Judges* 5:31). David, too, speaks about the destruction of the "enemies of God" (*Psalms* 92:10). It is only when one is truly concerned with the glory of God rather than with one's own feelings that one may rejoice in His exaltation when His enemies perish.

The concept that God does not ask anything of us which is beyond our means is pivotal in Judaism. Many have unfortunately deviated from Torah observance because they felt it to be too demanding. We may have to give up some conveniences in the observance of Torah, but we must know that we are fully capable of doing so.

One might raise the objection that the Torah does require that we show kindness even to an enemy, as when it requires that we return a lost item to him or help him unload a heavy burden from his mule (*Exodus* 23:4-5). True, we are capable of controlling our actions, and we are required to be of assistance to someone we do not like, but we are not required to love him, because feelings are not under voluntary control. We should do things that may help change our feelings, as when the Talmud says that if a friend and an enemy both require help at the same time, we should first help the enemy (*Bava Metzia* 32b). Why? Because this may lessen our animosity. We do have control of our actions and we can be asked to do something we would rather not do. In this case doing a favor for someone we dislike is indeed a challenge, but it is within our means. This action may help change our feelings toward him, which is different than asking us to eliminate our dislike of him and replace it with love.

This principle cannot be overemphasized. Indeed, in his last words to the Israelites, Moses tells them that observance of the Torah is well within everyone's capability (*Deuteronomy* 30:14). This is particularly important to remember if we think that it is too demanding to get up for morning *minyan,* to find time every day for Torah study, or to close one's ears to *lashon hara.* Once we dispose of the rationalization that it is too difficult, Torah observance becomes as easy as Moses says it is.

ד/כה] **אֱלִישָׁע** בֶּן אֲבוּיָה אוֹמֵר: הַלּוֹמֵד יֶלֶד, לְמָה הוּא
דּוֹמֶה? לִדְיוֹ כְתוּבָה עַל נְיָר חָדָשׁ.
וְהַלּוֹמֵד זָקֵן, לְמָה הוּא דוֹמֶה? לִדְיוֹ כְתוּבָה עַל נְיָר מָחוּק.

25.

אֱלִישָׁע בֶּן אֲבוּיָה אוֹמֵר
Elisha ben Avuyah says

This mishnah is fascinating, not so much because of its content, but because of its author.
Elisha ben Avuyah is one of the most tragic
figures in Jewish history. He was a Torah scholar of the highest magnitude, yet
he became a heretic. The Talmud cites several possible reasons for his defection.
One opinion is that he saw a young man honoring his father by fulfilling his
bidding to send away the mother bird before taking the eggs from the nest. These
are two mitzvos for which the Torah promises a reward of long life for their
observance (*Exodus* 20:12; *Deuteronomy* 22:7). Yet, the young man fell from
the trree and was killed. Another opinion is that Elisha turned against God when
the great sage Chutzpis was killed by the Romans. As great a scholar as Elisha
was, he could not accept that there were some things that were beyond his
capability to understand.

As we have noted, the mystery as to why the righteous suffer is beyond our
ability to resolve. The Midrash states that God showed Moses the great leaders
that would follow him, and when he saw that R' Akiva was tortured to death, he
asked of God, "Is this the reward for studying Torah?" God answered, "This is
the way it must be," and did not give Moses the explanation he sought. Elisha
could not make peace with this and rebelled against God.

There are many anecdotes of the devotion of the great sage, R' Meir, to his
teacher-turned-heretic. When Elisha fell sick, R' Meir pleaded with him to
repent. "Is it not too late?" Elisha asked, and R' Meir answered that a person's
teshuvah can be accepted even if it is with his last breath. Elisha began to weep,
and died while crying. "I believe my teacher died amidst *teshuvah*," R' Meir said.

Perhaps it is because he may have redeemed himself with *teshuvah* in the final
moments of life that the Talmud quotes his teaching. It is axiomatic that no Torah
teaching is accepted from a person who is not fully observant of Torah. Even the
wisest words of Elisha would not have been included in the Talmud if he had not
ultimately done *teshuvah*.

I believe it is possible and perhaps even likely that Elisha's repentance began
somewhat before his very last moments, and that the teaching in this mishnah
was from that period. It is unlikely that the Talmud would have quoted the words
of an apostate. There is reason to believe that this very teaching was the
beginning of his regretting his apostasy.

The Talmud relates that when Elisha would come into a *cheder* and see young
children studying Torah he would say, "Why are they wasting their time here?

25. **E**lisha ben Avuyah says: One who studies [Torah] while [he is still] a child, to what can he be likened? — to ink written on fresh [clean] paper. And one who studies [Torah] as an old man, to what can he be likened? — to ink written on smudged paper.

Let this one learn carpentry, and this one art, and this one to be a tailor," and the children would then leave the *cheder* and abandon their learning. In the statement of this mishnah Elisha recanted and emphasized that it is precisely at the tender age of youth that learning Torah is most effective.

Some people today repeat Elisha's mistake when they fail to give their young children a Torah education. If the firm foundations of Torah study are not laid during their childhood, it becomes increasingly difficult to excel in Torah. This is particularly important in our times, when the world is so bereft of stable values. We must give our children an early grasp of Torah principles. Those who say, "Let the child choose for himself when he grows up," are making a grave mistake. The child does not remain a vacuum, and in absence of Torah values, he will adopt the values that prevail in his environment. He does not remain "a fresh paper" for long, as the existing cultural concepts are impressed upon him. Should he later wish to change, he will find this more difficult because in order to espouse new ideas, he must uproot those he has held. A person can become "a smudged paper" at a relatively young age, and parents who think they are giving the child freedom to choose are in error. By not providing him with Torah principles, they are essentially choosing the values of his peers and environment for him.

A careful reading of the mishnah validates this point. The opposite of "fresh" or "new" paper should have been "old" or "stale" rather than "smudged." The choice of words indicates that the decreased effectiveness of Torah study begun later in life is because the old ideas are entrenched and must be uprooted. At the very best, there is some residual even after the eradication. Superimposing Torah teachings upon concepts that are alien to Torah may preclude a clear grasp of Torah principles.

Elisha's repentance toward the end of his life, after many years of apostasy, may well have been due to his having had an early exposure to Torah. But just as an early exposure to Torah can facilitate *teshuvah* for one who has deviated from Torah, so can an early exposure to secularism render one vulnerable to return to the prevailing morals and ethics even if one has learned Torah in the interim.

יֶלֶד . . . זָקֵן
A child . . . an old man

Youth and age are not necessarily determined by numbers. One can have a youthful spirit even as a senior citizen, and one can feel exhausted and worn out in the prime of life.

At a chassidic gathering, a slight elderly gentlemen pushed aside two people

[כו] **רַבִּי** יוֹסֵי בַּר יְהוּדָה אִישׁ כְּפַר הַבַּבְלִי אוֹמֵר: הַלּוֹמֵד
מִן הַקְּטַנִּים, לְמָה הוּא דוֹמֶה? לְאוֹכֵל עֲנָבִים
קֵהוֹת, וְשׁוֹתֶה יַיִן מִגִּתּוֹ. וְהַלּוֹמֵד מִן הַזְּקֵנִים, לְמָה הוּא
דוֹמֶה? לְאוֹכֵל עֲנָבִים בְּשׁוּלוֹת, וְשׁוֹתֶה יַיִן יָשָׁן.

---

and jumped over the bench to the vacant space. "They think I am an old man of 93. Actually, I am three young men of 31."

The Rabbi of Bobov was conversing with a group of *chassidim*, when someone mentioned that this was a special day that warranted a bit of celebration. They agreed that they should have some refreshments, and looked around for whom they might send to get them

"Why don't you give me the money," the Rabbi said, "and I will send my boy." They did so, and after a lengthy interval the Rabbi returned, having gone himself for the refreshments. The embarrassed *chassidim* said, "We thought you were going to send your boy."

"I did," the Rabbi said. "As I grew older, I decided I would never abandon my youth, and I brought my 'boy' along with me to my old age."

Youth is characterized by energy and fervor. In our younger years we strive for great accomplishments. Some people, as they grow older, feel that their best years are behind them, and they lack the enthusiasm and motivation of their youth. We should never lose these qualities, and even as octogenarians we should dream and strive. There *is* a fountain of eternal youth. It is right within us.

26.

הַלּוֹמֵד מִן הַקְּטַנִּים, לְמָה הוּא דוֹמֶה?
לְאוֹכֵל עֲנָבִים קֵהוֹת . . .
וְהַלּוֹמֵד מִן הַזְּקֵנִים, לְמָה הוּא דוֹמֶה?
לְאוֹכֵל עֲנָבִים בְּשׁוּלוֹת

*One who learns [Torah] from the young,
to what can he be likened? —
to one who eats unripe grapes . . .
one who learns [Torah] from the old,
to what can he be likened? —
to one who eats ripe grapes*

According to some interpretations of this mishnah, there is some risk in learning from the young, because their immature thinking may be flawed, and one can develop erroneous concepts. This would seem to be in contradiction to the statement of Ben Zoma in the opening mishnah of this chapter, that a wise person is one who learns from *everyone*. This should not exclude someone much younger and immature. How are these two statements to be reconciled?

Perhaps a personal experience may shed some light on this. I was privileged to have a correspondence with the Steipler *Gaon* for many years. When I encountered some difficulty in my Talmud study, I would write it to him, and

26. **R**abbi Yose bar Yehudah of Kfar HaBavli says: One who learns [Torah] from the young, to what can he be likened? — to one who eats unripe grapes or drinks unfermented wine from his vat. But one who learns [Torah] from the old, to what can he be likened? — to one who eats ripe grapes or drinks aged wine.

---

he responded with an explanation that clarified it for me. At the bottom of the letter there would be a postscript: "If it is not too difficult for you, I would appreciate having a copy of this letter, because I am very protective of any *chiddushim* (insights) in Torah which God has granted me." Some time later, a new volume of his expositions on Talmud would appear, and I would find a discussion of the problem I had posed, but the explanation was much different than the one he had written me initially. The latter had been the first flash of insight that had occurred to him when he considered the problem, but he would not publish an insight until he had reexamined it and had given it considerable thought. After all, to publish an explanation on the Talmud for students and scholars to read is an awesome responsibility! In other fields, if a scientist publishes a concept which is erroneous, it is not catastrophic. When the error is discovered, one simply publishes the results of the new findings. This is not so with Torah, because of the axiom in Talmud that once a mistaken concept is absorbed, it may be very difficult to uproot (*Peschaim* 112a). The initial flash of insight may be compared to a lightning bolt which indeed brightly illuminates the sky, but does so only for a fraction of a second. If one tries to navigate by the brightness of the lightning, one can be in serious trouble. A more steady light, even if it is much less bright than the lightning, can allow a person to proceed safely.

What the Steipler *Gaon* would do was to rethink his explanation and reexamine it in the light of his vast knowledge of the Talmud and its commentaries. He would then refine it and edit it, and I am certain that it underwent numerous revisions before he allowed it to be published. The final product may have lacked the brilliance of the initial insight, but he felt it was his obligation to present what was true rather than to demonstrate his brilliance. It is a lesson in Torah study to compare the final version with the initial insight. I could see that the latter was essentially a seed or a blossom which grew into a plant. It may indeed be thought of as "unripe grapes." We should realize that ripe grapes do not appear fully formed, but begin as tiny, sour grapes, which mature into delicious fruit.

Ben Zoma was correct in saying that we must learn from everyone, even from those whose wisdom is much inferior to our own. R' Yose cautions us, however, not to take the knowledge that we learn from them *as the finished product.* Rather, consider it as being "unripe grapes" which must be allowed to

ד/כז-כח [כז] **רַבִּי** מֵאִיר אוֹמֵר: אַל תִּסְתַּכֵּל בַּקַּנְקָן, אֶלָּא בְּמַה
שֶּׁיֶּשׁ בּוֹ; יֵשׁ קַנְקַן חָדָשׁ מָלֵא יָשָׁן, וְיָשָׁן
שֶׁאֲפִילוּ חָדָשׁ אֵין בּוֹ.

[כח] **רַבִּי** אֶלְעָזָר הַקַּפָּר אוֹמֵר: הַקִּנְאָה וְהַתַּאֲוָה
וְהַכָּבוֹד מוֹצִיאִין אֶת הָאָדָם מִן הָעוֹלָם.

---

mature. Indeed, you may take the insights of the young, but reexamine them
and make the necessary corrections and revisions so that the conclusions you
reach are true. We should not be misled by the bright flash of lightning,
because it is not a reliable illumination. Rather, capture the energy of the
lightning bolt and develop it into a source of light that is steady.

There are some difficult portions of the Rambam's works which may be
clarified by brilliant interpretations. In one such case, the commentary, *Maggid
Mishneh,* offers an interpretation, but admits it is a difficult one. If one
compares this interpretation to another, more dramatic interpretation, one
may find the latter more acceptable. However, some correspondence from the
Rambam was later discovered, in which he responds to the question about his
statement with the "difficult" explanation that the *Maggid Mishneh* proposed.
The more dramatic interpretation was indeed brilliant, but the more subdued,
difficult one was correct.

We recite the blessing over Torah, referring to it as *Toras emes,* a Torah of
truth. The criterion is truth rather than brilliance, and this is the intent of R'
Yose's statement.

27.

אַל תִּסְתַּכֵּל בַּקַּנְקָן
Do not look at the jug

We have already noted that R' Meir accepted
Torah teaching from Elisha ben Avuyah, and
that he came under criticism for this. The Talmud
explains that R' Meir had the unique capacity to "eat the fruit and discard the
peel"; i.e., he was able to take what was good from Elisha and reject anything
that was tainted with his heretical concepts. R' Meir was unique in being given
this latitude. For everyone else the rule remains intact: One does not accept
Torah teaching from anyone who does not live a Torah-true life.

It is of interest, therefore, that R' Meir tell us not to judge a book by its cover,
except that he uses the wine-containing metaphor instead. Is R' Meir saying
that if the content is good, the character of the person who conveys is irrelevant? Is he giving *carte blanche* to emulate him and accept Torah teaching from
someone who is not Torah observant?

Hardly. R' Meir knew only too well the risks involved, and that the attitude
of his peers was critical of him. The Talmud states that R' Meir stood head and

27. **R**abbi says: Do not look at the jug, but at what is in it; there is a new jug filled with old wine, and an old jug that does not even contain new wine.

28. **R**abbi Elazar HaKappar says: Jealousy, lust, and glory remove a man from the world.

---

shoulders above his peers, who could not fathom the depth of his reasoning (*Eruvin* 13b). Being aware of his great capacities, R' Meir felt that he could safely extract the good from this enormously learned scholar who had deviated from Torah observance. His case was an exceptional one, not to be followed by others.

The metaphor R' Meir is using in our mishnah, that of old versus new vessels, refers to outward appearance only. There are some people who are charismatic and are excellent orators, hence they may give the impression of being extremely learned. On the other hand, there are those who are extremely humble, and to look at them one might never guess that they were great scholars. One of the greatest pre-Holocaust Talmudists was R' Menachem Ziemba, who was the proprietor of a hardware store in Warsaw. Few people knew of his erudition. It was only when the Rabbi of Gur told him that the Torah world was in need of his knowledge that he was essentially forced out of hiding.

We must be aware that the humility of Torah scholars may cause them to conceal their scholarship. Appearances may indeed be deceiving.

28.

הַקִּנְאָה וְהַתַּאֲוָה וְהַכָּבוֹד
מוֹצִיאִין אֶת הָאָדָם מִן הָעוֹלָם
Jealousy, lust, and glory
remove a man from the world.

The commentaries explain that these three drives are insatiable, hence the frustration resulting from their endless pursuit can be fatal. The validity of this statement may not be fully appreciated by everyone.

I am reminded of the dialogue between R' Shlomo Eiger, a great 18th century Talmudist and his son. He was not sympathetic to the chassidic movement and was very distressed when his son, R' Leib Eiger, became a follower of the Rabbi of Kotzk. When R' Leib returned home after a long stay in Kotzk, R' Shlomo, who thought *chassidim* were not adequately diligent in Talmud study, asked his son, "What did you learn in Kotzk?"

R' Leib responded, "I learned that God rules the world."

"And for that you had to spend all that time in Kotzk?" R' Shlomo asked. He then called in the maidservant and asked her, "Who rules the world?" The maidservant answered, "Why, God, of course!" "See," R' Shlomo said, "she says that without having spent many months in Kotzk."

"Yes, Father," R' Leib said, "she *says*, but I *know.*"

That is how I feel about R' Elazar's statement. People who recite *Ethics of the Fathers* on Shabbos may read this mishnah without concentrating adequately on it. Even those who do may accept it intellectually may not fully appreciate it. Like R' Leib Eiger, I feel that others *say,* whereas I *know.*

The reason I make this statement is because for the past 35 years I have been treating addicted people. Many times each day I encounter people who were destroying themselves as well as harming those they loved by pursuit of something that could never be satisfied. The more they tried to satisfy the craving, the more intense it became, and this could even result in their death. People who become addicted to alcohol or drugs embark on a pursuit of gratifying a pathological craving which can never be satiated. The more they drink or use drugs, the more intense their craving becomes. Their ever-increasing need for these chemicals results in widespread destruction, as they impoverish themselves and their families, violate the law, inflict severe emotional pain on everyone, ruin their health, and not infrequently die as a result of their chemical abuse. This is the prototype of the pursuit of any insatiable craving. This is as true of jealousy, lust, and glory as it is of any number of drugs.

As with drugs, so it is with the pursuit of these other cravings. The person is unable to recognize that what he is doing is self-destructive. The intense craving renders him blind to reality, and even when it is clearly demonstrated to him that he is destroying himself, he is unable to see this. A person may read the wonderful works of *mussar* and listen to lectures on *middos,* yet walk away as though these teachings do not apply to him. The intensity of the denial is truly frightening.

It is not unusual for a person to see these traits in others, yet be completely oblivious of them in himself. A person may feel that he is very firm in his convictions, but he may consider anyone else who is "firm in his convictions" as being obstinate as a mule. Or he may pride himself on being accommodating and flexible, but think of others who are like that as being spineless jellyfish.

There is a well-known anecdote about a man who was reciting the confession on Erev Yom Kippur in which he was declaring his self-effacement and humility by reciting, "I am a nothing." Nearby him stood another man, a rather simple, unassuming person. As the former overheard him reciting the same phrase, he turned to a friend and said, "Just look at who thinks he is a nothing!" His verbalization of humility was lip service, and had not decreased his vanity and feeling of superiority over others even one iota.

Ironically, there is a saving grace in alcohol or drug addiction, because eventually the condition precipitates some kind of crisis that shocks the person into reality. At this time he may accept treatment for his condition and turn his life around. Unfortunately, with jealousy, lust, and glory there is not likely to be any crisis that may bring a person to his senses. People may have these self-destructive traits for their lifetime, which, as R' Elazar states, may be shortened by these futile and endless pursuits.

The pursuit of glory is a problem which can generally be traced to feelings of low self-esteem. A person who has unwarranted yet intense feelings of inferiority may have transient relief from these when he receives honor and acclaim. This gives him a feeling of worthiness. "If others think highly of me, I must really be good."

This attempt to compensate for feelings of inferiority yields only temporary relief. It is possible for a person to compensate for a defect that exists in reality, as when a blind person develops an acute sense of hearing or touch to compensate for his inability to see. However, if in fact one does *not* have a defect in reality, but *thinks* he is defective, no amount of reassurance will be of any duration. Trying to compensate for an imagined deficiency is like trying to fill a bottomless pit. All efforts are futile, and the person exhausts himself trying to do the impossible.

It is quite likely that jealousy and lust may also be at least in part the result of low self-esteem. Feelings of inferiority may be extremely painful. Inasmuch as a person generally does not know that his emotional distress is the result of low self-esteem, he may attribute his unhappiness to not having the things that others have. "I would be much happier if I had a nicer house, a luxury automobile, or more money." This may result in his being jealous of those who do have these things. On the basis of my clinical experience, I can tell you that I have come across people who have all of the above and even more, yet are most unhappy. Similarly, just as a person may seek relief from discontent by use of alcohol or drugs, so he may also try to escape into physical indulgences. All of these do not produce lasting contentment, and their endless pursuit may indeed "remove a man from the world."

A healthy self-esteem, based on a true self-awareness, a sense of purpose in life, and behavior which is directed toward fulfilling that purpose, may keep a person in the world. There are numerous passages in the Talmud where sages who lived to a very old age were asked, "How did you merit such longevity?" Their answers varied, but all describe how they each pursued their goal in life, by virtue of which they eliminated those things which R' Elazar points out that "remove a man from the world."

We do not have to go all the way back to Talmudic times for this phenomenon. Very close to our own times, there was the Chofetz Chaim, the sage of the past century who lived into his 90s. His lifestyle was most austere, his denial of worldly pleasures bordered on asceticism, and his rejection of acclaim and glory is legendary. In fact, the Chofetz Chaim quoted our mishnah and pointed out that it is not only the relentless *pursuit* of glory that is harmful, but that the mishnah states that glory per se is toxic. When any honor was accorded him, he refused to accept it, stating that this was simply self-preservation.

Did the Chofetz Chaim have good self-esteem? He wrote the *Mishnah Berurah*, which may well be the definitive work on the *Shulchan Orach Orach Chaim* (Code of Jewish Law) until the end of time. Unless he was fully aware of his encyclopedic knowledge and thorough understanding of everything

[כט] **הוּא** הָיָה אוֹמֵר: הַיִּלוֹדִים לָמוּת, וְהַמֵּתִים לִחְיוֹת,
וְהַחַיִּים לִדּוֹן — לֵידַע לְהוֹדִיעַ וּלְהִוָּדַע
שֶׁהוּא אֵל, הוּא הַיּוֹצֵר, הוּא הַבּוֹרֵא, הוּא הַמֵּבִין, הוּא הַדַּיָּן,
הוּא הָעֵד, הוּא בַּעַל דִּין, הוּא עָתִיד לָדוּן. בָּרוּךְ הוּא, שֶׁאֵין
לְפָנָיו לֹא עַוְלָה, וְלֹא שִׁכְחָה, וְלֹא מַשּׂוֹא פָנִים, וְלֹא מִקַּח
שֹׁחַד; שֶׁהַכֹּל שֶׁלּוֹ. וְדַע, שֶׁהַכֹּל לְפִי הַחֶשְׁבּוֹן. וְאַל יַבְטִיחֲךָ
יִצְרְךָ שֶׁהַשְּׁאוֹל בֵּית מָנוֹס לָךְ — שֶׁעַל כָּרְחֲךָ אַתָּה נוֹצָר,
וְעַל כָּרְחֲךָ אַתָּה נוֹלָד; וְעַל כָּרְחֲךָ אַתָּה חַי; וְעַל כָּרְחֲךָ
אַתָּה מֵת; וְעַל כָּרְחֲךָ אַתָּה עָתִיד לִתֵּן דִּין וְחֶשְׁבּוֹן לִפְנֵי
מֶלֶךְ מַלְכֵי הַמְּלָכִים, הַקָּדוֹשׁ בָּרוּךְ הוּא.

---

there was to know in halachah, how could he have taken on the awesome
responsibility of being the final authority in halachah? Obviously, the Chofetz
Chaim knew his capabilities, yet this not deter him from a humility and
self-effacement that was comparable only to that of Hillel. That is what is
meant by healthy self-esteem.

29.

הַיִּלוֹדִים לָמוּת, וְהַמֵּתִים לִחְיוֹת
The newborn will die;
the dead will live again

In this mishnah Rabbi Elazar gives a summation
of reality, some of which is reality as it is perceived, e.g., all those born will one day die;
people are born without willing to be born, and
people die without willing to die, and reality as it is taught by Torah, e.g., the
dead will again come to life; there will be an accounting before God on Judgment Day.

Ethics of the Fathers is a guide to proper living, and it should be obvious that
a person cannot make an optimum adjustment to life unless he has an accurate
perception of reality. A psychotic person whose perception of reality is distorted by delusions or hallucinations cannot possibly make an optimum adjustment to life.

The first words of the mishnah, that all humans are destined to die and that
the dead will come to life, is a combination of perceived and believed reality.
I can attest to the value of these perceptions from my experience as a rabbi and
as a psychiatrist.

As a rabbi, it was my function to officiate at funerals. Halachah requires that
burial be in a simple coffin, and that the mourners remain at the graveside until
the grave is completely filled with earth. Not infrequently, coffins are fashioned

29. **H**e *[Rabbi Elazar HaKappar] was accustomed to say: The newborn will die; the dead will live again; the living will be judged — in order that they know, teach, and become aware that He is God, He is the Fashioner, He is the Creator, He is the Discerner, He is the Judge, He is the Witness, He is the Plaintiff, He will judge. Blessed is He before Whom there is no iniquity, no forgetfulness, no favoritism, and no acceptance of bribery, for everything is His. Know that everything is according to the reckoning. And let your Evil Inclination not promise you that the grave will be an escape for you — for against your will you were created; against your will you were born; against your will you live; against your will you die; and against your will you are destined to give an account before the King Who rules over kings, the Holy One, Blessed is He.*

---

of bronze and quilted with silk. Some families go to great expense "to give the departed the finest." Unfortunately, some families would leave the cemetery before the coffin was lowered, and when I explained that this was not in keeping with halachah, people explained that this was to spare the mourners the emotional pain of witnessing the entire burial process of their loved one.

Years later, as a psychiatrist, I treated any number of patients who were experiencing emotional difficulty because of unresolved grief reactions. Invariably these were people who had not gone through the grief process at the time of their loss, a time when this was a normal and healthy reaction. The delayed grief emerged at a time when they were unprepared for it. The normal emotional response at the time of the loss, the sadness and crying, were understood by the mourner and by everyone in the environment. Unresolved grief feelings that emerge months and even years later in a variety of symptoms totally bewilder the patient, who has no inkling why he is feeling this way, and those around him cannot understand what is happening to him.

Let's face it. Parts of reality are unpleasant and may be extremely painful. Death of a loved one can be devastating, but if it occurs, it is a reality that cannot be denied. There are no two ways about it: Denial of reality is delusional, and cannot result in an optimum adjustment to the reality in which a person must live.

Halachah recognizes this and deals with it frankly. There is no denying of what happened nor disguising it. There are no frills that can eliminate the pain subsequent to the loss of a loved one. The painful reality must be acknowl-

רַ**בִּי** חֲנַנְיָא בֶּן עֲקַשְׁיָא אוֹמֵר: רָצָה הַקָּדוֹשׁ בָּרוּךְ הוּא
לְזַכּוֹת אֶת יִשְׂרָאֵל, לְפִיכָךְ הִרְבָּה לָהֶם תּוֹרָה
וּמִצְוֹת, שֶׁנֶּאֱמַר: "יהוה חָפֵץ לְמַעַן צִדְקוֹ, יַגְדִּיל תּוֹרָה
וְיַאְדִּיר."

edged, accepted, and overcome so that one can proceed with life. To provide
a departed person with a quilted coffin, as though he could feel its comfort, is
nothing less than a denial of his death. Witnessing the covering of the grave
may indeed be painful, but it brings closure to the episode. This is followed by
the week of *shivah,* during which the mourner may not go to work or
participate in anything that would distract him from the sad reality. A person
has no choice whether or not to have a grief reaction. The only choice is
whether to have it at the proper time when it can best be handled, or to put it
off in the deceptive hope that it can be avoided.

Some people have a mistaken concept of kindness. It is not unusual in the
hospital, when relatives are told that a loved one has died, for a nurse to offer
them a tranquilizer. This is a serious mistake. All that tranquilizers can do is dull
a person's sensations to prevent him from perceiving reality correctly and
dealing with it effectively.

Survivors may be comforted by their faith. We believe that our life in this
world is but a sojourn. As we have seen in an earlier mishnah (4:21), it is a

Rabbi Chanania ben Akashia says: The Holy One, Blessed is He, wished to confer merit upon Israel; therefore He gave them Torah and mitzvos in abundance, as it is said: HASHEM desired, for the sake of its [Israel's] righteousness, that the Torah be made great and glorious (Isaiah 42:21).

---

period in which we can prepare ourselves for an eternal existence. While death is indeed a painful separation, it is only a transient one. Eventually there will be a reunion of souls that will remain uninterrupted. This combined perception of the two realities may forestall the distress of unresolved grief reactions.

Rabbi Elazar goes on to point out that life has meaning, and that every person has a mission in life. It is for this reason that there is accountability as to whether one fulfilled his mission or was derelict in its performance. Precisely because one must be in optimum condition to execute one's mission on earth, one cannot afford to indulge in deceptive comforts which will later result in dysfunction, any more than one can take a narcotic to relieve the pain of an inflamed appendix. Such misguided attempts at comfort can have serious consequences.

In the previous mishnah, R' Elazar cautions against destructive traits which can "remove a person from the world." In this mishnah he provides valuable advice as to how we may stay in it.

פרק חמישי ‎&§
Chapter Five

כָּל יִשְׂרָאֵל יֵשׁ לָהֶם חֵלֶק לָעוֹלָם הַבָּא, שֶׁנֶּאֱמַר: „וְעַמֵּךְ כֻּלָּם צַדִּיקִים, לְעוֹלָם יִירְשׁוּ אָרֶץ, נֵצֶר מַטָּעַי, מַעֲשֵׂה יָדַי לְהִתְפָּאֵר."

All Israel has a share in the World to Come, as it is said: And your people are all righteous; they shall inherit the land forever; a branch of My plantings, My handiwork, in which to take pride (Isaiah 60:21).

[א] **בַּעֲשָׂרָה** מַאֲמָרוֹת נִבְרָא הָעוֹלָם. וּמַה תַּלְמוּד
לוֹמַר? וַהֲלֹא בְּמַאֲמָר אֶחָד יָכוֹל
לְהִבָּרְאוֹת? אֶלָּא לְהִפָּרַע מִן הָרְשָׁעִים, שֶׁמְּאַבְּדִין אֶת
הָעוֹלָם שֶׁנִּבְרָא בַּעֲשָׂרָה מַאֲמָרוֹת, וְלִתֵּן שָׂכָר טוֹב

Chapter Five

1.

בַּעֲשָׂרָה מַאֲמָרוֹת נִבְרָא הָעוֹלָם . . .
אֶלָּא לְהִפָּרַע מִן הָרְשָׁעִים

With ten utterances the world was created . . .
This was to exact a payment from the wicked

The obvious problem addressed by the commentaries is whether we are to understand the mishnah to mean that the wicked will be dealt with more harshly because they are ruining a world which was created with ten rather than one utterance. This is incompatible with our understanding of Divine justice, let alone Divine mercy. It appears unfair to set up conditions which will increase the gravity of a transgression.

Several commentaries, most prominently *Ruach Chaim*, provide a different interpretation of the mishnah. If we pay close attention to the wording in the mishnah, we will note that it refers to the *reward* for the righteous, but does not state the logical opposite, i.e., *punishment* for the wicked. Rather it uses the term לְהִפָּרַע, which means "to exact payment." In other words, the world was created with ten utterances in order to give the sinful an opportunity to repay or make amends for their wrongs, and it is thus an example of Divine mercy.

The Midrash points out that in the account of Creation, the pattern is "God said . . . and it was so." The one exception is, "God said, 'Let there be light, and there was light.'" Why does the Torah not say, "and it was so"? The Midrash explains that the initial light of Creation was a wondrous light, one which enabled a person to see "from one end of the earth to the other." However, inasmuch as God knew that there would be sinful people who would be undeserving of this wondrous light, he concealed it "for the righteous in the World to Come," and replaced it with a lesser light. Hence, the Torah does not say, "and it was so," which would indicate that the original light of Creation remained. Rather, "God said, 'Let there be light,' and there was (another) light." According to this Midrash, the sinful were responsible for a negative change in Creation.

Inasmuch as the Divine utterance for creation of light did not contain any other elements of Creation, nothing else was affected. Those responsible for this unfavorable change do not bear an overwhelming liability, hence it is within their means to atone and make amends. Had there only been a single utterance for Creation, the negative effect of the sinful would have had a much broader

1. **W**ith *ten utterances the world was created. What does this come to teach us? Indeed, could it have not been created with one utterance? This was to exact a payment from the wicked, who destroy the world that was created with ten utterances, and to bestow goodly reward*

---

impact, and it might have been beyond their capacity to atone for this. The division of Creation into ten utterances was therefore in *consideration* of the sinful, to minimize the consequences of their wrongdoings.

There is a novel, ingenious interpretation of this mishnah which also follows the theme that the Creation of the world with ten utterances rather than one was to mitigate the retribution of the sinful. It is based on the principle that God does not deviate from His system of justice, as it is said, "The King establishes His land by the law." While there is forgiveness, this can only be within the system of justice, which provides for forgiveness when there is adequate *teshuvah*. However, one may not say, "Never mind. God will overlook this" (see *Bava Kamma* 50a). There is no overlooking, as R' Elazar said above, "Everything is according to the reckoning" (4:29). However, since God is merciful, He devised ways in which the punishment of wrongdoers can be mitigated within the system of justice.

God therefore created the world with ten utterances in order to give greater reward to the righteous. It would appear then that the punishment that has been designated for the sinful should be correspondingly severe, since they violated the world that was created with ten utterances. This, however, provides the sinful with a cogent defense; i.e., "Just because You created the world in a manner to give greater reward to the righteous is no reason to deal with us so harshly. Had You created the world with just one utterance, our misdemeanors would not have called for that severe a punishment." Inasmuch as this is a reasonable argument, God can mitigate the retribution of the sinful, yet remain within His system of justice.

There is a principle that once God gave the Torah to man, He will not change it. Indeed, God abides by the halachah based on the interpretations of Torah by Torah scholars. This interpretation of the mishnah is thus adopted by God as part of His system of justice, and results in His extending mercy to those who would otherwise face a harsh sentence on Judgment Day.

הָרְשָׁעִים, שֶׁמְּאַבְּדִין אֶת הָעוֹלָם
שֶׁנִּבְרָא בַּעֲשָׂרָה מַאֲמָרוֹת
**The wicked, who destroy the world
that was created with ten utterances**

There are those who complain that some of the laws of Torah are too restrictive, and they seek to change Torah in order to accommodate themselves. This attitude is based

on a lack of understanding of Torah.

לַצַּדִּיקִים, שֶׁמְּקַיְּמִין אֶת הָעוֹלָם שֶׁנִּבְרָא בַּעֲשָׂרָה מַאֲמָרוֹת.

[ב] **עֲשָׂרָה** דוֹרוֹת מֵאָדָם וְעַד נֹחַ, לְהוֹדִיעַ כַּמָּה

Zohar (Vayeitzei) teaches that the Torah was the instrument wherewith God created the world: ("He looked into the Torah and created the world.") By this it is meant that the laws of Torah are the fundamental basis for the *laws of nature*, and are as inexorable as the law of gravitation. Torah laws cannot be amended or repealed any more than one can amend or repeal the law of gravitation. Inasmuch as the world was designed to operate according to the laws of Torah, any violation thereof exerts a negative effect on the world.

We can better understand this than our forebears could. As a result of our rather reckless conduct, we have not only polluted our air and water, but have also tampered with the ozone layer, which is causing global warming. This is held responsible for the widespread devastation caused by El Niño, which has resulted in the loss of many thousands of lives and in property damage into the many billions. When we drive our automobiles and emit fumes from the exhaust, or when we use a spray can that emits a fine mist, we may say, "Of what significance can this possibly be? This tiny bit of material can hardly exert any kind of effect on the world." Yet, the cumulative effect of these actions threaten the very existence of humanity. When laws to restrict these abuses are adopted and enforced, there are loud outcries of protest from those who feel inconvenienced by them, and they may petition their legislators to repeal these restrictive laws. Is it not the height of folly and gross irresponsibility to do so? Can the decision of the legislatures and courts prevent the impact on the atmosphere resulting from our behavior?

This is how we must understand the relationship of Torah to the world. Torah laws are not rituals that were superimposed upon the world, but are rather the very laws of nature according to which the world optimally operates. Neglecting these laws or tampering with them has an inexorable effect, and rabbinical rulings cannot prevent such an effect.

The wording of the mishnah is thus valid. The violation of Torah law *destroys* the world, just as does reckless conduct that upsets the delicate balance of world ecology.

2.

עֲשָׂרָה דוֹרוֹת מֵאָדָם וְעַד נֹחַ
There were ten generations from Adam to Noach

The commentaries raise the question: What is the intent of this mishnah? If it is to tell us about the extent of God's patience, we may ask: Why did it come to an end after ten generations?

This mishnah has an extremely important message, which is most vital for us today. God's patience is not time limited to any number of generations. He is

upon the righteous, who sustain the world that was created with ten utterances.

2. T*here were ten generations from Adam to Noah — to*

---

as patient with the most severely sinful as with those less sinful. But whereas God's patience is infinite, it is contingent on one thing: the possibility that the sinful person will do *teshuvah*. We say this in the closing prayer of Yom Kippur: "You desire the *teshuvah* of the wicked and You do not wish their death." This is clearly stated in Scripture, " 'Do I desire at all the death of the wicked men?' declares God. 'Is it not rather his return from his (errant) path that he might live?' " (*Ezekiel* 18:23). This concept is so important, that it is repeated several times (*Isaiah* 55:7; *Ezekiel* 18:32, 33:11). As long as there is even the slightest possibility of *teshuvah,* God is patient.

Whereas the ten generations that preceded the Deluge were most sinful, God was patient with them, because there was the possibility of *teshuvah*. This situation changed with the generation of the Deluge.

The Talmud states that the fate of the generation of the Deluge was sealed because of the sin of robbery. In other words, their gross immorality and corruption, as serious as it was, did not yet warrant their destruction, but the sin of robbery did. Why was this sin so grave that it precluded God's patience?

The answer lies in the way robbery was committed. The Talmud describes three types of thievery: (1) the *ganav*, the thief who steals in stealth, under cover of darkness; (2) the *gazlan*, the armed robber; and (3) the *chamsan*, one who takes away an item from its owner by force, but gives him the money it is worth. One might think that the *chamsan* is the least sinful of the three, because he compensates the victim for his loss, but the opposite is actually true. The *ganav* and *gazlan* have a greater possibility of *teshuvah*. Their conscience may so trouble them that they may return the stolen object. The *chamsan* is most unlikely to do *teshuvah* because he thinks he did nothing wrong. "Why should I return the item? After all, I paid for it, didn't I?" He sees his act as a legitimate purchase rather than as a crime. His conscience is clear, which makes *teshuvah* virtually impossible.

Close attention to the words of Scripture indicate that the generation of the Deluge engaged in *chamas* (*Genesis* 6:11), i.e., compensated robbery. For this sin there was no possibility that they would do *teshuvah*. The Midrash also tells us that they would steal something the value of which was below the amount for which the owner could have recourse in court. Because this was not enforceable by law, they saw it as not being a sin. Again, if it was not recognized as a sin, there could be no *teshuvah*. It is this that distinguished them from the sinful of the previous generations. In the absence of any possibility that they might mend their ways, there was no option other than that they be destroyed.

We find a similar occurrence in the destruction of Sodom. Here, too, there was no possibility of *teshuvah*. As the Midrash tells us, the laws of Sodom were

אֶרֶךְ אַפַּיִם לְפָנָיו; שֶׁכָּל הַדּוֹרוֹת הָיוּ מַכְעִיסִין וּבָאִין, עַד שֶׁהֵבִיא עֲלֵיהֶם אֶת מֵי הַמַּבּוּל.

[ג] **עֲשָׂרָה** דוֹרוֹת מִנֹּחַ וְעַד אַבְרָהָם, לְהוֹדִיעַ כַּמָּה אֶרֶךְ אַפַּיִם לְפָנָיו; שֶׁכָּל הַדּוֹרוֹת הָיוּ מַכְעִיסִין וּבָאִין, עַד שֶׁבָּא אַבְרָהָם אָבִינוּ וְקִבֵּל שָׂכָר כֻּלָּם.

---

corrupt. According to their laws, what we consider to be criminal acts were rewarded, whereas anyone who did an act of benevolence was punished. When crime is legitimized, there can be no *teshuvah*.

This is a concept which is of great relevance in our time. Our legislatures and courts have legitimized actions that should be considered wrong. Just several years ago, when the first physician-assisted suicide was publicized, there was an outcry of protest and outrage. As more cases occurred, we became rather indifferent to this. Several states have recently adopted laws sanctioning this detestable act. For years marijuana has been known to be a drug that can have very harmful effects. Young people especially may lose their motivation to educate and advance themselves during the most propitious years of their lives. There is a movement to legalize marijuana (and even heroin and cocaine!), and under the guise of medical use, California has essentially done so. This kind of thinking essentially constitutes a surrender to what is wrong, with the attitude being, "Since you can't stop it, legalize it." This is a trend which may have far-reaching consequences. As long as something is considered wrong, there is hope that a person may come to his senses. Once he believes that what he is doing is right, there is little or no hope that he will change.

That is the lesson of this mishnah. The sins of ten generations may have been grievous, but as long as they were not legitimized, God was patient. As we noted in the quotes from Scripture, He hopes that the sinful can avert destruction by mending their ways. When people commit wrong deeds but are unable to recognize the true nature of their acts because they have given them social sanction, they are contributing to their own destruction.

3.

עֲשָׂרָה דוֹרוֹת מִנֹּחַ וְעַד אַבְרָהָם
There were ten generations from Noah to Abraham

All of *Ethics of the Fathers* is intended to serve as a guide for us to live an ethical life. How does the knowledge that Abraham received the reward of the past generations promote this goal? As with the previous mishnah, we find an important teaching here.

We have earlier alluded to the teachings in both chassidic and *mussar* writings, that there is no character trait that needs to be totally rejected. Rather, we

5/3   *to show the degree of His patience; for all those generations angered Him increasingly, until He brought upon them the waters of the Flood.*

3. **T**here *were ten generations from Noah to Abraham — to show the degree of His patience; for all those generations angered Him increasingly, until our forefather Abraham came and received the reward of them all.*

---

should be able to channel our traits toward desirable rather than undesirable goals. Whereas we think of anger as being bad, it is good if it is directed towards injustice. Envy of another's belongings is bad, but envy of those who have achieved great spirituality is good. Obstinacy is bad, but being firm and unyielding on moral principles is good. We noted a Midrash wherein Moses is quoted as having said that he was born with some very undesirable character traits, but that he redirected them to be refined and noble.

Abraham was not created fully formed, like Adam. His father, Terach, was a pagan, and other ancestors were not paragons of virtue. They presumably passed on to Abraham some very undesirable character traits, which, in their hands, were very objectionable. Like Moses, Abraham was able to convert and redirect these traits toward the service of God.

The chassidic writings state that *chesed* (benevolence) and "love" are outflows of the same Divine emanation. When directed properly, the love is expressed in love of God, love of Torah, love of one's fellow man, love of justice and righteousness. When misdirected, love can result in gratifying all one's animalistic desires, as when one indulges in food because one "loves" it, when one is greedy, or when one hoards money because one "loves" it, etc.

Paganism is replete with intemperance, and the deities the pagans worshipped indulged in sensualism. This was the inheritance of Abraham, which he was able to redirect so that he reached the zenith of *chesed*. In history we read about the alchemists who sought to convert base elements into gold. Abraham was a "spiritual alchemist." He took the base desires which he inherited from his ancestors and converted them into a desire for closeness with God. He took the "love" which they used for self-gratification and converted it into *chesed*. Abraham received the reward of the past ten generations, because they were derelict in that they failed to use their traits and energies properly. When Abraham did direct them toward *kedushah*, he reaped the reward that they might have earned had they done so.

There is more to this than admiring the greatness of the Patriarch. There is a rather prevalent belief that we are to a very great extent the product of how our parents raised us. While there is no question that our parents certainly have a significant impact on us, we are not wooden puppets whom they fashioned. We do not act because they are pulling the strings. We have the ca-

ה/ד־ו ‏[ד]‏ **עֲשָׂרָה** נִסְיוֹנוֹת נִתְנַסָּה אַבְרָהָם אָבִינוּ וְעָמַד בְּכֻלָּם,
לְהוֹדִיעַ כַּמָּה חִבָּתוֹ שֶׁל אַבְרָהָם אָבִינוּ.

‏[ה]‏ **עֲשָׂרָה** נִסִּים נַעֲשׂוּ לַאֲבוֹתֵינוּ בְּמִצְרַיִם וַעֲשָׂרָה עַל
הַיָּם. עֶשֶׂר מַכּוֹת הֵבִיא הַקָּדוֹשׁ בָּרוּךְ הוּא
עַל הַמִּצְרִים בְּמִצְרַיִם וְעֶשֶׂר עַל הַיָּם.

‏[ו]‏ **עֲשָׂרָה** נִסְיוֹנוֹת נִסּוּ אֲבוֹתֵינוּ אֶת הַקָּדוֹשׁ בָּרוּךְ הוּא
בַּמִּדְבָּר, שֶׁנֶּאֱמַר: „וַיְנַסּוּ אֹתִי זֶה עֶשֶׂר
פְּעָמִים, וְלֹא שָׁמְעוּ בְּקוֹלִי.‟

---

pacity to make changes in ourselves, even revolutionary changes. To patients who claim that all their problems are the fault of their parents, I say, "Even if you are what your parents made you, if you stay that way, that is your own decision."

Ethics of the Fathers is not a history book, but a guide to correct living. It tells us that Abraham did not turn out to be what Terach raised him to be. This teaches us that our early life experiences notwithstanding, we all have the capacity to become that which we should be.

4.

עֲשָׂרָה נִסְיוֹנוֹת נִתְנַסָּה אַבְרָהָם אָבִינוּ
Our forefather Abraham
was tested with ten trials

While it is indeed good to know the greatness of our forefather Abraham, it is not quite clear what the teaching is for us. Furthermore, is it not possible that Abraham withstood the ten trials because of fear of God or out of loyalty to God rather than because of his love for God?

Both of these questions are resolved if we understand the principle that God never places a greater burden upon a person than one is capable of carrying (*Avodah Zarah* 3a). One has greater expectations of a scholar and pious person than of someone unlearned and coarse. As Solomon states, "As knowledge increases, suffering increases" (*Ecclesiastes* 1:18). A person of scant spirituality will not be severely tested, whereas a person who has advanced to spiritual heights and can withstand greater tests may indeed be subjected to greater challenges.

The Patriarch Abraham perceived the pattern. As he drew himself closer to God, his trials became increasingly more severe. A person of lesser mettle would have said, "Enough! There is no purpose in my advancing myself spiritually, because this will only result in my subjecting myself to greater ordeals. Let me stop where I am, and spare myself further agony." But

5/4-6   4. Our forefather Abraham was tested with ten trials and he withstood all of them — to show the degree of our forefather Abraham's love for God.

5. Ten miracles were performed for our ancestors in Egypt and ten at the Sea. Ten plagues did the Holy One, Blessed is He, bring upon the Egyptians in Egypt and ten at the Sea.

6. [With] ten trials did our ancestors test the Holy One, Blessed is He, in the Wilderness, as it is said: They have tested Me these ten times and did not heed My voice (Numbers 14:22).

Abraham did not halt his spiritual progress. His love for God was so intense that he continued to draw himself ever closer to God, with the full knowledge that he was thereby rendering himself vulnerable to more strenuous trials. This could only be done out of love, and not out of fear or loyalty.

The message for us is clear. We, too, may come to be aware that we may encounter greater challenges in life as we advance spiritually. The Rabbi of Kotzk commented on the above verse in *Ecclesiastes*, "Suffer if you must, but be wise!" If we hesitate to advance spiritually, the logical conclusion is to become as ignorant as cows in the pasture, who seem to be very contented. Our pride as human beings should motivate us to maximize our capacities for spiritual development, even if this comes at a price.

5-6.

עֲשָׂרָה נִסִּים נַעֲשׂוּ לַאֲבוֹתֵינוּ . . .
עֲשָׂרָה נִסְיוֹנוֹת נִסּוּ אֲבוֹתֵינוּ אֶת הַקָּדוֹשׁ בָּרוּךְ הוּא
Ten miracles were performed for our ancestors . . . [With] ten trials did our ancestors test the Holy One, Blessed is He

Again, since *Ethics of the Fathers* is not a history book, what is the point of telling us that our ancestors were the beneficiaries of miracles?

Some people who struggle with *emunah* (belief in God) may say, "If only He were to give me a sign! If only we saw miracles the way our ancestors did." This sounds logical enough, but the fact is that the aphorism "seeing is believing" is not always true. It is possible for a person to witness a manifest Divine revelation and still not be a believer.

Let us look at the account of the Israelites in the Torah. Moses told them that God had sent him to deliver them from enslavement, and he performed miracles before their eyes. After the third of the ten plagues, Pharaoh's magicians admitted that Moses was exhibiting Divine powers. While the plagues

[ז] **עֲשָׂרָה** נִסִּים נַעֲשׂוּ לַאֲבוֹתֵינוּ בְּבֵית הַמִּקְדָּשׁ: לֹא
הִפִּילָה אִשָּׁה מֵרֵיחַ בְּשַׂר הַקְּדֶשׁ; וְלֹא
הִסְרִיחַ בְּשַׂר הַקְּדֶשׁ מֵעוֹלָם; וְלֹא נִרְאָה זְבוּב בְּבֵית
הַמִּטְבָּחַיִם; וְלֹא אִירַע קֶרִי לְכֹהֵן גָּדוֹל בְּיוֹם הַכִּפּוּרִים; וְלֹא
כָבוּ הַגְּשָׁמִים אֵשׁ שֶׁל עֲצֵי הַמַּעֲרָכָה; וְלֹא נִצְּחָה הָרוּחַ אֶת
עַמּוּד הֶעָשָׁן; וְלֹא נִמְצָא פְסוּל בָּעֹמֶר, וּבִשְׁתֵּי הַלֶּחֶם,
וּבְלֶחֶם הַפָּנִים; עוֹמְדִים צְפוּפִים, וּמִשְׁתַּחֲוִים רְוָחִים; וְלֹא
הִזִּיק נָחָשׁ וְעַקְרָב בִּירוּשָׁלַיִם מֵעוֹלָם; וְלֹא אָמַר אָדָם
לַחֲבֵרוֹ: „צַר לִי הַמָּקוֹם שֶׁאָלִין בִּירוּשָׁלָיִם."

---

devastated Egypt, the Israelites suffered no casualties. During the three days when the Egyptians were immersed in total darkness, the Israelites basked in the sunlight. When all the Egyptian firstborn died, not a single Israelite died. And finally, when the Israelites were trapped between the sea and the oncoming Egyptian army, the waters of the sea divided, and the Israelites crossed over a dry sea bed. Yet, the Talmud tells us, the *idol of Micah* accompanied the Israelites as they made their way between the walls of water. How is it possible to cling to idolatry when one has seen the undeniable hand of God at work?

We are not yet finished. Within days after the revelation at Sinai, the Israelites worshipped the Golden Calf. Every day fresh manna came down from the skies, and if anyone gathered more than his allotted amount it rotted. In the arid desert, Moses brought forth abundant water from a rock. Yet, all these striking miracles notwithstanding, the Israelites questioned the presence of God time after time.

This teaches us an important psychological concept. *If you wish to believe, then you will believe without miracles, and if you are determined to doubt, all the miracles in the world will not convince you.*

This is frequently evident clinically. If someone has a need to believe something, you will not be able to disprove it. There is an anecdote about a person who developed a delusion that he was dead, and absurd as it was, no one could convince him otherwise. One psychiatrist asked him, "Do dead men bleed?" The man answered, "Of course not." The psychiatrist said, "I want you to repeat aloud one hundred times, 'Dead men don't bleed.'" After the completion of the recitation, the psychiatrist pricked the man's finger, causing it to bleed. "There!" he said triumphantly. The patient responded, "Dead men *do* bleed."

On the other hand, if someone has the need to deny something, he will do so even if it is right in front of his eyes. Day after day I see people, often highly educated and very successful, who deny the incontrovertible evidence right before their eyes that they have lost control of alcohol, of drugs or of gambling.

The upshot of all this is that in order to stay in touch with reality, we often need

7. **T**en miracles were performed for our ancestors in the Holy Temple: (1) No woman miscarried because of the aroma of the sacrificial meat; (2) the sacrificial meat never became putrid; (3) no fly was seen in the place where the [sanctified] meat was butchered; (4) no seminal emission occurred to the High Priest on Yom Kippur; (5) the rains did not extinguish the fire on the Altar pyre; (6) the wind did not disperse the vertical column of smoke from the Altar; (7) no disqualification was found in the Omer, the Two Loaves, or the Show Bread; (8) the people stood crowded together, yet there was ample space when they prostrated themselves; (9) neither serpent nor scorpion ever caused injury in Jerusalem; (10) nor did any man say to his fellow, "The space is insufficient for me to stay overnight in Jerusalem."

---

an objective observer, perhaps a friend or a therapist who is not affected by our bias to spell out reality for us. This does not mean that we should blindly accept other's opinions, but rather that we should recognize that our convictions may be subject to our wishes, and that we must critically examine some of our certainties.

7.

עֲשָׂרָה נִסִּים נַעֲשׂוּ לַאֲבוֹתֵינוּ בְּבֵית הַמִּקְדָּשׁ
Ten miracles were performed for our ancestors in the Holy Temple

This mishnah, too, is not a historic narrative, but a lesson in living.

Mishnah 5 refers to the miracles of the Exodus — manifest and dramatic suspension of the laws of nature, whose supernatural character could not be denied, at least at the moment they occurred. This mishnah lists ten miracles, all of which were supernatural phenomena, but their true nature could be overlooked. The fact that a woman did not miscarry from the aroma of the sacrificial meat is not a stunning event, nor is the absence of flies in the room where slaughtering took place. It takes a bit of introspection to recognize that all the occurrences listed in the mishnah are not just natural phenomena.

David says, "God performs miracles alone" (*Psalms* 136:4), which the Talmud interprets to mean that only God knows that these happenings are miraculous, and not just natural events. We often refer to unusual happenings as "coincidental," but in fact there are no coincidences. It has been correctly said, "Coincidences are really miracles in which God preferred to remain anonymous."

Although dramatic miracles are impressive, any disruption of nature is transient. Miracles which occur under the guise of natural phenomena are of much

ה/ח [ח] **עֲשָׂרָה** דְּבָרִים נִבְרְאוּ בְּעֶרֶב שַׁבָּת בֵּין הַשְּׁמָשׁוֹת,
וְאֵלּוּ הֵן; פִּי הָאָרֶץ, וּפִי הַבְּאֵר, פִּי הָאָתוֹן,
וְהַקֶּשֶׁת, וְהַמָּן, וְהַמַּטֶּה, וְהַשָּׁמִיר, הַכְּתָב, וְהַמִּכְתָּב,

---

greater durability. It is for this reason that the Talmud gives great importance to Purim, considering it superior in some ways even to Passover. This is precisely because the miracle of Purim did not involve any suspension of the laws of nature. God's manipulation of the world was no less miraculous than when He divided the waters of the Red Sea, but it was not clearly evident.

It has been said that when King Ahasuerus had Queen Vashti executed, two Jews were conversing, and one said, "Did you hear what went on in the palace yesterday? The king was drunk, and was so provoked by the queen's behavior that he had her executed." Whereupon the other person said, "Don't bother me with that. I'm not interested in listening to meaningless gossip." Who could know then that this event would be the precursor to Esther being chosen as queen, and that this would lead to the salvation of Israel?

In his work, *Kedushas Levi*, R' Levi Yitzchak of Berditchev expands upon this theme. He explains why miracles that are within nature are superior to those that suspend the laws of nature. He explains why listening to the *Megillah* takes priority over Scriptural mitzvos, and why Purim is so important. This is because we must recognize that everything that happens in the world is directed by God, even events that seem to happen naturally. The Baal Shem Tov emphasized this by saying, "If you see a leaf blown by the wind from one place to another, it is because God wills it to be there." The concept of *hashgachah pratis* (Divine providence) is that with the exception of doing good or evil, which God has left to man's free choice, everything in the universe is under Divine control.

Some may ask: Is it not absurd to maintain that God will occupy himself with keeping a fly away from the Temple, or to care where a leaf lies? The answer to this lies in understanding the concept of infinity.

If one were to compare both a thimble full of water and a small lake to the Pacific Ocean, one may say that whereas the ocean is so many times greater than the lake, it is many, many times greater than the thimble full of water. This is because both are being compared to something finite. Whereas the Pacific Ocean is indeed vast, it nevertheless has boundaries and limits. However, when you compare anything to something infinite, large and small are equal. Thus, one divided by zero is infinity, and 50 billion divided by zero is also infinity. One infinity cannot be greater than another infinity. Greater or smaller apply only to things that have limits.

If one asserts that a leaf is too insignificant to warrant God's attention, can he assume that a super galaxy is so enormously great that it is important enough for Divine attention? In relationship to infinity, a leaf and a supergalaxy are equal. Either God is interested in everything or He is interested in nothing. To say that some things are too small to warrant God's attention but that others are

8. **T**en things were created on Sabbath eve, at twilight. They are: the mouth of the earth, the mouth of the well, the mouth of [Balaam's] donkey, the rainbow, the manna, the staff, the shamir worm, the script, the inscription,

---

large enough to be important indicates a failure of awareness that God is infinite.

The subtle miracles that the mishnah lists are no less momentous than the dramatic wonders of the Exodus. In ancient times there were people who believed in Creation, but felt that after God created the world He abandoned it because it is too unimportant to warrant His attention. The Talmud considers this *avodah zarah* (idolatry), because this leads to the conclusion that He turned the world over to underlings who should be worshipped. To assign relative importance to items large or small in relation to God's infinity is essentially making the same mistake. The mishnah teaches us the concept of *hashgachah pratis*. We, tiny humans, who are not even a microscopic speck on the celestial map, are very much the object of God's attention.

8.

עֲשָׂרָה דְבָרִים נִבְרְאוּ
בְּעֶרֶב שַׁבָּת בֵּן הַשְּׁמָשׁוֹת
Ten things were created on
Sabbath eve, at twilight

We have noted that in contrast to the other chapters of *Ethics of the Fathers* which clearly refer to the desirable *middos* that a person should develop, this chapter lists things of historical value; i.e., ten generations, ten trials, ten miracles, ten tests, and now ten things that were created the moment before the onset of Shabbos. We have seen, however, that all these "historical" mishnahs carry important ethical concepts. Certainly this mishnah is no exception.

Various explanations have been given as to why these items were created on the last moment of the Six Days of Creation. Perhaps the mishnah means to tell us that these were not created until after Adam's sin.

The chassidic works state that had Adam not sinned, the world would have become the *olam hatikun*, a world in which everything was right. There would not have been a *yetzer hara* and people would not have sinned. As a result of Adam's sin, we must wait until after the ultimate Redemption for the *olam hatikun* to come about.

The majority of the ten things listed in this mishnah would not have been necessary had people not sinned. The course of history would have been much different had the *olam hatikun* come about soon after Creation. But inasmuch as Adam did sin, all humans after him were vulnerable to sin. It was therefore necessary that the earth open to swallow Korach when he rebelled against Moses. It was necessary that there be manna and water in the desert for the Israelites who had to wander there for 40 years because of the sin of

וְהַלּוּחוֹת. וְיֵשׁ אוֹמְרִים: אַף הַמַּזִּיקִין, וּקְבוּרָתוֹ שֶׁל מֹשֶׁה, וְאֵילוֹ שֶׁל אַבְרָהָם אָבִינוּ. וְיֵשׁ אוֹמְרִים: אַף צְבָת בִּצְבָת עֲשׂוּיָה.

[ט] **שִׁבְעָה** דְבָרִים בְּגֹלֶם, וְשִׁבְעָה בְּחָכָם. חָכָם אֵינוֹ מְדַבֵּר לִפְנֵי מִי שֶׁגָּדוֹל מִמֶּנּוּ בְּחָכְמָה

---

the spies. It was necessary that there be a rainbow following the Deluge brought about by that sinful generation, etc. All the commentaries agree that the reason God did not wait to create all these things until they were needed was because the entire work of Creation was to be completed in the six days. God did not create an imperfect world, hence these ten items had to be provided for before Creation was completed.

But why were they created the moment before Shabbos? This was because Adam was given *bechirah* (free will), to sin or not to sin. Had he not sinned, all the items that were needed because of the human capacity to sin would not have been needed at all. Thus, their creation did not come about until after Adam's sin.

But then they could have been created immediately after Adam's sin. Why did God wait until the very last moment of Creation? Because there was still a possibility for the *olam hatikun* to come into being had Adam done *teshuvah*. The Midrash states, however, that Adam did *not* do *teshuvah,* and in fact, when God reprimanded him for eating from the Tree of Knowledge, Adam said, "I ate from it and I will continue to eat from it," and was defiant toward God (*Bereishis Rabbah* 19:22). But even then there was still the possibility that Adam would do *teshuvah* before the Six Days of Creation came to a close. The Midrash (*Bereishis Rabbah* 22:28) states, however, that Adam was un- aware of *teshuvah* until much later, when he met his son Cain, and asked him, "What was the result of your judgment (for having killed Hevel)?" Cain answered, "I did *teshuvah* and I reached an accommodation with God." Adam then said, "Woe is me! I did not know that *teshuvah* is so powerful (that it can remove a sin)." It was not until after the Six Days of Creation that Adam did *teshuvah*. But by then it was too late. The period of Creation had been completed, and the opportunity to bring about the *olam hatikun* was lost. It was then that God provided for those things that would be the consequences of man's sin.

What is the teaching of this mishnah? It is that God waited until the very last second for Adam to do *teshuvah* and bring about the *olam hatikun*. All it would take for *teshuvah* was one moment, as the Talmud says (*Kiddushin* 49b), if a person marries a woman with the understanding and condition that he is a total *tzaddik*, then the marriage must be considered binding even if he were known to be a *rasha* (sinful person) of the worst kind. Why? Because of

and the Tablets. Some say also the destructive spirits, Moses' grave, and the ram of our forefather Abraham. And some say also tongs, which are made with tongs.

9. **S**even *traits characterize an uncultivated person and seven a learned one. A learned person does not begin speaking before one who is greater than he in wisdom*

---

the possibility that for a moment he thought to do *teshuvah.* Think of it! Here is a person who regularly violated Shabbos publicly, and ate *tereifeh* on Yom Kippur, yet, if he had a sincere thought of *teshuvah* he would be considered a complete *tzaddik!* Similarly, all that was needed for Adam to bring about the *olam hatikun* was just a moment of *teshuvah.* Since this is a matter of *bechirah* which God has left to man, God waited patiently for this moment of *teshuvah* to occur. It was only when night was about to fall and the period of Creation was coming to its very end, and seeing that Adam had not done *teshuvah* and that man would therefore be prone to sin, that God created those things that were necessary because of man's sins.

The Talmud (*Avodah Zarah* 17a) tell of Elazar ben Doradia, a profligate person who was immersed in the coarsest of sins his entire lifetime, and because he did *teshuvah* shortly before he died, he was granted *Gan Eden.*

The message of this mishnah is thus clear: Man always has the capacity to do *teshuvah,* a single moment of sincere *teshuvah* can remove one's sins, and God is infinitely patient, never giving up the hope that a person will do *teshuvah* until it is no longer possible for him to do so (cf. mishnah 2). And not only can *teshuvah* atone for a sin, but it can even convert sin to a merit (*Yoma* 86b), which would have enabled the *olam hatikun* to come about. This, then, is the power of *teshuvah,* and this teaching is certainly appropriate for *Ethics of the Fathers.*

9.

שִׁבְעָה דְבָרִים בְּגֹלֶם . . .
*Seven traits characterize
an uncultivated person . . .*

I have often been asked, "With your busy schedule, where did you find time to write 30 books?" My answer is that I did not write 30 books. Rather I wrote *one book* in 30 different ways. I am fixated on the idea that *all* psychological problems, with the exception of those that are primarily a result of a biochemical imbalance, can be traced to a single primary source: *the lack of self-esteem.*

The concept of self-esteem must be properly understood. Every person has a self-concept or self-image, and he functions according to this concept. A person who thinks of himself as dull is not going to aspire to go to a top-rated school, nor will he undertake anything that he feels is beyond his capacity to

וּבְמִנְיָן; וְאֵינוּ נִכְנָס לְתוֹךְ דִּבְרֵי חֲבֵרוֹ; וְאֵינוּ נִבְהָל לְהָשִׁיב; שׁוֹאֵל כָּעִנְיָן, וּמֵשִׁיב כַּהֲלָכָה; וְאוֹמֵר עַל רִאשׁוֹן רִאשׁוֹן, וְעַל אַחֲרוֹן אַחֲרוֹן; וְעַל מַה שֶּׁלֹּא שָׁמַע אוֹמֵר: „לֹא שָׁמַעְתִּי‟; וּמוֹדֶה עַל הָאֱמֶת. וְחִלּוּפֵיהֶן בַּגֹּלֶם.

[י] **שִׁבְעָה** מִינֵי פֻרְעָנִיּוֹת בָּאִין לָעוֹלָם עַל שִׁבְעָה

---

do. Furthermore, the way a person sees himself is how he believes others see him. This is the obvious teaching of the statement of the spies Moses sent to scout Canaan: "We saw giants there. We were as grasshoppers in our eyes, and that is how we appeared to them" (*Numbers* 13:33). I.e., the way a person thinks of himself is the way he is certain others perceive him.

Many people have a faulty self-image, in that they see themselves as less than they are in reality. They may think of themselves as unattractive, boring, dull, incompetent, inadequate, or negative in any one or more ways, while the reality is that the exact opposite is true. In fact, the most profound feelings of inferiority are likely to occur in people who are the most gifted. I expanded on this theme in *Let Us Make Man* (CIS Publications) and *Life's Too Short* (St. Martin's Press), and I suggested possible reasons for this phenomenon and gave examples of a variety of symptoms and inappropriate behaviors that may result from the self-image distortion.

The manifestations of low self-esteem are the result of a person either resigning himself to the status of inferiority or defending himself against this distressing feeling in any number of ways. One of these defenses may be to try to show that he is *not* inferior. Earlier, I presented the thesis that *gaavah* (vanity) is a desperate attempt to avoid the pain of feeling inferior. In contrast to the impression we may have that a vain person thinks of himself as the greatest, the fact is that he actually feels very *inadequate*. His vanity is but a shield to protect him from this feeling. He may also be supersensitive, thinking that his inadequacy is apparent to everyone. I was most pleased to discover this very concept in the works of Rabbeinu Yonah.

The seven traits that this mishnah lists of a *golem* (an uncultivated person) can all be seen as manifestations of the defensiveness of a person with a poor self-image. He may try to show how wise he is, and rather than listen to wise people, he tries to seize the stage. He may interrupt others, thereby indicating " I already know what you are going to say," or "what I have to say is more important." He is impetuous in his responses, because assuming that he knows it all, he does not take the time to deliberate. He is so preoccupied with himself that he does not pay attention to what others say. His questions may be off the mark or his response to a question may be inappropriate because he never bothered to hear it. By the same token, he does not weigh his thoughts to respond in an orderly fashion. He will *never* say, "I was not aware of that,"

or in years; he does not interrupt the words of his fellow; he does not answer impetuously; he asks relevant questions, and replies appropriately; he discusses first things first and last things last; about something he has not heard he says, "I have not heard"; and he acknowledges the truth. And the reverse of these [traits] characterizes an uncultivated person.

10. **S**even types of punishment come to the world for

---

because he cannot admit that there is anything he does not know. Finally, he cannot admit the truth, because he is absorbed with seeing everything in a way that would put him in a positive light. How things are in reality does not concern him.

Why is this person referred to as a *golem?* *Golem* is the raw material of which an object is made, or an incomplete object. A person who lacks a true self-awareness is an "incomplete" person. A complete person knows the truth about himself, both his strengths and his weaknesses, and he can exercise the former and seek to improve upon the latter.

A wise person behaves in just the opposite ways of a *golem.* He is not threatened that his "inadequacies" will be discovered. The truly wise person can afford to be humble. The sage of the last generation, the Chofetz Chaim, clearly was aware of his encyclopedic knowledge of the Talmud and halachah, else he would not have written the authoritative work on halachah, the *Mishnah Berurah.* Yet, his humility was legendary. People who knew the Chofetz Chaim were eyewitnesses to his manifesting the seven traits of a wise man that the mishnah lists.

We should realize that a person can adjust properly to reality only to the extent that he has a correct perception of reality. We should also realize that a person's self is a major part of one's reality. A person must perceive himself correctly in order to function optimally. That is the message of this mishnah.

10.

שִׁבְעָה מִינֵי פֻרְעָנִיּוֹת בָּאִין לָעוֹלָם
Seven types of punishment come to the world

It is one of the thirteen principles of Judaism that God rewards those who do His will and that He punishes those who transgress it. Nevertheless, anticipation of reward and fear of punishment should not be the reasons for performing mitzvos and avoiding sin, as was stated in Chapter 1 mishnah 3.

When God does punish someone it is only for that person's benefit. If a small child runs into the street, the father may accompany his reprimand with a *patsch* (smack) duly applied to the site which was designed to receive it. This

ה/יא גוּפֵי עֲבֵרָה: מִקְצָתָן מְעַשְּׂרִין וּמִקְצָתָן אֵינָן מְעַשְּׂרִין, רָעָב
שֶׁל בַּצְּרֶת בָּא, מִקְצָתָן רְעֵבִים וּמִקְצָתָן שְׂבֵעִים; גָּמְרוּ שֶׁלֹּא
לְעַשֵּׂר, רָעָב שֶׁל מְהוּמָה וְשֶׁל בַּצְּרֶת בָּא; וְשֶׁלֹּא לִטּוֹל אֶת
הַחַלָּה, רָעָב שֶׁל כְּלָיָה בָּא;

[יא] **הֶבֶר** בָּא לָעוֹלָם – עַל מִיתוֹת הָאֲמוּרוֹת
בַּתּוֹרָה שֶׁלֹּא נִמְסְרוּ לְבֵית דִּין, וְעַל פֵּרוֹת

---

is *not* child abuse. The child cannot understand the danger of running into traffic, and may wish to retrieve his ball that has rolled into the street,. The father must therefore impress upon the child that he dare not do so. If the child is at the age where a verbal reprimand is not understood, the *patsch* that is given out of love may be life-saving.

In *Deuteronomy* (8:1-10), Moses instructs the Israelites to observe the Torah in order that they may live and prosper, and points out the care which God provided for them during the 40 years of their sojourn in the desert. He then states, "You should know in your heart that just as a father disciplines his child, that is how God disciplines you." Divine discipline derives from God's love for us. We are much like the child, and because we may not understand that transgressing God's will is to our own detriment, God may have to deliver a *patsch,* something that we can understand, in order to protect us from harming ourselves. Hopefully, we will reach a level of maturity to understand that the mitzvos are for our own benefit.

In this mishnah, the Talmud tells us that there are specific punishments for certain transgressions, and that these should serve as a deterrent until we reach the point when we observe the word of God because we understand that it is for our own good to do so.

However, there is another concept of punishment, which holds that the punishment may not be directly inflicted by God but is rather a natural consequence of violating His will. The child who disobeys the father and is struck by a car when he runs into the street is not being punished by the father, but is suffering the natural consequences of disobeying him.

King David says in *Psalms* (34:22), "The deathblow of the wicked is evil"; i.e., the very wrongs that the sinful person commits will destroy him. Like the disobedient child who is struck by a car, this is not "punishment" in the usual sense of the word.

The *Zohar* states that the Torah was a blueprint for Creation: "God looked into the Torah and created the world accordingly" (*Zohar, Vayeitzei*). Just as there are physical laws of nature that are evident to us, there are also other laws of nature that are equally inviolable, although we cannot perceive them with our senses or grasp them with our limited human intelligence. The harm that results from tampering with the delicate balance of nature is not a "punish-

5/11   *seven kinds of transgressions. a) If some people tithe and others do not, a famine caused by lack of rain ensues; some go hungry and some are satisfied; b) if all decided not to tithe, [general] famine caused by armed bands and drought ensues; c) if [they also decided] not to separate challah, a famine caused by fatal drought ensues.*

11. d) P*estilence comes to the world for death penalties prescribed by the Torah that were not carried out by the court, and for [illegal use of] fruits of*

---

ment," but a natural consequence. Similarly, transgressing the Divine will results in a disruption of the normal functioning of the world, although we may not be able to associate cause and effect.

In Scripture we are warned against adopting the practices of the pagans of Canaan, because the Holy Land cannot tolerate these abominations. This could not have been stated with greater clarity than in *Leviticus* (18:27-28). After prohibiting immoral acts, the Torah says, "All these abominations were committed by the inhabitants of the land that preceded you, and the land was defiled. Let not the land expel you if you defile it as it expelled the people that preceded you." The Holy Land cannot harbor immoral people just as Antarctica cannot harbor giraffes and palm trees. The expulsion of Israel from the Holy Land does not have to be seen as a Divine punishment, but rather as a natural consequence.

This is equally true of other transgressions. The Torah associates pagan practices with expulsion from the Holy Land, and in this mishnah the Talmud reveals several other cause and effect associations. There are many more harmful consequences that result from violation of the Torah which we may not be able to perceive as cause and effect. We must know, however, that this is indeed the case. This is why those who try to amend the Torah for whatever reasons are as foolish as if they wished to amend the law of gravitation.

This, then, is the teaching of this mishnah. "Seven types of punishment *come to the world. . .,*" i.e., they are not necessarily inflicted as retribution, but are natural consequences of violating the laws according to which, as the *Zohar* says, the world was designed to function.

11-12.

דֶּבֶר בָּא לְעוֹלָם . . .
בְּאַרְבָּעָה פְּרָקִים הַדֶּבֶר מִתְרַבֶּה
Pestilence comes to the world . . .
At four periods pestilence increases

It is noteworthy that all the transgressions that are listed in these two mishnahs as the reasons for disastrous occurrences are all *bein adam la'chaveiro* (offenses against other

שְׁבִיעִית; חֶרֶב בָּאָה לָעוֹלָם – עַל עִנּוּי הַדִּין, וְעַל עִוּוּת
הַדִּין, וְעַל הַמּוֹרִים בַּתּוֹרָה שֶׁלֹּא כַהֲלָכָה; חַיָּה רָעָה בָּאָה
לָעוֹלָם – עַל שְׁבוּעַת שָׁוְא, וְעַל חִלּוּל הַשֵּׁם; גָּלוּת בָּאָה
לָעוֹלָם – עַל עוֹבְדֵי עֲבוֹדָה זָרָה, וְעַל גִּלּוּי עֲרָיוֹת, וְעַל

---

people), with the apparent exception of *chilul Hashem* (desecration of the Divine Name) and *avodah zarah* (idolatry). Even the violation of *Shemittah* (the Sabbatical year) is a sin that affects others, because the crops of the Sabbatical year are to be left for all to share. Depriving the poor is certainly a grievous sin. But how do *chilul Hashem* and *idolatry* fit into this pattern? These appear to affect only the relationship between man and God.

We have already noted that Torah and mitzvos were given for the refinement of man, as the Midrash says, "Of what difference is it to God how an animal is slaughtered? The mitzvos were given to refine man." God is absolute perfection and does not need anything from humans. "If you have sinned abundantly, how have you affected Him? . . . If you were righteous, what have you given Him?" (*Job* 35:6-7). The emphasis on *kevod Shamayim* (honor and respect of God) is so that we should accept His sovereignty and fulfill His commandments, which are to our own advantage.

While it may seem that the gravity of idolatry is because it is an insult to God, the fact is that God is not concerned about His honor for His own sake. "I wish they would not bother with Me, and rather observe My Torah" (*Jerusalem Talmud*, *Chagigah* 1:7). Just as a loving father is concerned that his child, who lacks an understanding of what may be harmful to him, should not endanger himself, so does God care that we should not do anything that would harm us. God has given man total freedom of choice in matters of good or evil, and desires that we do not act foolishly to our own detriment.

The Talmud states that although Scripture relates that the Israelites deviated to idol worship, this was not because they believed in the least that the idols were of any substance. As we know, Jews, by nature, are skeptical, and are hardly so credulous as to think that an idol has any powers. Rather, says the Talmud, they were looking for a dispensation that would permit them to gratify the desires that the Torah forbids. Idol worship was no more than an attempt to grant public sanction to gratification of their temptations (*Sanhedrin* 63b).

This phenomenon has repeated itself throughout history. When people feel that the Torah is too restrictive, they seek to find defects in the Torah. By challenging the legitimacy of Torah, they feel free to reject its laws. With or without a statue, tampering with the Torah to suit one's whim is no different than idolatry.

All of Torah is to refine man, whose limited intelligence cannot distinguish true good from evil, any more than a small child can know that playing with a sharp instrument can be very harmful. Hillel stated it succinctly, "All of Torah is 'Do not do to others what you would not have others do to you' " (*Shabbos* 31a). This

the seventh [Sabbatical] year; e) the sword [of war] comes to the world for the delay of justice, for the perversion of justice, and for rendering decisions contrary to the halachah; f) wild beasts come upon the world for vain oaths and for Desecration of God's Name; g) exile comes to the world for idolatry, for immorality, for blood-

---

was reiterated by R' Akiva who said, "The all-encompassing rule of Torah is 'Love your fellow man as you do yourself' " (*Jerusalem Talmud, Nedarim* 9:4).

How does one's consumption of *tereifeh* foods affect behavior toward others? How does avoidance of *tereifah* refine a person's character? We are unable to fathom Divine wisdom just as a child cannot understand that what his parents restrict him from doing is for his own welfare. We must have faith that inasmuch as the mitzvos of the Torah are not for the benefit of God, they can be only to our advantage, even though we may not understand how this is so.

The gravity of idolatry is that it provides a person with a way in which he can justify all his desires, corrupt or base as they may be. Idolatry can be used to sanction immoral behavior, infanticide, and any act which is morally reprehensible. Hence, idolatry can very profoundly affect a person's conduct toward others.

This is equally true of *chilul Hashem*. Reverence for God is a *sine qua non* for moral behavior. The Patriarch Abraham said to Abimelech, "Because there is no reverence for God here, I feared that they might kill me in order to take my wife" (*Genesis* 20:11). Even a cultured and sophisticated society is not beyond abominable behavior, as was so painfully proven by the inhuman atrocities of Nazi Germany. Any demonstration of lack of reverence for God diminishes people's resistance to sin. Any practice which causes a person to lose respect for Torah may divert people from proper ethical behavior as set forth in the Torah.

Both *avodah zarah* and *chilul Hashem* therefore belong to the category of *bein adam l'chaveiro*, because they undermine the foundation on which proper behavior is built.

גָּלוּת בָּאָה לְעוֹלָם . . .
Exile comes to the world . . .

In the Haggadah *From Bondage to Freedom* (Mesorah), I point out that the repeated reference to the Exodus in our liturgy is to emphasize that a person should not be enslaved to anyone or anything, neither to a ruthless despot nor to one's innate drives. A person who cannot control an urge, whether it be to drink, to use drugs, to smoke, to eat to excess, to gather wealth, to seek acclaim, or to react in rage, is essentially a slave. True freedom consists of a person being a master over his behavior, and not being subject to any compulsion. A person who cannot resist smoking a cigarette even though he knows it endangers his health, and he certainly wishes to preserve it, is as much a slave as his ancestors who were under the whips of Pharaoh's taskmasters.

ה/יב   שְׁפִיכוּת דָּמִים, וְעַל שְׁמִטַּת הָאָרֶץ.

[יב] **בְּאַרְבָּעָה** פְּרָקִים הַדֶּבֶר מִתְרַבֶּה: בָּרְבִיעִית,
וּבַשְּׁבִיעִית, וּבְמוֹצָאֵי שְׁבִיעִית,
וּבְמוֹצָאֵי הֶחָג שֶׁבְּכָל שָׁנָה וְשָׁנָה. בָּרְבִיעִית, מִפְּנֵי מַעְשַׂר
עָנִי שֶׁבַּשְּׁלִישִׁית; בַּשְּׁבִיעִית, מִפְּנֵי מַעְשַׂר עָנִי שֶׁבַּשִּׁשִּׁית;
בְּמוֹצָאֵי שְׁבִיעִית, מִפְּנֵי פֵּרוֹת שְׁבִיעִית; בְּמוֹצָאֵי הֶחָג
שֶׁבְּכָל שָׁנָה וְשָׁנָה, מִפְּנֵי גֶּזֶל מַתְּנוֹת עֲנִיִּים.

R' Shalom of Belz said that there are three types of *galus* (exile). The first is when Jews are in exile and oppressed by other nations. The second and more serious is when Jews are oppressed by other Jews. The third and most serious is when a person is oppressed by himself; i.e., when he is enslaved by his internal drives. While breaking free from a despotic ruler is difficult, history is replete with nations that have achieved their independence. People who were under the thumb of their own countrymen have been able to secure their freedom. The most difficult enslavement is when a person is unable to control his actions and is under the domination of his innate drives. He is indeed in *galus*, and this is the most difficult yoke to throw off.

The sins listed in this mishnah: idolatry, immorality, murder, and violation of *Shemittah* are the result of a person being driven to act by his lustful, hostile, and acquisitive drives. This indeed constitutes a *galus*, an oppression from which it is most difficult to break loose, because one is not likely to even be aware that he has lost control of his behavior.

The Torah teaches us to be truly free, and the comprehensive Torah literature, particularly that which focuses on *middos* (character traits), teaches us how to achieve true freedom.

וְעַל שְׁמִטַּת הָאָרֶץ
And for working the earth during the Sabbatical year.

These mishnahs attribute grave consequences to the violation of *Shemittah*, and indeed, the Torah states explicitly that the expulsion from the Holy Land will be a result of the sin of working the land on *Shemittah* (*Leviticus* 26:34). What is it about this particular mitzvah that gives it such great significance?

When the Israelites left Egypt, the provisions they took with them miraculously lasted for weeks, until the manna decended. The commentaries indicate that the reason the miracle of the manna was instituted prior to the giving of the Torah at Sinai was to impress upon the Israelites that not only was their physical sustenance dependent upon God, but also that each person would receive exactly enough for the needs of his household and not the slightest bit more. Each person was instructed to gather a fixed amount for each member of his

shed, and for working the earth during the Sabbatical year.

12. **A**t four periods [of the seven-year Sabbatical cycle] pestilence increases: in the fourth year, in the seventh year, in the year following the Sabbatical year, and annually at the conclusion of the [Succos] festival. In the fourth year [of the Shemittah cycle] for [neglecting] the tithe of the poor in the third; in the seventh year for [neglecting] the tithe of the poor in the sixth; [immediately] following the Sabbatical year for [violating the laws of] the Sabbatical produce; annually, at the conclusion of the festival [of Succos], for robbing the poor of their gifts.

---

household, and if anyone gathered more, the excess would spoil. On the other hand, if one gathered less, the measure filled on its own. In addition, any manna that was put away for the next day decayed. The message was clear: One will receive just what one needs, and God will provide anew every day.

This trust that God would care for one's needs had to precede the Torah, because only with this faith in God could one be expected to observe those Torah commandments that are in opposition to one's inborn acquisitive drives. Parenthetically, there is an aphorism that an infant is born with clenched fists, which indicates that he is driven to seize whatever he can, whereas when a person dies, his palms are outstretched, indicating that after all his toil, he takes nothing with him.

There are many mitzvos that require suppression of the acquisitive drive: not to steal, not to lie, not to cheat, not to swear falsely, not to covet, not to take usury, to tithe, to give *tzedakah,* etc. The only way one can properly fulfill these mitzvos is with a belief that one will not be impoverished thereby, and that God will provide for one's legitimate needs. On the other hand, any effort to take more than one was allotted will be futile. This basic trust therefore had to precede the giving of the Torah and was taught by the blessing of the manna.

The acid test of the strength of faith is the mitzvah of *Shemittah.* Not only is it required that one leave his farm and orchard fallow for an entire year, which could be viewed as placing his income in jeopardy, but even those who do not earn their living by tilling the land are dependent on the produce of the land. Their faith, too, is tested by the land being left fallow. *Shemittah* is thus not only a test for the individual, but also for the entire nation. Failure to observe *Shemittah* indicates a lack of faith and trust in God for both the individual and the nation as a whole.

Much of human behavior is motivated by the degree to which we yield to or restrain our acquisitive drive. The fundamental principle of the Torah, as stated

ה/יג [יג] **אַרְבַּע** מִדּוֹת בָּאָדָם. הָאוֹמֵר: "שֶׁלִּי שֶׁלִּי וְשֶׁלְּךָ שֶׁלָּךְ," זוֹ מִדָּה בֵּינוֹנִית, וְיֵשׁ אוֹמְרִים: זוֹ

---

by Hillel, is to care for one's fellow man. We are told that love and unity among Jews makes them invincible, and there is nothing that can undermine unity as much as yielding to one's acquisitive drive. It is for this reason that *Shemittah* is accorded so crucial a role.

13.

אַרְבַּע מִדּוֹת בָּאָדָם. הָאוֹמֵר:
"שֶׁלִּי שֶׁלִּי וְשֶׁלְּךָ שֶׁלָּךְ"
There are four character types
among people: a) One who says, "My
[property] is mine, and yours is yours"

The two opinions in the mishnah about the person who says, "What is mine is mine, and what is yours is yours," are not really all that divergent. The first opinion is not pejorative, and merely states a fact: The average person, i.e., the most common character type, has an essentially isolationist attitude. He does not wish to take anything that belongs to others, but neither is he willing to share with others. The second opinion renders a judgment. It is a mistake to think that just because this type of person is not criminal in that he does not steal from others, this is a viable option. To the contrary, failure to be considerate of others may actually be self-destructive and can result in the collapse of society, just as Sodom was destroyed. If your neighbor's house catches fire and your attitude is, "That is no concern of mine. Let my neighbor worry about it," you are putting your own home in jeopardy, because the fire can spread to your property.

No person is an island, nor is any nation an island. Diseases that threaten the whole world often began in some obscure location. We have discovered that economy is a global issue, and that when the economy of other countries fail, our own suffers as well. The sooner we realize our interdependence, the sooner we will discard our isolationist attitude, not out of altruism, but simply for self-survival. The mishnah states the regrettable fact that most people fail to recognize the reality of interdependence, and think they can be secure within their own boundaries. This is an illusion. The aphorism attributed to Benjamin Franklin is valid: "We either hang together or we will hang separately."

The second category, "What is mine is yours, and what is yours is mine," i.e., doing away with the concept of private property, is indicative of ignorance. This is essentially the theme of communism, which appeared to many people as a lofty ideal, but proved to be a dismal failure.

Anecdotally, a friend told me that he took a group for a visit to Russia before the demise of communism, and when he sought to reserve rooms in a hotel, he was told there was no vacancy. He contacted someone who bribed the

13. **T**here are four character types among people: a) One who says, "My [property] is mine, and yours is yours," is an average character type, but some say this is

---

hotel manager, and they were given the rooms. Once there, he discovered that the hotel was virtually empty! He asked the hotel manager why he was told there was no vacancy, and the latter said, "Why should I take in customers? It makes no difference to me whether the hotel is full or empty. I don't gain anything by renting out the rooms, and all I have is more work. Let the rooms stay vacant. I don't care!"

A person may be motivated to do something l'shem Shamayim, because he wishes to obey the Divine will, or for personal gain. The atheistic and economic communist concepts deprived people of all motivation. All they were left with is the fear of not complying with the government. When fear is the only motivation, a person will try and do the bare minimum necessary to ward off punishment.

While we can expect a person to be charitable and to share with others, human nature is such that the elimination of private property must backfire. The amusing book, Animal Farm, describes the deception inherent in communism, which gives rise not only to an elitist group, but also to one which is despotic and cruel. As Orwell put it so succinctly, the initial ideal of "All animals are equal" underwent a gradual change to "All animals are equal, but some are more equal than others." The Soviet experiment clearly demonstrated this.

Poverty can be eliminated, but not by this naive approach. The Torah states, "May there be no destitute among you" (Deuteronomy 15:4), yet goes on to say, "For destitute people will not cease to exist within the Land" (ibid. 15:11). Rashi reconciles these two verses by pointing out that the elimination of poverty will be the result of God's blessing, as is clearly stated in the first passage, ". . . because God will surely bless you." When we live according to the Torah, we merit the Divine blessing, and there will be no poor. If we behave in a way that does not merit the Divine blessing, there will always be poverty. The mishnah states that anyone who believes that poverty can be eliminated by the manipulation of economics is simply ignorant

The third category, "What is mine is yours, and what is yours is yours," is that of a pious person. This does not mean that a person must give away everything he owns. The halachah puts a limit on tzedakah of 25 percent of one's earnings. Exceeding this limit is discouraged, because one may impoverish himself and become dependent on others for survival.

There were tzaddikim who excelled in this trait. It is told of the Chofetz Chaim and of other great Torah personalities that if something of theirs was stolen, they declared it hefker, i.e., they divested themselves of the ownership of the stolen item so that the thief should not be guilty of keeping another's property. This is the characteristic of the truly pious.

The wicked person's greed and his actions to take everything for himself needs no comment. We are unfortunately fully aware of criminal behavior, whether it be that of an individual or of a country.

Clearly, it is unethical to be wicked, ignorant, or isolationist. Given the above definitions of the four types, we have no option other than to try to be pious. This is not a formidable challenge. As we noted, "What is mine is yours, and what is yours is yours" does not require total self-sacrifice, but rather following the halachah on giving *tzedakah* properly.

Of course, there are degrees of piety, depending on how one sees one's role in the world. I have already told this story but it bears repeating.

My great-grandfather, Reb Motele of Hornostipol, lived a very austere life, even though he had a huge income from his *chassidim*. One time, my great-grandmother asked him for some money for household expenses, and he said he had none. Later that day, she saw that he had been visited by one of his wealthy *chassidim*, and she knew that this *chassid* must have given the Rebbe a tidy sum. Immediately after the *chassid* left, she came in and asked for money, but Grandfather again told her he had none.

"How can that be?" Grandmother asked. "I'm sure that this *chassid* gave you a handsome *pidyon*" (donation).

Grandfather nodded and then showed her that his vest had two pockets. "This one is for my own needs, and this one is for *hachnasas kallah* (enabling poor girls to marry) and *pidyon shevuim* (ransoming Jews from the dungeons where the feudal lords had imprisoned them). The money this *chassid* gave me went into the second pocket and does not belong to me.

"You see," Grandfather continued, "for reasons known only to Him, God did not distribute wealth evenly. Some people have much, some have little. He has given us a precious mitzvah of *tzedakah* and has assigned some people to convey the *tzedakah* of the 'haves' to the 'have nots.' For fulfilling this assignment, one is entitled to a reasonable wage.

"I am one of those people who are assigned this task, and I am permitted to keep some of the money for myself as my wage. If I would take more than I have coming to me, this would be embezzlement. I would then be dismissed from this job, and we would have no income at all. Certainly you would not want me to jeopardize our income."

Grandmother had to agree with this logic. She had been well trained by her father, the *Tzaddik* of Sanz, whose *tzedakah* is legendary.

As with other *middos* of *tzaddikim*, we may find this level difficult to achieve. Nevertheless, if we are aware of what constitutes perfection of *middos*, we have an ideal which can serve as our guide.

5/13 *characteristic of Sodom; b) "Mine is yours, and yours is mine," is an unlearned person; c) "Mine is yours, and yours is yours," is scrupulously pious; d) "Yours is mine, and mine is mine," is wicked.*

הָאוֹמֵר: ,,שֶׁלִּי שֶׁלִּי וְשֶׁלְּךָ שֶׁלָּךְ
a) One who says, "My [property] is mine, and yours is yours"

The chassidic master, the Maggid of Kozhnitz, gave this mishnah a novel interpretation.

The average person on the street dichotomizes life. Part of life is religious; i.e., observance of the mitzvos, like Shabbos, tefillin, matzah, shofar, etc., and part of life is secular; i.e., working, doing business, sleeping, washing the car, mowing the lawn, etc.

"Mitzvos belong to God, and mundane things belong to me. What is Yours is Yours, and what is mine is mine."

This is not the appropriate Torah view of life, which is "Know Him (God) in all your ways" (*Proverbs* 3:6). One eats and sleeps to be healthy so that he can do the mitzvos and study Torah. One engages in activity to earn a living to provide for his family, to give *tzedakah*, to pay the tuition for the children to learn Torah, etc. Since cleanliness is important (*Avodah Zarah* 20b), washing the car can be in the Divine service. Lest anyone say that Jews live slovenly, keeping one's lawn attractive can be a *kiddush Hashem* (to the greater glory of God). With the proper attitude, everything one does can be considered in the category of mitzvos. Hence, the pious person says, "Not only what is obviously Yours (the mitzvos) is Yours, but also that which is mine (mundane activities) is also Yours."

The ignorant person does not realize that everything in life is controlled by God, except the choice between right and wrong, good and evil, which is left to man. How much one will earn is predetermined, but whether one will study Torah and perform mitzvos is up to man. Not realizing this, the ignorant person spends most of his time trying to make more money and leaves little time for spiritual pursuits. This is futile because he cannot make more than what was decreed for him. He thus confuses his priorities, essentially saying, "What is really Yours, i.e., how much I will earn, is mine, i.e., that is where I will put my effort. But what is really mine, i.e., my spiritual pursuits, that I will leave to You."

The wicked person is a hypocrite. He has no desire to do the will of God. Everything in his life is self-centered. If it is to his advantage to give people the impression that he is observant of mitzvos, he may do them for show, and exploit mitzvos for ulterior motives. "Not only what is mine is mine, but even what should be Yours (mitzvos) are also mine," i.e., performed only when it is to my advantage to do so.

Putting things in proper perspective will allow every person to become a *chassid*.

ה/יד [יד] **אַרְבַּע** מִדּוֹת בְּדֵעוֹת: נְוֹחַ לִכְעוֹס וְנְוֹחַ לִרְצוֹת,
יָצָא שְׂכָרוֹ בְּהֶפְסֵדוֹ; קָשֶׁה לִכְעוֹס וְקָשֶׁה
לִרְצוֹת, יָצָא הֶפְסֵדוֹ בִּשְׂכָרוֹ; קָשֶׁה לִכְעוֹס וְנְוֹחַ לִרְצוֹת,
חָסִיד; נְוֹחַ לִכְעוֹס וְקָשֶׁה לִרְצוֹת, רָשָׁע.

14.

אַרְבַּע מִדּוֹת בְּדֵעוֹת: נְוֹחַ לִכְעוֹס . . .
There are four types of temperaments:
a) One who is angered easily . . .

Management of anger occupies a pivotal place in ethics. In his famous letter to his son, Ramban begins with an instruction on anger. Control of anger, says Ramban, will lead to humility, which is the finest of all character traits. It is noteworthy that Ramban does not recommend this "finest of all traits" as the starting point of character development. As long as one has not achieved mastery over anger, it is impossible to achieve humility. This is why the mishnah gives special attention to this emotion.

In *Lights Along the Way* (Mesorah 1995) I pointed out that there are three phases of anger, and that although the Hebrew language uses the word *kaas* to refer to all three, it is important that we distinguish between them.

The first phase of anger is the emotion that occurs when a person is provoked. This is virtually a reflex action which is not within a person's voluntary control. The second phase is the reaction to this emotion, which can range from total silence and restraint through a broad spectrum of responses all the way to frank violence. The third phase is the retention of anger or bearing a grudge. The second and third phases are within a person's capacity to control.

To avoid confusion, let us refer to these three phases by different terms. We will refer to the emotion evoked by provocation as *anger*, the response to the provocation as *rage*, which can be mild or severe, and the continued retention of the emotion as *resentment*.

Inasmuch as the pure sensation of anger is not under voluntary control, it is not the subject of ethics. Our mishnah is therefore concerned with the second and third phases, *rage* and *resentment*.

The validity of our definition is evident from two statements that appear in the Talmud and in *Zohar*. The *Zohar* states, "One who is angry is as though he worshipped idols" (1:27), whereas the Talmud states that "One who tears his clothes or breaks things in a fit of anger is as though he worshipped idols" (*Shabbos* 108b). It is obvious that they are both referring to the same thing, and that the *Zohar* is referring to what we have termed "rage."

The mishnah states that if a person is easily provoked to rage, even though he may quickly be appeased, the negative obscures the positive. The threaten-

14. **T**here are four types of temperament: a) One who is angered easily and pacified easily, his gain is offset by his loss; b) one who is hard to anger and hard to pacify, his loss is offset by his gain; c) one who is hard to anger and pacified easily is pious; d) one who is angered easily and hard to pacify is wicked.

---

ing or insulting words and the physical harm resulting from the rage reaction cannot be reversed by remorse. Furthermore, people who are in a relationship with someone who is easily enraged may feel terrorized and may "walk on eggs" for fear of provoking an outburst. The fact that one quickly apologizes for his rage is not an adequate compensation.

The second temperament is that of a person who is not easily provoked to rage, but harbors resentments for an extended period of time. The latter is indeed undesirable, but does little harm to others. Inasmuch as the Torah forbids acting out a grudge, both actively and passively (*Leviticus* 19:18), harboring a resentment does not affect others. Rather, it is the bearer of the grudge who feels its negative effects, as it ferments within him and disturbs his peace of mind. Resentments may even contribute to a number of physical illnesses, such as migraine, high blood pressure, and heart disease. Solomon was therefore wise in calling the person who harbors resentments "a fool" (*Ecclesiastes* 7:9). It is the height of folly to punish oneself because of another person's inability to restrain his expression of anger. Since others suffer little from one's bearing a grudge, the positive trait of restraining one's rage outweighs the negative.

Let us jump to the fourth type, one who is both easily provoked and harbors resentments. This needs no explanation. One who is easily enraged and retains his anger indefinitely is clearly a *rasha*, since he has made no effort at self-mastery.

The third type of temperament, one who is difficult to provoke and readily divests himself of resentments, is a *chassid*. This person not only exhibits self-mastery but may even succeed in eliminating the initial emotion of anger. Although the latter is essentially a reflex reaction and not under voluntary control, it is possible to mitigate the sensation. For example, one may not feel anger at being provoked by a small child who is not aware of what he is doing. It is also possible that a grown-up may have been the victim of circumstances that distort his judgment. He may therefore be in a state of mind similar to that of a child. It is also possible that a person may not be aware that his actions are provocative. Judging people favorably (1:6) may lessen the feeling of anger upon provocation.

Although one cannot extirpate the initial feeling of anger on his own, a person may pray to God to lift this emotion from him. Unless one has done

[טו] **אַרְבַּע** מִדּוֹת בְּתַלְמִידִים: מָהִיר לִשְׁמֹעַ וּמָהִיר
לְאַבֵּד, יָצָא שְׂכָרוֹ בְּהֶפְסֵדוֹ; קָשֶׁה לִשְׁמֹעַ
וְקָשֶׁה לְאַבֵּד, יָצָא הֶפְסֵדוֹ בִשְׂכָרוֹ; מָהִיר לִשְׁמֹעַ וְקָשֶׁה
לְאַבֵּד, זֶה חֵלֶק טוֹב; קָשֶׁה לִשְׁמֹעַ וּמָהִיר לְאַבֵּד, זֶה חֵלֶק
רָע.

---

one's homework in trying to mitigate this feeling by being more considerate of others and by mastering the second and third phases of rage and resentment, one has no right to expect God to intervene and remove the feeling of anger.

The Chofetz Chaim was often seen entering the *shul* in the early hours of the morning. Some students, curious to know what he was doing there, concealed themselves in the *shul*. They noted that the Chofetz Chaim would open the ark and pray fervently and tearfully for God to remove the emotion of anger from him.

Ramban closes his letter by assuring his son that on the day he reads this letter, his prayers will be answered. One might protest that one has read the letter many times and has prayed to become wealthy, but that his prayers have not been answered. I believe that the Ramban knew his son to be beyond the status of praying for wealth. He knew that his son was striving for spirituality. The end of the letter therefore is referring to its beginning. A person who reads the letter and takes it to heart will wisely pray, like the Chofetz Chaim, for God to remove the unpleasant emotion of anger. This sincere prayer is certain to be answered.

15.

אַרְבַּע מִדּוֹת בְּתַלְמִידִים
There are four types of students

The previous mishnahs describe character traits that are largely under a person's control, such as his attitude towards property or his management of anger. Similarly, the subsequent mishnahs refer to degrees of charitability and attitudes toward study. In as much as *Ethics of the Fathers* is essentially a manual for character development, these mishnahs are instructive. However, our mishnah refers to the capacity to absorb or retain material, which is essentially an innate feature. While there are indeed varying degrees of ability to absorb and retain, what purpose is there in telling us this in *Ethics of the Fathers*? If one was born with a poor memory, is there really anything he can do to significantly improve it?

Lev Avos provides an interpretation which reveals a profound understanding of the learning process. It is indeed true that some people are born with a quicker grasp and better memory than others, yet there is much that a person does that increases or decreases his learning capacity. The latter *can* be affected by his attitude.

We can all recall teachers whom we loved and admired. Consequently, we

15. There are four types of students: (a) One who grasps quickly and forgets quickly, his gain is offset by his loss; (b) one who grasps slowly and forgets slowly, his loss is offset by his gain; (c) one who grasps quickly and forgets slowly, this is a good portion; (d) one who grasps slowly and forgets quickly, this is a bad portion.

---

hung on to every word they said and we readily grasped the material. However, if the subject material was not important to us, we did not retain it for long. We were attentive to the instructor because of our feeling for him, hence we absorbed quickly. However, the material "went in one ear and out the other" because we did not value it.

We may also recall some instructors for whom we had little liking. Perhaps we did not like the person himself, or perhaps it was his method of teaching that displeased us. Sitting in his classroom was a chore and was usually boring, and this diminished our attentiveness. However, since the subject matter was important to us, we made an effort to review it and retain what we learned.

Let me digress to tell you about an analogous phenomenon. When I was in medical school, the lectures on pediatrics were given on Shabbos, which, of course, I did not attend. On Sunday I would find out from the other students what the subject of the lecture was, and I read the texts on it.

The professor of pediatrics was an excellent physician, but the most boring lecturer imaginable. His monotone quickly put many students to sleep, or at least encouraged daydreaming. Because these students relied on the lectures, their knowledge of the subjects was relatively meager. On the other hand, I had gathered my knowledge from studying the texts, and thus had a much better grasp of the material. Consequently, although I had not attended any of the lectures, I received a much higher grade on the exams than the students who did attend!

Inasmuch as a person *can* change his attitude toward a teacher and *can* change his valuation of the subject matter, he can profoundly affect how readily he absorbs material and how well he retains it. Insofar as Torah is concerned, *Ethics of the Fathers* instructs us how to develop the desirable attitudes in Chapter Six.

But, you may say, Chapter Six is limited to Torah study. What are the guidelines for more effective learning of subject matter other than Torah?

Let us consider the latter. We may ask: Inasmuch as this tome has established that our goal in life is knowledge and implementation of Torah, why should we have any interest in any other subject matter at all? The answer is that there are types of knowledge which can serve us to earn a living, or which can be applied to some aspects of Torah. Thus, if we adopt the principle of "Know Him in all your ways" (*Proverbs* 3:6), which means that everything we

[טז] **אַרְבַּע** מִדּוֹת בְּנוֹתְנֵי צְדָקָה: הָרוֹצֶה שֶׁיִּתֵּן וְלֹא
יִתְּנוּ אֲחֵרִים, עֵינוֹ רָעָה בְּשֶׁל אֲחֵרִים;
יִתְּנוּ אֲחֵרִים וְהוּא לֹא יִתֵּן, עֵינוֹ רָעָה בְּשֶׁלּוֹ; יִתֵּן

ido should be directed toward God, then earning a living in order to fulfill the Torah obligations to provide for our families, to support Torah scholars, and to give *tzedakah* become accessories to Torah. If one needs to know astronomy n order to calculate the calendar, then astronomy becomes an accessory to Torah (above, 3:18). If one masters mathematics or the physical sciences because they can be applied to halachah, then these become accessories to Torah. If knowledge of the wonders of nature enhances reverence for and love of God, as Rambam says (*Yesodei HaTorah* 2:2), then this too is an accessory to Torah. Rambam said that his study of science was only that it be "a handmaiden to Torah." When acquiring secular knowledge is subordinated to Torah, the principles of Chapter Six apply to this as well.

But what if one wishes to acquire secular knowledge that is not subordinated to Torah in the above ways? What are the guidelines for more effective learning in this area? The answer is that there is no justification for attaining anything that is not in some way relevant to Torah. As the mishnah says above: "The day is short, the task is abundant" (2:20). We do not have the luxury of spending time on anything that does not contribute in some way toward the ultimate goal of Torah living.

It is of interest that this mishnah uses the expressions "gain" and "loss" in regard to study habits, terms that are usually employed in commerce. Perhaps the mishnah wishes to impress upon us that at the very least we should relate to Torah study the way we do to our business affairs. Of what good is earning much money if one quickly dissipates it? On the other hand, if one earns meagerly but saves his earnings carefully, he may yet end up with a tidy sum.

The Talmud was well aware that our experiences in everyday living can serve as models for our attitudes toward Torah. For example, R' Yochanan ben Zakkai responded to his disciples request for his blessing by saying, "May you fear God as much as you fear people" (*Berachos* 28b). In many *siddurim* there is the admonition that one should not hurry through the prayers, but "should say the words slowly as if one were counting money." We cannot escape our limitations and values as mortals. We can, however, sublimate them and develop them as accessories to Torah.

16.

אַרְבַּע מִדּוֹת בְּנוֹתְנֵי צְדָקָה
There are four types of donors to charity

Even a cursory reading of this mishnah raises an obvious question. The mishnah refers to four types of *donors,* among which is someone who does *not* donate but wishes that others would, and

16. **T**here are four types of donors to charity: (a) One
who wishes to give himself but wants others not
to give, he begrudges others; (b) that others should give
but that he should not give, he begrudges himself; (c) that

---

also someone who does not donate nor does he wish others to do so. How can
these two be considered to be "donors" if they do not donate?

Rabbi Moshe Aleshkar explains that all four categories in the mishnah refer to
people who do indeed donate to charity, but their attitudes vary. Thus, the first
type of donor is one who prefers that no one else should give, so that he may
claim the entire credit of a project for himself. It has rightly been said that much
more could be accomplished in the world if people did not care who received
the credit for it.

This type may also refer to a person who donates, but by his donation may
cause others to withhold. It is customary, when an appeal for funds is made,
that a major donor announces his pledge first. If he is able to donate handsomely and announces a pledge of $10,000, he has set the tone and standard
for others, who will donate proportionately. If he announces a much smaller
amount, then others will follow suit, thinking, "If Mr. A. gives only $1,000,
then it is enough if I give $25." Thus, by his giving a lesser amount than he
should, he causes others to give less.

If we pay close attention to the wording of the mishnah, it describes the
second type as "one who wishes others to give, but he himself does not give."
The mishnah places the givers first, and the "nongiver" last, and this refers to
someone who is indeed a donor, but his attitude is "let others give first, and I
will then give whatever necessary to meet the goal." I.e., he does ultimately
donate, but is a nongiver at the start. This might be thought of as commendable, since he is assuring that the objective will be met.

The Talmudic sages are critical of this approach, whose precedent occurred
when the Israelites were constructing the Sanctuary. While everyone donated
the gold, silver, and other essential materials, the leaders of the tribes said, "Let
everyone donate first, and we will then make up any lack." They later donated
the precious gems for the High Priest's breastplate, yet the Talmud censures
them for their dereliction. Although their gift may have actually been more
valuable, their failure to seize the opportunity to be among the first donors
indicates that they did not adequately appreciate the value of the mitzvah.
Similarly, if one would have a proper concept of the greatness of *tzedakah*,
one could hardly restrain oneself from being the first donor.

The fourth category also refers to a donor, but one who gives grudgingly.
Furthermore, he does so in a manner that reveals that he considers the recipient or project to be undeserving. This disparaging attitude discourages others
from donating.

Giving *tzedakah* should not be considered an obligation, but rather a privi-

וְיִתְּנוּ אֲחֵרִים, חָסִיד; לֹא יִתֵּן וְלֹא יִתְּנוּ אֲחֵרִים, רָשָׁע.

[יז] **אַרְבַּע** מִדּוֹת בְּהוֹלְכֵי בֵית הַמִּדְרָשׁ: הוֹלֵךְ וְאֵינוֹ עוֹשֶׂה, שְׂכַר הֲלִיכָה בְּיָדוֹ; עוֹשֶׂה וְאֵינוֹ הוֹלֵךְ, שְׂכַר מַעֲשֶׂה בְּיָדוֹ; הוֹלֵךְ וְעוֹשֶׂה, חָסִיד; לֹא הוֹלֵךְ וְלֹא עוֹשֶׂה, רָשָׁע.

---

lege. Torah literature is replete with the inordinate greatness of *tzedakah*. As we see in this mishnah, it is not only the act of giving that is important, but also the attitude with which it is given and the consideration one has for the recipient of *tzedakah*.

The chassidic master, the *Tzaddik* of Sanz, was renowned for his *tzedakah*, and often pawned his *kiddush* cup to get money to give to the needy. One time, shortly before sunset on the eve of Succos, he sent a messenger to a wealthy citizen in the community to borrow a large sum of money. The man provided the requested funds, but wondered, "What could the rabbi be doing with this money now? All the stores have closed and there is no way one could purchase anything for the festival." Curious, he followed the messenger, who delivered the money to a person for whom he knew the *Tzaddik* had already provided money for the essentials of the festival. He asked the *Tzaddik* why he gave him additional money.

The *Tzaddik* explained, "The Torah states that one should celebrate the festival with food and drink, and that one should rejoice. True, he has enough money for food, but how can he rejoice when he knows that immediately after the festival his creditors will be hounding him? He will be worried all through the festival that he will not be able to face his creditors. I therefore gave him money so close to sundown that he could not possibly spend it, and he can now have some peace with the knowledge that he will be able to pay some of his debts after the festival.

"The Torah requires that we provide the poor with *all* their needs. This man has a need for the joy of the festival, which we are obligated to provide for him."

This anecdote indicates the importance of the thoughtfulness and consideration that should go into the mitzvah of *tzedakah*. It is this attitude toward the giving of *tzedakah* that the mishnah is describing.

17.

עוֹשֶׂה וְאֵינוֹ הוֹלֵךְ
One who studies [at home]
but does not attend [the house of study]

Some commentaries interpret the word *holech* to mean "progressing," and they point out that in contrast to angels who are static (*omdim*), a human being should grow and advance in character

he should give and that others should give is saintly; (d) that he should not give and that others should not give is wicked.

17. There are four types among those who go to the house of study: (a) One who goes but does not study has the reward for going; (b) one who studies [at home] but does not attend [the house of study] has the reward for accomplishment; (c) one who goes and studies is pious; (c) one who does not go and does not study is wicked.

---

development. The second category of this mishnah refers to someone who is *oseh*, who seemingly does what he is supposed to do, yet he does not appear to be advancing in spirituality and improving himself in any way. This question arises not infrequently. Why are there observant people who seem to be deficient in *middos* (fine character traits)?

The mishnah provides an answer to this question. In *Twerski on Spirituality* I pointed out that the human spirit is comprised of all the traits and capacities that are unique to humans and are not found in any other living things. One of the distinguishing features of people is that they are capable of being considerate of others and doing things for others even at some cost to themselves. A human being can also dedicate himself to the service of God, and can deprive himself of many things that are pleasurable. Animals cannot do either of these, because they are impulse driven to provide their body with whatever gratification it desires. In a word, animals are selfish and cannot be otherwise, whereas a person can look away from himself and be outwardly directed.

In Chapter 1 mishnah 3 we are told, "Be not as servants who serve the master for the sake of receiving reward." A person who does mitzvos for the sole purpose of being rewarded may indeed be doing the right things, but since his motivation is self-centered, i.e., with an eye toward reward, he is not advancing himself spiritually.

We can now understand the interpretation of this mishnah by the *Maggid* of Mezeritch. "If a person does what he is supposed to, yet is not a *holech*, i.e., does not progress spiritually, it is because שְׂכַר מַעֲשֶׂה בְּיָדוֹ, he has the reward for acomplishment, i.e., *all that he has in hand* is the reward for his actions, and he has not looked beyond his self-interests. While he may be observant of Torah, he is not doing it in such a manner that will foster spiritual growth."

This interpretation also clarifies why the mishnah refers to a *holech v'oseh* as being a *chassid*. If the meaning is only that one goes to the house of study and studies, why is he considered a *chassid*? He is simply complying with the basic requirements of Torah, whereas a *chassid* is a person who does more than

[יח] **אַרְבַּע** מִדּוֹת בְּיוֹשְׁבִים לִפְנֵי חֲכָמִים: סְפוֹג, וּמַשְׁפֵּךְ, מְשַׁמֶּרֶת, וְנָפָה. סְפוֹג, שֶׁהוּא סוֹפֵג אֶת הַכֹּל; וּמַשְׁפֵּךְ, שֶׁמַּכְנִיס בְּזוֹ וּמוֹצִיא בְזוֹ; מְשַׁמֶּרֶת, שֶׁמּוֹצִיאָה אֶת הַיַּיִן וְקוֹלֶטֶת אֶת הַשְּׁמָרִים; וְנָפָה, שֶׁמּוֹצִיאָה אֶת הַקֶּמַח וְקוֹלֶטֶת אֶת הַסֹּלֶת.

---

is required. However, if we understand *holech* to mean spiritual progress, then we can see why a person who seeks to advance himself spiritually is considered a *chassid*. He is doing more than just complying. This is why the mishnah does not say what kind of reward the *holech v'oseh* has, because a *chassid* is not motivated by reward, and seeks only to grow spiritually and bring himself closer to God.

We may further understand why the mishnah refers to the fourth category, a person who is neither a *holech* nor an *oseh* as a *rasha*, which is a rather denunciatory term. The reason for this is that human beings are not static. Given the strong biological drives that arise from our physical nature, a person either tries to master them or yields to them, either progressing or regressing spiritually. A person who actively seeks spiritual advancement will make significant progress. One who does not actively pursue such advancement but at least complies with the mitzvos which restrain one from giving free rein to one's impulses has the potential for spirituality in that he is not regressing. A person who neither seeks to become more spiritual nor abides by mitzvos is defenseless against his impulses. He will act out his biological drives, which will indeed cause him to be a *rasha*.

It has been pointed out that the Hebrew word for man, *adam,* is philologically related to the word *adamah,* earth, and also to *adameh,* to be similar, which refers to *adameh l'Elyon,* being akin to God. The latter is what was meant by man being created in the image of God. Man has the option to be either lowly as earth, or supreme and Godlike. *Ethics of the Fathers* is a manual on how to achieve the latter.

18.

אַרְבַּע מִדּוֹת בְּיוֹשְׁבִים לִפְנֵי חֲכָמִים
There are four types among those who sit before the sages

Mishnah 16 described the various degrees of absorbing and/or retaining knowledge. This mishnah addresses the variety of discriminatory abilities among students, comparing them to a sponge, a funnel, a strainer, and a sieve. Everyone agrees that the sponge represents one who absorbs everything indiscriminately, and that the funnel represents one who essentially absorbs nothing or retains nothing. There is some difference of opinion as to the

18. T*here are four types among those who sit before the sages: a sponge, a funnel, a strainer, and a sieve — (a) a sponge, which absorbs everything; (b) a funnel, which lets in from one and lets out from the other; (c) a strainer, which lets the wine flow through and retains the sediment; (d) and a sieve, which allows the flour dust to pass through and retains the fine flour.*

---

symbolism of the strainer versus the sieve.

There is general agreement that the "sponge," i.e., the student who absorbs and retains everything indiscriminately, is at a disadvantage. He may just as easily retain falsehoods as truth. It appears from the commentaries that the danger in being spongelike is that one may absorb erroneous data. There is yet another important symbolism of the sponge, which is particularly relevant today.

I often feel uneasy upon walking into a library, and seeing the many thousands of books there. I realize that if I spent all 24 hours of the day reading, I could not read more than a fraction of those books in my lifetime. I have a thirst for knowledge, and there is so much that I cannot possibly know! However, I invariably make peace with reality, and borrow the book or two that I wish to read.

This feeling of futility and being overwhelmed by what there is to know that one can never know has been magnified many times by the advent of the Internet. At one's fingertips lies a virtual universe of information. Even if one narrows the search to one's particular interest, there is still a formidable fund of data. For example, I looked up a particular subject, and found that there were 18,764 references to it! There was just no way I could deal with this. Perhaps if I were more proficient on the computer I might have found a way to be selective, but since my skills in this area are limited, I abandoned the computer and sought my sources in the references provided in an article on the subject.

The human mind has been compared to a huge warehouse, which may be able to contain much, but is nevertheless limited in how much it can hold. Once it is filled to capacity, one cannot put in any new material until one removes some of the existing material. This means that a person must prioritize, and decide what it is that is most important for him to retain. Thus, the flaw of the sponge is not necessarily that it will retain *objectionable* material, but rather that it will retain *irrelevant* material which will prevent access to important material. It is therefore important that a person not only avoid erroneous information, but also that he not clutter up his mind with irrelevant material. I suspect that the genius of many of our Torah scholars may have been due to their being able to exclude anything other than material pertaining to Torah from their minds.

כל [יט] אַהֲבָה שֶׁהִיא תְלוּיָה בְדָבָר, בָּטֵל דָּבָר, בְּטֵלָה אַהֲבָה; וְשֶׁאֵינָהּ תְּלוּיָה בְדָבָר, אֵינָהּ בְּטֵלָה לְעוֹלָם. אֵיזוֹ הִיא אַהֲבָה שֶׁהִיא תְלוּיָה בְדָבָר? זוֹ אַהֲבַת

The mishnah's use of the similes of strainer and sieve are relevant to our thinking as well as to our learning. At any one moment, we are subjected to countless stimuli, but we are conscious of only a few. Thus, if you are reading a book, you are aware of the material in the book. If there happens to be music in the background, you may also be aware of that. If you were to draw your attention to your hands, you could become aware of the tactile contact between your fingers and the book. Within your peripheral field of vision, there is the picture on the wall which you are indeed seeing but you are not really aware of it. There is also a point of contact between your shoes and the floor, of which you are oblivious unless you concentrate on it. If you decided to listen, you would certainly hear the noises of the cars passing by. In fact, if you really concentrated, you could feel the tactile contact of your wrist and your wristwatch. All these and countless other stimuli bombard us every moment of the day. Fortunately, our mind acts as a filter, as a sieve if you will, and enables us to focus on what is important at that moment and block out everything else. If you heard the siren of a fire truck and went to the window, you would become unaware of the book you are holding and focus on the fire truck. It is the filtering system that allows our mind to function. If the filtering system were to fail and a person would become overwhelmed by all the stimuli to which he is subject, it would be impossible for him to think. Indeed, it has been suggested that some types of severe mental illness are due to the failure of the filtering system to block extraneous stimuli.

An efficient filtering system enables us to discriminate and prioritize. A *chassid* was once asked, "What do you think is the most important thing to your Rebbe?" He responded, "Whatever he happens to be doing at the moment." If there were anything more important, the Rebbe would be doing that instead. I recently saw a bumper sticker which proclaimed, "The main thing is to know that the main thing is the main thing." We have some control over our filtering system and can adjust it to the amount of extraneous material we wish to filter out.

What would our lives be like if we fine-tuned our filtering system to admit to our minds only that which is really relevant? There is no question that we would be far more efficient. However, this presupposes that we have a concept of what is truly important to us and what we consider to be the purpose of our lives. Only then would we have a criterion by which we could judge what is or is not relevant.

All of *Ethics of the Fathers* constitutes a manual for correct living. This particular mishnah is of pivotal importance. By applying the teaching of this

19. A*ny love that depends on a specific cause, when that cause is gone, the love is gone; but if it does not depend on a specific cause, it will never cease. What sort of love depended on a specific cause? — The love of*

---

mishnah, we may be able to use all the teachings of this book to filter out what is irrelevant to our goal in life.

19.

כָּל אַהֲבָה שֶׁהִיא תְלוּיָה בְדָבָר
Any love that depends on a specific cause

Come, world! Open your ears to the truth! Divest yourself of your muddled thinking and bring some sanity into your lives. Come to the fountain of truth, the teachings of *Ethics of the Fathers*. How can you expect to communicate effectively and have healthy relationships when you are not even aware of the meaning of the words you are using? This mishnah is nothing more than a dictionary. It defines a word that is used so freely and frequently, a word that is the drive behind much of human behavior, yet we so often do not know what it means: LOVE.

R' Mendel of Kotzk saw a young man clearly enjoying eating a tasty dish of fish. "Why are you eating the fish?" the rabbi asked. The young man was taken aback by the strange question. "Because I love fish," he said.

"And it is because you love the fish so much that you killed and cooked it," the rabbi said. "If you really loved the fish, you would have let it live in the water. You love *yourself,* young man, and because the fish gratifies your appetite, you killed and ate it."

Our civilization is awash in "love," yet marriages are disintegrating at an unprecedented rate. This is because love in western civilization is "fish love" and therefore the word love is empty.

The concept of love in Judaism is based on its use in regard to love of God, something which can be defined as "devotion." Just as there can be devotion to God which is not self-centered, there can also be a love of *devotion* to another person. Of course, in marriage the relationship does bring gratification to the people involved, but the fulfillment of one's desires should not be the entire or even the primary basis for the relationship.

When the love is of the devotion type, it is much more likely that each partner will be more tolerant if the other displeases them in any way. In a self-oriented relationship, sacrificing one's comfort for the other partner is unlikely. Incidents that might result in disruption of a "fish-love" relationship can be taken in stride and worked through with empathy and consideration. Devotion relationships can withstand both internal and external stresses.

The mishnah wisely cites an example of self-oriented love as the passion of

אַמְנוֹן וְתָמָר. וְשֶׁאֵינָה תְלוּיָה בְדָבָר? זוֹ אַהֲבַת דָּוִד וִיהוֹנָתָן.

[כ] **כָּל** מַחֲלֹקֶת שֶׁהִיא לְשֵׁם שָׁמַיִם, סוֹפָהּ לְהִתְקַיֵּם;
וְשֶׁאֵינָה לְשֵׁם שָׁמַיִם, אֵין סוֹפָהּ לְהִתְקַיֵּם. אֵיזוֹ
הִיא מַחֲלֹקֶת שֶׁהִיא לְשֵׁם שָׁמַיִם? זוֹ מַחֲלֹקֶת הִלֵּל וְשַׁמַּאי.
וְשֶׁאֵינָה לְשֵׁם שָׁמַיִם? זוֹ מַחֲלֹקֶת קֹרַח וְכָל עֲדָתוֹ.

Amnon for Tamar, where his lust was intense, yet after it was gratified it turned to bitter hatred: "Amnon despised her with great hatred. Indeed, his hate exceeded his prior love in its intensity" (*II Samuel* 13:15). This is not an infrequent phenomenon. Sometimes a person may have an ambivalent attitude toward an object, but his desire for gratification may outweigh his negative feelings. When the impulse is gratified, nothing remains but the hostility, which is magnified by the guilt over his failure to resist his impulse.

According to the kabbalists, the feeling of love is a derivative of the Divine emanation of *chesed* (loving-kindness). *Chesed* is of supreme importance in Judaism. The father of Judaism, the Patriarch Abraham, is cited as the pillar of *chesed*. Indeed, the Divine intent in bringing the world into existence was that there be the possibility of *chesed* (*Psalms* 89:3). The Divine *chesed* is described as *chesed* of (*emes*) truth (*Exodus* 34:6). Inasmuch as God is perfect and has no personal needs, His *chesed* is true and absolute, devoid of any self-interest. Man receives this Divine emanation, but inasmuch as he has *bechirah* (freedom of choice) and is capable of deviating from truth, he may misdirect this positive force into a spurious *chesed*. He may turn it inwardly so that he becomes the object of his *chesed* and the Divine emanation of love is distorted into self-love.

Abraham's championing of true *chesed* is consistent with his rejection of idolatry and paganism. The latter are nothing but the attempt of man to sanction gratification of his animal impulses by creating an authority that condones them. The worship of idols is devoid of devotion.

We may think that an enlightened civilization such as ours could not possibly regress to the folly of paganism. However, what is the drive to legalize destructive practices other than a pagan ritual to sanction self-gratification? What is the attempt to eliminate Torah commandments that interfere with one's comfort and convenience other than a regression to the principles of paganism, albeit in a more sophisticated form? If contentment becomes the goal of one's life, one may seek to remove all obstructions to contentment.

It is little wonder that in a society where self-love rather than the love of devotion prevails, there is an epidemic of family dissolution. Listen to the timeless words of our sages: *Any love that depends on a specific cause, when that cause is gone, the love is gone.*

In contrast, the love of devotion endures. The love of Jonathan for David was not one of self-gratification. Jonathan knew that David would succeed to the

Amnon for Tamar. And what did not depend upon a specific cause? — The love of David and Jonathan.

20. **A**ny dispute that is for the sake of Heaven will have a constructive outcome; but one that is not for the sake of Heaven will not have a constructive outcome. What sort of dispute was for the sake of Heaven? — The dispute between Hillel and Shammai. And which was not for the sake of Heaven? — The dispute of Korach and his entire company.

---

throne instead of him. Self-love would have converted the relationship to one of bitter hatred. Instead, Jonathan remained devoted to David until the very last.

This mishnah has both defined true love and has given us guidelines for achieving lasting relationships.

20.

כָּל מַחֲלֹקֶת שֶׁהִיא לְשֵׁם שָׁמַיִם
Any dispute that is for the sake of Heaven

A number of commentaries translate this mishnah as "Any dispute that is for the sake of Heaven *will endure*." The endurance of the dispute appears to have a positive value. They explain that disputants that are not motivated by self-glorification but rather by pursuit of truth will give rise to opinions that will stand the test of time.

R' Yisrael of Salant gives a rather novel interpretation to the first portion of the mishnah. He states that people are often motivated to assume a particular position because it is to their advantage. They may be so "bribed" by the benefits they expect to derive that they convince themselves that their position is indeed correct. Although it may be somewhat difficult to convince them otherwise, it is nevertheless possible that by showing them their bias and the validity of the other position they may retreat from their own.

R' Yisrael says that the most difficult bias of all to overcome is when a person is convinced that he is championing the greater glory of God. He may not even have a personal stake in maintaining his position, and if he does, he is oblivious to this. He dupes himself into believing that he is only interested in promoting the glory of God.

Motivations that are ostensibly *l'shem Shamayim* can result in paradoxical behavior. As an example, R' Yisrael cites the case of a young man who made his way through a crowd, rudely pushing people aside so that he could get to the front of the room to be near the speaker who was to deliver a *mussar* lecture. His rude behavior is the very antithesis of *mussar*, yet he thinks he is advancing himself spiritually by getting closer to the lecturer, so dedicated is he

[כא] **כָּל** הַמְזַכֶּה אֶת הָרַבִּים, אֵין חֵטְא בָּא עַל יָדוֹ; וְכָל הַמַּחֲטִיא אֶת הָרַבִּים, אֵין מַסְפִּיקִין בְּיָדוֹ לַעֲשׂוֹת תְּשׁוּבָה. מֹשֶׁה זָכָה וְזִכָּה אֶת הָרַבִּים, זְכוּת הָרַבִּים תָּלוּי בּוֹ, שֶׁנֶּאֱמַר: "צִדְקַת יהוה עָשָׂה, וּמִשְׁפָּטָיו עִם יִשְׂרָאֵל." יָרָבְעָם בֶּן נְבָט חָטָא וְהֶחֱטִיא אֶת הָרַבִּים, חֵטְא הָרַבִּים תָּלוּי בּוֹ, שֶׁנֶּאֱמַר: "עַל חַטֹּאות יָרָבְעָם אֲשֶׁר חָטָא, וַאֲשֶׁר הֶחֱטִיא אֶת יִשְׂרָאֵל."

---

to learn *mussar*! He is unlikely to accept a reprimand because after all, he was simply trying to assure that he hears *mussar*, wasn't he?

Much the same happens in a dispute, says R' Yisrael, when the disputants believe that they are motivated *l'shem Shamayim*. They may be most difficult to convince that they should yield. If it were their personal honor that was at stake, they say, they would gladly surrender their own position. "I am not obstinate," they say, "but whereas I have a right to be self-effacing, I have no right to compromise on the honor of God!"

This mishnah bemoans the divisiveness that has plagued our people since our very inception as a nation. When the dispute is *l'shem Shamayim*, says R' Yisrael, it is likely to endure, because each side is self-righteous that they are defending the honor of God.

Obviously, R' Yisrael did not mean this to be the actual interpretation of the mishnah, since the examples the mishnah provides are inconsistent with this interpretation. However, he does take advantage of the first portion of the mishnah as an independent statement to emphasize this important point. Not only is this type of *l'shem Shamayim* dispute likely to persist, but to our great sorrow, its effects endure even when the disputants are long gone. We are in exile today and without a Sanctuary because of the bitter divisiveness that prevailed at the time of the Second Temple.

Have we learned from the history of the past? Obviously not, else we would have been redeemed and returned to our homeland with a *Beis HaMikdash*. In every community there is fragmentation, with splinter groups separating from the congregation to form their own *shul*. Among observant people, a perfectly reliable *hechsher* (supervision assuring that a food product is kosher) may be shunned, because a faction insists on its own *hechsher*. In communities where there is an *eruv*, some people will deny its reliability not because of any halachic considerations, but because they are at odds with the rabbi who approved it. Even families may be torn asunder because of obstinacy that a particular tradition must prevail, all ostensibly *l'shem Shamayim*!

The mishnah also tells us about the insidiousness and deceptiveness of divisiveness. As an example of a dispute that is not *l'shem Shamayim* the mishnah cites the uprising of Korach against Moses, but instead of naming

21. **W**hoever influences the masses to become meritorious shall not be the cause of sin; but one who influences the masses to sin will not be given the means to repent. *Moses was meritorious and influenced the masses to be meritorious, so the merit of the masses was to his credit, as it is said: Carrying out God's justice and His ordinances with Israel (Deuteronomy 33:21). Jeroboam ben Nebat sinned and caused the masses to sin, so the sin of the masses is charged against him, as it is said: For the sins of Jeroboam that he committed and that he caused Israel to commit (I Kings 15:30).*

Korach and Moses as the disputants, the mishnah says, "Korach and his company." The commentaries tell us that there was disunity between Korach and his own followers. They were united only in their opposition to Moses. Korach's group may have indeed thought that they were of one mind, but actually each one was really involved with his own ego. Had they succeeded in their rebellion against Moses, they would have splintered apart into numerous factions. This is a phenomenon that has repeatedly occurred in our history, whether in politics or in a community.

When will we ever learn?

21.

כָּל הַמְזַכֶּה אֶת הָרַבִּים
Whoever influences the masses
to become meritorious

Several commentaries point out that the mishnah states that someone who influences the masses to be meritorious shall not be the cause of sin, or, as some translate, will be kept from sin. The mishnah then cites Moses as an example of one who influenced the masses favorably, but it does not follow through with a source that indicates that Moses was therefore protected from sin. We may also ask: Inasmuch as every person has *bechirah* (free choice) at all times, how can one "be kept from sin"? It is also noteworthy that the literal translation of the mishnah is "that no sin will come to his hand"; i.e., he will not have the *opportunity* to sin.

Perhaps we may understand this mishnah with a comment of R' Mendel of Kotzk who said, "The reason a person should not sin is not because it is forbidden. Rather, he should be so occupied with doing mitzvos that he simply does not have the time or opportunity to sin."

Earlier we cited the Talmudic statement that a person should think of himself as being evenly balanced between mitzvos and sins. Performing a single

מִי שֶׁיֵּשׁ בְּיָדוֹ שְׁלשָׁה דְבָרִים הַלָּלוּ, הוּא [כב] **כָּל**
מִתַּלְמִידָיו שֶׁל אַבְרָהָם אָבִינוּ; וּשְׁלשָׁה דְבָרִים
אֲחֵרִים, הוּא מִתַּלְמִידָיו שֶׁל בִּלְעָם הָרָשָׁע. עַיִן טוֹבָה,

mitzvah will now weigh the balance in his favor and cause him to be considered a *tzaddik*, whereas a single sin will cause the sins to dominate and he will be considered a *rasha*. Furthermore, he should think of the world as being evenly balanced between *tzaddikim* and *reshaim*, so that if he is a *tzaddik*, the majority of the world is now comprised of *tzaddikim* and will be judged favorably. A person thus has the capacity to bring great merit to the entire world

If a person succeeds in following this Talmudic advice, he will *always* be occupied in doing mitzvos. As the Rabbi of Kotzk says, he will never have an opportunity to sin. Furthermore, it is only when a person is motivated by self-interest that he may sin in gratifying a desire. Someone who has totally divested himself of self-interest and is totally devoted to doing for others is simply not at risk of doing a sin.

Moses' devotion to caring for *Klal Yisrael* was absolute. The Torah states that Moses descended from the mountain to the people, upon which Rashi comments that he went directly to the people and did not attend to any of his own needs. Meticulous attention to the words of the mishnah supports this interpretation. The word זָכָה means "pure." Hence, *Moshe zachah* means that Moses purified himself; i.e., cleansed himself of any self-interest. Moses was motivated by absolute *chesed* and he truly emulated God, Who, of course, has no needs whatever. It is not that Moses was kept from doing sin as a Divine reward, because he always retained his *bechirah*. Rather, the verse quoted by the mishnah, "Carrying out God's *tzedakah* (justice or righteousness)," refers to Moses' total abstention from any self-interest and, like God, caring only for others. It was this absolute selflessness and complete preoccupation with his mission that kept him away from sin.

The mishnah is thus cohesive in citing Moses as an example of someone who is devoted to caring for others, particularly to "purify" them and elevate them spiritually. Anyone who follows in Moses' footsteps will similarly "be kept from sin" in that "no sin will come to his hand"; i.e., he will not have an opportunity to sin.

There is also cohesiveness in the latter part of the mishnah. Again, the mishnah states that one who causes others to sin will not have the opportunity to do *teshuvah*. The mishnah quotes Scripture which states that Jeroboam caused others to sin, but does not cite a source that Jeroboam was denied *teshuvah*. Furthermore, we know that no person is denied *teshuvah* (*Jerusalem Talmud, Peah* 1:1). Why would a person who caused others to sin and did sincere *teshuvah* not be forgiven?

Let us consider: Why would a person wish that another person should sin? One may be driven by his own temptation to sin, but what gain is there in

22. **W**hoever has the following three traits is among the disciples of our forefather Abraham; and [whoever has] three different traits is among the disciples of the wicked Balaam. Those who have a good eye,

---

causing others to do so?

It is only an ego drive that can lead a person to cause others to sin. In the case of Jeroboam, he was motivated to establish an idol cult and a new place of worship for fear that if his subjects made the pilgrimage to Jerusalem they would recognize the king of Judah as the authentic king of Israel. Similarly, anyone who wishes to cause others to sin is ego driven. His guilt feelings for his own improper behavior are mitigated if others sin along with him. Just as a person who takes a narcotic to alleviate abdominal pain will not have an inflamed appendix removed and may die of peritonitis, so a person who relieves his guilt by causing others to sin along with him will lose the motivation for *teshuvah*.

The mishnah does not state that one who causes others to sin is *denied* the right to do *teshuvah*. Indeed, if he does sincere *teshuvah* he too will be forgiven. It is just that this person is unlikely to do *teshuvah* because he eliminates the sensation of guilt, the distressful feeling that motivates a person to *teshuvah*.

This mishnah provides an important insight into the motivation of a person. It tells us what one can do to avoid sin, and what can prevent a person from having remorse for errant behavior.

22.

כָּל מִי שֶׁיֵּשׁ בְּיָדוֹ שְׁלֹשָׁה דְבָרִים הַלָּלוּ,
הוּא מִתַּלְמִידָיו שֶׁל אַבְרָהָם אָבִינוּ
Whoever has the following three traits is among the disciples of our forefather Abraham

Rashi explains the trait of a "good eye" as not being jealous of others, i.e., not begrudging them what they have. Please note: In Hebrew this is referred to as עַיִן טוֹבָה, and in Yiddish this is translated by a single word, to *fargin*. Both are *positive* terms denoting a positive feeling of being pleased about another person's good fortune. In English, however, there is no equivalent of עַיִן טוֹבָה or *fargin*, and we must describe this trait in negative terms; i.e., the *absence* of jealousy or *not begrudging* another's good fortune. Is it not strange that in a language that is so rich in vocabulary, the massive Webster's unabridged dictionary does not have a word that is equivalent to *fargin*, i.e., a positive trait rather than the absence of a negative trait?

If we were to represent a positive trait as a plus and a negative trait as a minus, the absence of a negative trait can only be at the zero point, but does not constitute positivity. What does this signify?

וְרוּחַ נְמוּכָה, וְנֶפֶשׁ שְׁפָלָה, תַּלְמִידָיו שֶׁל אַבְרָהָם אָבִינוּ.
עַיִן רָעָה, וְרוּחַ גְּבוֹהָה, וְנֶפֶשׁ רְחָבָה, תַּלְמִידָיו שֶׁל בִּלְעָם
הָרָשָׁע. מַה בֵּין תַּלְמִידָיו שֶׁל אַבְרָהָם אָבִינוּ לְתַלְמִידָיו
שֶׁל בִּלְעָם הָרָשָׁע? תַּלְמִידָיו שֶׁל אַבְרָהָם אָבִינוּ אוֹכְלִין
בָּעוֹלָם הַזֶּה, וְנוֹחֲלִין הָעוֹלָם הַבָּא, שֶׁנֶּאֱמַר: ‚‚לְהַנְחִיל
אֹהֲבַי יֵשׁ, וְאֹצְרֹתֵיהֶם אֲמַלֵּא.״ אֲבָל תַּלְמִידָיו שֶׁל בִּלְעָם
הָרָשָׁע יוֹרְשִׁין גֵּיהִנָּם, וְיוֹרְדִין לִבְאֵר שַׁחַת, שֶׁנֶּאֱמַר:
‚‚וְאַתָּה אֱלֹהִים תּוֹרִדֵם לִבְאֵר שַׁחַת, אַנְשֵׁי דָמִים וּמִרְמָה
לֹא יֶחֱצוּ יְמֵיהֶם, וַאֲנִי אֶבְטַח בָּךְ.״

Much can be learned about a culture by a study of its language. A culture will devise words only for the concepts with which it is familiar. For example, neither in Hebrew nor in Yiddish is there a word equivalent to the English "fun." There are words for pleasure, enjoyment, play, and amusement, but not for fun. This is because the concept of fun is alien to Jewish ideology. Fun denotes an activity which has no purpose, as is evident from the popular phrase "for the fun of it." If you see someone engaged in an activity which appears to serve no purpose and you ask why he is doing it, he is likely to respond, "just for the fun of it." One might also respond, "just for the heck of it." Again there is no equivalent for "heck" in Hebrew or Yiddish. A culture that has a concept of "fun" or "heck" is one that condones purposeless actions. The reason there is no equivalent to "fun" or "heck" in Hebrew or Yiddish is because such actions are alien to Jewish thought. It is inconceivable that one would do anything that has no purpose.

In Yiddish we can *fargin*. When someone buys a new house or a new automobile or has great *nachas* from his children or grandchildren, we can say, "I *fargin* him." One can even say, "I *fargin* him wholeheartedly." It is rather awkward to say, "I don't begrudge him wholeheartedly."

As descendants of the Patriarch Abraham, or as converts to the faith of Abraham, we have the capacity of עַיִן טוֹבָה. We have the positive trait of *farginning*. Perhaps this is because we have the companion trait of רוּחַ נְמוּכָה, an undemanding soul; i.e., to be satisfied with what one has. The Talmud considers a person with this trait as being truly wealthy (above, 4:1). One who is discontented with his lot will find it difficult to *fargin* others what they have.

But note! The fact that we have the term means that we have the *capacity* to *fargin*. This is a capacity that must be cultivated so that we indeed become *farginners*. Indeed, all the commendable traits cited by Ben Zoma in the opening mishnah of Chapter 4 are essential prerequisites for *farginning*. As we have noted in our discussion of that mishnah, these traits and values differ from those that prevail in the secular world. In order to *fargin*, we must tear ourselves

5/22 *a humble spirit, and an undemanding soul are the disciples of our forefather Abraham. Those who have an evil eye, an arrogant spirit, and a greedy soul are the disciples of the wicked Balaam. How are the disciples of our forefather Abraham different from the disciples of the wicked Balaam? The disciples of our forefather Abraham enjoy [the fruits of their good deeds] in this world and inherit the World to Come, as it is said: To cause those who love Me to inherit an everlasting possession [the World to Come], and I will fill their storehouses [in this world] (Proverbs 8:21). But the disciples of the wicked Balaam inherit Gehinnom and descend into the well of destruction, as it is said: And You, O God, shall lower them into the well of destruction, men of bloodshed and deceit shall not live out half their days; but as for me, I will trust in You (Psalms 55:24).*

---

away from prevailing cultural concepts and adopt those that will merit our being true disciples of Abraham.

In the discussion of spirituality (*Twerski on Spirituality,* Mesorah 1998) I pointed out that Abraham is noted primarily for his *chesed,* his dedication to doing things for others. *Chesed* requires that one be able to look away from one's own needs and be concerned for others. Hedonism and *chesed* are mutually exclusive. It is because Abraham excelled in the traits listed in this mishnah that he was the pillar of *chesed.*

We take pride in being the children of Abraham. To merit this honor we must emulate the Patriarch in his espousal of *chesed,* and we can achieve this by developing the three positive traits of this mishnah.

Why does the mishnah not begin with enumerating the desirable character traits? What is the purpose of the introduction that possessing three certain traits renders one a disciple of Abraham?

As we have noted, we do not come into the world with noble character traits. The newborn infant has only self-gratifying urges. As he grows and matures, he must refine these urges, directing them into proper channels (cf. *Tiferes Yisrael,* end of *Kiddushin*). This requires much effort, denying oneself fulfillment of various innate drives. This can be achieved only if one is adequately motivated.

A philosophical understanding of the desirability of certain character traits does not suffice to warrant the required self sacrifice. As children, we are taught about the lives of the Patriarchs, and we pray to "the God of Abraham, Isaac, and Jacob." Our initial motivation is to emulate the *middos* (traits) of the Patriarchs. We must aspire to achieve the spirituality they manifested. The

[כג] **יְהוּדָה** בֶּן תֵּימָא אוֹמֵר: הֱוֵי עַז כַּנָּמֵר, וְקַל כַּנֶּשֶׁר, רָץ כַּצְּבִי, וְגִבּוֹר כָּאֲרִי לַעֲשׂוֹת רְצוֹן אָבִיךָ שֶׁבַּשָּׁמָיִם.

[כד] **הוּא** הָיָה אוֹמֵר: עַז פָּנִים לְגֵיהִנֹּם, וּבֹשֶׁת פָּנִים לְגַן עֵדֶן. יְהִי רָצוֹן מִלְּפָנֶיךָ יהוה אֱלֹהֵינוּ וֵאלֹהֵי אֲבוֹתֵינוּ שֶׁיִּבָּנֶה בֵּית הַמִּקְדָּשׁ בִּמְהֵרָה בְיָמֵינוּ וְתֵן חֶלְקֵנוּ בְּתוֹרָתֶךָ.

Sages say that a person is obligated to say, "When shall my deeds reach those of my ancestors?" (*Tanna DeVei Eliyahu* 5).

The mishnah therefore begins with the statement that there are three traits that characterized the Patriarch Abraham. If someone wishes to emulate the Patriarch's lifestyle and become his disciple, there is reason to proceed to discuss these. If he is not so motivated, it is pointless to enumerate the traits that can be attained only with much self-denial.

It is of interest that Balaam, whom the mishnah cites as the polar opposite of Abraham, was well aware of Abraham's greatness, and even aspired to die as noble and as spiritual a person as Abraham (*Numbers* 23:10). However, Balaam did not want to *live* the life of Abraham, preferring instead a life of indulgence.

The mishnah goes on to state that the disciples of Abraham enjoy both this world and the World to Come, whereas the disciples of Balaam have neither. It might be argued that while self-indulgent people may not merit Paradise, they seem to partake heartily of worldly pleasures. Why does the mishnah deny this?

The desires of those who lust for earthly pleasures may be either fulfilled or unfulfilled. If unfulfilled, they remain frustrated and discontented. However, fulfillment may not bring them contentment either.

A young man consulted me because of a feeling of futility with life. His father was very wealthy, and his own share of the wealth was considerable. "I think my father is crazy," he said. "He has more money than he could consume if he lived to be a thousand years old, but he still goes to the office every day to make more money. I already have all the money I can use. I have a condominium on the Riviera and another on the west coast. I have a stable of horses. I have or can get everything a person could possibly want. I just don't have any taste for living. It is all meaningless. To tell the truth, I've often thought of suicide."

There is a Chinese curse, "May all your wishes come true." I never understood why this is a curse until I met this young man. If you have everything you want and you lack for nothing at all, what can motivate you to go on living?

23. **Y**ehudah ben Tema says: Be bold as a leopard, light as an eagle, swift as a deer, and strong as a lion, to carry out the will of your Father in Heaven.

24. **H**e [Yehudah ben Tema] was accustomed to say: The brazen goes to Gehinnom, but the shame-faced goes to the Garden of Eden. May it be Your will, HASHEM, our God and the God of our forefathers, that the Holy Temple be rebuilt, speedily in our days, and grant us our share in Your Torah.

You have nothing toward which to strive!

I asked the young man why he does not use his money to provide for the needy. "Give away my money? Why would I want to do that?" he said. With all his interests directed only inwardly, he had lost all zest for life.

The inordinate lusts of the disciples of Balaam condemn them to a life of discontent. It is only the disciples of Abraham who can truly enjoy this world, as well as merit Paradise.

Someone observing the lifestyle of Balaam's disciples may think that they are happy with their indulgence. One need only observe a heroin addict under the influence of the drug. He is in a state of incomparable euphoria. However, there is no *Gehinnom* that can compare to the misery of the addict's lifestyle. One recovering addict said, "The worst day of my sobriety is far better than the best day of my addiction."

As the children of Abraham, we should also be his disciples. We can truly enjoy the world, as well as merit *Gan Eden*.

23-24.

הֱוֵי עַז כַּנָּמֵר . . . עַז פָּנִים לְגֵיהִנֹּם
Be bold as a leopard . . .
The brazen goes to Gehinnom

Several of the commentaries interpret this mishnah as instructions to a *baal teshuvah*, to one who wishes to change his lifestyle to a more spiritual one.

The first stage requires boldness. One's peers may mock him for abandoning his pursuit of pleasures. "What's happened to you? Are you becoming a saint? Do you think you are better than us? Come along with us for some fun!" The memories of pleasurable pastimes may exert a strong attraction, and one must be bold to resist both the temptation and the jeers of one's friends.

Bold, yes. Arrogant and insulting, no. The lightness of the eagle refers to its ability to hover and descend gently. The eagle does not swoop down upon its nest in a crescendo. The response to those who are critical of one's *teshuvah*

ה/כה [כה] **הוּא** הָיָה אוֹמֵר: בֶּן חָמֵשׁ שָׁנִים לַמִּקְרָא, בֶּן עֶשֶׂר שָׁנִים לַמִּשְׁנָה, בֶּן שְׁלֹשׁ עֶשְׂרֵה לַמִּצְוֹת, בֶּן חֲמֵשׁ עֶשְׂרֵה לַגְּמָרָא, בֶּן שְׁמוֹנֶה עֶשְׂרֵה לַחֻפָּה, בֶּן עֶשְׂרִים לִרְדּוֹף, בֶּן שְׁלֹשִׁים לַכֹּחַ, בֶּן אַרְבָּעִים לַבִּינָה, בֶּן חֲמִשִּׁים לְעֵצָה, בֶּן שִׁשִּׁים לְזִקְנָה, בֶּן שִׁבְעִים לְשֵׂיבָה, בֶּן שְׁמוֹנִים לִגְבוּרָה, בֶּן תִּשְׁעִים לָשׁוּחַ, בֶּן מֵאָה כְּאִלּוּ מֵת וְעָבַר וּבָטֵל מִן הָעוֹלָם.

must be courteous. One should not return a jeer with acrimony.

Particular caution and sensitivity must be exercised when parents disapprove of their child becoming a *baal teshuvah*. Parents may interpret their child's adoption of "Yiddishkeit" as a repudiation of their values and a personal affront. One must bear in mind that respect of parents is a major tenet of Torah. One may indeed differ with one's parents, but this must be done with utmost respect and consideration of their feelings.

The swiftness of the deer refers to the diligence in doing mitzvos. One must overcome inertia and indolence, and do the mitzvos with enthusiasm. Swiftness does *not* mean that the *baal teshuvah* should take giant leaps in transforming his lifestyle in a radical manner. Sudden changes may be counterproductive. The *baal teshuvah* should be guided by a halachic authority in his adaptation to a Torah-observant lifestyle.

Finally, the *baal teshuvah* should have the strength of a lion. The Talmud says that as a person progresses spiritually, his *yetzer hara* increases in strength proportionately (*Succah* 52a). The challenges confronting the *baal teshuvah* may become greater as he embraces Torah living. The initial introduction into a Torah lifestyle may be comparatively easy. The going may get rougher as one proceeds.

In some texts mishnah 24 is part of mishnah 23. Yehudah ben Tema wishes to clarify the boldness that he recommended. It is indeed essential to be firm in one's convictions in defiance of one's peers. However, such boldness must not be allowed to degenerate into arrogance. Humility is the calling card of a Torah lifestyle. Arrogance and insensitivity should not be permitted to accompany the adoption of Torah. Such behavior constitutes a *chilul Hashem* (desecration of the Divine Name). Insolence indeed warrants *Gehinnom*.

The translation בּוֹשֶׁת (*boshes*) as "shamefaced" may be misleading. A more correct translation is "modesty," which is the opposite of arrogance. Technically, there is a difference between "guilt" and "shame." Guilt is a distressing feeling resulting from awareness that one has done wrong. Such guilt can be constructive because it leads to correcting one's behavior and doing proper *teshuvah*. "Shame" is a feeling that one is bad in essence, even in absence of any wrongdoing. Shame is not eliminated by *teshuvah* and is depressing. The

25. H*e [Yehudah ben Tema] was accustomed to say: A five-year-old begins Scripture; a ten-year-old begins Mishnah; a thirteen-year-old becomes obliged to observe the commandments; a fifteen-year-old begins to study Gemara; an eighteen-year-old goes to the marriage canopy; a twenty-year-old begins pursuit [of a livelihood]; a thirty-year-old attains full strength; a forty-year-old attains understanding; a fifty-year-old can offer counsel; a sixty-year-old attains seniority; a seventy-year-old attains a ripe old age; an eighty-year-old shows strength; a ninety-year-old becomes stooped over; a hundred-year-old is as if he were dead, passed away and ceased from the world.*

---

desirable trait is *modesty*, which is the correct translation of בּוּשָׁה in the mishnah. Modesty is an outgrowth of humility. As Ramban says in the letter to his son, humility and modesty are the foundation of all commendable character traits.

Although Yehuda ben Tema's advice may have been directed to the newcomer to Yiddishkeit, it is equally valid for everyone. Indeed, inasmuch as we should all be seeking to improve ourselves, our spiritual growth should render the spirituality of the past as inadequate. We should all be *baalei teshuvah*.

25.

בֶּן חָמֵשׁ שָׁנִים לַמִּקְרָא . . .
A five-year-old begins Scripture . . .

I distinctly remember my first lesson when I was 5. My teacher opened the book of *Leviticus*, where the word וַיִּקְרָא was printed in large letters, except for the diminutive א. He explained that I was beginning to learn the third of the Five Books of Moses rather than *Bereishis* (*Genesis*), because *Leviticus* is about the sacred offerings in the Sanctuary. Since I was now beginning to learn the holy Torah, I too was sacred, and even dearer to God than the offerings in the Sanctuary.

I was of course curious why the *aleph* was so much smaller than the other letters. My teacher told me that knowing that I am holy should not cause me to be vain. The diminutive *aleph*, the first letter of the alphabet, teaches us that one can retain Torah only if one is humble.

What a wonderful way to introduce a child to Torah! I am privileged to have seen my children and grandchildren celebrate this ancient ritual of beginning Torah study at age 5, with the invaluable teachings contained in the very first word they learn.

The child then proceeds to *Genesis*. He learns that the universe was

[כו] **בֶּן** בַּג בַּג אוֹמֵר: הֲפָךְ בָּה וַהֲפָךְ בָּה, דְּכֹלָּא בָהּ; וּבָהּ תֶּחֱזֵי, וְסִיב וּבְלֵה בָה, וּמִנַּהּ לָא תָזוּעַ, שֶׁאֵין לְךָ מִדָּה טוֹבָה הֵימֶנָּה. בֶּן הֵא הֵא אוֹמֵר: לְפוּם צַעֲרָא אַגְרָא.

❧ ❧ ❧

---

created. The world is not the result of a haphazard accident, but was created by God for a purpose. In a purposeful world he, too, has a purpose. He learns about the Patriarch Abraham, the father of Judaism, whose incomparable *chesed* (kindness to others) should be our basic character trait. Later in the child's Talmudic studies this will be reinforced by Hillel, who taught that the essence of Torah is to love others as you do yourself.

At age 10 the child is introduced to the study of the mishnah, and soon begins discussing intricacies of halachah that parallel in complexity the subjects taught in law school.

The mishnah states that at 13 (12 for a girl) a youngster becomes an adult. The transition from a minor to an adult occurs in a fragment of a second, at the precise moment of sunset on the last day of the 12th (or 11th) year.

Judaism does not recognize the phase of adolescence created by Western civilization. We are just now beginning to understand the folly of this artifact. In Judaism the parents are culpable for the misdeeds of their minor child. At the moment of Bar or Bas Mitzvah, the transformation is complete and the youngster is responsible for his/her actions. There is no hiatus of responsibility of adolescence, when the child is too old for the parents to be held responsible, but is not yet old enough to be held responsible himself/herself. The artifact of adolescence has led to the development of "juvenile law." Young people who commit heinous crimes know that they will not be subject to the punishment warranted by their actions. It is only recently, when 11-year-old children have committed terrible crimes such as killing their teachers and classmates, that the wisdom of "juvenile law" is being questioned.

The Torah definition of adulthood is simple and uniform. In the United States the age of majority varies from state to state. Even within a state there is one age of majority for voting, another for driving, another for marriage, and yet another for drinking. Little wonder that there is confusion about the age of responsibility.

At first glance this mishnah may appear to be out of place in a work on ethics. It might be more appropriate in one of the tractates dealing with legal issues. A closer understanding reveals its crucial role in ethical behavior. Judaism begins teaching ethics at 5, and enforcing it at 13 or 12.

5/26

26. **B**en Bag Bag says: Delve in it [the Torah] and [continue to] delve in it, for everything is in it; look deeply into it; grow old and gray over it; do not stir from it, for you can have no better portion than it. Ben Hei Hei says: The reward is in proportion to the exertion.

❧ ❧ ❧

26.

בֶּן בַּג בַּג
Ben Bag Bag

Midrash Shmuel states that the names Ben Bag Bag and Ben Hei Hei were pseudonyms to disguise the identities of these scholars who were descendants of proselytes. Another authority states that they themselves were proselytes. In fact, since they were contemporaries of Hillel, he states that they were the pagans whom Hillel embraced.

The stories of the two pagans are well known. One came to Shammai, stating that he would convert to Judaism if he would be made High Priest. Shammai repelled him. He came before Hillel, who began teaching him Torah. He soon learned that even the greatest and most saintly scholar cannot aspire to the priesthood, which is assigned exclusively to the descendants of Aaron. He then embraced Judaism.

The second pagan challenged Shammai to condense the entire Torah into a few sentences, "As long as I can stand on one foot." Again, Shammai rejected him. Hillel told him that the entire Torah is contained in the single mitzvah, "Love your neighbor as yourself." The rest of Torah is an elaboration of that mitzvah. He, too, embraced Judaism.

According to this authority, Ben Bag Bag and Ben Hei Hei were these two converts. Both had come to a profound appreciation of the Torah. It is quite likely that prior to their conversion they had been highly educated. They were therefore in an ideal position to teach that all knowledge is contained in the Torah. It is not all on the surface, and one must exert oneself to reap the reward of this wealth of knowledge. Having been reared in the hedonism of paganism, their admonishment, "Do not deviate from Torah. It is the true and finest way to live," carries great weight.

This mishnah, which extols the virtues of Torah, serves as an introduction to the next chapter. Chapter Six is a collection of Talmudic passage appended to *Ethics of the Fathers* that elaborates on the teachings of Ben Bag Bag and Ben Hei Hei.

רַבִּי חֲנַנְיָא בֶּן עֲקַשְׁיָא אוֹמֵר: רָצָה הַקָּדוֹשׁ בָּרוּךְ הוּא לְזַכּוֹת אֶת יִשְׂרָאֵל, לְפִיכָךְ הִרְבָּה לָהֶם תּוֹרָה וּמִצְוֹת, שֶׁנֶּאֱמַר: ‏‫,,‬יהוה חָפֵץ לְמַעַן צִדְקוֹ, יַגְדִּיל תּוֹרָה וְיַאְדִּיר.‏‫"‬

Rabbi Chanania ben Akashia says: The Holy One, Blessed is He, wished to confer merit upon Israel; therefore He gave them Torah and mitzvos in abundance, as it is said: HASHEM desired, for the sake of its [Israel's] righteousness, that the Torah be made great and glorious (Isaiah 42:21).

פרק ששי

Chapter Six

כָּל יִשְׂרָאֵל יֵשׁ לָהֶם חֵלֶק לָעוֹלָם הַבָּא, שֶׁנֶּאֱמַר:
„וְעַמֵּךְ כֻּלָּם צַדִּיקִים, לְעוֹלָם יִירְשׁוּ
אָרֶץ, נֵצֶר מַטָּעַי, מַעֲשֵׂה יָדַי לְהִתְפָּאֵר.‟

All Israel has a share in the World to Come, as it is
said: And your people are all righteous; they shall
inherit the land forever; a branch of My plantings, My
handiwork, in which to take pride (Isaiah 60:21).

פרק ששי

שָׁנוּ חֲכָמִים בִּלְשׁוֹן הַמִּשְׁנָה. בָּרוּךְ שֶׁבָּחַר בָּהֶם וּבְמִשְׁנָתָם.

[א] **רַבִּי** מֵאִיר אוֹמֵר: כָּל הָעוֹסֵק בַּתּוֹרָה לִשְׁמָהּ זוֹכֶה לִדְבָרִים הַרְבֵּה; וְלֹא עוֹד, אֶלָּא שֶׁכָּל הָעוֹלָם

Chapter 6

> **בָּרוּךְ שֶׁבָּחַר בָּהֶם וּבְמִשְׁנָתָם**
> **Blessed is He Who chose them and their teaching.**

This chapter, often referred to as "The Chapter of Acquisition of Torah," is preceded by an expression of thanks to God: "Blessed is He who chose the sages and their teaching." This posits an important principle of Torah.

The validity and value of secular knowledge is independent of its discoverer, author, or inventor. We apply the law of gravitation regardless of the characters of Newton or Kepler who elucidated it. There is no need to know anything about the lifestyle of Fleming in order to use penicillin effectively. Scientific findings stand on their own merits.

This is not true of Torah. Regardless of how valuable a Torah teaching may be, it is not acceptable if its author was not thoroughly observant of Torah. Torah is often compared to life-giving water. The purest water will become contaminated if it is contained or passed through a dirty container. The apparent value of a teaching that emanates from a person whose character is incompatible with Torah principles is illusory. "Blessed is He Who chose *the sages* and (only afterward) their teachings." The teacher must first meet the criteria of Torah refinement before we will consider his teachings.

It is related that R' Levi Yitzchak of Berditchev ascended to heaven and found the heavenly host to be jubilant. He inquired as to the reason for this joy, and was told that it was decreed that all Jews should have abundant earnings, and that no one should suffer poverty. "Who initiated this decree?" he asked. He was told that it was Satan's idea. "Then the decree must be annulled," he said. "Nothing good can emanate from an evil source."

It is for this reason that Torah scholars must be able to withstand meticulous scrutiny of their character. Only then can we rely on the truth of their teachings.

1.

> **כָּל הָעוֹסֵק בַּתּוֹרָה לִשְׁמָהּ**
> **Whoever engages in Torah study for its own sake**

A variety of interpretations have been given to the expression תּוֹרָה לִשְׁמָהּ, assuming that the word לִשְׁמָהּ indeed means "for its own sake." There is general agreement that it excludes one who learns Torah in order to be respected as a scholar. Rambam and Shelah

*T*he Sages taught [this chapter] in the language of the Mishnah. Blessed is He Who chose them and their teaching.

1. *R*abbi Meir says: Whoever engages in Torah study for its
own sake merits many things; furthermore, [the cre-

---

define this term as meaning learning Torah in order to implement its commandments, which one could not do properly if he was ignorant of Torah. R' Shneur
Zalman explains that it refers to study of Torah as a means to attach oneself to
God, Who has "placed Himself within the Torah." R' Chaim of Volozhin defines
לִשְׁמָהּ as meaning to know and understand its contents.

The Rabbi of Kotzk suggests that we take the word לִשְׁמָהּ literally — not "for its
own sake," but "for its name." The word Torah means "to guide." Torah must be
seen as the guide, the *only* guide through life.

Some people conceptualize religion as an *ingredient* of life; an important
ingredient, but nevertheless only an ingredient. Food that is without salt may
indeed be tasteless because salt is an important ingredient. Nevertheless, the food
is edible without salt. If religion is an ingredient of life, then they view life without
religion as livable.

Although we use the term "Torah life," it is a redundancy. Life wthout Torah
is not a life that lacks an important ingredient. It is not life at all.

The Talmud says that those who reject Torah are considered lifeless even while
they live (*Berachos* 18b). In *Twerski on Spirituality* (Mesorah 1998), I pointed out
that the human being is a composite of a body and a spirit. The human body is
essentially an animal body, differing only in some relatively minor physiologic and
biochemical ways from other mammals. What gives a human being his distinction
and uniqueness and hence his *very definition* as a human being is the *spirit*, which
is the sum total of all the capacities that a person has that animals do not have. For
example, *chesed* is uniquely human. No tiger has ever thought, "I really should
leave some of this carcass for that poor hungry jackal." Animals are by nature
centripetal. All their drives are aimed at self-gratification. Consideration for others
even at the cost of self-deprivation is unique to humans. A person who functions
centripetally is, in that respect, animal in nature.

This is equally true of all the other features that distinguish a human being from
animals. To the degree that a person fails to implement the spirit, to that degree
he is deficient in humanity.

The Torah is *the manual* for spirituality. Rejection of the Torah is rejection of the
spirit. The person who rejects Torah may indeed be alive in the sense that he
breathes, moves about, and metabolizes, but his existence is essentially an animal
existence. The Talmud is correct in stating that *as a human being he is lifeless*. His
animal body exists, but his human spirit is dead.

This is what the Rabbi of Kotzk meant. Torah is the manual, the guide that gives
a person the distinction of being a true human being.

זוֹכֶה לִדְבָרִים הַרְבֵּה; וְלֹא עוֹד
Merits many things; furthermore

The wording of the mishnah, "further-more," indicates that the phrase זוֹכֶה לִדְבָרִים הַרְבֵּה, "merits many things," is an independent statement. It is not a rubric for all the detailed items that the mishnah enumerates. What are the "many things" that the true Torah scholar receives in addition to those enumerated?

The word דְּבָרִים can be translated as "words" as well as "things." Chasam Sofer therefore interprets this statement to mean that the words of an authentic Torah scholar are meaningful.

Following Chasam Sofer's translation, the mishnah may be conveying yet another thought. The Chofetz Chaim dedicated his life to the eradication of *lashon hara*, and his works are replete with many restrictions on speech. Indeed, it would appear that keeping silent is the only way to avoid the violation of *lashon hara*. One might think that the Chofetz Chaim was therefore a person of few words. People who knew the Chofetz Chaim, however, relate that he was an excellent conversationalist. The greatness of the Chofetz Chaim was not that he kept silent, but that he could engage in normal conversation without approaching the faintest tincture of improper speech.

A true Torah scholar is totally absorbed in Torah, both when he is studying Torah and when he is engaged in the normal activities of life. All his actions are dictated by Torah. His conversation, too, is dictated by Torah. He is therefore capable of speaking profusely without stepping beyond the realm of speech prescribed by Torah. The mishnah is thus asserting that the Torah scholar can indeed be a "person of many words."

The statement זוֹכֶה לִדְבָרִים הַרְבֵּה can have yet another interpretation. The word זוֹכֶה can also mean "to purify." The mishnah is then stating that the true Torah scholar can *purify* many things.

Chassidus teaches that the function of a Jew is to make everything sacred. The Rabbi of Kotzk cited the verse (*Psalms* 115:16): "The heaven, the heaven is to God, and the earth He gave to man," and remarked, "God made the heaven into heaven, and He gave the earth to man so that man should make *it* into heaven."

Everything on earth can be transformed into something sacred if its use is for an ultimately sacred purpose. A person who eats in order to have the nourishment necessary for optimum health so that he can observe the mitzvos is converting the food substance into something sacred. If one uses money for *tzedakah*, for support of Torah learning, or for the necessities of life that will enable him to fulfill the mitzvos, this money assumes a sanctity. Every material object that is used in any way that will contribute to the fulfillment of the Divine will becomes sacred. Every mundane object can undergo a purification when directed toward Torah goals.

This concept is contained in the words of this mishnah. The dedicated Torah scholar whose sole motivation is fulfillment of the Divine will can purify many things; i.e., virtually anything with which he comes in contact, because he will use them solely for Torah-specified goals.

שֶׁכָּל הָעוֹלָם כָּלּוֹ כְּדַאי הוּא לוֹ
The entire world is worth-while for his sake alone.

Chasam Sofer's translation is that for the true Torah scholar, "the entire world is adequate." His interpretation of this mishnah may be embellished by a personal anecdote.

I had often wondered why Moses began his review of the Torah by instructing the Israelites not to add nor take away from the mitzvos (*Deuteronomy* 4:1-2). It would appear more logical to instruct them on the most fundamental mitzvos first. After finishing the entire list he might then caution them not to tamper with the mitzvos. Why did he give precedence to this warning?

I received a gift of an attaché case with a combination lock, but after a brief use I set it aside. Many months later I used it to carry some important documents to the office. When I tried to open it, I did not remember the combination. I thought that I had probably chosen 613, because this would be easily recalled by my less-than-efficient memory. Alas! 613 did not open the lock. I was about to force the lock open, but decided to try my luck by moving the numbers at random. Lo and behold! The lock sprung open! I looked at the numbers. They were 613. Why had this combination not worked initially? Because my setting had been inaccurate. I had been off by one number, either 612 or 614, which of course did not work. I concluded that when the correct formula is 613, one more or one less will not work.

The answer to my question became apparent. Moses was telling the Israelites that God had provided them with the formula for life: the Torah. Its 613 mitzvos were the combination for proper living. Tampering with the formula would invalidate it. One cannot reject any of the mitzvos or create new ones.

A number of the mitzvos are contingent on the existence of the *Beis HaMikdash* (Temple) and on our dwelling in the Holy Land. How can we complete the requisite 613 mitzvos to make the Torah formula operational when we are in exile? The Talmud answers that when one studies the content and rules of the mitzvah in the Torah, this is equivalent to performing it (*Menachos* 110a). It is thus possible to fulfill the entire Torah formula, including those mitzvos which we cannot perform, by the study of Torah.

Chasam Sofer therefore interprets the mishnah to mean that for a true Torah scholar the entire world suffices for performance of the mitzvos. One who does not study Torah and who lives outside of the Holy Land or at a time when certain mitzvos cannot be actualized is lacking in compliance with the essential formula of 613. The Torah scholar can meet this requirement at any time in history and

א/ו אוֹהֵב אֶת הַבְּרִיּוֹת, מְשַׂמֵּחַ אֶת הַמָּקוֹם, מְשַׂמֵּחַ אֶת
הַבְּרִיּוֹת וּמַלְבַּשְׁתּוֹ עֲנָוָה וְיִרְאָה; וּמַכְשַׁרְתּוֹ לִהְיוֹת צַדִּיק,

in any place in the world via his Torah study. For him, "the entire world," both spatially and temporally, is adequate for observance of the complete Torah.

**אוֹהֵב אֶת הַמָּקוֹם, אוֹהֵב אֶת הַבְּרִיּוֹת,
מְשַׂמֵּחַ אֶת הַמָּקוֹם, מְשַׂמֵּחַ אֶת הַבְּרִיּוֹת**
*He loves the Omnipresent,
he loves [His] creatures,
he gladdens the Omnipresent,
he gladdens [His] creatures.*

The true Torah scholar is a person whose sole interest is to unite with God, and he achieves this by dedicating himself to Torah study. God has said, "I put Myself into the Torah." One who identifies with Torah has an intimate relationship with God. He is indeed beloved by God and by man, and gladdens both.

The Talmud relates that during a drought the people asked the sage Choni to pray for rain. Choni drew a circle around himself, addressing God: "Your children have asked me to intercede for them, knowing that I am on close terms with You. I swear that I will not step out of this circle until You have mercy on Your children." It rained sparsely, and Choni said, "Dear God, I meant abundant rain." It then rained profusely to the point of flooding. Choni then said, "Dear God, we cannot handle such abundance," and the rain fell normally.

Shimon ben Shatach rebuked Choni for his audacity in giving orders to God. "You deserve to be excommunicated for this, but what can I do? You are beloved to God as a child is to his father. Anything the child asks for, the father gladly gives him. The Scriptural statement, 'May the father and mother rejoice in their child' (*Proverbs* 23:25), refers to you" (*Taanis* 19a, 23a).

A *tzaddik* who is as dear to God "as a child to his father" gladdens both God and man when he elicits Divine mercy. The Talmud states that when Jews are in agony, God suffers along with them. Elijah pointed out to the sages that there were two people who had earned *Gan Eden* (Paradise). The sages asked the men what virtuous acts they had done to merit *Gan Eden*. "We circulate in the marketplace, and when we see someone whose spirits are low because he has not earned anything, we try to cheer him up." *Maharsha* states that they merited *Gan Eden* because by relieving the sadness of people, they relieved God of His suffering (*Taanis* 22a).

The true Torah scholar is devoid of self-centeredness. His devotion is therefore to others, to God and to his fellow man.

וּמַלְבַּשְׁתּוֹ עֲנָוָה
*[The Torah] clothes
him in humility*

The expression "clothes him in humility" is specific. Humility is to be a garment which can be removed when necessary. Earlier (1:1), it was pointed out that misguided humility can be destructive. There are times when a person must be firm and assertive. A true Torah scholar knows when he must set aside his humility and assume a position of leadership.

6/1   *he loves [His] creatures, he gladdens the Omnipresent, he gladdens [His] creatures. [The Torah] clothes him in humility and fear [of God]; it makes him fit to be a tzaddik,*

Many *tzaddikim* took the term "clothed in humility" literally. They shunned rabbinic apparel, dressing in a simple fashion. People who did not know R' Zundel or the Chofetz Chaim would not be able to pick them out of a crowd. On the surface, they were indistinguishable from others. There are abundant anecdotes about their being mistaken for ordinary lay people.

The apposition of humility to the love of others is not coincidental. A Torah scholar may well be aware of his erudition and achievements, yet he does not consider himself superior to others. R' Bunim of P'shische cites the halachah that if someone is ordered to kill another person or be killed himself, he must sacrifice his life because, "What makes you think that your life is more precious than another person's life?" (*Pesachim* 25b). Even if the greatest scholar and public benefactor is ordered to kill the lowliest person, he must forfeit his life. He has no right to think that his life is of greater value than another's. The Torah concept of humility indeed fosters the love of and respect for other people.

The humility of our great Torah personalities was genuine. The two great Torah luminaries, R' Akiva Eiger and R' Yaakov of Lisa, once spent a Shabbos together. At the Torah reading, R' Akiva Eiger was called to the portion of the Torah that is traditionally accorded to the leading Torah scholar. When he realized that he had been called instead of R' Yaakov, he fainted. No one knew what had happened to him.

The only one who understood what had happened was R' Yaakov. R' Akiva felt that by giving the first honor to him, R' Yaakov was offended. He did not think of himself as being as deserving as R' Yaakov.

R' Yaakov knew that R' Akiva would not be appeased if he told him he was not in the least offended, and that R' Akiva was indeed most deserving of this honor. When R' Akiva regained consciousness, R' Yaakov said to him, "Your community of Posen is much larger than my community of Lisa. It was only fit to accord the honor to the representative of the larger community." Only then did R' Akiva approach the *bimah* (pulpit) for the Torah reading.

וּמַכְשַׁרְתּוֹ לִהְיוֹת צַדִּיק
It makes him
fit to be a tzaddik

The words of this mishnah are carefully chosen. Proper learning and implementation of Torah does not make one a *tzaddik*. Rather, it *prepares* one to become a *tzaddik*. In other words, a true Torah scholar never considers himself to be in a state of completion. To the contrary, the fact that Torah is infinite makes it impossible for anyone to grasp it in its entirety. The more Torah one learns the greater is his understanding of its infinity. A Torah scholar is therefore in a constant state of *becoming*. He is always advancing toward a goal which he knows is unreachable.

The works of *mussar* and *chassidus* emphasize this concept. Until the very last day of life a person should be progressing. The *yetzer hara* never slackens. It may indeed change its tactics, enticing the aged in ways other than it does youth, and the scholar in ways other than a simpleton, but it never relaxes its effort to lead a person into sin. The struggle against the unrelenting *yetzer hara* never ends. A person who believes that he has achieved a state of spirituality so great that he is beyond sin has fallen prey to the *yetzer hara's* deepest pit: vanity.

One of the chassidic masters said that a person should think of the *yetzer hara* as an enemy who holds a sharp sword over one's head and wishes to behead him. One *chassid* asked, "What if I cannot think this way?" "Then it has already succeeded in beheading you," the master said.

The chassidic master, R' Elimelech of Lizhensk, said, "People think that I am a *tzaddik*. This is not true. I know myself best and I know that I am not a *tzaddik*. Even if the prophet Elijah would say that I am a *tzaddik* I would not believe him. If God Himself said I was a *tzaddik*, I would have no choice but to believe Him. However, I would believe Him for only that moment. The moment afterward I would return to my conviction that I am not a *tzaddik*."

This is what is meant by the earlier mishnah (2:21). One is not expected to reach a stage of completion, but one is obligated to progress as far as possible.

**וּמַכְשַׁרְתּוֹ לִהְיוֹת צַדִּיק,
חָסִיד, יָשָׁר, וְנֶאֱמָן**
*It makes him fit to be a tzaddik,
chassid, yashar, and ne'eman*

This statement poses a major problem for us: Just what is a *tzaddik*? What is a *yashar*? What is a *chassid*? What is a *ne'eman*? The Talmud does not have superfluous words. Clearly, these four appellations apply to four distinct levels of spirituality. However, this is rather bewildering. Is *tzaddik* not an inclusive term? Can one be a *tzaddik* yet not be a *yashar*, *chassid*, or *ne'eman*? Can one be a *chassid* yet not be *ne'eman*? It would seem that a *tzaddik* has all the other three characteristics, as do all the other terms.

These terms lend themselves to a variety of definitions, and we have no way of knowing which is correct. What is clear is that there are *qualitative* as well as quantitative differences in spirituality. For example, the Talmud says that if R' Shimon ben Lakish was seen conversing with someone, people would trust that person enough to transact business with him without witnesses (*Yoma* 9a). The Talmud does not say this of any of the other sages. Or, we find that Rav never spoke an unnecessary word in his entire lifetime, and that he never had a meal that was not considered a *seudas mitzvah* (*Chullin* 95b). Again, this is not said of others. Various different statements are made about other sages.

Perhaps the Talmud means that while all were exceedingly spiritual, each one had a particular trait in which he excelled. In this particular trait he was superior to others. Or perhaps all possessed all the commendable traits, but revealed of themselves only that which they considered essential.

It is important that we have a proper concept of our great Torah personalities.

They were all paragons of virtue and spirituality. They were not at the mercy of their inborn traits, but were masters of their characters. The Talmud states that in comparison to us, the sages of yore were angels. What we know of their personalities is only what they allowed us to know.

It is of interest that in the last generation, the Chofetz Chaim, whose knowledge of Torah was encyclopedic, was thought of more as a great *tzaddik* than a great scholar. Other contemporary Torah personalities were thought of primarily as great scholars and only secondarily as *tzaddikim*.

It is related that because of his profound humility, the Chofetz Chaim had prayed that people should not think of him as a *gaon* (Torah genius), and his prayers were answered. Why, then, did he not also pray that people not think of him as a *tzaddik*? Because the possibility that he might be considered to be a *tzaddik* never even occurred to him!

In the final analysis, we are at a loss to understand this mishnah. The differences between these four categories may be measured in microns. Our minds may be no more capable of grasping these concepts than it is of hearing sound waves above or below the frequency within the range of the human ear.

We sometimes find ourselves in disagreement with a Torah authority. Although we may have some Torah knowledge, we should realize that we are not in the same league with any of them. We may indeed accept a different ruling of another Torah authority, but we must be most cautious to avoid making judgments on our own which are at variance with those of Torah authorities.

וּמְרַחַקְתּוֹ מִן הַחֵטְא
It moves him away from sin

Again, the words of this mishnah warrant careful scrutiny. Profound Torah study can discourage one from sin and encourage one to virtuous acts, but it does not eliminate the possibility of sin or compel one to virtue. Every human being, at any moment of his life, has *bechirah* (freedom of choice). The Talmud relates that Yochanan served as the High Priest for 70 years, and toward the end of his life defected to the Sadducees.

I often use examples derived from my work in treating alcoholics. Alcoholism is an excellent example of a self-destructive behavior that may hold a person captive. Indeed, Scripture frequently uses drunkenness to portray inappropriate behavior; e.g., "they were drunk albeit not with wine, they wandered aimlessly although without ale" (*Isaiah* 29:9). There is much that we can gather from the observation of the alcoholic that is applicable to ourselves. For example, an alcoholic who became sober does not refer to himself as "recovered," but rather as "recovering." He is aware that at any moment he is vulnerable to fall back into destructive drinking. One such person said, "I am always recovering. If I die sober, only then can I be considered to have recovered." Indeed, when he died at 83 after 42 years of sobriety, the news of his death was conveyed as "John has recovered."

לִידֵי זְכוּת. וְנֶהֱנִין מִמֶּנּוּ עֵצָה וְתוּשִׁיָּה, בִּינָה וּגְבוּרָה,
שֶׁנֶּאֱמַר: „לִי עֵצָה וְתוּשִׁיָּה, אֲנִי בִינָה, לִי גְבוּרָה.״ וְנוֹתֶנֶת

As we have repeatedly noted, life is a constant struggle with the *yetzer hara*. We must always remain on the alert. We must adhere to the many precautions that halachah dictates. The Talmud cites cases of great people who thought themselves to be incapable of sin. They were lax in exercising halachic precautions because they considered them unnecessary as deterrents to sin. Despite their advanced spirituality, they fell prey to sin.

Today's world is replete with indecency in the various types of media. It is a mistake to think that we are so spiritual that exposure to these will not corrupt us. We must always remember our human vulnerability, and distance ourselves from all impropriety.

וְנֶהֱנִין מִמֶּנּוּ עֵצָה וְתוּשִׁיָּה
From him people enjoy counsel and wisdom

Torah scholars are indeed people from whom one may seek counsel and wisdom. Regrettably, their expertise is not exploited often enough. It is related that a rabbi notified his community that he was resigning. "Why are you leaving us?" some people asked. "Because," the rabbi said, "this is the first *she'eileh* (halachic inquiry) I was asked since I have been here." It is difficult to serve a community that does not have recourse to its rabbi for Torah teaching and counseling.

I can identify with that rabbi. As a youngster, my aspiration had been to follow in my father's footsteps. His study was regularly frequented by people who sought his counsel. I was ordained in 1951. Following World War II, psychiatry and psychology had a meteoric rise and became immensely popular. I soon realized that people were not seeking my services as a counselor or as a teacher of Torah. Rather, I was expected to officiate at rituals: bar-mitzvahs, weddings, funerals, unveilings, and whatever other ceremonial events there might be. I was not satisfied with this superficial role, and in order to be the counselor I had aspired to be, I became a psychiatrist.

Many people today consult their rabbi primarily for a *"berachah"* (blessing). There is nothing wrong with this. Unfortunately, not many people seek the rabbi's advice on how to improve their spiritual life. Rather few people ask the rabbi how to achieve better *kavannah* (concentration) in their prayers, or what they might do to feel greater spirituality in the performance of mitzvos. Few people confide in the rabbi that they have been remiss in their observance of Torah and what they should do for proper *teshuvah*.

The chassidic master, R' Nachum of Chernobel, was once challenged by someone who asked him why he dispensed *berachos*. "What makes you think you have the capacity to give potent *berachos*?"

R' Nachum answered, "The Torah states that before the Israelites went out to war, the *Kohen* (priest) addressed them. He said that anyone who had built a new home and had not yet moved into it is exempt from army duty and should

and draws him near to merit. From him people enjoy counsel and wisdom, understanding and strength, as it is said: "Mine are counsel and wisdom, I am understanding, mine is strength."

---

return home. This exemption also applied to someone who had betrothed a woman, to someone who had planted a vineyard and had not reaped its first fruits, and to someone who felt that his sins might deprive him of Divine protection in battle (*Deuteronomy* 20:1-9).

"The only one who was really at risk of falling in battle was the sinful person. However, if this were the only exemption, then anyone excused from service would immediately be identified as a sinner. This would be very humiliating, and a sinful person might be afraid of this exposure. To protect the anonymity of the sinful person, several other exemptions were added. This way, no one could know why anyone had been excused from the army.

"So it is with me," R' Nachum said. "My primary function is to help people do *teshuvah* for their sins or inadequate performance of mitzvos. If that was the only function I had, people might be reluctant to be seen consulting me, since that would identify them as sinners in need of *teshuvah*. I therefore give *berachos*. This way, it can be assumed that people consulting me are not sinful, but desire a *berachah*."

The primary function of a rabbi should be to teach Torah and to instruct people on spiritual issues: how to do proper *teshuvah* and enhance their performance of mitzvos. Unfortunately, the rabbi's true function is often relegated to a secondary position, and he is consulted primarily for *berachos*.

A chassidic rabbi remarked, "People often ask me whether they should buy a house or undertake a business venture. They are likely to accept my opinion even though I have no expertise in real estate or commerce. My expertise is in matters related to Torah. However, if I speak to them about the need to increase the quality of Torah observance, which is my area of expertise, my opinion is often ignored."

The mishnah states that the Torah scholar is a resource of counsel and wisdom. We should exploit this resource to improve the spiritual aspect of our lives.

„לִי עֵצָה וְתוּשִׁיָּה"
"Mine are counsel and wisdom"

The qualities enumerated by this mishnah are not characteristic of just anyone with Torah knowledge, but only of a Torah scholar who learns Torah *lishmah*, with total dedication.

The validity of this position was made evident to me. A woman who was suffering from a postpartum depression consulted me. I recommended a medication and referred her to a psychiatrist in her area. Her condition improved markedly. Because of the risk of the effect of the medication on a fetus, she consulted a halachic authority and was permitted to avoid pregnancy for a period of time. Several months later her husband called. She had become pregnant and he was concerned that she may suffer a relapse of severe depression. I told him to consult a *posek*, and that I would give the *posek* the medical facts of the case.

Several days later I received a call from R' Moshe Feinstein. "Is it the pregnancy per se that constitutes a danger to her health? Suppose that she were a Rockefeller and could afford adequate help with the care of her children and the household duties. She would then be able to rest adequately and avoid stress. Would she still be at risk?" he asked. I replied that if these were her circumstances, the pregnancy would not pose a danger.

"Well then," R' Moshe said, "it is not the pregnancy that is the culprit, but the lack of money for adequate help. I will undertake to see that enough money is raised to get her the help she needs. I will also prevail on her husband to spend more time helping at home." This was indeed done, and the woman had a safe pregnancy. She remained in good emotional health after the baby was born.

How many people, even people with some Torah knowledge, would have thought this way? How many might have looked for a simpler solution? How many might not have fully appreciated the gravity of another solution?

R' Elchanan Wasserman explained that every Torah scholar obviously has some Torah wisdom. However, he also has other things that help form his opinion: his own desires, his family's wishes, advice of friends, community opinion, etc. His Torah knowledge may comprise perhaps 25 percent of his opinion-making resources. This may be obscured by the 75 percent contributed by the non-Torah sources. It is only one who has no sources other than Torah who can provide counsel that is totally Torah wisdom.

The mishnah rightfully states that real wisdom and understanding is the domain of the truly dedicated Torah scholar.

There are numerous anecdotes about Torah personalities who, when their advice was sought, would study a portion of Torah before giving their response. This was the customary practice of R' Chaim of Volozhin. In other words, it was not just that having a Torah mindset enabled them to counsel wisely. They realized that the Torah was an actual source of wisdom.

When R' Chaim, the *Tzaddik* of Sanz, was a child of 10, his father took him to the Seer of Lublin. The Seer had great affection for the young boy, who he predicted would be a stellar Torah personality.

Many people continuously filed into the Seer's study. Abruptly, the Seer asked that the doors be closed as he needed some solitude. The young Chaim concealed himself in a closet in the Seer's study. He noticed that the Seer paced to and fro, reciting several mishnahs by heart. The Seer then opened the closet and brought the young Chaim out of his hiding place.

"You see, Chaimke," the Seer said, "people come to ask my advice. How can

I counsel them correctly? The Midrash says that the original light of Creation was one that enabled a person to see from one end of the world to the other. God concealed this light because mankind was undeserving of it. Where did He conceal this light? In the Torah. When one studies Torah properly, one can gain great insights as a result of this powerful light.

"After I had given advice to a number of people, I felt that I had depleted my capacity for insights and that I needed it renewed. That is why I took some time to review several mishnahs.

"You will one day be a great leader, Chaimke. Remember what I told you," the Seer said.

There are numerous accounts of incidents of our great Torah personalities that appear to be due to superhuman wisdom, virtually prophetic insights. They regularly denied that they were Divinely inspired. Rather, these were the result of being enlightened by Torah study, something which they felt was within everyone's reach.

Yes, this is indeed achievable by everyone. However, one must meet the qualification stated by the mishnah: that one must study Torah *lishmah.*

וְנוֹתֶנֶת לוֹ מַלְכוּת, וּמֶמְשָׁלָה
[The Torah] gives him kingship and dominion

Various interpretations are given to this mishnah based upon the Talmudical designation of Torah sages as kings (*Gittin* 62a). Although undoubtedly correct, true Torah scholars do not aspire to kingship or dominion.

There may be yet another interpretation of this mishnah, which reverts back to the statement (4:1) that the truly powerful person is one who is master over himself. Indeed, Solomon states that "one who is master over himself is superior to one who conquers a city" (*Proverbs* 16:32). The mastery to which a Torah scholar aspires is to be master over himself, and not a pawn at the mercy of his drives.

It is of interest that the mishnah refers to two types of rulers, מֶלֶךְ and מוֹשֵׁל. The distinction is often made that *melech* refers to a king who rules with the consent of the populace, whereas *moshel* is one who occupies the position by force.

The teachings of the Torah apply to all times. The mishnah may be telling us that there are two ways in which the Torah scholar can achieve self-mastery. The first is by subjugating his body by sheer force, denying it all of its desires. This was characteristic of the *tzaddikim* of yore, who fasted frequently and tormented the flesh until all earthly desires were eradicated.

In the more recent ethical writings, this method is not recommended for the average person. Instead of destroying a drive, it is recommended that it be sublimated and channeled toward proper goals. This is perhaps because a person who deprives himself of everything may come to think that because of his self-sacrifice he has become a *tzaddik*. This would constitute vanity, the worst of all traits.

The *Maggid* of Mezeritch said, "Anyone who causes a small defect in his body causes a large defect in his soul." Along the same line is the admonition of a Rebbe to a *chassid* who practiced self-flagellation as a means of *teshuvah*. "You are really doing a complete job," the Rebbe said.

The *chassid* was pleased that the Rebbe apparently approved of his practice. "No," the Rebbe said. "What I mean is that first you sinned and damaged your *neshamah*. Now you are intent on damaging your body as well. That is indeed a complete job."

One can become master of his body as a *melech*, in which case one enlists the body's cooperation, or one can wield force over the body, as a *moshel*. The true Torah scholar knows which is appropriate for him.

וְנוֹתֶנֶת לוֹ . . . וְחִקּוּר דִּין
[The Torah] gives him . . .
analytical judgment

Is analytical judgment unique to the Torah scholar? Do not many thinkers have analytical judgment?

What the mishnah is referring to is true analytical judgment which the Torah scholar can apply in a ruling of law. All one need do is listen to the arguments of the prosecution and the defense in any case before a secular court. Each side may present a very convincing argument. Both are capable of keen analysis, but this does not reflect the truth. The analytical judgment provided by the Torah enables the Torah scholar to rule justly. This is what is meant by "God is present in the court of law" (*Psalms* 82:1).

I have told you that the students of R' Yechezkel Landau (*Noda BeYehudah*) presented him with a problem of halachah. Following his response, the students showed him that the majority of authorities disagreed with him. R' Landau explained, "You presented me with a hypothetical case. My judgment in theory may indeed be wrong. When an actual case is brought before me, it is not only my own judgment that is at work. The Torah itself guides me to a proper decision."

This principle was applied by R' Moshe Feinstein to the case of a woman who remarried after the Holocaust, having assumed that her husband had died. Several years later, it was discovered that her husband had escaped death. The consequences of her remarriage were therefore grave.

The woman stated that after the war she had sought a halachic ruling from a noted Torah authority in Europe, who gave her a *hetter* (permission to remarry). This rabbi had since died, and she unfortunately had lost the document of her *hetter*.

R' Feinstein repeatedly questioned the woman, and she finally admitted that she had never received a *hetter*. She had fabricated the story, knowing that the rabbi she cited was deceased and could not contradict her. Bystanders at the scene felt that the detection that her story was false indicated that R' Feinstein had been Divinely inspired.

R' Feinstein dismissed this with a wave of his hand. "It has nothing to do with Divine inspiration," he said. "In all the cases where I have issued a *hetter*, it has never occurred that the husband was later found to be alive. The rabbi this woman cited was far superior to me in halachah. I was certain that regardless of what information was given to him, he never would have issued a *hetter* if the husband was still living. His Torah *lishmah* would have precluded such an erroneous judgment."

Regardless of the degree of genius, the human mind is subject to erroneous analysis. Torah *lishmah* assures access to the truth.

וּמְגַלִּין לֹו רָזֵי תֹורָה
The secrets of the Torah
are revealed to him

The secrets of the Torah are revealed to one who learns Torah *lishmah* and *only* to one who learns Torah *lishmah*. One does not reveal secrets except to someone who is beloved and trustworthy. As we have seen, these are characteristics of one who learns Torah *lishmah* .

Some Torah authorities have pointed out that the essence of the Torah lies in the concealed portion. They note that the treasures of the earth — soil nutrients, diamonds, gold, silver, oil, etc. — are all deep beneath the surface of the earth. However, since one cannot walk or build on these, there is the earth's surface which provides the place for people and buildings. Similarly, the "surface" of the Torah or its revealed portion is accessible to all and allows us access to its hidden treasures.

It is axiomatic that one should not delve into the concealed portion of the Torah until one has reached maturity and has a thorough and comprehensive knowledge of the revealed portion. One does not study Kabbalah until one is "saturated with Talmud and halachah."

It is of interest that many of our great Torah scholars who excelled in Talmud and did not particularly study Kabbalah were nevertheless quite proficient in Kabbalah. They manifested the fulfillment of the mishnah's statement that the secrets of the Torah *are revealed* to one who learns Torah *lishmah*.

The corollary to this is that if a person is not "saturated" with Talmud and halachah, he is totally unprepared to grasp Kabbalah. The attempt to learn Kabbalah without a proficiency in Talmud and halachah is as futile as trying to learn differential calculus without knowing elementary arithmetic.

There seems to be a fascination with Kabbalah, and bookstores display many volumes on the subject. The word "Kabbalah" means "to receive." True knowledge of Kabbalah was *received* from competent teachers, and its transmission was from teacher to student. Only then could one benefit from the written works on Kabbalah.

I regret to disillusion those who believe they have learned Kabbalah from books. Schools of higher learning do not allow a student to take certain courses until he has mastered the prerequisites. It is the same with Kabbalah.

וְנַעֲשֶׂה כְמַעְיָן הַמִּתְגַּבֵּר, וּכְנָהָר שֶׁאֵינוֹ פוֹסֵק; וְהֹוֶה צָנְוּעַ,
וְאֶרֶךְ רוּחַ, וּמוֹחֵל עַל עֶלְבּוֹנוֹ. וּמְגַדַּלְתּוֹ וּמְרוֹמַמְתּוֹ עַל כָּל
הַמַּעֲשִׂים.

וְנַעֲשֶׂה כְמַעְיָן הַמִּתְגַּבֵּר, וּכְנָהָר שֶׁאֵינוֹ פוֹסֵק
He becomes like a spring flowing stronger
and stronger and like an unceasing river.

Earlier we noted that there are two types of highly productive people. One is ambitious, and the other has a need to prove himself. This is true of teachers as well. A teacher who feels he must defend his fragile ego by demonstrating how much he knows may *resemble* the teacher whose knowledge is so abundant that it overflows. The former is tormented by insecurity, while the latter thoroughly enjoys sharing his knowledge with others. The mishnah's metaphor of the steadily strengthening spring aptly describes the true Torah scholar.

Furthermore, the more water one draws from the spring, the more it produces. This is why Torah teachers are so reluctant to lose a student. The student's drawing upon the teacher's knowledge stimulates and increases it. The Talmud relates that when R' Shimon ben Lakish died, R' Yochanan grieved bitterly. He had lost the primary stimulus that generated his Torah knowledge.

The Torah refers to spring water as "living water." In contrast to stagnant water, each drop is fresh. The Torah scholar may review a portion of the Talmud countless times, and each time will discover a new meaning. He is excited over his new discovery as if he had never learned that passage before.

The metaphor of the river is interesting. The Talmud states that when the flow of a river is increased by rain or melted snow, "for each amount of water that is added from above, the springs feeding the river produce twice that amount" (*Taanis* 25b). For the true Torah scholar, the acquisition of Torah is exponential. The Talmud relates that two of the greatest sages, R' Eliezer and R' Akiva, began their study of Torah very late in life, yet surpassed all their contemporaries. Because their learning was *lishmah,* every bit of Torah knowledge blossomed and bore fruit.

The Talmud states that during intrauterine life an angel teaches the fetus the entire Torah. Prior to birth, the fetus is made to forget it. Of what purpose, then, is the learning? Although there is no conscious awareness of Torah at birth, it has been stored in the deep recesses of the mind. Subsequent active study of Torah can produce a recall phenomenon, much the same as a "booster shot" of vaccine can recall the immunization in infancy and stimulate the production of huge quantities of antitoxin.

The true Torah scholar is much like a river. For every bit of knowledge he gains by active study, he acquires many times that amount from the hidden sources within him.

6/1   *he becomes like a spring flowing stronger and stronger and like an unceasing river. He becomes modest, patient, and forgiving of insult to himself. [The Torah] makes him great and exalts him above all things.*

There may be skeptics who look upon this concept as a theological fantasy. If they find it difficult to accept the teachings of the Talmud, perhaps they might be convinced of its truth by recourse to a secular philosopher. I suggest they read Plato, who demonstrates quite convincingly that *all* knowledge is essentially recall.

וְהֹוֶה צָנוּעַ, וְאֶרֶךְ רוּחַ, וּמוֹחֵל עַל עֶלְבּוֹנוֹ.
וּמְגַדַּלְתּוֹ וּמְרוֹמַמְתּוֹ עַל כָּל הַמַּעֲשִׂים

He becomes modest, patient, and forgiving of insult to himself. [The Torah] makes him great and exalts him above all things.

Chapter Six is not an integral part of *Ethics of the Fathers*. It is a collection of teachings of the sages that was appended to the tractate. It is entirely concerned with the beauty and infinite value of Torah. Some of the passages in this chapter are therefore repetitions of teachings in the first five chapters. We have discussed the virtues of modesty, patience, and forgiving of insults above.

It is extremely difficult to escape the influence of one's environment. Indeed, the Psalmist attributes the Israelites' deviation from Torah to "They mingled among nations, and they learned from their actions" (*Psalms* 106:35). Total absorption in Torah may minimize these deleterious effects.

The environmental influences in today's world are particularly threatening. The printed and graphic media have shed all restraints, and under protection of the First Amendment, concepts of corruption, violence, and immorality are widely disseminated. Youngsters who might have developed into decent and upright people are awash in decadence.

I am often asked, "What is there that a family can do to prevent their children from being influenced by our toxic environment?" My answer is that whereas in past years it might have been sufficient for a Jew to be observant of halachah, today's world puts a much greater burden upon him. If we wish to save our children from the prevailing decadence, we must achieve what the mishnah says — "to be exalted above all things." We must elevate ourselves to a level of spirituality where we are so far above our environment that its toxic behavior cannot reach us. This requires us to observe Torah *lishmah*. We must strengthen and purify our study of Torah and we must enhance our performance of mitzvos.

The demands upon us are much greater than those made of our ancestors. If an enemy attacks with spears and arrows, shields may serve as an adequate defense. If the enemy is firing missiles, our defenses must be increased accordingly.

[ב] **אָמַר** רַבִּי יְהוֹשֻׁעַ בֶּן לֵוִי: בְּכָל יוֹם וָיוֹם בַּת קוֹל יוֹצֵאת מֵהַר חוֹרֵב, וּמַכְרֶזֶת וְאוֹמֶרֶת: "אוֹי לָהֶם לַבְּרִיּוֹת, מֵעֶלְבּוֹנָהּ שֶׁל תּוֹרָה! שֶׁכָּל מִי שֶׁאֵינוֹ עוֹסֵק בַּתּוֹרָה נִקְרָא נָזוּף, שֶׁנֶּאֱמַר: "נֶזֶם זָהָב בְּאַף חֲזִיר, אִשָּׁה יָפָה וְסָרַת טָעַם." וְאוֹמֵר: "וְהַלֻּחֹת מַעֲשֵׂה אֱלֹהִים הֵמָּה וְהַמִּכְתָּב מִכְתַּב אֱלֹהִים הוּא חָרוּת עַל הַלֻּחֹת," אַל תִּקְרָא "חָרוּת" אֶלָּא "חֵרוּת," שֶׁאֵין לְךָ בֶּן חוֹרִין אֶלָּא מִי שֶׁעוֹסֵק בְּתַלְמוּד תּוֹרָה. וְכָל מִי שֶׁעוֹסֵק בְּתַלְמוּד תּוֹרָה הֲרֵי זֶה מִתְעַלֶּה, שֶׁנֶּאֱמַר: "וּמִמַּתָּנָה נַחֲלִיאֵל, וּמִנַּחֲלִיאֵל בָּמוֹת."

Today's environment is attacking us with morally lethal missiles of unprecedented power. If we wish to maintain our standards of decency, and if we wish our children to be morally and ethically upright, we must increase our defenses accordingly. This is indeed a great demand of us, but the challenges we face are formidable. We must strive for a level of spirituality that will put us "above all things."

2.

. . . בְּכָל יוֹם וָיוֹם בַּת קוֹל יוֹצֵאת מֵהַר חוֹרֵב
שֶׁאֵין לְךָ בֶּן חוֹרִין אֶלָּא מִי שֶׁעוֹסֵק בְּתַלְמוּד תּוֹרָה
Every single day, a Heavenly voice emanates from
Mount Horeb . . . for you can have no freer man
than one who is engaged in the study of Torah.

The Baal Shem Tov posed the obvious question: Inasmuch as we do not hear this voice, of what use is it? He explained that although the voice may not be audible, the *neshamah* does hear it. When a person feels he is spiritually deficient and that he must devote himself more to Torah, it is because at that moment his *neshamah* has heard the voice from Horeb.

The Baal Shem Tov's explanation is most understandable in the light of modern science. It has been proven that "subliminal stimuli" can profoundly affect behavior. A person may be subjected to stimuli which he cannot hear nor see, yet they can have an impact on his thoughts and feelings.

The Heavenly voice is an incentive for *teshuvah*. It is important that we recognize the source of the awakening to *teshuvah*. It is nothing less than God calling to us to reevaluate our goals in life and our lifestyle.

Responding to the call for *teshuvah* would necessitate that we make changes in the way we live. Some of these changes may impinge on our comfort and

2. **R**abbi Yehoshua ben Levi said: Every single day, a Heavenly voice emanates from Mount Horeb, proclaiming and saying, "Woe to them, to the people, because of [their] insult to the Torah!" For whoever does not occupy himself with the Torah is called, "Rebuked," as it is said: Like a golden ring in a swine's snout is a beautiful woman who turns away from good judgment (Proverbs 11:22). And it says: The Tablets are God's handiwork and the script was God's script charus (engraved) on the Tablets (Exodus 32:16). Do not read charus (engraved), but cherus (freedom), for you can have no freer man than one who is engaged in the study of the Torah. And anyone who engages in the study of the Torah becomes elevated, as it is said: From Mattanah to Nachaliel and from Nachaliel to Bamos (Numbers 21:19).

---

on our pursuit of pleasure. In order to maintain our status quo we may turn a deaf ear to the Heavenly voice.

In my work treating alcoholics I have repeatedly seen people who have been alerted to the self-destructive nature of their behavior and encouraged to abandon it. They have been offered help and support in doing so. However, their addiction to alcohol causes them to reject this helpful advice. They view giving up alcohol as too difficult a task for them, and they wish to continue its use to provide them with the state of comfort they seek. This pattern may continue until they arrive at a moment of truth and reach a crisis at which time they can begin their recovery. Once they recover they can see how their entire lives had been dominated by alcohol. They can realize that they had been enslaved by a ruthless taskmaster, and that they had lost every bit of free will. They did whatever the alcohol dictated.

The greatest pride of the human being is that he is unique and distinct from other forms of life in that he has freedom of choice. Animals are not free, because they must follow the dictates of the body, their innate drives. Man is the only creature that can refuse to follow the body's demands. Man can reflect on an impulse and decide whether it is morally and ethically right. He can defy the body in favor of morals and ethics. To surrender this unique capacity is to lower oneself to a subhuman level. No dignified person should permit this to occur.

The capacity to exercise free will was given to man by God. To all other peoples of the earth this capacity is contained within the seven categories of Noahide mitzvos. To the Jew it is contained in the Torah. The Talmud quotes

ו/ג

[ג] **הַלּוֹמֵד** מֵחֲבֵרוֹ פֶּרֶק אֶחָד, אוֹ הֲלָכָה אֶחָת, אוֹ
פָּסוּק אֶחָד, אוֹ דִבּוּר אֶחָד, אוֹ אֲפִילוּ
אוֹת אֶחָת, צָרִיךְ לִנְהָג בּוֹ כָּבוֹד. שֶׁכֵּן מָצִינוּ בְּדָוִד מֶלֶךְ
יִשְׂרָאֵל, שֶׁלֹּא לָמַד מֵאֲחִיתֹפֶל אֶלָּא שְׁנֵי דְבָרִים בִּלְבָד,
וּקְרָאוֹ רַבּוֹ, אַלּוּפוֹ, וּמְיֻדָּעוֹ, שֶׁנֶּאֱמַר: „וְאַתָּה אֱנוֹשׁ כְּעֶרְכִּי,
אַלּוּפִי וּמְיֻדָּעִי." וַהֲלֹא דְבָרִים קַל וָחֹמֶר: וּמַה דָוִד מֶלֶךְ
יִשְׂרָאֵל, שֶׁלֹּא לָמַד מֵאֲחִיתֹפֶל אֶלָּא שְׁנֵי דְבָרִים בִּלְבָד,
קְרָאוֹ רַבּוֹ אַלּוּפוֹ וּמְיֻדָּעוֹ – הַלּוֹמֵד מֵחֲבֵרוֹ פֶּרֶק אֶחָד,
אוֹ הֲלָכָה אֶחָת, אוֹ פָּסוּק אֶחָד, אוֹ דִבּוּר אֶחָד, אוֹ אֲפִילוּ
אוֹת אֶחָת, עַל אַחַת כַּמָּה וְכַמָּה שֶׁצָּרִיךְ לִנְהָג בּוֹ כָּבוֹד!

God as saying, "I created man with a yetzer hara (temptation), and I created Torah as its antidote. If you observe the Torah, you will not be subject to its domination" (Kiddushin 30b). For the Jew there is no other antidote against the yetzer hara, no other defense against its powerful seductive force other than Torah.

In the Haggadah From Bondage to Freedom (Shaar Press) I pointed out that we do not celebrate the Exodus from Egypt as an Independence Day. Passover does not represent political freedom, but rather a repudiation of enslavement. Shortly after the bonds of the Egyptian taskmasters were broken, the Israelites stood at Mount Horeb (Sinai) where they received the Torah. It is the Torah which can give man the freedom that dignifies him as being superior to all other creatures.

The mishnah states this clearly. The Heavenly voice that our ancestors heard at Sinai still speaks to us, albeit in a subliminal way. It tells us that we need not, nay, dare not be slaves. It is all the same whether one is enslaved by a cruel despot, by alcohol, by other drugs, or by one's bodily and ego drives. "One who engages in the study [and application] of Torah becomes elevated," the mishnah says. Elevated, indeed. It raises him above the level of the beasts of the jungle that are under the domination of the body and cannot exercise free choice.

We think of the ten plagues as miraculous phenomena. We think of the parting of the Red Sea as a great miracle. However, the greatest miracle of all was taking a people that had been enslaved and crushed both physically and spiritually, that had every vestige of dignity drained from them, and within seven weeks transforming them into a spiritual people, "a sacred nation" (Exodus 19:6). This miracle could be achieved only through their receiving and adopting the Torah at Horeb. This was the only path to freedom then, and it is the only path now.

3. **H**e who learns from his fellowman a single chapter, a single halachah, a single verse, a single Torah statement, or even a single letter, must treat him with honor. For thus we find in the case of David, King of Israel, who learned nothing from Achitophel except for two things, yet called him his teacher, his guide, his intimate, as it is said: You are a man of my measure, my guide and my intimate (Psalms 55:14). One can derive from this the following: If David, King of Israel, who learned nothing from Achitophel except for two things, called him his teacher, his guide, his intimate — one who learns from his fellowman a single chapter, a single verse, a single statement, or even a single letter, how much more must he treat him with honor!

3.

הַלּוֹמֵד מֵחֲבֵרוֹ פֶּרֶק אֶחָד . . .
אוֹ אֲפִילוּ אוֹת אֶחָת, צָרִיךְ לִנְהָג בּוֹ כָּבוֹד

He who learns from his fellowman a single chapter . . . or even a single letter, must treat him with honor

The Tzaddik of Sanz had a huge following. The Friday night meal was attended by many chassidim who came from afar to share the Shabbos experience with the Tzaddik and listen to his homilies on the Torah portion of the week.

One time the Tzaddik greeted one of the guests with great aplomb. He sat him at the head of the table and made certain that he was served handsome portions. This lavish honor continued throughout the entire Shabbos. As this was a rather simple person of limited scholarship, the chassidim did not understand why he merited such great honor.

After the man left, the chassidim expressed their bewilderment. Was this man perhaps one of the hidden tzaddikim who masqueraded as a simple person?

"Not at all," the Tzaddik said. "He was my first teacher of aleph-beis. The Talmud says that if someone learns even one letter from a teacher, he is obligated to honor him. This man taught me the entire aleph-beis. There is no limit to the honor I must show him."

The word of this episode spread, and came to the ears of the man who had taught the Tzaddik Talmud as a child. In his desire to be lavishly honored by the Tzaddik, he made his way to Sanz. The Tzaddik greeted him politely and indeed showed him much respect, but it fell far short of the reception given to the first teacher.

After Shabbos the man asked the Tzaddik, "Perhaps it was wrong of me to seek honor. But I cannot understand why you accorded so much more honor

וְאֵין כָּבוֹד אֶלָּא תוֹרָה, שֶׁנֶּאֱמַר: „כָּבוֹד חֲכָמִים יִנְחָלוּ"; „וּתְמִימִים יִנְחֲלוּ טוֹב" וְאֵין טוֹב אֶלָּא תוֹרָה, שֶׁנֶּאֱמַר: „כִּי לֶקַח טוֹב נָתַתִּי לָכֶם, תּוֹרָתִי אַל תַּעֲזֹבוּ."

[ד] **כָּךְ** הִיא דַרְכָּהּ שֶׁל תּוֹרָה: פַּת בַּמֶּלַח תֹּאכֵל,

---

to the other teacher. After all, it was I who taught you Talmud, whereas he only taught you *aleph-beis*."

The *Tzaddik* smiled. "My dear teacher," he said. "I do indeed respect you. However, what the other teacher taught me was that this letter was an *aleph*, this one a *beis*, this one a *gimmel*, and so on. What he told me was the absolute truth. Even today I recognize these letters to be what he said they were.

"You did indeed teach me Talmud. However, as I came to learn more, I realized that the interpretations you had given me of the Talmud were erroneous. I cannot make any use of your teachings today. I indeed respect you for your effort, but this does not compare to the truths I received from my *aleph-beis* teacher."

The *Tzaddik* of Sanz was right. If we learn even one letter from someone, but it is the truth, then we are obligated to show him great honor. The slightest morsel of truth is priceless.

There is further significance in one letter of truth. We have cited the Talmudic statement that God gave Himself to us in the Torah. The *Zohar* states, "Israel, the Torah, and God are one." Since God is identified with Torah, every letter of Torah is Godliness. Since God is perfect unity and cannot be fragmented, where there is *any* of God there is *all* of God. Thus, each letter of the Torah is Infinite God. To know a single letter, and to know in truth, is to embrace the *Ein Sof* (the Infinite).

This abstract concept may be a bit difficult to grasp. It is related that when the *Maggid* of Mezeritch began expounding on Torah, R' Zusia would hear the first word and repeat it hundreds of times. He never heard the remainder of the *Maggid's* lecture. Yet, he knew it all.

The key word here is *absolute* truth. God is identified with truth, as we say at the end of the *Shema*, "God, your God, *is* true." The Midrash quotes God as saying, "Give me an opening the size of the tip of a needle, and I will open portals like the doors of a banquet hall." The Rabbi of Kotzk said, "The opening may be as tiny as the point of a needle, but it must pierce through and through." This is essentially the above concept. A single letter, a tiny bit of absolute truth, can contain everything.

כְּבוֹד חֲכָמִים יִנְחָלוּ
The wise shall inherit honor

This mishnah appears to give *kavod* (honor) a positive value. Yet we previously learned the very harsh statement that "Jealousy, lust, and (pursuit of) glory remove a man from the world" (4:28).

And honor is due only for Torah, as it is said: The wise shall inherit honor (Proverbs 3:35); and the perfect shall inherit good (ibid. 28:10). And only Torah is truly good, as it is said: I have given you a good teaching, do not forsake My Torah (ibid. 4:2).

4. *This is the way of the Torah: Eat bread with salt,*

This apparent contradiction is rather easily resolved. Many Torah scholars, upon entering the study hall, would carry a volume of Torah with them. When students arose to show their respect for them, they were able to rationalize that they were showing respect for the Torah volume instead of for them.

This was not an affectation on their part. Clearly, Torah scholars are aware of their erudition. How else could they assume the responsibility of writing authoritative works on halachah? However, they do not feel that they warrant admiration for what they see as simply fulfilling the mitzvah of Torah study. They will attribute any honor accorded to them to something else.

R' Akiva Eiger was a hunchback. When he came to Warsaw, people stood on the porches to be able to get a glimpse of this outstanding Torah scholar. When R' Akiva saw the many people looking at him, he remarked in all sincerity, "I did not realize that my deformity was so great that it attracts so much attention."

Pursuit of honor is indeed deleterious. Honor is due only to Torah. Of course, we show our great respect for those who have devoted themselves to Torah. These people, however, separate their Torah knowledge from themselves. While recognizing that it is Torah that deserves honor, they are capable of removing their own person from the picture.

4.

פַּת בְּמֶלַח תֹּאכֵל
Eat bread with salt

There are various interpretations given to this mishnah. For example, that the mishnah does not actually mean that one must live on the meagerest of subsistence in order to excel in Torah. Rather, that he must be ready to do so if circumstances necessitate such austerity. If he cannot make peace with living on the bare essentials, he may be distracted from his Torah studies in order to better his condition. If, however, one is able to subsist on the bare necessities, greater comforts will not distract him. Similar interpretations have been given, all of which indicate that the mishnah is not to be taken literally.

I have begun to wonder whether perhaps this mishnah *was* meant to be taken literally after all. In the United States we have been fortunate to have had a proliferation of Torah education. We have had dedicated scholars who have spent their entire day in Torah study. There are scholars who have little interest

ו/ה וּמַיִם בַּמְּשׂוּרָה תִּשְׁתֶּה, וְעַל הָאָרֶץ תִּישָׁן, וְחַיֵּי
צַעַר תִּחְיֶה, וּבַתּוֹרָה אַתָּה עָמֵל; אִם אַתָּה עוֹשֶׂה כֵּן,
"אַשְׁרֶיךָ וְטוֹב לָךְ": "אַשְׁרֶיךָ" – בָּעוֹלָם הַזֶּה, "וְטוֹב לָךְ"
– לָעוֹלָם הַבָּא.

[ה] **אַל** תְּבַקֵּשׁ גְּדֻלָּה לְעַצְמְךָ, וְאַל תַּחְמֹד כָּבוֹד;
יוֹתֵר מִלִּמּוּדְךָ עֲשֵׂה. וְאַל תִּתְאַוֶּה לְשֻׁלְחָנָם

---

for anything other than their Torah study, and who do not live in luxury by any means.

Yes, we have indeed produced some fine Torah scholars. Yet we must recognize that we have not produced a single Torah scholar of the caliber of R' Moshe Feinstein on American soil. Reliable accounts of pre-Holocaust Europe indicate that there were many outstanding Torah scholars. Why have we not been able to achieve this degree of excellence? Is it possibly because in America the most austere student does not live on a ration of bread and a measure of water? The Steipler *Gaon* often slept on a bench for lack of a bed, and there were days on which he had little or no food. The Talmud says that retention of Torah requires that one deprive himself of all but the bare necessities to remain alive (*Berachos* 63b).

Why did our great Torah personalities — the *Gaon* of Vilna, the *Shaagas Aryeh*, R' Elimelech of Lizhensk, among many others — why did they leave their homes to wander among villages, subsisting on mere morsels of food and sleeping in the most wretched accommodations? It can only be because they felt that to the degree that they provided comfort for the body, to that degree they diminished the capacity and efficiency of the *neshamah*.

The prototype of the Torah genius is Hillel. He chopped wood for a living, earning a small amount each week. Half of this meager earning was to provide for his family, and the other half to pay the gatekeeper to allow him into the study hall. One winter evening when he could not pay the gatekeeper, he climbed on the roof and put his ear to the skylight to hear the Torah lectures, and he was almost frozen to death. We span 2,000 years to a contemporary, the Steipler *Gaon*, who once sent for his students and gave his *shiur* (lecture) while lying in bed. It was later discovered that he was not ill, but that he owned only one pair of trousers which were at the tailor for repair. He could not leave his bed for lack of clothes.

It is unrealistic to expect that Torah students today will adopt such a lifestyle. They could not do so even if they wished to. Our culture is such that even the impoverished are not permitted to live the sparse life of the *gedolim* (great Torah personalities) of the past. This is not an admonition nor a recommendation to live an ascetic life. It is merely a suggestion that perhaps we do not have to offer any interpretations of this mishnah. It may mean exactly what it says.

6/5 *drink water in small measure, sleep on the ground, live a life of deprivation — but toil in the Torah! If you do this, You are fortunate and it is well with you (Psalms 128:2). You are fortunate — in this world; and it is well with you — in the World to Come.*

5. **D**o *not seek greatness for yourself, and do not crave honor; let your performance exceed your learning. Do*

,,אַשְׁרֶיךָ'' – בָּעוֹלָם הַזֶּה, ,,וְטוֹב לָךְ'' – לָעוֹלָם הַבָּא
You are fortunate — in this world; and it is well with you — in the World to Come.

How can a person who exists on bread and water and sleeps on the ground be considered fortunate in this world?

One of the chassidic masters encountered a man who was not observant of Torah. He was well to do and partook heartily of the goods of the world.

"Where is your *olam hazeh* (worldly reward)?" the rabbi asked.

"What do you mean, rabbi? Don't you see that I have an abundance of *olam hazeh*?" the man replied. "I lack for nothing."

"You don't understand me," the rabbi said. "You are using up your *Olam Haba* (reward in the Eternal World). What I asked you is where is your *olam hazeh*?"

The Talmud says that God does not withhold the reward due anyone. If a person does not observe Torah, but has to his credit a few scant mitzvos, he is given his reward in this world, and comes empty-handed to the Eternal World. On the other hand, a person who lives a thorough Torah life may have inadvertently committed a transgression. Justice demands that a transgression does not go unchastened. He may therefore be subjected to deprivation on earth, and reap the abundant reward for his mitzvos in the Eternal World.

The awareness that the reward one has accrued will be bestowed in the Eternal World can indeed provide happiness for one who is deprived of worldly pleasures.

5.

אַל תְּבַקֵּשׁ גְּדֻלָּה . . . יוֹתֵר מִלִּמּוּדְךָ עֲשֵׂה
Do not seek greatness . . . let your performance exceed your learning.

As was noted, some of the selections of this chapter are restatements of those in the earlier chapters. In 4:28 the disapproval of vanity and pursuit of honor were discussed. In Chapter 3 mishnah 22 we were instructed that our deeds should exceed our learning. This selection may have been added because of the latter phrase.

Chapter Six stresses the overriding importance of Torah study. One might

שֶׁל מְלָכִים, שֶׁשֻּׁלְחָנְךָ גָּדוֹל מִשֻּׁלְחָנָם, וְכִתְרְךָ גָּדוֹל
מִכִּתְרָם; וְנֶאֱמָן הוּא בַּעַל מְלַאכְתְּךָ, שֶׁיְּשַׁלֶּם לְךָ שְׂכַר
פְּעֻלָּתֶךָ.

---

therefore think that a scholar who is totally occupied with Torah study is exempt from performance of mitzvos. This mishnah points out the fallacy of this. "Let your performance exceed your learning." The more one knows of Torah, the greater is his obligation to implement his knowledge in the performance of mitzvos.

Yalkut Yehudah cites a dialogue between the two sages, R' Elazar ben Parta and R' Chanania ben Teradyon, both of whom were imprisoned by the Romans. R' Chanania was burned at the stake, and it is of him that the Talmud relates that he was wrapped in a Torah scroll. As the scroll was consumed by the flames, R' Chanania said to his disciples, "The parchment may burn, but the letters take wing in the air" (*Avodah Zarah* 18a). Torah is not destroyed when its enemies burn the yeshivos.

R' Chanania said to R' Elazar, "You are fortunate that you were imprisoned because of your *gemilas chassadim* (acts of kindness) and by virtue of these you were spared. I was involved only in Torah study." The Talmud comments that R' Chanania also had to his credit *gemilas chassadim*. It was precisely because he surpassed R' Elazar in Torah scholarship that it was incumbent upon him to surpass him in *gemilas chassadim* as well. Because he did not do so, this detracted from his merits (*Avodah Zarah* 17b). These are the extraordinary standards to which our sages were held!

The requirement for our deeds to exceed our learning may be symbolized by the mitzvah of *tefillin*. The *tefillin* on the arm represents action, and is to remind us that all our actions must follow the teachings of the parchments contained within it. The *tefillin* worn on the head represents our intellect, which should be primarily directed toward the parchments within it. The *tefillin* on the arm is put on first and taken off last. We thus wear it a bit longer than the headpiece. This symbolizes the teaching of this mishnah. Our actions and our performance of mitzvos should exceed our knowledge of Torah.

וְכִתְרְךָ גָּדוֹל מִכִּתְרָם
And your crown is greater than their crown

Let us compare the achievements of kings to those of Torah scholars.

Kings are primarily remembered by statues and monuments. One may read about them in history texts, but they offer us nothing. The grandeur and opulence of monarchs may have been impressive in their time, but contribute nothing to the betterment of our lives.

It is related that a visitor to one of the royal burial grounds was impressed by the beauty of the monument on the grave of a king. The sculpture was breathtaking. Overcome with wonderment he said, "That's what I call living. Kings

not lust for the table of kings, for your table is greater than theirs, and your crown is greater than their crown, and your Employer is trustworthy to pay you remuneration for your deeds.

---

sure knew how to live!"

We do not remember King David by a lifeless statue or monument, but by his *Tehillim* (*Psalms*). The sages of the Talmud, Rashi, Rambam, and all our great Torah scholars are very much alive. They speak to us in their Torah writings. Indeed, when we learn the teachings of the sages, "their lips move in their graves" (*Yevamos* 97a).

The crown of Torah is far greater than that of kingship.

6.

גְּדוֹלָה תוֹרָה יוֹתֵר מִן הַכְּהֻנָּה וּמִן הַמַּלְכוּת

Torah is even greater than priesthood or royalty

In Chapter 4 mishnah 17 we were told that there are three crowns. This chapter, which is dedicated to Torah study, tells us why the crown of Torah is superior to the other two. The Talmud lists 30 privileges enjoyed by the king and the 24 gifts that the Torah confers upon a *Kohen*. Torah is acquired by 48 qualities.

It is noteworthy that kingship and priesthood are distinguished by the *privileges* of the king and priest. Torah, on the other hand, is unique for its *prerequisites*. Exclusive of the numbers, Torah surpasses the other two because of the refinement of character it requires. Historically, we have had kings and priests whose character left much to be desired. Our Torah personalities, however, are paragons of *middos* (fine character traits).

It is clear that if there are 48 prerequisites, then having 47 will not prepare a person adequately for acquisition of Torah. However, it is simply not true that every Torah scholar has perfected himself in these 48 traits.

The mishnah does not state that these 48 qualities are essential for *knowledge* of Torah, but rather for the *acquisition* of Torah. This term refers to an absorption of and an identification with Torah. The Talmud states that at first a scholar learns the Torah of God, and only after much effort does it become *his own* Torah. It is the latter that requires the achievement of the enumerated traits. Indeed, the Talmud says that when Moses initially learned Torah from God he would forget it. He later *acquired* Torah when it was given to him as a gift (*Nedarim* 38a). This occurred when he had elevated himself to a level of spirituality where he became identified with the Torah.

This also answers the question: Insofar as one cannot achieve the 48 qualities without the guidance of Torah, and if one cannot acquire Torah until *after* he possesses the 48 traits, where does he begin? The answer is that one begins

ו/1 [ו] **גְּדוֹלָה** תוֹרָה יוֹתֵר מִן הַכְּהֻנָּה וּמִן הַמַּלְכוּת,
שֶׁהַמַּלְכוּת נִקְנֵית בִּשְׁלֹשִׁים מַעֲלוֹת,
וְהַכְּהֻנָּה נִקְנֵית בְּעֶשְׂרִים וְאַרְבָּעָה, וְהַתּוֹרָה נִקְנֵית בְּאַרְבָּעִים
וּשְׁמוֹנָה דְבָרִים, וְאֵלּוּ הֵן: בְּתַלְמוּד, בִּשְׁמִיעַת הָאֹזֶן,

---

with the *knowledge* of Torah. This enables him to achieve the requisite qualities. One can then rise to the position of having Torah as an *acquisition*.

Some of the Talmudic sages were occasionally addressed as "Moshe." This
was because they had elevated themselves to a very high spiritual level. Like
Moses, they *acquired* Torah.

**וְהַתּוֹרָה נִקְנֵית בְּאַרְבָּעִים וּשְׁמוֹנָה דְבָרִים,
וְאֵלּוּ הֵן: בְּתַלְמוּד**

**But the Torah is acquired by means of
forty-eight qualities, which are: Study**

To say that study is essential for
acquisition of Torah appears
superfluous. We would hardly
have thought that one can acquire
Torah by some magical means.

The term "study" in the mishnah connotes diligence, perseverance, and
indefatigability. This is especially important today, when the influence of modern technology has impacted upon us. Many things that in the past required
much labor and effort are now accomplished with relative ease and with much
greater speed. Acquisition of Torah has remained unchanged.

There are abundant anecdotes about the ways in which our Torah giants
toiled over Torah. A student of secular subjects who becomes weary with study
is likely to take a break or a short nap. He feels his mind cannot absorb in his
state of tiredness. Certainly if he has a headache he will put aside his books.
This is not true of our Torah scholars. We need not go back to the great
scholars of yore. I remember diligent Torah students who forced themselves to
remain alert by putting their feet into a pan of cold water as they continued to
study. I recall someone who did not leave his studies because of a headache,
but rather put an ice bag to his forehead and remained glued to the Talmud.

The study to which the mishnah refers is a devotion to Torah so complete
that one does not permit a single moment to go to waste. Eyewitnesses relate
that when R' Aaron Kotler spoke on the telephone, he held the receiver in one
hand and a *Mishnah Berurah* in the other. If there was even a momentary
delay in the conversation — let alone a prolonged "hold" — his eyes promptly
shifted to the *Mishnah Berurah*.

R' Moshe Feinstein's grandchildren once visited him, and found him to be
studying Talmud. Not wishing to interrupt him, they waited patiently outside
his study. The Rebbetzin walked by and said, "If you're waiting for him to take
a break from his learning, you'll be standing here all day." Stories abound
about the total devotion of our great scholars to Torah.

We are privileged today to have Torah tapes of various kinds available. We

6. **T**orah is even greater than priesthood or royalty, for royalty is acquired along with thirty prerogatives, and the priesthood with twenty-four [gifts], but the Torah is acquired by means of forty-eight qualities, which are: Study, attentive listening,

---

can listen to *shiurim* (lectures) at our leisure, and we can utilize driving time constructively by putting a Torah tape in the car's tape deck. This is indeed wonderful. Let us remember, however, that Torah *knowledge* is distinct from Torah *acquisition*. The latter is not achieved without much toil and effort.

That true Torah acquisition is not accomplished without toil and effort is indicated in the following story:

R' Shmelke of Nikolsburg was an outstanding Torah scholar, and his homilies reflected his vast Torah erudition. In Nikolsburg there was a man of unrefined behavior who would regularly interrupt R' Shmelke with challenges to his homilies. The community was puzzled by the incongruity of this man's lack of *middos* and his encyclopedic knowledge of Torah.

One time R' Levi Yitzchak of Berditchev visited Nilkosburg, and R' Shmelke complained about the agony this man was causing him. R' Levi Yitzchak met with the man and said, "The Talmud tells us that when the infant is in its mother's womb, he is taught the entire Torah. Before he is born, an angel touches his lips and he forgets everything. He can reclaim his knowledge only with diligence in Torah study.

"Even an angel is not infallible. It may occur that the angel may fail to touch an infant's lips. However, I am in a position to correct the angel's dereliction." R' Levi Yitzchak leaned over and touched the man's lips, following which the man was totally ignorant, to the point of not even recognizing *aleph-beis*.

Torah that is acquired with diligent study can transform a person's innate base traits. Knowledge of Torah that was not acquired by effort may not impact upon a person's character.

This is why the mishnah begins with the need for "study" as the first step in Torah acquisition. Perhaps not everyone is capable of the total absorption in Torah study that characterized our great Torah scholars. However, to whatever degree one does make the effort to learn Torah, to that degree the Torah will enhance his *middos*.

בִּשְׁמִיעַת הָאֹזֶן
With attentive listening

There are varying degrees of attention. We may think we listen attentively, but . . .

Prior to Rosh Hashanah, the Chofetz Chaim delivered a speech on *teshuvah*. One of his students, R' Sholom of Aishishok, said to his friend, R' Elchanan Wasserman, "This is the exact talk the Rabbi gave last year, word for word."

"No," R' Elchanan said, "This time *there were eight additional words.*"

That is attentive listening.

"Attentive listening" is a loose translation of בִּשְׁמִיעַת הָאֹזֶן. The literal translation is "with listening of the ear."

I recall my father commenting on the verse in the Torah where God changed the name of the Patriarch from Avram to Avraham by adding the letter ה. My father said that the Patriarch was striving to perfect himself so that his body should not desire anything other than to do the Divine will. He indeed achieved this goal in terms of his actions, but he continued to strive for greater perfection. The Patriarch wished his body to be so devoted to God's will that all five senses would be subject to it. In other words, that his eyes would not see anything improper, that his ears would not hear anything improper, etc. The letter ה has the numerical value "five." When Avram reached this extraordinary level of spirituality, God added the letter ה to his name, indicating that he had become master over his five senses.

If the sounds of *lashon hara* or other improper speech enter our ears, they become less receptive to Torah teachings. The true Torah scholar masters the listening of his ear. Acquisition of Torah requires that we "turn off the receiver," so that we do not hear what we should not hear. This is what the mishnah is referring to.

בַּעֲרִיכַת שְׂפָתַיִם
With articulate speech

Many commentaries explain that a deeper understanding and better retention of Torah requires verbalization. One must speak the words aloud and hear what one is studying. Silent study is inadequate.

My friend Dr. Jacob Greenwald told me that on one of his visits to the Steipler *Gaon* there was no response to the knock on the door. (The Steipler *Gaon* was hard of hearing.) Dr. Greenwald pushed the door open a bit, and saw the Steipler sitting and mumbling something to himself. Curious, he tiptoed over and heard the Steipler reciting the thirteen principles of faith and translating them from Hebrew into Yiddish. "*Ani maamin*, I believe, *b'emunah shleimah*, with complete faith, etc."

This story electrified me. Firstly, because of the Steipler's feeling that a meaningful grasp of the principles required not only saying them out loud, but also translating them into Yiddish, his first language. Secondly, because this great Talmudic scholar who never allowed a moment to go without Torah study, felt that it was essential for him to reinforce his belief in the basic principles of Yiddishkeit. This was so important that it warranted taking away precious time that he could have spent in Torah study in order to strengthen his *emunah* (faith).

Few people are anywhere near the total devotion to Torah of the Steipler. How many of us ever think that we are not sufficiently secure in our *emunah* and that we must do something to strengthen it? It seems strange that the only people who do not take their *emunah* for granted are those who have the greatest right to do so.

Several commentaries translate בַּעֲרִיכַת שְׂפָתָיִם to mean "with preparation of speech." In the letter to his son, Ramban instructs him to pause and reflect upon what he wishes to say before he speaks. This is extremely good advice. Scripture refers to speech as "an arrow" (*Jeremiah* 9:7). Just as an arrow cannot be retrieved once it is released from the bow, neither can spoken words. Words that were not given adequate consideration before being spoken are often the cause of much distress.

There is yet another type of preparation of speech. R' Yechezkel Abramsky once delivered a lecture on Talmud, and an impatient student interrupted him, remarking that there is another passage in the Talmud that contradicts his position. Rabbi Abramsky responded, "Yes. I gave that challenge some consideration, and I was able to reconcile the apparent conflict. Inasmuch as I was not planning to discuss that resolution today, I did not prepare the way in which I wished to present it. I will do so at a later date."

R' Abramsky knew the answer to the student's question. However, inasmuch as he had not formulated the precise words he wished to say, he withheld his response. The clarity of our great Talmud teachers was due to their preparation of their lectures to the point where every word was carefully weighed.

בְּבִינַת הַלֵּב, בְּשִׂכְלוּת הַלֵּב
With intuitive understanding,
with intuitive discernment

The literal translation of בְּבִינַת הַלֵּב, בְּשִׂכְלוּת הַלֵּב is "understanding of the heart and the intellect of the heart." These are rather strange terms, since we think of the heart as being associated with emotions, and that understanding and intellect are related to the mind rather than to the heart. However, the mishnah is very specific in its terminology.

Neither intellect nor understanding are immune to bias. It has been found that even serious scientific researchers may ignore findings that cast doubt on their theories. This is by no means conscious deception. Rather, the emotional investment in one's theories can render even the most sincere scientist oblivious to anything that threatens to disprove his position. The phenomenon of unconscious denial can affect anyone, and presents a formidable obstacle to reaching the truth. The only defense against this pitfall is to be especially vigilant to note precisely those findings that tend to disprove one's theory.

The Talmud states that the reasons the opinions of the school of Hillel were accepted rather than those of the school of Shammai were: (1) The school of Hillel were easy; (2) they were forbearing; and (3) *they always quoted the opinion of the school of Shammai before their own* (*Eruvin* 13b). It is the last of these qualities that gave the school of Hillel the upper hand. Once you state your own opinion, you may be blinded to any opposing opinion.

R' Chaim Shmulevitz states that this is the reason why a judge is not permitted to listen to one litigant unless the other litigant is present. He may try to keep an open mind in the knowledge that he will hear an opposing opinion. However, once the position of the first litigant has entered his mind, he may be unable to be truly objective to the opposing opinion.

The mishnah is right on target with requiring "an intellect of the heart"; i.e., that one overcome any emotional influences in order to set the intellect free from bias. This may be done by techniques such as that of the school of Hillel, to give the opposing opinion due consideration *before* asserting your own.

A similar approach must be taken toward *binah* (understanding). *Binah* is the deductive capacity, or the ability to derive from premises. If the derivatives are such that they may bring about any distress or discomfort, the deductive capacity may be inactivated. This is clearly stated by *Isaiah*: "This people is fattening its heart, hardening its ears, and sealing its eyes, lest it see with its eyes, hear with its ears, and understand with its heart, *so that it will repent and be healed*" (*Isaiah* 6:10). The healing the prophet refers to is abandoning the corruption and indulgence into which the Israelites had sunk. Acceptance of the truth would of necessity require relinquishing their decadent behavior. The desire to continue in their ways therefore set up a resistance to hearing the truth.

Just as one can be rendered oblivious to facts that contradict one's position, so can one be rendered oblivious to principles whose acceptance would lead to some discomfort. The mishnah therefore requires *binas halev*, i.e., that *binah* be set free from emotional influences.

The Torah scholar in search of truth must be aware that his emotions might impact upon his thinking. The qualities listed in this mishnah result in greater objectivity.

בְּאֵימָה, בְּיִרְאָה
With awe,
with reverence

The Torah is the very heart of Judaism. A surgeon performing an open heart operation is well aware that even a slight error may result in the patient's death. The Torah scholar must be aware that an erroneous interpretation of the Torah is of equal gravity. He must stand in awe of the Torah he is studying.

"Fear of God" does not refer to fear of punishment. The latter may be necessary as a first step for those of limited understanding. As was noted earlier, a father may spank a small child who runs into the street to retrieve his ball. The child cannot grasp the danger of being harmed by oncoming traffic, and it is therefore necessary to discourage his running into the street by associating it with a punishment. As soon as the child is mature enough to recognize the danger, punishment is no longer necessary. The concept of Divine punishment for a transgression is for those who lack the capacity to understand that transgression of Torah is self-destructive. The mature fear of God is the fear that one might be seduced by temptation to do something that is self-destructive.

The *Beis HaLevi* addresses the question, "How can we be commanded, 'Do not covet'? Is desire under voluntary control?" He answers that if a person were pursuing an intense passion and ran into a life-threatening situation, his concern with self-survival would obliterate the passion, at least momentarily. To put it in current terms, assume someone was en route to satisfy an impulse of passion and his car hit an icy spot, causing it to spin around and careen out of control. His awareness that he might be killed would eliminate the most intense passion. That, says the *Beis HaLevi*, is how one should feel at the first hint of a forbidden desire. The awesomeness of transgressing the word of God should make improper coveting impossible.

This is the concept of awe and reverence that is required for the *acquisition* of Torah.

בַּעֲנָוָה
With modesty

The pivotal role of modesty and humility has been addressed in the earlier chapters. I will simply add several anecdotes to reinforce this vital concept.

R' Moshe Schreiber (*Chasam Sofer*) was a prolific scholar, whose writings on all aspect of Torah abound. When asked why he was not publishing his writings, he replied, "For those who know more than me or are of equal erudition, my writings will add nothing. It is hardly worthwhile to go through the bother of publishing for those few who know less than I do. I am required by Torah to write my thoughts. If anyone thinks they are worthy of being published, he is free to do so."

R' Shlomo Kluger, an outstanding Torah personality, wrote in his will: "No terms of praise should be used in my eulogy. All that may be said of me is 'This man served the public for many years. It is in order that people should pray that he be shown mercy and that his sins be forgiven, so that he may merit the Eternal World.' "

R' Avraham Shmuel Binyamin Schreiber (*Kasv Sofer*) secluded himself on his 54th birthday. One of his former students was bold enough to enter his room, and found his teacher in tears. "Why are you crying?" he asked.

"My dear student," the rabbi answered, "Today I am 54 years old. What do I have to show for these 54 years? I know so little of Torah. I lack wisdom. I have no piety. How can I not cry when I see that so many years have passed and are irretrievable, and I have made so little use of them?"

These *tzaddikim* and many others like them did not feign humility. Even though they were aware of what they knew, they felt they were derelict in not having achieved much more.

Genuine humility is the hallmark of a true Torah scholar.

בְּשִׂמְחָה
With joy

I shall never forget the scene. It was before my bar mitzvah, and my *melamed* came across a difficulty in a *Tosafos* (commentary on the Talmud). When the commentaries appended to the Talmud did not clarify the point, he began searching among the volumes in the bookcase. After paging unsuccessfully through several of them, he suddenly exclaimed, "*Oy!* here it is!" He repeatedly kissed the volume, then hugged it and began dancing with it. The difficulty in the *Tosafos* had been resolved, and his joy knew no bounds.

It has been asked: How can the requisite feelings of *eimah* (awe) and *simchah* (joy) coexist? It would seem that fear would severely dampen joy.

"Not so," said the Baal Shem Tov. "It is clear that the two can indeed coexist. The psalmist states, 'Rejoice with trembling' (*Psalms* 2:11). This may be understood by his statement 'I rejoice over Your words like one who has found a great treasure' (*Psalms* 119:162). Think of a person who comes across a huge horde of gold coins, but has only a small container. He fills the container, runs home and empties it, then runs back to get more. He is overjoyed with his good luck at finding the treasure, but knows that with his small container he cannot possibly get the entire treasure. He is at once elated, but also fearful that he will leave so much behind.

"So it is with Torah," the Baal Shem Tov said. "One rejoices over having some of it, but knowing its infinity, he realizes that he will leave the world with only a small fragment of it."

R' Shneur Zalman explains the verse, "Your statutes were music to me" (*Psalms* 119:54), as follows. The term for laws in this verse, *chukim*, refers to those laws for which we cannot find a logical reason. If a person hears an enchanting melody, it plays over and over in his mind until he begins to sing it. That is how the Torah scholar feels about even those portions of Torah that are beyond his understanding.

R' Baruch Ber Lebovitz said, "I cannot fathom how a person who grasps an explanation of a Talmudic concept by R' Akiva Eiger can restrain himself from dancing." This is the attitude of *simchah* to which the mishnah refers.

בְּטָהֳרָה
With purity

"Purity" in this mishnah does not refer to being free of *tumah* (ritual contamination), but rather to *purity of motivation and purpose*. R' Moshe Chaim Luzzatto devotes an entire section on "Purity" in *Path of the Just*. He defines purity and gives instructions on how it may be attained. I provided some commentary to this in *Lights Along the Way* (Mesorah 1995). At this point I only wish to cite from the fifth of Rambam's *Eight Chapters*, his introduction to *Ethics of the Fathers*:

"A person must subjugate all his capacities to the principles we have presented. He should have only a single purpose, which is to reach God to whatever degree is humanly possible. All his behavior should be directed toward this goal. His intentions in eating, drinking, sleeping, marital relations, moving about, and resting should be only to achieve optimal health. The desire for optimal health, in turn, should be that it will enable him to acquire the wisdom, character traits, and intellect that will lead him toward the above goal."

In these few sentences the Rambam sums up the concept of purity referred to in this mishnah.

בְּשִׁמּוּשׁ חֲכָמִים
With ministering
to the sages

The Talmud derives many laws from nuances in the wording of a phrase in the Torah. An extra letter is not without significance. Yet in the episode where the Patriarch Abraham sends Eliezer to find a wife for Isaac, the Torah relates at great length Eliezer's detailed account of how he was led to choose Rebecca. Why is the Torah so liberal with this narrative? The Talmud answers, "The conversation of the servants of the Patriarchs is of greater importance than the learned discussions of their descendants" (*Bereishis Rabbah* 50:11). No amount of learning can equal an eyewitness account of someone who was in constant contact with the Patriarch. This person saw Torah in action. Ministering to the sages can convey Torah teachings even more than learning from their works (*Berachos* 7b).

R' Yosef Bloch (*Shiurei Daas*) states that the superiority of the education one derives from ministering to the sages is evident in an episode related in the Talmud. A maidservant in the house of R' Yehudah *HaNasi* witnessed a father beat his grown-up son and she excommunicated him. None of the sages dared remove the excommunication, although they were scholars of enormous stature. Since the maidservant had the opportunity to observe R' Yehudah, they felt that by watching his behavior she had gained a degree of Torah knowledge that surpassed their learning! They considered themselves incapable of removing a ban which she had pronounced (*Moed Katan* 17a).

This is as true of contemporary *tzaddikim* as it is of the sages of yore. Anyone who was privileged to observe the Steipler *Gaon* had the opportunity to see how every move of his was filtered through halachah.

We are privileged to have biographies of many of our great Torah personalities. These provide a rich source for practical application of Torah principles.

בְּדִקְדּוּק חֲבֵרִים
With closeness
with colleagues

There are two versions of this mishnah: "closeness" (בְּדִבּוּק) with colleagues and "careful choice" (בְּדִקְדּוּק). They are interdependent. It is precisely because Torah study requires a close relationship with colleagues that one must carefully choose his colleagues.

Scholars who study Torah together cannot but influence one another. Studying with someone who does not have the proper attitude toward Torah, who is indolent, or whose logic is distorted can impair one's learning. In addition, one may be infected if one associates with someone who has undesirable habits.

Parents should take special note who their children's friends are. Peer pressure is a formidable force. Children tend to conform to their friends. Furthermore, children spend more time with their friends than they do with their parents.

Guiding children to choose proper friends may not be easy. Disapproval of a youngster's friends may be met with the objection that the parents are judging someone unfairly and are discriminatory. What is worse is that young people may seek to clandestinely associate with friends of whom their parents disapprove. We may tell our children that we are not discriminating nor sitting in judgment in disapproving of their closeness with certain friends any more than we would be considered discriminatory if we discouraged them from avoiding closeness with friends who had colds. Habits are as contagious as viruses. Unfortunately, such lectures are not always effective.

As with other things we wish to teach our children, we can do so most effectively by modeling. If parents associate with friends of whose lifestyles they disapprove, it is difficult to expect the children to be different. We should be courteous toward everyone, and we should not be discriminating when it involves consideration of others or helping others. We should certainly not be snobbish. However, if we wish our children to choose good friends, our own close friendships should be with people whose lifestyles and *middos* we respect.

בְּפִלְפּוּל הַתַּלְמִידִים
with sharp discussion with students

The Talmud states, "I learned much from my teachers, more from my colleagues, and most of all from my students" (*Taanis* 7a). Explaining a concept to students requires that the teacher clarify it for himself. Challenges by the students cause the teacher to rethink the material and modify it if necessary.

There is yet another advantage to interacting with students. A scholar may have formed an opinion which does not permit him to see the subject in any other way, regardless of how hard he may try. A student may know far less than the teacher, but may bring a fresh look to the subject.

R' Chaim of Volozhin once came to Vilna on a Friday, and was preparing himself for Shabbos when he was told that the *Gaon* wished to see him promptly. He dropped everything and hurried to the *Gaon*. The *Gaon* appeared haggard, and had a cloth tied around his forehead. "My dear R' Chaim," the *Gaon* said, "please help me understand this most difficult passage in the Jerusalem Talmud."

R' Chaim was taken aback. "How can my master expect me to understand something which defies the master's incomparable understanding?"

The *Gaon* replied, "Solomon says, 'Two are better than one. . .If one stumbles, the other can help him up' (*Ecclesiastes* 4:9-10). A weaker person can lend a helping hand to a stronger person who has fallen."

R' Chaim looked at the difficult passage and said, "Perhaps if we approached it from a different angle, the difficulty would be resolved." He began to interpret the passage as he understood it, then said, "The master can now go on with it."

The *Gaon* was ecstatic, removed the compress from his forehead and thanked R' Chaim profusely. He then asked for some food. R' Chaim later learned that the *Gaon* had not been able to take any food for three days!

Wise teachers can benefit greatly from their discussions with their students.

בְּיִשׁוּב
With deliberation

The word *yishuv* refers to a calm, unhurried train of thought. We may have a bright idea and be inspired by a new insight, but we should not jump to conclusions. First impressions may be exciting but may also be misleading.

I have mentioned that in my correspondence with the Steipler *Gaon* I posed a question about a passage in the Talmud. His reply was brilliant. He requested that I send him a copy of his letter, because he had not recorded the answer to my question.

Two years later, another of his many volumes on Talmud appeared. I found that he cited my question, but his answer was markedly different from that he had written to me. There was only a faint reference to the brilliant insight. It was clear that the Steipler had reviewed and rethought the issue many times, and the final version was what he felt to be correct. The initial insight was indeed brilliant and exciting, but brilliant and exciting ideas are not necessarily true.

Yishuv also means focusing on the issue at hand. Sometimes our thought processes diffuse, and we cannot concentrate properly on a single item. True Torah scholarship requires the capacity to eliminate all extraneous thoughts.

Closely associated with focusing is "orderliness." The Chofetz Chaim said that a *masmid* (diligent student) is not necessarily one who spends a great deal of time studying, but one who studies in an orderly fashion. Our great Torah scholars were orderly both in their lifestyles and in their study habits. The Talmud says that when R' Yehudah *HaNasi* was studying one subject, he did not wish to be asked questions pertaining to a different subject (*Shabbos* 50b). Although his knowledge was encyclopedic and he could have easily addressed any other question, he did not wish to be distracted.

As we said, a *chassid* was asked, "What is most important to your Rebbe?" He answered, "Whatever he happens to be doing at that time. If something else were more important, he would be doing that."

Focusing and orderliness prevent the confusion which can result in muddled thinking. This type of study has a much greater impression on one's mind, and enables greater retention. The legendary retention of Torah which our great scholars had was undoubtedly due to the intensity with which they focused on one subject. This retention of Torah is necessary for its *acquisition*.

ו/ו בְּמִקְרָא, בְּמִשְׁנָה, בְּמִעוּט סְחוֹרָה, בְּמִעוּט דֶּרֶךְ
אֶרֶץ, בְּמִעוּט תַּעֲנוּג, בְּמִעוּט שֵׁנָה, בְּמִעוּט שִׂיחָה,

בְּמִקְרָא, בְּמִשְׁנָה
With [knowledge of]
Scripture [and] Mishnah

We are blessed with many excellent expositions on the Talmud, and many yeshivah
students try to be proficient in these. However, if
they are asked to find a particular verse in the
Chumash, they may be bewildered. There is particularly scant knowledge of
the Prophets.

This is regrettable. The Chofetz Chaim had a small volume of the *Tanach*
(the entire Scripture) in his *tallis* bag. When he studied a subject in the Talmud
he would first consult the *Chumash* to find its original source. If he did not
understand the derivation from the verse in the Scripture, he would review the
latter, consulting the major commentaries on *Chumash* until he understood
the derivation.

Our great Torah scholars were proficient in Scripture. Anyone reading R'
Yaakov Kamenetzky's writings on Scripture can see that he accounted not
only for every single letter, but also showed how the meaning of a verse
requires an understanding of the musical notes in Scripture. During his last
years he was deeply upset because he was unable to recall the precise wording
of a Scriptural verse. "That I should not remember a verse in *Tanach*," he
lamented.

The mishnah is the basis of the Talmud. The mishnah was compiled before
it was permitted to record the Oral Law. In order to facilitate its retention, the
mishnah had to be condensed. The elaborate discussions in the Talmud are
essentially expositions on the mishnah. It is not too difficult to memorize the
compact mishnah, which then allows one to have greater recall of the deliberations of the rest of the Talmud.

The Hebrew letters of "mishnah," משנה, can be rearranged to spell
neshamah, נשמה, (soul). It is therefore customary to learn the mishnah for the
souls of the departed. However, the mishnah is at least equally important for
the *neshamah* of the living. The Shelah states that R' Yosef Karo merited
Divine inspiration and became the halachic authority in Judaism because of his
profound study of mishnah.

The true Torah scholar utilizes the mishnah to facilitate his retention of all
that he has learned.

בְּמִעוּט סְחוֹרָה
With limited
business activity

The Talmud states that a person's earnings are predetermined for him on Rosh Hashanah (*Beitzah* 16b). He
cannot exceed his prescribed amount regardless of how
much effort he exerts. On the other hand, a person's
spiritual gains are totally within his own hands. A true awareness of this will
result in a person devoting the majority of his time to those things that he can

accomplish with his own effort. He will minimize the expenditure of effort where it will make little difference. The true Torah scholar therefore keeps his business activities to a minimum.

The Chofetz Chaim supported himself by operating a small store. When he had earned enough for that day, he closed the store and devoted the rest of the day to Torah study. Our lives have been greatly enriched by the Chofetz Chaim. His works are widely studied and his portrait graces many Jewish homes. There were contemporaries of the Chofetz Chaim who were indeed successful business people. Who were they? What did they contribute to the world? Those people who wish to perpetuate themselves for posterity might compare the true Torah scholar and the successful businessman.

Yes, we pray in the morning, and many people go to *shul* daily for morning services. Heaven forbid if the one who leads the services is a bit slow and the service takes 34 minutes instead of the usual 30. After all, one must get to the office, where he may spend the next nine hours.

Acquisition of Torah requires having one's priorities in order.

בְּמִעוּט דֶּרֶךְ אֶרֶץ, בְּמִעוּט תַּעֲנוּג
With limited sexual activity, with limited pleasure

The human being was given a variety of biological drives and appetites. He shares many of these with other forms of life. His uniqueness and perfection is not in indulgence in the biological drives, but in the development of that portion of him which is uniquely human: the spirit. The biological drives are there to serve a purpose, and they should be satisfied to the degree that this contributes to a person's optimal functioning *as a dignified human being.* Indulgence, even if permissible, is discouraged. Indeed, Ramban considers spiritual growth to be a Scriptural requirement, and he interprets the verse, "You shall be holy" (*Leviticus* 19:2), to mean that one should abstain from permissible indulgences. We should be guided in these by the principles of propriety found in Torah teachings.

The quality of "limited pleasures" has been mentioned (6:4). I have come across a recorded conversation of the Steipler *Gaon* on the value of austerity which I wish to share with you.

In the past, we grew up in the villages in extreme poverty. We became accustomed to the facet that we cannot get everything we want. A child who came home from "cheder" hungry and did not find anything to eat in the house learned to tolerate hunger. The food we did have was simple. Fruits were a rare delicacy. We got new clothes very infrequently.

Poverty and suffering are a beneficial training. If, in the course of life, a person does not attain what he wants, he accepts that as normal. Deprivation does not affect him appreciably.

Today, a child learns at an early age that his parents will give him whatever he wants. Food is plentiful. It is rare that a house is without food, fruits, and confection. Children are extremely well dressed.

In contrast to the physical goods given to the child, his spiritual training is neglected. Father leaves home for work and cannot pay attention to the children. When he returns home, he is exhausted and tense, and he cannot devote time and thought to providing spiritual training for the children.

Furthermore, having been accustomed since childhood to get whatever they want, any deprivation or adverse occurrence in adulthood results in nervousness and depression.

Parents give their children adequate food and clothes, but they do not provide them with self-esteem. If they lack self-esteem and see other children as being more gifted, they are consumed with envy. The craving for recognition torments them, since they have become accustomed that all their desires are met. They gradually deteriorate to the point of crisis.

This would not occur if they had been immunized in childhood to withstand deprivation. The vicissitudes of life would not result in nervousness and depression.

In addition, children who grow up under very austere conditions appreciate anything they receive. Everything that is just a bit better than their usual fare brings them much joy.

Today, when even the poor have many comforts that in the past were restricted to the wealthy, there is very little joy in life. Nothing brings them joy, because everything is taken for granted. It takes some outstanding occurrence to make someone happy. . . (Of the Fathers, vol. 4, p.109).

The Steipler *Gaon's* summation requires no further comment.

בְּמְעוּט שֵׁנָה, בְּמְעוּט
שִׂיחָה, בְּמְעוּט שְׂחוֹק
With limited sleep, limited
conversation, limited levity

There is, of course, a need for sleep. However, it is not uncommon to exceed the amount necessary for optimal functioning. Some people find it very difficult to arouse themselves early. It is very conducive to Torah study to arise early and begin the day with Torah, even before morning services.

On the other hand, depriving oneself of adequate sleep is wrong. The Chofetz Chaim would come into the study hall late at night and send the students off to bed. He said that inadequate sleep detracts from mental acuity.

Some of our great Torah scholars did indeed function with a bare minimum of sleep. The *Tzaddik* of Sanz hardly slept at all, but he explained: "A swift runner may cover a long distance in a fraction of the time it would take the average person. I happen to be a swift sleeper. I can accomplish in minutes of sleep what may take others hours."

Modern science is learning much about sleep. There are various stages of sleep. For instance, REM (rapid-eye-movement) sleep occurs for very brief periods during the night. The REM phase is extremely important, and it does not come on until one has had a longer period of other phases. It is conceivable that if a person could get into a REM stage immediately, he could get along with much less sleep. It may also be possible to gain control of sleep phases with techniques such as biofeedback. In other words, the *Tzaddik's* claim that he was a "swift sleeper" may have scientific validity.

The importance of limiting one's conversation was previously mentioned (1:17). The *yetzer hara* is particularly efficient in stimulating conversation during study time as well as in *shul*. I recall that several students were engaging in conversation while the volumes of Talmud lay open before them. Their teacher passed by and said, "If you must talk, please show your respect by closing your volumes of Talmud." One student's joking comment contained some truth. "There is no pleasure in talking if the *gemaras* (books of Talmud) are closed."

One of my friends developed a throat ailment which required him to be silent for weeks. He would communicate with us by writing. Of course, the written communication was far less than the verbal would have been. When he was again permitted to talk, his conversation was scant. "I found out how so much of what we say is unnecessary."

While an upbeat attitude is highly desirable, levity is discouraged. There is no harm in exchanging witticisms, but one must be cautious to maintain an attitude of due respect for Torah. One does not crack jokes when one is doing delicate eye surgery, nor when one is sitting at the controls about to send people into orbit. These are activities which require close and undivided attention. This is equally true of Torah study. The Talmud relates that Rabbah would preface his lecture with something that would bring mirth to the students, but once Torah study was begun, they would sit with awe and reverence (*Pesachim* 117a).

By "limited," the mishnah means "judicious." King Solomon summed it up well. "There is a proper time for everything" (*Ecclesiastes* 3:1). The true Torah scholar exercises careful judgment in all his activities.

בְּאֶרֶךְ אַפַּיִם
With slowness to anger

The issue of anger is discussed in Chapter 5 mishnah 14. Suffice it to say that Moses, the greatest of all Torah scholars, erred in halachah when he became angry (*Sifri, Mattos* 48). The vulnerability to err when angry occurs even if the anger is justified.

In our discussion of anger, we pointed out that there are several phases to anger. The propensity to err in judgment is a consequence of *rage*. We have no precedent that the third phase, *resentment*, predisposes to error. However, it is evident that this is so from Solomon's statement, "Anger rests in the bosom of a fool" (*Ecclesiastes* 7:9). Solomon is clearly referring to the *retention* of anger as rendering one a fool. Acquisition of Torah requires wisdom for correct analysis and proper judgment. If one is a fool, one lacks wisdom.

The Torah not only forbids acting out a grudge, but also explicitly forbids harboring hatred toward another person (*Leviticus* 19:17-18). It is extremely difficult to make a clear separation between hostile feelings. Except in the case of feelings about a very beloved person, anger and hatred usually go together. Harboring feelings of hatred is not only foolish, but also constitutes a Scriptural transgression. Anyone who is in frank violation of the Torah cannot possibly acquire it.

An important insight into the defective trait of *rage* is provided by R' Yerucham Levovitz (*Daas Chochmah U'Mussar* vol. 6, p. 189). R' Levovitz alerts us to the precise words of the Talmud, "One who comes *to the capacity* of rage comes to *the capacity* of error" (*Rashi, Numbers* 31:21). It is not the actual rage that predisposes to error, but rather the "capacity" to become enraged. Just what is this "capacity"?

R' Yerucham says that a person who has complete trust in God is in a state of calmness. This attitude of serenity will enable him to prevent the feeling of anger upon provocation to progress to rage. Failure to control one's anger indicates an imperfection in one's faith.

R' Yerucham supports his position by pointing out an apparent conflict. The Midrash states that Moses' transgression was that he became enraged when the Israelites demanded water (*Bamidbar Rabbah* 19:5). Yet in the Torah we read that God reprimanded Moses, "Because *you lacked faith* in Me" (*Numbers* 20:12). R' Yerucham states that these two statements do not conflict. As difficult as it is for us to conceptualize that the faith of Moses was lacking in perfection, we can come to no other conclusion than that in a most minute and delicate way, this was so. It was this faint trace of imperfection in faith and trust in God that resulted in the *capacity* for rage.

Following R' Yerucham's thesis, the more perfect one's faith is, the more complete is his mastery of anger. The acquisition of Torah is dependent on a profound degree of faith. Hence, the scholar who learns Torah *lishmah* will be slow to anger.

בְּלֵב טוֹב
With good-heartedness

In Chapter 2 mishnah 13 it was pointed out that "a good heart" is comprehensive and is the source of all other commendable traits. The role of a good heart in the acquisition of Torah is symbolized by the connecting letters of the last verse of the Torah to the first. As is evident on Simchas Torah, when we complete the reading of the Torah we immediately go to its beginning. The last letter of the Torah is *lamed*, and the first letter is *beis*. These two letters make up the word *lev* (heart).

The circular pattern of our reading of the Torah indicates that it is without end. The acquisition of Torah, integrating the infinite within our finite beings, is accomplished by *lev,* by good-heartedness.

There is no denying that people come into the world with varying dispositions. Some people seem to be naturally kindhearted from infancy on. Others may have a cruel streak evident very early in life. R' Shneur Zalman states that emotions can be altered by the intellect, and a person who is not innately kindhearted can make himself so. However, this requires much dedication and effort.

A student of the chassidic master, R' Shlomo of Karlin, complained that he was unable to develop the emotions requisite for spirituality and the acquisition of Torah. "What can I do, my son?" the Rabbi said. "I have been unable to find the key to open your heart."

"Who needs a key?" the student cried. "Open it with an ax!"

"Never mind," the Rabbi said. "Your heart has just been opened."

R' Shneur Zalman was right. An intense desire to develop salutary emotions can bring them about.

בֶּאֱמוּנַת חֲכָמִים
With faith in the Sages

The essence of faith in the sages is that they are the authentic interpreters of God's word. The prototype of faith in the sages is the faith of the Israelites in Moses (*Exodus* 14:31). Moses conveyed the Divine will to the Israelites, and true Torah scholars have occupied that position of authority throughout all ages. As we noted, some of the Talmudic authors would address Torah scholars as "Moses" (*Shabbos* 101b).

Tzaddikim were concerned that the admiration of their followers might cause them to feel that the *tzaddik* had independent powers to perform miracles, and they discouraged this type of faith.

A woman came to R' Mordechai of Chernobel, complaining that after many years of marriage she was still barren. She pleaded with the Rabbi to bless her that she might bear a child. To everyone's astonishment, the Rabbi refused to give his blessing. The woman left brokenhearted.

The Rabbi noticed that the onlookers were puzzled by his refusal to bless her. He sent his *shammas* (assistant) to call the woman. When she returned, the Rabbi asked, "What did you do when you left here?"

The woman answered, "I turned my eyes to heaven and said, 'Master of the Universe. Even the holy Rabbi cannot help me. You are the only One Who can help me."

The Rabbi smiled and said, "Go in peace. You will be blessed with a child."

The Rabbi then said, "This woman had thought that I have some magical powers to grant wishes. She was turning to me for help instead of to God.

When I refused her, she prayed intensely to God. Her prayer will now be answered."

There is certainly nothing wrong with asking for the blessing of a *tzaddik*. Rashi cites the Midrash which states that God gave Abraham the power to give blessings (*Genesis* 12:2). However, one must realize that the fulfillment of the blessing emanates from God.

There are countless stories about the sincere faith that people had in *tzaddikim*. The *Gaon* of Vilna was once so involved in his studies that he did not see a man enter the room. After a long wait, the man left. He later asked the *Gaon*, "Why did you ignore me?" The *Gaon* apologized profusely explaining that he simply had not seen him. "You are very dear to me," the *Gaon* said. "May you live to be 100 years old."

When the man was 98, he fell ill, and his family summoned a doctor. The man refused to let the doctor examine him. "I don't need a doctor. I know I will get well. I still have two more years to live." Indeed, the man died on his 100th birthday.

The true Torah scholar trusts that the *tzaddik's* teachings and instructions are authentic. R' Yitzchak Meir of Gur was an outstanding Torah scholar. He composed a commentary on a section of the *Shulchan Aruch* (Code of Jewish Law), and showed it to the Rabbi of Kotzk, who reviewed it and said, "It is excellent. In fact, it is too good. The accepted commentary on the *Shulchan Aruch* is that written by the *Shach*. If you publish this, it is likely that people will use this commentary instead of the *Shach*. That must not happen. I suggest you destroy the manuscript."

R' Yitzchak Meir did not hesitate. He said, "It is a mitzvah to obey the words of the sages," and threw the manuscript into the fire.

That is how a true Torah scholar has faith in the sages.

בְּקַבָּלַת הַיִּסּוּרִין
With acceptance of suffering

This is undoubtedly one of the most difficult challenges a person faces. Avoidance of pain is instinctive, and is present in all forms of life that have a sensory system. The Torah does not demand of us anything which is beyond our capacity. It is only natural for a person to avoid pain. Yet, the instinctive reaction of avoiding pain and the acceptance of suffering are not contradictory.

"Pain" and "suffering" are generally thought to be synonymous. If someone says, "I'm in such pain," you know he is suffering. Technically, however, there is a difference between the two.

If a person in severe pain is given morphine, he may say that the pain is totally gone. If he is questioned carefully and told to focus on the sensation, he may report that the sensation of pain is still there, *but that it does not bother him.* This is also true of the anesthetic effect that can be induced under hypnosis. The person may say that he is very comfortable. Again, if he draws his attention to the sensation that had caused him discomfort, he may say that he still feels it but that it does not "hurt" him.

Although it is somewhat difficult to grasp, the fact is that "suffering" occurs when the brain *interprets* that "pain" sensation as discomfort.

Just as morphine or hypnosis can prevent the brain's interpretation of pain as suffering, so can a person's attitude or state of mind. A person with a very profound love of God and *emunah* (trust) that God will never allow any real harm to befall him may be able to feel the pain sensation, yet not be "suffering."

However, very few people are able to accomplish this. For most of us, pain and suffering are inseparable.

Neither physical nor emotional pain can always be safely relieved by medication. There are times when we have no other choice but to adjust to suffering.

Of all living things, human beings are the most subject to emotional pain. The Talmud says, "I have never seen any creatures experiencing suffering in their search for their sustenance" (*Kiddushin* 82b). It is precisely the intelligence of the human being that makes him vulnerable to suffering. Indeed, Solomon says that "suffering increases proportionally to intelligence" (*Ecclesiastes* 1:18). It is clear, says R' Yerucham Levovitz, that God gave man the unique capacity of suffering. Why this is so is beyond us, knowable only to the Divine wisdom (*Daas Chochmah U'Mussar* vol. 6, p.88).

It is patently simple: When suffering is unavoidable, it must be accepted. We have the option of experiencing suffering with bitterness and anger, or accepting it with serenity.

I was very moved by the account of a couple who longed for a child, but the wife did not conceive until 17 years after their marriage. When she was expecting, they were overjoyed. "Imagine my bitterness and anger when the child that I longed for so many years was born mentally challenged. I was angry at God. 'Why did You do this to me?'

"We loved this child. Every night we stood over the crib and prayed fervently. 'Almighty God, we know that You can do anything. You have done so many miracles. We ask You for just one more miracle. Change him.' One day the miracle occurred and our prayers were answered. God changed *us*. We had been praying for the wrong thing. God transformed our prayers into prayers for acceptance, and He then answered them." Of course one makes every effort to eliminate suffering, but when we cannot change reality, we must pray for the help to accept it.

Some people say that suffering is a Divine punishment for our sins. That is too broad a generalization. The fact is that we do not understand the reason for suffering. The Talmud states that Moses asked God why innocent people suffer, and God told him that this was something that is beyond human understanding.

It may be argued that suffering as a punishment is evident from the account of King David in Scripture. David had to flee from the rebellion led by his son Absalom (*II Samuel* 15). When he was a fugitive, he was attacked and cursed by Shimi ben Geira. David's general wanted to kill Shimi, but David restrained him. "He is but an agent of God. God sent him to curse me" (ibid. 16:5-10). Does this not prove that all adversity is a Divine punishment?

This is not so. David made this interpretation because he recognized the rebellion as the Divine punishment which the prophet had predicted would transpire because of David's transgression involving Bathsheba (ibid. 12:4). This does not mean that all suffering is punishment. There is a concept of "suffering inflicted because of Divine love" (*Berachos* 5a), a concept which we must accept by faith.

The faith of the true Torah scholar enables him to accept suffering with serenity. There are countless accounts of our great *tzaddikim* who persisted in their study of Torah even when they were experiencing much physical pain. Their acceptance by virtue of their faith enabled them to do so.

הַמַּכִּיר אֶת מְקוֹמוֹ
Knowing one's place

Some of the commentaries interpret this to mean realizing that the place one happens to be in, i.e., this world, is not one's permanent place. The true Torah scholar's world is the Eternal World.

The mishnah may also refer to the colloquial "knowing one's place"; i.e., not pushing oneself where one does not belong. At an assembly, it is not unusual for people to push their way forward to the dignitaries in order to be seen in their company and perhaps even appear in a picture with them. This reflects a need to bolster a fragile ego and to give an artificial lift to one's impoverished sense of self-esteem. A person who has good self-esteem has no need for such tactics.

In Chapter 4 mishnah 3 it states that there is "no person without his hour and you have no thing without its place." One of the chassidic masters said that it is logical to assume that every person also has his place. The problem is that many people are dissatisfied with their own place and wish to be in someone else's place. This is the envy which Scripture refers to as "the rot of the bones" (*Proverbs* 14:30). The person who recognizes that his own place is indeed proper for him is free of envy.

The Torah scholar who is genuinely humble may seek an inauspicious place. However, when his leadership is essential, he recognizes that he must occupy a position of prominence. He "knows his place," recognizing where he belongs at different times.

וְהַשָּׂמֵחַ בְּחֶלְקוֹ
Being happy with one's lot

This quality has been discussed in 4:1 and also in this mishnah in regard to austere living.

The more a person understands that his *neshamah* is Divine and that he can unite with God, the less he will be concerned with earthly needs. A person who may be annoyed by a headache and discovers that he has won a huge amount of money in a sweepstakes promptly forgets about his headache. Any earthly deprivations a person may experience are totally overshadowed by the good fortune of having the Torah and developing a close relationship with God. Earlier in this mishnah, *simchah* was listed as a prerequisite for acquisition of Torah. Being happy with one's lot leads to greater acquisition of Torah, which in turn increases the happiness with one's lot. The true Torah scholar thus has a positive self-reinforcing cycle.

A more accurate translation of this mishnah is "being happy with one's *portion*." This lends itself to a unique interpretation by R' Shlomo Kluger (*Magen Avos*).

In the *Amidah* we pray for the welfare of the *tzaddikim* and that they receive their due reward. This is followed by the phrase "and put our portion with them." It would seem that we are asking God to reward us along with the *tzaddikim*. Is it not chutzpah to expect that we should share reward with *tzaddikim* who are totally devoted to the Divine service? What right do we have to make such a request?

The Arizal explains that if a person sins to the degree that he forfeits his share in *Gan Eden* (Paradise), his share is given to a deserving person. The average person will gladly accept an additional portion of *Gan Eden*. A *tzaddik*, however, does not want any reward which he did not earn by his own effort. The *tzaddik* will therefore reject the forfeited share and return it to the sinner. This is what is meant by the prayer "put our portion with them (with the *tzaddikim*)." We think of ourselves as being sinful and forfeiting our share of *Gan Eden*, and we therefore ask that our portion be given to *tzaddikim*. They are certain to return the forfeited portion to us.

This is what the mishnah means. The true Torah scholar is happy with his own portion in *Gan Eden*, and does not accept a portion that he receives because it was forfeited by another. He is happy only with the reward that he earned by his fulfillment of Torah and mitzvos.

וְהָעוֹשֶׂה סְיָג לִדְבָרָיו
*Making a [protective] fence
around his personal matters*

In Chapter 1 mishnah 1 we read that the Men of the Great Assembly said that one should "make a protective fence for the Torah." This was essentially an instruction to halachic authorities to add precautionary measures that will prevent a person from committing Scriptural transgressions. In this mishnah we are told that a true Torah scholar sets up additional precautionary measures for himself as he deems necessary. For example, although halachah prescribes a waiting period between meat and milk foods, Mar Ukva said that his father did not eat any dairy foods on the day he had eaten meat. This was a personal precautionary measure, and is not binding on anyone else.

We all have different tendencies. A wise person, who recognizes that he is particularly vulnerable in one area, may take extra precautionary measures that are not required by halachah.

Let me cite an example from my work in treating alcoholics. Ted is a stock broker who was treated for alcoholism. In the treatment center he developed a friendship with Tom, who worked in a nearby office building. They both had come into recovery at the same time. Two years later I met Tom, and in our conversation he told me that Ted was going to ridiculous extremes. They had been walking down the street, and as they approached a tavern, Ted crossed the street. "I don't even want to be near those places," he said. Tom thought this was foolish. He passes taverns numerous times and does not have an urge to go in. I told Tom that it was not Ted who was foolish, but he. The risk of relapse in alcoholism is significant, and the realization of this warrants taking extra precautions.

Twenty years have since passed. Ted is still sober. Tom went back to drinking and is having a very difficult time maintaining sobriety. Tom never appreciated the intensity of the drive to drink, nor the grave consequences of falling back into that destructive pattern. If we understand the gravity of transgression and know that we have a propensity to do so, we will take precautionary measures.

Some commentaries translate the mishnah as "making a protective fence around his *words.*" This is in keeping with the dictum of Chapter 3 mishnah 17, that silence is a protective fence for wisdom. Our great Torah personalities were very watchful of their words. Indeed, the Talmud says that even the ordinary conversation of Torah scholars is instructive (*Avodah Zarah* 19b).

A lecturer once spoke for $1^1/_2$ hours. He was later approached by someone in the audience who introduced himself as a television producer. "I think your message is important, and should reach many people. I would like to fit it into a television broadcast. You realize that every second of television time is very costly. Do you think you could condense the essence of your lecture into three minutes?"

The speaker thought for several moments. "Yes, I think I could," he said.

"Then why in heaven's name didn't you do so?" the man demanded.

If we think carefully about what we really wish to convey, we are sure to discover that we can trim our conversation down to the bare essentials. We may also discover that there are things that are better left unsaid.

The Torah scholar is particularly watchful of what he says. Realizing that people will take his words as authoritative, he tries to prevent the possibility of his words being misinterpreted. He follows the teaching of Avtalyon (1:11).

The Chazon Ish was once handed a letter from a group of rabbis about a particular *kashrus* issue. He refused to read the letter and explained: "If I answer this question in the negative, the very fact that I gave it consideration will result in some people contending that this is a question which can be debated. Since I do not wish to reply to this letter, there is no point in my reading it." Time proved the Chazon Ish to have been right.

Whether the mishnah is referring to actions, words, or both, the concept of making protective fences gives weight to both word and deed. It conveys a sense of responsibility for one's behavior that is necessary for the acquisition of Torah.

הַמַּכִּיר אֶת מְקוֹמוֹ . . .
וְאֵינוֹ מַחֲזִיק טוֹבָה לְעַצְמוֹ, אָהוּב . . .

Knowing one's place, . . . claiming no credit for himself, being beloved . . .

As we noted, Chapter Six is not a continuation of *Pirkei Avos* but was appended to it. There are therefore a number of repetitions: being happy with one's lot (4:1), making a protective fence (1:1), and not claiming credit for oneself (2:9). However, if we scrutinize the wording of the mishnah, we may find that it is not just repetitious.

In the first part of the mishnah, the traits are preceded with the letter ב (*beis*) meaning "with." I.e., Torah is acquired *with* study, *with* attentive listening, etc. After many traits are enumerated, the *beis* is dropped, and the mishnah begins to enumerate the character traits of the scholar. I.e., he is *one who* knows his place, *one who* is happy with his lot, etc. The mishnah then makes another change, eliminating "one who" and just says *that he is* beloved, *loves* God, etc.

What the mishnah may be saying is that the true Torah scholar who has implemented all the enumerated qualities that are requisite for acquisition of Torah, is *one who* knows his place, etc. In other words, the character traits are *consequences* of his having studied Torah *lishmah*, exercising all the requisite qualities in his study. Proper study of Torah refines a person and has great impact on his character. The mishnah then goes on to say that a scholar who has these commendable character traits *is* in turn beloved and loves God, etc. The latter traits are consequences of the former

Not every Torah scholar achieves the distinction of being widely beloved. Sometimes a person who "makes protective fences" and is more stringent in the way he observes mitzvos may elicit a negative reaction from some people. They may think of him as having a "holier-than-thou" attitude. This does not occur with a person who does not claim credit for himself. The latter is likely to be very modest, and the extra precautions he takes are usually not even noticeable to others.

We have been privileged to have been eyewitnesses to the validity of this mishnah thusly interpreted. We have observed some outstanding Torah scholars, how they studied Torah, what their character traits were like, and how they were perceived. There were indeed many, but I will mention only two about whom there are many revealing anecdotes.

The unfaltering devotion to Torah study with all the requisites enumerated in the mishnah was characteristic of R' Moshe Feinstein and R' Shlomo Zalman Auerbach. Both were extremely humble and shunned acclaim, both lived austere lives and were happy with their lot, both were extremely cautious with words, both did not claim any credit for their enormous erudition, and both were beloved by all.

Before Yom Kippur, R' Moshe Feinstein, then advanced in age, was taken with a wheelchair into an elevator. A man in the elevator, his head not covered with a *yarmulke* (skullcap), wished the rabbi a happy New Year. The rabbi returned the greeting, whereupon the man leaned over and said, "and a healthy one." R' Feinstein smiled and said with great feeling, "May you too have a healthy year. May you enjoy great success and have much *nachas* from your children."

The man later remarked, "The rabbi could see that I am not an observant Jew. But to him I am a somebody."

A similar comment was made by an African-American nurse who attended a training session at Brooklyn's Maimonides Hospital. When the lecturer cited a ruling by Reb Moshe on a medical issue, she was heard to remark, "Oh, R' Feinstein. He's a *real* rabbi!" When she was asked what she knew about R' Feinstein she said, "I helped out as a nurse when his great-grandson was born. Before he left the *bris* ceremony, he turned his wheelchair around to say good-bye to me. To him I was a somebody."

In his later years, Reb Moshe had a police escort when he went to *tashlich* (a *teshuvah* ritual of the Days of Atonement). The police sergeant asked Reb Moshe for a *berachah*. "My mother told me to always ask for a blessing from a holy man." Other police officers followed suit, and Reb Moshe obliged, giving them all individual blessings. Even non-Jews recognized him as a *tzaddik*.

Someone asked Reb Moshe to what he attributed his great popularity. He shrugged, as if the latter were not factual. "Perhaps," he said, "because I have never in my life knowingly hurt anyone."

It was not just the absence of feeling negative feelings toward anyone. It was the positive feelings he had for everyone. R' Moshe Feinstein was beloved by all because he felt love for everyone. He dedicated his life to teaching people that everyone could achieve a closeness to God if they made a sincere effort at it.

It is well known in Jerusalem that if one wishes to learn something about the character of R' Shlomo Zalman Auerbach, one must ask the taxi drivers. Many of them have stories to tell. Two rabbis were in a taxi when the driver, who was not wearing a *kippah*, abruptly asked them, "Did you know R' Auerbach?" When he learned that one of his passengers was R' Auerbach's grandson, he became very excited.

"I would drive the rabbi to the yeshivah early in the morning. Let me tell you, I never met so pleasant a person. He was always with a smile, always with a warm greeting, always inquiring about my family. I asked the other cabdrivers to give me exclusive rights to drive him to and from the yeshivah. In my 30 years as a cabdriver I never met another person like him.

"After we had become very friendly he once said, 'I don't want to interfere with your lifestyle, but I do wish you would not work on Shabbos.' He said this with great sensitivity and consideration. I could tell that it really hurt him that I was working on Shabbos, but he was hesitant to intrude in my personal life. There was no way I could refuse him. Since then I do not work on Shabbos."

The city built a new path that provided a much shorter walk from R' Shlomo Zalman's home to the *shul*. He refused to use that path, and continued to use the longer route. He explained, "The new walk is very close to several homes and one can look into the windows on passing. That is an intrusion on people's privacy. It might make them uncomfortable."

Another non-observant Jew who came to know R' Shlomo Zalman was Ehud Olmert, the mayor of Jerusalem. He would visit R' Shlomo Zalman on the festivals. He said, "In a world whose values are power, acclaim, and honor, it may be difficult to understand the secret of this man's enormous influence and the esteem in which he was held by all. His house and furnishings were plain and his demeanor was humble and unassuming. He was respected and loved by all."

Over 300,000 people participated in R' Shlomo Zalman's funeral. The drivers of the taxis which served his neighborhood were in tears. "We lost a dear friend."

Anyone familiar with Jerusalem traffic is well aware of how impatient many taxi drivers can be. The slightest delay or blocking of traffic may result in a cacophony of horn tooting. The unprecedented crowd that attended R' Shlomo Zalman's funeral blocked many streets. Not a single horn was sounded. Everyone showed the utmost respect for this outstanding Torah personality.

It is unfortunate that we do not have better accounts of the great Torah personalities of the past millennium. How inspiring it would be to know how Rashi lived! We are fortunate in that we do have accounts of *tzaddikim* of the past century. We would be wise to read about them. Their lives can inspire us to strive for greater spirituality.

אָהוּב, אוֹהֵב אֶת הַמָּקוֹם, אוֹהֵב אֶת הַבְּרִיּוֹת,
אוֹהֵב אֶת הַצְּדָקוֹת, אוֹהֵב אֶת הַמֵּישָׁרִים,
אוֹהֵב אֶת הַתּוֹכָחוֹת

Being beloved, loving God, loving [His] creatures, loving righteous ways, loving justice, loving reproof

We can continue our interpretation of this mishnah as meaning that these character attributes are those that result when one learns Torah with the requisite qualities.

Being beloved, loving God and loving His creatures are intertwined. In 3:13 it states that God is pleased only with those with whom people are pleased.

R' Eliyahu Lopian related that one of the supporters of his yeshivah was not at all observant. R' Eliyahu asked him why he was so devoted to the yeshivah. The man answered, "Because I know that you were close to the Chofetz Chaim."

"When I was a boy," the man continued, "I was interviewed for admission to the Chofetz Chaim's yeshivah in Radin. I was a freethinker and my ideas were unacceptable to the yeshivah. I was told to return home, but there were no more trains that day.

"I had nowhere to sleep, and the Chofetz Chaim took me into his home and let me sleep in the loft. The house was cold. Late at night I heard the door open. The Chofetz Chaim thought I was asleep. He took off his fur coat and covered me with it.

"I still feel the warmth of that fur coat 60 years later."

One who loves others is beloved. King Solomon says that just as water reflects one's image, so does one heart reflect the feeling of another (*Proverbs* 27:19).

R' Michael Ber Weissmandl happened to be visiting a rabbi when a young man and his sister came in. The young man said that he wished to marry a non-Jewish girl, and that his mother insisted he consult the rabbi. The rabbi was very abrupt with the young man and sent him on his way. R' Michael Ber followed the two and engaged them in a conversation. Being a Holocaust survivor, he gently and patiently explained to the young man that we had lost so many Jews to the Nazi murderers, we could not afford to lose any more to intermarriage. He arranged to meet them again at a particular time.

Shortly thereafter, R' Michael Ber was hospitalized with a heart attack. He had a friend contact the young man's sister and explain why he could not meet them. The young woman burst into tears. "The rabbi is in intensive care with a heart attack and he thinks of us!"

Many people think that "love of righteous ways" refers to going beyond the call of duty and doing more than what is required by halachah. They may think of *tzedakah* itself as being *beyond* the call of duty. This is an error. Those who translate *tzedakah* as charity are equally wrong. *Tzedakah* means "righteousness." It is only right to give of oneself and of one's belongings to those in need. We should love to do that which is right.

Some people may give *tzedakah* grudgingly. Unfortunately, when someone rings the doorbell and asks for *tzedakah* he is not always greeted with a smile. Sometimes a person gives a *meshulach* (charity collector) some money, and when he leaves, mumbles, "I find it difficult to handle these people who make a living by *schnorring.*" This is not only a frank violation of Scriptural law which states, "You should not feel badly when you give to the needy" (*Deuteronomy* 15:10), but also conveys the wrong message to members of one's household. Parents may try to teach their children that they must share and not fight over things. Such teachings are undone if the parents give *tzedakah* grudgingly

As pointed out, these character traits are an outgrowth of the qualities in the first part of the mishnah. The person who is satisfied with the bare necessities of life and avoids excesses is not likely to begrudge giving *tzedakah*. Indeed, he loves *tzedakah* and welcomes the opportunity to give it.

"Love of justice" characterized R' Yosef Dov Soloveitchik (*Beis HaLevi*) from his earliest years on. As a child of 7 he was in *cheder* when two young students, Shlomo and David, got into a fistfight. Shlomo, who came from a wealthy family, told the *melamed* (teacher) that David, who was the child of a poor widow, started the fight. The *melamed* promptly slapped David.

The young Yosef Dov said to the *melamed*, "I saw what happened. It was Shlomo that started the fight. You did not even bother to get to the truth because Shlomo's father is a prominent citizen and pays full tuition. David's mother is a poor helpless widow.

"The Torah requires us to be especially considerate of an orphan and widow. It tells us not to distort justice. I refuse to learn Torah from a teacher who does not obey the Torah." With that he left the *cheder*.

Although the teacher apologized, Yosef Dov's father and grandfather could not prevail on him to return to the *cheder*. Already at 7 the child exhibited the trait of a true Torah scholar. Little wonder that he founded the Torah dynasty of Brisk.

Some people bristle when they are reprimanded, and others may accept constructive criticism more graciously. The true Torah scholar *loves* reproof. He realizes that a person is often oblivious to his own shortcomings and is totally dependent on others pointing them out to him. Think of how you would feel if you drove into a gas station and asked how far it was to your destination. The attendant raises his eyebrows and says, "How far? Why, you're heading in the wrong direction! Turn around and head back." Would you not feel thankful? If not for his pointing out your error, you would be going away from your destination instead of toward it. That is exactly how one should feel when reprimanded.

We have already related this story of the chassidic master, R' Bunim of P'shische, who once told his master, the Yehudi *HaKadosh*, that someone had sharply rebuked him and had given him a dressing down such as he had never received before. The Yehudi *HaKadosh*, who knew that his disciple R' Bunim was a *tzaddik*, became enraged. "What did you say to him?" he asked.

"I took hold of him, kissed him, and held him to my heart." He then showed the master a work of *mussar* he had been reading. He saw the teachings of *mussar* as sharp reprimands of his deficiencies in proper observance of Torah. The reproof was as dear to him as the very air he breathed.

One of R' Bunim's disciples was R' Yitzchak Meir of Gur. This outstanding Torah scholar was initially a disciple of the *Maggid* of Kozhnitz. The *Maggid* had great love for R' Yitzchak Meir, and one time embraced him. Thereupon, R' Yitzchak Meir left the *Maggid* for the school of R' Bunim. He revered the *Maggid* greatly, but said, "I do not need a master who adores me. I need a master who will make me tremble."

"Love of reproof" also refers to *giving* reproof with love. The above anecdote of R' Shlomo Zalman's telling the taxi driver to observe Shabbos is an

וֹ/ו וּמִתְרַחֵק מִן הַכָּבוֹד, וְלֹא מֵגִיס לִבּוֹ בְּתַלְמוּדוֹ,
וְאֵינוֹ שָׂמֵחַ בְּהוֹרָאָה, נוֹשֵׂא בְעֹל עִם חֲבֵרוֹ,

example of reproof that was effective because it was given with love.

A *maggid* (preacher) who had delivered a sermon of harsh rebuke and had raised his voice complained to the Chofetz Chaim that he felt his reproof was not well received. The Chofetz Chaim asked, "When you put on *tefillin* this morning did you shout the *berachah* or say it quietly? Giving reproof is indeed a mitzvah, but you do not shout when you fulfill the mitzvah of *tefillin* . Neither should you shout when giving reproof."

Many *tzaddikim* were concerned that because people looked up to them no one would be bold enough to give them reproof. The *Gaon* of Vilna asked the *Maggid* of Dubno to give him reproof. R' Zusia also hired someone for that task.

One Friday night the chassidic master, the Shpoler *Zeide*, turned to his *chassidim* and said, "I am tormented by the thought that I may have lit the Shabbos candles a bit too late in the day." (Many of the chassidic masters lit Shabbos candles in the study.)

The *chassidim* tried to cheer him up. "That cannot be possible," they said. They quoted such passages as, "No sin can befall a *tzaddik*" (*Proverbs* 12:21), or Talmudic statements such as, "God will protect a *tzaddik* from inadvertent sin" (*Yevamos* 99b).

The *tzaddik* was not consoled. He turned to R' Refael Bershid, whose devotion to truth is legendary. "Refael," he said, "you are a dear friend. Tell me the truth."

R' Refael responded, "One cannot dismiss a question of possible violation of Shabbos so lightly. The Rabbi must do *teshuvah.*"

The *tzaddik* turned to his *chassidim*, "Your comforting words could have resulted in my dying without having done *teshuvah*. It was only Reb Refael that saved me."

The Book of *Proverbs* is replete with references to the fact the wise welcome reproof, whereas fools reject it (*Proverbs* 1:7, 1:20-33, 9:8, 12:1, 15:5, 17, 31, 25:12). The wise accept advice, while fools believe they know it all (*Proverbs* 12:15, 13:20, 15:14, 17:16, 18:15, 26:12). The Torah scholar is truly wise. He not only accepts advice and reproof, but seeks it and loves it.

וּמִתְרַחֵק מִן הַכָּבוֹד, וְלֹא מֵגִיס לִבּוֹ בְּתַלְמוּדוֹ, וְאֵינוֹ שָׂמֵחַ בְּהוֹרָאָה
Keeping far from honor, not being arrogant with his learning, not enjoying halachic decision-making

In the earlier chapters much attention was given to the overriding importance of humility. This mishnah stresses that the true Torah scholar, having achieved enormous Torah erudition, does not allow it to turn his head. The prototype of this was Moses, who spoke to God "face to face, as one would speak to a friend" (*Exodus* 33:11).

Yet the Torah states that Moses was the most humble "of all men on earth" (*Numbers* 12:3). Contrary to what we often see in the secular world, where one's high academic status may make him proud, it is just the reverse with Torah. The greater the acquisition of Torah, the more profound is the humility.

As a youngster, R' Menachem of Vitebsk had one day successfully mastered seven pages of Talmud, and was walking with his *yarmulke* tilted a bit. His master, the *Maggid* of Mezeritch, said to him, "Mendele, if seven pages of Talmud results in such pride that you tilt your *yarmulke*, how many pages of Talmud will it take before you remove your *yarmulke* altogether?" These words penetrated to the very heart of the young scholar. For the remainder of his life, he signed his name, "the truly lowly Menachem Mendel."

One might think that referring to oneself as humble is self-contradictory. This is not necessarily so. R' Refael of Bershid said, "I am so grateful that vanity is not a mitzvah. If it were, I could never fulfill it. What do I have to possibly be vain about?"

The humility of R' Mendel was not simulated. Like R' Refael, he felt he was truly lowly.

One Simchas Torah the Chofetz Chaim entered the yeshivah to participate in the *hakafos* (festive circuits with the Torah). The *simchah* was intense. Students gathered around the sage and he expounded on various references on the incomparable value of Torah. Suddenly some of the students began singing the melody, "The *tzaddik* will blossom like the date-palm," a song with which students glorify their Torah mentors.

The Chofetz Chaim turned pale. He covered his eyes as if to become oblivious to the scene before him. It was clear that this acclaim hurt him deeply. Those nearby heard him mumble to himself, "Be strong! One must suffer humiliation to give honor to the Torah." He followed the teaching of the mishnah to its logical conclusion. The true scholar not only avoids honor and arrogance, but actually feels pain when he is honored for his Torah knowledge.

People who knew the Steipler *Gaon* knew that his humility was genuine. When he published his first volume of commentary on the Talmud, he received an endorsement from the acknowledged Torah leader, R' Chaim Ozer Grodzinsky of Vilna. This endorsement would have significantly popularized his work among scholars who had no knowledge of this budding young *gaon*. The endorsement was omitted because of the flattering terms R' Chaim Ozer used about him. When he became the acclaimed Torah scholar of the generation, his humility remained just as profound.

It is an understatement that a Torah scholar does not enjoy making halachic decisions. It is ironic that today some self-anointed Torah "authorities" claim expertise in halachah. In the responsa of the truly outstanding Torah scholars of the past, we often find a closing comment: "What I have said is just my humble opinion. It is not to be taken as halachah until two other Torah scholars concur with it."

Dr. Barnard related that when he performed the world's first heart transplant and saw the vacant cavity in the patient's chest, he was overcome with an awe that bordered on panic. He had removed a person's heart! If his new procedure was unsuccessful he would have killed a human being! This is how a Torah authority feels when giving a halachic opinion. He feels he is dealing with the very heart of the Jewish nation, and that erring in an interpretation of Torah would be catastrophic.

I was privileged to have studied ever so briefly with R' Elkanah Zoberman, who was a Holocaust survivor and came to the United States after the war. One time there was a gathering of halachic authorities who were grappling with a thorny issue. Various opinions were stated and discussed. During the entire proceeding R' Zoberman was silent. When he saw that the discussion was about to end without a clear resolution to the problem, he said, "May I suggest something?" He then proceeded to discuss the issue with a lucidity that left all the attendees stunned. He was later asked why he had not spoken up earlier. He answered, "I was certain someone else would say this." He did not wish to display his scholarship. When it was obvious that the meeting would disband with the problem being unresolved, it was only then that he felt obligated to give his opinion.

Yes, our great Torah scholars did indeed follow in Moses' footsteps.

___

נוֹשֵׂא בְעֹל עִם חֲבֵרוֹ
Sharing his fellow's yoke

R' Yerucham Levovitz devotes an entire essay to this trait (*Daas Chochmah U'Mussar* vol. 4, pp.29-32). He states that this trait is not a derivative of the mitzvah of loving one's fellow man, but rather *extends* it. Furthermore, it is the *very basis of Torah and mitzvos*. It is fulfilled only when a person feels another's pain *as if it were his own*.

R' Yerucham states that he was once asked whether he has any idea how many times he turns from side to side when asleep. He thought the question was absurd. The inquirer stated that he had just visited a sick person who had to maintain one position and could not turn from side to side. R' Yerucham says that he realized at that point that he had never properly fulfilled the mitzvah of *bikur cholim* (visiting the sick). It had not occurred to him to think of how limited a sick person may be in doing what everyone takes for granted, something as simple as turning from side to side. "How great is the suffering of the sick person who cannot do this! I had never given it any thought. I did indeed visit the sick, but I was remiss in not sharing their suffering."

R' Yerucham goes on to say that feeling the burden and suffering of another person underlies all of the mitzvos "between man and fellow man," and probably also those "between man and God."

The degree with which our great Torah personalities identified with others and felt their pain is mind-boggling. My great-grandfather, the Rabbi of Hornostipol, said, "When any of my people feel even a slight pain in their little finger, I feel that pain too." When the *Gaon* of Tshebin was told that his wife had died, he wept. He abruptly interrupted his crying and asked, "What about the other woman in her room? Was she adversely affected by the death of the person who shared her room?"

A tearful father brought his young son to R' Moshe Feinstein. Doctors had diagnosed his child as having bone cancer and said that amputation of his leg was the only hope for his survival, but they could not guarantee the results even then. R' Feinstein began to weep along with the father. He took the father's hand between his two hands and said, "The gates of tears in heaven are never closed. May our tears come before God, and may your child have a *refuah shleimah* (complete recovery)."

In his younger years, while still in Volozhin, R' Chaim Soloveitchik demonstrated his *chesed*. When a huge fire engulfed the city, he broke through the flames to save children who were in the houses. He then ran around town finding children who had fled from the flames and delivered them to their distraught parents.

Perhaps this was just a *chesed*. After all, stories of such heroism are not uncommon. What distinguishes R' Chaim is that later in Brisk, following the fire in 1895 which destroyed many homes, R' Chaim worked tirelessly for the restoration of the homes. During this time, he slept on the floor of the *shul*. His family's entreaties that he come to sleep were refused. "I will not sleep in my bed until every Jew in Brisk has a roof over his head."

There were times in Baranovich when there was not enough money to buy adequate food for the yeshivah kitchen. On those difficult days, R' Elchanan Wasserman took no food or drink. He could not eat when yeshivah students went without adequate food. Some wealthy relatives advised him to give up a yeshivah which was so difficult to finance, and they would support him. He declined, stating that he could not conceive of living in comfort when others were destitute.

Our chronicles are replete with stories such as these. This mishnah came to fulfillment in the lives of our great Torah personages, who *acquired* Torah by their extraordinary feelings for others.

וּמַכְרִיעוֹ לְכַף זְכוּת, וּמַעֲמִידוֹ עַל הָאֱמֶת
Judging him favorably,
setting him on the truthful course

Let me share with you an anecdote that I heard from my teacher, R' Chaim Kreiswirth.

R' Kreiswirth visited the Chazon Ish, and told him of an insight he had that resolved a puzzling conflict in the

Rambam, who appeared to contradict himself. The Chazon Ish listened patiently and made no comment. Their conversation continued for a while, and when R' Kreiswirth arose to leave, the Chazon Ish escorted him to the door. Just as he was about to step out, the Chazon Ish said, "Incidentally, your resolution of the conflict in the Rambam is not correct." He then went on to point out the error.

R' Kreiswirth said, "The Chazon Ish could have corrected me immediately. However, he followed a Talmudic precedent to judge me favorably; i.e., that I might discover my error on my own. When I had not done so and was about to leave, he felt obligated to correct me and set me on the true path."

This is an example of how sensitive a true Torah scholar is to the feelings of other people.

וּמַכְרִיעוֹ לְכַף זְכוּת, וּמַעֲמִידוֹ
עַל הָאֱמֶת, וּמַעֲמִידוֹ עַל הַשָּׁלוֹם
Judging him favorably,
setting him on the truthful course,
setting him on the peaceful course

In the previous chapters, the values of truth, peace, and judging others favorably were cited individually. In this mishnah we may see that they are intertwined. Let me share with you a clinical example, which may serve as an example to be followed in other situations.

I was consulted by a man who stated that his father, who lives with him, complains that when he goes to *shul*, people are constantly doing things intentionally to annoy him. He demands that his son put a stop to this. The son said that when he tells his father that this is not true and that he is imagining it, his father becomes very angry with him. "To keep peace in the house, perhaps I should go along with his idea and tell him that I will do whatever I can to stop this." My advice to him was to tell his father gently that this is not true, even though it may make him angry. Why? Because one should not reinforce a delusion. Doing so will not help his father, and indeed, may cause him to become more delusional. One must stay with the truth, even if it upsets him.

"Judging a person favorably" may also mean making judgments that will be favorable to that person. One should indeed try to keep the peace, but not at the price of compromising the truth.

One may cite the oft-quoted Talmudic statement that "one may lie to promote peace." The fact is that the Talmud does not say this. Rather it says "that a person may *alter* things for the sake of peace" (*Yevamos* 68b). The words of the Talmud are carefully chosen. Had it meant that one may frankly lie, it would have said so. For the sake of peace, one may "alter" a statement which might have a double meaning, as we find when Sarah said, "My master is too old (to father a child)," and God quoted her as saying "I am too old" (*Genesis* 18:13, *Rashi*). One of the commentaries interprets this as God saying that Sarah doubted His capacity to perform the miracle of her bearing a child in her old age, as though God had "grown too old" to perform such feats. Sarah's statement "my master is too old" could apply to either Abraham or to God. To keep the peace, God chose the latter interpretation. One may stretch the truth to keep the peace, but not to frankly lie. Rashi indeed states that Joseph's brothers did lie to him in conveying a message from their father (*Genesis* 50:17), but does not say that this was proper.

The message of the mishnah is that we must indeed try to preserve the peace, but we should exercise great judgment on how far we may stretch the truth.

וּמִתְיַשֵׁב לִבּוֹ בְּתַלְמוּדוֹ
Thinking deliberately in his study

An excellent example of careful deliberation in Torah study is provided by the following anecdote.

R' Yaakov of Lisa and R' Aryeh Leib Heller each wrote excellent expositions on the *Shulchan Aruch*. The *Ketzos HaChoshen*, R' Aryeh Leib's work, became immensely popular among Torah scholars. The *Nesivos HaMishpat* of R' Yaakov is no less a work of genius, but did not achieve the wide acceptance of the *Ketzos HaChosen*. The latter is a standard text in all yeshivos.

When they met, R' Yaakov asked R' Aryeh Leib why it was that his *Ketzos HaChoshen* enjoyed greater popularity than the *Nesivos HaMishpat*. "When do you do your writing?" R' Aryeh Leib asked.

"I do my writing first thing in the morning, when I am well rested and my thinking is clear," R' Yaakov said.

"Perhaps that explains it," R' Aryeh Leib answered. "When I wake up in the morning well rested, and can think clearly, I review what I wrote the day before."

Both were eminent Torah scholars, but R' Aryeh Leib's deliberation and rethinking of what he had written earlier made it the superior work.

שׁוֹאֵל וּמֵשִׁיב
Asking and answering

What is so special about "asking and answering"? Everyone asks questions, and everyone responds to a question when asked. Perhaps this is the reason that other texts read "asks pertinent questions and answers to the point." Some students may ask questions that are not related to the topic under discussion, and teachers may sometimes give evasive answers, particularly if they are stumped by the question. It is one of the attributes of Rashi that he does not hesitate to sometimes state, "I don't know" (e.g., *Genesis* 43:11).

However, our text must also have meaning. Perhaps it means that when a Torah scholar asks a question, it is posed so clearly that it provides the answer. There is an aphorism, "The question of a wise man is half the answer." A question may sometimes be the result of incomplete understanding of the subject. Properly formulating the question may clarify the issue, so that the answer becomes obvious.

One of the best ways of resolving a problem in Torah study is to write it down as if one were posing the question to another scholar in a letter. In the process of formulating the question with lucidity, the answer often becomes obvious.

It is said that when students pose a difficult problem to a teacher, both are pleased. The student is pleased because he has discovered a difficulty in the subject that may not have been previously detected. The teacher is pleased because in providing an answer to the question, he feels he has revealed his erudition. When a difficult problem was posed to R' Chaim of Brisk, no one was pleased. R' Chaim would not provide an answer to the question. Rather, by going over the subject material with the student, he would so clarify it that the question would disappear. The student would realize that he had not understood the subject well enough, which is hardly anything to be proud of. R' Chaim would not be particularly pleased because he felt he had done nothing other than to explain the material. He did not feel that he had contributed anything new.

A question in Talmudic study may appear to constitute a problem only because the student did not have a clear understanding of the material. Given his misunderstanding, the question may indeed have been ingenious. A teacher will not be critical of the student's failure to understand the issue. On the contrary, he will praise him for his acuity in raising the question, then proceed to resolve the problem by setting the student straight.

Pointing out an error to a student may sometimes come across as criticism. One of my Talmud teachers would often respond to a student's question by what appeared to be an amusing contradiction. He would say in his less-than-perfect English, "You 100 prozent right. Now I going to show you where you wrong!" The student was encouraged by the teacher's appreciation that his question was indeed thoughtful even if his premise was in error.

שׁוֹמֵעַ וּמוֹסִיף
Listening and contributing to the discussion

Again, this translation is not literal. The literal translation is "listens and adds."

Obviously, a scholar who listens adds to his knowledge. In what way is this attribute to be considered special in the acquisition of Torah?

A difficulty in understanding a particular portion of Torah may be due to insufficient knowledge of other information that would elucidate this particular problem. Trying to analyze the question at hand may be futile because of lack of pertinent information. This is what the *Jerusalem Talmud* means when it says, "Words of Torah may appear obtuse in one place, but are lucid in another place" (*Rosh Hashanah* 3:5).

This is why someone who may have acquired Torah knowledge in the yeshivah and may be considered a fine *talmid chacham* (Torah scholar) should not assume that he knows enough to make halachic decisions. The latter requires a degree of clarity and understanding that is attained only by one who knows all of the Talmud. Anyone who falls short of this may think that he fully understands a particular subject. However, his understanding may be incomplete because he lacks important relevant information that is contained in the part of the Talmud which he has not learned.

This is what the mishnah means. Of course a student who listens to any lecture adds to his knowledge. The Torah scholar is unique in that whatever he learns adds to his knowledge *exponentially* rather than linearly. Any new learning may shed light on a variety of other subjects.

הַלּוֹמֵד עַל מְנָת לְלַמֵּד,
וְהַלּוֹמֵד עַל מְנָת לַעֲשׂוֹת
*Learning in order to teach,
learning in order to practice*

A student once presented his instructor with what he felt was a novel approach to the *halachos* of evidence. This insight would resolve a thorny problem in *Tosafos* (commentary on the Talmud).

"Tell me," the teacher said, "would you apply this novel concept to make questionable evidence acceptable in the case of an *agunah* (a woman whose husband is missing and it is not known if he is living or not)?"

"No, of course not," the student said. "I just meant it as a theoretical concept."

"Then don't bother with it," the teacher said. "If it is not sufficiently strong to be applied in halachah, it is not worth considering."

The teacher's point was that "Torah" means "guidance." If a Torah teaching is so abstract that it cannot be applied as a practical guide, it is not true Torah.

There is a version of the mishnah that reads, "asks pertinent questions and responds according to halachah." Perhaps this is what the mishnah means. The true Torah scholar provides answers that can be implemented in halachah.

In the letter to his son, Ramban instructs him, "When you finish a session of Torah study, see what there is in what you have learned that you can apply in what you do."

The first *berachah* we recite for Torah in the morning is that God has commanded us "to engage in the words of Torah." It is noteworthy that we do not refer to the mitzvah of "learning" Torah but rather of "engaging" in Torah. This means that we are to conduct ourselves according to Torah.

Some people have an erroneous notion that we act according to Torah law when we observe Shabbos, put on *tefillin*, avoid non-kosher foods, etc. However, they may think that the acts of daily life are not directly concerned with Torah. Nothing could be further from the truth.

הַמַּחְכִּים אֶת רַבּוֹ, וְהַמְכַוֵּן אֶת שְׁמוּעָתוֹ, וְהָאוֹמֵר דָּבָר בְּשֵׁם אוֹמְרוֹ. הָא לָמַדְתָּ, כָּל הָאוֹמֵר דָּבָר בְּשֵׁם אוֹמְרוֹ, מֵבִיא גְאֻלָּה לָעוֹלָם, שֶׁנֶּאֱמַר: "וַתֹּאמֶר אֶסְתֵּר לַמֶּלֶךְ בְּשֵׁם מָרְדֳּכָי."

A farmer is immersed in Torah observance throughout his workday. When he plows, he may not use two animals of different species to pull the plow. He may not intermix various plants. When harvesting, he may not pick up stalks of grain that have fallen or retrieve sheaves that have been forgotten. He must leave a corner of his field for the poor. He must tithe. He may not muzzle the ox in threshing grain. In the seventh year he may not work his farm at all. These are but some of the Torah laws that apply to farming.

The businessman must be careful that his weights are accurate. He may not mislead a customer. He may not lend or borrow money on interest.

In any walk of life, a person must guard his speech to avoid even a trace of *lashon hara* (speaking badly of someone). A person may not pass by a lost article, but must pick it up and seek out its owner. The Torah prescribes how to relate towards parents, toward the elderly, and toward scholars. One must at all times speak the truth. One may not stand by idly if one can prevent harm to another person. One may not seek revenge or harbor a grudge.

These are just some of the mitzvos that apply to daily activities. Of course, there are also the mitzvos of prayer, of the blessings before and after partaking of food, of learning Torah, and of teaching Torah to one's children. The early morning *berachah* is meant to set the tone for the day. We are to "engage" in Torah, and to conduct ourselves according to Torah in everything we do.

We sometimes hear youngsters complain that they are bored by Torah study. If this is so, it is due to the failure of the teacher to make Torah come alive. If Torah is approached as an abstract study, it may indeed be boring.

The two qualities cited above are related. The person who learns Torah with the intent to apply it is also one who can teach it effectively.

הַמַּחְכִּים אֶת רַבּוֹ
Making his teacher wiser

We have noted the Talmudic statement, "I learned much from my teachers, more from my colleagues, but most of all from my students" (*Taanis* 7a). A diligent student insists on his teacher clarifying concepts for him, and in doing so, the teacher gains a much better grasp of the material. Torah teachers held their diligent students in high esteem.

The Torah scholar, R' Eizel *HaCharif* (the brilliant), wished to acquire a superior Torah scholar as a husband for his daughter. He went to one of the leading yeshivos and gave a lecture, in which he raised a very difficult problem

making his teacher wiser, pondering over what he has learned, and repeating a saying in the name of the one who said it. For you have learned this: Whoever repeats a thing in the name of the one who said it brings redemption to the world, as it is said: And Esther said to the king in the name of Mordechai (Esther 2:22).

---

in a particular Talmudic subject. He stated that any student who could resolve the difficulty would be considered as a candidate to become his son-in-law. Various students proposed solutions to the problem, but he refuted all of them. When no one presented a satisfactory answer, R' Eizel left the yeshivah.

As his coach pulled away, R' Eizel heard a shout and saw that one of the students was calling to him. The student was breathless as he overtook him. "Did you find the answer to the problem?" R' Eizel asked.

The student said, "No, I did not. It does not concern me whether I become your son-in-law. But I must know the answer to the problem. Please tell it to me."

R' Eizel told the student the answer and said, "You are the one I desire for my daughter. Of all the students, you are the only one who could not be at peace without knowing the answer." R' Eizel appreciated the value of a student whose thirst for Torah knowledge was intense. Students such as this, who persist in attaining an understanding of Torah, do indeed make the teacher wiser.

An alternative translation of this phrase is "appreciating the wisdom of his teacher" (*Midrash Shmuel*). In the secular world, students often feel they have surpassed their teachers. With new scientific information and more advanced technology available, progressive generations feel superior to their predecessors. Our Torah scholars held their forebears and teachers in high esteem, and never felt equal to them.

My older brothers were students of R' Shlomo Heiman. One time R' Heiman delivered a brilliant discourse on a difficult Talmudic question. His reasoning appeared to be flawless. He sighed and said, "Although my answer to the question appears valid, I am afraid it is not so. You see, the question was posed by R' Akiva Eiger, who commented that he could not find a satisfactory answer. I cannot conceive that I was able to find an answer that escaped the mind of R' Akiva Eiger."

R' Elchanan Wasserman asked the Chofetz Chaim, "How do we know when a particular era ends and a period of lesser authority begins? In the Talmud there was the era of the *Tannaim* (authors of the Mishnah) followed by an era of *Amoraim* (compilers of the Gemara). Then came the period of the *Geonim* followed by the *Rishonim* and the *Acharonim*. What determines the closure of an era?"

The Chofetz Chaim responded, "At the end of every era there is one individual who is clearly of such vast and comprehensive knowledge of Torah that he is capable of organizing all that preceded him. At the closure of the Tannaic era there was R' Yehudah *HaNasi* who organized the Mishnah. At the end of the Amoraic period there was Rav Ashi, who did the same for the Gemara. Rav Hai *Gaon* closed the Geonic period, and so on."

R' Elchanan stated that the Chofetz Chaim's humility was such that he was not aware that he himself was the Torah personality that brought the recent era to a close.

R' Elchanan was well qualified to assess the magnitude of Torah scholars. "There is no one," he said, "who can grasp the enormity of the Chofetz Chaim's Torah knowledge."

In secular studies, we often find later philosophers and scientists who refute the opinions of their forebears. Not so in Torah writings. The Torah scholar who may disagree with an opinion of a scholar of the previous generation says, "I have not merited to understand him."

וְהַמְכַוֵּן אֶת שְׁמוּעָתוֹ
Pondering over what
he has learned

There are a number of translations of the phrase הַמְכַוֵּן אֶת שְׁמוּעָתוֹ. I might take the liberty of translating the word מְכַוֵּן to mean "giving direction," as when one directs an arrow toward a target or toward a specific point. The quality which the mishnah is citing is the capacity to focus on a particular issue, and not allow oneself to be distracted by any extraneous thoughts.

The power of focusing and directing all one's energies toward a specific point has been demonstrated in karate. Under usual circumstances, a person's energies are diffused throughout his entire system. If he can learn how to gather all his energies and bring them to bear at one specific point, he can accomplish unusual feats, such as breaking a brick with the stroke of his hand. An analogous phenomenon occurs with the laser beam. Normal light is comprised of a number of light rays of varying wavelengths. If one can concentrate all the light rays to one wavelength, the result is a beam of light that can penetrate solid objects.

This is also true of Torah. A scholar may have his thoughts diffused over a number of subjects. If he can avoid such diffusion, and bring his mind to concentrate on a single issue, the intensity of his thinking can be as penetrating as a laser beam. I suspect that our great Torah scholars did just that. They dismissed anything that was not immediately pertinent to the topic at hand. They thereby developed an acuity and clarity of thought which made a profound impression on the mind. This may well account for their phenomenal memories.

We have a tendency for our thoughts to drift. If we can focus our attention on the issue at hand, we may be surprised at our mental acuity.

וְהָאוֹמֵר דָּבָר בְּשֵׁם אוֹמְרוֹ
And repeating a saying in the name of the one who said it

To take credit for another person's idea is frank plagiarism, which is universally condemned and is forbidden by law. This mishnah is enumerating qualities that characterize a true Torah scholar. It hardly seems likely that there is a need to say that a Torah scholar should not be a plagiarist!

Perhaps the mishnah is referring to the importance of ascribing a saying to whoever *one believed to be* its author. This may help establish the authenticity of the statement.

A student once related to R' Issar Zalman Meltzer something that he read in the *Pri Megadim* (a commentary on the *Shulchan Aruch*). R' Issar Zalman remarked, "The *Pri Megadim* did not say that." The student was about to reach for the *Pri Megadim* to find the source, when R' Issar Zalman restrained him. "Let us first see whether it is possible for the *Pri Megadim* to have said that." He then proceeded to explain the *Pri Megadim's* method of analysis, and showed the student that this particular statement would be inconsistent with the *Pri Megadim's* approach. When he finished he said to the student, "Now you may consult the work to find your source." Of course, there was no such statement in the *Pri Megadim*.

"Do not think that I know the *Pri Megadim* by heart, because I do not," R' Issar Zalman said. "However, knowing the approach a Torah scholar has in Torah enables one to know what kind of statements he may have made."

In a similar vein, R' Shlomo Zalman Auerbach permitted the use of a hearing aid on Shabbos. Someone who disagreed with him said that the amplification of the hearing aid is no different than a microphone. He quoted R' Aaron Kotler as having said that one may not converse on Shabbos with someone wearing a hearing aid, just as one may not speak into a microphone.

R' Shlomo Zalman said, "If you wish to debate the point, I will be glad to do so. However, please do not quote R' Aaron Kotler in support of your position. It is simply impossible for him to have made that statement." R' Shlomo Zalman knew that it would have been inconsistent for R' Kotler to have given that opinion.

We have concluded the 48 prerequisites for the *acquisition* of Torah. We are told that God gave the Torah in the desert to indicate that just as no one has exclusive ownership of the desert, neither is the Torah the exclusive possession of any individual or group. This is in sharp contrast to other faiths, where the authentic knowledge of the teachings of the faith was a closely guarded secret, usually restricted to the priestly class. Torah is available for everyone to take.

There is another distinction between Torah knowledge and other bodies of knowledge. Torah requires that one have the proper character traits. A

[ז] **גְּדוֹלָה** תוֹרָה, שֶׁהִיא נוֹתֶנֶת חַיִּים לְעוֹשֶׂיהָ בָּעוֹלָם
הַזֶּה וּבָעוֹלָם הַבָּא, שֶׁנֶּאֱמַר: „כִּי חַיִּים הֵם
לְמֹצְאֵיהֶם, וּלְכָל בְּשָׂרוֹ מַרְפֵּא." וְאוֹמֵר: „רִפְאוּת תְּהִי
לְשָׁרֶּךָ, וְשִׁקּוּי לְעַצְמוֹתֶיךָ." וְאוֹמֵר: „עֵץ חַיִּים הִיא
לַמַּחֲזִיקִים בָּהּ וְתֹמְכֶיהָ מְאֻשָּׁר." וְאוֹמֵר: „כִּי לִוְיַת חֵן הֵם
לְרֹאשֶׁךָ, וַעֲנָקִים לְגַרְגְּרֹתֶיךָ." וְאוֹמֵר: „תִּתֵּן לְרֹאשְׁךָ לִוְיַת
חֵן, עֲטֶרֶת תִּפְאֶרֶת תְּמַגְּנֶךָּ." וְאוֹמֵר: „כִּי בִי יִרְבּוּ יָמֶיךָ,
וְיוֹסִיפוּ לְךָ שְׁנוֹת חַיִּים." וְאוֹמֵר: „אֹרֶךְ יָמִים בִּימִינָהּ,
בִּשְׂמֹאולָהּ עֹשֶׁר וְכָבוֹד." וְאוֹמֵר: „כִּי אֹרֶךְ יָמִים וּשְׁנוֹת
חַיִּים, וְשָׁלוֹם יוֹסִיפוּ לָךְ."

---

person's genealogy or social status does not render him privy to Torah. It is one's *middos* that determine whether or not he will acquire Torah.

It is, of course, possible for a person who lacks *middos* to read Scripture and Talmud and even to achieve some proficiency in them. However, that knowledge is not Torah. Torah is a teaching and a guide, and is such only when it is implemented.

One might ask: If Torah is contingent on *middos*, and *middos* are attainable only by implementing Torah, do we then have a "Catch-22" situation? The answer is that one may begin acquisition of Torah with rudimentary *middos*, with the hope that the Torah he learns will enable him to develop his *middos* to the fullest.

I am not aware of any body of secular knowledge that requires the student to have proper character traits as essential attributes for mastering that body of knowledge. Yes, Torah is different. *Very* different.

7.

גְּדוֹלָה תוֹרָה, שֶׁהִיא נוֹתֶנֶת חַיִּים
Great is the Torah, for it confers life

The mishnah cites seven verses in support of the statement that Torah confers life. Why so many? Would not one or two verses have sufficed?

The term *Toras Chaim* is often translated as "a Torah of life" or "a living Torah." These terms fail to convey the concept of this mishnah. What the mishnah is saying is that the term "chaim" is not an adjective which describes Torah, but rather a noun, which is identical to Torah. In other words, *Toras Chaim* means a "Torah which is life."

Earlier we cited the Talmudic statement that the wicked are considered dead even when they are alive" (*Berachos* 18 a,b). We pointed out that the human being is a composite creature. He is comprised of a body which is essentially an

7. **G**reat is the Torah, for it confers life upon its practitioners, both in this world and in the World to Come, as it is said: For they [the teachings of the Torah] are life to those who find them, and a healing to his entire flesh (Proverbs 4:22). And it says: It shall be healing to your flesh and marrow to your bones (ibid. 3:8). And it says: It is a tree of life to those who grasp it, and its supporters are praiseworthy (ibid. 3:18). And it says: They are a tiara of grace for your head and necklaces for your neck (ibid. 1:9). And it says: It will give to your head a tiara of grace, a crown of glory it will deliver to you (ibid. 4:9). And it says: Indeed, through me [the Torah] your days shall be increased, and years of life shall be added to you (ibid. 9:11). And it says: Lengthy days are at its right, and at its left are wealth and honor (ibid. 3:16). And it says: For lengthy days and years of life, and peace shall they add to you (ibid. 3:2).

---

animal body, and a *neshamah*. The human body has drives and cravings which are no different than those of other forms of life. He indeed has an intellect which is superior to that of animals, but if he utilizes this intellect merely as a tool to gratify his animalistic drives, it, too, remains subhuman. Man's qualitative distinction from other forms of life is the *neshamah*. When a person functions according to the needs of the *neshamah*, he is functioning as a human being. If he neglects the needs of the *neshamah* and is occupied with gratifying his physical drives, he is alive *as an animal*, but his human component is dead.

All human beings have a *neshamah*. The *neshamah* of the Jew is fulfilled when he observes all the mitzvos of the Torah. The *neshamah* of the non-Jew is fulfilled when he observes the seven categories of the Noahide mitzvos. In either case, failure to actualize the *neshamah* renders a person *spiritually lifeless*. As a unique human being, he is considered dead even though he breathes and metabolizes, *even though he may compose great literary works and operate highly sophisticated technological apparatus*.

The Torah states that man was created "in the image of God." This refers to his *neshamah*, which is of Divine origin. We are considered "children of God" (*Exodus* 4:22), and as such we have some resemblance to our Father.

I am indebted to Rebbetzin Feige Twerski for the following anecdote. Prior to Passover, mothers were taking their children to the clothing store to have them outfitted for the festival. One child whose family could not afford new clothes peered through the store window at the other children who were getting

[ח] **רַבִּי** שִׁמְעוֹן בֶּן יְהוּדָה מִשּׁוּם רַבִּי שִׁמְעוֹן בֶּן יוֹחַאי
אוֹמֵר: הַנּוֹי, וְהַכֹּחַ, וְהָעֹשֶׁר, וְהַכָּבוֹד,
וְהַחָכְמָה, וְהַזִּקְנָה, וְהַשֵּׂיבָה, וְהַבָּנִים – נָאֶה לַצַּדִּיקִים
וְנָאֶה לָעוֹלָם, שֶׁנֶּאֱמַר: „עֲטֶרֶת תִּפְאֶרֶת שֵׂיבָה, בְּדֶרֶךְ

---

suits, dresses, and shoes. As one woman emerged from the store, she saw the expression of pain on this child's face. She took the child into the store and bought him a suit and shoes.

The child looked up at his benefactor and said, "Are you God?" The woman was taken aback by the child's question but managed to answer, "No. I'm just one of His children." The child nodded and said, "I knew you must be related!"

Yes, when we do *chesed* we are in the image of God, and we are indeed related.

In the account of Creation, man is given dominance over all living things. Indeed, the Talmud states that a beast could not overcome a human being "unless the latter appeared to it as an animal" (*Shabbos* 151b). In other words, man maintains his dominion over animals only as long as he is "in the image of God." If this is in any way defective, he becomes subject to the strength of beasts. It is written that Daniel's survival in the lions' den was not a miracle. Rather, because Daniel's "image of God" was completely intact, his dominion over animals was a natural phenomenon, in keeping with the superiority given to man in Creation.

Man's *neshamah* is Godly, and this makes it possible for man to identify with God. Ramban states that while technical observance of all 613 mitzvos is mandatory, the identification with God does not occur as long as man indulges himself, even if he is not in frank violation of Torah. God states, "You shall be holy, because I, your God, am holy" (*Leviticus* 19:2). Man's holiness is dependent on his becoming spiritual, on fulfilling the needs of the *neshamah*.

The Talmud states that R' Tarfon said to his colleague, R' Akiva, "Akiva, anyone who separates from you is separating from life itself" (*Kiddushin* 66b). Knowing that R' Akiva's interpretation of Torah was valid, he considered being deprived of authentic Torah teachings as being deprived of life.

This also explains why the mishnah says that Torah provides life in the Eternal World. It is generally assumed that in *Gan Eden* (Paradise) there are no physical bodies. It is the *neshamah* that exists in *Gan Eden*. A *neshamah* which was properly nurtured with Torah continues to live in the Eternal World.

We may now have another insight into the introductory passage to *Ethics of the Fathers*: "All Israel has a share in the World to Come." As noted, every person is comprised of two portions, the body and the *neshamah*. Everyone therefore has a share of his being, a *neshamah*, which will have an existence in the Eternal World.

Most people equate life with the period of time when a person's mind and

8. **R**abbi Shimon ben Yehudah says in the name of Rabbi Shimon ben Yochai: Beauty, strength, wealth, honor, wisdom, old age, hoary age, and children — these grace the righteous and grace the world, as it is said: Ripe old age is a crown of splendor, it can be found in the path of

---

body are functioning. They think of death as the cessation of such functioning. The concept of human life as being the life of the spirit rather than that of the body may be difficult to grasp. This is why the mishnah cites repeated references from various portions of Scripture, to stress the concept of human life as being that of the *neshamah*.

8.

הַנּוֹי, וְהַכֹּחַ . . .
נָאֶה לַצַּדִּיקִים וְנָאֶה לָעוֹלָם
Beauty, strength . . . these grace the righteous and grace the world

A more accurate translation of this mishnah is that all these attributes *grace tzaddikim and grace the world.* The mishnah wishes to tell us that these attributes are beneficial to the world *only* when they belong to the righteous. The same attributes in the wrong hands can be very harmful to the world.

I once heard Rabbi Eliezer Silver comment on the miracle of Moses' rod turning into a serpent. He said that Moses' rod was an instrument of many beneficial phenomena, dividing the waters of the Red Sea to save the Israelites and bringing forth water from a rock in the desert. However, the rod was a benevolent tool only when it was in the hands of Moses and Aaron, who were spiritual people. When it left the hands of spiritual people, this same rod became a venomous serpent.

Today the wondrous rod is represented by science and technology, which have indeed wrought many miracles. However, the world can benefit from science and technology only when they are the instruments of responsible, spiritual people. Nuclear fission can provide undreamed-of sources of energy. Radiation can be used to diagnose and cure deadly diseases. These very tools can also be used to wipe out an entire population in seconds. The Internet can be used to bring unprecedented sources of valuable information to every man, woman, and child. It can also supply them with obscene material. Television could have been an excellent vehicle for education and appropriate amusement, but instead has become a wellspring of immorality and violence. The beauty of the human body could be an example of the beauty in creation. Instead it has been corrupted to appeal to man's basest drives.

"These grace the righteous and they grace the world." All the attributes in the mishnah are indeed advantageous to the world, but only when they are in the possession of spiritual people.

צְדָקָה תִּמָּצֵא." וְאוֹמֵר: "עֲטֶרֶת זְקֵנִים בְּנֵי בָנִים, וְתִפְאֶרֶת בָּנִים אֲבוֹתָם." וְאוֹמֵר: "תִּפְאֶרֶת בַּחוּרִים כֹּחָם, וַהֲדַר זְקֵנִים שֵׂיבָה." וְאוֹמֵר: "וְחָפְרָה הַלְּבָנָה וּבוֹשָׁה הַחַמָּה, כִּי מָלַךְ יהוה צְבָאוֹת בְּהַר צִיּוֹן וּבִירוּשָׁלַיִם, וְנֶגֶד זְקֵנָיו כָּבוֹד." רַבִּי שִׁמְעוֹן בֶּן מְנַסְיָא אוֹמֵר: אֵלּוּ שֶׁבַע מִדּוֹת, שֶׁמָּנוּ חֲכָמִים לַצַּדִּיקִים, כֻּלָּם נִתְקַיְּמוּ בְּרַבִּי וּבְבָנָיו.

[ט] **אָמַר** רַבִּי יוֹסֵי בֶּן קִסְמָא: פַּעַם אַחַת הָיִיתִי מְהַלֵּךְ בַּדֶּרֶךְ, וּפָגַע בִּי אָדָם אֶחָד. וְנָתַן לִי שָׁלוֹם, וְהֶחֱזַרְתִּי לוֹ שָׁלוֹם. אָמַר לִי: "רַבִּי, מֵאֵיזֶה מָקוֹם אָתָּה?" אָמַרְתִּי לוֹ: "מֵעִיר גְּדוֹלָה שֶׁל חֲכָמִים וְשֶׁל סוֹפְרִים אָנִי." אָמַר לִי: "רַבִּי, רְצוֹנְךָ שֶׁתָּדוּר עִמָּנוּ בִּמְקוֹמֵנוּ וַאֲנִי אֶתֵּן לְךָ אֶלֶף אֲלָפִים דִּינָרֵי זָהָב וַאֲבָנִים טוֹבוֹת וּמַרְגָּלִיּוֹת?" אָמַרְתִּי לוֹ: "אִם אַתָּה נוֹתֵן לִי כָּל כֶּסֶף וְזָהָב וַאֲבָנִים טוֹבוֹת וּמַרְגָּלִיּוֹת שֶׁבָּעוֹלָם, אֵינִי דָר אֶלָּא בִּמְקוֹם תּוֹרָה." וְכֵן כָּתוּב בְּסֵפֶר תְּהִלִּים עַל יְדֵי דָוִד מֶלֶךְ יִשְׂרָאֵל: "טוֹב לִי תוֹרַת פִּיךָ מֵאַלְפֵי זָהָב וָכָסֶף." וְלֹא עוֹד אֶלָּא שֶׁבִּשְׁעַת פְּטִירָתוֹ שֶׁל אָדָם אֵין

9.

אָמַר רַבִּי יוֹסֵי בֶּן קִסְמָא
R' Yose ben Kisma said

The dialogue between R' Yose ben Kisma and the man who met him has given rise to many interpretations. It is clear that the mishnah wishes to emphasize the importance of living in a Torah environment. But of what significance are the details of "once I was walking on the road," and "he greeted me"?

We have repeatedly emphasized the importance of *middos*, and stressed that courtesy and respect are prerequisites for Torah (*Vayikra Rabbah 9:3*). However, we have also noted (3:21) that "In the absence of Torah, there can be no *derech eretz* (proper ethical conduct)." These prerequisites must quickly be reinforced by Torah. Formal courtesy and etiquette that are not supported by Torah are merely a window dressing that contribute nothing to a person's character. No country was as well versed in proper decorum as prewar Germany, whose expressions such as *"bitte"* and *"danke schoen"* did nothing to prevent them from behavior that was far beneath that of brute beasts.

righteousness (Proverbs 16:31). And it says: The crown of the aged is grandchildren, and the splendor of children is their fathers (ibid. 17:6). And it says: The splendor of young men is their strength, and the glory of old men is hoary age (ibid. 20:29). And it says: The moon will grow pale and the sun be shamed, when God, Master of Legions, will have reigned on Mount Zion and in Jerusalem, and honor shall be before His elders (Isaiah 24:23). Rabbi Shimon ben Menasya said: These seven qualities that the Sages attributed to the righteous were all realized in Rabbi and his sons.

9. **R**abbi Yose ben Kisma said: Once I was walking on the road, when a certain man met me. He greeted me and I returned his greeting. He said to me, "Rabbi, from what place are you?" I said to him, "I am from a great city of scholars and sages." He said to me, "Rabbi, would you be willing to live with us in our place? I would give you thousands upon thousands of golden dinars, precious stones and pearls." I replied, "Even if you were to give me all the silver and gold, precious stones and pearls in the world, I would dwell nowhere but in a place of Torah." And so it is written in the Book of Psalms by David, King of Israel: "I prefer the Torah of Your mouth above thousands in gold and silver." Furthermore, when a man departs from

---

The Talmud stresses the importance of initiating a greeting (Above, 4:20). Yet, the man who met R' Yose preempted him and greeted the sage first! Clearly a person of distinguished behavior! He then asked R' Yose, "What city do you come from?" The Chofetz Chaim said that the intent of this question was, "Do you mean that in your community they allow a person of your stature to travel on foot and unaccompanied? Why, in our city we would never allow that to occur. We know how to respect people of distinction. You would fare better living with us." He then offered R' Yose a huge sum of money to take up residence in his community.

R' Yose understood that this person's concepts of superficial manners and his overvaluation of money are related. He responded to the question as to why he was traveling on foot and unaccompanied. He explained that there are very many outstanding Torah scholars in his community, hence it is not feasible to

מְלַוִּין לוֹ לְאָדָם לֹא כֶסֶף וְלֹא זָהָב וְלֹא אֲבָנִים טוֹבוֹת
וּמַרְגָּלִיּוֹת, אֶלָּא תוֹרָה וּמַעֲשִׂים טוֹבִים בִּלְבָד, שֶׁנֶּאֱמַר:
„בְּהִתְהַלֶּכְךָ תַּנְחֶה אֹתָךְ, בְּשָׁכְבְּךָ תִּשְׁמֹר עָלֶיךָ, וַהֲקִיצוֹתָ
הִיא תְשִׂיחֶךָ.‟ „בְּהִתְהַלֶּכְךָ תַּנְחֶה אֹתָךְ‟ – בָּעוֹלָם הַזֶּה;
„בְּשָׁכְבְּךָ תִּשְׁמֹר עָלֶיךָ‟ – בַּקֶּבֶר; „וַהֲקִיצוֹתָ הִיא תְשִׂיחֶךָ‟
– לָעוֹלָם הַבָּא. וְאוֹמֵר: „לִי הַכֶּסֶף וְלִי הַזָּהָב, נְאֻם יהוה
צְבָאוֹת.‟

[יא] חֲמִשָּׁה קִנְיָנִים קָנָה הַקָּדוֹשׁ בָּרוּךְ הוּא בָּעוֹלָמוֹ,
וְאֵלּוּ הֵן: תּוֹרָה – קִנְיָן אֶחָד, שָׁמַיִם וָאָרֶץ
– קִנְיָן אֶחָד, אַבְרָהָם – קִנְיָן אֶחָד, יִשְׂרָאֵל – קִנְיָן אֶחָד,
בֵּית הַמִּקְדָּשׁ – קִנְיָן אֶחָד. תּוֹרָה מִנַּיִן? דִּכְתִיב: „יהוה קָנָנִי

supply them all with travel means and escorts.

R' Yose did not stop at this point. The invitation to come to this man's community was obviously to become its spiritual leader. R' Yose pointed out to the man that he lacked the basic underpinnings of spirituality.

Many people have an intellectual understanding of spiritual concepts, but it may not impact on their emotions and behavior. For example, everyone knows that one does not take along any of his wealth after death. It is not unusual for people to comment at the funeral of a wealthy person, "Here at the cemetery, the rich and poor are all alike." They then return home and promptly absorb themselves in the pursuit of wealth. I have often told people that I have never heard a person in the last days of life say, "My only regret is that I did not spend more time at the office." People only lament not having spent more time with the family. Everyone in the audience nods their head in the affirmative, and then they go on with their usual pattern. This is because their intellectual understanding does not filter down to an emotional understanding. Superficial concepts do not impact upon behavior.

I have pointed out to many people that their lifestyle is not too dissimilar from the self-destructive lifestyles of the people I treat for addiction. Every addict knows intellectually that the chemical he uses is harmful, just as the smoker knows that cigarettes are toxic. Yet, these people are driven by a compulsion to use drugs or smoke. When a person is compelled to do something that he intellectually understands to be harmful, this must be recognized as an addiction. The person who knows that it is most important to spend more time with the family, yet cannot tear himself away from the office, bears a similarity to the addict.

R' Yose's teaching can apply to many people. When we know something to be right, we must adopt it in our behavior.

this world, neither silver, nor gold, nor precious stones nor pearls escort him, but only Torah study and good deeds, as it is said: "When you walk, it shall guide you; when you lie down, it shall guard you; and when you awake, it shall speak on your behalf." "When you walk, it shall guide you" — in this world; "when you lie down, it shall guard you" — in the grave; "and when you awake, it shall speak on your behalf" — in the World to Come. And it says: "Mine is the silver, and Mine is the gold, says HASHEM, Master of Legions (Chaggai 2:8)."

10. **F**ive *possessions did the Holy One, Blessed is He, acquire for Himself in His world, and they are: Torah, one possession; heaven and earth, one possession; Abraham, one possession; Israel, one possession; the Holy Temple, one possession. From where do we know this about the Torah? Since it is written: God acquired me [the Torah]*

10.

חֲמִשָּׁה קִנְיָנִים
Five possessions

If we allow ourselves a bit of homiletic license, we can give this mishnah a rather novel interpretation. Indeed, it seems that this is the way it was understood by *Sfas Emes.*

The psalmist states, "How many are Your deeds, O God! You have made them all with wisdom. The world is full of Your acquisitions" (*Psalms* 104:24). One of the chassidic masters translated this verse as, "The world is full *of ways in which to acquire You.*" This follows Rambam's assertion that one who looks at the marvelous structure of the world intelligently will come to the realization and love of God. If this was true in Rambam's time, how much more so in our time. Powerful microscopes and telescopes have given us unprecedented access to both the microcosm and the macrocosm. We can appreciate the majesty of God as never before.

We may interpret this mishnah along the same lines. I.e., there are primarily five ways in which man can acquire God. These five ways provide the means whereby one can be aware of God's existence and one can develop a relationship with Him.

The first way is Torah. As we have noted earlier, God put Himself into the Torah. When we embrace Torah we are embracing God. Study of the Torah and performance of the mitzvos is the bridge that spans the gap between finite man and infinite God.

רֵאשִׁית דַּרְכּוֹ, קֶדֶם מִפְעָלָיו מֵאָז." שָׁמַיִם וָאָרֶץ מִנַּיִן?
דִּכְתִיב: „כֹּה אָמַר יהוה, הַשָּׁמַיִם כִּסְאִי, וְהָאָרֶץ הֲדֹם רַגְלָי,
אֵי זֶה בַיִת אֲשֶׁר תִּבְנוּ לִי, וְאֵי זֶה מָקוֹם מְנוּחָתִי"; וְאוֹמֵר:
„מָה רַבּוּ מַעֲשֶׂיךָ יהוה, כֻּלָּם בְּחָכְמָה עָשִׂיתָ, מָלְאָה הָאָרֶץ
קִנְיָנֶךָ." אַבְרָהָם מִנַּיִן? דִּכְתִיב: „וַיְבָרְכֵהוּ וַיֹּאמַר, בָּרוּךְ
אַבְרָם לְאֵל עֶלְיוֹן, קֹנֵה שָׁמַיִם וָאָרֶץ." יִשְׂרָאֵל מִנַּיִן?
דִּכְתִיב: „עַד יַעֲבֹר עַמְּךָ יהוה, עַד יַעֲבֹר עַם זוּ קָנִיתָ";
וְאוֹמֵר: „לִקְדוֹשִׁים אֲשֶׁר בָּאָרֶץ הֵמָּה, וְאַדִּירֵי כָּל חֶפְצִי
בָם." בֵּית הַמִּקְדָּשׁ מִנַּיִן? דִּכְתִיב: „מָכוֹן לְשִׁבְתְּךָ פָּעַלְתָּ
יהוה, מִקְדָּשׁ אֲדֹנָי כּוֹנְנוּ יָדֶיךָ"; וְאוֹמֵר: „וַיְבִיאֵם אֶל גְּבוּל
קָדְשׁוֹ, הַר זֶה קָנְתָה יְמִינוֹ."

[יא] **כָּל** מַה שֶּׁבָּרָא הַקָּדוֹשׁ בָּרוּךְ הוּא בְּעוֹלָמוֹ לֹא

The second method is heaven and earth. This refers to the knowledge of the intricacies of the microcosm and macrocosm, the terrestrial and the celestial. And the psalmist says, "The heavens relate the glory of God, and the firmament bespeaks the works of His hands" (*Psalms* 19:2). The intricate design and function of a leaf is a testimony to the Creator.

Study of the function of the human body reveals it to be nothing less than a miraculous machine. A four-story fully computerized factory could not duplicate the function of the liver. All the computers in the world combined pale in comparison before the human brain, whose 14 billion cells are multiply interconnected. The motor and sensory activates of the brain are staggering, and science has no understanding yet as to the way the brain generates thought. That this miraculous being develops from a single cell is an undeniable testimony to the infinite wisdom of the Creator.

The third way is that of the Patriarch Abraham, who represents *chesed*. The Talmud states that the way one can be close to God is by emulating Him. "Just as God is merciful, you too should be merciful" (*Shabbos* 133b). By doing *chesed* one follows in the Patriarch's footsteps, and one can thereby achieve intimacy with God.

The fourth way is Israel, i.e., *ahavas Yisrael*. The Baal Shem Tov stated that the royal path to develop love of God is though love of man.

The fifth way is the Holy Temple, site of the Sanctuary. Although the Sanctuary was the site of the Immanent Presence of God, the Torah states, "Let them make for Me a Sanctuary and I will dwell within them." The Torah commentaries point out that God did not say, "I will dwell within it," but rather, "I will dwell within them." By fulfilling the mitzvah of the Sanctuary, Israel

6/11   *at the beginning of His way, before His works in time of yore (Proverbs 8:22). From where do we know this about heaven and earth? Since it is written: So says God. The heaven is My throne, and the earth is My footstool; what House can you build for Me, and where is the place of My rest? (Isaiah 66:1). And it says: How abundant are Your works, God, with wisdom You made them all, the earth is full of Your possessions (Psalms 104:24). From where do we know this about Abraham? Since it is written: And He blessed him and said: Blessed is Abram of God the Most High, Who acquired heaven and earth (Genesis 14:19). From where do we know this about the people Israel? Since it is written: Until Your people passes through, God, until it passes through — this people You acquired (Exodus 15:16); and it [also] says: But for the holy ones who are in the earth and for the mighty all my desires are due to them (Psalms 16:3). From where do we know this about the Holy Temple? Since it is written: Your dwelling place which You, God, have made; the Sanctuary, my Lord, that Your hands established (Exodus 15:17). And it says: And He brought them to His sacred boundary, to this mountain which His right hand acquired.*

11. **A**ll that the Holy One, Blessed is He, created in His world,

---

achieves the presence of God within each person.

This chapter is referred to as *Kinyan HaTorah*. Mishnah 6 enumerates the 48 ways in which a person con acquire Torah. The chapter closes with the five ways in which a person can acquire a relationship and an identity with God.

11.

כָּל מַה שֶׁבָּרָא הַקָּדוֹשׁ בָּרוּךְ הוּא
**All that the Holy One,
Blessed is He, created**

This mishnah is a fitting closure of *Ethics of the Fathers*. It states the principle that underlies all Creation. The universe and all that is within it should proclaim the majesty of God.

This concept is mentioned elsewhere, yet is rarely given adequate consideration. At the marriage ceremony, the very first *berachah* that is recited after the man and the woman have been joined in wedlock is, "that God created everything for His glory." We have all attended many weddings. How often

בְּרָאוֹ אֶלָּא לִכְבוֹדוֹ, שֶׁנֶּאֱמַר: ,,כֹּל הַנִּקְרָא בִשְׁמִי וְלִכְבוֹדִי בְּרָאתִיו, יְצַרְתִּיו אַף עֲשִׂיתִיו"; וְאוֹמֵר: ,,יהוה יִמְלֹךְ לְעוֹלָם וָעֶד."

❦ ❦ ❦

רַבִּי חֲנַנְיָא בֶּן עֲקַשְׁיָא אוֹמֵר: רָצָה הַקָּדוֹשׁ בָּרוּךְ הוּא לְזַכּוֹת אֶת יִשְׂרָאֵל, לְפִיכָךְ הִרְבָּה לָהֶם תּוֹרָה וּמִצְוֹת, שֶׁנֶּאֱמַר: ,,יהוה חָפֵץ לְמַעַן צִדְקוֹ, יַגְדִּיל תּוֹרָה וְיַאְדִּיר."

---

have we reflected on the relevance of this *berachah* to the marrige ceremony?

Modern life has unfortunately been plagued with an unprecedented number of marriages that have failed. Even in marriages that last, there is often far too much strife and discord.

The natural inclination of human beings is self-gratification. Deprivation of gratification may result in frustration. If a person enters a marriage relationship with the primary expectation that it will satisfy his/her physical and emotional needs, that relationship is on a precarious foundation. Optimum function as a spouse and as a parent not infrequently requires setting aside one's own needs and desires.

If a husband and wife each have their own agenda, the unity of the marriage is weakened. If they both strive toward a common goal, the unity is

He created solely for His glory, as it is said: All that is called by My Name, indeed, it is for My glory that I have created it, formed it, and made it (Isaiah 43:7). And it says: God shall reign for all eternity (Exodus 15:18).

❦ ❦ ❦

Rabbi Chanania ben Akashia says: The Holy One, Blessed is He, wished to confer merit upon Israel; therefore He gave them Torah and mitzvos in abundance, as it is said: HASHEM desired, for the sake of its [Israel's] righteousness, that the Torah be made great and glorious (Isaiah 42:21).

---

strengthened.

The very first message that husband and wife receive is that all of Creation is solely for the glory of God. Their marriage, too, should be directed toward this purpose. When husband and wife, father and mother, can make the glory of God the primary goal of their marriage and all other considerations secondary, that marriage has great staying power.

Just as in marriage, so in every other aspect of a person's life, the primary goal should be to enhance *kevod Shamayim*, the greater glory of God. The teaching found here may indeed require much restraint of one's drives and much effort to give the primacy to spiritual rather than physical needs. The final mishnah tells us how this can be accomplished: by dedicating one's life to further the goal of Creation, the greater glory of God.

৵ঌ Epilogue

E*thics of the Fathers* was introduced with the passage, "All Israel has a share in the World to Come." We have noted that the human being is a composite entity, comprised of a body and spirit. The human body is much like the animal body in terms of its drives and impulses. What gives man his distinction is the spirit, which is his unique feature.

Most authorities agree that the Eternal World is an *olam haneshamos,* a world where the spirit exists rather than the body. It is therefore the *spirit* which should be prepared for existence in the World to Come. This is what is meant by, "All Israel has a share, i.e., part of their being or the *spirit* which will exist, in the World to Come." *Ethics of the Fathers* provides the guidelines and teachings whereby the spirit can be prepared for the World to Come.

In *Eight Chapters,* the Rambam's introduction to *Ethics of the Fathers,* he states, "Such achievement requires that a person use all the powers of his soul to the single ideal of knowing God. Whatever he does, whether great or small, and whatever he says, must be geared directly or indirectly to a higher spiritual purpose. Such a person considers before he acts or commits a single deed whether it will bring him closer to that goal, and proceeds to act only if the answer is that it will . . . Such striving is what the Almighty demands of us when He says, 'Love God with all your heart, with all your soul, and with all your might' (*Deuteronomy* 6:5), meaning with all the powers of your soul. In other words, infuse each faculty of your soul with the love of God . . . Our sages summed up the idea briefly, concisely, and clearly with this ethical precept, 'Let all your deeds be for the sake of Heaven' (Above, 2:17). When you consider how they have encapsulated a great and momentous idea with a few words, while others have written books without adequately explaining it, you recognize that the sages undoubtedly spoke with Divine inspiration" (*Eight Chapters* §5).

This is indeed an appropriate introduction to *Ethics of the Fathers,* but it serves equally well as a summation.